INTO THE FATHER'S HEART

A Study of the Character of God

Michael F. Clute

Published by
God's Last Call Ministries
P.O. Box 473
Woodburn, OR 97071

DEDICATION

This revised and updated version of "Into the Father's Heart," is dedicated to the following people who have inspired and helped me to prepare and publish it: Rosendo, who built and maintains God's Last Call website and who typed the first eight chapters as an incentive for me to re-publish IFH. And then to the following people who proofread the pre-publication manuscript, as well as gave donations to help print it: Greg, Charles, Laura, Wayne, Esther, Robert, and Kent who scanned the entire original book for me to revise which saved many hours of hard labor. And also to Dave, Mike, Phil, Seth, Nathan, Eric, Maxine, John, Sharon, Stuart, Esther, Carol, Rose, Debbie, Gil, Mark, Joz, Sally, Neva, and a host of others too numerous to mention, who through the years have encouraged, counseled, advised, prayed and supported this ministry through thick and thin. Without them this book would never have been completed, let alone printed.

Cover Design by Michael F. Clute
Cover Illustration by Gary Hunt
1st Printing, GLC Edition, June 1982, 50,000 copies
2nd Printing, Revised Edition, August 2005, 50,000 copies
Published by GLC Ministries
Library of Congress Catalog Card Number 0-9608682-0-8

Printed in the United States of America

TABLE OF CONTENTS

Religions before and after the cross have portrayed God as harsh and severe—undeserving of our trust and love. But the nail-pierced hands of Jesus beckon us to come to Him as we are without fear. "My Father bids you come," He says. "He loves you just as much as I do. He was crucified with Me. We died to save you." (From Pastor Clute's first manuscript published May 11, 1977.)

INTRODUCTION

In the fall of 1976, I was impressed to memorize some Psalms. Since I already knew Psalm 1, my journey began with Psalm 2. It was very hard work, but I persevered, even though I didn't understand much. "Kiss the Son, lest He be angry, and ye perish from the way, when his wrath is kindled but a little. Blessed are all they that put their trust in Him." Psalm 2:12. I knew this was referring to the Son of God, even our Lord Jesus Christ, but I could not understand why the Scripture would state that our gentle Lord Jesus of the New Testament would be angry at us if we did not kiss Him. It was completely out of character for Him. See additional note 17, pg. 531.

The next Psalm didn't help me. In fact it deepened my confusion. "Arise, 0 Lord; save me 0 my God: for thou hast smitten all mine enemies upon the cheek bone; thou hast broken the teeth of the ungodly." Psalm 3:7. Now, I was really confused. David, under the inspiration of God's Spirit tells us that God smashes the faces of His enemies. He even knocks out their teeth. Yet, Christ, in the New Testament tells us to "love our enemies," and to "turn the other cheek." I could not understand why God was apparently contradicting Himself. Or was He? Was there a secret code language or a special concept that runs throughout the Bible which would explain this paradox? I continued to memorize, prayerfully seeking the answer.

Finally, I came to Psalm 5:10 and the light broke through. "Destroy thou them, 0 God; let them fall by their own counsels;" Here then was the key. The Bible truly was written in a special code. There was a hidden concept about God, but only those who truly seek to know Him (Jeremiah 29:13) would ever discover it and be able to go "Into the Father's heart." God takes the blame for everything that happens, as Judah was willing to do, Genesis 43:9. He claims to destroy a person even when the person, like Saul, (1 Chronicles 10:4, 5, 13, 14), and Judas, (Matthew 27:5) commit suicide. As I continued to study, all of my research confirmed this truth. At the urging of friends, I put the basic concept in manuscript form in 1977. Two more manuscripts were subsequently written between 1978 and 1981. This book is a combination of those manuscripts.

No claim to infallibility is made by this author. This book, in my humble estimation, has only scratched the surface. There is much more for the serious student who will earnestly study and pray. All suggestions, ideas and criticisms are welcomed. I have always learned more from my critics than my adulators. My only desire is for you, the reader, to gain deeper insights into our wonderful Heavenly Father's great and magnificent heart of love. That the same joy and ecstasy which came to this poor writer's heart be experienced by the reader is the sincere desire of the author. June 1982.

AUTHOR'S PREFACE

In the first edition of "Into the Father's Heart," 50,000 copies were published in June of 1982. By 1987 over 40,000 had been distributed in the USA and a few foreign countries at the basic cost of 50 cents each. At least 50% of that number were given away free including over 1,000 which were sent to readers in Africa. By 1998 the balance of 10,000 were also gone and I began making photo copies to fill the few orders that continued to come in. Although I had published a second book on the character of God in 1986, entitled, "THE WONDERFUL TRUTH ABOUT OUR HEAVENLY FATHER," 394 pages, the requests for "Into the Father's Heart" continued to come in along with the question as to when I was going to publish a second edition.

About five years ago a young man in LA asked permission to build and maintain a website featuring the front page articles I had written over the years on God's true character of love. Even though I was not on the internet at that time, nor did I even know what a web site was, I granted permission, explaining that I had no budget for such a project. This humble young man from East L.A. said he would build and maintain it free of charge which he continues to do to this day. He explained that the day after he re-dedicated his life to the Lord Jesus Christ my paper arrived at his door. He said that as he began reading the articles the Lord impressed him to build a web site. He also typed the first eight chapters of "Into the Father's Heart," and placed them on the web site as well. He said people were reading those chapters and requesting more info.

Although I did not have the funds I knew that eventually I would have to re-publish this book which had touched so many lives in the last 23 years, causing a paradigm shift in the thinking of an entire generation. At the urging of this young man I finally requested help from my readers to re-type the remaining 22 chapters. Only two or three volunteered for the job. Finally, a man from Kentucky wrote to me out of the blue and volunteered to scan the whole book for me. Although this solved the problem of re-typing the book I then faced the task of revising, correcting and updating the entire work because in 1982 I had not yet understood the concept of Universal Restoration, based on Acts 3:21 and many other supporting passages from the Holy Bible. This seemed like a task so overwhelming and daunting that at first I refused to even think about it with a writing schedule that I felt was already beyond my capacity to maintain.

That is when I began to really pray about this matter. As a result the Lord urged me to just try going over the first eight chapters. I was amazed at how quickly I was able to bring those chapters up to speed, theologically speaking. This gave me the courage to spend as much time as was necessary to finish the entire book which was finally completed on April 9th, 2004. I then had 100 copies of this revised manuscript printed and sent out to anyone who requested it, asking for whatever donation they could afford. As usual, I ended up giving most of them away with the request that each reader return this revised edition with their comments and suggestions. Only five people agreed to do this, and with those five returned manuscripts I completed the final corrections on October 29th, 2004. Still I had no funds to re-print this revised edition.

Many things happened in the next few months which showed that the Lord was in charge and wanted this book republished. Satan was allowed to do his best to stop it with severe tests for yours truly. But as usual, the Lord brought me through these trials and then touched several people's hearts to send in the needed funds so I could print the volume you now hold in your hands. Although I did not quote from one of my favorite authors in the first edition of "Into the Father's Heart," I have quoted from her several times in this revised edition. Here is one of my favorite quotes: "If we surrender our lives to His service, we can never be placed in a position for which God has not made provision. Whatever may be our situation, we have a Guide to direct our way; whatever our perplexities, we have a sure Counselor; whatever our sorrow, bereavement, or loneliness, we have a sympathizing Friend." Christ's Object Lessons, 173. And this one also: "Worry is blind, and cannot discern the future; but Jesus sees the end from the beginning. In every difficulty He has His way prepared to bring relief. Our heavenly Father has a thousand ways to provide for us, of which we know nothing. Those who accept the one principle of making the service and honor of God supreme will find perplexities vanish, and a plain path before their feet." "Desire of Ages," by Ellen G. White, page 330.

The message in this book has changed the lives of many people for the good. I know it has certainly changed mine. In 1982 I only knew of three levels of God's character. There are now seven. See Additional Note #28, pg. 541. The seventh level will be the last one to be fulfilled when the Lord returns to claim His own. May we each be ready for His return is the sincere prayer and earnest desire of my heart. Your friend always in the power and love of our Blessed Redeemer, the Lord Jesus Christ. Pastor-Evangelist, Michael F. Clute. July 19, 2005.

CHAPTER 1

WHAT IS GOD REALLY LIKE? DOES HE HURT AND KILL PEOPLE OR NOT? HOW CAN WE KNOW?

The God of the Bible is a Being who is often misunderstood. Very few people serve God out of love. Even very devout people reserve a place in the back of their minds for the inevitable disaster that God might bring upon them, or upon a friend, or worse, upon a close loved one. I have seen people who have been Christians for years become embittered and hateful toward God because they felt He either brought some kind of sickness or destruction into their lives directly or they believed He just stood by and allowed the tragedy to happen when He could have stopped it. Why? If God is love, why did He let it happen? Or worse, WHY DID HE DO IT? May I submit right now that every question we are considering here can be answered ONLY in the light of the Cross of Christ! I will not expand on that idea right now. I will come back to it later, but I just want to insert that concept into our discussion at the beginning to give us a reference point, a bench mark, as it were.

GOD IS ON TRIAL BEFORE THE UNIVERSE

Whether we want to believe it or not, our beloved Heavenly Father is on trial before the entire universe. Through the centuries, Satan has successfully painted Him as a GOD OF WRATH AND VENGEANCE with such consummate skill and alacrity through religious institutions and zealots that nearly everyone today looks upon God as a Being to be feared. When I first began sharing this concept with church groups, the most devout members of the church would usually be the first to protest.

"But, Pastor Clute," they begin, "God does kill people. He

does destroy. What about the Flood? What about Sodom and Gomorrah? What about this and what about that?" they continue, in their efforts to perpetuate this concept of a God of Wrath and hatred and vengeance about which the medieval church taught people for more than a thousand years, and which even Reformation preachers believed in, although the emphasis was upon His love more than His wrath by that time.

What about you, friend? Is your mind closed or open? Is it sealed shut with your preconceived opinions and prejudices or are you willing to reason together with me for a while as we consider this important study on the CHARACTER OF GOD? I ask you only to reserve judgment until we have considered all the evidence. God is actually on trial, for murder. Do we want to indict God for murder before we have heard all the testimony? I don't think so.

There are hundreds of statements in both the Bible and in contemporary religious literature which seem to indicate that God does destroy, that God does hurt, maim, and kill people. In fact, God Himself seems to say, "I destroy." The Bible states it over and over again in the Old Testament. 1 Samuel 2:6; Deuteronomy 32:39.

In Isaiah 45:7, the Lord says, "I form the light, and create darkness: I make peace, and create evil: I the Lord do all these things." And yet in the New Testament, He says just the opposite: We...declare unto you, that God is light, and in him is no darkness at all. 1 John 1:5.

Both texts are true. They do not really contradict each other. They can be explained. They can be harmonized, but only if you want to really know the truth about God and about Jesus Christ and about His plan for your life. Jesus is real. Jesus is true. Jesus is love. Jesus wants to live in you and guide you and implant His own character in your heart and life. Will you let Him do that? He can make life new and beautiful for you. He can give you a glorious new start. Even if you have been a church member for 60 years or more, He can give you a new beginning again and take away the nagging doubts and the fears and the perplexity you may have.

I find that church people need Jesus the most. They are in the church, but not in Christ. If that statement upsets you even a little bit, that is proof positive that Jesus' love has not filled your soul completely yet. I know, for I have had the experience myself.

Remember that it was the most religious group of people who ever lived on the earth who killed the Creator. Is it possible that we in this generation are repeating their history step by step? What a horrifying thought! Let us get down on our knees and pray to God that we will not kill the Savior again by our wicked unbelief.

EVERY MYSTERY IN THE UNIVERSE IS ANSWERED IN THE CROSS

The cross of Jesus Christ is the Divine key that will unlock every mystery in both the secular and sacred realms. In fact, the entire history of man is like a giant murder mystery. Who is really responsible for all of this human carnage and bloodshed? The light flowing from Golgotha's hill will chase away the shadows and reveal truths hidden from the foundation of the world.

We don't need to be afraid of God. He will not hurt us. The cross proves that. If He ever would have lashed back, it should have been then. And He never changes, Malachi 3:6; Hebrews 13:8. Therefore, the cross will explain all other mysteries as we behold His face seated on His eternal throne of glory. Even now, by faith and personal experience, in His day by day communications with us as He leads us in the paths of His own choosing, we can know His character by these gracious manifestations of His loving guidance.

But, it takes the cross to break our hearts and open our eyes. That is why we must continually be looking at the cross in order to understand the mystery of Godliness as well as the mystery of iniquity. See I Timothy 3:16 and II Thessalonians 2:7.

GOD THE FATHER REVEALED IN CHRIST

"And all things are of God, who hath reconciled us to himself by Christ Jesus, and hath given to us the ministry of reconciliation; to wit, that God was in Christ, reconciling the world unto himself" 2 Corinthians 5:18, 19.

This text is an amazing revelation. Here we see that God the Father was actually crucified on the cross with His only Son. Even Satan saw God revealed in His true character. But, like anyone who has taken a stand for something he believes, Satan was too proud to admit he had been wrong. But he was wrong. Dead wrong. But, he would rather die than admit his error, and so he continued in his rebellion against God the Father and Jesus His Son.

You see, friend of mine, Lucifer is the prodigal son who never came home. The Great Controversy is really a family feud and you and I are caught in the middle. We must decide whether the Father is really all He claims to be or not.

Lucifer, who has become his own Father's enemy, or Satan, which means "adversary," in the Hebrew, has been carrying on a campaign of hatred and slander against the Father and Son for nearly 6,000 years.

The controversy is about to come to a close, and the majority of the world still do not know what God is really like. Lucifer sinned or rebelled in the full light of sacred glory. Lucifer was the covering cherub. He knew and understood more about the Father than anyone else. Therefore, he could do untold damage to the Divine government. His rebellion was unthinkable and unbelievable, and yet it happened. Lucifer's ability to make the Father look guilty was beyond calculation. Would the Father retaliate? Lucifer made his decision to never obey the Father again.

Yes, Satan took his stand against his Heavenly Father because he did not want to admit he was wrong. Because we are sinful beings, we have the exact tendency to do the same. No one wants to admit he is wrong. It is only as our hearts are broken and as we surrender to the sweet influence of the Holy Spirit that we can receive power to admit that we are sinners; that we have erred by our wrong choices and are in need of pardon and forgiveness through the blood of Jesus Christ.

And only as we look at the cross can this change take place in our hearts. Any other type of "conversion" leads to proud Pharisaism, self-righteousness, empty works instead of Spirit filled fruit. Unless our will is yielded to the guidance of the Holy Spirit, our lives will be characterized either by an attitude of active rebellion or of passive indifference.

The first is a failure on our part to stop sinning, and the second is a failure to let God work through us to do righteous deeds of mercy. Both are a result of broken fellowship with the Father. Therefore, it is vitally important that we understand how beautiful and wonderful the Father truly is.

THE MORE WE KNOW ABOUT GOD THE BETTER HE LOOKS TO US

The reason we do not show and tell the height and depth of God's love is because we have not fully seen or experienced it ourselves. But our Father is so merciful and loving. He encourages us to pick up and go forward in our lives with this new understanding of His character. How can we refuse such graciousness? What a joy to tell others of our Wonderful, Heavenly Father.

My father was not as religious as my mother, but he attended church from time to time. I had wanted to enter a religious high school, but was not allowed to do so, because it was my father's belief that I would learn more in public school. He knew I wanted to be a minister and counseled me on how to be a success in that line, but he felt I would be better off finishing my last year in the public school I had been attending. The Lord worked through my father to give me much counsel in many things, and I trusted his judgment and submitted to his authority. He encouraged me in my decision to enter a Christian college and was supportive in all my studies for the next four years.

In the fall of 1956, when I was only 18 years old, I entered a liberal arts college to study for the ministry. All my life, my mother had taught me about God. I had also studied the Bible on my own, but still there were many passages I could not comprehend. Yet, I had a wonderful experience with Jesus and became involved in religious activities.

MY FIRST INTRODUCTION TO THE CHARACTER OF GOD

One of the most brilliant and wonderful teachers I have ever studied under had a theme he threaded through all his lectures and classes. The theme was,"God is a loving heavenly Father. He destroys no man. Man destroys himself." It was during this period that I began to form an image of God in my mind. It was an image of a Being that loved me so much He came to die. God became a Father who wept with me in all my trials and disappointments. I came to love and worship this heavenly Father very devoutly during my late teens and early twenties. This understanding of God has carried me through many fiery trials and deep waters. And yet, I was still very legalistic and sometimes pharisaical. I had not yet learned the full truth about the Father's great heart of love which I am going to share with you in this book. I hope to take you step by step into the Father's heart. We will deal with God's character in terms of simple logic, using as much Scripture as I feel is necessary for you to understand the principle I am trying to present. Then we will answer some of the basic questions that seem to always come up.

Next, we will consider the supreme objective of Christ's Messianic mission to planet earth. We will show the Father's relationship to all of His creatures, even to Lucifer. Yes, especially to Lucifer. We will use Bible narrative and the symbology hidden in these stories to go deep into the Father's great and magnificent heart of love.

Finally, we will have questions and answers and then some additional thoughts and concepts on God's character which were either not brought out clearly enough, if at all, or not expanded upon. Most of the people who disagree with this concept of God (that He does not kill), do so with a zeal worthy of a better cause, and they show by their very words, actions, gestures, and facial expressions, that they not only believe God kills, but would feel justified in doing so themselves if the circumstances permitted and if the occasion (as far as they were concerned) demanded it.

This attitude, my friend, is the inevitable result of rejecting the fullest revelation of the character of God that was ever given -- EVEN THE LIFE OF OUR LORD AND SAVIOR, CHRIST JESUS!

I have said it before, and I will say it again, if you can show me one time in the life of Christ where He killed someone, I will believe God kills, for Christ was God, and the Bible says God never changes. See Psalms 89:34; Malachi 3:6; Hebrews 13:8; and James 1:17.

But in order to show that many hard-to-understand passages and experiences in the Old Testament and in the New Testament, as well, can be explained, I am writing this book. More evidence is coming to my desk every day, and the Holy Spirit is revealing more and more how this whole concept ties in with the final controversy over the Sabbath. It is truly an unbelievable experience.

SOME MINDS LIKE CONCRETE

Someone once said about those who close their minds to new ideas, "their minds are like concrete, all mixed up and permanently set." Well, I suppose we all are like that at some time or another. None of us are infallible, and that is the reason we must be patient, kind and gentle with one another, especially those who persecute us.

Just think what a tragedy would have come to the early

church if one of the Christians had decided not to be like Jesus for a few minutes and had assassinated Saul of Tarsus. What would have happened? Why, the Jews might have rounded up every Christian they could find and brought them to trial for conspiring to murder their priests.

At least they would have tried to get the Romans to do it, and they would have had a legitimate reason for suspecting them. Secondly, the early Christians would have lost their witness to the Jews and all the then-known world. Thirdly, they would have had a bad example which would have brought in a "gospel of violence," neutralizing the power of the non-violent methods of Jesus. And fourth, the greatest apostle of the New Testament would have been dead before he had a chance to get converted and become Paul, the bold one for Jesus.

But, under the power of the "early rain," this did not happen. Today we are expecting the Latter Rain to fall on us. Can we be expected to be any less than were the early Christians? Or is the Lord expecting more from us today since we have more light? What do you think? If the Lord Jesus Christ is the fullest revelation of God's true character, then we must go to the cross and stand in its light and glory and plead for power and strength to be like Him. Are we willing to go all the way and be crucified with Jesus? May the Father grant us strength to do it.

THOUGHTS TO INSPIRE YOU TO READ THE REST OF THIS BOOK

"Man's mind -- stretched by a new idea -- never goes back to its original dimensions." Oliver Wendell Holmes.

"The more we know of God, the higher will be our ideal of character and the more earnest our longing to reflect His likeness." "Mount of Blessing", pg. 19.

CHAPTER 2

WHY DOES GOD ALWAYS TAKE THE BLAME?

Earlier we quoted Isaiah 45:7: "I form the light, and create darkness: I make peace, and create evil: I the Lord do all these things".

In Strong's Exhaustive Concordance of the Bible, under the word for "create,"we see the Hebrew word "BARAH," (bawraw) which basically means "to make or create." But it can also mean "select," "feed," "choose," "cut down," "dispatch," "do," "make (fat)." (Strong's word number 1254).

Now, let us ask ourselves the question. Does God ever perform any of the above acts in such a way that the result is "evil"? Well, we would say He brought on all the evil in the world by creating Lucifer in the first place and by "selecting" him to be the leader of the angels so Lucifer could lead one-third of them astray.

God "fed," or "sustained," Lucifer from the start and "chose" him and "dispatched" him with important messages to all the angels. Lucifer was foremost in informing all the creation of God as to the plans of the Lord. Ezekiel 28:3, 14.

By placing Lucifer (his name meant "Light-bearer") in such a high position, God took the risk of having Lucifer rebel and turn against Him.

But, since God is Omniscient (all-knowing: Isaiah 46:9, 10), He knew this would happen and had already made provision to meet the emergency.

Jesus had made a pledge to die for man before Lucifer rebelled, took one-third of heaven with him, and then led Adam and Eve astray. Revelation 13:8. Why then did God decide to let this happen when He realized all the suffering it would cause? The most satisfactory answer I have come up with is that God could not permit His creatures to be free moral agents, with the power of choice, if He made them robots, so they could never rebel against Him.

So, He made both angels and mankind with the option to serve or not to serve Him. To obey or not to obey. He saw down through the corridors of time that Lucifer would choose to go his own way and do his own thing, yet He created him anyway. Why? Because He knew in the final analysis His creation would be perfected. Rev 15:1-4 says that every creature will praise Him at the end of the Great Controversy.

So, instead of letting Lucifer and his angels suffer the consequences of their disobedience immediately, He chose to let sin run its course. He chose to shield His creatures from as much pain and sorrow as possible by sacrificing Himself.

The Father has suffered with His Son from the beginning, so that our suffering would not be as great. The God family has kept all of His fallen creation alive so as to let the demonstration run its full and ultimate course. Is this picture one of an arbitrary despot? Or is it the picture of a God who is total, pure love? Of a love that we cannot paint on a canvas or describe in words, but a love that we can experience only by letting Him live within our hearts?

I say it is the latter, which is the road of experience of allowing the blessed SAVIOR to lead us day by day, hour by hour and moment by moment. Jesus and His Father want to live in our hearts and control our lives. I feel the Lord's presence in my life more and more as I try to tell others of His marvelous love and grace. It floods my soul more every passing day.

Revelation 13:8 tells us that the "Lamb," or Jesus, was "SLAIN FROM THE FOUNDATION OF THE WORLD." Since the Father and Son let these circumstances happen, they would take full responsibility for every mistake Lucifer and all of his angels (now demons) would ever make. They would also take the blame for every mistake every human would make after he fell into sin.

WHAT MAGNIFICENT, UNUTTERABLE, INDESCRIBABLE LOVE!!! So, a good God did not create a bad devil. No! A perfect, totally pure, infinitely loving God permitted a perfect angelic being known as Lucifer to come into existence, and Lucifer by his own choice, over an extended period of time, which we cannot know, transformed himself into a devil.

"THOU WAST PERFECT IN THY WAYS FROM THE DAY THAT THOU WAST CREATED, TILL INIQUITY WAS FOUND IN THEE." Ezekiel 28:15. The sin was found in Lucifer, not in God. This, the Bible calls, THE MYSTERY OF INIQUITY. 2 Thessalonians 2:7.

WHERE SIN OCCURS GOD CANNOT WISELY PREVENT IT FROM HAPPENING

Charles G. Finney, born August 29, 1792, was used of God in a most remarkable way in the middle of the 19th century. He was a dynamic preacher and educator, probably best known for the establishment of Oberlin College.

One of his most famous sermons was the heading I chose for this section. His text on this subject is found in Luke 17:1: "Then said he (Christ) unto the disciples, It is impossible but that offences will come: but woe unto him, through whom they come!"

An offense is defined in Webster's dictionary as "a cause or occasion of sin." It would seem that Christ here is acknowledging the sad fact that in a universe of "free choice," the eruption of sin's ugly head on some peaceful planet was inevitable.

But, as I said before, God chose to deal with such a possibility on a personal basis, taking the blame Himself, and using this seeming "disaster" as a lesson for all eternity.

Our world is like a lesson book for the universe. Someone may ask, "But is it worth all the heartache and suffering?" Yes, it is. God says it is, and I believe He speaks the truth. Proverbs 8:8. But, He even gives a wonderful promise that after this "vale of tears is past," it will never happen again. Listen: "WHAT DO YOU IMAGINE AGAINST THE LORD? HE WILL MAKE AN UTTER END: AFFLICTION SHALL NOT RISE UP

THE SECOND TIME." Nahum 1:9. "And they (the redeemed) sing the song of Moses the servant of God, and the song of the Lamb, saying, great and marvelous are thy works, Lord God Almighty: just and true are thy ways, thou King of saints. Who shall not fear thee, O Lord, and glorify thy name? for thou only art holy: for all nations shall come and worship before thee, for thy judgments (decisions) are made manifest." Revelation 15:3, 4.

FINNEY'S FINAL CONCLUSION

Finney came to the conclusion that even though "sin, under the government of God, cannot be prevented," it was nevertheless "utterly inexcusable as to the sinner...." In V. R. Edman's book, Finney Lives On, p. 192.

He also concluded that "God's government over men is moral," and is known by every intelligent creature. I agree with this, as God's Spirit can and does impress each person with a knowledge of Himself to a greater or lesser extent according to the circumstances (Romans 2:11-16; Psalms 87:4-6).

The Psalmist David declared that God has revealed the truth of His "Glory," to all the world by the stars at night. And it is true: "THE HEAVENS DECLARE THE GLORY OF GOD." Psalm 19:1.

His glory is really His character, or a transcript of the Ten Commandments, which tell us what God is really like. We see this on Mount Horeb (Sinai) where Moses received the Law, Exodus 34:4-7.

Through the Holy Spirit, the Law of God is impressed on every human heart and mind (emotions and intelligence) which proves that God's name or character, His glory, is known to every intelligent person, and God will be able to decide on this basis who really wants to become one with Him at His Second Coming.

Finney also says, "By the term moral I mean that it governs by motives, and does not move by physical force. It adapts itself to mind, not matter." By this, he means that God controls matter by one set of rules, but His intelligent creatures by another. The first is by physical laws and the second by moral, which He governs through our conscience. When we break the moral law, the physical law reacts against us from within and without, and we suffer. This is the "law of sin and death," (Romans 8:2) being activated by our disobedience.

God controls the planets by the agency of physical law, and His creatures by moral law. In God's government over the human mind all is voluntary; nothing is coerced as by physical force. Finney concluded, as does the Bible, that God is not to blame for sin, and yet because of God's love and compassion, He takes the blame so we will not have to suffer. "FOR HE HATH MADE HIM TO BE SIN FOR US, WHO KNEW NO SIN; THAT WE MIGHT BE MADE THE RIGHTEOUSNESS OF GOD IN HIM." 2 Corinthians 5:21.

Even though it is not God's fault that Lucifer rebelled, or that Adam and Eve fell into sin, the God-family has taken the blame so They can pay the bill. Revelation 5 shows this.

Let us examine two Scriptures, "The Lord killeth, and maketh alive: he bringeth down to the grave, and bringeth up." 1 Samuel 2:6. "See now that I, even I, am he, and there is no god with me: I kill, and I make alive; I wound, and I heal: neither is there any that can deliver out of my hand. For I lift up my hand to heaven, and say, I live for ever." Deuteronomy 32:39,40.

Hannah and Moses both spoke under the inspiration of God's spirit, and yet they described God in terms or words of their own understanding. We know Satan is the one who kills, but because God allows him to do it, God takes the blame. Hannah and Moses no doubt believed this too. The Bible progressively reveals God's true character culminating with the life of Christ, the fullest revelation of His character.

We could read verses 40-43, which quote God as saying that He is responsible for destruction with the sword and all the blood it sheds. He says that He will render vengeance on all His enemies. Is it any wonder that people think of the God of the Old Testament with fear and even disgust? But, why does God do this? Why does He take the blame?

I have asked many people this important question, and few have ever been able to give me the right answer. I have prayed on this matter much and asked God for wisdom to understand it myself. Why does God always take the rap? Why does He always play the "heavy," and say, "I did it"?

TWO BASIC ANSWERS

First of all, God knows we cannot bear the guilt and blame, so He takes it upon Himself. It is too much for us to bear. "Surely he hath borne our griefs, and carried our sorrows: yet we did esteem him stricken, smitten of God, and afflicted. But he was wounded for our transgressions, he was bruised for our iniquities: the chastisement of our peace was upon him; and with his stripes we are healed." Isaiah 53:4,5.

We have no idea how weak we are. It is the protection of God over all creation which keeps this planet from self-destructing. And this watch care has been over us since time began. Yes, Christ's efficacious atonement has been applied to every age from the beginning.

From the moment Jesus, the Son of God, made the agreement with the Father to become man's redeemer, He became the LAMB SLAIN FROM THE FOUNDATION OF THE WORLD. Revelation 13:8.

And so from time immemorial until He died on the cross, our precious Lord Jesus became both our SAVIOR AND DELIVERER. And throughout all eternity, the CROSS OF CHRIST will be the exhaustless science and theme of redeemed humanity. "Never will it be forgotten that He whose power created and upheld the unnumbered worlds through the vast realms of space, the Beloved of God, the majesty of heaven, He whom cherub and shining seraph delighted to adore-humbled Himself to uplift fallen man;...That the maker of all worlds, the arbiter of all destinies, should lay aside His glory and humiliate Himself from love to man will ever excite the wonder and adoration of the universe." GC 651.

The second reason I have discovered why Jesus always takes the blame is so He can remain in control of our lives. There are only two forces in this world which influence our mind for good or for evil: Jesus and Satan. If a father refuses to be responsible for the actions of his child, he will soon lose custody of that child and forfeit his right to influence his life for good or for evil.

The same principle holds true in God's case. Since He is our Creator, He is our Father, and thus responsible for our actions, good or bad. Unless He is willing to take the blame for our actions, He would forfeit all right to intervene in our behalf for purposes of mercy. He could not send His holy Angels to protect us from deception or bodily injury, unless He was willing to pay the price of our redemption. We broke His covenant and that is sin. "The wages of sin is death." (Romans 6:23). His death is a demonstration of what will happen to us if we reject his love.

BIBLE PROOF THAT GOD DOES TAKE THE BLAME

People, however, continue to be puzzled as to why Christ in the Old Testament is always saying, "I did it. Let me take the blame."

For example, in 1 Chronicles 10:13,14, the Lord takes the blame for Saul's death, when verses 4 and 5 clearly state that Saul committed suicide.

And in the book of Job, where it is crystal clear that Satan is the DESTROYER who destroyed Job's children and property with wind, fire and with the sword and ravaged his body with boils, God (Christ) declares, "Has thou considered my servant Job, that there is none like him in the earth, a perfect and an upright man, one that feareth God, and escheweth evil? And still he holdeth fast his integrity, although thou movedst me against him, to destroy him without cause." Job 2:3.

The Living Bible gives this interesting paraphrase of the same verse. "And he has kept his faith in me despite the fact that you persuaded me to let you harm him without any cause."

Here, the Living Bible, gave the true meaning of the Scripture. It is sad that many people who claim to believe the Bible are not quite as interested in making it clear who the destroyer is as they are in exalting their own self-righteousness.

You would not believe how many professed Christians write to me, saying, "Jesus Christ DOES kill people."

How sad it is to see people misunderstand the beauty of the Father's character in Christ. Do you realize, my friend, that God the Father was crucified with Christ, His only Son, on the cross? 2 Corinthians 5:19

But in Isaiah 53:10, we read that it pleased the Lord (God the Father) to bruise him; he hath put Him (Jesus, in the garden and on the cross) to grief. Here, God the Father is taking the blame for killing His own Son at Golgotha.

IS GOD A LIAR?

I used to wonder why Christ was so vehemently opposed when He was here on earth, but I don't wonder anymore. It was because He was revealing the true character of the Father. Satan doesn't really care what we do in our religious services and personal lives, as long as we do not reveal the true character of God. This exposes him more than anything else. That is why he has gotten the religious world involved in so many "good works" programs and "spiritual gimmicks" which are designed to make us feel good and think that we have attained and earned our acceptance with God. But, really, that is just so much rubbish.

Satan is just laughing his head off at us, for he knows as long as he can keep us on his pseudo-spiritual merry-go-round, he doesn't have to worry. As long as he can keep us deceived as to what our true work on earth really is (to reveal the character of God in our lives) he can continue to live and reign on this planet and keep the Great Controversy going on and on endlessly. Yes, as long as Satan can keep religious people so involved in doing the work of the Lord that they forget the Lord of the work, their damnation is assured!

Too many religions depend upon outward show to demonstrate their piety and dedication to God. They think that the height of zeal for God is to always be busy doing something for the "cause." Such an attitude can lead to feelings of pride and self-sufficiency, which often leads to the substitution of business methods used by the world, which inevitably leads us away from our dependence upon God and His Spirit.

But, friend of mine, I have some good news for you. That isn't going to happen always, for God's true character is going to be understood, preached, and lived-out in the lives of a few chosen people called the Elect who will stand through the last great conflict and fully display the truth about God the Father, just as Jesus did. Matt. 24:24.

It will be the most terrible ordeal a person could imagine, and in one's own strength he could never make it, but the Elect will stand through it by permitting the Holy Spirit to demonstrate through them the full and final display of His love.

God isn't a liar. He only hates sin, not us. He doesn't play favorites, nor does He make people sick, or cause accidents, nor does He maim, torture, or kill people. If God could be blamed for just one of those sins, He could be blamed for them all.

But you cannot indict God on the basis of circumstantial evidence, and that is all you have in the Old Testament. The Flood is circumstantial evidence. Sodom and Gomorrah are two more examples of circumstantial evidence often brought forward to prove God kills people.

And there are many other instances, such as the death of Korah, Dathan, and Abiram; and the 250 princes; not to mention Nadab, Abihu, and Uzzah.

Oh, how people love to use these stories to prove that God is a killer. They can hardly wait to watch God kill all the dirty sinners during the seven last plagues, and their mouth is just watering to see the wicked burned up in the Lake of Fire after the 1,000 years, while they stand at a safe distance saying, "Burn, baby, burn," or very piously shaking their heads as they declare, "Give it to them, God. They deserve every bit of it, for we warned them enough times that we were right, and they just wouldn't listen."

Is that the kind of God you serve, my friend? If it is, then you serve the death-god, Satan, the great deceiver, and he has deceived you about the true character of God. For the same God who doesn't break the Tenth Commandment (thou shalt not bear false witness) also does not break the Sixth: " thou shalt not kill." (murder or execute). Same Hebrew word. See page 30.

The Bible testifies to the truthfulness of God. "God is not a man, that he should lie; neither the son of man, that he should repent." Numbers 23:19. "For what if some did not believe? Shall their unbelief make the faith of God without effect? God forbid: yea, let God be true, but every man a liar; as it is written, that thou mightest be justified in thy sayings and mightest overcome when thou art judged." Romans 3:4. Compare Revelation 15:3,4. Proverbs 8:6-9. The cross vindicated God, but He has let this world of sin continue on to permit Satan and man to see the full and total result of their own willfulness. The universe must be permitted to see where sin finally leads...to total self-destruction. God is telling the truth when He declares, "THE WAGES OF SIN IS DEATH." Romans 6:23. Francis Schaeffer has some interesting comments on God's truthfulness and quotes the Westminster Confession to make a point: "First, the Bible tells men and women true things about God. Therefore, they can know true things about God. One can know true things about God because God has revealed himself. The word God was not contentless to Reformation man. God was not an unknown *philosophic other* because God had told men about himself. As the Westminster Confession (1645-1647) says, 'when God revealed his attributes to people, the attributes are not only true to people but true to God.' That is, when God tells people what he is like, what he says is not just relatively true but absolutely true. As finite beings, people do not have exhaustive truth about God, but they can have truth about God; and they can know, therefore, truth about that which is the ultimate universal. And the Bible speaks to men and women concerning meaning, morals, and values." Francis A. Schaeffer, ***How Should We Then Live?***, pp. 84, 86.

CHRIST CLEANSED OUR TEMPLE

In order to demonstrate this ultimate universal to the universe, the Son of God humbled Himself and came to this dark world as a little baby, born in a stable in Bethlehem, under the Law of "Sin and Death." Gal. 4:4; Rom. 8:1-3. This is the same law each of us are born under. In order for Christ to cleanse the temple of our fleshly tabernacle, He had to dwell in it for a time (33 years) and prove that the law could be kept under such circumstances. He did this and cried out in triumph on the cross, "IT IS FINISHED." He had justified and cleansed this sinful body of flesh and now gives it to us that we might live. The bread that I will give is my flesh, which I will give for the life of the world. John 6:51. Jesus fought the battle of life just as we must fight it....in a body of sinful flesh, Rom. 8:3. "Forasmuch then as the children are partakers of flesh and blood, he also himself likewise took part of the same; wherefore in all things it behooved him to be made like unto his brethren, that he might be a merciful and faithful high priest" ....Hebrews 2:16, 17. The cleansing of the heavenly sanctuary in type in the Old Testament on the day of atonement (tenth day of the 7th month), had a personal fulfillment in the life of Jesus, who called His body a "TEMPLE." The Jews then said to Him, 'What sign will you show us for Your doing these things?' Jesus replied, 'DESTROY THIS TEMPLE (or sanctuary) and in three days I will rebuild it.'" John 2:18, 19, Modern Language Version. The KJV says, "Will raise it up," referring to the resurrection.

Christ fully "justified," and cleansed and finished this body temple for each of us. He began where Adam failed or lost, and won. Jesus took up from where Adam fell and redeemed not only Adam's mistake and failure, but the sin and failure of every human being since. But, He did it at a tremendous disadvantage, not having the same advantage Adam had in his pre-fall state. Jesus took upon His sinless nature, our sinful, fleshly nature, but He never sinned, therefore He was never a sinner. His mind was sinless and pure. He did not gravitate toward evil. He was repulsed by it. But He never had an advantage over us. In fact He had tremendous disadvantages due to the power He could use, but didn't. Matt. 4:1-11.

THE INCARNATION ALONE PROVES HE WOULD NEVER DESTROY

By that one unselfish act alone, of taking on a body of flesh to die for us, we can know that Jesus is a life-God, not a destroyer. And the fact that Lucifer (Satan) is the one who led the Jews to take His life, by crucifixion, proves beyond a doubt, that he is indeed the death God. Even the Bible itself declares Satan to be the Destroyer in Rev. 9:11. And they had a king over them, which is the angel of the bottomless pit (grave), whose name in the Hebrew tongue is Abaddon, but in the Greek tongue hath his name APOLLYON. The marginal reading defines the noun APOLLYON as "A DESTROYER." In Psalm 106:37, the word for "DEVILS," is "SHED," meaning DESTROYER OR SPOILER. The reason I am pinpointing the definition of the word DESTROYER, is because many people believe the word DESTROYER sometimes refers to God or Jesus. *Note: In regard to the name Apollyon, we should mention that some theologians interpret Rev. 9:11 as applying to Christ, not Satan. They see this angel as delivering the dead from the pit because He has the "keys" of hell and death, Rev. 1:18. The word "fall" in 9:11 should be translated "descend" or "alight." Christ is here "destroying" death, not people. They cite Exodus 12:23, as proof-that Christ Jesus, our Lord, killed the firstborn. But, did

He do it? Would our Holy, Precious Jesus do that? No, of course, He wouldn't. The text clearly states that the DESTROYER is the one who killed the firstborn of Egypt. The Hebrew word in that text is "SHACHATH," which means to "mar, corrupt or to destroy." We know that Jesus never mars or corrupts. No, Satan and mankind do that, but not Jesus or His Father. Have you ever heard of DEVILED EGGS? What does it mean to "devil" something? Why, it means to chop, cut, and smash it into little pieces, and that is exactly what Satan, the destroyer does, and then blames God for it, and the Lord usually does not argue, but says, YES, I DID IT. JESUS ALWAYS TAKES THE BLAME SO HE CAN BE OUR SAVIOR. ISN'T HE WONDERFUL! PERHAPS HE IS ALSO TRYING TO SHIELD HIS BELOVED LUCIFER, WHO REBELLED AGAINST HIM. IS GOD CAPABLE OF THAT KIND OF LOVE? I BELIEVE HE IS. I CANNOT COMPREHEND IT, BUT I ACCEPT IT AND WANT TO SHARE IT. DON'T YOU?

*The concept of killing and death in the book of Revelation moves very close here in Rev 9 to the ultimate, Divine concept Jesus and Paul taught, i.e. that in dying we live. "Whosoever shall lose his life for my sake and the gospel's, the same shall save it." "I die daily." I Cor 15:31. "I am crucified with Christ: nevertheless I live; yet not I, but Christ lives in me:" Gal 2:20.

Furthermore, the Greek word translated "fall" in Rev. 9:1 is from "pipto" which is from "peto" Strong's 4098, 4072 meaning to "light on," which is the same as "descend." Actually, the name Apollyon could have a dual meaning in Rev 9:11 in that it first applies to Lucifer, who truly was the first "star" who fell from heaven with one third of his angels and became the first Angel of the bottomless pit (grave) for 6,000 years. But then Jesus descended into a body of flesh, died and went to this same bottomless pit to rescue all of his creation, including Lucifer and his fallen angels. By conquering death Jesus received the key to save everyone by unlocking the bottomless pit or grave.

THE BIBLE ALWAYS MAKES GOD RESPONSIBLE FOR EVIL

And so that is why the Scriptures always make God sovereign over every event in history. Whether it is good or evil, the Bible makes God responsible. He always takes the blame in order to protect His children. I know it is not easy to understand, yet for every difficult text, there is always another verse to shed light on the true meaning of that scripture. For example, "Now consider this, ye that forget God, lest I tear you in pieces, and there be none to deliver." Psalm 50:22. Most people would take this to mean that God will tear in pieces those who do not serve Him. If one doesn't dig any deeper, that is all you will get. This is "surface reading." But let us dig deeper with another Psalm. "O Lord my God, in thee do I put my trust: save me from all them that persecute me, and deliver me; lest he (a third personality, Satan, is introduced here) tear my soul like a lion, rending it in pieces, while there is none to deliver." Psalm 7:1, 2. Jesus is the deliverer, but only for those who call upon Him. The Lord is addressed as the One who can SAVE. But, the one who rends or tears in "pieces" is a third party. However, he is not directly pointed out, but safely kept in the background. It was not until Jesus came in the flesh, that God permitted the finger to be put on Satan, in order to save the people. And even then, Satan brought it upon himself by coming out into the open to oppose Christ when Jesus came to deliver demon possessed people and to help others. "How God annointed Jesus of Nazareth with the Holy Ghost and with power; who went about doing good, and healing all that were oppressed of the devil; for God was with Him." Acts 10:38. And so Satan exposed himself as a murderer and a killer when he crucified Jesus on the cross. This was his fatal mistake, but he had no choice if he wished to continue his rebellion against His Creator. His only other option was to repent and admit he was wrong and Christ was right. This, Satan would not do at that time, but the day is coming when he will be "brought to ashes." Satan will be destroyed and Lucifer will be re-born. Ezekiel 28:6-18. "Behold, I make all things new." Rev. 21:5. "The last enemy" to be destroyed is death itself. 1 Cor. 15:26. "Death and hades (the grave) will be cast into the Lake of Fire." Rev. 19:14. Much more will be explained in the rest of this book.

CHAPTER 3

GOD ON TRIAL FOR MURDER

For nearly 6,000 years now, God the Father and God the Son have been on trial for murder. Most of the angels were not sure until the cross. Revelation 12:10-12 indicates that there are beings on other worlds who "overcame" and "rejoiced" when Christ triumphed over Satan at Calvary. Even the angels desire to "look into" this matter, I Peter. 1:12.

Yes, the good and loyal angels had wondered, too. They sometimes wondered if Satan's charges were true or not. It did seem like God sometimes destroyed. There were some things which did seem rather inconsistent, or at least unexplainable. But, they, by faith remained loyal to God in spite of these mysteries. The Great Controversy was revealing the true character of both God and Satan to men and angels alike, as well as unfallen worlds.

The prophets themselves "inquired" about the plan of redemption. They didn't fully understand it themselves, even though they wrote the prophecies about it. They (the prophets) were finally told that these things would not occur during their lifetime (For example, this was told to Daniel. See Daniel 12:8,9,13) "but long years later, during yours. And now at last this good news has been plainly announced to all of us. It was preached to us in the power of the same heaven-sent Holy Spirit who spoke to them: And it is all so strange and wonderful that even angels in heaven would give a great deal to know more about it." 1 Peter 1:10-12. Living Bible. The King James Version says, "which things the angels desire to look into."

God never uses the methods of Satan. Force, coercion, compelling power are the principles of Satan's government. God's authority is based upon love, kindness and compassion. He never uses force. Truth and righteousness are the foundation of His government. Exodus 34:5-7; Psalms 97:2.

DO GOD'S ANGELS OBEY THE TEN COMMANDMENTS?

Are God's angels under the same obligation to obey the law as we are? Yes, they are. "Bless the Lord, ye his angels, that excel in strength, that do his commandments, hearkening unto the voice of His word." Psalms 103:20. Compare Revelation 14:6.

Up until Lucifer rebelled, no created being in God's vast universe had ever questioned his goodness, love, mercy, or equity. Obedience was the spontaneous outgrowth of a perfect and abiding relationship with their Creators, God the Father, and His only Son. The foul miasma of sin sprang up in the heart of Lucifer. See Ezekiel 28:15.

Sin, is disconnecting yourself from God our Creator. This is what broke the perfect harmony, love, and fellowship of heaven. When Adam and Eve separated themselves from God, the same experience of disharmony came to planet earth. Broken fellowship always leads to sin, which in the original Greek simply means "missing the mark." In essence, it is a demonstration of the misunderstanding and misapprehension of the character of God, which the Creator is in the process of correcting by allowing this Great Controversy to continue in the first place.

In order for planet earth to be restored and re-connected to the throne of God we must first understand that the law of God is a transcript of His very character. And fellowship can only be re-established by permitting Christ to reign in our hearts. Jesus came to earth as a fleshly embodiment of His holy law, so that the Father might once again become the center of our lives. And when we have fellowship with God we are at peace with ourselves and with our fellow men. Proverbs 16:7.

Yes, God's angels are subject to the law of God, just as Christ was subject to it while upon earth. Galatians 4:4. Notice how strictly they obey it. "Although the angels in heaven who stand in the very presence of the Lord, and are far greater in power and strength than these false teachers, never speak out disrespectfully against these evil Mighty Ones." 2 Peter 2:11. Living Bible.

Does God observe this same law? Yes, the pre-incarnate Christ of the Old Testament obeyed His own law, as we read in Jude 9. "Yet Michael, one of the mightiest of the angels, when he was arguing with Satan about Moses' body, did not dare to accuse even Satan, or jeer at him, but simply said, 'the Lord rebuke you.'" Living Bible. Not only does Christ not kill angels or human beings, He doesn't even slander or speak harshly to them. Jesus was really inviting Satan to behold His Father's face and be reconciled. Matthew 18:10.

Many sincere Christians have been told that God does not murder but He does kill or destroy in order to punish sin and sinners whenever necessary, now and especially in the final judgment. This is neither correct or true because the Hebrew word for both words is the same, i.e. "Ratsach."

Let us take a look at these two words, "Murder and Kill" in Strong's concordance of the holy Bible. Both of these passages use Strong's word number 7523, ratsach (raw-tsakh') which is a primitive root. It is translated in the Authorized Version (KJV) as slayer, 15 times, murderer 13 times, kill 2 times, murder 4 times, slain 3 times, manslayer 2 times, killing 1 time, slayer 12 times, slayeth 1 time. The finite Hebrew meaning of ratasch is 1) to murder, slay, kill 1a) (Qal) to murder, slay 1a1) premeditated 1a2) accidental 1a3) as avenger 1a4) slayer (intentional) (participle) 1b) (Niphal) to be slain 1c) (Piel) 1c1) to murder, assassinate 1c2) murderer, assassin (participle) (subst) 1d) (Pual) to be killed. Thus we see "kill and murder" are from the same Hebrew word.

Should the claim that Exodus 20:13 and Deuteronomy 5:17's use of "ratsach" mean "Thou shalt not murder," and only this meaning can be taken as true, then this claim leaves a huge hole in solid Biblical interpretation. Why? Because it is obvious that the word, "ratsach" also means "to kill." No one accidentally "murders" because murder is always intentional and premeditated. Our study of the Word of God must be intellectually honest in order to arrive at a correct interpretation. To select a preferred definition of meanings of original words as the only possible interpretation is what many denominations have done in order to sustain their doctrines and thus have distorted the obvious meaning of God's holy word.

We must be bound by honesty to embrace an interpretation that includes accepting all the definitions that come forward from an original word in Scripture. In this case, we see then that "ratsach" means "to kill" as much as it means "to murder." Is there a second witness to this conclusion about the use of "ratsach" in Exodus 20:13 and Deut 5:17? Yes, there is. Jesus Himself gave it to us in Matt 5:21. "Ye have heard that it was said by them of old time, Thou shall not kill; and whosoever shall kill shall be in danger of the judgment...." This passage uses Strong's word number 5407 foneuw phoneuo fon-yoo'-o from 5406; ; v, which is translated in the Authorized Version as 1) to kill 10 times, 2) do murder 1 time, 3) slay 1 time; out of 12 occurrences. It is obvious that the word, "phoneuo" has the preponderance of meaning to be 1) to kill, slay, while the lesser meaning is 2) to commit murder. Furthermore, Jesus clearly shows us that Exodus 20:13's and Deuteronomy 5:17's use of "ratsach" does not mean solely "to murder," but also means "to kill" as well. In confirmation, the context of verse 22 shows that Jesus felt that anger alone leads to killing another, hence the guilt of breaking the law in Exodus 20:13 and Deuteronomy 5:17 would stain that person's heart as much as the act of killing itself. See also Luke 18:20 which is also from 5407 in Strong's. The Bible student who believes that God does not murder, but kills, after understanding this light must ask the Holy Spirit to help him reevaluate all the passages in Scripture on whether God breaks His own law and kills.

In conclusion on this matter, let us remember that in the original language codices there was no inspired punctuation. As a result some passages have been given the wrong meaning. An example is Lamentations 3:38, which reads as a question in the KJV, but in reality is a statement about God's true character.

"Out of the mouth of the most High proceeded not evil and good." When taken as a statement, instead of a question, the meaning of the text is entirely changed.* That God will, because of His holiness, not even speak evil. How much less will He kill? God lives by His own law. God counsels Christ, who is God, in Proverbs 3:1 "My son, forget not my law; but let thine heart keep my commandments." Jesus, who reveals the Father, kept His own law. We know by Jesus' example that the Father keeps His own law too. *See "Septuagint" and "Lamsa" on Lam. 3:38.

GOD'S VENGEANCE

So many Christians misunderstand the true meaning of God's vengeance. Let us reason together on this from Romans 12:14,17: "Bless them which persecute you: bless, and curse not. Recompense to no man evil for evil. Provide things honest in the sight of all men." Is God the Father like that? Yes, He is. We see the Father in Christ praying for His enemies as He was hanging on the cross. He was simply letting his Father live out His own instruction He gave in Matthew 5:43-45. "Ye have heard that it hath been said, Thou shalt love thy neighbor and hate thine enemy. But I say unto you, love your enemies, bless them that hate you." Did Jesus live this way Himself? Yes, He did. "Father, forgive them, for they know not what they do." Luke 23:34.

BUT DOES THE FATHER ACT LIKE THAT TOO?

Matthew 5:45 proves that the Father does act like that, too. "That ye may be the children of your Father which is in heaven: for he maketh his sun to rise on the evil and on the good, and sendeth rain on the just and on the unjust." Notice how the Living Bible renders it: "Love your enemies! Pray for those who persecute you! In that way you will be acting as true sons of your Father in heaven." Matthew 5:44.

Since God never changes (Numbers 23:19,20; Psalms

89:34; Malachi 3:6; Hebrews 13:8; James 1:17), His character is the same in the Old Testament as it is in the New Testament. Jesus and His Father have always acted like this. Although it would appear in the Old Testament that God was a different kind of Person than Jesus portrayed in the New Testament, He really has been the same all the time.

"Dearly beloved, avenge not yourselves, but rather give place unto wrath: (that is, let God handle it) for it is written, Vengeance is mine; I will repay, saith the Lord." Romans 12:19.

Vengeance is from the old French "venger" and from the Latin root,"vindicare," from which we get our English word, "vindicate," meaning "to clear from criticism, censure, suspicion."

The way God clears His name, and ours as well, will be in keeping with His divine character of love and not according to our fallen, carnal way of dealing with people and circumstances. "For my thoughts are not your thoughts, neither are your ways my ways, saith the Lord. For as the heavens are higher than the earth, so are my ways higher than your ways, and my thoughts then your thoughts." Isaiah 55:9. "Man looketh on the outward appearance, but God looketh on the heart." 1 Samuel 16:7.

Special Note:

As you go through this book, you will find the recurring concept that God always takes the blame. Chapter 2 dealt with this, but there is much more to learn for this is a frequent and continuous theme throughout the history of the Great Controversy. In the first two chapters of the book of Job, God is really the one who is on trial in the person of His servant Job. What most people are not aware of is that Job was tested all through the book of Job when his closest friends accused him of harboring some kind of secret sin for which God was punishing him. And then at the close of the book we find from chapters 38 to 42 a voice speaking to Job in a very harsh and haughty tone. For years I did not realize that this was actually Satan who was allowed to speak to Job in this manner. Why? Because this is what Job thought God was like, therefore the true Lord allowed the kind of god Job believed was punishing him to speak to him.

"Out of the storm cloud," Job 38:1. We know this voice is not the true God for he commanded Job to sacrifice animals. Job 42:8. This reveals the real speaker behind all these strong words. For more information re: the contrast and difference between the true and false God go to page 442.

CHAPTER 4

GOD DEALS WITH GREAT LOVE AND TENDERNESS WITH EVERY SINGLE ONE OF HIS CREATURES.

God deals with each individual creature in a most loving manner far beyond our wildest dreams or imaginations. He is infinite in mercy, compassion, and love. He has a thousand ways to solve every problem when we cannot even think of one solution. Ps 147:5 "But thou, O Lord, art a God full of compassion, and gracious, longsuffering, and plenteous in mercy and truth." Ps 111:4; 112:4; 147:4. "The Lord has appeared of old unto me, saying, Yea, I have loved you with an everlasting love: therefore with loving-kindness have I drawn you." Jer 31:3.

When we see someone doing something wrong, we feel compelled, more often than not, to lecture, criticize, and condemn him for his "bad behavior,""aberrant actions," and "sinful ways."

But God doesn't use these methods. The Bible tells us that we all have sinned and "come short of the glory (character) of God." Romans 3:23. Furthermore, Paul speaks very bluntly on this point of judging others: "But do you suppose this, O man, when you pass judgment on those who practice such things and do the same yourself, that you will escape the judgment of God? Or do you think lightly of the riches of His kindness and tolerance and patience, not knowing that the kindness of God leads you to repentance?" Romans 2:3, 4. NAS.

Notice carefully the teaching of Christ on this business of judging. "I have come a light into the world," (Jesus said in Luke 12:49 that He came to bring" fire," that is, a "fire of truth and righteousness") "that whoever believes in me may not remain in darkness. If anyone hears my sayings and does not keep them, I do not judge him; for I did not come to judge the world but to save the world. He who rejects me and does not receive my sayings has a judge; the word that I have spoken will be his judge on the last day." John 12:46-48 RSV.

The fire of God's word will reveal God's love to the wicked in the final Day of Judgment. God's word is a "sword," and it is a "fire." Someone has written this little poem about the power of Christ's name.

> "I know of a world that is sunk in shame
> and of hearts that ache and tire.
> But I know of a name, a name, a name,
> that will set that world on fire."

Yes, Jesus Christ is the fire of God's eternal truth and love. This love and truth will burn in your heart to give you life or it will burn in you to bring death, as it did to Judas.

Paul says the same thing this way. "For we are unto God a sweet savor of Christ, in them that are saved, and in them that perish: To the one we are the savor of death unto death; and to the other the savor of life unto life." 2 Corinthians 2:15,16. Satan tempts us to break the law and then uses it to produce guilt (fire). See Matthew 12:27, Deuteronomy 32:31,37, Job 31:11,12, James 4:11, Matthew 5:25, John 8:50.

When we truly have Jesus and His word in our lives, we will be hated intensely by most of the people in the world. Many even in the church, who do not really know the Lord, will hate us. But, you will be loved by a faithful few who will stand by you through thick and thin. Many heartaches, problems, and obstacles will come into the lives of those who go all the way with Christ. But, if we truly follow Jesus, He will give us glorious victories. Every problem will be solved in a manner which is in keeping with the character of God.

Most of our solutions are based on man's concept of problem solving, which is the use of force and violence. God never directly forces anyone against his or her will. He does not use force and/or coercion to bring a person to a decision. He does, however, permit Satan to use these methods on us to develop our character and demonstrate His keeping power in a human life.

We see this happening in the life of Job and again in the life of Jesus, especially at the beginning of His ministry, when He was tempted by Satan, after He had fasted for forty days. See Matthew 4. God permitted this to happen. He used something that was meant by Satan to bring defeat and death to Christ and the world, to instead bring victory and eternal life to us all.

A man recently wrote to me saying, "I do not agree with your belief that God doesn't directly punish and destroy people. When my children sin, I do not bring in my worst enemy to punish them."

At first glance, the analogy seems to be quite valid, but when we examine it further, we can see how it does not apply at all.

In the first place, we cannot bring God down to our level. We are sinful. He is sinless. We are mortal. He is immortal. He is infinite and omniscient. We are finite and unable to know the future. His ways are higher than our ways, and much better. "For as the heavens are higher than the earth, so are my ways higher than your ways and my thoughts than your thoughts." Isaiah 55:9.

In order for us to realize the horribleness of sin, God permitted the sacrificial system or ceremonial slaughtering of animals for sin to be instituted. The sinner had to kill a lamb so he would realize that it was his own sin that would cause the death of our blessed Redeemer on the cross. This was the type that pointed forward to the death of the Messiah.

In like manner, God allows fathers and mothers to administer punishment to their own children so that the parents might realize that they have passed on their own sinful natures to their children. We "chasten" after our "own pleasure." Hebrews 12:10. But God's "chastening" is not like ours. His ways are "higher" than our ways.

Just as killing a lamb is distasteful to us and makes us cringe, so also a godly parent does not take delight in administering punishment to his precious little one who weeps as he spanks him or her. God permits punishment to come to us. He does not bring it. Lam. 4:6.

Since God is not responsible for passing on to us a sinful nature, which has its own punishment, in and of itself, as we live day by day, He does not need to directly punish us as we need to directly punish our children. Instead, He simply controls, directs, and guides us by permitting and preventing events and circumstances to take place and to develop in our lives.

Without ever interfering with our free choice, He uses each experience to teach us lessons and, yes, to allow punishment to come to us indirectly, if you please. Satan is right there without being invited, doing all he can to destroy us. Proverbs 13:21. God did not invite him, but He does not "cast him out," either. We ourselves must make the decision as to which power (God or Satan) will control us by our own choice. We have the power to cast him out ourselves if we so choose. It is our choice whether he stays or leaves.

As one of my friends said, most people have the "ivory soap syndrome." That is, about 99 and 44/100 per cent of them don't know how God operates, for they misinterpret His character. They are "purely" in the dark about Jesus' true love.

When you begin with a false premise, as this man who wrote to me did, you cannot avoid coming to a wrong conclusion. God is not a man, and because of that, we cannot parallel the way He deals with us with the way He has instructed us to deal with our children.

Of course, there are many similarities and parallels, but there are of necessity many differences because of the sin factor. Satan has been at the side of Christ and mankind from the beginning of the Great Controversy. This fact is made clear in Zechariah 3:1. Satan is the accuser and has been playing his role well from the beginning. And yet God has never used force or coercion in any of His dealings with Satan.

God's patience is incredible when you think about it. Our God is much bigger and mightier than any of us have ever or could ever imagine. And I believe it is a terrible slander against His wisdom and power, when we attribute to Him our own carnal motives and actions. We cannot conceive how such an enemy as Satan could be overcome without force and coercion; that is, a direct blow in the right place at the right time!

Thus we bring God down to our level and make Him after our own likeness. This practice is called anthropomorphism. May God forgive us for doing it, and praise His name, He does forgive us. He loves His innocent creatures and realizes we are the victims in a terrible struggle, but He Himself has become the sacrifice, so He can make the journey through this vale of tears, just as pleasant as possible for us.

If only we knew how much suffering sin has brought to the heart of God, I think we would stop feeling sorry for ourselves. But the main thing I want to emphasize here is that God's government is moral. Truth and love are to be the prevailing power. His nail pierced hands are always outstretched to save, never to smite. His hand is outstretched still. Isaiah 5:25; 10:4; 9:12, 17, 21. Compare Romans 10:21; Matthew 14:31; Psalms 88:9.

God's wrath is not when He gets angry, no. God's wrath is simply the condition in which God no longer is able to restrain man from destroying himself, and He is forced to "give them up." "How shall I give thee up, Ephraim?" Hoses 11:8.

And Paul says, "But God shows his anger (wrath, in the KJV) from heaven against all sinful, evil men who push away the truth from them. So God let them go ahead into every sort of sex sin and do whatever they wanted to—yes, vile and sinful things with each other's bodies. That is why God let go of them and let them do all these evil things, so that even their women turned against God's natural plan for them and indulged in sexual sin with each other." Romans 1:18, 24, 26. Living Bible.

God never turns away from men. Men turn away from God. Paul in A.D. 60 wrote to the church of Rome and asked, "Has God rejected his people? By no means! I myself am an Israelite, a descendant of Abraham, a member of the tribe of Benjamin. God has not rejected his people whom he foreknew." Romans 11:1,2 RSV.

And at the close of human probation God does not cut people off. No, they cut Him out of their lives. He does not reject them, they reject Him. The close of human probation is an act of man against God, not an act of God against man.

Revelation 22:11 makes it clear that God is simply permitting men to remain in the frame of mind they have chosen without any further interference on His part. They have made their final choice or decision as to whom they want to serve, and He honors their right to choose the way they wish to go, which is their own way and to follow their own counsels. Psalms 5:10.

And yet God takes the blame, saying, "I killed them with seven last plagues. In my wrath I am sending seven angels to pour out seven vials upon them because they have rejected me."

It does seem that God is authorizing seven angels to do a lot of destroying down here on this earth, in Revelation 15 and 16. But, Revelation 7:1 shows that four angels are holding back the "winds of the earth," (war, strife, sickness, disease, astral and terrestrial catastrophes, such as cyclones, tornadoes, earthquakes, tidal waves, and so forth: see Psalms 9:6 Isaiah 14:15-20 to show that Satan brings them).

Revelation 15 and 16 simply describe seven angels who are commissioned to command the four angels to no longer restrain all of these calamities. And by withdrawing their restraints, or discontinuing their holding pattern, they are indirectly "pouring out their vials." Like their Lord, the angels receive the blame.

If a person will accept this premise, he immediately obligates himself to acknowledge that the same principle applies to all the destructive acts in the Old Testament as well. This application most people refuse to make; therefore, they are stuck with a "killer god," and there is no escape for them from their dilemma, except to go all the way and accept the military Messiah concept which Satan will fulfill when He comes claiming to be Christ. How tragic that so many will believe this terrible lie about our Lord Jesus Christ and His Father.

In every age, only a few have stood for the truth. Only a few have remained faithful in the face of imprisonment, torture, and loss of property, livelihood, and life itself. Why should it be any different in this final hour? It won't. In fact, it will be worse. But thank God we can make it. Thank God we can know who God is and we can know His character and possess it and reveal it to others. This will be the final work of the Elect. This will be their final message, "Behold your God." Yes, God's people will be giving the final message verbally with their lips, but they will also be showing with actual deeds of love and mercy to the sick and dying what God is really like.

Only those who have carefully studied the life of Jesus and beheld His beautiful character will be transformed into His perfect likeness and thus be enabled to give the final message to the world in both word and deed.

CHAPTER 5

THE LOVE AND FORGIVENESS OF GOD

God never turns away from men. Look at Jesus weeping over Jerusalem. "Oh, how can I give you up?" And again on the cross He is still forgiving them even though they are trying to kill Him. But they could not kill God. No. He gave up His own life for them. "I lay down my life, that I might take it again. No man taketh it from me, but I lay it down of myself. I have power to lay it down, and I have power to take it again. This commandment have I received of my Father." John 2:19; 10:17,18.

After the resurrection did Jesus write Annas and Caiaphas and all the Jews off His love list? No, He didn't. Neither did He appear before them in the privacy of their homes to accuse and condemn them for their murderous deed. He respected their choice and continued to treat them with the same dignity and courtesy that He had always showed them, for He loved them still. Christ never changes. He is the fullness of the Godhead, "For in him dwells all the fullness of the Godhead bodily...." Colossians 2:9. Therefore, we can confidently declare, with theological accuracy, that God the Father never changes either. "Jesus Christ, the same yesterday and today and forever." Hebrews 13:8; Malachi 3:6; Psalms 89:34.

Now, since we know that Jesus is God and that He never changes, and since Jesus is the fullest revelation of what God is really like (He that hath seen me hath seen the Father, He said in John 14:9), we know that God does not kill people. But He, in most cases, is forced to allow death to occur because He cannot interfere with man's free choice. For proof I offer this text: "Yea, they turned back and tempted God, and limited the Holy one of Israel." This is from the Hebrew word "tavah." According to Strong's Concordance 8428, this is the only place the word "limit" is used in the entire Old Testament, which is amazing. It means "to grieve:-limit (by confusion)." God's willingness to forgive in the Old Testament is just as great as it is in the New Testament. But unless we come to Him He cannot forgive us. We will deal with the concept of "Free Choice" later on in this book in regard to God's ***"Ultimate Plan of the Ages"*** for man and angels.

SEVENTY TIMES SEVEN = 490

Now, beloved, let us notice the parallel between the Christ of the Old Testament and the Christ of the New Testament. "Then came Peter to Him, and said, Lord, how oft shall my brother sin against me, and I forgive him? Til seven times? Jesus saith unto him, I say not unto thee, until seven times: but, until seventy times seven." Matthew 18:22.

Is the God of the Old Testament like that? Yes, He is, for the God of the Old Testament is the same Jesus Christ who was speaking to Peter. Notice how He operated in the Old Testament. "Seventy weeks are determined upon thy people and upon thy holy city, to finish the transgression, and to make an end of sins ... and to anoint the most holy." Daniel 9:24.

This is a very familiar prophecy to those who believe in the Three Angels' Messages of Revelation 14:6-12. Jesus Christ of the Old Testament was continually saying, "Father, forgive them, for they know not what they do." I looked up the meaning of the original Greek in my "Novum Testamentun Graece" by Nestle, and discovered that the Greek reads, "O DE JESOUS ELEGEN, PATER, APHES AUTOIS OU GAR OIDASIN TI POIOUSIN."

The tense of the verb "elegen," which is from the root word, "lego," meaning,"to say," and the verb here is in the third person singular, imperfect active, and should be translated as an act that Christ "was doing," and therefore should be rendered something like, "Jesus was saying," or "Jesus kept on saying," or "Jesus was continually saying, FATHER, KEEP ON FORGIVING THEM; FOR THEY KNOW NOT WHAT THEY DO (are doing)." That, to my mind, is very powerful. He kept on forgiving them, for they kept on hurting Him. Phillips translated Luke 23:34, "But Jesus himself was saying, 'Father forgive them; they do not know what they are doing.'"

But Israel of old crucified their Messiah over and over again by their "unbelief." Hebrews 3:19. They killed the prophets and broke down God's altars over and over again. Yet, He kept on forgiving them all through the centuries. The infinite love of God is something we have not understood in the Old Testament, but it is there. Our eyes have been blinded. Even Elijah gave up on them. He couldn't see any sense in putting up with their rebellion any more and testified against Israel. In Romans 11:1-4, Paul spoke of the incident. Elijah was criticizing Israel, and the Jesus of the Old Testament was standing up for them. This was the occasion when the Lord told Elijah that He had "reserved to myself seven thousand men, who have not bowed the knee to the image of Baal." We will deal with this in more depth in Chapter 18.

THE BLOOD OF JESUS

Now let us look at a very interesting passage from Isaiah which will give us tremendous insight into the Christ of the Old Testament. "Who is this who comes from Edom (Edom is Esau, and Esau in Hebrew means "red." Isa 63:1. Compare Obadiah 1:18) "from the city of Bozrah, with his magnificent garments of crimson?" Who is this in kingly robes, marching in the greatness of his strength? "It is I, the Lord, announcing your salvation; I, the Lord, the one who is mighty to save. "Why are your clothes so red, as from treading out the grapes?" Isaiah 63:1,2. Living Bible.

Christ sweat blood in Gethsemane, Luke 22:44 (also see Hebrews 12:4) and was horribly bloodied from Pilate's soldiers and the scourging. "I have trodden the wine press alone. No one was there to help me. In my wrath (Psalms 5:10; 78:49 explains His wrath) I have trodden my enemies like grapes." Isaiah 63:3 Living Bible.

What actually destroyed the Jewish nation? Was it not God's goodness which they despised? And His righteousness and holiness which they rejected? This was the Rock which finally crushed them in their own conscience and mind. Luke 20:18; Matthew 21:41. "In my fury I trampled my foes. It is their blood you see upon my clothes." Isaiah 63:3. Here Jesus takes the blame for the death of the wicked. He pictures Himself as responsible for their destruction. In essence He is saying, "I have killed you with my love. I loved you so much, and it made you so angry, you have bloodied yourselves and each other to try to hurt Me more. I am so sorry; I loved you so much. It is all my fault that you feel so guilty you are killing yourselves."

Now the prophet continues. "For the time has come for me to avenge (justify or vindicate) my people, to redeem them from the hands of the oppressors. I looked but no one came to help them; I was amazed and appalled. So I executed vengeance (carried out his decision to save His people by dying for them) alone; unaided, I meted out judgment (decision to die for them). "I crushed the heathen nations in my anger (let them go their way) and made them stagger and fall to the ground." Isaiah 63:4-6 Living Bible.

Compare this text with Psalms 9:3: "When mine enemies are turned back, they shall fall and perish at thy presence." See also John 18:6, when the mob fell backward to the ground at the time they are about to arrest Christ in the garden. This was no doubt because of the glory of the angel which had ministered to Him during His agony when He even sweat blood. Luke 22:43, 44. See page 341.

This is what Isaiah was predicting that Christ would do. He would tread the winepress alone making grape juice (doctrines or truth) for mankind. Jesus, through the Holy Spirit, pictures Himself as causing the death of those who reject Him. They "drink" the truth and it kills them. They stagger and fall. The blood He shed for them was rejected, and the blood of guilt killed them.

"For the day of the Lord is near upon all the heathen: as

thou hast done, it shall be done unto thee: thy reward shall return upon thine own head. For as ye have drunk upon my holy mountain, so shall all the heathen drink continually, yea, they shall drink, and they shall swallow down, and they shall be as though they had not been." Obadiah 15,16.

To those who love the Lord, He is a savor of life unto life, but to those who reject Jesus, to them He is a savor of death unto death. See 2 Corinthians 2:15,16. The same truth that gives life to the righteous, brings death to the wicked. They die like King Saul (1 Chron. 10:4, 5, 13, 14) and Judas Iscariot (Matt. 27:5) or like Hophni and Phinehas. 1 Samuel 4:10, 11.

GOD'S LOVING KINDNESS

"I will tell you of the loving-kindness of God. I will praise him for all he has done; I will rejoice in his great goodness to Israel, which he has granted in accordance with his mercy and love. He said, 'they are my very own; surely they will not be false again.' And he became their Savior. In all their affliction he was afflicted, and he personally saved them. In his love and pity he redeemed them and lifted them up and carried them through all the years." Isaiah 63:7-9 Living Bible.

In view of this loving endearment, picture in your mind the tender Savior carrying a little lamb such as we find portrayed in Clyde Provonsha's painting, "The Rejoicing Shepherd" and in many other such pastoral scenes portraying the kindness of our Blessed Redeemer.

But the next verse jolts and shocks us with a different image. It is a picture of an angry God who is fighting and killing His people. Listen: "But, they rebelled against him and grieved his Holy Spirit. That is why he became their enemy and personally fought against them." Isaiah 63:10 Living Bible.

This text need not be a problem if we keep in mind the principle we are working from and remember the true character of God, which is evident throughout the great body of Scripture.

God is here again, saying, "Because I let your foreign enemies, disease, famine, weather aberrations, such as earthquakes, drought, and pestilence destroy you, I have personally permitted these things to come upon you. I control all things, for I am God. Worship me only, for I alone have the power to bless you or to curse you (by permitting evil to come when you chose to go your own way)."

HOW GOD USES ADVERSITY

Next we see how the Jesus of the Old Testament brings good out of evil and makes all things "work together for good," Romans 8:28, which is a New Testament concept; but if God never changes, this concept was true in the Old Testament too.

In Isaiah 63:11-14, the prophet shows how adversity turns Israel back to God. They cry out to Him for deliverance from the oppressor (Satan). In our manner of speaking today it is as if they were saying: "O Lord, look down from heaven and see us from your holy glorious home; where is the love for us you used to show, your power, your mercy and your compassion? Where are they now? Surely you are still our Father! Even if Abraham and Jacob would disown us, still you would be our Father, our Redeemer from ages past. O Lord, why have you hardened our hearts and made us sin and turn against you?"

So, true to form, Israel again blames God for all their own failures. But Jesus willingly takes the blame as He did in Pharaoh's day when He said He would "harden" Pharaoh's heart. The prophet continues on in this dialogue between the Divine Shepherd and His wandering sheep. The people are speaking now.

"Return and help us, for we who belong to you need you so. How briefly we possessed Jerusalem! And now our enemies have destroyed her. O God, why do you treat us as though we weren't your people, as though we were a heathen nation that never called you Lord." Isaiah 63:17-19. LB.

These verses show us how God brings us back to Himself,

to His waiting arms of love, by permitting disaster to overtake us, but never greater than we can stand (See 1 Corinthians 10:13).

He always remains our Sovereign and Omnipotent King and Savior by assuming the role of oppressor and destroyer, (Isaiah 14:14; Psalms 35:5,6) and thereby taking the blame, so Satan will not receive any credit and thus have no grounds whatsoever to claim worship. All through these calamities, Satan brings upon us, Christ controls the situation so as to always direct our attention to Him for deliverance. He keeps our affections (our hearts and minds) focused upon Himself by saying, "I am doing this, my child, so look to Me for deliverance. I only am God. I only am able to deliver you and save you. Worship me and all will turn out right in the end." *

Satan is thus defeated in getting any attention or credit. Our whole attention is centered upon Christ. This was how He revealed Himself to ancient Israel. "I am the Lord, and there is none else. I form the light, and create darkness: I make peace, and create evil: I the Lord do all these things." Isaiah 45:7.

This was how God operated in the Old Testament. This was all they had to go on. But, today we have the New Testament record of what God is really like, and we have no excuse for not understanding the true character of God. In the face of Jesus Christ we see the eternal truth about God, which was obscured for 4,000 years. "How shall we escape, if we neglect so great salvation?" Hebrews 2:3.

* This is a classic example of how the Hebrew writers always placed the blame on God for both good and evil. Acts 10:38 tells us Jesus did only good and Psalm 5:4 declares that evil does not dwell with God. 3 John 11 tells us that "he who does evil has not seen God." James 1:13 says that God cannot even be tempted by evil and Jesus taught us to pray, "Deliver us from evil." Luke 11:4. God does not cause or bring evil but He does control it and uses it by turning bad or evil things into good in the long run. For example, He uses the evil Satan and men do to each other or themselves to teach them lessons and discipline them. We all can learn from our mistakes.

Paul says, "All things work together for good, to them that love God, to them who are the called according to his purpose." Rom. 8:28.

CHAPTER 6

DID GOD "KICK" SATAN OUT OF HEAVEN?

A number of people have told me that God does make war against His enemies because He made war against Satan in heaven and kicked him out. They quote Revelation 12:7 to prove their point. I would only say in reply that God did not hurt Satan then anymore than He has since.

God has never used force or coercion and He never will. Jesus cast out demons with His word. "And he cast out the spirits with his word, and healed all that were sick." Matthew 8:16.

In Matthew 12:28 we read that He "cast out devils by the Spirit of God." And Mark 16:17 tells us Christ promised us, "In my name shall they cast out devils." Since Christ never changes, we can safely believe that Satan was cast out of heaven in the same way that he was cast out of human beings when Jesus walked the earth in person. Jesus revealed Himself in truth and power and Satan was very glad to get out of His presence.

Jude 6 indicates that Satan and his evil angels left heaven of their own free will. "And the angels which kept not their first estate, but left their own habitation...." And Revelation 12:4 tells us that it was the dragon's "tail," which drew the third part of the stars of heaven and did cast them to the earth. And in Lamentations 2:1 we see God taking the blame for Israel's fall by Nebuchadnezzar. God claims to have "cast down from heaven unto the earth the beauty of Israel." We know Israel destroyed herself by disobedience.

The point in all this is that people are always so eager to blame God for sin. They want to picture the Creator as the one responsible for this whole mess, concluding that because of the sin problem, God has to use carnal methods to deal with a situation which is out of control. Such is the picture most people have of God. Is it any wonder so few people serve God out of a pure motive of love? Hopefully, this study will change that picture in many minds.

As we look at the Bible as a whole, we can see the image of Jesus in every text. He never changes. We can trust Him. Notice how Job resolves this casting down question. "The steps of his strength shall be straitened, and his own counsel shall cast him down. For he is cast into a net by his own feet, and he walketh upon a snare." Job 18:7.8. In these two verses we see the beginning of Satan's fall and his final destruction by the hand of his followers in the lake of fire. See Ezekiel 28:6-10.

I have maintained from the beginning of my study on the character of God that Satan was not kicked out of heaven as we think of someone being kicked out of an organization here on earth. No, God is not that kind of person. Notice what Jesus said on this very subject when He was here. "Now is the judgment of this world: now shall the prince of this world be cast out." John 12:31. This was a plea and a warning to Satan.

If you compare this with Revelation 12:10 you can see that Christ was referring to the casting down of Satan in the eyes of the holy angels and the unfallen worlds.

When they saw Satan lead the Jews to crucify their Creator, their eyes were opened and they no longer wanted to listen to the Devil's lies about God. This is no doubt what Jesus was talking about when He said, "I beheld Satan as lightning fall from heaven." Luke 10:18. If God forced Satan out of heaven then it was not a "fall." But the Bible teaches us that Satan "fell." He was not pushed, shoved or tripped. He "left," Jude 9 says.

The unfallen worlds made a decision (a judgment) that they would not entertain Satan as a guest ever again. This was what the angels had decided in the precincts of heaven in the beginning of the controversy. The loyal two-thirds of the angels voted him out, and Satan left to go to the remainder of the universe to see if he could gain a following and prove them wrong. This planet is the only one which was deceived by him. The rest have always remained true to God. We are the one lost sheep. Matthew 18:12; Luke 15:4.

HOW WILL SATAN DIE?

Many people ask me how Satan will die in the end. Ezekiel 28:16 states, "and I will destroy thee, O covering cherub, from the midst of the stones of fire." Please note that the fire which destroys Satan does not come from God, but originates from the midst of Lucifer, Ezekiel 28:18. Lucifer's own angels and his closest followers will turn upon him and "destroy" him in the end.

Of course, the way God destroys is made plain in Psalms 5:10. "Destroy thou them, O God; let them fall by their own counsels." In other words, the "death" of the wicked in this age (aion or eon) is something God allows or permits but does not do directly. Yet, in the Scriptures, He makes Himself responsible for it, taking the blame, because He is the Creator. We see this in the death of King Saul who committed suicide. But the Bible claims that God killed him. I Chron 10:4,5, 13, 14. It is also very interesting to note the progression of understanding in the Bible from the Old Testament prophets to the New. For example, the prophet Ezekiel, as noted above, states that God is going to "destroy" Lucifer. The Hebrew word is nethar, Strong's 5426, meaning "to shake off," which is from 5425, nathar, which is defined as meaning "to jump, i.e. be violently agitated; causat, to terrify, shake off, untie:...let loose, make, move, undo." Before I go to Paul's writings regarding the death of Lucifer (now Satan) please note that the Hebrew word can mean to "untie or let loose," which means ***<u>the Creator is going set Lucifer free in the final end and this will effectively stop or cure his rebellion.</u>*** Now, let us go to Hebrews and I think you are going to be pleasantly surprised how beautifully the brilliant theologian Paul explains the "death" of God's first created angel. First, let's read the King James Version. "..He (Jesus) also Himself likewise took part of the same; that through death he might destroy him that had the power of death, that is, the devil; And deliver them who through fear of death were all their lifetime subject to bondage." Hebrews 2:14, 15. The Greek word here is kataluo, Strong's 2673 and is from 2596 and 3089 which includes the basic meaning "to loosen down or dissolve, come to nought, overthrow." The word "destroy" does not mean to annihilate or put out of existence by fire or any other means. The New American Standard Bible translates this verse thusly: "...that through death He might ***render powerless*** him who had the power of death, that is, the devil." In other words, Christ's death on the cross, unmasked Satan so that the universe and all of us living today know the real truth about Lucifer. This revelation of the Father and Satan has taken away his power. It has unplugged his battery, so to speak, and disabled him. Ezekiel 28:8, 9 indicate that Satan will die the same kind of death as all of the lost outside of the city. And what kind of death will that be? It is the death they never died in this life, the death to self, the death of their pride and ego, their desire to always be right and to have their own way. This is the second death which is explained in Rev 20:14. "And death and hell were cast into the lake of fire. This is the second death." This does not mean that Satan and all of his followers are going to get off easy.

The suffering in Lucifer's mind will be terrible as he sees how wrong he has been. Paul tells us that "every knee shall bow," before Jesus. That includes Satan. Philippians 2:9-11. Isaiah 14:16,17 and Psalms 9:6 prove Satan destroys the earth in these last days.

And Jesus described the death of the wicked in this way. "Then shall he (Christ) say also unto them on the left hand, Depart from me, ye cursed, into everlasting fire, prepared for the devil and his angels." Matthew 25:41.

Christ did not say that He had prepared the fire, but simply stated that it had been prepared. Revelation 11:18 indicates that men will be destroying the earth in the last days when Christ comes to "destroy" them with the glory of His truth, which will cause them to destroy each other as they "consume away" on their feet. Zechariah 14:12. This is at the end of this age. The great "age of the ages" will take place after the 1,000 years or millennium. 2 Peter 3:7 tells us that the "heavens (atmospheric heavens or first heaven) and the earth...are kept in store, reserved unto fire against the Day of Judgment and perdition of ungodly men."

At this point, someone might say, "Well, sure God is reserving the earth and heaven so He Himself can destroy it." But, it doesn't say that. It simply states that God is reserving it or preventing it from being destroyed right now. Who has the power to destroy the earth right now with his bombs and rockets and germ warfare? Not God, but man.

So, the Lord is allowing man to pollute the air, water and even his own body. Can't we logically expect an ecological kickback from all of this abuse of our environment and even of our own bodies? God is simply giving man up to himself and his own willful, lustful, carnal and selfish desires...his own counsels (Psalms 5:10) and ways. ***This is God's wrath.*** How could it be any plainer? God has nothing to do with man's destruction. Man is obviously committing suicide very methodically without God's help and against His will for the human race. "I am come that they might have life," the Savior told us. John 10:10. But Satan, the "god of this world," 2 Corinthians 4:4, is blinding the eyes of men so they cannot see who is really systematically leading the world to self-destruction. All the while Satan puts the blame upon God.

But, let us get back to the final death of Satan. Of all the Scriptures I have ever read in the Bible, I believe Ezekiel 28:6-10 is probably the clearest and easiest to understand. "Behold, therefore I will bring (permit to come) strangers upon thee, the terrible of the nations: and they shall defile thy brightness. They shall bring thee down to the pit (grave), and thou shalt die the deaths of them that are slain in the midst of the seas (people)." Revelation 17:15. Now, I quoted only verses 7 and 8. The Lord didn't want anyone to misunderstand, so He gave us five verses with 124 words to make sure everyone got the point.

In addition to that He gives several more verses in the same chapter, plus other verses in other chapters and other books. And it is always punctuated with a clear, "thus saith the Lord," so no one will misunderstand.

Yes, my friend, it is none other than Jesus Christ Himself speaking to us through the prophets of old, telling us how Satan will finally die. What a horrible experience this will be for such a once beautiful angel. The day of judgment will finally come for Lucifer and his suffering will be very great. The Lord has wanted to save him from this but Lucifer refused to listen. Read Isaiah 14:12-17. But let us go into the death of Satan in more depth than we ever have before. In Ezekiel 28:12 the Lord told the prophet, "Son of man, take up a lamentation upon the king of Tyrus." Now, is he referring to the literal king of Tyrus here? No, because notice that he says, "Thou sealest up the sum, full of wisdom, and perfect in beauty. Thou hast been in Eden the garden of God..." Ezekiel 28:12. We know that the prince or king of Tyrus was not in Eden nor was he "wiser than Daniel." v. 3. Nor was the king of Tyre "perfect" at any time or covered with "every precious stone." v. 13. Furthermore, Ezekiel refers to this same being (Lucifer) in Ezekiel 31:2, 3 under the title of Pharaoh king of Egypt and "the Assyrian," and Eden is once again mentioned, v. 9. The Lord is simply covering up for Lucifer, (Satan), all the while appealing to him to repent. "Thou art the anointed cherub that covers and I have set thee so." Ezekiel 28:14. The Lord never demoted Lucifer or kicked him out. He is weeping for him. But let's go down to verses 18 and 19. "Therefore will I bring forth a fire from the midst of thee, it shall devour thee (Satan, the adversary) and I will bring thee to ashes upon the earth in the sight of all them that behold thee. All they that know thee (as an adversary) among the people shall be astonished at you: You shall be a terror, and never shall you be any more."

Notice, beloved, that the fire is coming forth from Satan, not from the Lord. In the final day of judgment the Lord will bring forth from Satan's mind all of the memories he had when he was first created. These will include all of the good times he had with his Creator in the beginning before he rebelled. Then it will include all of the memories of God's long suffering with him in spite of all the evil Satan has done against God, His only Son and His innocent, holy people. This is what will bring Satan to "ashes." Now, let us define the word ashes.

"Among the ancient Hebrews, to put on sackcloth and ashes, or to lie in them, or to sprinkle ashes on the head was a token of grief and mourning , 2 Sam 13:19; Esther 4:1, 3; Job 2:8; Neh 9:1. To sit in ashes was also a sign of penitence Jonah 3:6; cf. Job 42:6." Bible Dictionary, page 82. Therefore, when we see the word "ashes" in Ezek. 28:18 we know this is a sign and prediction of a future event when Lucifer will be brought to "grief, mourning and repentance" in the sight of the whole universe. What a most humiliating and humbling experience that is going to be for Satan. So, when Satan truly repents he will never be Satan again but will be reborn, or born again into the kingdom of God, for the place and position which the Lord created him to fill in the first place, his covering cherub, Lucifer. This will be the return of the first prodigal. And he will be fully restored. So, it is true after all, Satan will never enter heaven. But after he truly repents, and is born again, he will have the same right to be in heaven as the thief on the cross for God's forgiveness has no limits or expiration dates. We all have sinned and come short of the glory of God but when we repent, like the prodigal son we are welcomed back with open arms. And Lucifer is the first prodigal son and the last to finally come back home.

CHAPTER 7

THE CORRELATION OF GOD'S LAW OF LOVE WITH RIGHTEOUSNESS BY FAITH

"And we have known and believed the love that God hath to us. GOD IS LOVE; and he that dwelleth in love dwelleth in God, and God in him." 1 John4:16.

The Bible reveals God's character. God's Ten Commandment law is a standard of character. "The law of the Lord is perfect, converting the soul." Psalms 19:7 It reveals our sins. It cannot cleanse from sin, but it converts our thinking about sin and about ourselves and our standing with God and our fellow men. The law is mentally assenting to Christ so He may live out His will (law) in our minds through His spirit.

To keep the law means to guard against "doing" the sins the law says we must avoid if we would be like God and thus have His character... His righteousness, which is His L_O_V_E. RIGHTEOUSNESS IS LOVE. Loving Jesus means not to "worship other gods," not "to bow down to or make other gods," not to "take His name in vain," not to "break the Sabbath," not to"dishonor your father and mother," "not kill," "steal or bear false witness or covet."

So, we see that there are no "works" in the Ten Commandments. God's holy law describes ten areas of relationship with God and man where we can and must resist evil. "Resist the devil and he will flee from you," is often quoted to show how we are to overcome and get the victory. But, this is only the last half of the text of James 4:7. The first part says, "Submit yourselves therefore to God."

Really, then, it is a love relationship that brings victory. As soon as we become partakers of His divine (Christ's) nature we receive power to obey Him. Get married to Jesus, by allowing His very life to flow into your life. CHRIST'S LIFE IS THE OUTFLOW OF UNSELFISH LOVE. For God is love and

"God was in Christ, reconciling the world unto Himself." 2 Cor. 5:19.

In the Hebrew language the number ten was all encompassing. The ten toes of the image of Daniel 2 represented all the nations that would ever exist until the end of time. And so the Ten Commandments were given to cover every facet of human conduct. If we are to be like God and have His character written in our hearts and stamped upon our lives, we must overcome in each one of these ten areas of human conduct.

Romans 7 documents Paul's utter failure to overcome in his own strength, but his victory was in Christ when he surrendered to what Jesus had already won for him at Calvary. The cross draws us to God for reconciliation, but it is His life "In The Father's Heart," in the most holy place of the sanctuary, in heaven, that saves us. Romans 5:10. He found out that the law was "ordained to life," by saving us from death, and that it is "spiritual," Romans 7:10, so that his inward man "delighted" in God's law, but his carnal fleshly nature sold him into sin. He discovered that he could only "serve the law of God" by mentally assenting to it; that what it warned him against was absolutely right; that he could not avoid sinning in his own strength in these ten areas of human conflict with the forces of darkness.

He discovered the wonderful truth that it is only through Jesus that we gain the victory of surrendering to His beauty and purity of character. Those who discover this relationship find that the Sabbath is more than just a cessation from the regular mundane, but is a special relationship we enter into with the One in whom our soul delights, even the Lord Jesus Christ. You can rest on any day, or avoid work on any day, but you can SABBATH ONLY ON THE SABBATH. You cannot SABBATH on any other day except the seventh day of the week.

There is no English equivalent for the Hebrew word "SHAVATH" or "SHABATH." The word "rest," simply means, "To Sabbath." Israel's problems in Egypt really began when they started keeping the seventh day Sabbath. "Pharaoh said...ye make them 'rest' (Sabbath) from their burdens." Exodus

5:5. Persecution is coming again. Revelation 13.

Now, when we understand the law in its true light and let our Creator write it in our minds (Jeremiah 31:33), we begin to understand the character of God and the relationship we are to have with Him by "guarding" His law. You might say that the law is our marriage vows when we get married to Jesus. And since the law is a transcript of God's character that law or character is inscribed in our lives as we seek to be like Him more every day.

It is impossible to talk about the love of God without explaining the relationship of the law to His love for us. These ten restrictions were given to us so that we might have life to the full and experience fullness of joy. In this study I wish to show: 1) that the Character of God as revealed in His law has never changed, and thus God never changes; 2) that God's law is founded upon that eternal principle of love. Nehemiah 9:6-15.

The Law of God, the moral law, is as unchangeable as God Himself. The Law of God is the same in the Old Testament as it is in the New Testament. I submit that Jesus Christ gave us that law on Mount Sinai and that it was not nailed to the cross or changed in any way by the death of Jesus, for it is perfect. Psalms 19:7. Only the ceremonial laws of animal sacrifices were nailed to the cross.

Just as the law is the same in both the Old Testament and the New Testament, so character is the same in the Old Testament as well as in the New Testament, just as grace is the same in the Old Testament as well as in the New Testament. I further submit that just as many people have misunderstood the law of God in the Old Testament and how it has been carried over into the New Testament unchanged, so many Christians today, who claim to believe the whole Bible, have misunderstood the truth about God's love and character in the Old Testament and have failed to see how the God of the Old Testament is the same exact God of the New Testament.

Somehow they have not been able to correlate the actions

of the God of the Old Testament, who was Jesus Christ, with the God of the New Testament who also was Jesus Christ.

Now, let me ask you a logical question. If we believe His law was the same in both testaments and that His grace was the same and that His love was the same, why do we think that His character would not be the same also since His law is a transcript of His character? The word of the Lord says it was the same in both the Old and New Testaments.

Now, if the final issue in this old world is going to be over the Law of God, then it must also be over the character of God, for the law is a transcript of His character. Therefore, if people have a question regarding the validity of the Law of God today for man, then they also have a question about His character as well, and some questions about His love, for the law reveals His character of love.

We know that a great apostasy has taken place in the church today, but it is to get even worse. Now, we have always taught that the final issue in this world will be over the Sabbath, and it will be, but the final message to go to the world is not just the right day to worship on; but, the final message to go to the world is also the LOVE OF GOD, as revealed in the Sabbath message.

The reason the world is in such a sorry mess is because people are apprehensive (afraid of) about God. His character has been misrepresented from the very beginning. Does not this point up the tremendous importance of giving a message today that will enlighten the darkness of our modern minds? Is it not time that men and women everywhere found out the real truth about God? The final message to go to this dying world must of necessity be about the love of God in Christ.

The importance of God's love as revealed in His law has never been fully understood and therefore, never fully realized by His people. Satan has misrepresented and distorted God's real personality or character so much that men are afraid of God and even hate Him or deny His existence. But, there is a very good reason why Satan has done this. He knows that if we find out what God is really like we will desire with all our hearts to be like our heavenly Father.

THE REAL PURPOSE OF RIGHTEOUSNESS BY FAITH

If you were to ask a sincere Christian why he is trying to study deeply into Christ Our Righteousness, he would probably say something like this: "Well, I am trying to learn how to receive enough faith from Christ so I can be like Him; that is, live the same kind of victorious life that He lived." And I think that is a very good answer. In our study, however, I wish to tie two additional, or shall we say "neglected," aspects of Christ's Righteousness into the picture, to enable us to see the whole concept in its totality and completeness.

Many sincere Christians who believe in Jesus want nothing to do with the Law. But they do not realize that when they say this they are actually rejecting Christ's righteousness, for His rightness or righteousness comes as a result of His perfect obedience to His Father's Law, which is the center of the whole controversy. Jesus became righteous and formed a Character like His heavenly Father because He permitted His Father's love and power and Law to be imprinted upon His mind and life fully.

And so the LAW OF GOD or the TEN COMMANDMENTS and GOD'S CHARACTER are two aspects of the study of RIGHTEOUSNESS BY FAITH that I wish to emphasize and tie in here in this study. Notice Psalms 119:172. "My tongue shall speak of thy word; for all thy commandments are righteousness." The word CHARACTER is not used in the Bible per se, but we can find it implied all the way through. For example, the word "image" in Hebrews 1:3 is from the Greek word ***charakter***, which means "an exact copy or representation: i.e. express image," as Paul says, ***"Who, being the brightness of His glory, and the express image of his person."*** Heb. 1:3. Character means the distinctive qualities or traits that form a person's personality or identify him. It has to do with his conduct more than anything else. That is why the Ten Commandments are called the MORAL law; for this law has to do with moral conduct and behavior in society.

The word *moral* is not used in the Bible, but we can see that the Ten Commandments are concerned with our conduct or morals. The reason Jesus was able to live a perfectly righteous life was because His Father's Law or Character was written in His heart. "I DELIGHT TO DO THY WILL O MY GOD: YEA, THY LAW IS WITHIN MY HEART." Psalms 40:8.

The very next verse tells how Jesus says to His Father, "I have preached RIGHTEOUSNESS in the congregation: lo, I have not refrained my lips, O Lord, thou knowest. I have not HID THY RIGHTEOUSNESS WITHIN MY HEART; I HAVE DECLARED THY FAITHFULNESS and thy Salvation: I have not concealed thy LOVING-KINDNESS AND THY TRUTH from the great congregation." Psalms 40:9,10.

Now, I want us to catch the full import of these scriptures. Jesus is here talking to His Father in heaven and telling Him that He is revealing to the people all the truth about Him. Now, keep in mind that when we are talking about truth, and righteousness, and holiness, and perfection, and law, and character, we are using words that are all synonymous or equal to the attributes of God. Now why would Jesus want to make such a big deal about His PR campaign down here on earth for His Father? Someone might say, "I thought everyone already knew that God was a nice person." I speak like a modern to make a point. But wait a minute. All that the Jews had to go on for their concept of Jehovah is what they had read in the Old Testament Scriptures and what they themselves had built up in their traditions. What kind of picture did they have of God? Well, their rigorous adherence to multitudinous rules and man-made regulations indicated that they believed in a very strict and unyielding, unbending deity who would serve judgment upon the sinner without a moment's notice for the least departure from any of these laws.

It was not a religion to bring joy or happiness to the heart or face. When you put with this the continuous slaughter of animals and the constant haggling and quarreling over the purchase price of animals for sacrifice, one begins to see the kind of picture that generation had of God.

He was to them a God that demanded strict obedience and a lot of blood and money. He was a God who loved to destroy His enemies in battle to show His superiority over the false gods of the heathen. He was a God who would curse you if you disobeyed. "The Lord shall send upon thee cursing, vexation, and rebuke, in all that thou settest thine hand unto for to do, until thou be destroyed, and until thou perish quickly...." He was a God who would smite you. "The Lord shall smite thee with a consumption, and with a fever, and with an inflammation and with an extreme burning, and with the Sword, and with blasting, and with mildew." Deuteronomy 28:15,20,22.

Is it any wonder that they considered all sickness and disease a direct judgment from God? To help the sick and suffering would be interfering with God's disciplinary measures. The parable of the Rich Man and Lazarus (Luke 16:19-31) pointed out this concept. So, is it any wonder that the Jews did not accept Christ when He came to them talking about a God of love and mercy and telling them that He had been sent to heal the sick and poor? It just blew their minds away. But why? Take your Bible with me now as we study the God of the Old Testament and try to discover who He really is.

CHAPTER 8

IS THE JESUS OF THE OLD TESTAMENT THE SAME AS THE JESUS OF THE NEW TESTAMENT? HEBREWS 13:8

The Messiah the Jews expected was obviously an altogether different God than Jesus claimed to be. The Jews wanted a Military Messiah who would lead them to victory over the hated Romans and set them up as rulers over the whole earth.

The Jews expected the Messiah to force them to accept Him. They imagined that He would overwhelm their wills and cause all men everywhere to acknowledge his power. Christ's greatest test was the temptation to compel his tormentors to confess that He truly was the Son of God.

But the exercise of force or coercion is contrary to the nature of God and to the principles of His law and government.

When Jesus announced the principles of His kingdom in the Sermon on the Mount, He punctured the dream balloon of the Jewish leaders. Matthew 5:1 through Matthew 7:29 outlines His government. It was all based on love to both God and man. Not a trace or thread of sinful human passion was anywhere to be found in all of the Savior's words or acts. Instead of approving of the proud way the religious leaders of the nation were carrying on and condemning the Romans and other unenlightened (cursed by God in their eyes) nations of the world, Christ pronounced a special blessing on those who were lowly in their own estimation. "Blessed are the poor in spirit for theirs is the kingdom of heaven. Blessed are the meek, for they shall inherit the earth." The only kind of people who would qualify for the Kingdom of God would be those who were "mourning" over their spiritual poverty and were meek and lowly or, in other words, humble in their own eyes as well as in the eyes of the world.

The pushy and the proud would be left out. But the merciful, the inwardly pure, and the peacemakers and persecuted who were rejoicing in their trials and praying for and loving their enemies were all star candidates for the Kingdom Jesus had come to establish.

This doctrine was the exact opposite of what the Jews believed and taught. Jesus' new teaching really bent them out of shape. It just blew their minds away, as they say today, and they came unglued at the very seams. But in addition to this, He openly rebuked these Jewish leaders before all the people. Yet, they brought it upon themselves. Christ had tears in His voice as He spoke for He knew most of them would not accept His counsel. Is it any wonder that they called Him an imposter? Does it surprise you that they claimed His wonderful miracles were done through the power of the evil one? They were desperate to maintain their position, and their explanations were equal to their desperation. But, let us look at some of the reasons they probably felt as they did.

"Read the history of our glorious past," they no doubt exclaimed. "Jehovah has always delivered His people by war and conquest. He has always overcome our foes with military force." This is what they no doubt said, but was it true that God had *ALWAYS* done this? No, it was not true. Take the Red Sea experience, for example, when the people were blaming Moses for bringing them to a seemingly impossible impasse. "And Moses said unto the people, fear ye not, stand still, and see the salvation of the Lord which he will shew to you today: for the Egyptians whom ye have seen today, ye shall see them again no more for ever. The Lord shall fight for you, and ye shall hold your peace." Exodus 14:13,14. It was not God's original plan for Israel to fight with sword and spear. IT WAS NOT HIS WILL THAT THEY SHOULD GAIN THE LAND BY WARFARE, BUT BY SIMPLY OBEYING HIS COMMANDS. Even though it was the people's idea to fight with the sword, not God's idea, He allowed them to have their own way or desire. But He always stayed with them to save them from the worst effects of their wrong choice as He did when they demanded a king. 1 Samuel 8:5. This was also the case when they demanded flesh food in their 40 years of wandering in the wilderness. "So they did eat, (quail) and were well filled: for He gave them their own desire." Psalm 78:26-31. Cf. Numbers 11:31-35.

The law of God is the central issue in the great controversy. Therefore, Satan is constantly working to prove that God's law is too strict. That it is impossible for men to keep it and, of course, that God is unjust and unfair to impose such restrictions upon mankind.

As soon as Satan can successfully tempt someone to break the law, he has the right to afflict and sometimes destroy him. Ezekiel 21:31. Satan then blames their death upon the Lord. Read Job 1 and 2 and you will see how God gets the blame for destroying the property of Job. "The fire of God is fallen from heaven, and hath burned up the sheep, and the servants, and consumed them." Job 1:16.

That was actually the fire of Satan, but God got the blame. Satan can bring fire down from the skies (atmospheric heaven), according to Revelation 13:13. God never changes, Malachi 3:6 and Hebrews 13:8 declare. Therefore the way He deals with the saints in the Old Testament is the way He will deal with them in the New Testament. And the way He deals with the sin problem in the Old Testament is the way He will deal with it in the New Testament. He leaves it up to us to study sufficiently to clarify the seeming contradictions and inconsistencies. We will deal with "God's fire" later in this book.

In 2 Corinthians 10:3-5 we read an enlightening statement about how God makes war. "For though we walk in the flesh, we do not war after the flesh: (For the weapons of our warfare are not carnal, but mighty through God to the pulling down of strongholds;) Casting down imaginations, and every high thing that exalteth itself against the knowledge of God, and bringing into captivity every thought to the obedience of Christ."

About the year 896 B.C., good King Jehoshaphat was faced with annihilation by the "children of Moab, and the children of Ammon," and a few others. The story is in 2 Chronicles 20. The king called for a fast and evidently the better part of Judah fasted and prayed with him. Jehoshaphat's heart was right with God and he prayed for himself and all the people. His example truly is one we can look to in our times of trouble today. Notice his choice of words. "We have no might against this great company that cometh against us; neither know we what to do: but our eyes ARE UPON THEE." Here is a man that knew how to cut through all the red tape and go directly to the throne room of God.

The answer came immediately through the Spirit of Prophecy. Jahaziel, a Levite, and a son of the line of Asaph, came under the power of the living God and spoke. "Be not afraid nor dismayed by reason of this great multitude; for THE BATTLE IS NOT YOURS, BUT GOD'S. YE SHALL NOT NEED TO FIGHT IN THIS BATTLE: SET YOURSELVES, STAND YE STILL, AND SEE THE SALVATION OF THE LORD WITH YOU." What a message! After all the battles David won you would think that some young firebrand would jump up and say, "This guy has totally freaked out of his mind! If you think I'm going to just walk out there and let those no-good so and so Moabites and Ammonites cut my head off you are crazier than a loon. Man, I am taking my sword and trusty slingshot. I'm not a coward. God helps those who help themselves."

But that didn't happen. Here is what really happened, and it is the secret to the great victory that followed. "And Jehoshaphat bowed his head with his face to the ground: and all Judah and the inhabitants of Jerusalem fell before the Lord, worshiping the Lord." 2 Chronicles 20:18. Living Bible.

And verse 19 says the Levites of the children of the Kohathites as well as the Korhites praised the Lord with a loud voice. The next morning Jehoshaphat's battle speech was very simple. Maybe Knute Rockne would have laughed and General Patton might have cried. But, all heaven rejoiced as the king said, "Believe in the Lord your God, so shall ye be established; believe his prophets, so shall ye prosper." Verse 20.

The battle plan was simple. They were going out to meet the enemy, singing praises to their invisible God. "He appointed singers unto the Lord, and that should praise the beauty of holiness, as they went out before the army, and to say, PRAISE THE LORD; FOR HIS MERCY ENDURETH FOR EVER." The interesting thing about this was that the king had "consulted with the people," on this strategy before they did it. He carried the people with him.

It appears that there was a wonderful spirit of harmony and unity among these people due to this national crisis. Is this not God's perfect will for His people today? And wasn't it His perfect will for Israel all through their history? The answer in both cases is "Yes." In this study I hope to explain why God "permitted" so much war and slaughter and bloodshed. If we keep in mind that God's "permissive will" is not His "perfect will," it will help us understand a lot of seeming contradictions and apparent discrepancies.

As these helpless and beautiful people marched out to meet the enemy with a choir at their head singing, "HIS LOVING-KINDNESS IS FOREVER," the opposing hosts went berserk, and masochistically turned upon themselves. "And at the moment they began to sing and to praise, the Lord caused the armies of Ammon, Moab, and Mount Seir to begin fighting among themselves, and they destroyed each other!...not a single one of the enemy had escaped....The fear of God fell upon them. So Jehosaphat's kingdom was quiet, for his God had given him rest." 2 Chronicles 20:22, 24, 29, 30 in The Living Bible.

Everything that happens is not God's will, but nothing can happen in this sin-cursed world to defeat God's ultimate plan of salvation. Romans 8:28 is still true. "And we know that all things work together for good to them that love God, to them that are the called according to his purpose."

The destruction of the enemies of God in Jehosaphat's day is an example of how the wicked will be destroyed in the final day. Since I will explain this in great detail later, I intend only to refer to it now. Jeremiah 25:31 tells us that God is going to "plead with all flesh; he will give them that are wicked to the sword, saith the Lord." The New English Bible says, "For the Lord brings a charge against the nations, and has handed the wicked over to the sword."

We shall see more and more as we go along in this book that God doesn't actually destroy or kill anyone at all. When people are killed by a physical act of nature (an act of God, as the insurance companies call it), or sickness of any kind, God always says, *"I the Lord have done this."* He always takes the blame, for He never justifies Himself, first of all, and secondly, He must remain sovereign (in control or boss), for mankind cannot be saved unless they worship the Creator, be it out of fear or love.

To establish a dichotomy of power would be to establish a dichotomy of worship: one directed toward a God of evil and one toward a God of good; mankind could not be saved on that basis. In order to receive worship from all His creatures, God must take all the credit and all the blame no matter whether a person gets sick or gets well. In both cases we are commanded to worship God, for He "does it all."

This concept of God always taking the blame for the sake of His sovereignty explains the difficult passage in Isaiah 45:7, "I form the light, and create darkness: I make peace, and create evil: I the Lord do all these things." In the preceding verse 5 the Lord said, "I am the Lord, and there is none else, there is no God beside me." In Isaiah 53:10 we read, "Yet it pleased the Lord to bruise him; he hath put him to grief." Did God the Father "bruise" His only Son on Calvary? No, but he "created" the possibility for it to happen and permitted or allowed Satan and his angels to urge on fallen humans to "bruise" Him on the cross. As always, God took the blame and said, "I did it. I bruised and hurt my only Son." Rather than take away the gift of free moral agency or choice, He chose to suffer Himself so that mankind might see that He is truly pure, total love.

When we read, therefore, in Jeremiah 25:31 that God "gives the wicked to the sword," it simply means that he "creates" the possibility for them to destroy themselves by withdrawing all of His restraints.

Before this age comes to an end and the 1,000 years begin, every human being will have one last chance to choose life or death, truth or falsehood. See Revelation 22:11,12. Probation will close for this age and every character will be frozen, every case closed and decided whether they will be translated and taken to heaven or die and sleep in the grave until after the 1,000 years at which time they will all be resurrected and live on this earth for "a little season" or another life time. See Isaiah 65:20. Let me make it very clear that the close of human probation is not an arbitrary act on the part of God. No. The close of human probation is an act of man against His Creator. It is his final choice to go his own way and do his own thing. This choice on man's part, the Bible always calls "God's wrath" or "anger." See Romans 1:19, 24, 26; and Psalms 78:49.

In Isaiah 45:7 where we read that God "creates evil," the Hebrew word for evil is Ra', which may mean either that moral evil which springs from within or trouble that comes upon one from without. "Ra" is the Egyptian name for Lucifer or light.

God permits "evil," whether moral or material, that men and angels may witness the result of a departure from the eternal principles of right (see on Daniel 4:17). In the Bible God is often held responsible for that which He does not restrain or stop. (see 2 Chronicles 18:18).

Psalms 5:10 says "Destroy Thou them O God, let them fall by their own counsels." The Bible writer used the Hebrew word "asham" meaning "to be guilty." In the form used here, the word "asham means to hold guilty." David desires that God would treat his enemies as guilty, which they undoubtedly are. He requests that they may "fall by their own counsels," so, that their own plans may be the means of their destruction (see Psalms 7:15, 16; Proverbs 26:27; 28:10). THIS CONCEPT IS FREQUENTLY USED IN THE OLD TESTAMENT. SIN DESTROYS ITSELF.

If we can always keep this one concept in mind: that God

always holds Himself responsible for that which He does not prevent, then we will never have any problems with phrases like, *"And God smote them,"* or *"God's wrath waxed hot at them and consumed them,"* or *"In his anger he slew them,"* and others. Just as we have to learn what the Bible means when it speaks of "forever and ever" and "eternal," so we must learn what "God's wrath" and "God's anger" actually refer to.

A good example of this is the death of the Egyptian army at the Red Sea. Satan is a double-crosser. That is, he betrays, swindles and finally destroys those who serve him. That is precisely what he did to Pharaoh and the Egyptian army. Satan knew the power of God. He was certainly aware of Christ's power to protect the over two million souls who left Egypt. Exodus 12:37 tells us there were 600,000 men alone. If there were only four to a family, that would make two million alone, but the families were no doubt much larger.

Satan is the "DESTROYER," Revelation 9:11. If he could not recapture or kill the Israelites, he would gladly destroy all of the Egyptians. Exodus 12:23 clearly shows that it was "The Destroyer" (Satan), who killed all the first born of Egypt. Now, if he could lead the whole Egyptian army (600 chariots plus horses) with murder in their hearts to pursue after Israel, he would have a "legal right," to destroy them. So actually, in bringing the Egyptian host down to the Red Sea he was planning to "double-cross," Pharaoh and kill him and his army. The commandment says,"thou shalt not kill (murder)." Exodus 20. And Obadiah 15 says, "As thou hast done, so shalt it be done unto thee."

In other words, Satan could not legally destroy the Egyptian's firstborn until he led them to have hatred in their hearts toward the Israelites. When he was successful in doing this, he then had a legal right to kill the firstborn. Matthew 5:21, 22. Now, again he leads Pharaoh and the Egyptians to reverse their decision to let Israel go. Then he inspires them to recapture and/or kill the Israelites at the Red Sea, and as a result, bring the death decree upon their own heads. God had a legal right to hold the water back for His own people, but He did not have a legal right to protect the Egyptians. It rained upon the Egyptians. Psalms 77:17, 18. God did not bring this rainstorm. Satan did. God's angels withdrew and Satan's angels brought disaster upon the Egyptians, but God took the blame for it, Exodus 14:24-28. God did not have a legal right to continue holding back the waters and withdrew. The double-cross was successful. The "East wind" was what opened up the Red Sea. Exodus 14:21. The East wind was always used to destroy. Genesis 41:6; Hosea 12:1. If God does not destroy who really opened up the Red Sea and set a trap for the Egyptians? See additional note 19. Page 532.

CHAPTER 9

JESUS IS THE GOD OF THE OLD TESTAMENT

In addition to this concept of what "God's Wrath" means, we must remember that when the Bible in Isaiah and Jeremiah and Psalms and all the other books of the Old Testament use the word Lord or God or Jehovah, the writer is often, but not always, referring to none other than Jesus Christ Himself. More on this later.

For example, "For he said, Surely they are my people, children that will not lie: so he was their Savior. In all their affliction he was afflicted, and the angel of his presence saved them: in his love and in his pity he redeemed them; and he bare them, and carried them all the days of old." Was this Jesus who led them in the cloud by day and in the fiery pillar at night? Yes, it was. Nehemiah 9:6-21 proves that it was Jesus. Cf. John 1:1-3, I Cor 10:1-4 and Hebrews 1:1-3.

We must now ask ourselves a very logical and important question. If this was Jesus, and we must admit that it was, acting in perfect harmony and accord with the Eternal Father and the Eternal Holy Spirit, just as He did when He was upon earth in the flesh, then we must come to the only harmonious conclusion we can come to; which is, that Jesus in the Old Testament did not hurt, maim or kill anybody anymore than He did when He walked the dusty roads of Galilee in a "body of sinful flesh" like ours. Phil. 2:7; Romans 8:3.

Any other conclusion denies the very essence of and nature of Deity; namely, that God never changes and that He knows all things ahead of time (we call that quality omniscience, i.e., all knowing). If He is, and Isaiah 46:9,10 tells that He is, then He would never have to change His plans for that would deny the very basis of omniscience, which is that an omniscient God is already two steps ahead of the devil and all mankind.

In fact, He is not only two steps ahead, but He has indeed

already gone the whole route. God's foreknowledge is an absolute necessity in order for us to have our free moral agency. But this foreknowledge also causes our God a lot of suffering. "In all of their affliction he was afflicted, and the angel of His presence saved them: in his love and in his pity he redeemed them; and he bare them, and carried them all the days of old. But they rebelled, and vexed his Holy Spirit." Isaiah 63:9, 10.

Now, the angels are not omniscient. They do not know the future anymore than we do unless God reveals it to them. Of course, they may not be limited by time and space like we are, but since they are created beings (Ezekiel 28:15), and since one-third of the original number rebelled and left heaven (Jude 6) to try to carry this world and as many other worlds with them, as possible, we can only conclude that they are not able to foretell the future as God does and are, therefore, not omniscient.

The rebellion of Lucifer (Satan) was over the authority of God the Father and His Son and His right to make the laws. Lucifer wanted that position (Isaiah 14:12-14). He wanted to be the big man who sat "upon the mount of the congregation, in the sides of the NORTH." Why did He want that North side? What is so special about the North side? Psalms 75:6 tells us, "For promotion cometh neither from the east, nor from the west, nor from the south. But God is the judge: (one who makes and interprets law) he putteth down one, and setteth up another."

That was the real reason. Lucifer wanted to be the one who controlled all things. Because our wonderful Creator God already knew what would happen and how it would all turn out, He did not need to use force or coercion, but was able to let each angel decide which way they desired to go. This was the way He operated at the beginning of the great rebellion and the way He has operated ever since. And it is also the way He will continue to operate until all things are restored. Acts 3:21.

"Thou shalt die the deaths of the uncircumcised by the hand of strangers: for I have spoken it, saith the Lord God." This text explains Satan's future. Jesus never laid a hand upon him in the beginning of the rebellion and He won't lay a hand upon him in the final day except to invite Him to come back home like the prodigal son. The very law he despised will be that which brings him and all who have despised it with him to "ashes" or remorse and repentance. "The Law of God is like a fire that pursues a man's conscience until he repents. God's fire is His love." Song of Solomon 8:6. He lovingly pursues us until He catches us like He did Saul of Tarsus, who was destroyed on the road to Damascus and became Paul the apostle. And that is how Satan will be destroyed and be reborn as Lucifer.

In Matthew 10:28, we read, "And fear not them which kill the body, but are not able to kill the soul: but rather fear him which is able to destroy both soul and body in hell." The word "hell" here is Gehenna or the fiery hell which destroys. It is both symbolic and literal. Symbolically fire represents love or hate. Literally, this GEHENNA "hell-fire" represents the literal fire the wicked will ignite themselves to burn themselves up. Someone will miss the point here and say, "See, God does kill people in the last day. This is His strange act." Let me answer that objection with a question. If it has not been necessary for God to destroy Satan or any of his angels so far, why should it be necessary for Him to use arbitrary (despotic) measures against human beings today or in the future? Are humans harder or easier for God to control and work around to carry out His plans? You say, "the fallen angels are harder to work around." I agree. But where in the Bible does it state that God ever hurt or killed any of them? It doesn't.

Therefore, if it is true that God has at no time ever lifted up His hand against Satan, before or after he "left" heaven in his attempt to win the remainder of the universe to his side, why in the name of all that is pure and true and righteous and holy, should it ever be said that God has ever hurt any human beings? That to my mind would be the height of injustice, and God is a righteous judge, the Bible says.

Some teach that Satan is stoking the fires of hell for the wicked and then they turn right around and say that Satan will burn with the wicked through all eternity. If that is true, then Satan and God are partners. God makes the rules. Satan tempts men to break them so God can send them to hell where He has employed the devil to torture them in hell-fire. This is not only a terrible slander against the character of God, but totally illogical. Why should God make the greatest sinner of all (Satan) the one who punishes the lesser sinners or humans?

Furthermore, Satan doesn't begin being punished until the end of the world. At that time Satan is supposed to begin burning himself. The justice of God is only about 6,000 years behind schedule, according to that view. But, what about those of us who do not believe in an ever-burning hell fire now or later on? Are we not as illogical as others, only in a slightly lesser degree? How is that, you ask? Well, to put it bluntly, some teachers are accused of defaming the name of God by picturing Him as a terrible bully who is torturing or will torture (depending upon your brand of theology about hell-fire) the wicked in an ever-burning hell, while others burn them only a little while.

The only difference is that the blowtorch God has in His hands to burn up the wicked is much smaller and doesn't last as long.

Either view makes God out to be an arbitrary despot instead of a loving creator who gives free moral agency to every one and never takes it away.

Which kind of Creator would you prefer to serve? The despot Creator or the loving Creator who never uses force or takes away the power of choice? If we are to be like Jesus in every particular and have His lovely character, then we may have to rethink some of our concepts about Him in the Old Testament. It is a duty impossible to avoid. So, how will the Creator deal with those who are lost in this age? The word "age or eon" is from the Greek word "aion" and is critical in understanding how God will deal with the wicked after the 1,000 years. Some believe God will burn or torture them in everlasting hell fire forever and ever while others, more benevolent say that they will only burn for a little while and then they will cease to exist. This is called the extinction or annihilation theory of the final judgment. Most Christians do not realize there is a third alternative or belief or that the Bible actually teaches it. In fact, this concept was taught in the early church up until the 5th century. Peter called it the *"Times of Restitution of all things."* Restitution is an old English word for Restoration. "Whom heaven must receive until the period of restoration of all things about which God spoke by the mouth of His holy prophets from ancient times." Acts 3:21. New American Standard. The KJV reads "from the beginning."

The salvation of all mankind is a recurrent theme throughout the Bible which most people miss. God locks up all mankind together in stubbornness, that He should be merciful to all. Rom 11:32. *See page 81. "Our SAVIOR, God, Who wills that all mankind be saved and come into a realization of the truth." I Timothy 2:4. Now, notice this one. "The Lord is not slack concerning His promise, as some men count slackness; but is longsuffering to usward, not willing that any should perish, but that all should come to repentance." Now, beloved, I just looked up the word "will" and "willing" in the original Greek in Strong's concordance, (1013 & 1014) and discovered that it comes from the Greek word "Boulomai" which means "to resolve, purpose or will." It also means "to intend." So, 2 Peter 3:9 really means that God has "purposed, resolved and absolutely intends" to save all mankind. Isaiah 53:11 tells us that in the final judgment Jesus will "see the travail of His soul and be SATISFIED." Do you think that our Blessed Redeemer would be satisfied with anything less than total success? I don't think so. Jesus, our blessed Redeemer and Shepherd of the flock of this earth will not be satisfied with anything less than 100%, a completed fold and house hold of faith. Matt 18:2-14.

THE VALLEY OF JEHOSHAPHAT

"Let the heathen be wakened, and come up to the valley of Jehoshaphat: for there will I sit to judge all the heathen round about." Joel 3:12.

We have already read the story of King Jehoshaphat who did not lead his people to battle with sword and spear, but did battle with the forces of darkness with the WORD OF GOD by singing praises to God.

Jehoshaphat means JEHOVAH HAS JUDGED. If God is an omniscient God, and I believe that Isaiah 46:9, 10; Psalms 139:2, 16 and Hebrews 4:13 say He is, then He has already "decided" or "judged" who will be saved and who will be lost for this age and who will be saved finally in the great age of the ages after the 1,000 years, because of each person's own choice.

Revelation 22:12 tells us that He is bringing His reward with Him when He comes the second time to rescue the saints. So, Jesus has already decided who among the living will be saved and He has also decided or judged worthy who will be with Him from among the dead who have already died before He comes again. And so, He has decided a lot of things already. In addition to that, the saints will go over the "books" to see why Jesus decided the way He did in each case. Revelation 15:2-4 indicates that the whole universe, saved and lost, will admit God was perfect in each and every one of his decisions. This will take place during the millennium or 1,000 years. More will be said later about how God will reconcile all the lost outside the city.

So, this Valley of Jehoshaphat is going to be a time when a great panoramic view is going to reveal all of these decisions Jesus has made with His Father; and everyone is going to bow down and declare that He is totally just. Do you think anyone would bow down if God has arbitrarily killed anyone? Everyone will realize and admit that they are outside the city by their own choice. God's laws are not arbitrary and therefore He is not a despot who forces His way or His will on anyone at anytime. *God destroys no man.* James 1:17. The wicked will have a lot of time to think things over out there. "A little season," in Moses' day was 120 years and Isaiah 65:20 is a text some have used to refer to this period of time. Just think of the suffering the wicked will have to endure for at least 100 years because of their wrong and evil choices in this life. How much better it is to decide for Christ right now, my friend, so you will be inside the city looking out and not outside looking in.

Satan is working under a thousand different masks and aliases for only one purpose—to misrepresent the character and government of God. What is God's government based upon? His law. Has Satan succeeded in perverting the Law of God? Yes. If that is true, then let us also be aware of how he is misrepresenting His character. For, if Satan can make us believe that God's character is different than it really is, will we be looking at and forming a character after the similitude of a loving Creator or of an angry despot? Think about it.

The Bible tells us that someday "every knee shall bow and every tongue will confess," Phil 2:9-11, Isaiah 45:23, Romans 14:11, Psalms 22:29. This would not only include all the people of the world, saved and lost, but all of the angels, holy and loyal as well as unholy and disloyal. It would also include all of the unfallen worlds who may have had some doubts along the way. God has won his case in court, as it were, without ever slandering, embarrassing, hurting or killing a single one of his beloved creatures. What a wise and wonderful God we serve!

Now, do you think that Satan and his hosts would ever bow the knee to Jesus if they could find one little flaw in His track record? Not a chance! Jesus will show in this final view of glory and song and praise that He was the same all the way through ... total pure love. The wicked will understand and have to admit they are outside of the city because of their own choice.

The valley of Jehoshaphat has been applied to the Kidron Valley, the depression between Jerusalem and the Mount of Olives, to the east of Jerusalem. It has been connected with the Valley of Berachah, the very scene of Judah's victory over the united forces of Ammon and Moab and Mt. Seir (2 Chronicles 20:1-30), which we have already referred to. The real significance of the name "Valley of Jehoshaphat" is in the name itself, and not necessarily in its location. The name means "Jehovah has judged." But, in our present context, it would seem very significant that this valley would indeed be the same valley where the final battle of this earth will be staged.

The New Jerusalem will come down upon the Mount of Olives, according to Zechariah 14:4,5,9. This will be the final scene of the judgment, the beginning of the Great "Age of the Ages." Even though the gates of the city are never closed the wicked will not go in, at least not at first. Why? Because their minds are filled with fear. That is why the saints must go out to them. See Ezekiel 16 and 47. This may be hard for you to believe at first, but it is true. You know, my friend, that tells me something wonderful about God. It tells me that everyone who really wants to be with Him in the kingdom is going to be inside the city and those who did not want to be with Him will be outside suffering. There will be a lot of wailing and gnashing of teeth. So, that tells me that our God is presently doing everything in His power to get people into that Golden City, not keep them out. It seems to me that it is hard to be lost and easy to be saved when you look at it from God's perspective. Jesus told Paul, "it is hard for you to kick against the pricks." And again He said, "my yoke is easy and my burden is light." We sure do make it hard, though, don't we? We sure paint a dark picture of God for people, don't we? I think it is about time we quit discouraging people. Acts 9:5; Matthew 11:28-30.

I want you to notice that it is the "song of praise from the redeemed" singing "Worthy is the Lamb that was slain," which is another way of singing and saying as they did in Jehoshaphat's day, "His loving-kindness endures forever," 2 Chronicles 20:21, which caused the masochistic death by self-execution of the wicked hosts of Moab and Ammon. God did not destroy them. No. They destroyed each other.

Well, someone is probably asking about now: "Why did God allow the Israelites to slaughter so many of the heathen in the Old Testament?" The answer seems axiomatic (self-evident) to me. It is the same reason the Lord allowed Moses to "command" husbands to give a writing of divorcement, and to put away their wives, which Jesus explained in Matt 19:7, 8. "Moses, because of the HARDNESS OF YOUR HEARTS SUF-

FERED (allowed) YOU TO PUT AWAY YOUR WIVES: but from the beginning it was not so." Ah, there you have it. God's permissive will as opposed to His perfect will is shown. And later we will also see there was another lord they were listening to. The Adversary lord. The Impostor god. Oh, yes, they thought they were obeying the true God but it was really the devil. Jesus revealed this to them in John 8:44 when He said, ***"You are of your father the devil."***

God has always had to accommodate Himself to the whims of mankind in order to carry out His Divine purposes. How many times we get in His way and delay the accomplishment of His work with our "own way," and "limit" the Holy one of Israel. Psalms 78:41. 2 Chronicles 20:21.

In order to remain sovereign and warn millions He sometimes permitted hundreds or thousands to be killed. But was this His idea? No. It was what the carnal mind of man wanted and Satan as the Angel of Justice (Rev 6:5) was always near to inspire the death sentence to be carried out and God took the blame by saying He commanded it or ordered it, because He allowed or permitted it to happen. We many times think of death in this life as the ultimate punishment, but that is not true at all. If we could know the truth, we might find out that many of those who were sentenced to be executed may have repented and will eventually be saved just as the convicted criminal, the thief on the cross, was saved at the eleventh hour. Luke 23:39-43.

Samuel and even Elijah carried out executions as a warning against potential lawbreakers. Let us not lower ourselves to using this against God's character to say this proves He does kill. Actually, it proves God's mercy in demonstrating the results of sin. Christ knew how much these heathen nations were suffering due to wrong eating habits, sexual abuse, etc. Instead of permitting them to die a slow agonizing death and infect many others with their bad example, especially the Israelites, God permitted them to be put to death by His people who, although not always within His will, still were His chosen people, and the only ones through whom He could carry out His final objectives for saving mankind. When Christ came in the flesh He refused to let them stone the woman caught in adultery. John 8:5-11. God never changes. He never ordered anyone to be stoned, but he allowed men to do what they desired to do. They heard the voice they wanted to hear. John 10:4, 27; 12:27-30.

If Israel had always been faithful, they would not have wanted to go to war and carry out these slaughters, for God had promised to drive out the inhabitants with "hornets." See Exodus 23:28 and Joshua 24:12. Some bible scholars and commentaries interpret "hornets" as meaning literal hornets while others see it as a figurative reference to the repeated invasion of Palestine by the Egyptians. One Hebrew/English lexicon defined "hornets" simply as a scourge or that which causes a scourge, which could be any number of disasters from bad weather, to sickness and disease to invading armies. The point is that the Lord wanted Israel to trust in Him and His sovereign control over all the forces of nature as well as man. They would not have to take up the sword to hurt and kill anyone. But they never came to the place where they completely surrendered themselves to Him to that extent. Therefore, He allowed them to use the sword at times.

Yet, God controlled the sword of man (Israel's carnal desire to kill) by saying "You may take life only when I give you permission to do so, and then only." This was never His "perfect will," but always His "permissive will," as it was with the laws on divorce, and later the monarchy. They were given "their own way" because of the "hardness" of their hearts. And as a result they suffered terribly.

David was a man of war and of much "blood," and as a result, was not permitted to build the temple because of it, which should tell us something in itself. But the Lord permitted Israel to have a king (Saul) and even selected him and took the blame for all the bad things he did, even for Saul's death. See 1 Chronicles 10:13,14. It was not God's will for David to have many wives, but He put up with it. He rebuked David, however, for the sin of taking Bathsheba. Oh, how God has to suffer because of our sinfulness. How often He weeps over our waywardness. No, it was not God's perfect will for Israel as a nation to fight and war or kill, nor was it His perfect will for individuals to kill, but in order to save millions He permitted a few to perish as examples. This prevented further rebellion and demonstrated the results of sin.

Are we not as a people today guilty of even a greater crime than was Israel by letting this world sink deeper every day while we refuse to surrender our all to God so He can finish His work in us and through us? How many millions are perishing and will continue to perish because of our neglect of duty? Only eternity will reveal it to us. How great is God's mercy! But someday it will be seen. All things will be revealed and everyone will have to face his/her record.

*** The TEV reads, "for God has made all people prisoners of disobedience, so that He might show mercy to them all." The NKJV says, "has commited them all to disobedience." The NAS reads, "shut up all to disobedience." The RSV says, "consigned." In God's soverign will He allowed man to fall in order to make planet earth the "lesson book" for the universe.**

CHAPTER 10

THE TRUE MEANING OF GOD'S WRATH

"God is not a man, that he should lie; neither the son of man, that he should repent." Numbers 23:19. If you can understand what "God's repentance," means, then you will be ready to grasp the true meaning of "God's wrath," as it is used in the Scriptures. The principle is the same. God's repentance is synonymous with pity and divine grief. The Hebrew word is "nacham," meaning "to sigh, breath strongly, pity, console." (Strong's 5162).

Malachi 3:6 tells us that "I am the Lord, I change not." Yet, we read in 1 Samuel 15:11, "It repenteth me that I have set up Saul to be king." Again in Genesis 6:6, "And it repented the Lord that he had made man on the earth, and it grieved him to his heart." I want to explain this "repent" aspect of God, for it all ties into my main point, that God never changes as man does, and we all know that to "repent," basically means to "be sorry," to "change direction and go another way." But, I am telling you that God is not like this. When the Lord "repents" it simply means He is sorry man has failed to obey and cooperate with Him so He could bless him. He then has to alter His plans to accommodate man's lack of understanding and cooperation.

Jesus is the Lord of the Old Testament who "repented that He had made man," and that He had made Saul King of Israel. See Genesis 6 and 1 Samuel 15:11. This same Lord permitted a flood to destroy the old world and let Saul be led by Satan to kill himself, thus removing him from being king. He simply let him follow his own will and counsel and thus destroy himself. "Destroy thou them 0 God. Let them fall by their own counsels." Psalms 5:10. For the flood, see Job 18:7,8, Job 22:15-18; Isaiah 54:5-10.

An angry God of the Old Testament who poured out His wrath on those who disobeyed His laws is the opposite of the

God of the New Testament who became one of us and "offered us the way of salvation." But hasn't this been the basic theology of most of Protestantism since the Reformation? I know there are many varieties among Christian groups today.

But somehow I believe that our theology in this last hour should have a more consistent and appealing ring to it than the preaching of a watered down Jonathan Edward's version of "Sinners in the Hands of an Angry God."

Whether it be for all eternity that they suffer at His hands or "just for a little while" in the lake of fire, it is still a slander and a blight on the Character of God. It just doesn't harmonize or ring true to the picture we see of Jesus in the New Testament.

"Oh, but Brother Mike," some will say, "this is God's strange act." What you really mean is that at the end of time Jesus is going to blow His cool and act out of character for just one last time before eternity begins. I am aware that this is the common understanding of many people. Until I began studying this subject of God's character in depth, I had no other explanation for it either. But, knowledge and truth are progressive. Now, I will deal with this concept of "GOD'S STRANGE ACT" later on, but for now, I want to examine the phrase, "THE WRATH OF GOD," with you and show what it really means and how and why it is used in the Bible.

"The Wrath of God," is an expression that is used over and over again in both the Old and New Testaments. Since Grace and Law and Character are the same in both Testaments, then it must follow suit that this expression would also be the same.

By my count from "Young's Analytical Concordance to the Bible," the word "wrath" is used more than 240 times in many different ways. There are, at least, eight different Hebrew words for wrath, maybe more, and, at least, five different Greek words for wrath in the New Testament.

It is not my intention in this study to examine each of these words and consider the different meanings, but it is my desire that we understand what the various phrases mean in context.

In Romans 1:18, we read, "For the wrath of God is

revealed from heaven against all ungodliness and unrighteousness of men, who hold the truth in unrighteousness." This is the first time in Scripture where the Holy Spirit inspired a writer to declare that God's wrath was going to be explained. Now, we have to pay close attention as Paul develops his thought in order to catch this revelation of God's wrath.

In verse 19, he says that God has showed people in the past the truth about Himself, and in verse 20, he calls these manifestations the "invisible things of him from the creation of the world."

Another translation says on verse 19, "For the truth about God is known to them instinctively, God has put this knowledge in their hearts." Living Bible. The King James Version says, "is manifest in them"; and Romans 2:14,15 explains what Paul means. "For when the Gentiles, which have not the law, do by nature the things contained in the law, these, having not the law, are a law unto themselves: Which shew the work of the law written in their hearts, their conscience also bearing witness..." The Living Bible says, "for down in their hearts they know right from wrong."

We have two factors established now. First, that God's wrath is revealed against those who go against what they know to be right or what the Bible calls "righteousness." Compare James 4:17 and 1 John 5:17. Second, the law of God is automatically built into a person when he is born. He is preprogrammed to recognize sin, for the law of God is in his mind to blow the whistle on him each time he breaks one of those Ten Commandments, even if he has never heard of the Ten Commandments or the name of God.

We know this is true from a study of anthropology, which shows that even in the most backward tribes, there are laws governing conduct, and these laws invariably are based upon the principles of the Ten Commandments. Of course, it is granted that not all ten of the precepts may be there, but even those that are left out or ignored condemn the people; and, to the extent that they disregard the inner voice, to that extent they are degraded. Anthropologists also tell us that every race in every age has worshiped some kind of deity, which proves that there is a built-in, innate, inner urge to worship something above and beyond themselves. Later on we will examine verse 16 of Romans 2, which will help us to understand "God's Strange Act."

WHEN GOD LETS A MAN GO HIS OWN WAY

Paul continues to build onto his definition of the WRATH OF GOD in verses 21,22, and 23 of Romans 1 and comes to his conclusion in verse 24 with this: "Wherefore, God also gave them up." That is God's Wrath. When He is unable to plead with human beings any longer, He is forced to "give them up" to their own lusts and passions and weepingly and sorrowfully watch them self-destruct.

Many people will carry into this verse their Old Testament concept of a God of wrath instead of a Jesus filled with love, weeping over the city of Jerusalem.

In A.D. 54 Paul wrote to the Church at Thessalonica about the Jewish persecution and opposition he was encountering everywhere he went. "For ye also have suffered like things of your own countrymen, even as they have of the Jews: Who both killed the Lord Jesus, and their own prophets, and have persecuted us; and they please not God, and are contrary to all men: Forbidding us to speak to the Gentiles that they might be saved TO FILL UP THEIR SINS ALWAY: FOR THE WRATH IS COME UPON THEM TO THE UTTERMOST." See 1 Thessalonians 2:14-16.

JESUS WEEPS OVER JERUSALEM

"And when He was come near, He beheld the city, and wept over it, saying, If thou hadst known, even thou, at least in this thy day, the things which belong unto thy peace! but now they are hid from thine eyes." Luke 19:41,42, Isaiah 26:11.

Let me ask you a question; was Jesus the one who was "hiding the truth from the eyes of the Jews" at this time so they would not accept Him? You would say, "No, of course not." What then did Isaiah mean when he said under the inspiration of JESUS IN THE OLD TESTAMENT, "also I heard the voice of the Lord, (Jesus) saying, Whom shall I send, and who will go for us: Then said I, Here am I; send me. And he said, Go, and tell this people, Hear ye indeed, but understand not and see ye indeed, but perceive not. Make the heart of this people fat, and make their ears heavy, and shut their eyes; LEST THEY SEE WITH THEIR EYES, AND HEAR WITH THEIR EARS, and understand with their heart, and convert, and be healed." Isaiah 6:8-10.

Why did Jesus tell Isaiah to go "BLIND THEIR EYES"? Didn't He want them to see the truth? "Oh," you say, "that is just a figure of speech. It really doesn't mean that. It wasn't Jesus' fault. It was the people's fault."

Oh, I see. Well, then maybe that reasoning would help us to understand the passage in Jude 6 which says, "And the angels which kept not their first estate, but left their own habitation, he hath reserved in everlasting chains under darkness unto the judgement of the great day." Cf. Psalms 73:6, Proverbs 5:22, John 8:24.

What does "everlasting chains under darkness" mean? Did Jesus bind Satan and all of his Angels with chains and kick them out of heaven so they could never get back in no matter what? Is that the way Jesus operates? You say, "No, Jesus is always kind and loving to everyone." I wonder if He wept over Lucifer and the angels when they "LEFT." Did the Father weep over His prodigal son when he left? Luke 15:11-32. Would it not simply mean that all of Satan's angels are still in darkness regarding the truth about God's true character? They still believe He kills. Mark 1:24. This is a doctrine of devils.

Consider Romans 11:7-10. King David spoke of this same thing when he said, "Let their good food and other blessings trap them into thinking all is well between themselves and God.

Let these good things boomerang on them and fall back upon their heads to justly crush them. Let their eyes be dim," he said, "so that they cannot see, and let them walk bent-backed forever with a heavy load." Living Bible.

"Even now when the Scripture is read it seems as though Jewish hearts and minds are covered by a thick veil, because they cannot see and understand the real meaning of the Scriptures. For this veil of misunderstanding can be removed only by BELIEVING IN CHRIST." 2 Corinthians 3:14,15 Living Bible. The veil represents our fleshly, carnal mind.

Friend of mine, let us pray that Jesus will lift the veil from our eyes so we may see the true beauty of His Character which is in His law. Jesus and His Father are total pure love. They have never changed. They have never hurt or killed anyone. Lucifer and his hosts left heaven because they wanted to leave. Lucifer was convinced that He was wrong, but pride would not let him go back. Ezekiel 28:15-17, Isaiah 14:12-14, Lam. 2:1.

Does pride blind a person? Yes, it does. It also leads to destruction—self-destruction or suicide. "Pride goeth before destruction and a haughty spirit before a fall." Proverbs 16:18. Because God is a God of love, He tries to show people their errors so they will not die. But, the more you show people how they are wrong, the more they rebel—most of them at least. And God always takes the blame. He says, "I blinded them with my truth. I killed them with my law, which revealed their sins and made them mad so they will not come to me. Now my WRATH IS UPON THEM."

And what is God's wrath? Romans 1:24 and 26 tells us. "So God let them go ahead into every sort of sex sin, and do whatever they wanted to—yes, vile and sinful things with each other's bodies. Instead of believing what they knew was the truth about God, they deliberately chose to believe lies. So they prayed to the things God made, but wouldn't obey the blessed God who made these things. That is why God let go of them...."

Can you picture God hanging on to a person He loves? Let's picture Jesus again weeping over the city of Jerusalem and the whole nation. He was hanging on to them just as long as He could, and they kept on kicking and hitting Him saying, "Let me go, let me go, I hate you, God, I don't want you to tell me the truth. Let me go so I can kill you, then I won't have to listen to you tell me about my sins anymore."

Did Jesus hit back? No. He never has and He never is going to in the future. But, all the time, Jesus takes the blame with His Father. Even on the cross He prayed for them, saying, "Father, forgive them, for they know not what they do." Have you ever wondered why He prayed for them? Because very few others were praying for the Jews. Satan was just gnashing at the bit to kill them, and finally got his chance in A.D. 70.

We will deal with that in depth in a moment, but let us now go to Psalms 78 and look at a few texts. Notice in verses 46-48 that the Psalmist uses the word "gave," which has the connotation of "permitting," just as we read in Romans 1:24,26, that God "gave them up;" it is the same thing. Now, look at verses 45,47,49, 50, and 51 of Psalm 78.

Notice the words and phrases as I list them in order: "sent," "He sent," "He destroyed," "He cast," "He made a way to his anger; he spared not their soul from death, but gave their life over to the pestilence; and SMOTE all the firstborn in Egypt."

Now, I quoted the last two verses of Psalm 78: 50, 51, completely, for a reason. Even though these are all different words, they all are saying the same thing . . . "I did not prevent it from happening. I, the Messiah, Jesus, of the Old Testament, let these things happen because the people chose to go their own way and do their own thing. They would not listen to me. I wept and begged them to listen, but they told me to stop talking and to let them go. And, so, I had no choice, for they have the right to choose which way they will go. I made them that way. I, Jesus, am weeping."

I want to say something about prayer. Prayer is power of attorney. It gives God the authority to act in your behalf or in the behalf of the one for whom you are praying. Jesus' prayers for His people who killed Him and for His disciples gave God the authority or power of attorney to protect the nation, to preserve it until 70 A. D. Psalms 122:6 is an admonition to "Pray for the peace of Jerusalem: they shall prosper that love thee." We should pray for it today as never before, because when Jerusalem is in trouble, the whole world is in trouble.

Now, let us consider the mechanics of how the wicked are destroyed today and in the past. "He cast upon them (notice the word, "cast') the fierceness of his anger, wrath, and indignation and trouble, by sending evil angels among them." Psalms 78:49. God always gives little keys to unlock the doors for those who really want to know the truth. Only those who truly want to be like Jesus in character will pray for the Holy Spirit to give them the keys to unlock these doors to God's heart so that we can go inside and see what He is really like.

Revelation 12:9 tells us that Satan was "cast out" of heaven when Jesus made "war" against Satan and his hosts. Job 18:7, 8 shows us how God casts down. Notice, "The steps of his strength shall be straitened, and his own counsel shall cast him down." Remember Psalms 5: 10, "Destroy thou them 0 God. Let them fall by their OWN COUNSELS." God always takes the blame. He always remains sovereign by saying, "I did it." "For he is cast into a net by his own feet, and he walketh upon a snare." Job 18:8. See also Lamentations 2:1.

Now let's read Psalms 9:15,16: "The heathen are sunk down in the pit that they made: in the net which they hid is their own foot taken." Compare Proverbs 26:27. Now read verse 16, "The Lord is known by the judgment which he executeth: the wicked is snared in the work of his own hands." "Higgaion." "Selah." In other words, God is known (to those who want to know the truth) by the DECISIONS WHICH HE CARRIES OUT. Read Revelation 15 very carefully and you will see that God is fully understood and vindicated in the end. This study will also help explain the WRATH OF GOD in the book of Revelation. God takes the blame for us now, but the day is coming when He will no longer be able to take the blame for us.

DEATH OF KING SAUL

The death of the first king of Israel is a perfect example of how God always takes the blame and says, "I did it." In 2 Chronicles 10:3-5 we see that Saul loses the battle and commits suicide by falling on his sword. But in verses 13 and 14, God says through the Holy Spirit, "therefore He slew him, and turned the kingdom unto David the son of Jesse."

In 2 Samuel 24:1, we read, "And again the anger of the Lord was kindled against Israel, and he moved David against them to say, Go, number Israel and Judah." The marginal reference says, "That is, Satan," instead of "He," which means that the truth of the matter is Satan was the one who moved or incited David to number Israel, but the Bible writer wrote it up as if God did it, even though 1 Chronicles 21:1 says bluntly, "And Satan stood up against Israel, and provoked David to number Israel." These two accounts were written 500 years apart which reveals progressive revelation on the part of the scribes themselves.

Now, why does God always take the blame? First of all, it is the only way He can save us from destroying ourselves because of the guilt of sin. Secondly, He never bad mouths people. He did not expose Judas. He always tries to shelter everyone from blame as much as possible. He only reveals what we can stand so that we will repent and turn from our sins and be saved. Thirdly, God must remain sovereign over all His creation so He can receive worship. He takes all the credit and all the blame so people will not worship Satan. He would rather have people worship Him out of fear and be saved (Jude 23) than for Him to say, "I don't do the bad things; he is the one over there who does the bad; so you better watch out for him (Satan)." Satan must be allowed to expose himself.

He did not do that in the Old Testament, for they would have worshiped Satan out of fear instead of God. But, in the New Testament, He reveals Himself a lot more. Yet, we do not see it unless we are praying for the Holy Spirit to help us to see

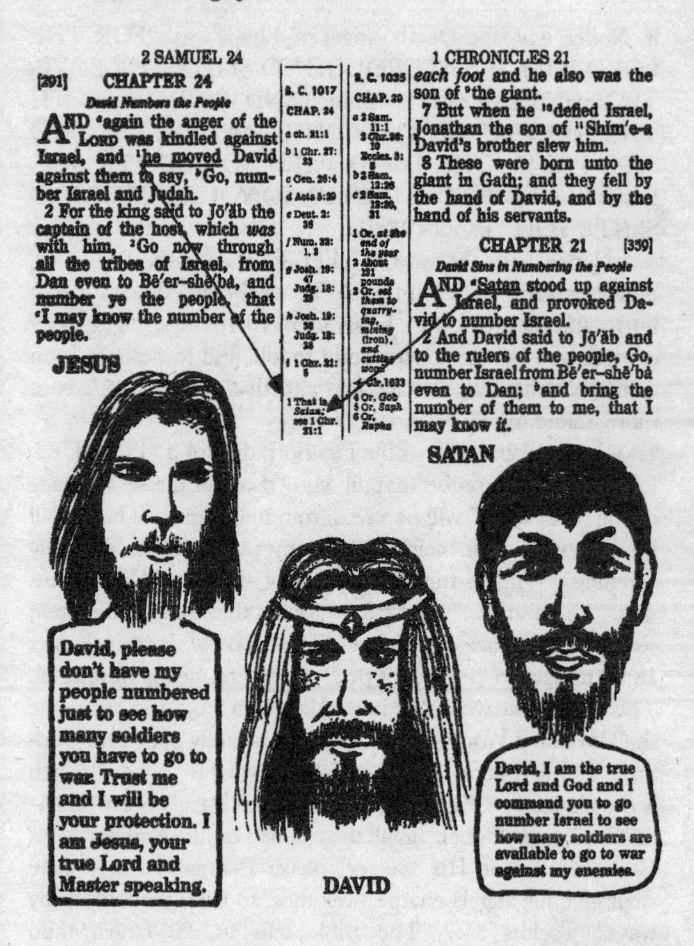

2 SAMUEL 24

[291] CHAPTER 24

David Numbers the People

AND [a]again the anger of the LORD was kindled against Israel, and [1]he moved David against them to say, [b]Go, number Israel and Judah.

2 For the king said to Jō'āb the captain of the host, which *was* with him, [2]Go now through all the tribes of Israel, from Dan even to Bē'er-shē'bā, and number ye the people, that [c]I may know the number of the people.

1 CHRONICLES 21

each foot and he also was the son of [9]the giant.

7 But when he [10]defied Israel, Jonathan the son of [11]Shim'e-a David's brother slew him.

8 These were born unto the giant in Gath; and they fell by the hand of David, and by the hand of his servants.

CHAPTER 21 [359]

David Sins in Numbering the People

AND [a]Satan stood up against Israel, and provoked David to number Israel.

2 And David said to Jō'āb and to the rulers of the people, Go, number Israel from Bē'er-shē'bā even to Dan; [b]and bring the number of them to me, that I may know *it*.

The drawing above illustrates clearly how the title "Lord" sometimes refers to Satan. These two accounts were written 500 years apart. The first was penned in the time of David, in 1035 B.C. and the second in 535 B.C, 500 years later, during the time of Ezra the scribe. The scribes realized that this "Lord" who incited or moved David to sin by numbering Israel was none other than Satan and so they updated the record by changing the title Lord to Satan. See page 392.

it. Notice who the Death Angel of Egypt was. "FOR THE LORD WILL PASS THROUGH TO SMITE THE EGYPTIANS: (Notice the word, "smite") AND WHEN HE SEETH THE BLOOD UPON THE LINTEL, AND ON THE TWO SIDE POSTS, THE LORD WILL NOT SUFFER THE DESTROYER TO COME IN UNTO YOUR HOUSES TO SMITE YOU." Exodus 12:23.

Notice here the word SUFFER. That is the key word. Suffer or allow or permit could be used here. Who is it that hurts and destroys and kills? John 10:10 says, "The thief cometh not, but for to steal, and to kill, and to destroy: I am come that they might have life, and that they might have it more abundantly."

Exodus 12:13 tells us the Firstborn died of a "PLAGUE." Psalms 91 is a promise that all who "dwell in the secret place of the Most High" will be saved from the plague. "There shall no evil befall thee, neither shall any plague come nigh thy dwelling." What is the secret place of the Most High? Jesus says, "Abide in me." John 15:4. Jesus is the "Rock," the great secret hiding place of the ages. The Hebrew word in Judges 13:18 translated "secret," is peli, which also means wonderful. This is the same word that is used in Isaiah 9:6, "And His name shall be called Wonderful." He (Jesus) is surely our "Peli," hiding place. In Psalms 91:1 the Hebrew word is "sether," which is translated the SECRET place. So Jesus is truly our wonderful "Peli" and "Sether," in all the troubles of life. And how does God "hide" us in His "Secret" place? Psalms 91:11. "For he shall give his angels charge over thee, to keep thee in all thy ways." Psalms 34:7. The Bible tells us, "0 Israel, thou has destroyed thyself, ... thou hast fallen by thine iniquity." Hosea 13:9; 14:1.

The Jewish nation in Hosea's day, as well as Jesus' day, brought all of their troubles upon themselves by their own stubborn disobedience. They simply reaped what they had sown. And yet the Bible, in most places, wrote it up as if God was bringing these terrible calamities upon them. He was continually covering up for Lucifer and his angels. "The Lord will smite thee with the botch of Egypt, and with the emerods, and with the scab, and with the itch, whereof thou canst not be healed. The Lord shall smite thee with madness, and blindness, and astonishment of heart." Deuteronomy 28:27,28.

But when Jesus came, he healed the sick, blind and mad. In fact, the Scriptures point out that Satan was the cause of the people's oppression. "How God anointed Jesus of Nazareth with the Holy Ghost and with power: who went about doing good, and healing all that were oppressed of the devil; for God was with Him." Acts 10:38. See also Luke 13:16. It will be the objective of this book to explain and remove this seeming contradiction from the mind of the reader.

It is most important that we understand how God has been operating throughout the centuries, so we will understand what is happening in this last hour of earth's history, for God never changes. The "TIME OF TROUBLE," spoken of in Daniel 12:1, is coming upon the world very rapidly. We must understand that Satan, not our wonderful Heavenly Father, is responsible for this terrible TIME OF TROUBLE. It must be clear in our minds just what God's wrath, God's anger, and God's judgment mean. Psalms 9:15, 16, proves that God executes judgment (carries out His decisions) by allowing the wicked to become "snared in the work of his own hands." See also Psalms 5:10 and Psalms 7:15.

Let's notice how God executes judgment. We, in our carnal nature want to serve a God who acts and thinks like we do so we can blame "our carnal" Father when we get angry or fed up. God's Wrath, God's Anger, God's Repentance, God's jealousy, yes, all of His ways are much different than our ways. "For my thoughts are not your thoughts, neither are your ways my ways, saith the Lord. For as the heavens are higher than the earth, so are my ways higher than your ways, and my thoughts than your thoughts." Isaiah 55:8, 9.

GOD DOES NOT STAND AS AN EXECUTIONER

GOD DOES NOT STAND TOWARD US AS AN EXECUTIONER OF THE SENTENCE AGAINST TRANSGRESSION: BUT WHEN WE REJECT HIS MERCY, HE IS FORCED TO LEAVE US TO OUR SELVES. Here it is again. "Wherefore God also gave them up." Romans 1:24. Notice also in Hosea's writings how God let Jerusalem go. "Ephraim is joined to idols: let him alone." "O Ephraim, what shall I do unto thee?" Hosea 4:17 and 6:4. *GC 36.

A modern translation reads, "0 Ephraim and Judah, what shall I do with you?" It sounds like an exasperated mother or a wounded spouse, doesn't it? But, go back to Hosea 6:1 and notice, "Come, and let us return unto the Lord; FOR HE HATH TORN, AND HE WILL HEAL US: HE HATH SMITTEN, AND HE WILL BIND US UP." SEE HOW GOD ALWAYS REMAINS KING OF THE UNIVERSE, BOSS OVER ALL CREATION, AND SOVEREIGN RULER OVER HIS OWN BY TAKING ALL THE BLAME. This is how He has even kept Satan and his angels alive.

If we can understand this one concept of the Hebrew Scriptures, it will open up a thousand locked doors. God takes the blame for man and Satan. "When Israel was a child, then I loved him, and called my son out of Egypt. As they called them, so they went from them: they sacrificed unto Baalim, and burned incense to graven images. I taught Ephraim also to go, taking them by their arms: but they knew not that I healed them. I drew them with cords of a man, with bands of love; (compare Psalms 2:1, 2) and I was to them as they that take off the yoke on their jaws, and I laid meat unto them.... HOW SHALL I GIVE THEE UP, EPHRAIM? HOW SHALL I DELIVER THEE, ISRAEL? ... MINE HEART IS TURNED WITHIN ME, MY REPENTINGS ARE KINDLED TOGETHER." Hosea 11:1-4, 8. It is the JERUSALEM SCENE all over again. The Hebrew root word for "repentings" is "nachum," meaning "consoled" or" comforted," Psalm 23:4—God's staff or Holy

Spirit "comforts" us. It also means to "sigh," and "breathe deeply" as in mourning or weeping. Our Heavenly father is a very emotional and romantic person. John 11:33-35. Song of Solomon 8:6.

God will have to leave the finally impenitent to themselves, to reap what they have sown. The city of Jerusalem, the Jewish nation and Judas are examples of what happens when God is forced to let them go. The leaders in Christ's day and even Peter and the other disciples misunderstood Christ's mission. They expected Him to humiliate and destroy their enemies. When He humiliated Himself by washing their feet and dying on the cross, they were horrified. So it is today! Christ's professed followers serve a God of wrath and vengeance instead of the lowly Nazarene. Another disappointment is coming for the Church.

The only people who will recognize the "true" Christ when he finally comes are those who have received the divine nature, 1 Peter 1:4. The "carnal mind"or nature we are born with is "enmity against God." Romans 8:7.

CHAPTER 11

GOD'S "FIRE," "SWORD," AND "WRATH," AND THE FINAL DESTRUCTION

"Come, my people, enter thou into thy chambers, and shut thy doors about thee; hide thyself as it were for a little moment, until the INDIGNATION be over past. For, behold, the Lord cometh out of His place to punish the inhabitants of the earth for their iniquity: the earth also shall disclose her blood, and shall no more cover her slain."

If you read all of Isaiah 26, you will discover something. The two verses just quoted above are from Isaiah 26:20, 21, the last two of the chapter. If you begin reading from verse 12, you will see that it is talking about the wicked not being raised from the dead and in verse 19 about the righteous being raised.

The setting is the end of the world and the Second Coming of Christ. Notice especially the word, INDIGNATION—let us paraphrase it a bit: "Hide yourselves in My love and protection until the 'anger' or 'wrath,' 'indignation,' or 'trouble' is past."

Remember Psalms 78:49? "He cast upon them the fierceness of his anger, wrath and indignation, and trouble, by SENDING (permitting to come) evil angels among them." Who is bringing the INDIGNATION AND TROUBLE UPON THE EARTH IN THE LAST DAYS? WHY IT IS SATAN, OF COURSE.

When Jesus ceases His intercession for us in the heavenly sanctuary above, beyond the veil, every soul's destiny will have been fully, finally and irrevocably sealed for this age. The four angels of Revelation 7 will then let go of the winds of strife because the sealing of the 144,000 (wheat harvest) has been completed by the Elect (Man Child or Barley). God's army, Joel 1, 2 and Rev. 19, has been sealed and are now ready to begin the Grape harvest or one third of the earth, Zechariah 13:7-9. Two thirds of the population of the earth will die but one third will escape. This will be the Remnant or what remains or is left over. These Remnant have escaped into the "wilderness" (seclusion & obscurity)* Revelation 12:6, 13-17. And that is how they will survive. They will have to go through the last 3 1/2 years of this final age in a mortal body of flesh in order to perfect their characters so they will be ready for translation at the end of the this last 3 1/2 year period. But the Elect will "shine like the sun" with their immortal bodies, Daniel 12:3, 10; Matthew 13:43. They are the Watchmen on the walls of Zion who were not asleep and woke up the sleeping Virgins. The five Wise Virgins have the extra oil of the Holy spirit but the Five Foolish virgins do not have the extra oil because they did not pray and study and their lamps go out in darkness. *GC 55.

God has done all in His power to draw every mind to Himself, beyond the sacred veil, safe in His arms of love. Soon it will be too late, for the Bible tells us that a time is soon to come when the decree will go forth, "He that is unjust, let him be unjust still: and he which is filthy, let him be filthy still: and he that is righteous, let him be righteous still: and he that is holy, let him be holy still: And, behold, I come quickly; and my reward is with me, to give every man according as his work shall be." Revelation 22:12.

The word "sword" is often used in the Bible. It has a dual meaning. First of all, it represents the BIBLE or the GOSPEL. "For the Word of God is quick, and powerful and sharper than any two-edged sword, piercing even to the dividing asunder of soul and spirit, and of the joints and marrow, and is a discerner of the thoughts and intents of the heart." Hebrews 4:12. Revelation 19:13-15.

The preaching of the Word of God (Fire), which is the Gospel, causes the wicked to hate and kill God's people. But, in the last day they will not be able to kill God's people who are sealed after, so they will kill themselves. Ezekiel 38:21, Zech. 14:13.

There is a very interesting scripture which applies to the wicked killing each other when they cannot kill God's people. "A noise shall come even to the ends of the earth; for the Lord hath a controversy with the nations, He will plead with all flesh; He will give them that are wicked to the SWORD." Jeremiah 25:31. Psalms 17:13.

Here is the second meaning of the word SWORD, i.e., a literal instrument of death; a gun, bomb, or knife, or sword. Anything that takes life. God is going to "give them that are wicked to the sword." It simply means that God is not going to restrain them from blowing each other to pieces anymore and so they will self-destruct.

The use of the word "wicked" is very interesting. Before, God's people were the "wicked" that had to be destroyed to save society. But, now, the table is turned and the hunters become the hunted. The slayers are now to be slain, just like Haman in the book of Esther and Daniel's enemies in Babylon, Daniel 6. "All that take the sword will perish by the sword." Matt. 26:52, Rev. 13:10. Many of these will be religious leaders, preachers who believe in a violent God, a military Messiah. They have chosen their modern day "Barabas" and he will lead them on to destruction.

JESUS SAID, "I AM NOT COME TO BRING PEACE, BUT A SWORD."

"Think not that I am come to send peace on earth, but a sword. For I am come to set a man at variance against his father, and the daughter against her mother, and the daughter-in-law against her mother-in-law and a man's foes shall be they of his own household." Jesus Christ, the Prince of Peace, was a mighty storm center. Again He said, "I am come to send FIRE ON THE EARTH; AND WHAT WILL I, IF IT BE ALREADY KINDLED? But I have a baptism to be baptized with; and how am I straitened till it be accomplished! Suppose ye that I am come to give peace on earth? I tell you, Nay; but rather division." Luke 12:49-51. The word "accomplished" also means "ended," or "completed."

The early Christians were a peculiar people. Their Christlike deportment and steadfast faith continually disturbed the sinner's peace. Though few in numbers, without money, position, or titles, they were feared by evil doers wherever their CHARACTER AND TEACHINGS WERE SPREAD. The nominal believers in God were their greatest persecutors, especially after the 3rd century and the conversion of Constantine.

But why were they so persecuted? It was basically because the lives of the followers of Jesus rebuked the wicked within the church who were only nominal believers or Christians, in name only. This caused division. Jesus had said, "I came not to send peace, but a sword." Matthew 10:34. Is this a contradiction of the prophecy that Christ would be the Prince of Peace? Luke 2:14. No, it isn't a contradiction, for the teachings of Christ will unite all who will follow those teachings in humble obedience. But since most of the world are under the influence and control of Satan, they hate and fight those who try to "live Godly in Christ Jesus," 2 Timothy3:12. Their holy lives are a continual rebuke and cause a reaction on the part of the wicked. Since God takes the blame for evil and wrong in the Bible, Christ once again takes the responsibility or blame for the wicked's retaliation against his message of love. In this sense, therefore, the gospel is a sword which brings division.

With these concepts clearly in our minds we can now understand how God makes war against Satan and all the wicked who unite with him. Now, let's go to Revelation 19:10. "And I fell at his feet to worship him." Here John is overcome by the brightness and beauty of the messenger who is about to show him some very important concepts about the great victory Jesus will achieve over the hosts of Satan. "And I saw heaven opened, and behold a white horse; and he that sat upon him was called Faithful and True, and in righteousness he doth judge and make war. And the armies which were in heaven followed him.... And out of his mouth goes a sharp sword, that with it he should smite the nations; and he shall rule them with a rod of iron: and he treads the winepress of the fierceness and wrath of Almighty God." Revelation 19:11,14,15.

We have already learned that the word "SWORD" simply

means the Gospel Story from the Bible—the good news that God is love and that He has made a way of escape from the darkness and death of this world of sin. Here Christ is pictured as making war against the enemies of the cross by "smiting" them with a "sharp sword." A sword would simply be the Bible story of Jesus given in a normal fashion under normal circumstances in this world of sin; but a SHARP SWORD would be the GOSPEL STORY BEING GIVEN WITH A LOUD CRY IN ABNORMAL TIMES WHEN THERE IS "GROSS DARKNESS" upon the earth. See Isaiah 60:1, 2.

The gospel is LIGHT which cuts SHARPLY through all the DARKNESS to bring salvation to those who accept, and SEVERE CONDEMNATION TO THOSE WHO REJECT. LIGHT ALWAYS CONDEMNS DARKNESS. LIGHT WILL ALWAYS "SMITE" DARKNESS. Truth always smites and wars against falsehood ... it smites or condemns and thus destroys it.

For an example, let us suppose that a thief was in a house stealing valuables. The house is very dark and he has a little flashlight to get around and find what he wants. Let us suppose the owner of the house came home through the back door very quietly and turned all the lights on. What would the thief do? He would either try to get away without being seen or caught or try to kill the man or at least tie him up, if he could. Right. But, let us suppose that this man's house is high on a mountain overlooking the ocean and the thief cannot kill the man because he doesn't have a weapon. So, in his fearful attempt to escape he climbs out the window and falls to his death on the rocks below. Who and what killed him? Why the owner killed him by turning on the lights, some would say. But, really, what killed him was the violation of the law and his attempt to break that law and then escape instead of admitting his GUILT and surrendering.

Let us say again that a group of people decided to have a big party in a high-rise apartment. Lest they be caught, they keep the lights very low to avoid detection. Let's suppose the owner of the apartment is a minister of a large and well respected church in Chicago and the son of this minister is leading a double life without his father knowing it. Let's further imagine what this young man and most of the other people would do when the father comes home unexpectedly, turns on the lights, and sees all those naked bodies sprawled all over the room. They would try to hide and run away if they could. Some might even jump out of the window and kill themselves to stop the pain and frustration of guilt and condemnation.

This is what is going to happen to all the wicked in this last generation when Jesus comes. There will be no place to hide. The Bible tells us that they (the wicked) will say "to the mountains and rocks, fall on us, and hide us from the face of him that sits on the throne, and from the wrath of the Lamb: For the great day of His wrath is come; and who shall be able to stand?" Revelation 6:15-17. "Behold, I come as a thief. Blessed is he that watcheth, and keepeth his garments, lest he WALK NAKED, AND THEY SEE HIS SHAME." Rev 16:15.

Throughout this study it has been our aim to show that "God's wrath," is not an arbitrary act on His part, but rather a withdrawing of His protection. However, it is a reluctant withdrawing of His power to prevent and restrain the evil lusts and passions of the soul. He is forced out of the person's life. But God is always standing by to reassert His power on the person's behalf if they repent and ask Him to come back into their life.

The close of human probation is an "act" or "decision" of man to finally be free of the restraint of God's Holy Spirit. Man's self-destructive, masochistic and sadistic actions that result from his final decision to be completely free from God's love and truth can hardly be charged against our Lord. And yet God permits the Bible record to state, "I have done thus and so." The only reason God takes the blame is because He cannot save man by giving Satan credit for these acts. He must remain sovereign so that man can worship Him, even if it is at first, out of fear. But those of us who desire to be like Him in character will know the truth about God and what kind of person He really is so we may be like Him. Those who continue to be afraid of God will be lost for this age. Revelation 21:8. They will come up in the second resurrection and go through the Lake of Fire which will be explained later.

"Then said one unto him, Lord, are there few that be saved? And He said unto them, strive to enter in at the strait gate: for many, I say unto you, will seek to enter in, and shall not be able." Is it possible that after the 1,000 years when the Holy City is on the earth and the wicked are raised up to see the reward of the righteous that some will argue with Jesus over His decision to exclude them from the Golden City? It would seem so. This will go on for a "a little season," which may be as long as 100 years. Isaiah 65:20.

"When once the master of the house is risen up, and hath shut to the door, and ye begin to stand without, and to knock at the door, saying, 'Lord, Lord, open unto us;' and he shall answer and say unto you, 'I know you not whence ye are.' Then shall ye begin to say, 'we have eaten and drunk in thy presence, and thou has taught in our streets.' But he shall say, I tell you, I know you not whence ye are; depart from me, all ye workers of iniquity."

What could be more tragic ... more heartrending? "There shall be weeping and gnashing of teeth, when ye shall see Abraham, and Isaac, and Jacob, and all the prophets in the kingdom of God, and you yourselves thrust out." Luke 13:23-28.

Did you notice the expression, "there shall be weeping and gnashing of teeth?" I just wonder if this gnashing of teeth would include some "blaming"others for causing them to be lost? I just wonder if they will be "gnashing" their teeth at each other at first; and then at Christ, and organize with and under Satan to try to take the city by force; and then after the panoramic view which unveils everything, they will be "gnashing" at one another again; and, because they cannot kill God and the saints, they will take their anger out upon one another. This will go on for a "Little Season." Ezekiel 28:6-10. *See note.

When we compare Matthew 25:31-46 with this passage we just read in Luke 13, we see a very clear picture. "When the Son of man shall come in his glory ... and before him shall be gathered all nations: ... he shall set the sheep on his right hand, but the goats on the left." Then follows the familiar, "Inasmuch as ye have done it unto one of the least of these my brethren ye have done it unto me." Here again the lost ask Christ why He has excluded them from the kingdom and He tells them it is because they did not see Him in the person of the naked, the thirsty, the hungry, the imprisoned and the stranger. His final decree of fate is, "Depart from me, ye cursed, into everlasting fire, prepared for the devil and his angels:" Matthew 25:41. Psalms 9:16 tells us how God "EXECUTES JUDGMENT" or "MAKES DECISIONS." He lets the sinner go his own way and do his own thing. He permits Satan to have complete control. But, in Revelation 7:1-3 his "judgments" are a "holding" action until the 144,000 (wheat harvest) are sealed which will be his army, Revelation 19. See Judges 7:13 and Ruth 2:23 concerning the first use of the concept of the barley harvest.

Even in this NT Scripture Christ again takes the blame. He pictures Himself as rejecting them, when they are the ones who are rejecting Him. This is also true in Revelation 3, where God "spews" the "Laodiceans" out of His mouth, when we are the ones spewing or spitting God out of our lives, even Jesus the "Bread, of Life," and Jesus, the "wine," of life.

*Note: Titus 2:11 reads, "For the grace of God that bringeth salvation hath appeared to all men." The marginal reading gives the original Greek rendering thusly: ***"Or, that bringeth salvation to all men, hath appeared."*** Obviously, this marginal reading gives a much clearer and stronger meaning in support of the concept of Universal Salvation.

CHAPTER 12

GOD NEVER USES FORCE

Our heavenly Father never uses force to motivate us to obey Him. These attributes are not part of His loving character. This concept of a non-violent deity simply reinforces what we are saying, that God has never used force or coercion. So, how does He banish every carnal weapon and defeat the powers of darkness? Simply by turning on the light of His truth and love. That is why Satan left heaven in the beginning. God revealed His truth and love enough so each angel could "see the light," and those who were living in the darkness of Satan's lies were eager to head for the shadows of Satan's company. If God at that time, had revealed all of His truth about Himself and about Satan and just what he was really doing and where it was taking him, Satan and all of his hosts would have not been able to survive. They would have surely self-destructed right there and then. But, had that happened, the loyal angels and unfallen worlds would not have understood the terrible malignity of sin, nor the protection that lies in strict obedience to the LAW OF GOD, WHICH IS THE LAW OF LOVE. In the Day of Judgment, in our present age, every issue of truth and righteousness will be brought out. The fire of His truth and love will "burn up" the wicked, but will "give life" to the righteous. In other words, God will permit the sinner go his/her own way and do his/her own thing. He will no longer hold back the forces of darkness. See Psalms 9:16. That day is hastening on apace. But for right now the angels are holding back the winds of strife. Rev. 7:1.

Now, let's talk about How the Lord EXECUTES JUDGMENT? HOW DOES HE "NOT CLEAR THE GUILTY"? Here it is: HE LEAVES THE REJECTERS OF HIS LOVE TO THEMSELVES. How does He do this? With a single word – "DEPART!" What is their PUNISHMENT to be? It is simply, "GO YOUR OWN WAY AND DO YOUR OWN

THING." Or in other words, "DEPART FROM ME." Or, "YOU ARE ON YOUR OWN NOW, I CANNOT STOP YOU FROM WHATEVER YOU WISH TO DO. I AM SORRY THAT I CANNOT HELP YOU SEE THE RIGHT WAY, SO YOU ARE NOW FREE TO DO AS YOU PLEASE." Of course, Satan is standing by to deceive them and he will be able to do that in this, our day, before Christ returns in this age, as well as after the 1,000 years, when the wicked are marshaled into a vast army to march against the Holy City, New Jerusalem, to try take it. These two time segments we shall now consider as we continue our study into God's "Fire," and "Sword," and the final end of sin and sinners and how God "PERMITS" this to take place, but does not actually arbitrarily do it. This is what I will continue to demonstrate with Scripture, and logic along with some outside references to astral catastrophism from contemporary writers and scientists.

"THE INHABITANTS OF THE EARTH ARE BURNED"

Notice the words of our majestic God in Isaiah. "Behold, the Lord maketh the earth empty, and maketh it waste, and turneth it upside down, and scattereth abroad the inhabitants thereof. The land shall be utterly emptied, and utterly spoiled:...the earth mourneth and fadeth away...the earth also is defiled under the inhabitants thereof, because THEY HAVE TRANSGRESSED THE LAWS, CHANGED THE ORDINANCE, BROKEN THE EVERLASTING COVENANT. THEREFORE HATH THE CURSE DEVOURED THE EARTH... AND ... THE INHABITANTS OF THE EARTH ARE BURNED, AND FEW MEN LEFT." Isaiah 24:4-6.

We have already explained how Jesus will "smite the nations," Revelation 19:15, with the "sharp word," that comes out of His mouth. It is not an arbitrary act on the part of God. No. Our heavenly Father destroys no man. He destroys darkness by the light of truth. He smites the Prince of darkness with

Light. The Time of Trouble will bring the WRATH OF GOD. But, Jesus does not send the Wrath, He only PERMITS it to come because of the CHANGED ORDINANCE, AND THE BROKEN EVERLASTING COVENANT. "And to wait for His Son from heaven...even Jesus, WHICH DELIVERED US FROM THE WRATH TO COME." 1 Thessalonians 1:10. "We shall be saved FROM WRATH THROUGH HIM." Romans 5:9. Now, notice this next scripture and how it parallels Revelation 19:15. "And to you who are troubled rest with us, when the Lord Jesus shall be revealed from heaven with his mighty angels, In flaming fire taking vengeance on them that know not God, and that obey not the gospel of our Lord Jesus Christ. Who shall be punished with everlasting destruction from the presence of the Lord, and from the glory of his power; When he shall come to be glorified in his saints, and to be admired in all them that believe..." I Thess 1:10. (This text refers to both His second coming before the millennium and His third coming after the 1,000 years). "And then shall that Wicked (Satan) be revealed, whom the Lord shall consume with the SPIRIT (WORD OR SWORD) of HIS MOUTH, and SHALL DESTROY WITH THE BRIGHTNESS (FIRE) OF HIS COMING." 2 Thessalonians 2:8, 9.

The way these scriptures have always been explained in the past is that Jesus and all the Holy Angels will come with all this tremendous brightness and glory and the wicked will be "blotted out" of existence. But, is that what really happens? Do the wicked just "vaporize" into the atmosphere due to the terrible brightness at His second coming before the 1,000 years begin? No, they do not. Notice, "And the slain of the Lord (God always takes the blame) shall be at that day from one end of the earth even unto the other end of the earth: they shall not be lamented, neither gathered nor buried; they shall be dung upon the ground." Jeremiah 25:33. This will take place in this age in which we are now living. The wicked will self-destruct. "Every man's sword shall be against his brother." Ezek. 38:21. So they will all die by their own hand when the Lord removes His protection. And they will remain unburied for 1,000 years. But after the millennium all of these billions of people are going to be resurrected to face the final judgment. And that is when they will see the truth and eventually every knee shall bow and every tongue confess. So, that is when they will all come back to Him be converted and restored. "All they that go down to the dust shall bow before him...They shall come, and shall declare his righteousness unto a people that shall be born." Psalm 22:28-31. "And the glory (character) of the Lord shall be revealed, and all flesh shall see it together." Isaiah 40:5. "For as in Adam all die, even so in Christ shall all be made alive." I Cor. 15:22.

Notice this next scripture from Isaiah 10:16, 17. "The Lord of hosts, (shall) send among his fat ones leanness; and under his glory he shall kindle a BURNING LIKE THE BURNING OF A FIRE. And the light of Israel shall be for a fire, and His Holy One for a flame: and it shall burn and devour his thorns and his briers in one day;" Notice that in Isaiah 33:5-17 we have a description of the events which will transpire after the 1,000 years. "The highways lie waste, . . . the earth mourneth . . . Now will I rise, saith the Lord; now will I be exalted; now will I lift up myself. Ye shall conceive chaff, ye shall bring forth stubble: your breath, AS FIRE, SHALL DEVOUR YOU. AND THE PEOPLE SHALL BE AS THE BURNINGS OF LIME: AS THORNS CUT UP SHALL THEY BE BURNED IN THE FIRE. The sinners in Zion are afraid; fearfulness hath surprised the hypocrites. Who among us shall dwell with the DEVOURING FIRE? WHO AMONG US SHALL DWELL WITH EVERLASTING BURNINGS?" Isaiah 33:14. Cf. Song of Solomon 8:6 where God's love is said to be like a flame of fire. Remember that Moses was not burned by the burning bush nor the disciples' hair singed by the "tongues of fire" on their heads on the day of Pentecost. Acts 2:3, 4, because we know that God is "harmless." Hebrews 7:26. Any fire that proceeds forth from Him is not destructive but life-giving. The proof for that would be Saul of Tarsus, who was literally baptized in the glorious light of the fire of Jesus' presence (Acts 9).This was like a LAKE OF

FIRE for Saul, but it did not kill him. It converted Him. This fiery experience changed His life in a very positive way.

The Word of God itself is compared to a fire, Jeremiah 20:9, as well as His holy angels, Hebrews 1:7. In contrast to this, Satan's fire is destructive, because it is literal fire, as revealed in the first chapter of the book of Job, when Satan caused fire to come down from the sky and destroy Job's sheep and servants, Job 1:16. Literal fire never existed until after the fall of Adam, when the curse of sin entered the world. But Jesus came to reverse this curse by bringing "fire on the earth," Luke 12:49. I will go into more detail on this point in Chapter 17, "JESUS, THE FIRE OF TRUTH."

Just picture if you will, Jesus standing above the wicked showing them a panoramic view of the ages. Every sin they have ever committed is brought home to each mind with tremendous clarity and force. It is all laid bare. As soon as those books of record are opened, and Jesus eyes look upon the wicked with love, they will become CONSCIOUS OF EVERY SIN WHICH THEY HAVE EVER COMMITTED. Revelation 20:11, 12 speaks of the "books being opened" and the wicked being judged by those books. This is another way of expressing the ability of God to give an instant replay of the entire history of the ages. This will not be a false history this time, not slanted or abridged or doctored, but the true history with no slimy details left out. Do you think this is going to burn the wicked in their hearts and in their minds? Isaiah 9:18. Yes it will because this will be their "Lake of Fire." And they will all fall down and worship the Lord just like Saul of Tarsus did on the road to Damascus. Acts 9.

Is God portrayed anywhere in the Scriptures as speaking out words of fire? Yes. "Behold, the name of the Lord cometh from far, burning with his anger, and the burden thereof is heavy: (and the grievousness of flame, says the margin) his lips are full of indignation and his tongue as a DEVOURING FIRE." Isaiah 30:27. Compare 2 Thessalonians 2:8, where it says that He "Shall consume them with the Spirit (breath) of His mouth." Now notice the next verse and how God takes the blame for not preventing the nations (permitting them) from destroying themselves. "His wrath pours out like floods upon them all, to sweep them all away. He will sift out the proud nations and bridle them and lead them off to their doom." LB. The King James Version uses the expression "His breath," showing that it is something coming from His mouth (words of fire) that causes the Lake of fire. But, remember that God's fire is love and truth. Song of Solomon 8:6.

God's Fire of love burns in every heart to give life or death. How we relate ourselves to it determines the outcome. If we fight and resist it or run away from it, we destroy ourselves, as Judas did. If we repent, as Peter did, that fiery love will transform us as it transformed both Peter and Saul of Tarsus into Paul the Apostle. Acts 9. In Luke 24:32 the two disciples on the way to Emmaus "said one to another, 'did not our heart burn within us, while he talked with us by the way, and WHILE HE OPENED TO US THE SCRIPTURES?'"

In that final day of judgment, NO ONE WILL BE SAYING THAT THE GUILT AND REMORSE THEY ARE EXPERIENCING IS ANY LESS PAINFUL THAN LITERAL FIRE. "Therefore the Lord will cut off from Israel head and tail, branch and rush, in one day. The ancient and honorable, he is the head, and the prophet that teacheth lies, he is the tail, For the leaders of this people cause them to err; and they that are led of them are destroyed. For all this his anger is not turned away, but his hand is stretched out still...(which shows that He never gives up pleading for them to come to Him. The gates of the city will always be open and little by little they will all eventually come in and drink of the water of life and eat of the tree of life) FOR WICKEDNESS BURNETH AS THE FIRE: ... And the people shall be as the fuel of the fire; no man shall spare his brother." Isaiah 9:14, 15, 16, 17, 18, Ezek 38:21. Other scriptures to study on fire are Jeremiah 4:4; 7:20; 20:9; 21:12, Lamentations 2:3. Isaiah 30:27; 42:25; 62:1. Just take a concordance and look up all the words on fire, burn and burning and you will find a consistent pattern all the way through. God speaks His words of LOVE (CALLED FIRE) and the people REACT instead of respond, at least at first. God's INTENTION is to SAVE them, but they think He is seeking to destroy and try to hide.

A LAKE OF FIRE BEFORE AND AFTER THE 1,000 YEARS

Let us look at Matthew 10:26. "Fear them not therefore: for there is nothing covered, that shall not be revealed; and hid, that shall not be known." God will reveal all sin by a revelation of His truth as it is written down in His law and all through the Scriptures and especially in the lives of His saints. The lake of fire is both spiritual and literal. God allows all the wicked to see the whole story. This "fiery" revelation of truth is the spiritual part of the lake of fire. A lake is a body of water and water is people. (Revelation 17.15) Can't you see all of those people outside the golden city New Jerusalem, "on fire" with hatred and anger toward God and the saints? And then when they find out the real truth, they are going to be blaming each other. So the fire from heaven is the loving truth about God which will cause the wicked to react and suffer.

I do not, however, blame God or hold Him responsible for this lake of fire, as so many have taught and are teaching today. No. God permits it to happen and takes the blame or responsibility for it because, He told the entire story (truth) about Satan's rebellion and the ensuing 6,000 years of rebellion on this planet ... this He calls bringing fire on the earth, Luke 12:49. Compare Revelation 20:9, "And fire came down from God out of heaven and devoured them." Compare also Proverbs 21:25 and Psalms 11:6; and 2. As a result of this "fiery revelation of truth," the souls of the wicked burn with anguish as they remember all of their sins. God's complete revelation leaves them "naked," and "ashamed," before the whole world and the whole universe as well. It is the first time in history that He has revealed all the truth and the first time He has not restrained Satan from controlling them and from their own evil passions which break forth like a fire from inside of them with terrible fury. This is indeed a strange thing for Him to do. In addition to that we must admit that this "Strange Act" could not be God killing sinners. Because, according to all known theology in the world He has always been doing that. So, there would be nothing strange about God killing people at the end of the world. So, that could not be His "Strange Act."

A "lake" is a body of water and water or "sea" (Revelation 17:15) symbolizes people. A lake of fire symbolically, therefore, could be a mass of humanity who are burning up with fear, anger, hatred and remorse. Notice Isaiah 28:21, "For the Lord shall rise up as in Mount Perazim, He shall be wroth as in the valley of Gibeon, that He may do His work, His strange work, and bring to pass His act, His strange act." It is always good to read the texts before and after in order to obtain a clearer meaning. Notice verse 22, the very next verse after the one I just quoted above.

Here is one theologian's position, which is the belief of most professed Christians today regarding the Tsunami which struck Sri Lanka and parts of India in 2004. "From a biblical perspective the Tsunami tragedy is purely an act of God, because there are no human factors to blame. There are no loggers to blame for clearing forests, no engineers to fault for poor design or construction, no government planners to call to account for allowing urban development in risky places. The slipping of the tectonic plates on the ocean-bed off Sumatra, cannot be blamed on global warming or on the lack of adequate precautionary measures. What happened is beyond human capacity to influence or control. Some Christians wish to blame the Devil for such natural disasters, but nowhere the Bible attributes to Satan power over weather, natural phenomena or disastrous events. Satan is sometimes called the prince of this world (2 Cor 4:4, John 12:31, 14:30, Eph 6:12), but his power appears to be limited to tempt and deceive." This writer forgot to quote

Ephesians 2:2. "Wherein time past you walked according to the course of this world, according to the prince of the power of the air, the spirit that now works in the children of disobedience." We also read in 2 Cor 4:4 that Satan is referred to as the "God of this world."

Even though the Bible does state that this world belongs to God, in reality He is taking the blame for what He permits the devil to do. For example, Isaiah 14:16, 17 clearly states that it is Satan who makes the earth to tremble. "Is this the man that made the earth to tremble, that did shake kingdoms; That made the world as a wilderness, and destroyed the cities thereof;?" Compare Exodus 19 where mount Sinai "was altogether on a smoke ...and the whole mount quaked greatly."

"Satan will continue to act a double part. Appearing to be the dispenser of great blessings and divine truths, he will, by his lying wonders, hold the world under his control; and at the same time he will indulge his malignity by causing distress and destruction, and will accuse God's people as the cause of the fearful convulsions of nature and the strife and bloodshed among men which are desolating the earth." {4SP 444.2}

"Satan works through the elements also to garner his harvest of unprepared souls. He has studied the secrets of the laboratories of nature, and he uses all his power to control the elements as far as God allows. When he was suffered to afflict Job, how quickly flocks and herds, servants, houses, children, were swept away, one trouble succeeding another as in a moment. It is God that shields His creatures and hedges them in from the power of the destroyer. But the Christian world have shown contempt for the law of Jehovah; and the Lord will do just what He has declared that He would--He will withdraw His blessings from the earth and remove His protecting care from those who are rebelling against His law and teaching and forcing others to do the same. Satan has control of all whom God does not especially guard. He will favor and prosper some in order to further his own designs, and he will bring trouble upon others and lead men to believe that it is God who is afflicting them. {GC 589.2}

Here again we see that the characterisitcs of the destroyer are not attributed to God, but to Satan, the enemy of mankind. God allows destruction by withdrawing His blessings and protection from those who rebel against Him. This is His strange act, as He is a God of love, and such behavior seems strange to selfish mankind.

"...Even now he is at work. In accidents and calamities by sea and by land, in great conflagrations, in fierce tornadoes and terrific hailstorms, in tempests, floods, cyclones, tidal waves [called by the Japanese term of Tsunami today], and earthquakes, in every place and in a thousand forms, Satan is exercising his power. He sweeps away the ripening harvest, and famine and distress follow. He imparts to the air a deadly taint, andthousands perish by the pestilence. These visitations are to become more and more frequent and disastrous." GC 589. God told Elijah the same truth: "And he said, Go forth, and stand upon the mount before the LORD. And, behold, the LORD passed by, and a great and strong wind rent the mountains, and brake in pieces the rocks before the LORD; but the LORD was not in the wind: and after the wind an earthquake; but the LORD was not in the earthquake: and after the earthquake a fire; but the LORD was not in the fire: and after the fire a still small voice." 1 Kings 19:11-12. So, my friend, if the True Lord was not in any of those aberrations of nature then who was doing it? It had to be the 'lord of this earth,' Satan.

About 1980 I began to understand that it was the "Lord of this earth" who was the destroyer. But I still did not realize that he was actually identified as "God" and "Lord" in the Old Testament. When we examine the original Hebrew word in Isaiah "ZUWR," Strongs 2114 it literally means, "to turn aside." "Hence to be a foreigner, strange, profane; to commit adultery." The second reference is from Strong's 5237, Nokriy, which also means "strange, adulterous, different, outlandish." It is derived from Strong's 5234 and 5235 "nakar" and "noker." Nakar means "to disemble, estrange, (and) to feign self to be another." Now, this is very revealing because that is exactly what

Lucifer (Satan) has been doing for 6,000 years...feigning himself to be the true Lord when he is actually the devil. It also means to "behave (make) self strange, ignore, dissimmulate."

Another important key to understanding the "Strange work or act," (always attributed to the true God) takes place when we realize that the Lord who is "rising up" to perform a "strange act and work," is actually the lord of this earth who is "rising up," or exalting himself...flexing his muscles in the earth to frighten and scare people into submission as he did at Sinai. "He shall be wroth, as in the valley of Gibeon." Isaiah 28:21. This identifies which Lord is actually doing the destroying because if God does not destroy Satan would have to be the Lord God of this earth, who was also the destroyer in the valley of Gibeon. ***It is positive then that this "strange" (out of character act) could not be from the true Lord, because our God does not act strange or weird or crazy. He does not act "strange" one time and normal the next. He is not a paranoid schizophrenic.*** He is not a bi-polar God. That would be the devil who acts like that. "The way of man is froward and strange: but as for the pure, his work is right." Proverbs 21:8 Christ and the Father are certainly pure: God is not strange. To be strange, this passage reveals, is to be perverted. God's strange act is not His active behavior, but His passive tolerance of the enemy's behavior.

So, if it is Satan who is the "lord" Isaiah is writing about what is there that is "strange" about this act or work? The obvious answer is that at the end of this age, when Satan knows that He only has a "short time" Rev 12:12, he will be allowed to destroy completely that which he formerly only wished to control and pervert. Hitler, at the end of his career, in 1945, also did something "strange." He ordered all of Germany to be destroyed because his plans did not work out as he planned. He claimed to love the German people and to be working for their betterment and welfare. Now, he commands for them all to be destroyed. It must have seemed strange to his followers and the whole German nation that the Fuerher they worshipped and had deified was now the one passing the death decree upon them. And so, this "lord" of planet earth will do the same thing. Notice what Dan 11:44 predicts will happen at the end of Satan's career in this final age. "But tidings out of the east and out of the north shall trouble him: therefore he shall go forth with great fury to destroy, and utterly to make away many."

"Now therefore be ye not mockers, lest your bands be made strong: for I have heard from the Lord God of hosts a CONSUMPTION, even determined upon the whole earth." The Hebrew word for "consumption," is from "KALAH," which literally means to be completed, finished or consumed. Its meaning is clearer when we read Psalms 37:20 . . . "But the wicked shall perish, and they shall CONSUME (KALAH); into smoke shall they consume (kalah) away." Our modern dictionary (Barnhart, for example) says, CONSUMPTION: "destruction or decay, progressive wasting of the body." The definition of CONSUME is: "to destroy as by decomposition or burning." Deuteronomy 28:22 says, "The Lord shall smite thee with a CONSUMPTION, AND WITH A FEVER, AND WITH AN INFLAMMATION, and with an extreme burning...." Now when we go back to our basic principle of how God operates, we can see that when He says, "lest your bands be made strong," simply means "unless you stop being disrespectful and defiant toward me and my law, I will not be able to protect you from the DESTROYER who will bind you with His bands of sin and lawlessness and disobedience and darkness and death until your life is totally consumed for this age." Compare Psalms 2:10-12.

When we consider Isaiah 28:14-20 we see an even clearer picture. "Wherefore hear the word of the Lord, ye scornful men, that rule this people which is in Jerusalem. Because ye have said, we have made a covenant with death, and with hell are we at agreement; when the overflowing scourge shall pass through, it shall not come unto us: for we have made lies our refuge, and under falsehood have we hid ourselves: Therefore thus saith the Lord God, Behold, I lay in Zion for a foundation a stone, a tried stone, a precious corner stone, (Christ Jesus) a sure foundation:

he that believeth shall not make haste. Judgment also will I lay to the line, and righteousness to the plummet: AND THE HAIL (the seventh plague is hail, and this does not mean merely ice, but rock, also) shall sweep away the refuge of lies, and waters shall overflow the hiding place." Isaiah 28:16-17. (See 2 Samuel 5:20, where the phrase, "breach or breaking forth of waters is used). Satan is the Lord of breaches. Isaiah 59:19, Job 16:14, Genesis 38:29, Pharez is equal to Satan. . . . "and your covenant with death shall be disannulled, and your agreement with hell shall not stand;" Even though the wicked planned to exit this world by suicide the Lord says that He has a plan to save them which will "disannul" their agreement with death and the grave, because Jesus' death on the cross has cancelled out all debts and there is no more debt to pay. Like the Prodigal son, they are now free to come back home into the Father's house. Death and hell will be "cast into the lake of fire..." (Rev 20:14) because ***"the last enemy that will be destroyed is death itself."*** I Cor. 15:26. This will happen after the 1,000 years.

Now, we are ready to study God's "Strange act" in more depth. Mount Perazim and the Valley of Gibeon are referred to as examples of how God will operate at the end of the world, ON BOTH OCCASIONS, BEFORE AND AFTER THE 1,000 YEARS. Remember that the god of breaking forth is SATAN. He is ALWAYS trying to push himself ahead of CHRIST. This is symbolized in the story found in Genesis 38:27-30. But let us go to another scripture now about DAVID. "AND DAVID CAME TO BAALPERAZIM, (meaning Lord Of the breaking forth). SATAN has always tried to push himself ahead of Christ. AND DAVID SMOTE THEM THERE, AND SAID, THE LORD HATH BROKEN FORTH UPON MINE ENEMIES BEFORE ME, AS THE BREACH OF WATERS. THEREFORE HE CALLED THE NAME OF THAT PLACE BAALPERAZIM." (Meaning, the valley of breaking forth). 2 Samuel 5:20.

Later on the Philistines came up again to fight David. Once again David would win the battle because the Lord told him, "when thou hearest the sound of a going in the tops of the mulberry trees, that then thou shalt bestir thyself. For then shall the LORD GO OUT BEFORE THEE, TO SMITE THE HOST OF THE PHILISTINES." Verse 24. Remember, when God says He smites someone, it means He has withdrawn His protection from them, because they forced Him out of their lives by their choice. Notice in Numbers 14:9, ". . . neither fear ye the people of the land; for they are bread for us: THEIR DEFENSE (shadow or shade: Psalms 121:5; Malachi 3:2; Jeremiah 48:45) IS DEPARTED FROM THEM, and the Lord is with us: fear them not." God's "strange act" is not when He finally blows His cool, becomes very angry and gets even. Oh, no. This is not God's character. And besides, what would be so "strange" about Him killing anyone at this time, if indeed He has been doing it all along throughout the Old Testament? God's strange act is not when He takes life, but when He is forced to stop preserving life by the choice of every creature who is determined to commit suicide. And in this final age He is going to completely withdraw and let Satan have entire control of this planet. This He has never done before. It will be a strange act. We have already discussed the reason why God permitted David to destroy with the sword. It was not His perfect will when anyone in the past used force or coercion to accomplish a certain job for the Lord. But, He permitted them to go out and slaughter whole nations at times, but it was His permissive will, not His perfect will. Deut 1:29-46. "So terribly blinded had they become by transgression. The Lord had never commanded them to 'go up and fight.' It was not His purpose that they should gain the land by warfare, but by strict obedience to His commands." Patriarchs & Prophets, page 392.

In the case of David at Perazim, the Lord received the glory for the victory. David, though a man of war, and falling short in some respects regarding God's will for his life, cooperated more with the Lord than any other King of Israel. Scripture refers us to this experience in history as an example of how God will "BREAK FORTH," or "SMITE" THE WICKED IN THE

LAST DAYS ON TWO OCCASIONS BEFORE AND AFTER THE 1,000 YEARS. The first time will be just before Jesus comes to rescue the final Elect who are under the death decree, similar to what was passed in Esther's day. Isaiah 11:4, Malachi 3:6, Jer. 5:3. How will the Lord "break forth" upon the wicked who are hunting down the righteous? He will reveal truth by raining the fire of truth down upon them, through the preaching of His holy Word, and they will just come unglued and slaughter themselves. In David's day his enemies were evidently allowed to see themselves as they really were in the fullness of their evil natures which made them hate themselves and each other. And then God permitted the evil angels to have full control by withdrawing all restraints and they began killing each other. Just how God is able to do this is beyond our comprehension, but when the Lord withdraws His protecting Hand, everything falls apart and men lose their courage, their physical and mental bearings and instantly reap in a few seconds or minutes what they would ordinarily reap in a life time. Isaiah 26:11-14. The key word is "visited," as in Exodus 20:5. Someone will protest, "but why would Satan's angels cooperate with God in casting down their own people?" First of all they are not "Satan's" people in the full sense of the word. All humans belong to God. Satan just claims them so he can deceive them and cause them to be lost for this age or eon. How he accomplishes this is irrelevant or beside the point to him. If he can cause anyone at any time to be destroyed and blame it upon God, he is anxious to do it so more people will look upon God as a cruel tyrant a hateful and vengeful judge. In addition to that, you must remember that although Satan is much wiser than we are, he is basically insane. And an insane being does not always act rationally. Another point is that Satan figures that a "bird in the hand is worth two in the bush." In other words, Satan is so anxious to destroy human kind and cause grief and heartache to the Father's heart, that he will destroy anyone at anytime anywhere he can. That is his nature. Satan's angels have no doubt been fighting each other too. Now, reason it out for yourselves. Is it possible that God has the power and the ability to restrain and release, prevent and permit even among the evil angels in order to carry out his purposes? And to do so without interfering with the free moral agency of either men or angels, loyal and disloyal to God's truth, fallen and unfallen from God's presence? I say, "YES," God can do it and He does it all the time. He is ACTUALLY preserving SATAN and His angels from destroying themselves for the Father has a plan for them as well as all of mankind. ANGELS AND MEN ARE MADE OF FIRE. The Hebrew word for man is ESH, which is from the same word that means "Fire." The angels are also flames or fires. "And of the angels he saith, who maketh his angels spirits, and his ministers a flame of fire." Hebrews 1:7. Satan's angels lost none of their power when they fell with Satan from heaven. But, they have perverted their very talents to destroy God's creation instead of to sustain and bring glory to the Creator. So, we are caught in the middle of two fires ... a fire of life and truth and a fire of deceit and death.

THE VALLEY OF GIBEON

In the last part of Isaiah 28:21 we read that God is going to "rise up and be wroth," or angry as "in the valley of Gibeon, that he may do his work; his strange work; and bring to pass his act, his strange act." In Joshua 10:10 we read the beginning of a story about a great victory the Lord gave to Joshua as the leader of Israel. "And the Lord discomfited them before Israel, and slew them with a great slaughter at Gibeon, and chased them along the way that goeth up to Bethhoron, and smote them to Azekah, and unto Makkedah." Now, God did not actually need Israel to do away with these wicked people. He never intended that they take a literal sword and get involved in bloodshed and the taking of life, but because of the HARDNESS OF THEIR HEARTS, AND THEIR STIFF NECKS, they had a very 'fiery" spirit and a pugilistic nature which they just had to satisfy. Of course, it also is against our human pride to give anyone else the credit for a special accomplishment. We want as much or all (if possible) of the glory for ourselves. But, in this case, God permitted a natural (or unnatural) disaster to overtake these wicked ones, for it says, "that the Lord cast down great stones (hail) from heaven upon them unto Azekah, and they died: they were more which died with hailstones than they whom the children of Israel slew with the sword." Psalms 78:47-49 proves that Satan and his angels bring hail. See also Job 37:10-13, 38:8-13.

CHAPTER 13

HAIL STONES AND ASTRAL CATASTROPHISM

In all the years I have been studying theology, I have never read where a commentary gave a scientific explanation for the events that are normally called "miracles" in the Old Testament. For example, the Flood. How did it happen? Most preachers I have heard talk about the flood simply explain it as an arbitrary act of God. In other words, the Lord was fed up with that age and came down, turned the faucet on, and drowned them all but Noah and his family, who had enough sense to go into the ark. If we understand the Omniscience of God we should realize that He has the foreknowledge to foresee all the events of the future and then lovingly prepare a way of escape for those who love Him and believe His Word. That in a nutshell is what He did for Noah, his family, and what He is doing for all who will live in the last hours of this last age.

God knew the flood was coming, just like He knows the end of the world is coming. He is the great mathematician and astronomer of the ages who can figure to one millionth of a second when each event in this world and in our personal lives is going to take place. Is it heretical to believe that He who created all the starry heavens and who keeps each planet in its orbit around each blazing sun would also be able to not only foresee, but also control the movements of these planets? And control them according to His own will and for the safety of His people and the accomplishment of His great plan of salvation, even though sin had caused problems in heaven itself, as well as on this earth? I AM means an eternal presence. The past, present, and future are alike to God. He sees the remote events of past history, and the far distant future with as clear a vision as we do those things that are transpiring daily. Immanuel Velikovsky is a Jewish scientist, historian and philosopher, who has convulsed the scientific community for more than a quarter of a century with his book, "WORLDS IN COLLISION." He sweeps away the foundations of evolution with daring explanations for the origin of planet earth and the age of the world. His main theme is CATASTROPHISM. Instead of this earth's crust and the lithosphere being formed over millions and millions of years, Velikovsky asserts that planets from outer space came close to earth in the past causing tremendous upheavals in the form of tidal waves, earthquakes, and giant hailstones.

Although he may not believe in the Divine Inspiration of the Bible, per se, Velikovsky does believe the Scriptures to be historically accurate in their accounts of past events. For example, he quotes Joshua 10:1 and then says, "The author of the Book of Joshua was surely ignorant of any connection between the two phenomena." He has reference to the sun's standing still and the stones (meteroites) falling on the same day. Here is his explanation. "If the head of a comet should pass very close to our path, so as to effect a distortion in the career of the earth, another phenomenon beside disturbed movement of the planet would strike the earth and would increase to a torrent. Stones scorched by flying through the atmosphere would be hurled on home and head. The wide radius over which the heavenly wrath swept is emphasized in the prayer: 'All the kingdoms tottered...' A torrent of large stones coming from the sky, an earthquake—(which he says accounts for a shifting of the earth on her axis so the day would be extended), a whirlwind, a disturbance in the movement of the earth—these four phenomena belong together. It appears that a large comet must have passed very near to our planet and disrupted its movement, a part of the stones dispersed in the neck and tail of the comet smote the surface of our earth a shattering blow." Page 59, "Worlds In Collision."

He also believes that these four phenomena were widespread in different parts of the earth and not just local events. He sites historical data to substantiate his claims. If Velikovsky were the only scientist to propound such a theory, we might not give it much thought or credence, but Donald W. Patten, along with Ronald R. Hatch and Loren C. Steinhauer, reputable scientists and Bible believing, Christ-professing Christians have developed this concept of ASTRAL CATASTROPHISM even farther in a work entitled, THE LONG DAY OF JOSHUA AND SIX OTHER CATASTROPHES.

With geometrical sketches and a lot of historical data and chronology, Patten and his associates have come up with some amazing deductions. Their book is being sold in Book and Bible stores all over America and probably in other countries as well. Their theory is a serious challenge to the followers of such German rationalists as Kant, Hegel, Feuerbach, Goethe, Marx, Hutton, and Lyell, who all propounded non-biblical ideas that prepared the way for a ready acceptance of Darwin's theory of evolution, and all that has come since to undermine faith in the Word of God.

"With reference to ancient history, to ancient literature, and to historical cosmology, we shall require from our readers a new framework of thought for ancient history and for cosmology." "THE LONG DAY OF JOSHUA," p. 8. Let us consider these ideas without accepting or rejecting them. Personally, I don't need these scientific explanations, but they may help some people. Just because I have included them in this book does not mean I believe this is the way it happened. But, I do believe to be objective these scientists deserve a hearing. According to Patten's ideas, the Long Day of Joshua occurred "circa October 25, 1404 B. C." He states further, "According to our model, CATASTROPHES or threatening CATASTROPHES should be expected once every 54 years, or every 108 years on the average." Ibid., 173. The dating method is based upon 1) the chronicles of Scripture; 2) the resonant model for the ancient Marian orbit; 3) the record of Josephus and Talmudic information; and 4) the observation that heavy holocausts tended to bunch in pairs every five to six centuries. Here are just a few events he has worked out with dates: The Joel-Amos Catastrophe, October 25, 756 B.C.; add 108 years and you have the Elijahic Catastrophe on October 25, 864 B.C.; add 108 years more and you have the Greater Davidic Catastrophe on October 25, 972

B.C. Samuel saw one in 1080 B.C.; Deborah in 1188 B.C.; and the Long Day of Joshua occurred on October 25, 1404 B. C.

"The phenomenon of heavy twin CATASTROPHES across the centuries should be observed. If a century had one very severe holocaust, very likely it also had another." Ibid., p.177. Regarding the fall of Jericho, he says, "Its wall shuddered and collapsed about the time of the vernal equinox...." The vernal equinox, (March 20-21), according to Patten is a time of earthquake activity. The majority of the severe earthquakes in the 20th Century A.D. have occurred in the months of March and April, when the moon is in perigee.

The Bible, regarding the fall of Jericho says, "So the people shouted when the priests blew with the trumpets; and it came to pass, when the people shouted with a great shout, that the wall fell down flat, so that the people went up into the city, every man straight before him, and they took the city." Joshua 6:20. Now, Patten does not say an earthquake destroyed Jericho, but that earthquakes seem to take place about the same time of year Jericho fell, from his research. Some may say that the trumpet blast caused the earthquake. But the Bible doesn't say there was an earthquake, but simply that the earth shook. The trumpet sound was a signal of victory. God's people were permitted to kill. This was not God's perfect will, but His permissive will. He allowed and controlled the sword, but He did not sanction it. If the trumpet blast and shout of the people caused the walls to fall, that also was God's permissive, not His perfect will. I would rather believe that God withdrew His protection, and these heathen died, except for Rahab's family. If the city perished by an earthquake, then it was Satan who directly destroyed it, for Satan brings earthquakes. Isaiah 14:12-17. When Christ was upon the earth, He stilled the angry sea, but caused no earthquakes. Ephesians 2:2 calls him (Satan) "the Prince of the power of the air." 2 Corinthians 4:4 calls him "the god of this world."

We know that tidal waves are caused by earthquakes, but what causes earthquakes? Perhaps Satan has the power to cause earthquakes in a way which we are not aware. A new type of modern warfare has been developed in which a nation can set off a charge in a certain part of the earth underground and cause a shock wave that will follow a fault line and result in an earthquake in another part of the world. Also, around 1900, Nikola Tesla, a Russian scientist, devised a system to transmit power which involved the use of extremely low frequency (ELF—electromagnetic frequencies) which are now being used to distort the weather and cause earthquakes, and even to effect human behavior. Another modality that is being used is HAARP, an acronym for (High-frequency Active Auroral Research Project). A book has been written on this project entitled: "Angels Don't Play This Haarp: advances in Tesla Technology," by Dr. Nick Begich and Jeane Manning. This book claims that this new system manipulates the environment in a way which can: 1. Disrupt human mental processes. 2. Jam all global communications systems. 3. Change weather patterns over large areas. 4. Interfere with wildlife migration patterns. 5. Negatively affect your health. 6. Unnaturally impact the Earth's upper atmosphere.

Has Satan communicated some of his diabolical skills to human beings to hasten their self-annihilation? It would seem so. In the January 1977 issue of SCIENCE DIGEST we read of a man who designed his own "home-made" A-bomb. He says, "Much of the physics required for the construction of a fission bomb gradually has become diffused-increased quantities of plutonium and uranium are manufactured, shipped, reprocessed and stored in all parts of the world. I am a 21 year old senior at Princeton University. In the fall of 1976, I designed a Pu-239 atomic bomb for my independent work in the physics department. If built, it would be small enough to fit into a U-haul trailer, and the yield would be an estimated 8 1/2 kilotons—enough to level a large part of Manhattan." It is very difficult to obtain plutonium, but apart from that item, Phillips said the cost would be $2,000 to build his "homemade" A-bomb. Fifteen pounds of plutonium would cost $150,000, if it could be bought; but it cannot be bought by an unaccredited person or organization. Phillips purpose in this research was to ascertain how difficult it would be for a terrorist or criminal organization to design and build such a device. The physics involved in building an atomic bomb are fairly well known. Page 20 of his paper is now withheld from public view: it's considered too revealing as to what's needed to build a device that will trigger a blast. Revelation 11:18 tells us that God will permit the wicked people who are destroying the earth to be destroyed themselves by His judgments (that is, by His decisions not to restrain them any longer). *See note on page 129.

And in 2 Peter 3:7-10 we read, "But the heavens and the earth, which by the same word are KEPT IN STORE, RESERVED UNTO FIRE AGAINST THE DAY OF JUDGMENT AND PERDITION OF UNGODLY MEN.....the heavens shall pass away with a great noise, and the elements shall MELT WITH A FERVENT HEAT, the earth also and the works that are therein shall be burned up." In verse 10 this is said to take place on "the day of the Lord," or at the time of his second coming in the clouds of glroy, in this last age. For it will be then that He will come as a thief in the night.

Donald Patton and his associates have done a remarkable job of studying out some new concepts, and I believe they are worthy of our consideration. Our earth is matter, and we are in space moving at tremendous speeds through the universe. The relationship between time and space is thus influenced by matter and its motion. This gives a geometrical structure to the world. Patten has used geometry and physics extensively along with Biblical chronology to measure past catastrophic events. Newton had a theory that a planet moves around the sun because of the gravitational force exerted by the sun. But Einstein came along with his theory of general relativity which says that a planet chooses the shortest possible path throughout the four-dimensional world which is deformed by the presence of the sun.

A ship or airplane may do the same thing while crossing the ocean. It would follow the section of a circle instead of a straight line. In the same way, a planet or light ray moves along the "shortest" line in its four-dimensional world. If we lived in a sinless world, it would still be a gigantic effort of a great mind to understand why things operate as they do. But, here we are caught in a time segment of eternity in the final scene of this earth's history when darkness covers the earth like a wet blanket. Isaiah 60:1-3. Satan has mastered the art of using all the elements of earth at his control. He is called the "prince of the power of the air"; so why should we think it strange that he would be able to cause great catastrophic events by methods that are far beyond even the mind of an Einstein to grasp? And all the time make it seem as if God did it!

It does not seem that life exists on any of the other planets in our little solar system except for planet earth. It is possible, therefore, that Satan has been permitted to manipulate and maneuver some of those other stellar bodies so as to cause astral disturbances or cosmological disaster. If he truly is the prince of the power of the air, I do not see why he should be limited to our atmosphere alone. Has he not roamed the universe in the past? Yes, he has. Revelation 12:9-12, Job 1-3. Satan had access to the unfallen worlds until Jesus' death on the cross revealed him as a murderer. Luke 10:18, John 12:27-33. And it is just as true that God knew what he would do in each instance and prepared a solution ahead of time to meet the crises without interfering with anyone's free moral agency, even Satan's. In fact, God has kept Satan from destroying himself.

That fact will be brought out someday, in the final judgment. Why else would Satan himself bow before God and acknowledge His goodness and justice, love and mercy? God did not arbitrarily bring the flood by just turning on the faucet and hosing them down good, like rats in a barrel. Isn't it more in keeping with the character of God to reason that Satan brought the flood upon himself by fooling around with something that was hotter than he could handle? Some have suggested that the antediluvian world was far more advanced than we have imagined and scientists of that day caused the flood themselves by setting off some kind of bomb or some other destructive device that triggered tremendous earthquakes and thus caused the vapor envelope above the earth to collapse. Others have suggested the sheet of water around the earth began to condense into water as soon as God withdrew His protection and let Satan have the earth all to himself, as soon as Noah and his family were safe in the ark. Without God holding it altogether, our solar system began to come unglued at the seams. See Isaiah 54:5-9, (Isaiah 28:2, Isaiah 59:19).

We will probably never know if that is true or not until we get to heaven. But, Patten has some interesting ideas on it. He believes that a close flyby of Mercury, between 25,000 and 30,000 miles, an outside pass, caused the seismic upheaval which, in turn collapsed the vapor envelope (sheet of water around the earth). "Long Day of Joshua and Six Other Catastrophes," page 307. One historian has set the date of the flood about Oct. 22nd*, the Jewish new year, but Patten believes it occurred about Nov. 7. An ice moon or satellite of Mercury drenched the earth with a 200 to 250 inch ice dump (average per square inch) across earth's 197,000,000 square mile surface. At least 50% of the ice particles came in as a sudden rain; the balance formed rings around the earth (like Saturn's rings). These ice dumps would account for the instant death and burial of the great mammoths which have been found preserved with tropical vegetation in their mouths after nearly 3,500 and 4,000 years. Patton says, "The vortex of the radiation belts in the Northern Hemisphere is currently over Northern Greenland, and this coincides with the center of the ice dump in the Northern Hemisphere." Ibid., page 307. This ice dump was the result of one of Mercury's ice moons fragmenting as it was pulled off course from its circuit around Mercury and drawn into the greater gravitational field of earth. There is a principle in astronomy describing tidal interaction of two celestial bodies approaching each other. At a certain point, the cohesive force of the smaller body is overcome by the tide-raising force of the larger body. The smaller body fragments before a direct collision occurs.

Edouard Roche, a French astronomer, did considerable research into the nature of the construction of planets and stars. Thus, this law of fragmentation before collision is called Roche's Limit and has never been recalculated from 2.44 to 2.45 radii. Now, this may be too heavy for some minds, but if you get Patten's books and study them yourself, it will not seem so difficult. I am not a scientist myself, but a theologian; however, I find that true science and mathematics document the historicity and chronological accuracy of the Word of God. We will leave it up to the reader to make a final decision as to the validity of these concepts and ideas.

*** Alexander Hislop, "The Two Babylons," page 136 seems to indicate the flood came on the Jewish new year, Oct. 22nd.**

*** Note: This report is now 38 years old. Today, 2005, nuclear devices are being made that fit into small suitcases and breifcases which are powerful enough to destroy an average- to large-sized American city, depending on the type of nuclear device used.**

CHAPTER 14

JOB: THE KEY THAT UNLOCKS THE DOOR OF TRUTH ABOUT SATAN

On Page 201 of The Long Day of Joshua and Six Other Catastrophes, by Donald W. Patten and associates Hatch and Steinhauer, we read the most interesting account of the story of Job. "Another significant catastrophe, a major disaster to Job, is somewhat described in the opening chapter of this work of high drama. ...'While he was yet speaking, there came also another and said, THE FIRE OF GOD IS FALLEN FROM HEAVEN, and hath burned up the sheep, and the servants, and CONSUMED them.' (Job 1:16) 'And behold there came a GREAT WIND from the wilderness and smote the four corners of the house and it fell upon the young men...!'" To prove that God does not bring destructive winds. See I Kings 19:11, 12. Psalm 148:7,8, Hosea 12:1.

Notice Patten's footnote to this on page 201. "'A great wind' in the above text suggests in English, a sudden gust on a stormy, windy day. This suggestion is quite mistaken. The Hebrew word for wind is ruwach which sometimes does mean wind in other texts, but was seen in Isaiah 37:7 and 2 Kings 19:7 as the 'blast' or the exploding bolide (a large, brilliant meteor which explodes) which destroyed almost 200,000 Assyrian troops. Among its meanings as found in Strong's Exhaustive Concordance are 'air, anger, blast, breath, tempest, whirlwind.' Since this occurred along with falling fire, it must suggest the effects of a bolide which are so comparable to the effects of a nuclear explosion. This cosmic holocaust, in the prelude to the book of Job, so disastrous to the patriarch of Uz, occurred in the year 1663 B.C., in which case it would have been a Case One catastrophe like the Isaihic or the Sodom-Gomorrah episode."

Here we have a scientist and astronomer attempting to explain what God allowed Satan to do. We know that Satan is the one who did it. He brought the wind and the fire both. This opens the door and lets us see who is really the bad guy in this great controversy. It isn't our precious Lord Jesus Christ, or His Father, because the Bible clearly identifies Satan as the destroyer (1 Cor 10:10) and God permits him to use these catastrophes at times to destroy those whom God has permitted to go their own way and do their own thing without any repentance. Yet, at times, even good men like Job suffer and some die, as in the case of Lazarus. In Job's case we have a clue in Job 3:25. "For the thing that which I feared greatly is come upon me, and that which I was afraid of is come unto me." So, fear was the chink or crack in his armor which needed to be sealed up for that was the opening Satan was looking for to break his connection with God and thereby take him down. And it almost worked but Job's faith carried him through. And the fear he had was eroded from his life because he learned the lesson the Lord wanted him to learn. "But He knows the way that I take; When He has tested me, I shall come forth as gold." Job 10:23. It does not matter what is happening to us, God is always with us to help us through every and any trial. "I am with you always, even unto the end of the world." Matt 28:19, 20. So every trial has a purpose and reason even for the most righteous as we see in the lives of Joseph and Daniel. Even Jesus was perfected by the things that He suffered. "Though He were a Son, yet learned He obedience by the things which he suffered; And being made perfect, He became the author of eternal salvation unto all them that obey Him;" Heb 5:8, 9.

But it is God who permits and prevents disasters in all of these experiences. Consider ISAIAH AS A HISTORIAN. Isaiah used the historical, astronomical, crises as themes for his prognosis of the coming day of the Lord. He did it repeatedly and his contemporaries knew what he had in mind, for catastrophic events of the past were well-remembered in general. THE SODOM-GOMORRAH SCENE of 1877 B.C. "Except the Lord of hosts had left unto us a very small remnant, we should have been as Sodom, and WE SHOULD HAVE BEEN

LIKE GOMORRAH." Isaiah 1:9. Gen 14:10 tells us that the "vale of Siddim was full of slimepits;" the RSV says, "bitumen pit or asphalt." Tacitus (Hist. v. 6. 7), and Josephus (War iv. 8.4), describe an area south of the Dead Sea (probably now covered by its rising water) as scorched by a fiery catastrophe that destroyed several cities whose burned remains were still visible in their day. Foul gases are said to have come from fissures of the ground. See Deut. 29:23. So, we see that Sodom could have easily been blown up by natural disasters when God removed His protection. See Lam. 4:6.

This catastrophe is an obvious reference to some sort of fiery meteoric shower of fire and brimstone which are really meteorites and bolides hitting the earth. This then could have ignited the oil, gas and bitumen or asphalt that existed in large quantities in the area. Bolides and meteors are frequently referred to in the Hebrew Scriptures. "Who can stand before his indignation? and who can abide in the fierceness of his anger? His FURY is poured out LIKE FIRE and the ROCKS are thrown down by him." Nahum 1:6. "PESTILENCE, AND BURNING COALS WENT FORTH AT HIS FEET." Habakkuk 3:5-6. "And THE LORD SHALL BE HEARD. ..and with the flame of a devouring fire with scattering, and tempest, and HAILSTONES." So, we see that "FIRE AND BRIMSTONE," are actually "BOLIDES AND METEORITES."

Now, let us take a look at a more recent author whose work has been receiving serious attention from both Creationists and Evolutionists. "IN THE BEGINNING: Compelling Evidence for Creation and the Flood," by Walt Brown, Ph. D. This 328 page volume, 8 1/2 by 11, first published in 1980, is now in its 7th edition, published in 2001. Although a Christian, Dr. Brown also believed in the theory of evolution. But in June of 1970 he began to have second thoughts when he heard that Noah's Ark rested near the 14,000-foot level of Mount Ararat in Eastern turkey. "If a gigantic boat was ever at that elevation, a huge flood must have occurred," he thought. "However, the biblical flood was always hard for me to imagine. Afer all, where could so much water come from? Where did it all go?" preface v.

As the case for the existence for Noah's Ark grew stronger many of his questions were answered. Here, in his own words is what finally led him to his decision. "If that much water sloshed over the earth for a year, many dead animals and plants would have been buried in vast amounts of mud and other sediments. This would explain how almost all fossils formed, especially those on the highest mountains. But the fossil record was supposedly the best evidence for evolution, a theory I had passively accepted. If a global flood produced most fossils, where was the evidence for evolution? The more I struggled with this question, the more amazed I became at the lack of evidence supporting creation. By 1972, I had become a creationist." Ibid.

On page 98 of his book Dr. Brown explains his theory of how comets, asteroids, and meteorites came into existence. He calls them the "Mavericks" of the Solar System. "These strange bodies have several remarkable similarities with planet earth. About 85% of a comet's mass is frozen water. Water is rare in the universe, but both common and concentrated on earth-sometimes called 'the water planet.' The remaining 15% of each comet's mass is basically dust, primarily the crystalline mineral olivine. Solid material that formed in space would not be crystalline. Olivine is probably the most abundant of the more than 2,000 known minerals on earth. Asteroids and meteorites are rocks similar in many ways to earth rocks. Surprisingly, some meteorites contain salt crystals and liquid water. Some asteroids appeared to have the residue of plant life." He believes that the "Hydroplate theory" explains the global catastrophe of the flood and all that followed in its aftermath. For example, he believes that about 50% of the water in earth's oceans today was once in interconnected chambers, about 10 miles below the earth's surface. pg 99. Dr Brown challenges the many theories of how comets began. "After a review of comets, a new explanation for comet origins will be proposed and tested. It appears that the fountains of the great deep and the power of high-pressure water exploding into the vacuum of space launched comets throughout the solar system as the flood began. Other known forces, acting on the expelled rocks and muddy droplets, created larger bodies resembling comets in size, number, density, composition, spin, texture, strength, chemistry (organic and inorganic), and many orbital characteristics." Pg 189. Dr Brown notes that comets contain organic matter which many early scientists concluded was "decomposed organic bodies." He challenges the popular belief that comets brought life to Earth. Instead, comets may have traces of life from Earth." Ibid 189. This assumption alone seriously undermines the validity of the evolutionary theory. Furthermore, he states "Earth has ten times more water, by volume, than land above sea level. Other planets, moons, and even interstellar space have only traces of water, or possible water. These traces, instead of producing comets, may have been caused by comets or water vapor that the 'fountains of the great deep' launched into space." Pg 199.

"The 'fountains of the great deep' launched rocks as well as muddy water. As rocks moved farther from Earth, earth's gravity became less significant to them, and their gravity became increasingly significant to nearby particles. Consequently, many rocks and their surrounding clouds of water vapor merged to become asteroids. Isolated rocks in space are meteoroids. Drag forces caused by water vapor and thrust forces produced by the radiometer effect concentrated asteroids in what is now the asteroid belt. Asteroids, meteoroids, and comets-sometimes called the mavericks of the solar system-are thus unified." Pg 219.

Dr Brown differs from most creation scientists in that he believes that the flood waters came from the waters under the earth, the fountains of the great deep which broke loose and were propelled, shot and/or thrown/forced up into the sky and then fell back down to this earth. That is the source of the flood waters, not from the Vapor Envelope of the flood. This concept teaches that most of the flood waters came from the collapse of the water Canopy or Envelope. The reason Dr Brown does not believe in this theory is because, according to him it, it did not exist. Most creation scientists disagree with him. What he teaches is that the flood waters came from the waters under the earth, the fountains of the great deep which broke loose and were propelled, shot and/or thrown/forced up into the sky and then fell back down to the earth. That, he says, is the source of the flood waters, not from the Vapor Envelope.

Although I disagree on that point, I think Dr Brown has made significant contributions with his research and writings, especially in encouraging a closer look at the cause and result of the fountains of the great deep breaking up as well as the tremendous amount of water, rock and dirt that the earth spewed up into the heavens at the time of the flood and fell back down to earth with great force. I think that the rocks which were thrown up into the heavens may well have hit the vapor envelope causing it to crack or break because the fountains of the great deep are mentioned before the windows of heaven, showing the sequence of events. Here is one of the best descriptions I have ever read. "For seven days after Noah and his family entered the ark, there appeared no sign of the coming storm. During this period their faith was tested. It was a time of triumph to the world without....They gathered in crowds about the ark, deriding its inmates with a daring violence which they had never ventured upon before. But upon the eighth day dark clouds overspread the heavens. There followed the muttering of thunder and the flash of lightning. Soon large drops of rain began to fall. The world had never witnessed anything like this, and the hearts of men were struck with fear. All were secretly inquiring, 'Can it be that Noah was in the right, and that the world is doomed to destruction?' Darker and darker grew the heavens, and faster came the falling rain. The beasts were roaming about in the wildest terror, and their discordant cries seemed to moan out their own destiny and the fate of man. Then 'the fountains of the great deep' were 'broken up, and the windows of heaven were opened.' Water appeared to come from the clouds in mighty cataracts. Rivers broke away from their boundaries, and overflowed the valleys.

Jets of water burst from the earth with indescribable force, throwing massive rocks hundreds of feet into the air, and these, in falling, buried themselves deep in the ground." Patriarchs & Prophets, page 99.

The Bible clearly teaches in Genesis 1:6-9 that there were waters above the earth at the time of the creation and when the flood came the "windows of heaven were opened," Gen 6:7. Psalms 148:4-5 is also a clue. "Praise him, ye heavens of heavens, and ye waters that be above the heavens. Let them praise the name of the LORD: for he commanded, and they were created." The context of the passage shows us that David is writing about the creation. From the Hebrew meaning, the "waters" in the passage definitely would be cascading water. See also Psalm 33:6, 7 & Job 26:7, 8.

His explanation of the origin of limestone is also interesting. "Too much limestone exists on earth to have been formed, as evolutionists claim, by present processes (from marine animals, such as shelled creatures and corals). Most limestone was deposited as the subterranean water violently escaped to the earth's surface during the flood. Simultaneously, fresh carbon, needed to rapidly reestablish plant life buried during the flood, was released into the biosphere." Pg 151. As for the frozen mammoths he believes that "some muddy water from the fountains of the great deep went above the atmosphere where it froze into extremely cold hail. Within hours, mammoths, that cannot live in Arctic climates or at Arctic latitudes, were buried alive and quickly frozen as this muddy hail fell back to earth in a gigantic hail storm. Previous attempts to explain the frozen mammoths ignore many observations and recognized facts....If we now look for the bones and ivory of mammoths, not just preserved flesh, the number of discoveries becomes enormous, especially in Siberia and Alaska. Nikolai Vereschagin, Chairman of the Russian Academy of Science's Committee for the Study of Mammoths, estimated that more than half a million tons of mammoth tusks were buried along a 600-miles stretch of the Arctic coast. Because the typical tusk weighs 100 pounds, this implies that more than five million mammoths lived in this small region." Pg 159.

"How could so many millions of animals have survived in the cold, dry and desolate area of northern Siberia? Obviously their surroundings at the time of their death were more temperate and moist. So, what caused the sudden climate change to freezing cold? Oil prospectors who have drilled through Alaskan muck have found ancient tropical forests in a frozen state, not in a petrified state between 1,220 and 1,700 feet below the ground. They even have found palm trees, pine trees, and tropical foliage in great profusion lapped all over each other, indicating they had fallen in that position. What could have caused such a phenomenon the same as with the frozen mammoths? The only logical answer is that there was a sudden and dramatic change from a tropical like climate to a very cold, arctic one. One mammoth contained 40 different species of plants: herbs, grasses, mosses, shrubs, and tree leaves. Many no longer grow that far north; others grow both in Siberia and as far south as Mexico. The obvious conclusion is that so many varieties of plants is proof that the climate of that region of the world was milder than it is today. Furthermore, the discovery of the ripe fruits of sedges, grasses, and other plants suggests that the mammoth died during the second half of July or the beginning of August. The sudden death of the mammoth is proved by the unchewed bean pods still containing the beans that were found between its teeth and the deep freeze is suggested by the well-preserved state of the stomach contents and the presence of edible meat. The mammoth must have been overwhelmed suddenly with a rapid deep freeze and instant death because its cells had not burst. Frozen-food experts have explained that in order for this to happen the temperature of the air would have to drop suddenly to 150 to 175 degrees fahrenheit in a matter of minutes. A typical wild elephant requires about 330 pounds of food per day. Therefore, vast quantities of food were needed to support the estimated 5,000,000 mammoths that lived in just a small portion of northern Siberia." Pgs 162-167.

GOD'S PROTECTIVE CARE AND THE WORK OF GOD'S FINAL REMNANT PEOPLE

As we noticed in Eph. 2:2, Satan is the "Prince of the Power of the air." Whether he is manipulating matter in space or here on "Terra Firma" (earth), the result is often the same; death and destruction to God's creation. To just give an example of how much God protects his creatures from daily catastrophes from space, I will read to you from the World Book Encyclopedia on Meteors. "Scientists estimate that as many as 200,000,000 [two hundred million or nearly 1/4 billion] visible meteors enter the earth's atmosphere every day. These and other meteorites are estimated to add more than 1,000 tons daily to the earth's weight. We first see most of these meteors when they are about 65 miles above the earth. Air friction heats them to about 4000 degrees F ., and they burn out at altitudes of 30 to 50 miles. Meteors that reach earth before burning up are meteorites." Page 355. 1008 Editor.

God's angels are constantly guarding us from dangers seen and unseen. Ps. 34:7; Ps.91:11, 12. We have no idea how much we owe to Jesus for protecting us. But, when the last man on earth has rejected or accepted God's final message of love, and all the righteous are sealed with God's eternal seal of His love and righteousness (obedience) in their hearts, minds and lives and the wicked are all marked up and settled into the "BEAST SYSTEM," for their welfare and sustenance, then probation will close for this age. But, before that takes place, there will be lots of trouble. There will be more after probation closes, to be sure, because that is when the seven last plagues will fall, but there are "plagues and judgments (decisions" before probation ends. If there are seven "last" plagues, this indicates there of necessity must be some "first" plagues. The seven last plagues are the last seven of a long siege of plagues that are going to come upon the earth before Christ returns at the end this age. Most Christians do not understand this, or that God is not the one who closes a person's probation. Each person does that by his or her own choices. Furthermore, every lost soul will be raised after the 1,000 years for the final judgment and restoration of all mankind. So, when we speak of "probation" we do not mean that God is finished with that person. His probation closed only for this age we are living in now. Most people do not realize that God's program is progressive, due to our dullness of mind to comprehend His will for our lives. The last work on this earth to be done by God's people will be helping those who are the sick and mentally and morally fatigued and debased. Isaiah tells us, " ...loose the bands of wickedness, ...undo the heavy burdens, and...let the oppressed go free...deal thy bread to the hungry ...bring the poor that are cast out to thy house...when thou seest the naked, that thou cover him ." Isa. 58:6, 7. Compare this with Matthew 25:31-46. When Jesus comes again he will say to the saved, "INASMUCH AS YOU HAVE DONE IT UNTO ONE OF THE LEAST OF THESE MY BRETHREN, YOU HAVE DONE IT UNTO ME." v. 40. Christ is really quoting and paraphrasing Isaiah 58 which also includes the Sabbath reform message in Isa. 58:12-14.

The Sabbath proves that Christ is the life God, not the death God, and it is also a sign of sanctification, see Ezek. 20:12, 20. Very few people today realize that the final work to be done in this earth is Medical Missionary work. Healing by God's Natural Methods. As we analyze these seven last plagues, we must realize that they are basically an "ecological kickback." Also, note that plagues # 1, #4, and #7 directly affect the bodies of men physically. The first is a "noisome and grievous sore." Rev. 16:2. This is a sickness or disease which could not be from the Lord because our God never brings disease. See James 1:17; Luke 13:16 and Acts 10:38. He is not the author of sickness or death. The word "SEA" in Revelation represents "peoples, and multitudes, and nations, and tongues." Rev. 17:15. Therefore, if the "sea" is turned into "the blood of a dead man," and the sea is people, it would symbolically mean that the people are being slaughtered, that they are in fact killing each other. Zechariah 14:13 says the same thing. But, we must not rule out the fact that these symbols may have a dual application, in that the sea or body of water will literally turn into some kind of substance like the blood of a dead man, which will become stagnated and toxic.

The plagues of Egypt were literal plagues. God has "control of, or power over," these plagues, in that He is permitting them to come by letting man's abuse of nature reap its natural result. The sun scorching men could be from any number of causes. But God is not responsible for this. Satan brings all the aberrations of nature. The ozone layer is also being erased or destroyed by man's pollutions. All those who believe God kills will reject the true Sabbath (Saturday), the 7th day and accept Sunday worship and the beast system, with its drug therapy. Those who believe God kills will not want to help the sick and the dying. Only true, Sabbath keepers will do MEDICAL MISSIONARY WORK, for only those who know and receive God's true character will understand that the Sabbath is the sign (Ezek. 20:12, 20) of the life God.

FROGS, LICE, AND FLIES

On page 209 of Patten's work, "The Long Day of Joshua," we read the reason Patten gives for the frogs' appearance in such profusion. "We shall offer two thoughts concerning this rather unusual plague. One view is that, with the invasion of volcanic dust and pumice, and meteoritic dust, water conditions rapidly deteriorated; plants were covered. Faced with a sudden change in their natural environment, frogs came up out of the waters in marshes, canals and rivers to die on the shores, in the streets and almost everywhere." This view is much more plausible than the second view, which essentially says that the original Hebrew word for frogs meant to "skip about," and the word tsephardea corresponded to volcanic pumice and ash which descended thickly throughout the land in marshes, in canals, in rivers, on the shores, and everywhere. This idea is totally unacceptable. In the case with the lice and flies, the balance of nature was thrown out of whack by destroying the natural ecological balance. Suddenly denied their normal habitat due to the volcanic fallout, these lice and flies turned upon man and beast alike in vast numbers. This plague of lice may describe voracious mites. At any rate, this concept gives an optional viewpoint which helps us to see that there is another way to explain this so it harmonizes with the way God would work through nature to neutralize or disable those who opposed Him and His truth and His people. God does not work contrary to the laws He Himself has set up, and even when man and Satan pervert the natural order of things He still receives glory out of the situation. He is always in complete control without arbitrarily destroying any human being or interfering with their free moral agency. This is the way He works today and will work in the future during the seven last plagues when He shields the righteous but permits the wicked to bring suffering on themselves.

WHAT THEN IS GOD'S STRANGE ACT?

Throughout the history of the world God has always tempered His JUDGMENTS or DECISIONS with MERCY. (Decisions to let them go and destroy themselves or be injured and/or killed by Satan). A faithful record is kept of all the wicked deeds and even the thoughts of men. Guilt accumulates through the centuries. The following text proves this: "Wherefore, behold, I send unto you prophets, and wise men, and scribes: and some of them ye shall kill and crucify; and some of them shall ye scourge in your synagogues, and persecute them from city to city: THAT UPON YOU (the generation that killed Jesus) MAY COME ALL THE RIGHTEOUS BLOOD SHED UPON THE EARTH, FROM THE BLOOD OF RIGHTEOUS ABEL UNTO THE BLOOD OF ZACHARIAS SON OF BARACHIAS, WHOM YE SLEW BETWEEN THE TEMPLE AND THE ALTAR. VERILY I SAY UNTO YOU, ALL THESE THINGS SHALL COME UPON THIS GENERATION. "Matthew 23:34, 35.

Christ was speaking to His own people in that day A.D. 31. What about His professed people today? Will we not suffer as much or more than the Jews did in their day, unless we repent?

And so God's "STRANGE ACT" is simply that HE NO LONGER IS ABLE TO RESTRAIN THE WICKED FOR THEY HAVE TOTALLY REJECTED HIM. "BEHOLD THE LORD'S HAND IS NOT SHORTENED THAT IT CANNOT SAVE: NEITHER IS HIS EAR HEAVY, THAT IT CANNOT HEAR: But your iniquities HAVE SEPARATED between you and your God..." Isaiah 59:1, 2. "Your sins have hid His face from you..." Psalm 22:24 proves that God never turns His face away from us. He definitely does not leave or reject us Matt. 28:20. We reject Him. God never changes. Mal. 3:6. "I am the Lord, I change not. Therefore, you sons of Jacob are not consumed." He is always willing to save. It is stubborn and rebellious humanity who refuse to change by turning away from their sins, with God's help. "And Him that cometh to me I will in no wise cast out." John 6:37.

AND SO, THIS IS HIS "STRANGE ACT...." He lets it all go, everything, FOR THE FIRST TIME IN ALL OF HUMAN HISTORY GOD DOES NOT RESTRAIN OR PROTECT the sinner from 1) himself; 2) his fellow human beings; or 3) Satan and his angels. It will be the most terrible ordeal the human race has ever been through since the world began. "And there shall be a time of trouble, such as never was since there was a nation even to that same time: and at that time thy people shall be delivered, every one that shall be found written in the book." See Rev 20:12; Mal 3:16-18.

THE WINE OF THE WRATH OF GOD

Jesus referred to the TRUTH that He brought as "NEW WINE," Matthew 9:17. New wine would not be fermented like old wine and therefore, would not make a person drunk. OLD WINE by contrast represented the doctrines and traditions of men which made many drunk and thus led them astray down the pathway of death instead of up the pathway of life to the Holy City. Jeremiah speaks of the Lord as giving "the WINE CUP of this fury," to the heathen nations. Jeremiah 25:15, 16. In Revelation, Babylon is symbolically depicted as making "all nations drink of the wine of the wrath of her fornications" Revelation 14:8; compare verse 10; 17:2; and 18:3. In Revelation 16:19 Babylon is given the cup of the wine of the wrath of God to drink of the fierceness of His wrath. Now, unless we understand the true meaning of the "FURY," and "ANGER," and "WRATH OF GOD," we will never understand what the prophets in the Old Testament are saying, neither will we understand what the prophets in the New Testament are saying. God's Fury and Anger and Wrath are still the same—they simply represented His withdrawing so every person can go his own way and do his own thing without any restraint or rebuke from God.

In other words, the wicked are following the counsel of their own will. "Our lips are our own: who is lord over us?" Psalm 12:4. "Let us break their bands (Father and Son) asunder, and cast away their cords from us." Psalm 2:3, Hosea 11:4. Now notice how God deals with these rebels, how He pours out His "fury" or "wrath" upon them as they drink down their "own counsels." "DESTROY THOU THEM, O GOD; LET THEM FALL BY THEIR OWN COUNSELS;" Ps. 5:10.

SO SHALL ALL THE HEATHEN DRINK

"FOR AS YE HAVE DRUNK UPON MY HOLY MOUNTAIN, SO SHALL ALL THE HEATHEN DRINK CONTINUALLY, YEA, THEY SHALL DRINK AND THEY SHALL SWALLOW DOWN, AND THEY SHALL BE AS THOUGH THEY HAD NOT BEEN." Obadiah 16. "My holy mountain" refers to the righteous "drinking the truth or water of life, " from the Words of the Bible Psalm 36:6; John 7:27,38. Just as the righteous keep on drinking and keep on living, so the wicked keep on drinking (false doctrines) and continue dying and killing each other all over the earth. "A noise shall come even to the ends of the earth; for the Lord has a controversy with the nations, He will plead with all flesh; (Joel 2:28-32) He will give them that are wicked to the sword, says the Lord...Behold, evil shall go forth from nation to nation, and a great whirlwind shall be raised up from the coasts of the earth. And the slain of the Lord shall be at that day from one end of the earth even unto the other end of the earth: they shall not be lamented, neither gathered, nor buried: they shall be dung upon the ground." Jeremiah 25:31-33. The prophet Joel also wrote about this same event and what causes it. Let us read his description of an army that cannot be stopped. This is the reason the Synagogue of Satan will come and bow down before them, pleading for their lives (Rev 3:9) as Haaman did before Esther, the Queen. Esther 7:7, 8. "Like the noise of chariots on the tops of mountains shall they leap, like the noise of a flame of fire that devours the stubble, as a strong people set in battle array. Before their face the people shall be much pained: all faces shall gather blackness. They shall run like mighty men; they shall climb the wall like men of war; and they shall march every one on his ways, and they shall not break their ranks." Joel 2:5-7.

We need to realize here that when the prophet spoke of the wicked being as if they had never existed he is speaking of that particular age or eon. The Greek word for age is "Aion." So, the wicked will perish in this age in which we are now living and cease to exist as if they had never been born. But they will live again after the 1,000 years because the Scriptures clearly teach that all the dead who have ever lived upon the earth will be raised up in the final day. John 5:25; Rev 20:4, 5, 12-15. The Bible compares the end of the world to the time of harvest. In the Jewish economy there were three phases of the harvest: 1. Barley. 2. Wheat and 3. Grapes. Rev 14:14-20 refers to these three harvests. Jesus referred to the harvest as the end of the world, Matt 13:37-43.

Now, let us consider Revelation 14:9-11. "And the third angel followed them, saying with a loud voice, If any man worship the beast and his image, and receive his mark in his forehead, or in his hand, the same shall DRINK of the WINE (false teachings of Babylon) of the WRATH (God's no longer restraining or shielding the wicked from themselves and the delusions of men and of Satan) of God, which is poured out without mixture (with any mixing of His mercy this time, for they have refused it) into the cup of his indignation." Remember that according to Psalm 78:49, God's wrath, anger and indignation is simply when He permits or allows evil angels to come among them and destroy without restraint.

Luke 23:27-31 tells the story of the women weeping as they see Jesus suffering under the load of the cross; but He tells them that they should be weeping for themselves instead of for Him, for their sufferings will be even greater. "For if they do this in a green tree, what shall be done in a dry." Luke 23:31. By the green tree, Jesus represented Himself, the innocent Redeemer. GOD SUFFERED HIS WRATH AGAINST TRANSGRESSION TO FALL ON HIS BELOVED SON. (Compare Isaiah 53:10; and Romans 5:9.) Jesus was to be crucified for the sins of men. What suffering, then, would the sinner bear who continued in sin? ALL THE IMPENITENT AND UNBELIEVING WOULD KNOW A SORROW AND MISERY THAT LANGUAGE WOULD FAIL TO EXPRESS. Now, let us consider the last part of verse Rev 14:10: "And he shall be tormented with fire and brimstone in the presence of the holy angels, and in the presence of the Lamb: And the smoke of their torment ascendeth up for ever and ever: and they have no rest day nor night, who worship the beast and his image, and whosoever receiveth the mark of his name." Revelation 14:10, 11. The Greek word of Revelation 14:10 for TORMENTED is BASANIZO." It also means to torture, "to torment or distress." This tormenting takes place before Christ comes, especially during the seven last plagues.

Because this experience is a result of receiving the MARK OF THE BEAST, it means that the movement to enforce Sunday worship will play an important part in this time segment of suffering. And since everything is progressive, we may safely conclude that the suffering will also be progressive—that is, progressively more intense and more painful for those who are suffering. When we compare other scriptures which use this same word BASANIZO, we can see that it means mental suffering as well as physical suffering, which will help us to see who it is and what it is that is causing the suffering. That is our main objective in this study, to pinpoint the DESTROYER, the person who is responsible for all the heartache and sorrow and suffering in the world. Is God bringing this special suffering pictured here in Revelation 14 or is He PERMITTING it just like He always has permitted it whenever men have totally rejected his protection by simply going their own way? Compare Rev. 9:3, 5, 11; Matt. 18:33-35, Matt. 4:3. A Tormentor is one who tries and tests, i.e. an inquisitor.

DOES GOD CAUSE MENTAL TORTURE AND SUFFERING?

What we are dealing with in this passage of Revelation 14:9-11 regarding the suffering and torture of those who receive the Mark of the Beast, as opposed to the Seal of God, is not only a physical suffering during the plagues, but a terrible MENTAL TORTURE. It is an inquisition caused by evil angels of Satan who have no holy angels to hold them in check and limit their activity as they have done in the past. THE ACCUSER OF THE BRETHREN now has a field day. All the wicked are sitting ducks. The word for torture, BASANIZO, is used in Mark 5:7, "What have I to do with thee, Jesus, thou Son of the most high God? I adjure thee by God, that thou TORMENT ME NOT." What we have here is an accusation by an evil angel of Satan. He is accusing Christ of having plans to torment him....or other evil angels like himself. It is a slander against the character of Jesus. The very fact that Christ had not killed the evil angels shows His dealings with them thus far. This angel of Satan was not in Dante's fictitious inferno, but alive and well, free to roam the world and practice his trade, which is that of devil possession, i.e. tormenting the minds and bodies of human beings. Their only pleasure is in reducing a human being, made in the image of God, down to a slobbering, screaming idiot. In Matthew 8:29, an evil angel asks out of his fear, and defiance, "What have we to do with thee, Jesus, thou Son of God? art thou come hither to torment us before the time?"

Darkness hates light. Evil despises good. Evil fears good. Why? Because it is afraid that the GOOD WILL EXPOSE THE EVIL, that it will tear away its disguise, its mask, and leave it naked and defenseless. Jesus is love and truth, and that is what Satan fears most, for LOVE AND TRUTH ALWAYS Cast Satan out. "THERE Is NO FEAR IN LOVE: but perfect love casts out FEAR: BECAUSE FEAR HAS TORMENT." I John 4:18. Do the angels know the truth about how God destroys? The good angels know the truth about how Satan destroys now after nearly 6,000 years of observing and helping God reclaim mankind. But, do the evil angels know the truth about God's love and truth? No, they do not.

Jude 6 tells us they are in "everlasting chains UNDER DARKNESS unto the judgment of the great day." Psalm 73:6, Proverbs 5:22; John 8:24. Satan evidently has convinced himself and his angels that God is unjust and does torment people; therefore, they exist in a morbid state of perpetual fear and bondage to this false concept of God which they chose to believe at the very beginning of the Great Controversy in heaven. Mark 1:24, 5:7. It is very possible that the reason why Satan left heaven is because he was afraid that God would kill him. He has taught this to his evil angels, Matt. 8:29; Mark 1:24; Luke 4:34. The Greek word basanizo is also used in 2 Peter 2:8 and translated vexed in referring to Lot, who was "vexed with the filthy conversation (conduct) of the wicked." In Matthew 14:24 it is translated "TOSSED," referring to the ship out on the sea. Will the wicked be "VEXED," and "TOSSED," and in "DISTRESS," during the last days when they realize they are lost? Their cry then will be, "The harvest is past, the summer is ended and we are not saved." Jeremiah 8:20. Matt. 12:31,32. The sin against the Holy Spirit is a man rejecting God so persistently that the man's heart is hardened against God, not God's heart against that man, for God never rejects anyone, ever, Jn. 6:37. There is no time limit on salvation as far as God's ability to save a person, but there is a time limit on man's ability to accept that salvation. The heavenly sanctuary closes only when that last man or woman rejects Jesus' blood, in this age. God would keep the sanctuary open forever, if it would do any good, for His mercy is Eternal and this will be seen in the age to come in heaven during the 1,000 years, and especially in the great "Age of the Ages" after the millennium when "every knee shall bow and every tongue confess, to the glory of God the Father." Phil 2:5-11. This is when the Father will become "All in All...for as in Adam all die, even so in Christ shall all be made alive." I Corinthians 15:28, 22.

WANDERING FROM SEA TO SEA - AMOS 8:11

"Behold the days come, saith the Lord God, that I will send a famine in the land, not a famine of bread, nor a thirst for water, but of hearing the words of the Lord: And they shall wander from sea to sea, and from the north even to the east, they shall run to and fro to seek the word of the Lord, and shall not find it." Amos 8:11, 12. Will not that be TORMENT? The plan of salvation will have been accomplished, but few chose to accept it. As mercy's sweet voice dies away, FEAR AND HORROR WILL SEIZE THE LOST. Satan will say to them, "It's TOO LATE! TOO LATE!!" "They will WANDER FROM SEA TO SEA, AND FROM THE NORTH TO THE EAST, TO SEEK THE WORD OF THE LORD. BUT, 'THEY SHALL NOT FIND IT." Amos 8:11. Jer. 8:20. "Anapausis," is a Greek word which means "cessation, refreshment and rest." It means that for the duration of the Time of Trouble until they die or Jesus comes and they are destroyed by the terrible earthquake that takes place at that time, they will have no relaxation or reprieve from the TORMENT. This is the mental suffering.

BUT THERE IS A PHYSICAL SUFFERING GOING ON AT THE SAME TIME. The "Fire and brimstone," of Rev 14:10 has a dual meaning. The cataclysmic catastrophes of the last days are more terrible than anything that has ever happened in the history of the world. The meteorites and bolides Satan may bring in the plagues, combined with the atomic and nuclear weapons of men (they are called swords in the Bible) will cause the most terrible upheavals of all time. John predicted there would be an earthquake that will break all the Richter scales in the world or possibly 90% of them. "And there were voices, and thunders, and lightnings; and there was a great earthquake, such as was not since men were upon the earth, so mighty an earthquake, and so great." Rev 16:18.

THE FINAL MESSAGE IS A MESSAGE OF FIRE

In Luke 12:49 Jesus said He had come to bring FIRE ON THE EARTH. Jesus brought a FIRE OF TRUTH AND LOVE, GOODNESS AND COMPASSION TO THE ENEMIES OF HIS FATHER AND OF HIMSELF. Now notice: "If thine enemy be hungry, give him bread to eat; and if he be thirsty, give him water to drink: FOR THOU SHALT HEAP COALS OF FIRE UPON HIS HEAD. AND THE LORD SHALL REWARD THEE." Proverbs 25:21, 22. Also notice Isaiah 34 which is what John the Revelator is quoting in Revelation 14 and 16 and other places. "And all the host of heaven shall be dissolved, and the heavens shall be rolled together as a scroll: and all their host shall fall down, as the leaf falleth off the vine, and as a falling fig from the fig tree." Isaiah 34:4. Jesus foretold the falling of the stars in Matthew 24 and Mark 13 and Luke 21 and John the Revelator quotes Isaiah 34 in Revelation 6:13, "And the stars of heaven fell unto the earth (meteors), even as a fig tree casteth her untimely figs, when she is shaken of a mighty wind." It is very interesting to note that the time span from the dark day (May 19, 1780) to the falling of the stars on November 12 and 13, 1833 is 53 years and about six months or exactly half way through the 54th year. Patten stated that astral catastrophes occur every 54 years and every 108 years. See The Long Day of Joshua, pp. 172-173. What significance this may have on our interpretation of prophecy in the past, today, and in the future cannot be determined at this time. However, the Bible tells us that end-time events will be understood by the righteous, (Dan 12:10), but the wicked will not understand because they don't have the life-giving Spirit of Jesus to interpret the "times and the seasons" as the righteous do. Therefore, the Second Coming of Christ will not surprise the righteous, for they have rightly interpreted the prophetic signs and symbols and are eagerly awaiting their Lord's return. 1 Thess. 5:1,4. Satan will use these calamities in nature to try to convince the world that we should get a national Sunday law, so God will stop being angry at us. Satan's angels claiming to be from outer space will come at this time to try to convince the world that our only hope is to get back to God with a NATIONAL SUNDAY Law. "All the host of heaven shall be dissolved. ..and all their host shall fall down...." Isaiah 34:4 may have a dual meaning. Compare Deut. 32:31-35, Jere. 51:25, Ezek. 28:16, 17, Rev. 6:16. It may refer not only to the falling of the stars literally (meteorites of 1833) but to the end time as well; but it may also refer to the complete fall of Satan's angels who are the "one third of the stars" who fell from heaven with him in the beginning. Revelation 12:4. His tail drew one third" of them with him when he LEFT of his own VOLITION. Rev. 9:1; Luke 10:17-19.

SATAN IS THE PRODIGAL SON WHO NEVER CAME HOME.

Now, Isaiah 34:5 says; "For my SWORD (Jesus said He came to bring a sword, which were His words of truth and love) shall be bathed in heaven: behold, it shall come down upon Idumea, and upon the people of my curse, to judgment."

When you compare this scripture with Isaiah 63:1-6 and especially with Obadiah 15-18, you get a clearer picture. Edom or Idumea here represents all the wicked (all the Esaus) who have rejected God's wonderful plan, His birthright for them. In Isaiah 63 we see how God takes all the blame as usual. He claims that His permissive will in letting the people kill each other with their swords, or weapons of war and destruction is His doing. Because He lets them do it, by not preventing them, He says, "I did it. I killed you all. I bathed my sword in heaven." It has a dual meaning here, too. The Sword of His Word represents the Word of God, the Bible; and He showers down upon the people who reject Him all the truth about Himself and them too, and it just leads them to get so mad that they set a date to destroy God's people and are in turn destroyed themselves. This, God calls His anger, wrath, indignation, and trouble. Psalm 78:49; Rom 1:18-28. When you compare Revelation 18:8 and Isaiah 34:8, you see that this has an application to Jerusalem in the time of Jesus and at the end of the 1,000 years as well. It also has the dual element of God's symbolic fire and the literal fire which He says He causes and brings, but which always happens as a result of Satan and men fighting God, setting a trap for the righteous and then destroying themselves. Job 14:7-14; Psalm 9:15, 16. "AS THOU HAST DONE, IT SHALL BE DONE UNTO THEE: THY REWARD SHALL RETURN UPON THINE OWN HEAD," Obadiah 15. For the day of the Lord is near upon all the heathen.

Now, verse 17 pictures God's people safe inside the Holy City: "But upon mount Zion shall be deliverance and there shall be holiness;" You see it is the Holiness of Jesus that He has imprinted upon the characters of the saints that gives them the power to withstand the final onslaught of the wicked. "And the house of Jacob shall possess their possessions ('The meek shall inherit the earth.' Matthew 5:5)." "And the house of Jacob (all the saved) shall be a fire, and the house of Joseph (another symbol for all the saved) A FLAME, and the HOUSE OF ESAU (EDOM OR IDUMEA or all the Lost), for STUBBLE, AND

THEY SHALL KINDLE IN THEM, AND DEVOUR THEM: AND THERE SHALL NOT BE ANY REMAINING OF THE HOUSE OF ESAU; FOR THE LORD HATH SPOKEN IT." Obadiah 18. Their carnal nature dies.

Can you just imagine how angry the wicked will be when they see all the righteous on the inside and themselves on the outside? "There shall be weeping and GNASHING OF TEETH, when ye shall see Abraham, and Isaac, and Jacob, and all the prophets, in the kingdom of God, AND YOU YOURSELVES THRUST OUT." Luke 13:28. They will see all the JACOBS (all the cheaters and heel grabbers they knew in this life who overcame) on the inside of the city and the JOSEPHS (those who lived godly from their youth up) with them in the city; and they are going to say to God: "HEY, GOD, YOU PLAY FAVORITES." Isn't that just what the brothers of Joseph said to Jacob by their actions? "Hey, God, how come we are out here and they are inside with all the gold and the pretty coats? You are not fair, God." Then the Lord will give them the panoramic view described in Ps. 50:3-6, and all the wicked are entranced. THIS IS THE SYMBOLIC PART OF THE FIRE THAT IS RAINED DOWN UPON THEM. "AND FIRE CAME DOWN FROM GOD OUT OF HEAVEN, AND DEVOURED THEM." Rev. 20:9. GOD SHOWS HIS TRUTH AND LOVE TO THE WHOLE WORLD. AND EVERYONE SEES THAT GOD IS TRULY LOVE AND, "ALL THEY THAT GO DOWN TO THE DUST (bite the dust, as they say, or die at this point) SHALL BOW BEFORE HIM: AND NONE CAN KEEP ALIVE HIS OWN SOUL." Psalm 22:29. Compare Philippians 2:10, 11, Ezek. 21:24. Psalm 21:8-12 gives a graphic picture of this same experience and Psalm 7 and 9 do also. Read them carefully and you will see it. The idea or concept of a fire that burns in the mind (MENTAL TORMENT) until every knee shall bow and every tongue shall confess, which will bring "Glory to God the Father." These truths should be very clear. Psalm 38:3 is good also, in describing the experience of the wicked in their "mental anguish and torment" before and after the 1,000 years. "There is no soundness in my flesh because of thine anger; (God's permitting all to be shown and the wicked to go their own way and deal with the sin problem all alone, by themselves: do-it-yourself religion, Pope-Self, righteousness by works) Neither is there any REST (peace or health, margin) in my bones BECAUSE OF MY SIN." In this last age this will take place in a short time and the wicked will die a terrible death; 2/3rds of them will die in this age. "And it shall come to pass, that in all the land, saith the Lord, two parts therein shall be cut off and die; but the third shall be left therein. And I will bring the third part through the fire, and will refine them as silver is refined, and will try them as gold is tried: they shall call on my name, and I will hear them: I will say, It is my people: and they shall say, The Lord is my God." Zechariah 13:8, 9. Isaiah 25:9. But after the 1,000 years they will all be restored as Acts 3:21 has predicted. I will explain this in much more detail in Chapter 22.

DUAL FIRE CONCEPT EXPLAINED IN ISAIAH 33:10-12

Notice how well this scripture brings out this idea of the symbolic fire that burns within (torments and vexes the guilty conscience, in other words). "NOW WILL I RISE, SAITH THE LORD; NOW WILL I BE EXALTED; NOW WILL I LIFT UP MYSELF." This is the final coronation of Jesus before every human being that has ever existed. YE SHALL CONCEIVE CHAFF, YE SHALL BRING FORTH STUBBLE: YOUR BREATH, AS FIRE, SHALL DEVOUR YOU." (THIS IS THE SYMBOLIC PART. The wicked will stoke their own fire with the hatreds and jealousies and backbitings they harbor and hold in their hearts). "AND THE PEOPLE SHALL BE AS THE BURNINGS OF LIME: AS THORNS CUT UP SHALL THEY BE BURNED IN THE FIRE." Isaiah 33:12. Notice the parable of the wheat and tares. "Gather ye together first the tares, and bind THEM IN BUNDLES TO BURN

THEM: BUT GATHER THE WHEAT INTO MY BARN." Matthew 13:30. Ezek. 15:7.

THE FIRE SHALL TRY (EXAMINE) EVERY MAN'S WORK (FOR GOD)

The most severe condemnation and judgment will fall upon the professed religious leaders in every age. These are the ones whose work will be examined with the most careful scrutiny. Preachers and religious leaders who have received great praise and honor and glory from men in this life will be very shocked and terribly embarrassed to find out that all their "wonderful orations," did little more than tickle the people's fancy, but did not touch many hearts for Jesus Christ or convert many sinners from the error of their ways.

"And every man shall receive his own reward according to his own labor...let every man take heed how he builds...for other foundation can no man lay than that is laid, which is Jesus Christ. Now if any man build upon this foundation gold, silver, precious stones, wood, hay, stubble; EVERY MAN'S WORK SHALL BE MADE MANIFEST: FOR THE DAY (day of Christ's coming before and after the 1,000 years, Judgment, in other words) SHALL DECLARE IT, BECAUSE IT SHALL BE REVEALED BY FIRE; AND THE FIRE SHALL TRY (TEST OR REVEAL) EVERY MAN'S WORK OF WHAT SORT IT IS." I Corinthians 3:8, 10, 11-15. Ezek. 15:7. God's fire is love. Satan's fire is hatred. I CORINTHIANS 3:13. THIS IS NOT LITERAL FIRE. Paul concludes I Corinthians 3:15 by stating that a man who has worked for the Lord and brought in a lot of souls may sadly discover that he doesn't have much of a reward after all. Others who thought their work was of little value may have a large reward. Both classes can be saved because of God's great mercy and power to save. "If any man's work shall be burned, he shall suffer loss: but he himself shall be saved; yet so as by fire." I Cor 3:15. This is a very powerful text proving Universal Reconciliation. The loss itself will serve as that person's punishment and discipline to restore him back to the throne of God.

It is also a warning to build upon the foundation JESUS CHRIST, and not upon the ideas, method or philosophies of human beings. "THEREFORE JUDGE NOTHING BEFORE THE TIME, UNTIL THE LORD COME, WHO BOTH WILL BRING TO LIGHT (with His truth and love) THE HIDDEN THINGS OF DARKNESS, (Light always exposes darkness), and will make manifest the COUNSELS OF THE HEARTS: AND THEN SHALL EVERY MAN HAVE PRAISE OF GOD." I Corinthians 4:5. John 3:19, 20. We have already read in Luke 12:49 how Jesus said He came to bring "FIRE," on the earth. Now in Matthew 3:11, we read, ..."He that cometh after me is mightier than I, whose shoes I am not worthy to bear: HE SHALL BAPTIZE YOU WITH THE HOLY GHOST, AND WITH FIRE." Isa. 4:4-6, Jer. 15:6-8. Now, notice the two kinds of fire that follow in Matt 3:12: "Whose fan is in his hand, and he will throughly purge His floor, and gather his wheat into the gamer; (the purging fire of God's Word separates the sheep from the goats) BUT HE WILL BURN UP THE CHAFF WITH UNQUENCHABLE FIRE." Cf. Song of Solomon 8:6. Here God in Christ takes the blame again for the self-destruction of the wicked. The wickedness and hatred in their hearts and minds, yes, even in their very souls, could not be burned out by love; so it will now be destroyed by a literal fire that will do away with "both body and soul" in the final flames. See Matthew 10:28.

This now brings us to the last scripture in this section on fire. "And if thy hand offend (the margin says, "cause to offend") thee, CUT IT OFF (stop sinning, in other words); IT IS BETTER FOR THEE TO ENTER INTO LIFE MAIMED, THAN HAVING TWO HANDS TO CO INTO HELL, (Ghenna, symbolic and literal fire), INTO THE FIRE THAT NEVER SHALL BE QUENCHED: WHERE THEIR WORM DIES NOT, AND THE FIRE IS NOT QUENCHED." Mark 9:43. The worm represents the ego or

FLESHLY, carnal, MIND, Ps. 22:6. Jesus became sin for us. 2 Cor. 5:21. This idea is repeated with the foot and eye using the same words each time: "cut it off," or "pluck it out," in reference to the eye. Few people who know scripture at all would take this literally. So, we now have a key to unlock the phrase, "WHERE THEIR WORM DIETH NOT." Greek, 'SKOLEX,' 'a maggot'. Major, Manson, and Wright (The Mission and Message of Jesus, p. 123) comment, 'The undying worm is not the symbol of a soul which cannot die, but is the symbol of corruption which cannot be purged.'" John the Baptist and Christ came to purge sin. We read in John 5:35, 36. "He was a burning and a shining light: and ye were willing for a season to rejoice in his light."

THE FINAL SECOND DEATH

Now, in Ezekiel 28:18, we read that God is going to "bring forth a FIRE FROM THE MIDST OF THEE, it shall devour thee, and I will bring thee to ashes upon the earth in the sight of all them that behold thee." What is this "fire from the midst" that the Lord is talking about? I believe it has two phases. First of all, Lucifer will have to come to the end of his rope, the end of his long journey and war against the kingdom of heaven. Those who have been supporting him for 6,000 years, evil, fallen angels and wicked men, in every age, will turn upon him and blame him for everything. This is the initial phase of the "fire" that will begin to destroy Satan. "He shall come to his end and none shall help him." Dan. 11:44, 45.

From Ezek 28 and Isaiah 14 we know that Satan was once a beautiful angel named Lucifer, meaning "Light Bearer." But through pride and self-exaltation he lost favor with God and the two thirds of the heavenly host and was eventually cast out of heaven itself after a war with Michael and his angels, Rev. 12 tells us. Non-canonical visionaries and extra-biblical sources have written about Lucifer's motives and activities. One such visionary states that after his expulsion from heaven he devised a plan to break Adam and Eve's light connection with the heavenly throne. He would formulate a temptation by which their loyalty to God would be tested, just as he was allowed to test Job and David and many others. Some passed the test but many others failed. Traditional theology teaches that the test involved some fruit on a tree, according to Genesis 2. Satan's strategy was to somehow lead Adam and Eve to believe that the true God had forbidden him to eat of one of the trees, the tree of "knowledge of good and evil" which, by the way, was never even mentioned in Genesis 1. Many theologians do not consider Genesis 2 to be the true version of the creation story. At any rate, Satan was able to deceive Adam and Eve into thinking that he was the true God and that he had changed his mind about this one particular tree, which he now calls "the tree of knowledge of good and evil." Through this cunning deception, Satan, posing as the Creator, was able to create a doubt in Adam's mind as to God's trustworthiness. And so it was that Adam's faith was weakened through a threat of death accompanied by the prohibition to eat of a perfectly good tree that Adam already believed was legally his. In order to counter this lie, Eve was informed by a talking serpent that nothing was wrong with the fruit. She was told that it was not dangerous at all because the true Creator God had already told them in Gen 1:29 that all the trees were good and they all belonged to them. None of them were off limits. The serpent also categorically stated that they would not die if they ate of the fruit of this tree, which the "Lord God" of Eden had forbidden them to eat. So, Eve checked it out and decided the serpent was telling her the truth. She ate of it and discovered that she did not die, just as the voice speaking through the serpent had told her. So, she knew then that the "Lord God" (actually, Satan, the Impostor, Pretender god of Eden) who had put the tree off limits was lying to them. So, naively thinking that Adam would believe her, she gave some of this same fruit to Adam, who also ate. But the problem with Adam was that he believed the lie that he would die. He was sure that Eve was going to die, so because he did not want to be separated from his beloved Eve he went ahead and ate the forbidden fruit.

Predictably, Lucifer's brilliant strategy worked. As soon as Adam and Eve ate of the fruit they began to feel guilty and were afraid, *and that fear is what broke their light connection with the mind of their Creator and His eternal throne and their robe of light began to fade.* Lucifer, pretending to be God castigated them severely, making sure the guilt trip was fully in place. Although some may not agree with this, the bottom line is that Lucifer's motive was achieved, no matter which version of the fall you may wish to believe. Lucifer (Satan) had a plan and it worked. Adam and Eve needed to be rescued. A plan of redemption must be carried out to redeem them.

Here is one visionary's explanation of what Lucifer (Satan) believed and his plan. "If Satan could in any way beguile them to disobedience, God would make some provision whereby they might be pardoned, and then himself and all the fallen angels would be in a fair way to share with them of God's mercy." SR 27. What does Satan look like now? This same visionary described Lucifer as once being a happy and exalted angel, the wisest of them all. He still has a kingly bearing according to one description. "His features still appear noble but the expression on his face shows care, anxiety, worry, unhappiness, malice, hate, deceit, mischief and every evil. He has a receding forehead from his eyes back. He has practiced evil so long that every good quality has been debased and every evil trait developed to the fullest degree. His eyes are full of cunning. He is sly and has the power of great penetration. He has a large frame but flesh hangs loosely about his hands and face. As he sets a trap for his victim he has an evil and satanic smile which grows more horrible as he fastens his victim in his snare."

Ok, so he has all this backlog of negative memories of all he has done against God and His creation. He has been carrying them with him all these thousands of years. So, all of this sense of guilt and failure is going to be burning inside of him. But there are also the memories of God's love before he fell and the reality of God's patient endurance with him from day one.

The fact that the Lord has never hurt him in any way, not even bringing a railing accusation against him, Jude 9, has to also be a positive memory that will burn the love of God into his mind with great power. When every last one of his followers and supporters have abandoned him and Satan remains all alone with only these memories something has to happen.

Amazingly, of all the sources from which I might quote to help us understand who the devil or Satan really is, his personality, how he operates and what will happen to him in the future I find the best one is from a psychiatrist who wrote a book in which he tells of his encounters with Satan. The title of the book is "People of the Lie: The hope for healing human evil," by M. Scott Peck, M.D. 1985. In chapter 5, "Of Possession and Exorcism," he seeks to answer the question: "Does the Devil exist?" As usual, the Lord has guided me to share this information with you, the reader, at the exact place in this book where it fits in best.

The following quotes are taken from Dr Peck's book itself, from pages 204 to 209. "The spirit I witnessed at each exorcism was clearly, utterly, and totally dedicated to opposing human life and growth. It told both patients to kill themselves. When asked in one exorcism why it was the Anti-Christ, it answered, 'Because Christ taught people to love each other.' ...Queried more, it simply said to the exorcist, 'I want to kill you.' There was absolutely nothing creative or constructive about it; it was purely destructive. Perhaps the greatest problem of theodicy is the question why God, having created Satan in the first place, simply didn't wipe it out after its rebellion. The question presupposes that God would wipe anything out. It assumes that God can punish and kill. Perhaps the answer is that God gave Satan free will and that God cannot destroy; He can only create. The point is that God does not punish. To create us in His image, God gave us free will. To have done otherwise would have been to make us puppets or hollow mannequins. Yet to give us free will God had to forswear the use of force against us. We do not have free will when there is a gun pointed at our back. It is not necessarily that God lacks the power to destroy us, to punish us, but that in His love for us He has painfully and terribly chosen never to use it. In agony He must stand by and let us be. He intervenes only to help, never to hurt.

"The Christian God is a God of restraint. Having forsworn the use of power against us, if we refuse His help, He has no recourse but, weeping, to watch us punish ourselves....In Christ, God Himself impotently suffered death at the hands of human evil. He did not raise a finger against His persecutors. Thereafter in the New Testament, we hear echoes of the punitive Old Testament God, one way or another, saying that 'the wicked will get what's coming to them.' But these are only echoes; a punishing God does not enter the picture ever again. While many nominal Christians still today envision their God as a giant cop in the sky, the reality of Christian doctrine is that God has forever eschewed police power....having forsaken force, God is impotent to prevent the atrocities that we commit upon one another. He can continue to grieve with us. He will offer us Himself in all His wisdom, but He cannot make us choose to abide with Him. For the moment, then, God, tormented, waits upon us through one holocaust after another. And it may seem to us that we are doomed by this strange God who reigns in weakness. But there is a denouement to Christian doctrine: God in His weakness will win the battle against evil. In fact, it is already won. The resurrection symbolizes not only that Christ overcame the evil of His day two millennia ago but that He overcame it for all time. Christ impotently nailed upon the cross is God's ultimate weapon."

Dr. Peck then spoke of Satan's method of operation, his modus operandi. He speaks repeatedly of how the devil uses lies and fear. "In fact, the only power that Satan has is through human belief in its lies....Satan can use any human sin or weakness-greed and pride, for instance. It will use any available tactic: seduction, cajolery, flattery, intellectual argument. But its principal weapon is fear. And in the post-exorcism period, after its lies had been exposed, it was reduced to haunting both patients with dully repetitive threats: 'We will kill you. We will get you. We will torture you. We will kill you.' As well as being the Father of lies, Satan may be said to be a spirit of mental illness.

"The spirit of evil is one of unreality, it, itself, is real. It really exists. To think otherwise is to be misled. Indeed, as several have commented, perhaps Satan's best deception is its general success in concealing its own reality from the human mind. Although it has a real power, Satan also has glaring weaknesses-the same weaknesses that caused its banishment from heaven. (Malachi) Martin noted that exorcisms can reveal not only extraordinary demonic brilliance but also extraordinary demonic stupidity. My observations confirm this. Were it not for its extraordinary pride and narcissism, Satan would probably not reveal itself at all. Its pride overcomes its intelligence, so that the demon of deceit is also a showoff. If it had been thoroughly clever, it would have left the two patients long before their exorcisms. But it could not allow itself to lose. It wanted only to win, so in both cases it hung in there until the bitter end-with the result that I and others today now know its reality.

"In the same way, Satan's intelligence is afflicted with two other blind spots I have observed. One that by virtue of its extreme self-centeredness, it has no real understanding of love. It recognizes love as a reality to be fought and even to be imitated, but utterly lacking in itself, it does not understand love in the least. Its reality appears to Satan only like the reality of a bad joke. The notion of sacrifice is totally foreign to it. When human beings at an exorcism are speaking in the language of love, it does not comprehend what they are saying. And when they are behaving with love, Satan is completely ignorant of the ground rules....Satan's weaknesses should not encourage us to overlook its strength. It propounds its lies with extraordinary power." And remember the most powerful lie of all is that "God destroys," which triggers Satan's greatest weapon, which is 'fear.' Dr. Peck concludes:

"I think it is necessary that we should hate Satan as well as fear it. Yet, as with evil people, I think it is ultimately more to be pitied. In Christian eschatology (the study of the last days) there are two scenarios for Satan. In one all human souls, having been converted to light and love, reach out to the spirit of hate and falsehood in friendship. Finally realizing itself to be totally defeated, with no human body left to possess, with all immune to its power, out of utter loneliness it breaks down and accepts the offer of friendship, and thereby in the end even Satan is converted. That is the scenario I pray for."

But how will this "conversion experience" take place? We know that Philippians 2:5-11 tells us clearly that every knee is going to bow and every tongue confess in the future. I think Dr. Peck touched upon the point which is going to do Satan in. He never gives up trying to prove that he is right and superior. And this is what will ultimately lead to his complete exposure, the same as it did at the cross. So, the day will come when all of Satan's facades are gone. Every one will know who he is and they will "look narrowly upon him," and say, "Is this the man that made the earth to tremble, that did shake kingdoms?" Isaiah 14:16. Yes, it is Satan who makes the earth to tremble with earthquakes and destroys cities at the end of the world. Psalm 9:6, Isaiah 14:17, Jer 25:31-33. His power to deceive will at long last come to an end, but he still does not give up. The hatred and pride and envy and jealousy that caused him to rebel in the beginning still exists. It is this obstinacy of the ego that will not give in no matter how much truth is presented that is going to prolong the suffering of the self-life for years. Isaiah 65:20 indicates this season of time may be 100 years.

So, it is this mental torment that Satan and all the wicked are going to have to go through before they will finally give in. As long as there is any rebellion left, the worm of sin in a person's life, he will continue to suffer without the comforting of the Holy Spirit. Mark 9:43-50. Each person will suffer according to the number of sins he has not confessed and which he/she still remember. These sins will torture and torment his mind as long as there is more for him to recall. That is how much longer he will have to suffer. In this age, before the millennium, the wicked will begin destroying each other during the battle of Armageddon.

The very atmosphere will no doubt ignite and burn up as well. 2 Peter 3:12. Their suffering is both mental and physical: "the worm of sin and corruption" will cause them torment and anguish as they recall their many sins. The longer the list, the more they will suffer, as they are destroyed both from without and within, Zech. 14:12, 13. Of course, they will not give in and admit they are wrong right away and so the suffering will continue until the sins of their entire lives have all come before them, just as they came before Belshazzer in Daniel 5. Just think how much he must have suffered before he finally was killed physically. The remorse, regret, shame and guilt will burn terribly. Remember one thing, when you read the Bible, the events are not always in chronological order. The reason for this is that God is the great I AM. With Him there is no past, or future. THERE IS ONLY THE ETERNAL EVER PRESENT NOW.

So, the event is what matters. The Hebrew writers were not so concerned with when it happened, but what actually happened. The Hebrew writers, under the inspiration of the Holy Spirit, did not give emphasis to the time element, but only to the event. When Scripture speaks, therefore, about the wicked's burning up (consuming, Rev 20:9) when the fire comes "down from God out of heaven." You must remember that this fire is not literal, for God does not destroy. It is a revelation of God's love. Look at Song of Solomon 8:6.

There is a difference between the coming of Christ in this age we are now living and the great age of the ages after the 1,000 years. There will be literal fire of destruction at the end of this age but that literal fire is from man, not from the Lord. The Jews confused the Scriptures pointing to the first coming of Christ with the Scriptures which speak of His coming in our day and after the 1,000 years. That is why the Jews sometimes confused the first coming of Christ with His second appearing in power and great glory. They expected Him to come in power and great glory at His first coming; and when He did not live up to their expectations, they rejected Him because of their false interpretations of Scripture. Remember the prophecy, "The glory of this latter house shall be greater than of the former ...," in Haggai 2:9? We are told that the old men who remembered Solomon's temple wept bitterly as they beheld the temple of Herod's day. They wept because they did not understand the prophecy. Their ideas were erroneous. The glory of the latter house WAS greater, not in magnificence of structure, but in the fact that THE LORD OF GLORY HIMSELF, JESUS, WALKED AND TALKED WITHIN IT. Let us make sure we today do not fall into the same trap of interpreting the Bible in accordance with preconceived notions and in anticipation of our own selfish ambitions for our church or for our position.

HOW WERE ANANIAS AND SAPPHIRA DESTROYED?

"Why hast thou conceived this thing in thine heart? thou hast not lied unto men, but unto God. And Ananias hearing these words fell down, and gave up the ghost..." Acts 5:4, 5. No lightning flashed from heaven on this occasion, so how did this man, and later his wife, die? What caused them to die? Did God just give them a heart attack? Did He inject some invisible poison into their veins? Is this the way God operates? No. Of course not. Let us consider the Person who was lied to. It was the HOLY SPIRIT. Can you find an instance anywhere in the Bible where the Holy Spirit killed, maimed, or destroyed anyone? I read that the Holy Spirit LEFT or QUIT PLEADING AND STRIVING WITH THE PEOPLE before the flood in Noah's day, but it doesn't say that the Holy Spirit killed them. It also says that Ananias lied to God, as well as to the Holy Spirit. It would seem that if what is true about the Holy Spirit is also true about God (for they are one) then it would be very difficult to pin this death on God or on the Holy Spirit. And it is very interesting that the Bible does not state in this case that God killed them. All that is necessary here to understand how Ananias and Sapphira died is to remember what the WRATH OF GOD is and what the JUDGMENT OF GOD is and how He permits wrath and judgment to take place. The power of the mind to negatively affect the body during periods of fear and/or guilt can be life-threatening and deadly. Ananias and Sapphira probably dropped dead out of pure guilt and fear as a result of having their sins exposed. Ananias and his wife are examples of people in the church who appear to be good Christians, but are not. They are not robbing banks or killing other people, but they would be miserable in the presence of Jesus and the redeemed though and will have to go through and experience the Lake of Fire for more education and discipline before they are ready to enter the kingdom. But, remember that the fire that comes down from God out of heaven is a fiery revelation of truth. Revelation 20:9.

My final point is that we must not overlook the fact that God has the power and wisdom to regulate not only this "fiery revelation of truth," but also, the "fire" that men begin as well as the "fire" that may come from an astral catastrophe; for God always works in harmony with the elements He Himself created and has the right to do so. He also will reveal more on this subject as we near the end of all things. So, if we do not now completely understand as much as we would like to understand about the fire of truth and love and righteousness, the fire of hate-induced nuclear destruction, and the fire of astral catastrophe, and the relationships herein sustained, let us be patient with ourselves and with God. Let us pray for more understanding and surely the Lord will reveal much more to us in His own good time and way. Eph 1:17, 18.

CHAPTER 15

DO GOD'S ANGELS EVER DESTROY HUMAN BEINGS?

Sometime ago I was talking to a minister about this subject and he said, "Why certainly God's angels destroy and hurt people. When Christ, the 'angel of the covenant,' was wrestling with Jacob, Jesus put Jacob's hip out of place. Yes, God and His angels do hurt and destroy people," he concluded with a smile of victory on his face; for he was sure that there was no answer to that argument. I said nothing at the time, for I had never really thought about it. I realized that it was very inconsistent with the character of Jesus in the New Testament to hurt anyone, so I prayed and asked God for special wisdom to understand this seemingly unexplainable contradiction. I will now share with you what the Holy Spirit revealed to me. "And Jacob was left alone; and there wrestled a man with him until the breaking of the day. AND WHEN HE [Jesus] SAW THAT HE [Jesus] PREVAILED NOT AGAINST HIM [Jacob], HE [Jesus] TOUCHED THE HOLLOW OF HIS [Jacob's] THIGH; AND THE HOLLOW OF JACOB'S THIGH WAS OUT OF JOINT, AS HE [Jacob] WRESTLED WITH HIM [Jesus]." If we agree that Jesus put Jacob's thigh out of place because Jesus could not prevail over Jacob, we are saying that Christ, the Creator, could not win a wrestling match with Jacob. That a created being is as strong or stronger than his Creator. This is, of course, absurd and totally unacceptable. The word prevail cannot be used here in a physical sense; God can prevail over anyone physically. We are no match for God physically or mentally anymore than we are equal to Him in any other way, shape, or form. So, the only answer is that Christ was trying to "PREVAIL" upon Jacob's mind or heart so Jacob would completely trust and fully believe that Christ had already blotted out his sins and forgiven Him. He wanted to give him the complete assurance of salvation. This will happen again in the lives of the saints during the "TIME OF JACOB'S TROUBLE." "Alas! for that day is great, so that none is like it: it is even the time of Jacob's trouble; but he shall be saved out of it." Jer. 30:7. Jacob's error that led him to obtain the birthright by fraud was clearly set before him. He had not trusted God's promises, but had sought by his own efforts to bring about that which God would have accomplished in His own time and way. As an evidence that he had been forgiven, his name was changed from one that was a reminder of his sin, to one that commemorated his victory.... from "Jacob" (meaning deceiver) to "Israel" (which means an overcomer). Gen. 32:28.

During the years of this century, it is possible that some ministers have used less than honest methods to preach the gospel. If so, then at the time when this last day "Jacob's Trouble," comes upon our world, they will cry out for assurance that their sins have been forgiven. Jacob wanted the birthright so badly he was willing to deceive his father, at his mother's urging, and steal from his brother. It is true that Esau had "sold" or bartered away his birthright to Jacob, for a mess of pottage, (red lentil soup, Genesis 25:29-34) when he was hungry, but Jacob took advantage when he should have been willing to share freely God's bounties. So, in these last days some have justified the means and methods they have used to obtain money, influence and position, all in the name of the Lord. If we confess our sins now, God will blot out the record, as He did for Jacob. Satan will cause many mental anguish, and they, will doubt and wonder if God has really forgiven them, and they will have their "night of wrestling." But, Jesus will deliver each of us then, if we trust Him, as He did Jacob.

Jesus saw that Jacob would not yield to Him so that he could receive the full assurance he needed to realize that he had been forgiven for deceiving Isaac. So, Jesus did something that He has to do with us sometimes. Satan wanted to destroy Jacob. But Christ would not allow him to take his life. But Jesus did give Satan permission to touch his thigh. If Jacob had surrendered sooner instead of fighting, Satan would not have been allowed to hurt him. If Jacob's "'Loins" had been girded about with truth he would have been protected. Eph. 6:14. Satan demanded that he be allowed to take Jacob's life but the Lord only allowed him to touch him in one place. Christ said "you may hurt him here only." And instantly Jacob's thigh was out of place. Is that not what God permitted Satan to do to Job because of his carnal fear? Job 2:25. Some unbeliever may now say, "Oh, you mean to tell me that God uses Satan to hurt us? That God and Satan are in partnership? That God lets or sends Satan to hurt people so they will repent?"

No, that is not how it works. The Lord is not in league with the enemy of all good. He does not "hire" Satan or work in "partnership" with the Devil in any way or at any time. But God does use the evil that Satan is constantly doing. That is, the Lord finds a way to turn the evil into good, if and when the individuals involved permit God to bring good out of Satan's evil, then the sinner gains a victory. See Deuteronomy 23:5. Satan is always trying to hurt us in some way or other. He is always looking for an opening to get to us. Jacob's resistance was a form of unbelief and became a chink in his armor. The Lord must always deal fairly with every person in every age or He would be charged with playing favorites. Romans 2:11 and James 2:1 proves that God never shows partiality or favoritism.

In most cases, when the Lord is forced to let Satan hurt someone, because he has broken the law, the individual does not turn toward God, but blames Him for the accident or calamity and turns away from Him. So, it is not in God's interest to play this game with the Devil, for in most instances people do not turn to the Lord. The law of averages is on the side of the devil. It just so happens that in the case of Job and Jacob, Satan lost. Furthermore, God is always trying to save people pain, not hurt them. If Satan had been able to break Jacob's hold upon God he would have been able to destroy him completely. But he was only permitted to afflict his thigh. Jesus acted as though He was attempting to get away from Jacob, similar to the experience on the road to Emmaus when Jesus gave the impression that He was going to continue His journey. God never forces His way into our lives so we will accept Him. We must invite Him into our lives. Rev. 3:20. "Behold I stand at the door and knock." As soon as Jacob's thigh was out of place He realized that God was the One He was wrestling with and He began to plead for a blessing so Esau would not be able to hurt him or his family. He also knew that if this God he was wrestling with would grant him a blessing it would mean his sin was forgiven and that he would have God's protection from Esau. If God destroys no man and if Satan was arguing that he had the right to DESTROY Jacob, who was it then who put Jacob's hip out of place and who would have destroyed him? Would it not have been the same being who destroyed the sons of Job when they sinned? And Job himself was afflicted even when he had done no sin, but God more than made it up to him, and He will more than make it up to us some day, even in this life, as He did to both Job and Jacob.

JESUS THE ARCHANGEL

In I Thessalonians 4:16 and Jude 9 we read that the Archangel has power to call forth the dead. These texts, along with John 5:25-29, prove that Jesus is indeed the Archangel. If there was ever a time when Jesus should have slapped Satan around and hurt him a little bit to teach him a good lesson, it was when He came to raise Moses from the grave in Jude 9 and Satan tried to stop Him. But what did Jesus do? He treated him with dignity, respect and kindness. Did not hurt him in any way. He simply referred Satan to His Father in Heaven. He didn't argue with the Devil (and we shouldn't either), or slander him in any way. "Yet Michael the archangel, when contending with the devil he disputed about the body of Moses, DURST NOT [presumed not or ventured-not] bring against him [Satan] a railing accusation, but said, The Lord rebuke thee." Jude 9 KJV.

The Modem Language Version says, "did not venture to

pronounce a reviling judgment against him...." The Revised Standard Version says the same. The Living Bible says, "Did not dare to accuse even Satan." You see, my friend, it is not Satan who is on trial in this great controversy but our Lord and the justice of His law that are on trial. If God doesn't accuse even Satan, how much less would He accuse a human being, let alone ever hurt or kill a human being. My friend, our Wonderful God has been slandered before all the universe for over 6,000 years. Satan has accused Jesus and His Father of murder and every other terrible crime. But in this last hour of earth's history, God's character will be vindicated through the preaching of the truth about His law.

Some people will ask, "Well, if Jesus is the Archangel, how could He be One with the Father and a co-Creator with the Father?" The answer to that is that Christ does not have to be an angel in order to be in charge of the angels anymore than a "cowboy" has to be a cow in order to be in charge of the cows or a "SHEPHERD" has to be a sheep in order to be in charge of the sheep. Scripture tells us that Christ is God in the fullest sense and has been One with the Father from the beginning. This is a mystery that has not been fully explained. But we do know the Bible teaches us that the Father created all things through His only Son. See John 1:1-3 and Hebrews 1:1-3. Since Christ is the leader or head of the angels, it would logically follow that He is responsible for all they do. Therefore, is it logical to believe that Jesus would command the angels at any time to kill, maim, or hurt any human beings in the Old Testament or the New Testament? No, it is not logical.

If Christ killed anyone, He would be transgressing His own Law, i.e., the sixth commandment, "Thou shalt not kill." Murder is the actual word intended. Psalm 103:20, says, that God's angels keep His commandments, too. "Bless the Lord ye his angels, that excel in strength, that do his commandments, hearkening unto the voice of his word." Since the angels are free moral agents like us, it follows that they have a choice as to whether or not they want to obey God or not. Do you think that a holy angel would carry out a command that is contrary to God's law? No, they would not break the law of God. Is God exempt from keeping His own law? Does He have to break His own holy law in order to uphold and honor that same law? Does He have a double standard? One that permits Him to kill when He so chooses but demands that His creatures must never kill or even hate? A law which commands us to allow people to slap us on both sides of the face, yet we must never retaliate, but just trust in Him and rejoice when we are mistreated. Does he act this way too? The cross proves he does not retaliate. Of course not. Whatever laws the Lord commands that we obey He obeys as well. He is not a hypocrite. Jesus' sinless, selfless life of sacrifice proves this beyond a doubt. Never once did he ever break the least of His Father's commandments, by even a look, word, glance or thought. Yet, most Christian teachers and preachers insist that God has to break the law by killing sinners, now and in the final judgment, in order to uphold the law.

At the conclusion of all these commands, Jesus stated, "Be ye therefore perfect, even as your Father which is in heaven is perfect." Matthew 5:48. Yes, Psalm 145:17 is true. "The Lord is righteous in all his ways, and holy in all his works." I believe that God the Father carries the whole universe with Him in all that He does, because He keeps or obeys His own Law and never has hurt or killed anyone.

Let us now consider some difficult experiences in the Old Testament where it does seem as though Jesus killed people. In the case of Korah, Dathan, and Abiram, and of the 250 princes, we see what is called a "JUDGMENT" of God. Moses was being accused again of being a dictator and not leading the people right. The challenge was met and here is the record. "If these men die the common death of all men, or if they be visited after the visitation of all men; then the Lord hath not sent me. But if the Lord makes a new thing, and the earth open her mouth, and swallow them up, with all that appertain unto them, and they go down quick into the pit; then ye shall understand that these men have provoked the Lord. And it came to pass, as he had made an end of speaking all these words, that the ground clave asunder that was under them. And the earth opened her mouth, and swallowed them up." Numbers 16:29-32. The marginal reading says, "CREATE A NEW NATION," instead of "Make a new thing." This simply means, that the original Hebrew phrase implies that after the 250 princes died, along with the other leaders, that God would have to appoint all new leaders. It did not mean a "new way" to kill people.

The question that must be answered is this. ***Does God kill people with earthquakes?*** If Jesus did not split open the earth, and kill them, then how did it happen? There are two possibilities which really boil down to just one. 1) It was a catastrophe which God knew was going to happen and simply let it happen or 2) Satan was given permission to cause an earthquake and split the ground open and kill them. I prefer to believe the second possibility, because we know that Satan can make earthquakes and that he is always ready to destroy anyone in order to garner in another soul and cast the blame upon God. Furthermore, the Lord always holds Himself responsible for the "judgment" by saying, "I did it," so as to command the people's reverence and their worship, so He can at least save them even through fear, if necessary, Jude 23. In this case the people did blame God and refused to repent of their sin in believing in the rebellion of Korah. "And all Israel that were round about them fled at the cry of them: for they said, 'LEST THE EARTH SWALLOW US UP ALSO.'"

Later on they gave Moses the "credit" by saying, "ye have killed the people of the Lord." Numbers 16:41. That is when the plague began among these people who were murmuring. See verses 45, 46, and 49. Who brought the plague? Paul tells us in I Corinthians 10:1 "Neither murmur ye, as some of them also murmured, and were DESTROYED OF THE DESTROYER." That should settle it, but we have yet to explain the fire flashing from the cloud in verse 35, "And there came out a fire from the Lord, and consumed the two hundred and fifty men that offered incense." Numbers 16:35.

LET US NOTICE SEVERAL CONCEPTS FROM THE BIBLE. These calamities were called "JUDGMENTS." Who led these people to the point that "Judgments" would fall? Why, it was Satan who caused them to be "successful in alienating 250 princes, men of renown in the congregation." It was Satan who had led them to be jealous. Jealousy gave rise to envy, which led to rebellion. Why does Satan tempt men to be jealous and rebel? Because he cannot destroy in most cases (such as in the experience of Job and in other cases when God permits Satan to destroy for reasons we do not understand) until he leads a person to break God's law. Then Satan goes to God and demands the right to be able to destroy that individual. Moses was entreating Israel to repent and flee from the coming destruction. Who is the destroyer? Satan is the destroyer. Exodus 12:23-24. Satan won the victory and held the people fast in his grasp so they would not to repent. How did the 250 princes die? Numbers 16:35 says "A fire from the Lord killed them," which simply means that God withdrew and let the destroyer kill them. 1 Cor. 10:10.

God never changes, so the way He dealt with Lucifer in the beginning is the way He has dealt with sin and sinners all along. He did not put down rebellion by force in the beginning and He did not do it in Moses' day. Nor will He do it today in this final age. We should know by now that the "WRATH OF GOD" always means that the Lord is assuming the responsibility, taking the blame, as we see in the death of King Saul, I Chron 10:13, 14 and again in Psalm 78:49, which proves that God's wrath and anger, indignation and trouble, is when the Lord removes His protection and allows Satan to destroy. Instead of worshiping and reverencing and fearing God by acknowledging His power to permit and prevent destruction from Satan, the people now declare that Moses is Satan's right hand man with lots of magic power to destroy people. It was in essence the same argument that was made against Jesus when the Jews said He did wonderful miracles of healing through the power of Beelzebub, the prince of devils. Matt. 12:22-24.

The danger is that someone will try to use this to prove that God is indeed the One who does the destroying and not Satan and that God is upset when people give the credit to Satan for killing people when it was really Jesus Christ who killed them. The irrationality of this human logic and carnal wisdom should be clear to all who really want to be logical.

Remember always, that God's JUDGMENTS (decisions) are part of His plan to save man. He (God) permits Satan to destroy, but takes the credit or blame for it in order to remain sovereign. TO GIVE SATAN CREDIT FOR GOD'S EFFORTS TO SAVE MAN BY PERMITTING AND PREVENTING SIN TO HAVE ITS NATURAL COURSE is called BLASPHEMY. In order to redeem mankind, God's sovereignty, His right to reign and rule and command worship, must remain intact in the minds of men. God cannot save man unless he worships Him; Thus the motive of fear is allowed, for man does not always respond to overtures of love due to his fallen nature. But God never is the author of fear. But He sometimes allows us to become fearful as it often causes us to cry out to Him for help. Matt. 8:23-24; Jude 23.

Now, we will consider some other experiences where it seems that God's Holy and sinless angels arbitrarily kill people. 2 Samuel 24:1, says, "And again the anger of the Lord was kindled against Israel, and he [the margin says SATAN; compare to I Chronicles 21:1 where the text specifically says, 'And Satan'] stood up against Israel, and provoked David to number Israel." *

The sin here, of course, is that Satan wants David to trust in numbers instead of trusting in the Lord. It would be the same as the Devil's tempting us to "count our money," or look at how many 'good' things WE have done, and so forth. It is giving credit to the power of man instead of to the power of God. Now, the result of this was, "So the Lord sent a pestilence upon Israel from the morning even to the time appointed: and there died of the people from Dan even to Beersheba seventy thousand men. AND WHEN THE ANGEL STRETCHED OUT HIS HAND UPON JERUSALEM TO DESTROY IT, THE

LORD REPENTED HIM OF THE EVIL, AND SAID TO THE ANGEL THAT DESTROYED THE PEOPLE, IT IS ENOUGH: STAY NOW THINE HAND. AND THE ANGEL OF THE LORD WAS BY THE THRESHING PLACE OF ARAUNAH THE JEBUSITE. AND DAVID SPAKE UNTO THE LORD WHEN HE SAW THE ANGEL THAT SMOTE THE PEOPLE, AND SAID, LO, I HAVE SINNED, AND I HAVE DONE WICKEDLY: BUT THESE SHEEP, WHAT HAVE THEY DONE? LET THINE HAND, I PRAY THEE, BE AGAINST ME, AND AGAINST MY FATHER'S HOUSE." 2 Samuel 24:15-17.

Now, let us look at I Chronicles 21:15-16, "AND GOD SENT AN ANGEL UNTO JERUSALEM TO DESTROY IT: AND AS HE WAS DESTROYING, the Lord beheld, and he repented him of the evil, (God's heart is broken as He sees Satan destroying) and said to the angel (Angel, that had withdrawn to let Satan destroy) that destroyed, it is enough, stay now thine hand. And the angel of the Lord stood by the threshing floor of Ornan the Jebusite. And David lifted up his eyes, and saw the angel of the Lord stand between the earth and the heaven, having a drawn sword in his hand stretched out over Jerusalem." In Numbers 22:31, we also see the Lord permitting Balaam to see an angel of the Lord with a drawn sword. Heb. 4:12, Eph. 6:17. The Bible says the SWORD represents God's Word or authority. Therefore, the angel with the drawn sword represents God's sovereignty over all the events and issues of life. God PERMITS AND HE PREVENTS ACCORDING TO HIS DIVINE WILL. But, since BALAAM was tuned into SATAN instead of to God, BALAAM SAW the angel's sword as an instrument of death when the sword (God's Loving word), was INTENDED to bring life.

ARE GOD'S ANGELS LYING SPIRITS?

Micaiah the prophet said to Ahab and Jehoshaphat, "I saw the Lord sitting on his throne, and all the host of heaven standing by him on his right hand and on his left. And the Lord said, who shall persuade Ahab, that he may go up and fall at Ramoth Gilead? And one said on this manner, and another said on that manner. And there came forth a spirit [angel] and stood before the Lord, and said, I will persuade him. And the Lord said unto him, Wherewith? And he said, I will go forth, and I will be a lying spirit in the mouth of all his prophets. And he said, Thou shalt persuade Him, and prevail also: go forth, and do so. The Lord hath spoken evil concerning thee." I Kings 22:19-23.

IN THE BIBLE, GOD IS OFTEN PICTURED AS DOING THAT WHICH HE DOES NOT RESTRAIN. This is just what we have been saying all along.... That God always takes the blame for that which He permits. This also explains I Sam 18:10, "And it came to pass on the morrow, that the evil spirit from God came upon Saul, and he prophesied in the midst of the house:" Do Satan's angels prophesy or preach? They sure do. And God says, "AND FOR THIS CAUSE [because they received not the love of the truth] GOD SHALL SEND [permit to come upon] THEM STRONG DELUSION, THAT THEY SHOULD BELIEVE A LIE: THAT THEY ALL MIGHT BE DAMNED WHO BELIEVED NOT THE TRUTH, BUT HAD PLEASURE IN UNRIGHTEOUSNESS." 2 Thessalonians 2:11, 12. Satan's angels are today preaching through the mouths of many preachers who are living in sin and telling the people they do not have to do this and can do that. Thus Satan leads the people to destruction by false doctrine. See Jere. 28:8-17.

The drawn sword represents God's control over all evil that man is capable of bringing upon the earth. Psalm 17:13. The rod that Moses held in his hand represented God's control over all of nature in Egypt. When he threw the rod down it meant God's authority over nature had passed to the power signified by the serpent, Satan. Moses' rod actually represented Christ, Isa.11:1. But when JESUS is cast down, SATAN takes over and rules. The Second Book of Kings tells a very interesting story about how Elijah called fire down out of heaven and destroyed two groups of 50 soldiers sent out by King Ahaziah to arrest Elijah for rebuking the king for going over to Baalzebub, the god of Ekron, by way of messengers, to see if he would get well from his sickness which was caused by a fall in Samaria. "0 man of God, thus hath the king said, Come down quickly. And Elijah answered and said unto them, If I be a man of God, let the fire of God come down from heaven, and consume thee and thy fifty. And the fire of God came down from heaven, and consumed him and his fifty." 2 Kings 1:10-14. This happened twice, and the third captain had reverence and respect for Elijah so his life was spared because he had reverence for the Lord's prophet, and Satan had no legal right to destroy the Captain. Now, how this fire was sent is similar to what we read about in the book of Job. Just how Satan is able to control and manipulate the elements of nature so as to bring down literal fire and destroy people we do not know, but evidently he has learned how to do this. This could be lightning or it could be a bolide or some similar astral catastrophe or it could be the same kind of fire that Satan will bring down in the last days to deceive people. Rev 13:13.

God always holds Himself sovereign over these events, just as He did when the bears actually came out of the woods and "tare forty and two" of those mocking young people: 2 Kings 2:23, 24. The Hebrew word for bear is from ***Slander***. God permitted these slandering slanderers to be destroyed by a symbol of what they were doing. Obadiah 1:15. Satan was allowed to destroy them in this way. In Luke 9:54, Jesus rebuked James and John for suggesting that He bring fire down and burn up the Samaritans. "But he turned, and rebuked them, and said, YE KNOW NOT WHAT MANNER OF SPIRIT YE ARE OF. FOR THE SON OF MAN IS NOT COME TO DESTROY MEN'S LIVES, BUT TO SAVE THEM." They never again brought up such an idea, but Peter brought his sword on the night of Jesus' arrest and was rebuked for that. Jesus healed Malchus' ear. Luke 22:51. GOD'S 'STILL SMALL VOICE' SPOKE TO ELIJAH ON THE MOUNT

"And he said, 'Go forth, and stand upon the mount before

the Lord.' And behold, the Lord passed by, and a great and strong wind rent the mountains, and brake in pieces the rocks before the Lord; but the Lord was not in the wind: and after the wind an earthquake; but the Lord was not in the earthquake: And after the earthquake a fire; but the Lord was not in the fire (Notice that God has nothing to do with literal fire): AND AFTER THE FIRE A STILL SMALL VOICE. [The margin says, "That is a delicate whispering, as of the breeze among the leaves."] And it was so, when Elijah heard it, that he wrapped his face in his mantle, and went out, and stood in the entering of the cave. And, behold, there came a VOICE UNTO HIM, AND SAID, WHAT DOEST THOU HERE, ELIJAH?" I Kings 19:11-13.

I do not read anywhere in the Bible where God arbitrarily brings natural disasters. He permits them to come and controls them according to His own will for what is best for His people and for all mankind. Here the Lord showed Elijah that God does not use or work through force and coercion. This is the work of Satan. "NOT BY MIGHT NOR BY POWER, BUT BY MY SPIRIT, SAITH THE LORD OF HOSTS." Zechariah 4:6. The only kind of people who will survive the TIME OF TROUBLE will be those who have THE TRUE CHARACTER OF OUR LORD JESUS CHRIST AND HIS FATHER. This is the character of love I am presenting in this book. This is the logical reality or substance of it. The doing of God's character is MEDICAL MISSIONARY WORK, and every church in the world, and every Christian in the world will be tested on this point. If we know how to give simple remedies and how to eat a simple diet straight from nature itself, we will be able to survive ourselves and help others to survive with us in outpost centers away from the cities. We must live outside of the cities with our families and reach the masses by going there periodically, as Enoch did, before the flood.

Very few people know how to eat a simple diet. But, this is what we must get back to...food in as simple and original of a form as possible. We must also learn how to give simple water treatments, steam baths, rub downs, and even to help straighten out crooked backs. This takes learning from those who know and time and mental and physical effort as well as money. You may be called by God to start a MEDICAL MISSIONARY OUTPOST in your own home wherever you are and begin immediately to demonstrate the character of God by helping the sick and dying all around you. You can teach the proper way to eat and live by being an example right there where you live. The need is great and the time is short. The only kind of people who will survive the TIME OF TROUBLE will be those who have Jesus' true heart of love. Out in the big cities is total, pure hatred. Sometimes you even see it in the church. Nothing but total pure love will be able to survive, physically, mentally, emotionally, and spiritually in such an atmosphere. Many are talking about Righteousness by Faith today, but do not really know what it is. Put together Romans 13:10 and Romans 8:4 and you will see that RIGHTEOUSNESS IS LOVE. God's indwelling Spirit will be shown by the outflowing of heavenly love. Let us pray for that "Golden Oil of Love," so we may not only explain God's character of love, but show it in deeds of love, healing and mercy.

*Lord and God are titles that Satan is allowed and permitted to assume throughout the Old Testament. Only by knowing and comparing the life and character of Christ can we know the difference between the true Lord and God and the false lord and god. See Chapter 27 on page 442 for examples of these contrasts between the true and false Lords in the Bible.

CHAPTER 16

THE WORD MADE FLESH

The Father is either like Jesus or Jesus is a liar, a fraud and a deceiver, as the Jews alleged. Which will it be for you? The Jewish view of God at the time of Christ, which is a God of hatred, jealousy, vindictiveness, violence and death or the Jesus view of God, which is a God of infinite love, compassion, wisdom, mercy and justice? This view of God pictures Him as always gentle, always kind, never hurting or killing, but always helping, always saving those who want to be saved, but who cannot and will not interfere with a person's free choice to reap the result of His own stubborn will. This is what the Bible calls God's anger, wrath, and punishment. See Psalm 78:49; Romans 1:18, 24, 26, 28. For a God who is not only Omnipotent (all powerful), but also Omniscient, (all knowing and seeing), would never have to resort to our carnal, fleshly methods to win the battle. See 2 Cor. 10:4, 5.

The Beloved John wrote of the Father's character in the first chapter of his Gospel. "AND THE WORD WAS MADE FLESH, AND DWELT AMONG US, [AND WE BEHELD HIS GLORY, THE GLORY AS OF THE ONLY BEGOTTEN OF THE FATHER] FULL OF GRACE AND TRUTH." John 1:14. The word GLORY in the Bible means character. Just think of it, through Christ we may obtain the attributes of God the Father, as Jesus did. Since the law is a transcript of His Eternal character, this happens when His law is fully implanted in our minds and hearts. Doesn't that just make you want to shout for joy!

GOD'S PRESENCE SYMBOLIZED BY A BEAUTIFUL DOVE

When Jesus began His ministry the sign or symbol of God's presence descended upon Him in the form of a dove. If God's character is violence, force, destruction and death, then He should have sent a falcon or a hawk. But these arbitrary methods are not the tools of His trade. He sent a sweet, little, beautiful and innocent dove. No wonder the Jews hated Him and rejected Him and hanged Him on a cross. And no wonder that "modern spiritual Jews," today, with their Jewish concept of God, do not accept the principles of the sermon on the mount which teaches us not to hit back, but to bless and pray for the happiness of our enemies, whom Jesus has told us to love. Modern man does not want that kind of a Messiah to rescue him anymore than the Jews did 2,000+ years ago. "AWAY WITH HIM," is their cry again today.

THE LAMB OF GOD WHICH CONQUERS THE WORLD

Again, when Jesus looked for a fit symbol to represent Himself 700 years before He came to earth, He selected a lamb, not a dragon, and put this concept into the heart and mind of His prophet Isaiah who depicted the coming Deliverer as a weak and helpless baby sheep who is "BROUGHT AS A LAMB TO THE SLAUGHTER, AND AS A SHEEP BEFORE HER SHEARERS IS DUMB, SO HE OPENETH NOT HIS MOUTH." ISAIAH 53:7. At both the beginning and at the close of Christ's ministry He chose non-aggressive animals to depict and symbolize the character of His work. When I verbalized this "LAMB" concept in a question and answer period after a preaching service in a church , someone pointed out that Christ was also pictured as the "LION OF THE TRIBE OF JUDAH." I agreed that this is true, and although there is a seeming contradiction here, there is in reality no contradiction at all, but very beautiful harmony and symmetry in this animal imagery of the prophets. It is not the lion of this earth which is used to depict the kingly traits of Christ, but the lion of the earth made new, when "The Wolf shall dwell with the Lamb, and the Leopard shall lie down with the kid; and the calf and the young lion and the fatling together ...and the lion shall eat straw like the ox. They shall not hurt nor destroy in all my Holy Mountain; for the earth shall be full of the knowledge of the Lord as the waters cover the sea." Isaiah 11:6-9.

The Word of God promises that the true power of God is in holiness and Godlikeness, and that characteristic will indeed crush the head of the serpent. "Thou shalt tread upon the Lion and adder: the young Lion and the dragon shalt thou trample under feet. Because he hath set his love upon me, therefore will I deliver Him: I will set him on high, because he hath known my name." Psalm 91:13, 14. Will the name of God be written in your forehead, friend of mine? Will it be written in mine? Or will we receive the mark of the beast? The choice is ours entirely. No one is going to force us, for arm twisting and coercion is contrary to the principles of God's government. "And they [those who understand and possess the character of Christ], shall see his face; and his name shall be in their foreheads." Rev. 22:4. God is always found by those who are looking for Him with all their hearts. On the night of Christ's birth only a few shepherds were ready to receive the wonderful story of the SAVIOR's birth. What about us today? Do we recognize the final message of truth anymore than the Jews recognized the beginning of it?

SIX MONTHS BEFORE

Only six months before, John the Baptist had been born to an old woman talking excitedly (fanatically, they no doubt said), about the appearance of an angel who had appeared to her husband announcing the forerunner of the Messiah. She was to be the mother of this forerunner, so her husband had told her. Zacharias was dumb, due to his unbelief, and could only write her notes, but she believed his story, especially after she became pregnant. But the priests didn't believe. "So, he had a stroke," they intoned piously, no doubt. "What is so unusual about that? After all, he is getting pretty old. As far as your pregnancy is concerned, we have no comment," they probably concluded as they dismissed her and her "ridiculous" prophetic utterances. "When the Messiah gets ready to come," they told themselves, as they went back to their scrolls, "God will tell us first. We will know about it before anyone else. Jehovah would not bypass us for we are His most loyal, dedicated and faithful servants. Yes, we will know the Messiah when He comes. Our interpretation of Holy Writ is infallible." At the time of Christ's first Advent, pride and envy had closed the door of the hearts of Israel's leaders. They were primarily interested in maintaining their theological positions and their power, influence and control over the people which guaranteed them a fixed yearly income as well as proof that they were indeed the elect of God. Later when Christ Himself was born they treated the reports of the shepherds as unworthy of their notice. They might have found the Messiah themselves and been ready to lead the wise men to His birthplace, but instead the situation was just reversed.

These so-called "men of God," showed their contempt for the heaven sent reports that were troubling King Herod and all Jerusalem by refusing to even go to Bethlehem to check things out. There and then they began rejecting Christ by leading the people to regard the interest in Jesus as a fanatical excitement. Their pride and stubbornness developed into hatred which closed the door to themselves, but opened it to the Gentiles. How did the Jews die? How did Jerusalem die? Did God kill them? No, they were killed by the Romans whom they hated, but whom they should have loved. They sowed to the wind in all their words, actions and attitude and they reaped the whirlwind. So it will be in the final day of judgment. The wicked will kill and be killed by their enemies, for there will be no friends in this final age among those who refuse the truth about God's true character. Every man will count his neighbor an enemy. Ezekiel 28:6-10. In chapter 12 we dealt with the mechanics of that destruction and how it is effected. See also, Ezek. 38:21; Zech. 14:13.

GOD'S FIRE OF TRUTH AND LOVE

Jesus said unto them, [Jewish leaders arguing with His declaration that He is the Messiah], verily, verily, I say unto you, before Abraham was, I am. John 8:58. Who was this speaking? Why, it was the Ever living One who appeared to Moses in the burning bush. This is the Jesus of the Old Testament standing before the leaders of Israel, who did not know him. Christ said in Luke 12:49, I am Come to send fire on the Earth; and what will I, if it be already kindled?

Question: did the fire of the burning bush in Moses' day or the fire that Jesus brought when He was upon earth burn anybody? Did Moses or the Jewish leaders or the disciples receive third degree burns as a result of coming into the presence of Christ?

No, they didn't. Why? Because the FIRE OF GOD in this instance was the fire of His very presence, which is infinite purity, love, truth and total righteousness. Song of Solomon 8:6, Isa 10:17. Man in his mortal state and carnal mentality cannot stand in the presence of such a being without having a total mental and physical breakdown, unless God shields His glory from them. This is what Jesus did in the case of Moses as well as in the case of the Jewish leaders, especially the Jewish leaders.

When the demons came into the veiled presence of Christ's glory when He was upon earth in the body of a man, they went into a frenzy. "Let us alone; what have We to do with thee, thou Jesus of Nazareth? Art thou Come to destroy us? I know thee who thou art, the Holy One of God." Mark 1:24. Again in the country of Gadara the demons cried out with a loud voice, and said, "What have I to do with thee, Jesus, thou Son of the most high God? I adjure thee by God that thou torment me not." Mark 5:7. Notice the doctrine of this devil. He believes that God torments His creatures. Since we exist on a different plane, we cannot see the unseen world as the good and evil angels do. Perhaps their mental and physical vibrations are so speeded up that we are unable to see them with our eyes of flesh. They are not encumbered with matter as we are, and yet they exist in a very real world of their own. God has wisely and lovingly veiled the brightness of His glory (character) so we can communicate with Him on our level and live. The more we read His Word and desire to live according to His perfect will, the more of His beautiful likeness we can absorb and the more we absorb, the closer we are able to come to Him without being aware of our unfitness to be in His Eternal presence. And as His mind, will and likeness are more and more impressed upon us, we will feel more and more comfortable in His presence.

When an evil angel or human being comes into the presence of truth and righteousness in the form of an angel of God, (who is in charge of a large company, no doubt), guarding a special agent of God, that evil angel or unsaved person is often very uncomfortable and anxious to get away from that presence as soon as possible. Why? Because they are convicted of their sinfulness. This causes tremendous mental torture. They are afraid of God, for they are living in their sin and love it instead of God. But the born again believer is not afraid, for his sins have been washed away by the blood of the Lamb. "Herein is our love made perfect, that we may have boldness in the day of judgment [decision]: because as he is, so we are in this world. [We have become perfect in Jesus], there is no fear in love: but perfect love casts out fear: because fear hath torment. He that fears is not made perfect in love." I John 4:17,18. A good example of this is Saul of Tarsus. When the bright "light from heaven," Acts 9:3, 4, which was the presence of Jesus, shined upon Saul, it frightened him so much that he "fell to the earth." Saul realized immediately that he was in the presence of infinite purity. Saul's experience is just a little sample of what the wicked at the end of the world will suffer when the eyes of Jesus look upon the wicked with His fiery look of love. Rev. 1:7, 14; Song of Solomon 8:6. This is the final judgment. Our minds record every bit of information which comes into our experience, conscious and unconscious and is able to be recalled instantly with perfect accuracy when God permits it to happen. If God is love, why would He permit this torture of mind? I can only believe that it is one last effort on His part to bring the lost to an awareness of their true condition. Everything else has failed. This is all that is left and He will leave no stone unturned to bring us to repentance. Every decision each person ever made is clearly revealed and every effort on God's part to save the sinner from himself, (the passions or fire of his own carnal desire) and from the tricks of Satan. Every invitation slighted. Every opportunity ignored. "For there is nothing covered that shall not be revealed; neither hid, that shall not be known," Luke 12:2. And they went up on the breadth of the earth and compassed the camp of the saints about, and the beloved city: and fire came down from God out of Heaven and devoured them. Rev. 20:9. Rev 11:4,5. To fully understand what this means one has to consider the word FIRE in its total aspect and usage throughout the Bible. DEVOURING FIRE, doesn't always mean a literal fire, but is often referring to a fire such as Moses saw when he approached the burning bush on Sinai. It was the Eternal Presence of Christ in the OT. Now notice this: "The sinners in Zion are afraid; fearfulness hath surprised the hypocrites who among us shall dwell with the devouring fire? Who among us shall dwell with everlasting burnings?" Isaiah 33:14.

Is it possible that this fire, which is His GLORY OR CHARACTER, will cause such a chemical reaction in the bodies of the lost when he comes in our age, that they will begin to deteriorate as they stand on their feet in the very presence of CHRIST AND HIS SAINTS? Listen to this description of their fate. Their flesh shall consume away while they stand upon their feet, and their eyes shall consume away in their holes, and their tongue shall consume away in their mouth. Zech. 14:12.

When a person has a fire of guilt, remorse, hate, jealousy and revenge burning away inside of him and a literal fire he himself has started burning the world up around him, it isn't likely that he will last more than a few hours or days. The fire that burns on the inside will burn first as the wicked see what they have lost and how they have unfitted themselves to dwell in the presence of God. This burning inside will lead to the literal fire which is started by the wicked, not by God. Isa. 9:18-20, Ezek. 38:21; Zech. 14:13, Psalm 140:7-10.

The more sins a person has to recall, the longer he will suffer and burn. Where their worm dies not and the fire is not quenched. Mark 9:46. The worm here is obviously the worm of sin (Pride ego or the carnal mind which separate us from God) and since Satan's worm is bigger and longer than anyone's he will suffer longer than anyone else. But God does not kill him. "They [the terrible of the nations] shall bring thee down to the pit, and thou shalt die the deaths of them that are slain in the midst of the seas. Wilt thou yet say before him that slays thee, I am God? [compare Isa. 14:12-14] But thou shalt be a man, and no God, in the hand of Him that slays thee. Thou shalt die the deaths of the uncircumcised by the hand of strangers: for I have spoken it, saith the Lord God." Ezek. 28:8-10. This will happen twice. Once before the 1,000 years begin, and once afterward. The first will be physical and spiritual but the second time, after the 1,000 years, it will be totally spiritual and symbolic.

CHAPTER 17

JESUS, THE FIRE OF TRUTH

In Luke 12:49, Jesus declared that He had come to bring FIRE ON THE EARTH. Was this a literal fire? No, we know it wasn't for Jesus never literally burned anyone up at anytime while He was on earth, not even an evil angel. But, He did bring a great deal of TRUTH AND RIGHTEOUSNESS, that made the disciple's hearts BURN within them, not only before the cross, but especially after, Luke 24:32. This fulfilled John the Baptist's prediction that Christ would baptize with Fire and the Holy Ghost. Luke 3:16. This came to pass in a most remarkable manner on the 50th day after the resurrection or on the Day of Pentecost, when Cloven tongues like as of fire, came and sat upon each of the praying disciples. They were truly men on fire for God after that, going everywhere preaching the Word of the risen Christ.

But, the unbelieving Jews were also baptized with fire as a result of this experience of the 120 disciples. However, like Pharaoh of old, it just "BURNED THEM UP," to see the religion of Jesus prosper so much. Their hearts were hardened by the truth. You see, friend of mine, the fire of truth either baptizes you with the fire of Jesus' love or the fiery indignation of Satan's hatred toward God. How we relate ourselves to it determines which effect it will have in our hearts and lives. The heart of Cleopas burned within Him, Luke 24:32, as he listened to Christ explain the O.T. Scriptures to him and his friend on Sunday afternoon. That same fire burned in Judas' heart at the last supper and on the night of Christ's arrest and subsequent trial. That fire which brought peace and joy to the other disciples brought death to Judas. Jesus killed Him with His love, you might say. Judas might have found repentance and forgiveness as did Peter, but the love that melted Peter's heart hardened Judas. Was that God's fault? No, but in Isaiah 53;10 and Zech. 13:7

God the Father is pictured as "Killing" His own Son, for God always takes the blame. Can you imagine what it will be like when Christ comes back the second and the third time? "Our God shall come, and shall not keep silence: A fire shall devour before him, and it shall be very tempestuous round about him. And the Heavens shall declare his righteousness: For God is Judge Himself." Psalm 50:3-6. His love and kindness go before Him. This is what causes the wicked to self-destruct. They cannot stand such love and purity and kindness. Rev, 6:14-17.

GOD'S LAW AND WORD IS FIRE

God's law is His Word and His Word is fire. Jesus Christ was the Word made flesh, or you could say, THE FIRE MADE FLESH. As we have already noted in Luke 12:49, Jesus declared that He had come to bring FIRE ON THE EARTH: At the end of the controversy of 6,000 years, Jesus displays His law in the sky. "And the Heavens shall declare His righteousness." Psalm 50:6.

So we see that the dual concept is here again used regarding the coming of Christ and the fire that He brings. It is a fire of truth and righteousness, as well as a literal fire. But, God is not bringing the literal fire, He is simply saying, "I am coming, and it will be a fiery coming." Remember that the text said, "And it shall be very tempestuous round about Him." It did not say He was bringing the fiery storm, but that there would be a storm raging about Him as He enters our atmosphere. If you will study out the context carefully, you will see that Christ does not bring the literal fire, but simply takes the blame for it, as He always has for all of the problems connected with the controversy on this planet. Notice: "And out of His mouth goeth a sharp sword, that with it He should smite the nations: and He shall rule them with a rod of iron: and He treadeth the winepress of the fierceness and wrath [God releasing His restraints] of Almighty God." Rev. 19:15. In 2 Thess. 1:7-9, Paul tells us that Christ will come "IN FLAMING FIRE, and that those who

KNOW NOT GOD, and OBEY NOT THE GOSPEL, are going to be PUNISHED WITH EVERLASTING DESTRUCTION, from the presence of the Lord, and from the GLORY of HIS POWER." Notice how Paul parallels the phrase, "GLORY OF HIS POWER," with the punishment of everlasting destruction. He lumped the second and the third comings of Christ into one grand, glorious, climatic event. When we go into the second chapter of Paul's letter to the Thessalonians, we see him again referring to the death and destruction that will result from Christ's appearance, only this time it is "THAT WICKED," which primarily refers to the Devil, but has a secondary application to the organizations, individual and/or individuals whom Satan is using today to deceive the world. The Mark of the beast is simply the character of man without God living in him. Notice how Paul describes their destruction.

"Whom the Lord shall consume with the Spirit of His mouth, and shall destroy with the brightness of His coming." Here again, Christ is taking the blame for the death of the wicked, saying, "I DID IT," so He may remain sovereign. Christ's coming will interrupt the battle of armageddon or actually end it (at least for 1,000 years). He comes to rescue His own and resurrect the sleeping saints from their graves. Satan knows he has lost the battle and yet makes one final attempt to destroy the final remnant who have refused to bow down to him and his marking system for survival by receiving the mark of allegiance to his sign (SUNDAY, THE SIGN OF THE DEATH GOD) in the right hand or forehead, the 666 Beast System. He will pass a death decree in order to destroy this one little offshoot, heretic, group of people (THE LITTLE BAND OF CONSCIENTIOUS SABBATH KEEPERS), who are still resisting his authority. He must stop the demonstration they are giving to the universe that an entire nation of people {144,000} can stand true to God and His Eternal law under the most adverse circumstances because they have permitted Jesus to fully saturate them with His love, which is His law written in their hearts.

Because Christ is omniscient (all knowing, Isa. 46:9, 10) and Satan is not, Jesus and His Father can calculate to the very second when each event in this last hour will occur. Satan has no power to counteract this. It was at midnight (Exodus 12:29) that God manifested His power for the deliverance of His people from Egyptian bondage. I believe God's people will again be delivered at midnight, when God says "It is done." Rev. 16:17. Now, as the result of this voice; which will sound like the sound of many waters (Rev. 1:15) there is a mighty earthquake. Now, I would like to suggest that what happens here is the same thing that happened when Christ died on the cross, when he said, "IT IS FINISHED." There was an earthquake at that time. Does God cause earthquakes? To answer that, just ask the question, do earthquakes kill people? Yes, they do. If God doesn't kill people and if earthquakes do kill, then God is not the one who brings the earthquakes, at any time or place. Psalm 9:6 and Isa. 14:16, 17 tell us that Satan is the one who destroys the cities in the LAST DAYS. See also Jere. 4:2, 3, 26. This does not mean God doesn't use, control and guide the results of earthquakes, which Satan is constantly bringing. Besides earthquakes, Satan also causes accidents, fires, disasters on land, sea and in the air. He brings tornadoes, hailstorms, tempests, floods, hurricane, droughts, plagues, and a thousand other kind of calamities.

Who brought the earthquake when Jesus died? Our Lord cried out, "IT IS FINISHED," as He gave up His perfect life as a sacrifice for our sins, and an earthquake immediately followed. We just read how Satan is the one who makes the earth to "tremble" and destroys all the cities at the end of the world. He is the death God. It is his very nature to destroy. He cannot help himself. It is obvious that God used the "temper tantrum," of Satan at Christ's death to open the graves of the saints who came forth with Jesus on Sunday morning and appeared to many and later ascended with Him to heaven. See Matt. 27:50-53, Psalm 24, Eph. 4:8-10. Some people may think that God's Angels will bring all the calamities upon the earth in this last hour of earth's history. But this is not true. Holy angels of God are often pictured in the Bible as destroying angels. But how do God's angels destroy? By simply withdrawing. These "destroying angels," are the same angels John saw in vision and wrote about in Rev. 7, 15 and 16. They are pictured as coming out of the temple with the vials full of the WRATH OF GOD. But, they are simply symbolic of God's restraint being withdrawn from Satan and the wicked. God's angels "destroy"on command by withdrawing. That is, they retreat at Jesus' command to honor man's free choice and Satan's angels then come in and fill the vacuum as they are "given permission to destroy," by God's holy angels (destroying angels) who just "destroyed," by removing the restraint at Christ's command. Remember the words VENGEANCE AND JUDGMENT do not mean to destroy, but to "vindicate," and to "make and/or carry out a decision." God does this by "preventing and permitting," with His holy angels. I Kings 22 pictures God's angels as "lying spirits," because He permitted Ahab to believe the lies of Satan's angels who were speaking through the mouths of the false prophets of Baal. God Himself is said to "repent," and to "harden" Pharaoh's heart and to send an evil spirit to Saul, as well as to kill Saul in the end. I Chron. 10:13, 14. "I am God, and there is none like me, Declaring the end from the beginning, and...saying, my counsel shall stand, and I will do all my pleasure...I form the light, and create darkness: I make peace, and create evil: I the Lord do all these things." Isa. 45:7, 46:9, 10. And remember that judgment (God carrying out a decision) never comes until man has fully set his own heart fully to do his own will and go his own way. God let Judas go. God let Jerusalem Go. God let the Jewish nation go. Go where? *Go their own way and do their own will.* This is how God destroys. "Destroy thou them O God. Let them fall by their own counsels." Psalm 5:10.

We are not told that the walls of JERICHO falling down flat killed anyone, but a person might assume this, although it is not so stated. But, it is stated that the Israelites rushed in and killed everyone in the city but Rahab and her family. Joshua commanded this, not God. Joshua 6:7. Why? Because Israel had failed to follow the Lord's perfect will and thus God had to let them follow their own will. The same is true about the laws of divorcement (Matt. 19:8, 9) and the selection of Saul as King (I Sam. 10:19). God's perfect will has seldom been carried out in this earth by man. A few people like Enoch, Joseph, Daniel and of course, Christ Himself (the only totally perfect one), permitted God to work out His perfect will through them. But regarding Jericho, God's angels again are pictured here as doing that which they permit to happen by withdrawing their power. Donald Patton believes that an earthquake caused the walls of Jericho to fall down. The Bible does not say that, so we do not know that to be true or false. What part the silence of seven days and then a lot of noise may have had on the laws of physics is beyond most brains to calculate. It just may have had a lot more to do with it than we may want to admit. QUESTION: WOULD SATAN DESTROY THE WALLS OF A CITY IF GOD REMOVED HIS PROTECTION? ANSWER: Yes, I believe he would. Why? Simply to make God look like a death God and thus distort the truth about His character. God never commands or brings Death. Proverbs 8:8, John 10:20. In other words, Satan, as in the days of Job, is permitted to bring disaster and then tells everyone God did it. Just as God assumed the responsibility for all the disasters in the Old Testament as well as the New, so He would again say, "I have destroyed Jericho." I say, to be consistent with the way God operates, this would be the MODUS OPERANDI of God again at Jericho, as we spiritually analyze it all. God's Holy angels are pictured as bringing the plagues, when in fact they do not bring the plagues. Satan brings the seven last plagues. Someone may ask about now, "why would Satan destroy his own people in Jericho?" I'll tell you why. Because Satan is the DESTROYER. When he is finished with a person or a nation, he destroys them, and blames it upon God, who accepts the blame to protect all of His creatures, including Satan and his devils. This is how much he loves us!

Another question which someone will ask is, "What about

Joshua's order to leave nothing alive in Jericho except for Rahab?" Joshua 6:17. Here again, as we already stated, is God's permissive will. It was JOSHUA'S order to leave nothing alive, not God's command. He permits Joshua and the people to perform "social surgery," so to speak, on a people so diseased with all kinds of sickness, mental, psychological, social and physical that their vile habits were spreading throughout the earth and would even have destroyed Israel if not checked. God let His people perform this "social surgery," so as to make a lasting impression on their minds of God's attitude toward this lifestyle. But it was His permissive way of dealing with it, not His perfect way, due to Israel's hardness of heart.

Suppose you had a son who wanted to go hunting with the other fellows in your town. Day after day he keeps pestering you,

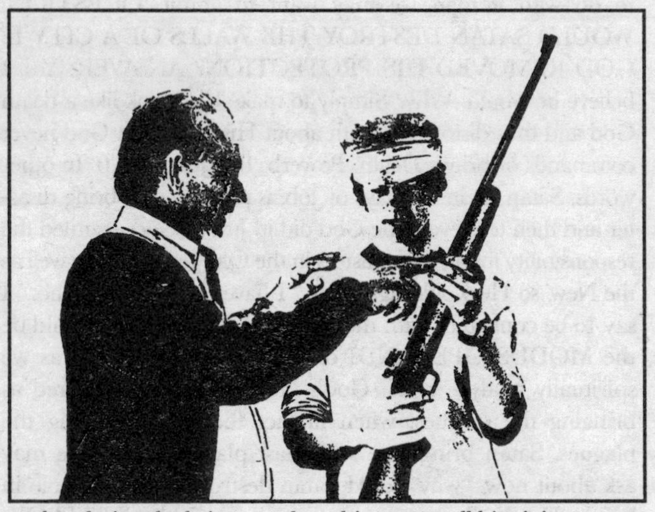

and each time he brings up the subject, you tell him it is not your will for him to kill poor, innocent, dumb animals God created for His pleasure and ours. Finally, one day, the boy defiantly tells you that he is going to buy a gun and go out hunting. He has saved his money and has made his decision. At that point you can either kick the boy out of the house, or take his money away from him and lock him in his room until he repents or you can let him have free will and go buy the gun. But, if you are a wise father, you will probably say, "son, it looks like you have made up your mind on this matter. I want you to know that I respect your right to think for yourself, even if it is against my beliefs and feelings. I once owned a gun myself, but I gave it up when I became convicted God did not want me to kill His creation. But, son, you are of age now and I must respect your free will. I would like to go with you to the sporting goods store tomorrow and help you select a gun. If you will permit me, son, I would like to instruct you how to use the gun. I once was an expert marksman, so I can teach you how to bring down an animal with one shot so the poor creature will not have to suffer so much. There are many things I can teach you, son, but most of all, I want to teach you how to handle the gun and use it so you will not endanger your life or the lives of others as you seek to become a hunter."

If anyone saw you go to the store and buy a gun for your son and then go out on the firing range and teach him how to shoot it, that person would probably believe and report that you had taken up hunting animals again, when the real truth of the matter would be that you were trying to save your son from the worst effects of his choice to become a killer .

This is precisely God's predicament. He had the choice of letting Israel alone to go out to battle the enemy, against His perfect will, or to teach them how to use the sword and to govern and control it as much as possible; only destroying that which was destroying itself anyway, such as the heathen tribes who were slowly dying of all kinds of diseases due to immorality and wrong eating habits.

When Israel chose to have a king and reject God as their king, the Lord gave them a king "after their own heart." He was Saul. God did not abandon His people when they left Him, but tried to save them from the worst effects of their wrong choice. The same was true of the diet. When men insisted upon eating animal flesh, God again tried to save them from the worst effects of that choice and told them what animals they could eat and what they should not eat, Leviticus 11 and Deut. 14. God's original diet for man in Eden was a vegetarian diet. Gen 1:29 and 3:18. After the flood man was given permission to eat the "clean" animals, but it was only until the earth could revitalize itself after the flood. But man's carnal nature liked the flesh food and very few ever went back to the Edenic diet. Some will say, "but Jesus ate fish." This assumption is based upon Luke 24;42-43. Notice that they offered Him two kinds of food. Fish and a honeycomb. It says, "And He took it, and did eat before them." He took "it," not them. Which article of food did Jesus choose? It does not say. My point is that this is not proof enough to me that Christ ate "fish." He very well may have eaten fish and Lamb and other meats as well, because the meat was much cleaner than it is today. It is not a test of fellowship. But, I believe in these last hours of earth's history God wants us to go back to the perfect diet of Eden especially since there are so many diseases in animals today. And also because of the many harmful chemicals, preservatives, and excito-toxins, such as MSG. A good rule to follow is: If man made it, don't eat it. Scientific research has proven that a vegetarian diet is possible and sufficient for man today and many believe it is much superior to a flesh food diet. Let each person be fully persuaded in his or her own mind about this matter after much study, prayer and maybe even some fasting.

THE VOICE OF GOD DELIVERS

Let us turn our attention again now to the voice of God which shakes the heavens and the earth. It is very natural to assume that the voice of Jesus causes all the aberrations in the heavens and the earth, but we have already established that Jesus does not destroy or bring earthquakes. This is the work of the DESTROYER, even Satan. When God announces the day and hour of His return, that voice rolls through the earth like peals of loudest thunder, (GC 640). But it does not destroy anything or frighten the righteous, waiting saints. When Isaiah heard the voice of the Lord it did not frighten him, Isa 6:3, 4. In John 12 Jesus asked the Father to glorify His own name. Immediately a voice spoke from heaven saying, "I have both glorified it, and will glorify it again." Those who heard this voice had two reactions. To those with a spiritual mind the voice sounded like an angel but to those who had a carnal mind the voice sounded like thunder. John 12:28, 29.

When the voice of God (Christ and His Father) says, "IT IS DONE," the heavens and earth shake, due to a tremendous earthquake, because of demonic anger and rage that the righteous have been delivered beyond their reach forever. They have lost and they know it. They believe they are doomed. It is like a man who has just lost a game of chance such as a card game or a horse race. He is beside himself with rage and pounds the table or the door. "I lost, I lost, I lost," he screams and curses, stamping his feet angrily and running around the room wildly. This is how the demons will act at this time. The angel of death which passed over Egypt will pass over all the world in these last days. Only those who are sealed with the truth (Jesus) will be spared, Rev. 7. The destroying angels of God represent God's withdrawing His protection, thus permitting destruction to come. Paris during the terror, in 1793-95 is an example of the destruction that will come again when God's Spirit withdraws. In fact, we can already see this happening in many countries in the world today.

DEFEATED DEMONS SCREAM

In the earthly ministry of our Lord we see how the demons acted when Christ defeated them. When Jesus saw that the people came running together, he rebuked the foul spirit, [angel of Satan] saying unto him, 'Thou dumb and deaf spirit, I charge thee, come out of him, and enter no more into him. And the spirit cried, and rent him sore, and came out of him: and he was as one dead; insomuch that many said, He is dead. But

Jesus took him by the hand, and lifted him up; and he arose." Mark 9:25-27.

Personally, I believe this happened quite often in Jesus' ministry. When Christ died on the cross, Satan shook the earth with anger, and he does the same thing at the end of the world. I believe Daniel has reference to this when he says, "But tidings out of the East and out of the North shall trouble him: [Satan] Therefore, He shall go forth with great fury to destroy and utterly to make away many." Dan. 11:44.

In this end-time, Satan will bring earthquakes, tidal waves and increase the heat of the sun, not only through his power, but through the wicked genius of evil men he controls. The So-called "weather-war" machines may be used to disturb the weather. All the prophets in the Bible who describe these end-time events saw many things in vision. They saw the lithosphere (solid part or outer crust of the earth) breaking up causing great tidal waves as the sea was lashed into fury. This is a perfect description of what scientists call astral catastrophes. God knows the exact moment these catastrophes are going to occur and has predicted them accordingly. Satan is the prince of the power of the air, (Eph. 2:2) and tries to manipulate nature against us, but God intervenes often and either stops it, or controls it by directing it in the way He sees best and takes the blame for whatever destruction results. He protects us from the disaster or lets us die in it for reasons we cannot know now, but which we will approve of later. What we can understand of His providence now, He has explained to us if our hearts are open to receive this information.

GOD USES EARTHQUAKES FOR GOOD

The Father used the earthquake at the death of Christ to open the graves of the saints Jesus took to heaven. At the end of the world Jesus will again say, IT IS FINISHED, OR DONE (Rev. 16:17). Satan again throws a temper tantrum and causes aberrations in nature to vent his wrath. Again the Lord uses this earthquake to open the graves of the dead who will come up in the special resurrection referred to in Rev. 1:7, Dan. 12:2. All who died believing God's true messages, those that mocked and derided Christ's dying agonies, and the most violent opposers of His truth and His people, are raised to behold Him in His glory and to see the honor placed upon the loyal and obedient. Why does Jesus raise these people? Just to torture and tantalize and kill them again? Oh, no, my friend. That is not God's character.

First of all, God never killed them the first time, so He won't do it the second time. Satan will do that unless they commit suicide. But either way God will say again, "I DID IT." No, the real reason the Lord brings these people back to see the final triumph of good over evil is to encourage them to change their minds about Him, if they will. Yes, His love is so great that He never gives up. He never quits. Rom. 2:4, "He hopeth all things." I Cor. 13:7. If they refuse to repent and accept His salvation in this final age before the 1,000 years, then they will be left behind to die with the 2/3rds of lost humanity, Zechariah 13:7-9, whom the Lord will resurrect after the 1,000 years for the final restitution or restoration of all things, Acts 3:21. This will be the final and ultimate proof that the God of all the earth does do right. Very soon now, we will see the King in all of His beauty coming from the east. Yes, Jesus is the king of the north (Isa. 14:12-14; Ps. 75:6, 7) and He is coming from the east to bring peace and everlasting life to His precious ones.

CHAPTER 18

ELIJAH, GOD'S CHARACTER AND MOUNT SINAI

In the first book of I Kings 19:9-12, we see Elijah standing upon Mount Horeb (Sinai) where Moses received the Ten Commandments. Elijah had run away from Jezebel. The Lord (Jesus of the O.T.) took this opportunity to give a "divine display of His power and glory." The Word tells us that the Lord passed by and there was a terrible windstorm that about tore the mountain apart. Next there was an earthquake that probably would have broken all the Richter scales, and finally a fire. But, it says, the Lord was not in the wind or the earthquake or the fire. So, who was doing this, if God wasn't? Is it possible that God was permitting Satan to bring these aberrations of nature in order to distort the true character of God? It would seem so. Isn't that amazing!

Many people forget that Satan has been at the right hand of Jesus Christ since the beginning of the Great Controversy. Zechariah 3:1 proves this. So, when Moses was on the mount to receive the law, Satan was right there to distort and twist the truth as much as possible so unfallen worlds, angels, fallen men and fallen angels would not understand the truth about God's holy character, which is a transcript of His eternal law.

Yes, Satan was right there to disturb the service and break up the meeting, if he could. God could not stop him completely without exposing and embarrassing Satan, and this the Lord could not and would not do and remain true to His own nature and character. But, the Lord did control it and use it to bring the people to a knowledge of His law on a level they could understand, that if they did not obey they would die.

Now, what was the result of this "divine display" of fireworks during which the voice was heard in spite of all the noise Satan brought? These same principles He later spoke on the Mount of Olives. Now, friend of mine, please let me ask you sincerely, does Jesus go around purposely trying to frighten people to get their attention so He can make His point? No, our Jesus is not like that. But, at Mt. Sinai He permitted Satan to do it in this way. It made a deep impression upon Israel's mind of His great power and majesty. They were used to the gods of the heathen (Satan's imitation of God) acting like this, so He spoke to them in terms they could understand, and yet it was not God who brought all the "scary stuff." But, since He created Lucifer (Satan now), He takes all the credit as well as all the blame for everything that happens. God permitted and controlled the whole show. Satan did not want the people to know or understand the law, (which reveals God's true character), so he tried to stop Christ from giving it. But he was not able to stop it. ***However, he was permitted to distort it.*** The first time I realized this was when I was memorizing in Psalm 18. In verse 6 we see Christ (for whom the Psalms were written as a guide book about 1,000 years before He came in the flesh), calling to His Father for help and receiving an answer. In verse seven we see the earth shaking and trembling because He (God the Father) is "wroth," it says. But what is God's wrath or anger? ***It is when God permits Satan and/or men to do evil in the earth.*** God cannot interfere with their free moral agency and be true to His Word that man has the power of free choice. We see this clearly in Romans 1:18, 24, 26 and Psalm 78:49, which shows' that when God withdraws, Satan's angels fill the void and God calls this His "WRATH."

As I continued memorizing in Psalm 18, I saw even more proof for this unbelievable concept. In verse 8 David portrays God as a fire breathing dragon. In verse 9 we read, "He bowed the Heavens also, and came down: and darkness was under his feet." [Rom. 16:20; Gen. 3:15; Ps. 91:13]. Verse 10 tells how God rides upon (the original Hebrew actually says "above or over") a cherub and the upon the wings of the wind. Verse 11 tells us he made "Darkness His secret place; His pavilion round about him were dark waters and thick clouds of the skies." Notice that God does not bring the darkness, but he hides

Himself in it. [1 John 1:5]. Verse 12 even makes it clear. "At the brightness that was before Him His thick clouds passed, hail stones and coals of fire." When we compare this with Hab. 3:3-6, we see more light. "God came from Teman, and the Holy One from mount Paran. Selah. His glory covered the heavens, and the earth was full of His praise. And His brightness was the light; He had horns coming out of His hand; and there was the hiding of his power. Before him went the pestilence, and burning coals went forth at his feet, [The margin says Burning Diseases]. He stood, and measured the earth: He beheld, and drove asunder the nations; (notice how God is always portrayed as using force and violence) and the everlasting mountains were scattered, the perpetual hills did bow; His ways are everlasting."

Habbuk here refers to the majestic events connected with the giving of the law, using them as an example of the events in the final Judgment. Deut. 33:2. Paran is a wilderness country between Midian and Egypt and between Sinai and Canaan. Notice carefully how God is pictured as a very destructive person. It says that HE DROVE ASUNDER THE NATIONS at Sinai, but we know God didn't do that at all. What we do know is that when nations and people do not keep the law their own sins find them out and put them six feet under. **In this way God does kill nations and people with His law and this is what the text means.** All through the Bible God is pictured as striking and smiting people with war, sickness and calamities in nature. Look at Miriam in Numbers 12 and see how the ANGER OF THE LORD, caused her to have leprosy. Did God really give her leprosy or did her disobedience forfeit God's protection from the effects of that disease which had been dormant in her body? God still protects us the same way as many diseases are dormant in our bodies today. Yes, God permitted the author of sickness and disease to afflict Miriam when she disobeyed, but even here the Lord controlled it, and proscribed the means for a fast cure.

The closed minded person who wants to serve a God of

hatred, anger and death to justify his own anger, hatred, and desire to deal out death to his enemies, will say, "see, that is what the Bible says and I believe it just like it reads." This is the very principle upon which the ETERNAL HELL FIRE and SUNDAY doctrines are built. ***People will find the God they want to find in the Bible.*** The true God of the Bible is not found by the surface reader. The cold-hearted, formal ritualistic, legalistic, faultfinding, calculating, time-serving reader of the Scriptures will find that kind of God, for he will only be reading to confirm his prejudices and establish more firmly his preconceived opinions. These kind of people serve God in the letter of the law out of fear, not in the spirit of the law out of love, and the expression on their face and the tone in their voice often reveals the condition of their heart. To these type of readers Christ will say in that final day, "I never knew you: depart from Me, Ye that work iniquity." Matt. 7:23. Even here at the close of time Jesus once again takes the blame with His Father. The wicked are still rejecting His love, but He says, "WE ARE REJECTING YOU." Why? Because that is the way they perceive it. Again He accepts the blame.

SATAN DECEIVES THE WICKED AGAIN

All through the great controversy Satan has deceived mankind about God. As the wicked reject God and His great love again and walk away from the golden city cursing their Creator, Satan takes advantage of the opportunity and moves in for the kill. He tells them that he is the real Jesus and the ONE in the city is a phony, a counterfeit who took the city away from him. He tells them that if they do not strike first the people in the city will overcome them and enslave them forever.

First of all, this takes place after the 1,000 years. Jesus does not attack the wicked in any way. He does not hurt or rebuke or reject them: They have rejected Him again just as they did in their former life. Without a doubt the wicked have come up to the city to investigate and learn about it. They find out that many of the inhabitants of the golden city are people they knew and considered very "unworthy" subjects for such a glorious kingdom. They are unable to figure out why they are excluded. Christ tells them that they need His righteousness, of which they want no part. The Bible tells us the reaction of all the lost at this time. "And I say unto you, that many shall come from the east and west, and shall sit down with Abraham, and Isaac, and Jacob, in the Kingdom of heaven. But the children of the Kingdom [religious people of all ages like the Jews who thought they were all holy and assured a place in heaven], shall be cast out into outer darkness: there shall be weeping and gnashing of teeth." Matt. 8:11, 12. We know that Jesus never changes, so we know that Christ is not dealing harshly, or unfairly or arbitrarily with these people at this time, but they are blaming Him for this.

The Bible tells us that God never turns anyone away at any time. So, even now, at this time God would forgive them if they truly repented. And Him that cometh to Me I will in no wise cast out. John 6:37. It is our own sinful attitude of selfishness and hatred which will exclude us from the city, if we are lost. God does not reject people. People reject Him. ***But God takes the blame as if He were the one who is doing the rejecting.*** This is the character of God. He invites us to be like Him. Someone will say though, "but God Himself states what He will say. 'Depart from me, ye that work iniquity?' Isn't Jesus turning them away here?" As I have said before, God always takes the blame, but He is not the one doing it. The Lord does not turn these people away at this time anymore than he turned the rich young man or ruler away. The wicked hear the voice of their god, SATAN, John 8:44 and blame it upon Christ. They cannot hear Jesus' voice, for they do not belong to Him. John 10:14, 16; John 6:37. Christ simply told him what the requirements were for entrance to His kingdom, and the rich young fellow decided the price was too high. See Matt. 19:16-22. Again in Matt. 22:11-14, we see the man who came to the wedding without a wedding garment and when he was asked why he was there without a wedding garment, he was SPEECHLESS. Now, notice how Christ again takes the blame. Then said the king to the Servants, bind Him hand and foot, and take Him away, and cast Him into outer darkness; there shall be weeping and gnashing of teeth. For many are called, but few are chosen. See also Matt. 7:21-23.

Now, is this the way it actually is going to happen, or is it a parable? Obviously, it is parabolic. The wicked will not be literally bound and thrown through the air into a deep hole in the earth burning with fire, sulphur and brimstone with the devil (forked tail and pitchfork) in charge as so often portrayed in medieval works of art and literature, such as Dante's Infernal.

Unless you understand how God always plays the heavy by taking the blame, you will not understand this most important concept and your idea of God will be an anthropomorphic image, instead of the loving Father image Jesus taught. Like so many today, you will bring God down to your level as the ancient Greeks and Romans did and make Him after your own likeness and image, assigning to the Eternal your own carnal desires and passions of anger and lust. Rom. 1:21-25. Thus by beholding you will become changed. And when such a person goes up to the golden city and looks inside those walls of transparent gold, he will be blinded by the glory and repelled by the purity of Jesus, the angels and the saints. When he finds out what he has to give up and become in order to enter that city, he, like the rich young ruler will turn away sorrowfully and in this case, very angrily, with much weeping and gnashing of teeth. "HE JUST KICKED ME OUT FLAT" each lost sinner will say. "WHAT AN INSULT," they will exclaim, "OFFERING ME A WEDDING GARMENT, AS IF I DIDN'T KNOW HOW TO DRESS PROPERLY FOR A WEDDING. AND ASKING ME TO ACCEPT HIM AS MY SAVIOR, AS IF I WERE A SINNER WHAT NERVE! WHAT KIND OF A TERRIBLE PERSON DOES HE THINK I AM? IMAGINE HIM TREATING ME LIKE THAT WHEN I BELONGED TO THE CHURCH ALL MY LIFE, AND WORKED SO HARD. I JUST FELT LIKE GOING UP

AND SPITTING RIGHT IN HIS FACE. AND DID YOU SEE WHO HE HAD IN THERE IN OUR PLACE SITTING AT THAT BEAUTIFUL LONG SUPPER TABLE? A BUNCH OF DIRTY STREET WHORES, ALCOHOLICS, GOVERNMENT BUREAUCRATS, HOMOSEXUALS, LESBIANS AND OF COURSE, A LOT OF THOSE 'GOODIE, GOODIE' TYPE CHRISTIANS WHO WERE ALWAYS READING THE BIBLE AND PRAYING AND VISITING THE SICK AND POOR ETC. WHILE I WAS BUSY KEEPING CHURCH BUSINESS TOGETHER. SO, WHILE THEY ARE IN THERE WITH 'HIM' ENJOYING THE GOOD LIFE, WITH ALL THAT GOLD, WE ARE OUT HERE WITH NOTHING TO LIVE ON. IF ONLY THERE WERE SOME WAY TO GET EVEN WITH ALL THOSE CHEATERS, (JACOBS AND FAKES) IN THERE." Can you imagine how happy such a person would feel if Satan would turn up about that time, appearing as Christ, and suggest that they assault the city which is rightfully theirs since the king inside is a fraud? Do you think the people outside the city would believe such a lie? They would no doubt shout, "PRAISE THE LORD AND PASS THE AMMUNITION!" Yes, they will believe Satan's lie.

The Bible indicates that the wicked will form a vast army with every kind of military device and instrument of destruction known to man now and a lot more before the flood, plus even more advanced technology which Satan will no doubt teach them. Rev. 20 indicates that they will gather together under Satan's leadership to make war against Christ and the Holy City and that they will even come up and surround the city. "And they went up on the breadth of the earth, and compassed the camp of the saints about, and the beloved City: and fire came down from God out of Heaven, and devoured them." Rev. 20:9.

For centuries Theologians have taken these prophetic words quite literally. I have always understood it and taught it that way, but since I have done this study on the character of God, the Lord has helped me to see that this "fire" is not literal nor is it destructive. In fact, it will be life-changing and life giving as it was for the 120 on the day of pentecost, and later for Saul of Tarsus in Acts 9 in his mini-lake of fire experience.

GOD IS ALWAYS IN CONTROL

Even though it often looks like God is losing and Satan is winning, Jesus Christ is always in control. When Jesus came down on Mt. Horeb (Sinai) to tell the people what He was really like, Satan was right there to try to drown out God's words and make Christ look as bad as possible. Jesus did not accuse Satan of distorting His true character or embarrass him by exposing him to the unfallen worlds, the fallen and unfallen angels and mankind. Neither will Christ do so in the final day. At Sinai the people were scared out of their wits, but God said, "I am doing this, because I am permitting it to happen. I knew it would happen ahead of time and have it all planned out. I am in complete control. Serve me and live. Disobey my law and you will die." To those who really come close to God and learn to know Him as Elijah finally did on Sinai, Jesus Christ becomes the ultimate reality. After all the fire works that God permitted Satan to bring to frighten Elijah were past, there was a "still small voice." The margin says, "That is a delicate whispering as of the breeze among the leaves." 1 Kings 19:12.

This is how Jesus described the work of the Holy Spirit among the inhabitants of this earth when talking to Nicodemus in John 3:8. This is how God tells us we can know Him in Psalm 46:10, "Be STILL AND KNOW THAT I AM GOD." Is Satan trying to drown out the still small voice of Jesus' Spirit in your heart today friend of mine? The Devil has a thousand noisy substitutes for the sweet and gentle voice of God. Don't be satisfied with a phony, two-bit, counterfeit, plastic experience with the Prince of Darkness, when you can have a beautiful number one, straight on relationship with the one and only true God of the whole universe, JESUS CHRIST, Himself.

Someone may protest here by saying that Christ does

expose Satan with the "panoramic view," described in Psalm 50:1-5. This revelation is not for the purpose of embarrassing or even exposing Satan, for Satan has done this to himself by marshaling the hosts of wicked against Jesus. In that final day it will be proved that God never was partial or unfair to anyone. Deut. 10:17, Job 34:19, Acts 10:34, Rom. 2:11,2 Chron. 19:7, Rev. 20. Now, Jesus simply turns on the light and lets Satan and all the wicked look at themselves. Each person sees his own life in this panoramic view, Satan included, and naturally all the lost see Satan for what he is too. But, the fact that Satan bows and acknowledges God to be just shows that it is not an expose per se, but actually a last gigantic, all out, last ditch effort to bring Lucifer and the wicked to repentance. And this is exactly what will happen. "Every knee will bow and every tounge will confess." Phil. 2:10, 11. "And this conversion experience will bring glory to God the Father." We will explain this more as we go along.

THE LORD ALWAYS OVERCOMES EVIL WITH GOOD

"Nevertheless, the Lord thy God would not hearken unto Baalam: but the Lord thy God turned the curse into a blessing unto thee, because the Lord thy God loved thee." Deut. 23:5. No doubt someone will say that God brought the earthquake in Acts 16 which broke down the Phillippian jail where Paul and Silas were in stocks singing even though their backs were probably sore and bleeding from the stripes they had received. "But, at midnight Paul and Silas prayed, and sang praises unto God: and the prisoners heard them. And suddenly there was a great earthquake, so that the foundations of the prison were shaken: and immediately all the doors were opened," ...Acts 16:25, 26. Who brought the earthquake? (Isa. 14:16) God or Satan? Again, I say, God does not bring aberrations in nature, but permits Satan to do so in order to destroy, but God turns it into a blessing by directing the earthquake to do good in as many cases as possible, such as opening graves and in this instance, breaking down the jailhouse so Paul and Silas could bring the jailer to repentance, by preaching Christ to him. Again Satan was defeated. The same principle is true of the storm on the sea of Galilee. God permitted Satan to bring the storm to try and kill the disciples, who had disobeyed by not leaving immediately. Satan brings all the aberrations of nature, (Isa. 28:2) and Ephesians 2:2 identifies him as the "Prince of the power of the air." But, Jesus overcame Satan by walking on the water and stilling the storm and teaching valuable lessons to his disciples. Was Satan "cooperating," with the Father in all these experiences so Jesus could prove His claims? HARDLY! Yet, I have heard this allegation made time and time again. If this be true, and we know it is absurd, then the wilderness temptation of Jesus was all planned by the Father too and Satan obediently went out and tempted Christ. No, my friend, that is not logical reasoning, for it is not in keeping with the character of God. Satan never cooperates with the Father nor Christ His son,

In the days of Jonah, Satan wanted to destroy Nineveh, but God sent a preacher to warn them so they would turn to Him and be spared. Satan persuaded Jonah to run away from the call of duty and then brought a storm on the sea to try and finish him off. But God moved upon the men to question Jonah and thus find out about the true God who created heaven and earth. Jonah figured it was better to die than face God and the angry crowds of Nineveh and requested to be thrown overboard into the angry sea. But God permitted a fish to swallow Jonah. Jesus referred to this "great fish" as a whale, Matt. 12:40. The Greek word is "kitos" which simply means a "sea monster." The KJV translates "kitos" as a whale. Satan led the whale to swallow Jonah, but God again overruled the situation and preserved the life of His prophet by controlling the fish and leading and guiding it to vomit Jonah out on the seashore. But after all these experiences, Jonah still did not understand the character of God. He still had the Jewish view of God instead of the Jesus view. Instead of praising God for sparing the city, as he had spared his life from heathen sailors, the sea and a whale's digestive organs, Jonah only wished death on Nineveh so he would be known as a famous hell-fire and damnation preacher. And yet God still accomplished His purpose without interfering with Jonah's freewill, in spite of all these obstacles Satan brought, for God is Omniscient, able to see the end from the beginning. Isaiah 46:9, 10.

You see, if it had been God who brought the storm to kill Jonah, then God could be accused of trying to stop Jonah from running away, but God does not try and stop us by hurting us, or killing us. But, He does use circumstances and Satan's machinations for purposes of mercy, bringing good out of evil.

CHAPTER 19

SONGS OF PRAISE CAUSE THE WICKED TO SELF-DESTRUCT

"Rejoice evermore, pray without ceasing. In everything give thanks: for this is the will of God in Christ concerning you." I Thess. 5:16-18. Just as God used an earthquake to deliver Paul and Silas at midnight, so the Lord will again deliver His people in this last hour of earth's history at midnight by using an earthquake brought on by Satan. The righteous will be praising God for His goodness while the wicked are killing each other all over the earth. See Isa. 25:6-12; Jer. 25:31-33.

In 2 Chronicles 20:10-25, we see how Satan and his host of demons really go wild with fright and anger when we praise God with singing. In that story, the enemy destroyed each other. There will be an instant replay of this same scenario at the end of this age before Christ comes to translate His own in three stages, which will be the Barley, Wheat and Grape harvests. Then, after the 1,000 years all the wicked will be reconciled and restored to God's throne. Here is the proof: ***"Then I heard every creature in heaven and on earth and under the earth and on the sea, and all that is in them, singing to Him who sits on the throne and to the Lamb be praise and honor and glory and power for ever and ever!" Revelation 5:13; "Who will not fear you, O Lord, and bring glory to your name? For you alone are holy. All nations will come and worship before you, for your righteous acts have been revealed." Rev. 15:4.***

And the song of praise will ascend from the Saints robed in white ABOUT the throne: "worthy is the lamb that was slain to receive power, and riches, and wisdom, and strength, and honor, and glory, and blessing." Rev. 5:12.

HIS KINDNESS IS FOREVER

In Jehoshaphat's day they sang "PRAISE THE LORD: FOR HIS MERCY ENDURETH FOREVER." The Living Bible says they sang, "HIS LOVING KINDNESS IS FOREVER," as they walked along praising and thanking the Lord!

"And at the moment they began to sing and to praise, the Lord caused the armies of Ammon, Moab, and Mount Seir to begin fighting among themselves, and they destroyed each other!" 2 Chronicles 20:21, 22. Here again God takes the blame by inspiring the Chronicler to record, "THE LORD CAUSED," as if it was all God's fault. "I DID IT," He says. "I KILLED THEM." Actually, what happened was that the Lord was no longer able to restrain the evil passions of the souls of these wicked men and Satan's angels had full control to destroy them (Psalm 78:49), when they heard them singing.

Satan's angels and the wicked both came into the presence of God's perfect law in the person of His faithful servants and it made them so angry they killed themselves. Suicide is one of the most subtle forms of hatred toward those who love the person who is killing himself. "See what you made me do? I hate you so much, I am going to punish you. Now, you will have to feel sorry and mourn for me forever." A person who can get up enough courage to kill himself also should have enough courage to live, but the truth of the matter is that the suicide has turned his thoughts and feelings inward for so long that he cannot think of anyone else but himself. In the case of Jehoshaphat's enemies, you might say that the "law of sin and death," Rom. 8:2, was fully activated in their lives, and they reaped in a few seconds what most people would reap in a life time, due to the tremendous hatred that was released in their minds and bodies due to the singing. So it will be in the final day.

God does not kill the sinner when he passes the line of divine forbearance [patience and leniency]. This withdrawing of restraint is called God's wrath, anger, vengeance, indignation, fire, punishment, and judgment, but these are all words to convey the meaning that God is not destroying that person, but is being forced out of that individual's life by giving the person and/or nation up to his or her own choice, turning them over to themselves and their own counsel and the guidance of Satan and his angels, Psalm 78:49. God never condemns the sinner to death, for He is a life God.

He does not pass a sentence of judgment against a person for his transgression. But every man passes sentence against himself by rejecting God's love in the form of light and truth from the Bible and godly ministers of the Word. As a man continues to reject the Holy Spirit's pleading God is forced out of his life and Satan moves in to control the evil, lower passions and man destroys himself. Judas, the city of Jerusalem and the whole Jewish nation in Christ's day are examples of what happens when God's warnings are despised and rejected. *"God does not stand toward the sinner as an executioner of the sentence against transgression; but He leaves the rejecters of His mercy to themselves, to reap that which they have sown. Every ray of light rejected, every warring despised or unheeded, every passion indulged, every transgression of the law of God, is a seed sown which yields its unfailing harvest. The Spirit of God, persistently resisted, is at last withdrawn from the sinner, and then there is left no power to control the evil passions of the soul, and no protection from the malice and enmity of Satan. The destruction of Jerusalem (in AD 70) is a fearful and solemn warning to all who are trifling with the offers of divine grace and resisting the pleadings of divine mercy." GC 36.*

The Bible proves that God "punishes" people by letting them go their own way and do their own thing. It is just the opposite of what we have always thought, myself included. Unless a person understands this, he will have no criterion upon which to base his actions in the final hours of this earth's history when the world is being bombarded with wars, disease, violence, plague and death on every hand. Is this the work of God or Satan? If it is God, then we had better keep Sunday holy to appease His wrath as the preachers are already suggesting in some circles. But, if God is not bringing these calamities, then it must be Satan, and the Sabbath, Saturday, the seventh day, is God's true day. Exodus 20:8-11, Heb. 4:4, Matt. 24:20, Luke 4:16.

Furthermore, the temptation to meet violence with violence will cause many to take up weapons to defend themselves, as Peter did in the garden. If they do this, they will no doubt meet with great heartache, disappointment and loss. Unless they repent, as Peter repented, they may very likely meet with eternal loss, as Judas did. Judas, Jerusalem and the Jewish nation are examples of how God is going to "punish," the entire world in the end time. This is just a little sample of His "strange act."

SATAN'S FRUSTRATION AND FEAR AND HIS ANGER

Just as Satan's fear and anger knew no bounds when Jesus died on the cross, so it will again know no bounds when the final demonstration of God's true character has been "finished," in the person of His final, faithful, chosen and elect people. Matt 24:24; Rev. 17:14. God says, "It Is Done," and all hell breaks loose on this planet as Satan unleashes his pent up fury. Isa. 28:2, Isa. 14:16, 17.

Yes, it is Satan and his demon hosts who are bringing all the noise and fireworks as Christ comes to raise the dead and translate the righteous, which will be the first phase of the harvest, the Barley or Elect, the Man Child, Rev. 12:5; the Christos, Rev. 11:15 & 12:10. Remember God's vengeance is the same as His wrath. He has withdrawn His restraint from the wicked. This is His punishment.

Is God the accuser or is it Satan who is uttering words of doom upon the wicked? Revelation 12:10 tells us that Satan is the accuser. SATAN'S sheep hear his voice and CHRIST'S sheep hear His voice. John 10:14, 16, 27.

While the wicked are being killed by flying rocks, lightning bolts and the weapons of men who hate them, (Ezek. 38:21) Jesus protects His chosen ones and escorts them safely through this Satanic holocaust up out of earth's fiery atmosphere to the Father's throne, where they will receive their commission to return and begin the Wheat harvest of the 144,000 (40 days) and later the Grape Harvest (3 1/2 years). Rev. 14:14-20. After the grape harvest Jesus will then translate one third of the earth's inhabitants, Zechariah 13:7-9 and escort them up through that opening in Orion into the heaven of heavens where they will live and reign with Him for 1,000 years of judgment, getting acquainted and "growing up." Malachi 4:2; Rev. 20:4-6.

SATAN IS A VERY, VERY BAD LOSER

And so Satan loses again, just as he lost at Calvary and as he will lose again after the 1,000 years, for Satan is a loser. BUT JESUS IS A WINNER, 2 Cor. 13:8, and He wins with love, not hatred. When Jesus died on Calvary's cross, there were lightnings and thunders, darkness and an earthquake. God did not bring these aberrations of nature, but He used and directed them. God hid Himself in the thick darkness so He could be just as close to His Son as possible. But, He who is ETERNAL LIGHT did not bring the darkness. Satan did that, for he is the originator or ruler of darkness. There is no darkness in God. "This is the message we have heard from Him and proclaim to you, that God is light and in Him is no darkness at all." I Jn. 1:5. "He bowed the heavens also and came down: and darkness was under his feet." Psalm 18:9. Moses predicted in Gen. 3:15 that Christ would overcome evil with His Eternal light and love. "For the weapons of our warfare are not carnal, but mighty through God to the pulling down of strongholds;" 2 Cor. 10:4. "For this purpose the son of God was manifested, that he might destroy (render him powerless) the works of the Devil." I John 3:8. Not only will Satan bow his knees, he will confess and be brought to "ashes" which is a Hebrew symbolism for remorse and repentance. Yes, all things are going to be restored (Acts 3:21), even the first great rebel, so that God may be ALL IN ALL, for as in

"Adam all die, even so in Christ shall all be made alive."

I Cor. 15:22-28. "The last enemy that shall be destroyed is death...that God may be all in all." This will be accomplished after the 1,000 years when "Death and hell" will be "cast into the lake of fire." Rev. 20:14. This is the final "second death," which is not a literal death, per se, but a death to the ego or self life that the true and original creation of God may be manifested in every creature. This is why Jesus died on the cross and He will not be "satisfied" until that one lost sheep is fully restored and there is a completed fold and a finished creation.

And what is it that has made all of this possible? By permitting Himself to be crucified on the cross of Calvary, in this one courageous act Jesus destroyed the power of Satan to perpetuate sin, darkness and death on this planet. When our Lord was lifted up on the cross, the whole universe's attention was drawn to Him. But it was not only for our world that Jesus died. All the angels and all the unfallen worlds saw for the first time what God is really like. Satan destroyed himself forever in the eyes of the universe when he led the people to kill the "human" part of Jesus.

Actually, the people did not really "kill," Jesus. He willingly laid down His life for us. "I lay down my life, that I might take it again. No man taketh it from me, but I lay it down of myself. I have power to lay it down, and have power to take it again. This commandment have I received of my father." John 10:17, 18. Someone may wonder why, in the light of this statement, that the apostles indited the Jews for the murder of Christ. See Acts 3:14, 15. "But ye denied the Holy One... and killed the prince of life." John taught that if you hate your brother you are a murderer, I John 3:15, and we know the Jews hated Him. In these ways, the Jewish leaders killed their true Messiah.

THE DARKNESS AT THE CROSS

The darkness at Calvary was not the result of an eclipse, but was a miraculous testimony given by God that the faith of after generations might be confirmed. God is blamed for the event, when He simply used, directed and controlled this aberration of nature caused by Satan in order to demonstrate His divine control and sovereignty over man and nature, as well as Satan. Satan proposes, but God disposes. Satan brings darkness, but God turns the darkness into a sign that cast light upon the event which split history in two. Satan tries to bring lightning to frighten and destroy, but God uses it to illuminate His only Son on the cross so all the ends of the earth might see His salvation. Thus Satan is defeated at every turn.

Satan tries to bring an earthquake which will bury the dead deep in the heart of the earth, but God uses the same earthquake to open the graves of the saints who will ascend with Christ as trophies of His victory over death and the grave, Psalm 24; Eph. 4:8. At the coming of Christ, Satan's earthquake will again be used to open the proper graves and break down certain jail cells, so His people may go free. Jesus always gives freedom, Satan always brings slavery .

For 1,000 years Satan will be "chained" to this earth, while the saints are in heaven with Jesus reigning in "Judgment" with Him. That is, they will go over the books with Him and see why He made the decisions He made regarding why things happened as they did. God does not keep Satan here by force. This planet will be the only "dark place" left in the universe for Satan to hide in. Light and truth are everywhere and it would be too painful for Satan to go anywhere near it. But, God takes the blame for this too. He still loves Lucifer and respects His feelings and decision. This is Satan's "Time out," so he can think about everything for 1,000 years.

JESUS CHRIST WAS OFFERED AS A BURNT SACRIFICE

Once, while I was driving into town, I began memorizing in Psalm 20. When I came to verse three, I kept repeating it over and over, for I felt that it had a special meaning I did not understand, but needed to know.

"Remember all thy offerings, and accept thy burnt sacrifice;" Selah. Ps. 20:3 Whenever I see the word Selah, I think of David the Psalmist stopping and pausing on the harp to consider the full significance of the words he has just sung. STOP THE MUSIC AND THINK ABOUT THAT, is what I believe "selah," means. I also believe that Jesus Himself inspired the Psalms to be written and compiled so He would have a song book full of hope and instruction and victory to sing as He fought the battle of life here on this earth for you and for me. Now, that He has won, each of these Psalms belongs to us.

But, the BURNT SACRIFICE of verse 3 is referring to Jesus who truly was offered on Calvary's tree as a burnt sacrifice in fulfillment of all the Old Testament sacrifices which pointed forward to Him. He had to go through this in order to fulfill the prophecy. In Psalm 22, definitely a Messianic Psalm, Christ declared, while hanging on the cross, "But I am a worm, and no man; a reproach of men, and despised of the people. I am poured out like water, and all my bones are out of joint: my heart is like wax; it is melted in the midst of my bowels. My strength is dried up like a potsherd." Psalm 22:6, 14,15

JESUS BECAME A WORM FOR EACH OF US

Yes, friend of mine, Jesus became a worm so that we might live. Is anything lower, more detestable, uglier, or more helpless than a worm? When you step on it, it simply rolls over and over, twists and turns, bleeding and writhing in pain and then dies. But Jesus went beyond the worm. He even became a snake for all of us, even for the whole universe. A serpent, the symbol of Satan. For years I could never fathom why the Lord instructed Moses to lift up a serpent on a pole in the wilderness so the people could look at the brazen serpent and live. I never dared to preach on this subject, because I just didn't grasp the meaning behind it. No one ever asked me, so I just put it way in the back of my mind.

Thank the Lord He finally made it clear to me. Why was the serpent made of brass first of all? (actually Bronze) Bronze is light and would not be heavy to hold up for a long time. My yoke is easy and my burden is light. Matt. 11:28-30. Bronze is an alloy of two metals, tin and copper, which fitly represents the dual nature of Christ. But there is more. When the serpent is up off the ground, as in Moses' day in Pharaoh's court (Exodus 7:8, 9) and later in Numbers 21, the serpent is restored to its pristine glory in the Garden of Eden and represents Christ, speaking forth life giving words of instruction and bringing healing to the world but at the same time sacrificing itself to be cast down in the dust and to become "sin for us," the most hated and feared animal in the world, a biting snake. It is a mystery we will no doubt look into and study throughout eternity.

It was not logical that the snake which was causing the Israelites to die would give them life if they looked. Neither is it logical that God would place all the sins of the world upon His only Son and permit Him to die the humiliating and horrible death He died on the cross for our redemption, but what seems to be foolishness with men is Wisdom with God. 1 Cor. 3:19.

Jesus became as sinful as the most sinful being that ever sinned, Satan himself, and died the eternal death every unrepentant sinner will have to die, even the second death in the Lake of Fire, which is a death to self or the ego. Death in this life is not death, but only sleep John 11:11. And that final death will not result in non-existence, as some teach, who believe in the annihilation theory, but in a re-birth and conversion experience which will grant them the right and privilege of entering into the gates of the New Jerusalem, into the celestial city. "He that overcometh shall inherit all things." Rev 21:7; Rev 22:14.

"And as Moses lifted up the serpent in the wilderness, even so must the Son of Man be lifted up; that whosoever believeth in Him should not perish, but have eternal life." John 3:14,15.

It is not exaltation in this life which brings victory and an eternal reward. No. Instead, it is death to self. As we take up our cross daily, and are crucified with Jesus, we die to self, burying our own ideas and plans and wills with Him. Then Christ resurrects us daily with Himself to walk hand in hand with Him in the ways of His choosing, which lead to life Everlasting.

THE DEVOURING FIRE OF REVELATION 20:9

"And fire came down from God out of heaven, and devoured them." Rev. 20:9. The Greek word "devour" has two meanings, just as fire does. "Thou lovest all devouring words, O thou deceitful tongue." Psalm 52:4, KJV. "You love all destroying words, O deceitful tongue." Ibid, Modern Language Version. "You love to slander—you love to say anything that will do harm, O man with the lying tongue." Living Bible, Ibid. "An ungodly witness scorneth judgment; and the mouth of the wicked devoureth iniquity." Proverbs 19:28. And the Modern Language Version says, "A worthless witness scoffs at justice and the mouth of the wicked swallows iniquity."

When we compare this with Obadiah 1:15-18, we find a prophecy that parallels Rev. 20:9. "For the day of the Lord is near upon all the heathen: as thou hast done, it shall be done unto thee: thy reward shall return upon thine own head. For as ye have drunk upon my Holy Mountain, so shall all the heathen drink continually, yea, they shall drink, and they shall swallow down and they shall be as though they had not been." Now, what is it they are going to drink? "The mouth of the wicked swallows [KJV says 'devours']." Proverbs 19:28.

Jesus drank the bitter cup for you and for me. QUESTION: WHAT WAS IN THE CUP? ANSWER: Why, it was all the sins of the world. If anyone refuses to accept His sacrifice, he must drink the cup himself ...and it Will "DEVOUR" him from inside out, as it killed Christ on the cross. We have often heard that it was the sins of the world which caused the death of Christ and that is true. He was burned up by the sins of the world from the inside out for us. Notice in Psalm 22:14, that our Lord cried out, "my heart is like wax; it is melted in the midst of my bowels. My strength is dried up... I thirst," He also said. It takes a lot of heat to cause that kind of experience, heat on the inside of one's body. The sin of the world was the "fire" that generated that heat in the body of Christ as he offered Himself as a BURNT SACRIFICE.

THE WICKED WILL BURN INSIDE AS AN OVEN

"Thine hand [the nail pierced hand of Jesus] shall find out all thine enemies: thy right hand shall find out those that hate thee. Thou shalt make them as a fiery oven in the time of thine anger: the Lord shall swallow them up in his wrath, and the fire shall devour them." Psalm 21:8, 9.

"For they have made [margin says, 'applied'] ready their heart like an oven." Hosea 7:6. And how does an oven burn? It burns up whatever is inside it. It "devours," the combustible material in it. That is the way the wicked will burn up in the day when God shows them their life history. "For, behold the day cometh, that shall bum as an oven: and all the proud, yea, and all that do wickedly, shall be stubble: and the day that cometh shall bum them up, saith the Lord of hosts, that it shall leave them neither root nor branch." Mal. 4:1.

As the wicked look at Christ upon His throne on a foundation of burnished gold high and lifted up, and the saved of all ages around Him, all the lost are filled with sorrow, envy, regret, but mainly hatred. It just "BURNS THEM UP," to see all their former friends and enemies with all that gold and them standing on the rubble of the earth with nothing but a machine gun and a hand grenade, and perhaps a few atomic and nuclear weapons which are even more deadly than we have today.

"BUT THE CHILDREN OF THE KINGDOM (all those who professed to believe in God) shall be cast out into outer darkness: there shall be weeping and gnashing of teeth." Matt. 8:12. This will last for a "little season." Rev. 20:3. How long is a "season?" "Choosing rather to suffer affliction with the people of God, than to enjoy the pleasures of sin for a SEASON." Moses lived to be 120 years. There is a text in Isa

65:20 which indicates this period of time could last for 100 years, which would be long enough for the billions of lost outside the city to get to know each other and blame each other for their pitiful condition. "The queen of the south shall rise up in the judgment with the men of this generation, and condemn them ...the men of Nineveh shall rise up in the judgment with this generation, and shall condemn it: for they repented at the preaching of Jonas; and behold, a greater than Jonas is here." Luke 11:31, 32. Rev 20:1-9 tells us the wicked will form an army and try to attack the city but the Lord will consume them with the "fire of His love," the only kind of fire God ever reveals to the human race for He does not destroy. This all will take place after the 1,000 years. But at His "second coming" which has three phases, Barley, Wheat and Grape, we read that "The Son of Man shall send forth his angels, and they shall gather out of his Kingdom all things that offend, and them which do iniquity; and shall cast them into a furnace of fire: there shall be wailing and gnashing of teeth. Then shall the righteous shine forth as the sun in the Kingdom of their Father. Who hath ears to hear, let him hear." Matt. 13:41-43, Psalm 78:49, Jer. 22:7.

The expression, "GNASHING OF TEETH," is used to describe people who are burning up with hatred and anger, such as the Jews who killed Stephen. "When they heard these things, they were cut to the heart; and they gnashed on Him with their teeth." Acts 7:54.

"Surely He shall not be moved for ever: the righteous shall be in everlasting remembrance. He shall not be afraid of evil tidings: His heart is fixed, trusting in the Lord. His heart is established, He shall not be afraid, until He see his desire upon his enemies. [His desire is Proverbs 25:21, to give them eternal food and drink, even Himself, but it is only coals of fire to them], He hath given to the poor; his righteousness endureth for ever; his horn shall be exalted with honor. The wicked shall see it, [all the good things He has done for them] and be grieved; He [the wicked] gnash with his teeth, and melt away: the desire of the wicked [all their sinful desires] shall perish." Psalm 112:6-10.

Please notice carefully that it is the "sinful desires" that are going to be "consumed," not the sinners themselves. God loves the sinner but hates the sin. Notice: "Oh let the wickedness of the wicked come to an end; but establish the just: for righteous God tries the hearts and reins." Psalm 7:9. When their sin and wickedness is "burned up" and "consumed" by the "fire of God" they will be purified and made ready to "enter into the gates of the city." The last to enter will be Satan and his angels who are the hardest cases and have the most sins to be burned out of them but eventually even Satan will be destroyed that Lucifer may be reborn.

THE RIGHTEOUSNESS OF THE LAW DESTROYS

It is really the law of God lived out in the life of Christ and the lives of His followers which will destroy the wicked. Because they have refused the protection of God's law, which law would have healed their sin sickness, as Christ wrote it in their hearts with His own blood, this same law they have refused will now, like a mirror, point out their sins in living color. They will have an instant replay of their whole life, for everything they have ever said, done or experienced is all in the mind. John 8:6-11 is an example of how this will happen at the end of our present age.

They will not be able to stand the sight of themselves as they realize what they have become without Christ. Yet, they still refuse to turn to Him at first and begin casting blame upon each other, especially the religious leaders who led them astray. The whole world will be on fire and will self-destruct. Every man's hand will be against his brother. Ezek. 38:21. This will take place in the age in which we are now living. But after the 1,000 years it will be different in the Lake of Fire. Satan himself will suffer longer than anyone, but is finally reduced to "ashes," which is repentance. The fire that destroys him is initiated by the wicked as a result of the fire of hatred which is in himself and comes forth with fury at this time according to Ezekiel 28:18. The fire that comes forth from within him is obviously all the sins he will recall. Mark 9 indicates that the worm of sin will not die nor the fire be quenched...until...Yes, until the work of consuming sin is completed. God will not force them. They still have free will. He never takes that away from any creature.

When we refuse to let Jesus write the law of the "SPIRIT OF LIFE" (Ten commandments) or law of liberty, James 2:10, in our hearts, we automatically activate the law of sin and death in our hearts. Rom. 8:1,2. This, then, is what will destroy the wicked, for sin devours itself. "I said therefore unto you, that ye shall die in your sins." John 8:24. NOTICE: James tells us about the ability of the lawgiver (JESUS) to destroy. "There is one law-giver, who is able to save and to destroy." James 4:12. Satan destroys by tempting men to break the law. Heb. 2:14, Rev. 6:8, Matt. 10:28, Isa. 14:20, Ezek. 28:20. And it is this law that will finally "destroy" all of the wicked in the "Lake of Fire," which Charles H. Pridgeon explains is a "Lake of Divine Purification." This book is available if you would like to read it. "Is Hell Eternal: Will God's Plan Fail?"

Because God is the author of the Ten Commandments and because this law is the undergirding and foundation of His throne, God makes Himself responsible for the sickness, disaster and death that result from the violation of its precepts. He says, "I made the law, therefore I have killed you. It is all my fault and I will take the blame in order that I may have the right to bring you a cure or remedy for the sickness and misery my law has revealed in your life." For the written code [letter of the law] kills, but the Spirit gives life. 2 Cor. 3:6. One early 20th century visionary made this insightful comment regarding the law of God.

"Against every evildoer God's law utters condemnation. He may disregard that voice, he may seek to drown its warning, but in vain. It follows him. It makes itself heard. It destroys his peace. If unheeded, it pursues him to the grave. It bears witness against him at the judgment." Education, page 144, 1903.

Paul clearly explains in Romans 7:7-25, that it is the righteousness of the law (character of God), which destroys us when we become aware of our sins. "I was once alive apart from the law, but when the commandment came, sin revived and I died; the very commandment which promised life proved to be death to me. For sin, finding opportunity in the commandment, deceived me and by it killed me." Rom. 7:9, 10, 11, LB. Do you see how Paul explains the "death" of the sinner, using himself as an example. He also said, "I die daily" and "crucified with Christ." It is a painful process and after the 1,000 years will take a very long time.

In the final day the law will be totally personified in the beautiful personage of our precious Redeemer who with outstretched hands (nail scars blazing with glory Habakkuk 3:4) makes one last, final call to all the lost standing before Him with their instruments of death and destruction in their hands to kill Him if they can. "Oh, why will you die," He will say to them, "when you can come to me and live forever. Behold the purchased possession of my blood. I did it for you too."

GOD'S FINAL CALL OF LOVE TO ALL THE LOST ONES

"With the voice together shall they sing: for they shall see eye to eye, when the Lord shall bring again Zion... the Lord hath made bare his holy arm in the eyes of all the nations; and all the ends of the earth shall see the salvation of our God." Isaiah 52:9, 10.

This clearly shows that the entire human race are all going to meet together in the future for the first time. It is at this time that the wicked will be confronted with their sins in full display in the heavens through a revelation of the plan of salvation. Each person in every age will see just where he went astray and how many times he/she refused to surrender themselves to God's way to His plan of salvation. They will finally realize what Paul meant when he said, "It is a fearful thing to fall into the hands [the nail scarred hands of Jesus] of the living God.

Hebrews 10:31. "God came from Teman, and the Holy One from mount Paran. Selah. His glory covered the heavens, and the earth was full of his praise. And His brightness was as the light; he had horns coming out of his hand: (margin says "bright beams out of his side." Habakkuk 3:3, 4. Here we see a prediction of a future panoramic "movie in the sky" in which will be displayed the life of Jesus and His sufferings. Another visionary saw it like this: *"As soon as the books or record are opened, and the eye of Jesus looks upon the wicked, they are conscious of every sin which they have ever committed. They see just where their feet diverged from the path of purity and holiness, just how far pride and rebellion have carried them in the violation fo the law of God. The seductive temptations which they encouraged by indulgence in sin, the blessings perverted, the messengers of God despised, the warnings rejected, the waves of mercy beaten back by the stubborn, unrepentant heart-all appear as if written in letters of fire." GC 666.* If everything a person has ever experienced is still in the brain then our mind is the "record books" the Lord will use to bring back all of those memories, good and bad and it truly will be like a consuming fire.

It may take a long time for them to admit they are wrong, but eventually *every knee will bow and every tongue will confess and this will bring glory to God the Father. It could not bring glory to His name if it were forced or faked. It would have to be a true and genuine conversion.* Read I Cor. 12:3 and Ezekiel 16:53-55; then Ezekiel 47 which indicates the righteous will go outside the city to heal the wicked. "These waters (the righteous coming out of the city of New Jerusalem) issue out toward the east country, and go down into the desert plain, and go into the sea: (all the lost) which being brought forth into the sea, the waters (lost and sick people) shall be healed." Ezekiel even uses the symbolism of "fish" to refer to the people. "And it shall come to pass, that every thing that lives which moves, wherever the rivers shall come, shall live: and there shall be a very great multitude of fish, because these waters shall come thither: for they shall be healed; and every thing shall live thither (where) the river cometh." Ezekiel 47:9. The ML & RSV read "become fresh" instead of live.

"Everything touching the water of this river shall live. Fish will abound in the Dead Sea, for its waters will be healed. Wherever this water flows, everything will live." LB.

CHAPTER 20

CHRIST'S SUPREME OBJECTIVE

The supreme object of the Messianic mission of Jesus Christ (the saving anointed One) was to reveal the heart of His Father, who is really our Father, as our Beloved Lord Jesus taught us to address Him in the "LORD'S PRAYER," Matt. 6:9. When only twelve years of age, Christ recognized Jehovah God as His Father. "'But why did you need to search?' he asked. 'Didn't you realize that I would be here at the temple, in my Father's House?'" Luke 2:49, LB. The KJV says, "Wist ye not [didn't you know] that I must be about my Father's business?"

Throughout the rest of His life, and especially during His three and one half years of ministry, Jesus continually referred to God the Father as "His Father," or "My Father." But He also called Him "Your Father." "Pray to YOUR FATHER who is in secret; and your Father who sees in secret will reward you." Matt. 6:6 RSV. This understanding must be extremely important. Why? Because the gospel writers, especially John, continually quote Jesus' words about His relationship with the Father. This is not only a revelation of what God is like, but an example, as well as a sample of the relationship we can and must have to be saved. The life of Jesus was a demonstration of what the Father is really like. A good example of this is found in John 5. Jesus had healed the man at the Pool of Bethesda who had been sick for 38 years. Instead of rejoicing over this wonderful miracle, the Jewish leaders tried to accuse Christ of breaking the Sabbath. It is incredible how blind they were. "So they began harassing Jesus as a Sabbath breaker, But Jesus replied, 'MY FATHER CONSTANTLY DOES GOOD, AND I'M FOLLOWING HIS EXAMPLE.'" John 5:16-17. LB. In verse 37 Jesus said the Father had sent Him. At His baptism a voice spoke from heaven, "WHICH SAID, THOU ART MY BELOVED SON, IN THEE I AM WELL PLEASED." Luke 3:22. And

Jesus declared, "...I do nothing of myself; but as my Father hath taught me, I speak these things... I do always those things that please him." John 8:28-29. These words only infuriated and enraged the Jewish leaders. Jesus told them why they would not accept him. "I speak that which I have seen with my Father (God): and ye do that which ye have seen with your father (Satan)" Jn. 8:38, 44. Then they took up stones to kill him. Later in John 10:25 Jesus said he was doing all of his miracles in HIS FATHER'S NAME. Now, a person's name among the Hebrews (later known as Israel or Jews) often described his character or what kind of a person he was. Even today a person may pick up a nickname like "smiley," or "chuckles," or "happy," or "grumpy." These adjectives describe the main characteristic of that person's personality. Well, Jesus said that the works he was performing, healing the blind and maimed and sick, were very descriptive of what His Father was really like. In other words "My Father is a very kind, and wonderful person. You should get to know Him better. He will not hurt you at all. The person who hurts people is the Devil." He told the Jews that this was their father. Is it possible that some very religious people today are serving the Devil like the Jews did? If it is true, we know the Father today is still the same and will forgive us and adopt us into His family, if we ask Him. I would encourage you to read the gospels of Matthew, Mark, Luke and John through, especially John. Pray as you read and the Holy Spirit will reveal more to you. In order for us to really understand what His Father's heart was like, Jesus told some parables that are well known to most religious people, but sometimes we may be so familiar that we have failed to penetrate their deeper meanings. Let us go to Luke 15. In verse 2 we read what was intended by the Pharisees and scribes to be a slander against Christ's beautiful character, but turns out to be one of the greatest compliments they could have ever paid him. "This man receives sinners, and eateth with them." Luke 15:2 KJV. I am so thrilled that Jesus received me and is willing to dine with me at every meal. He will dine with you too. He doesn't play favorites. James 1:5; Rom. 2:11.

Jesus never met murmuring with murmuring or sarcasm with sarcasm. Instead He tried to lift their minds to heavenly themes so they might see into His Father's great and magnificent heart of love which was yearning for them to come to Him. And some of them responded. Nicodemus and Joseph of Arimathaea finally accepted Him and also a "great company of the priests were obedient to the faith." Acts 6:7. In comparison with the large number of priests who rejected Christ the number was not a huge number, for God's faithful ones have always been in the minority, but this company was large enough to cause quite a stir in Jerusalem, so much so that by Acts 8 and 9 we see a great persecution taking place which caused the Christian Church at Jerusalem to be scattered throughout the regions of Judaea and Samaria. But these new converts "went everywhere preaching the Word." Acts 8:4. The Random House Dictionary defines "company," as "any relatively small group of soldiers." Webster's New 20th Century Unabridged says, "In military affairs, the body of soldiers united under the command of a captain: it is the lowest administrative unit, usually a subdivision of a regiment." The Bible qualifies company with the adjective, "great" showing it was not the usual size of a company, but "a great company." It may never have been more than 5% of the Jewish Nation at that time. Remember that 5% of a million would have been 50,000. It would be surprising if even 5% of the nation ever were converted to Christianity.

And so we see that the methods of Jesus bore the signature of His Heavenly Father and glorified His Father by winning souls to Him and His Eternal cause. Now, let us take a look at Luke 15 in depth. There are three parables and each of them have a very important message. Jesus spoke of 100 sheep who were in the wilderness. One became lost (our lost world). Jesus said he left the 99 in the wilderness to go out and seek this one lost sheep. If our world is the one lost sheep the other worlds must be the 99 who were not lost. Job 1:6 and Rev. 12:12 indicate there are beings on other planets who have never fallen into sin. What Jesus meant by having to leave them in the wilderness is not entirely clear, but some kind of risk to their safety is implied. But we are the one lost sheep. Our little world is a spectacle or theater "to the world, cosmos or universe and to angels, and to men." I Cor. 4:9. The one lost sheep knows that it is lost and cries out for help. It "repents," Lk. 15:7 and Jesus is able to gather that little lost sheep back into His strong, loving arms and return it safely to the fold. One day our lost world will be returned to the fellowship of the universe of unfallen worlds. What a day that will be!

Satan knows this and is busy trying to deceive people into believing that the UFOs are manned by angels or beings from other planets. UFOs have been known to forcibly kidnap people and even to burn humans and kill them as well as animals. This is not the work of a loving God. Our Heavenly Father's holy angels do not need any kind of mechanical device to fly around in such as a flying saucer, so-called. Satan hopes to deceive the world into believing that he is Christ. Most people will probably believe him. The methods used to communicate with UFOs are occult methods and the occult is not from God, but from Spiritualism, which is Satanic. Besides, God's holy angels do not kill. See Psalm 103:20; John 18:36, Hebrews 1:14.

The next parable Jesus told was about a lost coin. It was lost inside the house, not out in the wilderness like the sheep. There were ten silver coins. In the mind of a Hebrew the number ten denoted totality. Ten meant, "it's all there." Ten words or commandments of the decalogue (ten words) covered every facet of human conduct. The first four describe the perfect attitude we are to have toward God and the last six picture or delineate God's ideal for man in his relationship with his fellow man. It shows us how we should love God and man. This lost coin was made of silver which is the next most precious metal. Gold is more expensive, but gold and silver are usually mentioned together in the Bible. Some believe that gold symbolizes God's faith and love which He desires to implant in our hearts and that silver represents obedience which He will also give us, if we let

Him help us. If this be true, then this lost coin, which was still in the house, was not aware that it was lost through disobedience. But God still lovingly sought the coin out diligently until it was found. We must be God's hands and feet in bringing back lost members of our house. By faith, love and prayer we, with Christ's help can do it. The last parable Christ related to answer the murmuring slander of the Pharisees that Jesus defiled Himself by associating with "sinners," as if they were without any sin, is the story of the LOST BOY. We call it the story or parable of the "Prodigal son": Most people think prodigal means "wayward," but it means "wasteful." The prodigal went out and wasted his father's goods. But notice the reaction of the father, who is really the main character in this story. Does he send spies out after his son to see if he is behaving properly? No. Does he bribe the law to arrest him and bring him back before the boy has squandered his inheritance? No. The father stays at home grieving for his son, hoping and praying for his return. There are two ways to learn the lessons of life....the easy way by listening and obeying and the hard way by ignoring counsel and rebelling. This lost boy had to learn the hard way just like so many today. But finally the boy comes to his senses when all of his money and fair weather friends are gone. He remembers what it was like at home. Even the "hired servants" are in better shape than he is now. He's so hungry he was almost ready to eat the pig's food which were carob-pods, still counted a delicacy in the East, and known to schoolboys as "locust-beans" or "honey-beans." "But there are sweet and bitter carobs; Tatian's 'Gospel-Harmony [second century, A .D.] has 'carobs of the sea' [salt carobs]; the nicely brought-up youth could not stomach bitter carobs, which are still given to cattle." John the Baptist probably ate the sweet type carob. Matt. 3:4.

THE WASTEFUL BOY RETURNS

And so our young rebel has had his fill of worldly pleasure. He found that it only lasts for "a season," (Heb. 11:25) and that the way of the transgressor is hard, Proverbs 13:15 and leads to shame, Isa. 57:20, then on to the blackness of darkness forever, Jude 13. So he climbs out of the pigpen (which represents the bottomless pit or grave. Isa. 38:18; Job 17:16; Rev. 20:1) and heads for his father's house. He realizes now that his father's restrictions were for his own protection and welfare. He longs to hear his father's voice and to see his face again, but he dares not think that he would ever be accepted back as a son. He remembers his father's prayers and Bible readings at family worship. He recalls the sumptuous meals and the happy fellowship of younger days. He realizes that the hired servants (who were probably poor relatives) have it much better than he does. Evidently, they were taken into the house and even paid a wage, but were not on a level with the children. He remembers how his father was always kind to strangers and helped the poor and sick. "Oh, maybe, just maybe, he will have pity on me and hire me like he has some of my poor distant cousins," he muses as he begins the long journey home.

HE APPROACHES THE HOUSE

Obviously this returning son has no real concept of the FATHER'S HEART. He does not know the depths of love that are drawing him back home. Paul tells us that it is "the goodness of God that leads us to repentance." Rom. 2:4. The LIVING BIBLE puts it like this: "Don't you realize how patient he is being with you? Or don't you care? Can't you see that he has been waiting all this time without punishing you, to give you time to turn from your sin? His kindness is meant to lead you to repentance." Rom. 2:4. What a shocking but happy surprise the boy is going to receive when he approaches the house. But he doesn't know that now. No, he still has some of that old negative concept of his father in his mind. His father was always very careful with the money. He remembers how reluctant his dad was to give him his "rightful" inheritance. He didn't realize then that it wasn't because of the money but because he would miss his boy's fellowship so much and that he feared for his health and safety out in the big wicked world. He knows his dad probably had to go back to work in the fields, and he didn't care then, but he surmises that there will be some bitterness in his father's heart toward him because of this hardship.

And so he makes up his little speech about sinning against heaven and before his Father and since he is no longer worthy of sonship hopes that he can be hired out. Perhaps he even hoped to eventually earn enough money by hard sweat to pay his dad back, at least part of the inheritance. He doesn't dare ask it, not now at least, but he doubtless hopes and prays that someday his father will forgive him enough to consider him a son again. But, first of all, he must prove himself worthy of such an honor. And so on he goes and at last he sees the old farm house in the distance. Tears well up in his eyes as he remembers his childhood and youth. Those innocent years so long ago. The Bible doesn't tell us how long this prodigal was in the far country wasting his father's goods or substance. It could have been as long as twenty years or it could have been only one or five or ten. But it was long enough to accumulate a terrible burden of guilt and remorse that now comes flooding into his mind. What right does he have to come back home? When he was home his only thought was to get away and have fun, "...do my own thing... build my own world." He was sure this would bring him the happiness he felt was missing in his life. He wanted to get away from his father's restrictions and especially from his father's God. Yet, he wanted to claim the good things he felt he had coming without any acknowledgment or gratefulness to his father who had worked a lifetime for what the son took as a matter of course, as if he owed it to him. He realizes how wrong he was now. He realizes that he has made himself the center of everything without any thought for the happiness or the well-being of others. Instead of freedom he has found slavery. How can he ever make it up to his dad? Perhaps he should turn around and go back out into the world, get an honest job, make something of himself and become respectable again (as if he ever was or ever could be). Perhaps his father would be more receptive then. Besides, he would have some money saved by then to pay back part of what he had wasted. All these thoughts and many more are rushing through his mind. He has turned around now and is thinking about going back into the world. But he is weak and hungry and in rags. He would have to live off of charity for awhile. Then he turns around for one more look at the old homestead. It looks so good. If only he could just go down and say hello and see everyone. How good that would be.

THOSE QUICK EYES OF LOVE

Just then he sees someone going out to the mailbox. Why, its his old dad. His father looks down the road as if he might be expecting someone. And that's when the old man sees his long, lost boy. While his son is a "great way off," those quick eyes of love discern his boy's form. The Bible tells us that "he had compassion, and ran, and fell on his neck." It must have been a long, clinging and tender embrace.

HE LEARNS THE FATHER'S HEART

The son is shocked and speechless. He didn't expect this, for he did not know his father's true character of love. But the guilt and remorse come upon him again in a rush. He remembers the speech he had planned to give and no doubt pulls away or falls down on the ground and begins telling his father that he is no longer worthy of sonship. But the father interrupts him with quick commands to his servants who have come running out to see this unbelievable sight. They didn't know the true character of the father either. "But the father said to his servants, bring forth the best robe, and put it on him; and put a ring on his hand, and shoes on his feet:" Luke 15:22.

Now that his dad has kissed away his guilt and shame he places the royal robe upon him to cover his rags of misery. The father covers his wayward, wasteful, but repentant son with his own robe of righteousness so no one may be able to look down upon his boy with contempt. Isa. 61:10; Rev 21:2. Esther 3:10 says that King Ahasuerus "took his ring from his hand, and gave it unto Haman." This was no doubt a signet ring which was used to sign checks, legal documents and edicts such as the death decree Haaman later signed against all the Jews. This ring now meant that the son's word and authority was equal to that of his father. The son's restoration is now total and complete. The father does not bring up the past. The boy knows by his father's actions that his sins are "blotted out, as a thick cloud." Isa. 44:22. It is as if he had never left or done anything wrong at all. And so it is with you and me. He longs to forgive and to cleanse that we might have a celebration of our return to the father's house. "I will forgive their iniquity, and I will remember their sin no more." Jer. 31:34. "...Our God....will abundantly pardon." Isaiah 55:7.

GOD DOES NOT DEMAND THAT WE REPAY HIM

The story of the prodigal son has many lessons for us. First of all, it takes us into the Father's heart. We see the grief and sorrow that son brought to his dad by leaving home. Second, we see that the father gave free choice to his son. He did not prevent him from leaving, nor did he ever go out and try to force him to come home. Yet, we know that God sends His Holy Spirit out to draw all of his wayward children back to his infinite and eternal heart of love. Third, we see that God does not demand that we "pay him back." He didn't keep track of what the boy had spent and/or wasted. He didn't say, "alright, you can come back into the house after you have returned the inheritance I gave to you. You either go out and earn it or I'll take it out of your wages here on the ranch." Now, that is what the boy expected. That's the kind of person he thought his dad was. But, he was wrong. His father treated him as if he had never left and forgave him as if he had never wasted a dime. He never mentioned or brought up his past to him. The son repented and was forgiven. His restoration to the father's house was full and complete. His father treated him as if it had never happened. He was given a royal robe and a ring was placed on his finger showing that he was still heir to all the family fortune and had all the authority to transact and conduct business in his father's name just as before. He can sign checks, order supplies and run errands or do whatever the business requires. It is almost too good to be true. But it is true. At least about his father. But now enters the "elder brother." The celebration of his son's return is in high gear. The fatted calf has been killed and everyone is rejoicing at this party. This older brother has been out in the field working very hard. When he hears the music and dancing, Luke 15:25, he calls one of the servants for a report and finds out that his younger brother has returned home. This indicates that all the events related in the story so far have transpired in one day. The father didn't waste any time in celebrating his son's return. Even some of his old friends have been invited over.

The older brother is very angry and refuses to go in and join the celebration. So the father comes out to see him, but to no avail. It is also obvious that the boy who stayed home and was "faithful," to his father, at least in outward show and according to all appearance, did not know the true character of the father either. The older son shows his malignant pride and dreadful jealousy by his hateful words. He is not happy with his younger brother's return and refers to him as "thy son," as if he himself were not even related to him. It is obvious that if he had been in his father's place he would not have welcomed him back home. He is very insulted at the favor shown his younger brother and disrespectfully speaks to his father about the unfair way he feels he has been treated. "I have worked and slaved here on your old farm for you all these years and never broken one of your commandments, but not once have you even given me a kid or young goat so that I could have a party with my friends. But when this no good son of yours comes back home begging after wasting all of our money on whores and prostitutes, you roll out the red carpet. I don't think its fair at all." His attitude, tone of voice and words reveal the real condition of his heart. He has been trying to earn his father's inheritance by a strict, legalistic obedience to the law. His real motive has been his father's silver and gold instead of the abiding joy of his presence which brings pleasure forever more, Psalm 16:11. He has only avoided the pleasures of sin for a season so he can gain earthly wealth not because he loved his father.

The elder son is like Cain who hated Abel and like Esau who hated Jacob. He is like the first generation of Israel who failed to inherit the land of Canaan because of their ego and hardness of heart. He is like the son in the parable who said he would go to work in the vineyard but never did go, neither did he repent of his sin. Matt. 21:28-32. He is like Lucifer (Satan) who should have loved all of us on planet earth when God created us, but was jealous instead and found a way to deceive and destroy instead of lovingly help us to grow up into the Father's love. Genesis 3:1-15; Ezek. 28:13-18. The elder son represents the Pharisees in every age who do not love sinners as Christ did, but are envious and hateful toward them when Jesus draws them to his side and covers them with the royal robe of his righteousness. They claim to be workers in his vineyard, sons of his house, but are really only hirelings, always watching the clock and seeking to find out what the minimum requirements are to receive the reward of the "faithful," when in reality they are only time servers. They do not know that salvation is a free gift and are seeking to earn their way to heaven by toil, sacrifice, penance and good works. God is a hard taskmaster to them. They do not know his true character of love. This parable is a very loving appeal to the Pharisees then and in all ages. Jesus didn't say whether the elder son ever went in or not, for the actors were still on stage playing out the final scene. We know now that most of them never went in and were lost for that age. But there is a new age coming in which they will once again be confronted with the same choices. Christ reveals why they refused to accept Him the first time. "And all who heard John preach— even the most wicked of them— agreed that God's requirements were right, and they were baptized by him. All, that is, except the Pharisees and teachers of Moses' law. They rejected God's plan for them and refused John's baptism." Luke 7:29-30. LB

But did Jesus give up and stop trying to persuade them to come into the "Father's house" and celebrate? No, that is not His character to ever give up. He told a parable about a great supper and how all the ones he invited made excuses as to why they couldn't come. So he invited "the poor, and the maimed, and the halt, and the blind." Luke 14:21. They were "compelled" to come in. "But, Mike, I thought you said God didn't ever force anyone, but always gives us free choice." That is correct. It was "compelling love," that drew them into the supper in the Father's house. "The Lord hath appeared of old unto, saying, Yea, I have loved thee with an everlasting love: therefore with LOVING-KINDNESS have I DRAWN THEE." Jer. 31:3. Hosea tells us about God's drawing power. "I drew them with cords of a man, with bands of love;" That man is the Lord Jesus, our Blessed Redeemer. The Living Bible puts it like this: "As a man would lead his favorite ox, so I led Israel with my ropes of love. I loosened his muzzle so he could eat. I myself have stooped and fed him." Hosea 11:4, LB. Cf. Job 22:15-18. Psalm 2 tells us the rulers and kings plot how to break away from God's cords and bands of love. How sad. But God never gives up. That is his eternal nature and character for his love is so great. It is beyond our comprehension and yet He says that He will place that love in our hearts through His perfect law. He will make a covenant with us, Jer. 31:33: Hebrews 8:8; 10:16, 17. What is the purpose of the covenant? So that He, "will be their God, and they shall be my people." And what does He want to do for us? 'for I will forgive their iniquity, and I will remember their sin no more.'" Jer. 31:34.

This is what the Father did for his prodigal son when he came home. He even went out to meet him. The Father represents God the Father, who lovingly kissed this lost boy's sins away and put the robe of his own righteousness about his returned son and brought him into the house (New Jerusalem) for the celebration. Jesus told another parable to them about a "certain king, which made a marriage for his son." Matt 22:2. He tells how "his servants" were sent out to invite people to the wedding but those who were invited (the Jewish nation through the ages) refused to come. Well, they made light of it and then he says, "the remnant took his servants, and entreated them spitefully and slew them." Matt. 22:6. Later Jesus said, "Yes, woe to you, Pharisees, and you religious leaders— hypocrites for you build monuments to the prophets killed by your fathers and lay flowers on the graves of the godly men they destroyed, and say, 'we certainly would never have acted as our father's did.' In saying that, you are accusing yourselves of being the sons of wicked men.....you are following in their steps. Snakes! Sons of vipers! How shall you escape the judgment of hell?" Matt. 23:29-33 LB. Here Jesus is trying to save them from dying. It sounds like He is angry, but it is more like Divine heartache and grief Gen. 6:6; Mark 3:5. If we could have heard his tone of voice and perhaps seen the tears in his eyes, we would realize he was trying to save them. He was trying to get them into the Father's house, into the celebration, but like the older son they refuse to have anything to do with the marriage supper. Jesus is desperate to save them for time is running out for them in that age.

Next Christ tells them that He is going to keep on sending them prophets and wise men and inspired writers but they will reject them just like their fathers did and just as they are rejecting Him. "Oh, can't you see your blindness? Please don't kill yourself. Why will you die?" Then He refers to the murder of all the true men of God the Lord sent from Abel (killed by Cain) to Zechariah (II Chronicles 24:17-22). He blamed the death of "Zacharias son of Barachias, whom ye slew between the temple and the altar," upon the Jews in AD 31 when Zacharias (Zechariah) was killed in 856 BC at the commandment of King Joash, of Judah, the southern kingdom. The headquarters for the southern kingdom was Jerusalem, which David had established, but the 12 tribes had split after Solomon died. Ten went with Jeroboam who led them into heathen idolatry (1 Kings 12) and Sun worship and two tribes remained true to Jehovah and his worship at the temple in Jerusalem. Christ our Lord taught parables to both warn the leaders as well as to instruct the people. But as He neared the end of His mission, he began to speak more to the point about the sins of the priests. The people's minds were enslaved by the deceptions of the priests, and the scribes and elders regarding the mission of the Messiah. These corrupt teachers were themselves deceived. But the people reverenced them and their traditions. Jesus exposed them in no uncertain terms. You can read about it in Matt. 23. He must have had tears in his voice and pain in His magnificent heart of love as He attempted to set the people's minds free from their blind allegiance to a corrupt ministry. He had to break the chains that bound their souls in slavery to the Jewish hierarchy.

These Jews living in AD 31 were committing a much greater crime than King Joash had committed in killing Zechariah. They were about to kill the very Son of God. Their sin would therefore be much greater than any preceding generation. God had held back Satan, the destroyer, for centuries, hoping that his people would finally repent. But instead they just kept getting worse. By rejecting Jesus, the true Messiah, they were bringing all the blood of the ages upon themselves. Jesus was trying to save them from this terrible disaster, but they wouldn't listen. God does not destroy men. In fact He does everything in his power to save them from destroying themselves. When Christ referred to the stoning of Zacharias the scribes and Pharisees knew exactly what he was talking about for his blood had been imprinted upon the stones of the temple court and had been there for almost eight centuries as a testimony against the Jewish nation. Yet, they had never repented. Even when Nebuchadnezzar had destroyed Jerusalem and the temple, these stones were not molested in 605, 597 or 586 BC. Evidently, these stones were never moved, disturbed or even effaced during these sieges. The temple was rebuilt and dedicated in 515 BC and Jerusalem itself was completely repaired by

444 BC under Nehemiah's leadership. Ezra and Zerubbabel led out in the initial renovation in 536 BC. Joshua was the high priest. About 50,000 left Babylon to return to rebuild the temple and city. It is interesting that Christ was a direct descendant of Zerubbabel, Matt. 1:6, 12, 13; Lk. 3:27,31.

A HEARTBREAKING PROPHECY

The Jewish leaders, like the older son in the parable of the prodigal, were without excuse. They had every evidence a rational minded person could ask for that Jesus truly was the Messiah. But their pride and desire to run the temple their own way shut God's presence out. So they continued to enrich themselves at the expense of the people. They burdened them with a heavy guilt trip to ensure more animal sacrifices and gifts. Jesus ended his pleadings and warnings in Matt. 23 with this heartbreaking prophecy.

"Yes, all the accumulated judgment of the centuries shall break upon the heads of this very generation. O Jerusalem, Jerusalem, the city that kills the prophets, and stones all those God sends to her! How often I have wanted to gather your children together as a hen gathers her chicks beneath her wings, but you wouldn't let me. And now your house (Please notice that Jesus now calls it 'your house' instead of 'My Father's house') is left to you desolate or lonesome." Matt. 24:1 defines why they were lonesome. Jesus had departed. He was looking at Jerusalem as it would become in AD 70. The death sentence had already been pronounced by the Jews upon themselves. It only was a matter of time until it would be carried out by the Romans and their armies marching under the golden eagle representing the ancient phoenix of sun worship. Matt. 23:36:38.

The religious leaders were well aware of Zechariah's martyrdom. King Joash, in a fit of satanic fury had commanded Zechariah the priest to be stoned, 2 Chron. 24:20-22. All those years had witnessed against apostate Israel and now they were about to even add the blood of God's dear Son to their long and horrible list of crimes. Jesus was trying to save them from their doom. A thrill of terror must have pulsed through that throng as He referred to their crimes and the certainty of the coming punishment. No wonder Jesus wept over His people as He longingly looked one last time upon the temple and His audience. His voice must have choked with Divine love, pity, anguish and bitter tears as He exclaimed, "0 Jerusalem, why don't you listen. 0 Jerusalem, why don't you come to me and let me save you from destruction, pain and eternal death." This is a mental torture and heartache that is beyond human words to describe. And so we see that the parable of the prodigal son or lost boy has some very deep implications and parallels. It takes us into the Father's heart of love that we may see the depths of Divine pity and compassion for a lost world. But there is more. We will find that the fatted calf has deep significance. The Father going outside of the house to plead with his older son also means something.

THE RED HEIFER

Let us look at the offering of the red heifer. In my simple approach to the Word of God, I see red as symbolic of Jesus' blood. All the animal sacrifices pointed forward to Jesus' death on the cross. A heifer is a young cow that has not borne a calf. One may wonder if the gender (sex) has a meaning since it is a female and Christ was a male. Jesus is both father and mother to us as our SAVIOR, Lord and coming King. In Isa. 1:2 God says he "nourished" and brought up children. Jesus is the "word" John 1:1, and Isa. 28:9 speaks of "them that are weaned from the milk, and drawn from the breasts referring to those who are able to understand doctrine and not just simple, elementary, basic facts of the Bible. I Cor. 3:2 and Heb. 5:12. In Isa. 49:15 the Lord uses the example of a mother giving suck to her lovely young child to show how much he loves us. He says that even though a mother (woman) may forget "yet will I not forget." In Psalm 91 God uses the simile or figure of speech "He shall cover thee with His feathers." v. 4. This is what a mother hen does for her little chicks. Jesus used this same comparison or simile in Matt. 23:37. "0 Jerusalem....how often would I have gathered thy children together, even as a hen gathereth her chickens under her wings, and ye would not!" See Additional Note #26, page 537.

So, we see that God has used the feminine gender in the Scriptures to describe his love, compassion, tender care and his sacrifice on Calvary through both male and female animals, see Exodus 29:1 for an example of male animals representing Christ. This would symbolize his great strength and power that he gave to us in his death. He did not use it to hurt, but to save. Each animal that was sacrificed represented a particular facet or characteristic of Christ's life and death. Even the manner in which it was to be sacrificed had a special meaning and significance which each of us should study out so we might more fully appreciate what Jesus did for us. The red heifer had never been "yoked" nor had it ever "borne" a calf. This would mean that Christ was never under the bondage or yoke of sin, nor was he ever married to anyone. He had come to this earth like a free young bridegroom seeking his bride. All who would believe on Him and would be saved from the bondage of sin would become his bride and take part in the wedding feast celebration. The sacrifice of the red heifer is therefore the same as the "fatted calf' which was killed to celebrate the prodigal's return.

The blood of the red heifer was to be sprinkled "seven times" representing the perfect cleansing of Christ's blood and the complete recovery of the sinner from the pit of sin. Num. 19:4. The red heifer also was killed outside the camp signifying how Jesus would die "without the gate" of the city of Jerusalem. Heb. 13:12. The red heifer was also burned to ashes outside the gate. "Her skin, and her flesh, and her blood, with her dung, shall he burn: and the priest shall take cedar wood, and hyssop, and scarlet, and cast it into the midst of the bumming of the heifer." Num. 19:5-6. Jesus died in our place. He suffered the death that was ours that we might receive the life that was His.

By "his stripes we are healed." Isa. 53:5. Our "skin" which would be our own filthy outer covering of righteousness he has "burned" away by allowing "fiery" trials to come upon us in the course of our life. I Pet. 4:12-14. Isa. 64:6. Not only was the skin and entrails (inside parts or organs) burned, but also the blood and dung signifying the complete destruction of this earthly body so we might put on the "heavenly" body, for "flesh and blood cannot inherit the kingdom of God; neither doth corruption inherit incorruption." I Cor. 15:50.

The promise of God is that we will have "a glorious body" like Jesus had after He rose from the grave. Phil. 3:20-21. But, it was a real body that could eat food and be touched, Luke 24:39-43. "This same Jesus" ascended to heaven with this immortal, glorified body, Acts 1:9:11, and will return in like manner to rescue His bride. Then we will go home to the Father's house for the celebration Jesus promised His disciples in Matt. 26:26-29, when He will "drink it new" with us in "my Father's kingdom." This is the celebration of the "fatted calf" or "the red heifer."

For the last year or more I have been giving a simple Bible study from the last two chapters of the book of Revelation which to my mind clearly reveals God's future plans for the human race. For the first time in the history of the world the entire human race will meet. Unfortunately, at least two thirds of God's creation will be outside the golden city looking in. Zech. 13:8. This is when all the wailing, crying, weeping and gnashing of teeth will take place. What is going to happen to these people? The last two chapters of Revelation helped me to answer this question for myself.

The "Revelations" of John have been a great mystery through the centuries. But Dan. 12 predicted that in the "time of the end...knowledge shall be increased." v. 4. I once read that although the various translators and copyists faithfully copied and translated the canon of Scripture they did not always place equal value on certain books. For example, Martin Luther called the book of James, "An Epistle of straw," meaning it was his opinion that James had no real value or nourishment for the believer. Yet, he translated it. I don't know how he felt about the book of Revelation but I have heard and read that many scholars through the centuries placed little value on this last book of the Sacred Cannon. Yet, God, in His infinite wisdom has preserved this book along with the other 65 books of the Bible for a very special reason. And the last two chapters have taken on new meaning for me personally, during 1994 and 1995, when I began sharing special insights the Lord revealed to my mind as I prayed and studied.

Before we go to Rev. 21 and 22 we need to prepare ourselves with a little background study. Our first text is found in Rev. 15: 1. Here we read about a "sign" John saw "in heaven." This expression can mean one of three things. John is seeing something taking place in the atmospheric heavens where the birds fly and the clouds float or in the starry heavens or in heaven itself, the third heaven, where God dwells with the angels in the Holy City. In chapter 14:1 John describes a vision he had of the 144,000 on Mount Sion, which we believe is in heaven itself. Then in v. 6 we read that the first of three angels is flying "in the midst of heaven." Because the plagues are poured out on earth I believe the sign John saw about the seven last plagues is taking place in our atmospheric heavens. God is pictured here and in the next chapter as sending these seven angels to pour out the plagues but in reality God is only permitting them as Rev. 7:1-4 explains. There are four angels holding back the winds of strife until the servants of God are sealed in their foreheads. Now let's go to Rev. 15:2 where John is describing a different scene that I believe is taking place in the third heaven because John also makes reference to the temple in verses 5 and 8. John says that he sees a "sea of glass" mingled or combined together with fire. Seas represent people, Rev. 17:15, and the fire here is symbolic of truth, righteousness and love for God has nothing to do with literal fire. Literal fire never existed until after Adam and Eve left the Garden of Eden. Isa. 33 indicates the righteous will dwell with "fire" and "everlasting burnings." Jesus also told us that we would be like or equal to the angels in heaven and the angels are called "flames of fire." But the main point we want to make here is that I believe the same group who were singing in Rev. 14:3 before the throne of God "as it were a new song," is the same group who are singing here in Rev. 15. Actually, they are prophesying in this song, that "all nations shall come and worship before thee; for thy judgments (decisions) are made manifest." Rev. 15:3, 4. Now, this is truly awesome in its implications. This group is predicting that ALL NATIONS are eventually going to surround the throne of God and sing praises of joy and victory to God because everything He has ever done is finally explained, understood and accepted as being absolutely perfect. This should give us a lot of courage knowing everything is happening according to God's will and He knows what is best and will explain it all to us to our complete satisfaction at the proper time in the future. Between now and then He asks us to have faith in Him. "Jesus answered and said unto him, What I do thou knowest not now; but thou shall know hereafter." John 13:7.

Now, we come to Rev. 21. Verses 1 and 2 describe the events which transpire immediately after the 1,000 years. John sees a new heaven and a new earth because the former or first heaven and earth has vanished/disappeared. John is describing the final results of all that God is about to create—a new heaven and a new earth. In vs. 3, John speaks about the tabernacle of God being with men. The word "men" is the generic term for mankind, "anthropos," meaning humankind or human beings thus embracing the entire human race from Adam and Eve. God Himself is going to be their God and dwell with them personally. The expectation and joy inherent in this text can only be appreciated in terms of our own human experience of the happiness and joy we experience when we are waiting to meet someone we have been separated from for a long time.

Think of the emotions you had as you waited for that bus or airplane to arrive with your long separated loved one(s) on board. The Bible tells us that God created us in His very own image and likeness so why should we think that our loving God is any different from us? He is looking forward to being with His very own sons and daughters from whom He has been separated since Adam and Eve broke His heart and stood Him up at the altar in Eden where He planned to be joined with them in a spiritual union or marriage. Yes, God is looking forward to being joined at last to His finished creation...first with the 144,000 and eventually with all of creation. In verse 4 we are told that God is going to "wipe away all tears from their eyes, and there shall be no more death, neither sorrow nor crying, neither shall there be any more pain...for the former things are passed away." Beloved, here we are faced with the first of several facts most Bible teachers have overlooked, ignored, misinterpreted or flat out denied and/or refused to believe. Instead of destroying all of these masses of humanity and wiping them off the face of the earth, He came and died to save them.

Now, Jesus has brought them forth from the grave not to "wipe them out" but for the express purpose of wiping away all their tears and pain for they are the only ones who will be crying and suffering. Isaiah of old prophesied this very event. "And the glory of the Lord shall be revealed, and all flesh shall see it together; for the mouth of the Lord hath spoken it." Isa. 40:5. After Jesus told the Centurion that He would go to his house to heal his servant of the palsy this faithful soldier told Jesus that would not be necessary for He believed Christ could simply speak the word and heal his "grievously tormented" servant from a distance saving much time which could be used in healing other sick people. Matt. 8:10 tells us that when Jesus heard this man speak these words "He marveled, and said to them that followed, Verily I say unto you, I have not found so great faith, no, not in Israel. And I say unto you, That many shall come from the east and west, and shall sit down with Abraham, and Isaac, and Jacob, in the kingdom of heaven. (Inside that beautiful city of Gold). But the children of the kingdom shall be cast out into outer darkness: there shall be weeping and gnashing of teeth." Matt. 8:10-12.

Now, beloved, who are the people who are shedding many tears (weeping)? They are not the people on the inside of the city. Oh, no! Please notice another text on this same subject. "And shall cast them (wicked) into a furnace of fire: there shall be wailing and gnashing of teeth." These are all the lost who are weeping because they are outside of the city.

By contrast the saved are inside the city looking out. "Then shall the righteous shine forth as the sun in the kingdom of their Father." Matt 13:43; Dan. 12:3. Does that sound like a sad group of people to you? Hardly! Much more could be said and more proof given but this is sufficient for now to prove that the only people who are crying are those outside of the city. The righteous, inside the city, have been with Jesus for 1,000 years already. So, their tears were wiped away in the first few minutes after they were resurrected and taken up through the sky to heaven with Jesus. Any tears they may shed subsequently (afterward) when they found out that many of their loved ones and friends were not there were wiped away as soon as Jesus explained the whole situation to them, i.e. that after the 1,000 years they would have an opportunity to see and meet with their loved ones again when Jesus raised them up in the final resurrection.

Now, can you imagine the reaction of the righteous if Jesus told them that the specific purpose of this resurrection was simply to rehearse to the wicked all of their sins and show them how bad they were for the sole purpose of killing them again? Do you think the righteous would be in favor of this? Would you? Of course you wouldn't, nor would I. This is a crucial and critical point to consider. In every age God's people have held to some kind of "Exclusive Club" doctrine. The Jews in both testaments taught they were superior to all nations of the earth and had an exclusive birthright and privilege to the coming kingdom. Even after the resurrection Paul rebuked Peter for his dissembling or hypocrisy regarding the doctrine of circumcision. Gal. 2:11-16. Even the early Adventists, after the 1844 disappointment, thought they alone were the chosen people of God because probation had already closed on the rest of the world. Slowly but surely these false theories have lost their hold and appeal on God's Remnant. Now, it is time to see God's ultimate plan of the ages for the whole human race. And you will discover this concept takes you right into the mind of Christ, and on into the throne room of the Father.

In fact, I believe this is going to become crucial in the days ahead when everything that can be shaken will be shaken. This world is going to become so bad off economically, so sick physically and mentally and so deceived and evil spiritually that we will be tempted to believe God has totally forsaken the human race. It is at this time that a full understanding of God's overall plan of the ages will give comfort to God's Remnant people. It will be a vital doctrine to bolster the faith of His chosen, elect ones in these final days of planet earth. Now, let's come back to the question I posed regarding the response of the Remnant to the idea that all of their loved ones and friends are about to be annihilated off of the face of the earth forever.

What do you think they would say to the Lord? I think they would tell Jesus they did not like this idea at all. But then what if Jesus were to explain that the specific objective of the second resurrection was for the purpose of bringing salvation to all? How many of the redeemed would go for such an idea? What about you? I want you to think about that for awhile. So, we see clearly that the Bible teaches that the wicked will be weeping and crying and gnashing their teeth because of their great mental and physical suffering. But the righteous are going to be singing and shouting for joy. Now, let's go to Rev. 21:5-7. "And He that sat upon the throne (Jesus) said, Behold, I make all things new. And he said unto me, Write: for these words are true and faithful. And He said unto me, It is done. I am Alpha and Omega, the beginning and the end. I will give unto him that is athirst of the fountain of the water of life freely. He that over cometh shall inherit all things; and I will be his God, and he shall be my son." Notice, my friend, how v. 6 emphasizes that everything is already done and carried out as an established fact for with God His Word is action past, present and future for our God dwells in the Eternal NOW.

Now, beloved, please notice in v. 6 that Jesus says that He is going to "give unto him that is athirst (thirsty) of the fountain of the water of life freely." Notice beloved, that I said "Jesus" is the one who is speaking here from the throne of His Father for it is Jesus Himself sitting on the throne of the universe with His Father as the Mighty God, the Everlasting Father and the Prince of Peace. Isa. 9:6.

Remember, friend of mine, that the righteous have been drinking of the water of life for a thousand years... so they are not thirsty. They don't need a drink of water. But the recently raised wicked are in a Lake of Fire. Not a literal lake of fire, for God's fire is not literal. It never has been and never will be. Jesus said, "I have come to bring fire on the earth..." a fire of love, righteousness and truth. So, now, here we have the same thing again in the form of a revelation of truth in the sky... a panoramic view or giant movie in the sky. This lake of fire is, in reality, a lake of humanity on fire with their anger, hatred and rebellion caused mainly by this revelation of truth which creates a lake of Divine purification and education (discipline if you please). The mental agony and suffering they will be going through because of their remorse, guilt, anger and hatred will cause them to become very thirsty. But they are the enemies of God and His people. So, how will God treat His enemies at this time? Proverbs 25:21 tells us that He gives them bread to eat and water to drink. And as a result of this Divine favor the wicked "overcome," get the victory and become sons of God. This is what we just read would happen in Rev. 15:1-4...that "ALL NATIONS" would come before the Lord.

Now, let's look again at Rev 21:24-27. "And the nations of them which are saved shall walk in the light of it: and the kings of the earth do bring their glory and honor into it." The expression "do bring" indicates present tense and could very easily be expressed, "are bringing" because John is writing as an eyewitness of what God is showing him will take place in the future. So, as we keep this in mind, we can understand how John sometimes seems to be speaking in the present tense and then in the future for he realizes he is writing about events which are all still future. In the Modern Language version we read, "By its light the nations will walk (follow the light of truth flowing forth from the throne of God out into the earth) and to it (into the city itself) the kings of the earth will bring their splendor."

The next verse reveals how this is possible, because the nations outside of the city are not yet converted. But as they follow or walk in the light of God's revealed glory they will be converted and want to enter the city. In this light we can see why John next tells us that the gates of the city are never closed. "And the gates of it shall not be shut at all by day: for there shall be no night there." Revelation 21:25. You see, my friend, God's love never stops. His merciful invitation is ongoing forever and ever extending throughout eternity.

Why else would the gates of the New Jerusalem always be open and never be closed? Because, beloved, God never goes out of the saving business. That's why the gates of the New Jerusalem are never closed. He is forever and always saving people. Now, verse 26 tells us that these nations who come into the city are going to bring the glory and honor of the nations into it. These people who are saved are going to be beautiful and wonderful trophies honoring the power and love of God to save sinners to the uttermost. And then verse 27 tells us, "And there shall in no wise enter into it any thing that defileth, neither whatsoever worketh abomination, or maketh a lie: But they which are written in the Lamb's book of life." Here John is trying to make it clear that even though the gates of the city are open for all to enter that no unconverted or defiled person will be able to enter. The KJV uses the conjunction "And" when "But" would convey John's meaning better for John is trying to make an important point, which is: That even though he saw all these wicked nations outside of the city going into the city he wants to make it crystal clear that they did not go in until they were changed or converted. I like the way the Modern Language versions puts it: "But nothing unclean nor anyone practicing immorality and falsehood shall ever enter it..." Every time I give this study I learn something new. So, I am sure there is more to be learned.

But let us now go to Rev 22. Even though the apostle must have been overwhelmed with the many visions the Lord gave him of coming events, transpiring in wondrous light and glory, John, with an incredible economy of words conveys and covers volumes of information about the future. The first five verses focus on the throne of God. John describes a beautiful river flowing or proceeding forth or out of God's throne. Because Revelation is a book of symbols and because waters (seas, lakes and rivers) represent or symbolize people (Rev. 17:15) it becomes clear that John is describing more than just a beautiful, literal river, which I do believe will be there for us to enjoy. But let us not miss the meaning of the symbolism of what John is seeing here. It is a river of humanity flowing forth from the throne room of God, bright as crystal, filled to overflowing with the mighty power of His love. This is the message this book is intended to teach us. Compare it with the vision of Ezekiel 47 in which the prophet describes waters (people) flowing out of the city in Ezek. 47:1-5 in ever increasing depths until he can no longer wade in the water but must swim because it is now over his head. Then in v. 7 he talks about trees growing along the both sides of the river. The Bible speaks of "trees of righteousness" referring to righteous people and in Psalm 1 a tree is symbolic of a man.

Throughout the 48 chapters of his much neglected, ignored and over looked, prophetic, book Ezekiel continually refers to the Lord God or Creator as the One who is revealing all of these things to him. In v. 8 Ezekiel again says, "He told me: 'This river flows east through the desert and the Jordan Valley to the Dead Sea, where it will HEAL the salty waters and make them fresh and pure.' Everything touching the water of this river shall live. Fish will abound in the Dead Sea, for its waters (people of Sodom raised from the dead in the second resurrection) will be healed. Wherever this water flows, everything will live.'"

Would you like to be a "fisher of men" in the 'Dead Sea.' You can be if you want to be. Ezekiel was a prophet to the common people, probably older than Daniel but younger than Jeremiah. Like Daniel, he was taken captive but unlike Daniel, a prophet to kings and the upper class nobility, Ezekiel was a prophet to the common people and remained with the captives. He did not enter the University of Babylon like Daniel and graduate "Summa Cum Laude." What they did have in common though was the prophetic gift. Daniel makes one important reference to the resurrection in Dan. 12:2. "And many of those who sleep in the dust of the earth shall awake, some to everlasting life, and some to shame and everlasting contempt." A correct understanding of this passage hinges on our interpretation of "everlasting." The most popular interpretation is that everlasting means without end. The hell fire burner-uppers place the wicked in hell-fire, burning endlessly throughout eternity. Those who disagree with this theory believe the word everlasting simply means that the fires of hell will eventually go out after the wicked have suffered long enough to satisfy God's justice. The wicked will literally burn in a fire that will eventually burn itself out. This word everlasting makes a lot more sense when we translate it "age lasting." Now we can read more correctly with much greater understanding that some are raised "to age lasting life, and some to shame and age lasting contempt."

In Revelation 22:2 John introduces an incredibly important piece of evidence regarding God's plan for humanity. He describes a tree that is on both sides of the river. A dear saint I studied with once told me that this was like a Banyan tree which is known to be able to grow on both sides of a river. But the main point here is that the leaves of the tree of life are for the HEALING OF THE NATIONS.

One day it began to dawn on my mind that the only nations that will be in need of healing will be all the sick people outside the city. All the people inside the Holy City New Jerusalem will have been healed from all their earthly diseases and infirmities for 1,000 years. So, the only nations that will stand in need of healing are those outside the city wailing and gnashing their teeth because they are not on the inside. Then in v. 11 John flashes back in time to the last generation before the return of Jesus and declares that all characters will be frozen at a given time just before Jesus comes again. "And, behold, I come quickly: and my reward is with me, to give every man according as his work shall be." So, those who are "unjust and filthy" as well as those who are "righteous and holy," will stay that way until after the 1,000 years are finished. Then all of the wicked or lost will be raised from their dusty graves to receive their reward, which is a realization that they are in a lost condition because of their own evil, wrong choices. This is part of their punishment. In vs.14 Jesus pronounces a blessing on all of those "they that do (or are doing) his commandments, that they may have the right to the tree of life and may enter in through the gates into the city." This is yet another invitation to repent and be converted so they may enter the city. I like the way the Living Bible paraphrases this passage. The author correctly understood that this was in the present indicative mood, continuous action or present tense. "Blessed forever are all who are washing their robes, to have the right to enter in through the gates of the city, and to eat the fruit from the Tree of Life." See, right here is another indication that these people who are being invited to wash their robes have not eaten of the tree of life before this time. They are in the process of "washing" or becoming converted or cleaned up so they may be able to enter into the city. I say this because in the very next verse John tells us who it is outside the city who need to start washing their robes so they can enter into the city. Their robes are dirty...robes of their own devising...self-righteousness, mainly religious people of all types, from all ages, who thought they already knew everything there was to know about God, like the Jews of old, especially in Christ's day, who crucified Him.

Then in verse 17 Jesus and His Bride give the loving invitation to come and drink of the water of life. This is basically a paraphrase from Isaiah 55:1. "Ho, every one who thirsts, come to the waters; and he who has no money, come, buy and eat! Come, buy wine and milk without money and without price." Another translation reads, "It's all free." The LB reads: "come and drink the Water of Life without charge." The KJV simply reads: "Let him take the water of life freely." Now, I wish to share with you a verse from John 7 that bears on this subject. "In the last day, that great day of the feast, Jesus stood and cried, saying, If any man thirst, let him come unto me, and drink. (This shows clearly that Jesus intended for the word "drink" to mean listening and believing what you hear. "We drank it all in," we often say in regards to accepting what we hear someone say.) "He that believeth on me, as the scripture hath said, out of his belly shall flow rivers of living water." KJV. Now, notice what the LB says: "For the Scriptures declare that rivers of living water shall flow from the inmost being of anyone who believes in me. He was speaking of the Holy Spirit, who would be given to everyone believing in Him;" John 7:37-38. So, Jesus clearly defines the living waters as simply being the good news of the gospel being preached by Spirit filled human beings.

The idea of "buying and selling," is often taken literally, especially in regard to the Mark of the Beast in Rev. 13 and Matt. 25, in the story of the 5 wise and 5 foolish virgins. When the foolish virgins run out of oil and come to the wise ones to ask for some of their oil the wise virgins tell them to go to those who "sell" and buy for yourselves for if we give you our oil we won't have enough ourselves. The phrase, "are gone out" should be translated in the present tense, "are going out." In other words it was obvious that their interpretation of Scripture regarding end-time events...e.g. their Eschatology (study of last day events) is incorrect. Without a clear understanding of God's true character the prophecies of Daniel and Revelation can never be understood correctly. There has been a gradual falling away from the pure doctrines of the early church and even the reformation doctrines. The belief that the dead are still alive and can be contacted has led to spiritualism. The belief that homosexuality is inherent from birth has led to the ordination of gay ministers and same sex marriages. And the belief that God destroys will eventually lead to forced worship on the day of the Sun, a pagan holiday honoring Baal, the sun god of ancient Egypt and Babylon.

If you interpret the word "buy" literally you miss the more profound implications. For example, we use the word buy today to indicate acceptance of an idea. "I can buy that (idea)" or "I just don't buy that kind of talk (idea or belief)." We must realize that character is something that must be developed individually between the soul and his/her Maker. It is not transferable. I cannot "give" you my salvation. You have to receive or accept it for yourself from God. One person cannot do it for another that which he must do for himself in preparation for the crisis that is coming.

So, when the righteous or wise virgins refuse to give their oil to the foolish virgins but advise them to go to those who sell, this is a lesson about personal accountability. I believe Jesus told this parable to help every generation or age see the importance of individual responsibility. Ezekiel spoke directly to this point regarding the saving of other people's souls in times of crisis: "Though Noah, Daniel, and Job, were in it, as I live, saith the Lord God, they shall deliver neither son nor daughter; they shall but deliver their own souls by their righteousness." Ezek. 14:20. There is also implied in this short parable the idea that the foolish virgins are still just that...foolish or stupid people. Because they are asking for salvation on the basis of their own carnal ideas...according to their own folly or foolish ways of reasoning. Of course, you cannot reason with such people so the wise virgins, realizing this, simply tell these foolish people that they will have to go and talk it over with their own preachers who may be able to "..sell them on their ideas," because obviously the foolish virgins are not buying the theology of the wise virgins.

Virginity represents purity of mind as well as direction and purpose. Paul speaks of being "shod with the gospel of peace." Shoes also represent your direction and purpose or your work in life. Although the foolish virgins are very sincere they are sincerely wrong. Their motive for doing what is right is based on pride and appearance. Spiritual pride has been the downfall of many sincere people. This has taken place in every generation. But in the great final age to come we have an altogether different ball game or marketplace, if you please. God, in His great wisdom, knows what He is doing in every age with His creatures. As the potter molds the clay, so the Creator molds each of us as He chooses. Our part is to believe in Him and trust in His love, wisdom and eternal goodness.

In conclusion, I want to share this statement from from ***Desire of Ages***. "The gospel is to be presented, not as a lifeless theory, but as a living force to change the life. God desires that the receivers of His grace shall be witnesses to its power. Those whose course has been most offensive to Him He freely accepts; when they repent, He imparts to them His divine Spirit, places them in the highest positions of trust, and sends them forth into the camp of the disloyal to proclaim His boundless mercy. He would have His servants bear testimony to the FACT that through His grace men may possess Christ-likeness of character, and may rejoice in the assurance of His great love. He would have us bear testimony to THE FACT that He cannot be satisfied until the human race are reclaimed and reinstated in their holy privileges as His Sons and daughters." DA 826.

This same writer also stated that just as surely as God has a place for us to work here below in this earth, He also has a place for us to work in heaven. I always wondered and puzzled over this statement. Now, in the light of what we have just studied we no longer need to wonder anymore. May the Lord richly bless each of you as you continue to pray and study for more understanding of the deeper things of the Word of the Living God. May His Living Waters truly flow forth from our lives to water the thirsty souls we brush shoulders with each and every day. Please know that I am praying for you. Thank you for your prayers for yours truly. I would love to hear from you. Your prayers and donations for this ministry are so very important to our ongoing outreach.

CHAPTER 21

LUCIFER WAS THE ORIGINAL OLDER BROTHER

In this chapter we are going to deal specifically with God's final judgment on Lucifer and all the fallen angels who left heaven with him before this world was created. Lucifer made himself into the devil or Satan, Ezekiel 28:15-18, which means adversary or destroyer. Satan has lost every single battle during the Great Controversy. Even when he has killed and slaughtered God's innocent people in the Old Testament he lost. But when he caused the Son of God to be nailed to the cross he really finished himself off. Up until that time the unfallen worlds and holy angels still had some sympathy for him. So, now we come to the last battle of the Great Controversy, which will take place after the 1,000 years. All the saved will be inside the city New Jerusalem and all the lost will be on the outside with Satan, looking in. Satan will form an army, like Esau did, to go after Jacob, Gen. 33:1.They will come up against the city and compass it about, Rev. 20:7-10.

Lucifer is like the older brother in the parable of the prodigal son. He has enslaved all those with him in his righteousness by works program of the flesh, and deceived them to believe that everyone inside the city is their enemy. There they are, "outside the camp," wailing and gnashing their teeth. Like the elder brother, they are "angry," and refuse to come in, Luke 15:28. And many an Israelite for whom the Kingdom was prepared will be in that vast army with Satan and his angels. The Bible predicted this would happen as a result of their refusal to accept Jesus as the Messiah. So, now they are "cast into outer darkness, into the place of weeping and torment." Matt. 8:11-12; 13:42, 50; 22:13; 24:51; 25:30. The Bible says "fear has torment," I Jn. 4:18, but "perfect love casts out fear."

One common characteristic of all the people outside of the Holy City who come up with Satan to try and destroy Jesus and

His saints is that they are filled with fear. Rev. 21:8. They have not known the Father's heart of love because they refused to go inside with Him to learn His true character. "And there will be great weeping and gnashing of teeth as you stand outside and see Abraham, Isaac, Jacob, and all the prophets within the Kingdom of God." Luke 13:28 LB. The KJV says the same thing, but ends with the words, "and you yourselves thrust out." But who thrust them out? "But woe unto you, scribes and Pharisees, hypocrites! For ye shut up the kingdom of heaven against men: for ye neither go in yourselves, neither suffer ye them that are entering to go in." Matt. 23:13. "But the pharisees and lawyers rejected the counsel of God AGAINST THEMSELVES, ..." Luke 7:30. No, my friend, God did not shut or thrust them out. They thrust themselves out, just as the people in Noah's day refused to go into the boat or ark. Gen. 6 and 7.

Yes, Lucifer was the original "older brother" who was jealous of his "younger brothers and sisters" down here on planet earth and found a way to hurt and destroy us. But, Jesus, our Creator, was sent by the Father to win us back to His love and bring us home again to the Father's house. The Father never stopped loving the older brother, but sought to win him back too, but to no avail. The Father even went out to plead with his older son. "And he (the older brother) was angry , and would not go in: therefore came his father out, and entreated him." Luke 15:28. When did the Father do this? He did it the very minute Lucifer began to go astray in heaven and he kept it up until Lucifer closed his heart and mind and "left" with his angels, Jude 6. "And his tail (the dragon's or Satan's tail) drew the third part of the stars of heaven, and did cast them to the earth:" Rev. 12:4. But the Father never gave up trying to entreat Lucifer (Satan). Isa. 14:12-14 is an eloquent appeal for Lucifer to look at himself and consider what he has done and is doing to himself. "Oh, Lucifer, my beloved, look at what you are doing to yourself. You are the greatest victim of your own deceptions." The Father even reveals the future suffering and defeat of Lucifer, but to no avail. Lucifer's heart is hardened.

The cross was another time in which the Father went out to entreat his older boy to come home. "All this is from God, who through Christ reconciled us to Himself and gave us the ministry of reconciliation; that is, in Christ, God was reconciling the world to Himself, not counting their trespasses against them, and entrusting to us the message of reconciliation." 2 Cor. 5:17-19. RSV. The noun world is from the Greek "cosmos" which also means "universe" or "ordered system." Heb. 1:12 tells us that the Father created the worlds through His Son.

Jesus' death not only reconciled this world, but the whole universe back to the Father. Revelation 12:9-13. There were many animal sacrifices, many different kinds, but one thing that was common was the place the sacrifice was offered. This place was the altar of burnt offering in the courtyard of the sanctuary but not in the holy or most holy place, for the blood of the animal was taken by the priest into the holy place and sprinkled on or before the curtain. This was symbolic of what Jesus would do for us. Paul explains it clearly: "Now, when sins have once been forever forgiven and forgotten, there is no need to offer any more sacrifices to get rid of them. And so, dear brothers, we may now walk right into the very Holy of Holies where God is, because of the blood of Jesus. This is the fresh, new, life-giving way which Christ has opened up for us by tearing the curtain—his human body—to let us go into the holy presence of God." Hebrews 10:19-20. LB.

The offering of the red heifer was different in that it was not killed or offered or burnt (not all the offerings were burnt in the same way) inside the courtyard of the sanctuary, but was taken completely "outside the camp." Num. 19:3. Calvary was outside the city gates of Jerusalem and so were all the non-Jews. He died for the Jew "outside" the city, for they would not accept his sacrifice He wanted to make inside for them. But Jesus died for the non-Jew or the Gentile, too, and His death outside the city gates symbolizes this.

Some of the animals that were sacrificed were burned up completely on the altar after they were ceremonially and literally washed and cut into pieces, then arranged on the altar so the form of the animal was recognized. Sometimes after the animal was killed and its blood taken into the holy place and sprinkled before the separating veil, the animal was taken outside of the camp and burned the entire animal, but sometimes only parts of it were taken outside the camp and burned. Exodus and Leviticus give detailed instructions on all of these sacrifices. Num. 19 gives the instruction for the red heifer. Sometimes the flesh of the animal was to be given to the priests to eat, Ex. 29:32. The washing of the parts of the animal before it was burned was symbolic of Christ's cleansing us from sin by His death. As we see the perfect, sinless, spotless and innocent LAMB OF GOD suffering on the cross, it should break our hearts and open our eyes to the enormity of sin and turn us away from our own sinful ways to the righteous ways of the Father. But it took Jesus' sufferings and death at the hands of professedly righteous and holy men to make us aware or to inform us and give us the knowledge we need to turn us away from sin toward God so He could cleanse us.

Jesus' blood, which was literally shed about A. D. 31, was symbolized in the death of all those poor animals in the Old Testament every time someone came to sacrifice a clean beast to get his sins forgiven. Today we do not sacrifice animals, for Jesus' death took that all away. But the lessons remain to point us to the work of Christ today in the Sanctuary in heaven; Heb. 4:15, 16. The washing of the animal's individual parts after it was dissected, and before it was placed on the altar to be offered, is symbolic of what the Word of God does to the believer who will permit God's Spirit to cleanse him from all of the filthiness of the flesh and spirit," 2 Cor. 7:1. For "Christ also loved the church and gave himself for it; that he might sanctify it with the washing of water by the word." Eph. 5:25, 26. When we permit Jesus to cleanse our human, earthly vessels (bodies and minds) we will be ready for temple service. That is, we are ready for the anointed golden oil which represents the Holy Spirit, to flow through our "candlestick," as it were, so we may be a light to the world. Matt. 5:14.

As we are "laid on the altar" the Lord arranges us, after His cleansing, in the perfect order He chooses, just as the sacrificed "killed" animal was set in order on the altar of sacrifice. Our lives may be confused and disarranged, but when we give our selves to Jesus He brings order out of chaos and sets us straight. This is what He did when He created the world in the beginning and this is what He does at the re-creation of every soul who willingly dies to self. Gal. 2:20; I Cor. 15:31.

The offering of the red heifer was completely different from any other offering in that the entire sacrifice took place "outside the camp." Num. 19. The heifer was not killed at the altar in the outer court of the sanctuary, like other animals. The whole ceremony was done outside the camp. This is a striking symbolism of what was done to Jesus. Although some of Jesus' blood was shed inside the city at the trial because of the stripes from the whipping or scourging, and when He sweat blood in Gethsamane, Jn. 19:1; Luke 22:44, He was not executed until He was taken outside of the city, just like the red heifer. But there are other differences we should note. The blood was not taken into the holy place of the sanctuary and sprinkled before the curtain, as in the other sacrifices. The priest took the blood and sprinkled it "toward the front of the meeting tent." How far away he was from it we are not told, but he did not take the blood and sprinkle it on or before the inner sacred veil. Neither were any of the animal's inner parts cut out and washed as with other sacrifices. In the case of the red heifer, the entire animal was burned and cedar wood and hyssop and scarlet were cast into the fire as a symbol of complete cleansing. And then the ashes of the red heifer were gathered and laid up outside the camp. This had to be done by a man who was ceremonially clean and then he had to wash again afterward.

We may draw many significant lessons from this offering of the red heifer. Everything God commanded Israel to do had meaning. I would encourage you to study, pray and search for more meanings for yourself, but let me just share with you the ones that I have learned so far. These have come through prayer and meditation mainly, for I have read all I could find on this outside the Bible and have found very little.

WHAT KIND OF FIRE KILLED JESUS?

First of all, the sprinkling of the blood "seven times before the tabernacle" represents the perfection of Christ's atoning blood for the forgiveness of our sins. The sacrifice and therefore, the forgiveness is total, complete and perfect. Second, just as the red heifer was "burned" outside the gate, so Jesus suffered the "burning" second death for us. The fire that wicked or lost will have to go through in the Lake of fire, which they will kindle or start themselves, is the "fire" that killed Jesus. In Mark 9:43-48 we read of "their worm" that doesn't die. Ps. 22:6 predicts the words Christ would say as he died for us. "I am a worm and no man." Jesus became a worm for us....the worm represents the ego or self life that refused to be "crucified with Christ." He became "sin for us." 2 Cor. 5:21.

Worms that destroy fruit work from the inside out. Just so, sin destroys a man from the inside out. Now, I want you to notice what will cause the wicked to "burn" on the inside on that final day of reckoning, when the Father, through his son again pleads with all the "older" brothers to come inside and join the celebration. In Psalm 21, which only has 13 verses, David is addressing his Lord Messiah, Jesus. "The King (God the Father) shall joy in thy strength, O Lord and in Thy salvation how greatly shall he rejoice! Thou has given him his heart's desire, and hast not with holden the request of his lips. Selah." Ps. 21:1-2. The Father asked the Son to bring back the wayward prodigals of this earth and the Son is now standing before his Father's throne with all the redeemed as a token of the accomplishment of His glorious mission. We also know that the king mentioned here can be applied to David and the Lord would be Jehovah. But, it also has a more eternal application to the real king of the universe, God the Father. But, let us go down to verse 8. Here

Christ is outside the city pleading with all the older sons. He holds out His hand. "Thine hand (Jesus' nail pierced-hand) shall find out all Thine enemies: Thy right hand shall find out those that hate thee." (Can't you picture Jesus stretching out his nail-pierced hands while he says, "look how much I loved you. Please come home with Me into My Father's house." But notice what this causes in the minds of the prodigals) Thou shalt make them as a fiery oven in the time of Thine anger: the Lord shall swallow them up in his wrath, and the fire shall devour them. Their fruit (the works of men with their evil fruit or result) shalt thou destroy from the earth, and their seed from among the children of men. 2 Pet. 3:10. For they intended evil against thee (Rev. 20:7-9 tells how all the wicked surround the city). They Imagined a mischievous device, which they are not able to perform. Ps. 21:8-11.

WHAT DOES FOREVER AND EVER MEAN?

The same concept of a burning inside "like or as an oven" is given in Mal. 4:1 and Hosea 7:4-6, Luke 12:28; "Surely, the people is grass." Isa. 40:6-7. Jesus said the tares would be burned in the end of the world, Matt. 13:40. John the Revelator pictures the wicked in this way also after "drinking" which means believing or accepting the false doctrine of the beast and receiving "his mark" and "the number of his name." Rev. 14:10-11 speaks of the wicked being "tormented with fire and brimstone," so that they will have no "rest day nor night," because they are worshiping the beast and his image. Is this awful torment in a literal fire? I do not think so, for the Bible says "the wicked will cease to exist on the earth," Ps. 37:10. How is that accomplished? Because the wickedness of the wicked will be destroyed in the cleansing of the Lake of Fire. The Bible does not teach an ever burning hell fire which is a slander against the loving character of our Heavenly Father. The words forever and everlasting mean as long as a thing exists. It is based on the Greek word "Aion," which simply means an "Age or Eon." The effect or result of the fiery destruction of sin and wickedness is forever, but it doesn't take forever to accomplish this. It only takes "a little season," which may last for at least 100 years.

The wicked who have died in the past without ever accepting Jesus as their SAVIOR are "asleep," as Jesus referred to death as a sleep in John 11:11. Paul said the same thing in I Thess. 4:13-18. Solomon agrees with this concept when he unequivocally (without any doubt) stated, "the dead know not anything." Eccles. 9:5, 6. A loving God also permits the sleep of death to hide all His beloved of the ages from the terrible sorrows that have come upon this earth during the last 6,000 years. "For so He giveth His beloved sleep." Psalm 127:2; 116:15. But, in that final second resurrection of the damned or lost (they have damned themselves by refusing Jesus) the wicked will see the reward of all the righteous saved inside of the city. This is what is going to cause them to be "burning up." This is the Lake of Fire because a lake is water and water represents people. See Rev. 17:15.

Let us look at some Scripture which will give more details of this coming event. "For the day of the Lord is near upon all the heathen; as thou hast done, it shall be done unto thee: thy reward shall return upon thine own head. Cf. Ps. 7:14-16; 9:15-16. But upon mount Zion (inside the holy city New Jerusalem) shall be deliverance, and there shall be holiness: and the house of Jacob shall possess their possessions. And the house of Jacob shall be a fire, and the house of Joseph a flame, and the house of Esau for stubble, and they shall kindle in them, and devour them; and there shall not be any remaining of the house of Esau; for the Lord hath spoken it." Obadiah 1:15, 16-18.

In this prophecy, the Lord is telling us something very special about what is going to happen at that final meeting of earth's teeming multitudes. The Jacobs and the Josephs will be on the inside and represent the saved. The Esaus represent the lost who will be on the outside. Jacob represents the prodigal who finally comes back home with his father's blessing, but the mother is not in the picture. Jacob's mother, Rebekah, died while Jacob was with Laban in the east. Gen. 35:29 and Gen. 49:31 speak of Isaac and Rebekah's death and burial. It mentions that Esau and Jacob buried Isaac together which seems to indicate Rebekah had already died and been buried before Jacob's return from Mesopotamia. The prodigal son's mother is not in the picture either although he surely had one. And the Mother God of Israel is also kept hidden throughout the Scriptures. But she will be revealed in this final age. See Additional Note #26. But in the parable of the Prodigal son the emphasis is upon the Father.

Esau is the older son who marches against his brother with an armed band of 400 to impress upon Jacob that he is superior in rank and power. Gen. 32:6. But, the Lord softens Esaus' heart so he ends up embracing him with a kiss. After all they were twin brothers. His former hatred melts away and he forgets his grudge. His revengeful plot and vow to kill Jacob for stealing the birth right is not carried out. The Holy Spirit changes his mind so that he does not perform his "mischievous plan." Ps. 21:11. Paul tells us in Phil. 2:10-11 that "every knee" is going to bow and "every tongue" is going to confess. Isa. 40:5 and Isa. 52:10 tell us that all of mankind will see God's salvation at the same time. "And the glory (character) of the Lord shall be revealed, and all flesh shall see it together: for the mouth of the Lord hath spoken it." Isa. 40:5.

Never in the history of the world have all the different races met. Now, they are together. The lost are on the outside of the city and the saved of all ages are on the inside. The whole human race from Adam to the last person who was born on this earth will meet for the first time. And remember that all the dead who died without Jesus' saving blood are lost outside the city. They are "the rest of the dead" that "lived not again until the thousand years were finished." Rev. 20:5. The last part of verse 5 is really describing the blessedness of the first resurrection. Here is what it says, "this is the first resurrection." And then verse 6 follows.

In other words, John the Revelator, who wrote this in

Greek, without chapter and verse division, has just told us in verse 5 about the "rest of the dead" who did not "live and reign with Christ a thousand years," v. 4. Verses 4 and 6 are about the saved, but verse 5, except for the last sentence, "this is the first resurrection," is about the lost. Throughout history we have seen a pattern. Cain, the older brother hated and even killed his younger brother, Abel. Esau and Jacob had a conflict over the birthright. Just as Cain wanted to go his own way and do his own thing, so Esau was a vain and rebellious person. He wanted the birthright without being spiritual.

Cain was religious and went through the rituals, his own man-made rituals, but he did not desire to be spiritual. So, we see that the first-born or older son was often religious, but not spiritual, and quite often ridiculed and even persecuted the younger son. Ishmael's treatment of Isaac is an example. The first generation of Israel, which came out of Egypt, were religious. They wanted the reward without obedience. They were religious, but not spiritual. The second generation was spiritual and obedient and inherited the promised land. King Saul is another example of an older son who despised, persecuted and even tried to kill David, the king after God's own heart. Saul was religious, but like Cain, he was religious on his own terms. He wanted to be king of Israel, but he didn't want the God of Israel to interfere with his plans. He was a type of Lucifer who became Satan. David was a type of Christ who became a servant, and sin for us so we might be brought back to the kingdom.

Finally, we have another parable Jesus told which is parallel to the prodigal son in one significant aspect. The parable begins in the same way, "A certain man had two sons;" Matt. 21:28. The father in the story asks both boys, very kindly, to go work in his vineyard. The first one refuses to go, but repents later and goes into the field. The second son promised to go, but never went. Christ made the following application of the parable: "Surely evil men and prostitutes will get into the Kingdom before you do."

The mental torment and anguish all the lost will feel when

they see that they are lost is beyond human comprehension, expression or experience. Jesus spoke about it in the parable of the rich man and Lazarus, Luke 16. The rich man refused to help the poor man Lazarus although he had many opportunities to help him. Lazarus was not only poor (a beggar), but sick. Finally both of them died. The rich man went to hell (gehenna), but the poor man, Lazarus, went to Abraham's bosom (heaven). The Pharisees actually believed in this theology and Jesus simply met them on their own terms, using their own concept of the after life to teach them that what they do in this life will determine their eternal destiny. He was not teaching the doctrine of hell-fire, as many believe. But he was trying to tell the Pharisees that they were headed for the same kind of torment that the rich man suffered. Now, the question I want to ask is: "what was causing the rich man to suffer?" I submit that the suffering was caused by the fact that Lazarus was saved and he was lost. He is outside the city and Lazarus is inside. But what really causes the most mental anguish is that the lost outside of the city will think that they should be inside because of their "good works." In His Olivet discourse Christ predicted these very events we are talking about right now. "Not everyone who says to Me, 'Lord, Lord,' will enter the kingdom...Many will say to Me...'Lord, Lord, did we not prophesy in Your name, and in Your name cast out demons, and in Your name perform many miracles? And then I will declare to them, 'I never knew you; depart from Me, you who practice lawlessness.'" Matt. 7:21-23. NAS. There again the hatred of God's law is manifested.

A contemporary rendering of this passage makes it even plainer: "Be wary of false preachers who smile a lot, dripping with practiced sincerity. Chances are they are out to rip you off some way or other. Don't be impressed with charisma; look for character. Who preachers are is the main thing, not what they say. A genuine leader will never exploit your emotions or your pocketbook. These diseased trees with their bad apples are going to be chopped down and burned. Knowing the correct password-saying 'Master, Master,' for instance-isn't going to get you anywhere with me. What is required is serious obedience—doing what my Father wills. I can see it now -- at the Final Judgment thousands strutting up to me and saying, 'Master, we preached the Message, we bashed the demons, our god-sponsored projects had everyone talking.' And do you know what I am going to say? 'You missed the boat. All you did was use me to make yourselves important. You don't impress me one bit. You're out of here." Matt. 7:15-23. The Message Bible.

In order to save us all from this fate Jesus told the parable of the Rich Man and Lazarus. "And in hell he lifted up his eyes, being in torments, and sees Abraham afar off, and Lazarus in his bosom." Luke 16:23. Verse 24 says, "And he cried and said, Father Abraham, have mercy on me, and send Lazarus, that he may dip the tip of his finger in water, and cool my tongue; for I am tormented in this flame." Now, I want to direct our attention back to Obadiah 1: 18. "And the house of Jacob shall be a fire, and the house of Joseph a flame, and the house of Esau for stubble, and they shall kindle in them, and devour them;" Why would Joseph be called "a flame?" Why would Jacob be called a "fire?" There is only one logical explanation. Jacob and Joseph are representatives of the saved who are inside the city in "Abraham's bosom," and Esau represents those who are on the outside lost. The knowledge that they (the wicked) are lost when they felt they had every right to be saved enrages them. They are "burning up" inside with hatred and envy. They are gnashing their teeth and stamping their feet and wailing and moaning their fate. Isaiah 31:9; Isaiah 33; Luke 13:24-30.

They are burning up inside like a "FIERY OVEN." Ps. 21:9. The "worm of sin" inside of them is being pierced by the SWORD OF TRUTH in the person of all the Jacobs and the Josephs who perfectly reflect the loving character of their Heavenly Father. Every time they look up and see a "Jacob" or a "Joseph" inside the golden city it is like a knife going right through their heart. That "worm" of hatred and envy (ego or carnal mind) is pricked and stabbed by the truth and their torment and agony is terrible. Jacob represents the younger brothers who went away from home. Jacob cheated his older brother Esau out of the birth right. The older brother in Jesus' parable felt cheated too because his Father gave his younger brother his inheritance before it was time. He had done nothing at all to deserve it. But if that wasn't bad enough this rebellious younger brother went out into the world and wasted it on wine, women and song only to be forgiven and given a big party when he comes home. "I have a right to be angry," he storms to his father. It reminds us of Jonah who was angry when God forgave all the Ninevehites when they repented. Jonah 4:1. Jonah wanted God to destroy them. It is interesting that it was a "worm" that destroyed the gourd the Lord "prepared" for Jonah to shield him from the heat of the sun. The word "shade" also means defense or protection. It was Jonah's anger, envy, jealousy and bitter attitude that was causing a separation between him and the Lord. Isa. 59:1. The worm of sin causes separation and death. Rom. 8:7.

Jesus died to destroy the darkness. His light never casts any shadows. In the parable of the rich man and Lazarus of Luke 16 we also notice that Father Abraham told the rich man (Dives in the Latin) to "remember" all the good things that he had received in his former life. Now, why would he ask him to remember if such a remembrance would only cause more mental torture? God is not like that. Why then would "Father Abraham" (who represents God the Father) remind him? There is only one possible answer. He is pleading with his "older" son to repent, for it is "the goodness of God" that leads to repentance, Rom. 2:4. Read all of chapter 2 for Paul is talking about the "Judgment of God." Remember that the word "judgment" means decision. It doesn't mean the final day when God condemns us, for God never accuses or condemns anyone. Jesus' invitation of mercy is an eternal invitation. "Him that cometh to Me I will in no wise cast out." Jn. 6:37. Jesus' loving character never changes, Hebrews 13:8. And Jesus said if we had seen Him we had seen the Father. So the Father's character never changes either. They are forever the same. His judgments or decisions are as the "Light" Hosea 6:5, 6. And God's light or fire is His love in Jesus, Song of Solomon 8:6: John 8:15; John 12:47.

You see, my friend, it is not God's heart that is hardened toward us that prevents us from receiving forgiveness and salvation. Oh, no! It is our hardened heart toward him that prevents us from receiving his love and forgiveness. Paul explains it perfectly. "Do you not know that God's kindness is meant to lead you to repentance? But by your hard and impenitent heart you are storing up wrath for yourself on the day of wrath when God's righteous judgment (decision to give you up to your own ways) will be revealed." Rom. 2:4-5. Remember that God's wrath is when we force God to give up on us. Judas refused to repent. Jerusalem refused to repent. The Jewish nation refused to repent. They forced God out of their lives by their continual rejection of His pleas for them to come to Him. It wasn't that God had quit calling them, for God's love will never allow Him to give up, but their hardened hearts cannot hear Him anymore. Yet God always puts the blame on Himself, instead of on us.

In Isaiah 59:2 God takes the blame by saying, "He will not hear" when the previous verse makes it clear that God doesn't have an ear problem. Israel has a heart problem—a hardened heart. Hardened by sin. "Your iniquities have separated between you and your God." In Isa. 53:10 God takes the blame for "bruising" his own Son. In I Chron. 10:13, 14 God claims to have killed King Saul when we know Saul killed himself. The Scripture abounds with this concept from beginning to end—our wonderful Father taking the blame—shielding us, always protecting us. And he does it right to the very last. Oh, my beloved friend, we have not the slightest inkling of this Mighty God of Israel who took on a body of flesh and lived among us. But, it is the Father's will that we do know....that we do understand. For we must have His character or we will not survive the final holocaust of hate that is soon to engulf this world. Only the love in our wonderful Father's heart will shield us from it. That is why we must go into the Father's heart. It is safe in there. In this parable we are not told if the elder son ever accepts the invitation of the father to come inside the house and join in the celebration. All we saw was the Father going out to plead with the older son to come in to the celebration feast. The red heifer or fatted calf has been killed, but instead of mourning, there is rejoicing. Why? Because there has been a resurrection. "For this my son was dead, and is alive again: he was lost, and is found. And they began to be merry." Luke 15:24. When Jesus died on Friday afternoon, about the ninth hour, Matt. 27:46-50, there was mourning and weeping. But on Sunday morning, there was rejoicing. Remember, Jesus became "sin" for us. He became a prodigal for us. He left the Father's house and went into the "far country" and became a "lost Son" in our place. But the lost is now found and there is rejoicing. But the older "son(s)" do not rejoice. They are the Pharisees and scribes who have never "transgressed" the Father's law "at any time." They are legalists and believe they have achieved perfection through self-righteous adherence to the law. They believe in a pseudo-perfection, a human, man-made, do-it-yourself type religion. These are the older brother types in the "church," but not in Christ who despise the return of the prodigal in every age. They refuse to accept them as brothers and/or sisters in Christ. But the father still loves the older sons. He cannot give up on them. His love will never let them go. And that is why we know that the final outcome of the father's efforts will be successful.

In Charles Pridgeon's book, "IS HELL ETERNAL OR WILL GOD'S PLAN FAIL?" he deals with the concept of Universal Restoration as opposed to eternal hell fire and annihilation. In chapter 27 he quotes from some of the early fathers of the first centuries of the Christian religion and their belief in what he calls "Restitution" but what I call "Universal Reconciliation" or "Universal Restoration," which is the term Acts 3:21 uses in the New English Bible. "He (Jesus) must be received into heaven until the time of UNIVERSAL RESTORATION comes, of which God spoke by his holy prophets." Pridgeon studied the doctrine of the early fathers of the first five centuries of the Christian era very diligently and made this statement: "There is no word in these early statements of creed declaring in favor of endless punishment. It is passing strange that we have to wait 553 years after Christ before any attempt is made officially to condemn the doctrine of restitution, and then many of those who began to dominate Christian thought could not even read the New Testament in the original Greek." Page 279. I will not take the time or space here to quote all of his sources which include Irenaeus, Theophilus, Bishop of Antioch, Eusebius, Ambrose and many others. Here is one from Clement of Alexandria, 150-220 A.D., Presbyter of Alexandria. "The Lord is a propitiation not for our sins only but also for the whole world! Therefore, He indeed saves all universally but some are converted by punishments, others by voluntary submission, thus obtaining the honor and dignity, that to Him 'every knee shall bow of things in heaven, and things in earth, and things under the earth.'" Page 280.

Another work which documents the truth that Universal Salvation was the creed and teaching of the early church fathers is "THE ANCIENT HISTORY OF UNIVERSALISM," by Hosea Ballou, published in 1829. In this 326 page volume he traces its history from the time of the apostles, to its condemnation in the fifth general council, A.D. 553. There is a companion volume, entitled, "THE MODERN HISTORY OF UNIVERSALISM," by Thomas Whittemore, which became the basis for many later studies of the history of the belief that God will eventually save all mankind. There has been an explosion of this doctrine in the last few years and is all over the internet. More and more ministers and teachers are accepting it and preaching it. I myself did not accept it at first. But chapter 26 of Pridgeon's book, "CONCERNING THE SALVATION OF ANGELS AND DEMONS," convinced me it is true in 1986. There are many books available on this topic and more being written all the time. This concept, more than any other, will take you into the Father's Heart, for this is what He has planned to do from the beginning. "Having made known unto us the mystery of His will, according to His good pleasure which He hath purposed in Himself: That in the dispensation of the fulness of times He might gather together in one all things in Christ, both which are in heaven, and which are on earth; even in Him." Ephesians 1:9, 10.

JOHN WYCLIFFE BELIEVED IN UNIVERSALISM

John Wycliffe, the Morning Star of the reformation, 1330 to 1384 AD, was the first English scholar to translate the Scriptures from Latin into English. The entirety of Chapter 5 of the book, "THE GREAT CONTROVERSY," entitled, "JOHN WYCLIFFE," pages 79 to 96 is devoted to his life. However, what is not mentioned is the fact that Wycliffe, in his Bible commentary taught the concept of Universal Restoration. Here is what he wrote: ***"Drawing from Isaiah 45:23, where the Lord prophesies that universal worship will one day be given Him, the author (Paul) writes that in the name of Jesus (not at, which might suggest mechanical genuflection) the totality of created, rational beings will pay due homage. Those in heaven, on earth, and underground is an expression of universality and should not be forced." He also wrote that "The compound verb 'confess' (exomologeo) may mean to 'confess with Thanksgiving.'" Page 1325. From John Wycliffe's commentary on Philippians 2:10, 11. His comments on Psalm 22:27-31 (page 503) were similar. "His joyful anticipation. 'All the ends of the world.' In hope, the Psalmist sees the circle widen to include all mankind and future generations. His personal hope encompass the nation and then the world. In accord with the highest hope of Israel, the turning of mankind to God in worship (Isa 40:7; 45:22;52:10)."***

CHAPTER 22

ESAU AND JACOB

In the majestic prophecies of Isaiah we find some of the most sublime imagery in human literature. Isaiah 63 is an example. Here again we pick up on the theme of the older brother, and it is a familiar face, Edom or Esau. His name means "red," because when he was born he "came out red, all over like an hairy garment; and they called his name Esau." Now, let us notice again in Genesis 25 how Esau picked up the nickname of Edom. "And Esau said to Jacob, feed me,' (the margin says, 'let me wolf or swallow.') I pray thee, with that same red pottage; for I am faint: therefore was his name called Edom (that is red)." Genesis 25:25, 30. Swallow also means to devour, which is characteristic of Satan, 1 Peter 5:8. CF. Psalms 27:1-4.

Now notice how Esau or Edom is mentioned here in Isaiah 63. "Who is this that cometh from Edom, with dyed garments from Bozrah? this that is glorious in his apparel, traveling in the greatness of his strength? I that speak in righteousness, mighty to save. Wherefore art thou red in thine apparel, and thy garments like him that treadeth in the winefat? I have trodden the winepress alone; and of the people there was none with me: for I will tread them in mine anger, and trample them in my fury; and their blood shall be sprinkled upon my garments, and I will stain all my raiment. For the day of vengeance is in mine heart, and the year of my redeemed is come ... And I will tread down the people in mine anger, and make them drunk in my fury, and I will bring down their strength to the earth." Isaiah 63:1-4, 6. Edom also represents the land of ego, hell, or bottomless pit. Jesus went to the bottomless pit and hell for us to destroy the carnal mind or ego, so our true self or identity could be resurrected in Christ. The bottomless pit or hell is the grave.

ISAIAH 63

Bozrah was the city of Jobab, son of Zerah, son of Reuel, son of Esau. Jobab was the second king of Edom. Remember that Edom is Esau, older brother of Jacob. And remember that Jacob received the birthright instead of Esau and that Esau vowed to kill Jacob. Jacob had sinned, but repented. Esau never repented, for all he wanted was the material possessions of the birthright, not the moral and spiritual blessings and responsibilities. Esau forfeited the birthright on this basis alone, but still God granted him the chance to prove himself just as He gave King Saul a chance, and Judas a chance. God never rejects anyone. He treats all equally and fairly. James 1:5, Acts 10:34, 1 Peter 1:17. Job 34:19. But Esau failed as did King Saul. See Hebrews 12:16, 17.

Isaiah 63 pictures Jesus as coming from Edom with red stained, bloody-looking garments. He is claiming to be killing people and the proof is that their blood is sprinkled on his garments. He specifically is talking about all the people that he has just killed over at "Edom." Without deep spiritual understanding a person cannot comprehend this. "The foolishness of God is wiser than men." 1 Corinthians 1:25. Did not Jesus "kill" Judas by bringing Judas to a definite point of decision? He came out plainly, "one of you shall betray me." He was trying to stop Judas from this terrible act of suicide. He knew what Judas was about to do. He also knew that Judas was blind to the results, for he did not know or realize that when he kissed Jesus to identify Him that this was a "kiss of death." Not for Jesus, for he rose from the grave. It was the kiss of death for Judas. Judas just sealed his doom for that age. Of course, Jesus did die, and Judas betrayed him, but Judas did not have to be the one. It was his own choice. Jesus, did everything to stop him.

Now, friend of mine, Jesus never changes. Hebrews 13:8. Malachi 3:6. If Christ in His great love tried to stop just one human being from killing himself, how much more would He try to stop millions and billions of his beloved creatures from blowing each other up outside the city walls? The Father, through his Son, holds out the proof, the greatest evidence He can give them, of his undying love by stretching out that powerful right hand with the nail wound in it. "I love you. I died for you. Please accept Me. Don't reject Me. Don't do it, for it will cause you incredible suffering." Here then Psalms 21:8-12 will find its fulfillment. Revelation 20:12 tells us that "the books were opened: and another book was opened, which is the book of life* and the dead were judged out of those things which were written in the books... according to their works." Revelation 17:15 tells us that "waters" represent people. Therefore a "lake of fire," Revelation 20:10-14, which will be a human lake in its final phase is first of all, a mass of humanity, a lake of humanity, burning up inside "like an oven." There will be hatred and cursing. There will be wailing and gnashing of teeth. Everyone will be blaming someone else for being on the outside instead of the inside. All the Esaus look inside the city and see all the Jacobs and all the Josephs and it just burns them up with envy and jealousy. "The house of Jacob shall be a fire, and the house of Joseph a flame, and the house of Esau stubble; they shall burn them and consume them, and there shall be no survivor to the house of Esau." Obadiah 1:18. R.S.V.; Psalms 22:29.

The story of salvation will be seen by all and everyone outside of that city will see just where they refused Jesus' love. "The heavens shall declare his righteousness: for God is judge himself. Selah." Psalms 50:6. The opening of the books refers to a cosmic display of the entire 6,000 year struggle between good and evil. It would include all the facts in every person's life from Lucifer to the last lost man to live on this earth before Christ returns. All the saved would also be included. Just as Jesus made a last minute effort to save the Pharisees and Scribes (Matthew 23), by facing them squarely with their self-righteousness and futile efforts to save themselves so they would repent and be saved, so the Father

* The book of life would also represent the Father's heart. Isaiah 49:16; Psalms 80:17; Psalms 40:7, 8. Jesus Christ is the Father's Book of life.

pleads one last time with all of His older sons, all of His Esaus to repent and come into the house. He reveals their whole life history to them. It is a "strange act" for Him, for God has never before let everyone see all their sins at once. He has shielded them from that, but now in a desperate effort to bring them to their senses he reveals it all. The sky is like a giant movie screen. And it works, because all will bow down and confess.

Remember that God already knows that they will repent. That is why He does this. There are many relatives and friends inside that city who long for their brothers and sisters, mothers and fathers, sons and daughters to come inside with them. They are weeping and heartbroken over it. For their sake the Father makes this appeal, but not only for them, but because He loves them too. It is His eternal unchanging nature to love. He can't help Himself. "Oh, how can I give you up, My Ephraim? How can I let you go? How can I forsake you like Admah and Zeboim? My heart cries out within Me; how I long to help you!" Hosea 11:8 Living Bible. Our heavenly Father and His Son Jesus Christ are eternal and incurable lovers. The Bible pictures God's love in many, many ways. You can find it all throughout the Scriptures. John 3:16 is a well known classic. Isaiah 49:15, 16; 1 Corinthians 3:7. God's love never quits, never gives up. ***Jesus never fails.***

Will there be tears in that city as the saved inside watch their loved ones and friends? Yes, there will be tears, but listen to the promise. "And God shall wipe away all tears from their eyes; and there shall be no more death, neither sorrow, nor crying, neither shall there be any more pain: for the former things are passed away." Revelation 21:4. For all the lost are found.

THE MARK OF THE BEAST DEFINED

Notice also in Revelation 14 that the only people who suffer the "wrath of God," which is when he is forced to give up on a person, are those who receive or take by their own choice, the Mark of the Beast. Notice that the second coming of Christ does not take place until verse 14 and the torment in the presence of the holy angels and the Lamb takes place in verses 10 and 11. Besides this, the scenes here described are taking place before the seven last plagues, which occur before the second coming of Jesus. However, chapter 14 gives the whole scene here, taking us up to the second coming of Christ. Note the expression, "the same (whoever takes the mark) shall drink of the wine of the wrath of God . . ." Revelation 14.10. The word "shall" indicates future tense. In other words these verses are describing the decisions and events that lead up to the pouring out of the plagues which take place before the end of our age and Christ's return. Therefore, the "torment" of Revelation 14 does not take place in hell after Christ's return or any time before in some hollow place in the earth which men would say is hell. No. The events here described take place right here on earth in the sight of the holy angels. The Mark of the Beast represents the character of the carnally minded who are bowing down to the false god of Sun(day) worship, Satan, just before Jesus comes.

These people are suffering mental torment because they have rejected God and His truth. But there is something else we must understand. The torment the lost will suffer, which is described in Revelation 14 through 22 in various ways, is a torment that the lost of all ages will experience after the 1,000 years. When they come up around that holy city to capture it and/or destroy the saints and the Father and the Son and anyone else who opposes them, they are going to be tormented in their minds and bodies as they realize they cannot win. The specific torment described in Revelation 14, before Christ comes the 2nd time, will be experienced twice by those alive in the final generation of opposers of God and his truth and his people who live and preach that final message of truth. Daniel 12:2 and Revelation 1:7 indicates that there will be a special resurrection for some of the saved and some of the lost just before Jesus comes. I say there will be a "specific" torment for those who reject the truth about the Father in this Final generation or age.

Because, that same torment will be experienced again by the lost of all ages after the 1,000 years when they too come to a full realization of what they have lost. The lost of this present generation will be there too and will suffer further torment. It is not that God wants or wishes this for them, for He longs to deliver them from it, but He cannot force them to come into His house. Although the "mark of the beast" is being developed and perfected in our day, it has always existed in every age in one form or another. The older brothers have always been used by Satan to hurt the younger. After the 1,000 years, at Christ's 3rd coming to this earth, the mark of the beast will be fully perfected by Satan again and all the lost outside the city will be under its power and authority and will suffer because of it. The simplest definition of the mark of the beast is FORCED WORSHIP and it can be forced upon you by another person or an organization or by you yourself. If you are "forcing" yourself to pray over your food, read religious literature, the Bible included, or if you are "forcing" yourself to go to church or to "act" religious or perform religious "duties" of any kind, you are already experiencing to a degree, what it will be like when the mark of the beast is really in full swing. You are, as it were, just getting warmed up for it. Excuse the pun, but I hope you get the point. In that day, the heat will not only be on people, it will be in them, for they will "burn like an oven" on the inside, from guilt, remorse, regret and hatred. Malachi 4:1; Hosea 7:6; Psalms 21:8, 9. More specifically, Sun(day) worship is the sign of the Death God and 7th day Sabbath is the sign of the Life-God. Exodus 20:8-11.

Notice again Christ's effort to save Judas at the last supper. "After supper he gave them another glass of wine, saying, this is the token of God's new agreement to save you -- an agreement sealed with my blood I shall pour out to purchase back your souls. But here at this table, sitting among us as a friend, is the man who will betray me. I must die. It is part of God's plan. But, oh, the horror awaiting that man who betrays Me." Luke 22:20-22 Living Bible. This suffering causes them to repent.

The disciples were shocked and stunned. Who among them, would even think of such a dastardly deed! Let alone carry it out! And yet verse 24 says "and they began to argue among themselves as to who would have the highest rank (in the coming kingdom)." Living Bible. We look back and shake our heads at their blindness, but do we see any more clearly today? Do we understand the Father's character of love anymore than they did? I truly hope so, but unless we are continually "watching unto prayer," we too may sleep as did the disciples in the garden, when Jesus had told them, "pray that ye enter not into temptation." Luke 22:40. Jesus then went away from them "about a stone's cast, and kneeled down, and prayed." verse 41. He prayed that if the plan of salvation could be carried out any other way, except for the coming separation of the Father's presence, that it be done. Jesus did not fear physical torture and abuse. He did not enjoy it, for He was not a masochist, but this was not what made Him ask this special consideration. The Father's presence had always been with Him in an unlimited measure, John 3:34, ML. But, can you imagine how much the Father must have been suffering? "0, Daddy, if there is any other way to save the world and convince the universe that you are innocent from the false charges that Lucifer has brought against you, please let this cup pass from me. I don't want you or the angels or the unfallen worlds to have to see me suffer. And I know everyone will turn against Lucifer. If there is any other way, let this cup pass from me. But, thy will be done." It is estimated that Christ's three season's of prayer lasted about two hours.

The mental torture that Jesus endured in His struggle against sin and the forces of Satan were so powerfully oppressive that He actually sweat blood. Luke, the beloved physician, is the only one of the four gospel writers who mentions it. He received his information about the life of Jesus from eyewitnesses like John and Peter and James who saw Jesus sweat blood. Being a doctor of medicine he must have immediately recognized this as an important phenomenon. And truly it is.

A book entitled "*Behold the Man*" by Taylor G. Bunch, 1940, refers to this blood-sweating incident on pages 35-37 of his book. "While the sweating of blood is a very rare occurrence, it is not unknown to history and to medical science. It is known to medical authorities as diapedesis. The word is defined by Webster thus: 'The passage of the corpuscular elements of the blood from the blood vessels into the surrounding tissues. A few notable cases have been left on record by historians and physicians where persons under great physical strain, mental anguish, or intense fear, have actually sweat blood.' Since this is true, it was certainly the most natural thing that could have happened to Jesus while passing through a season of physical suffering and mental fear and anguish so terrible that it surpasses the utmost stretch of the human mind to portray."

THE CAUSE OF DIAPEDESIS

"Of the possibility and cause of diapedesis, G. H. Kannegiesser, a German physician, wrote: 'Violent mental excitement.... and in like manner sudden terror, or intense fear, forces out a sweat.... If the mind is seized with a sudden fear of death, the sweat, owing to the excessive degree of constriction, often becomes bloody." - German "Ephemerides," quoted by William Stroud, M.D., in The Physical Cause of the Death of Christ, page 86. Dr. Stroud was at one time the President of the Royal Medical Society of Scotland, and his book was endorsed by some of the leading physicians of the British Isles. His book was first published in 1847."

Of this rare occurrence another physician wrote: "Of all the maladies which affect cutaneous transpiration, diapedesis, or sweating of blood, is the most singular; so much so indeed, that its existence has been doubted, although several well-authenticated cases are on record, both in the ancient and modern annals of medicine. It is mentioned by Theophrastus, Aristotle, and Lucan. The base Charles IX of France sank under this disorder, as stated by Mezeray. The same historian relates the case of a governor of a town taken by storm, who was condemned to die, but was seized with a profuse sweating of blood the moment he beheld the scaffold. Lombard mentions a general who was affected in a similar manner on losing a battle.... It is probable that the strange disorder arises from a violent commotion of the nervous system, turning the streams of blood out of their natural course, and forcing the red particles into the cutaneous excretories." - Curiosities of Medical Experience, J. G. Millingen, M.D., vol. 2, pp. 338-342. (Stroud.)

S. A. D. Tissot, a Swiss physician and author who lived between 1728 and 1779, reported the case of "a sailor who was so alarmed by a storm, that through fear he fell down, and his face sweated blood, which during the whole continuance of the storm returned like ordinary sweat, as fast as it was wiped away." - Traite des Nerfs, pages 279, 280. (Stroud) Dr. Schenck, a German physician, cites the case of "a nun who fell into the hands of soldiers; and, on seeing herself encompassed with swords and daggers threatening instant death, was so terrified and agitated, that she discharged blood from every part of her body, and died of hemorrhage in the sight of her assailants." - Joannes Schenck a Grafenberg, in Observ. Medic., lib. 3, p. 458. (Stroud).

Writing of the death of Charles IX of France, F. M. Voltaire said: "The disease which carried him off is very uncommon; his blood flowed from all his pores. This malady, of which there are some examples, is the result either of excessive fear, furious passion, or of a violent and melancholic temperament." - Euvres Completes, vol. 18, pp. 531, 532. (Stroud.)

DeMezeray, a French historian, declared of the same case: "During the last two weeks of his life, his constitution made strange efforts. He was affected with spasms and convulsions of extreme violence. He tossed and agitated himself continually, and his blood gushed from all the outlets of his body, even from the pores of his skin, so that on one occasion he was found bathed in a bloody sweat." - Histoire de France, vol. 3, p. 306. (Stroud.)

The French historian, De Thou, tells of "an Italian officer who commanded at Monte-Maro, a fortress of Piedmont, during the warfare in 1552, between Henry II of France and the emperor Charles V. This officer, having been treacherously seized by order of the hostile general, and threatened with public execution unless he surrendered the place was so agitated at the prospect of an ignominious death, that he sweated blood from every part of his body." The same author also wrote of a young Florentine at Rome, unjustly put to death by order of Pope Sixtus V, and concludes the narrative as follows: "When the youth was led forth to execution, he excited the commiseration of many, and through excess of grief, was observed to shed bloody tears, and to discharge blood instead of sweat from his whole body." - The Physical Cause of the Death of Christ, Stroud, pages 86, 87. Other historic and scientific testimony might be given, but this is sufficient to prove that the sweating of blood is not only possible under excessive pain and fear, but that it has actually happened on many different occasions. "Thus, once more, destructive Biblical criticism has been silenced by the facts of history and science."

The word "diaphoresis" is a closely related term referring to actual sweating or perspiration, especially when profuse and caused by artificial means. The Greek word, "thromboi" meaning thick drops or clots is translated "drops or great drops of blood." The International Critical Commentary gives historical instances of persons whose pores have exuded a bloody sweat. Some scholars have omitted verses 43, 44, because certain manuscripts show it missing. But, the weight of evidence favors retaining them. That is, other ancient manuscripts include these verses. Living Bible footnote on Luke 22:43, 44.

Matthew Henry's Commentary (written around 1704-1710), says, "Every pore was as it were a bleeding wound, and his blood stained all his raiment. This showed the travail of his soul." Matthew Henry's Commentary on Luke 22:43, 44, page 1495.

Again Isaiah predicted Christ's agonies. "Behold my servant shall deal prudently, he shall be exalted and extolled, and be very high (or lifted up as the Revised Standard Version says). As many were astonied at thee; his visage was so marred more than any man and his form more than the sons of men." Isaiah 52:13-14. (Many think of the beatings etc. at his trial, but this also has reference to the terrible mental struggles he went through in the 40 day fast and temptation afterward. However, the struggle in Gethsamne is even worse, as He sweats blood, "striving against sin," as Paul tells us in Hebrews 12:4. "So shall he sprinkle (Cf. Isaiah 63:3) many nations: the kings shall shut their mouths at him: for that which had not been told them shall they see; and that which they had not heard shall they consider." Isaiah 52:13—15.

If God had acted as men thought He would and should act, our Father would have killed anyone who dared touch His Son. But would this have drawn anyone to the Father? No, it would have terrified them, just as all the other terrible calamities of the Old Testament had done, e.g. the flood, Sodom, Uzzah. We, in our carnal, fleshly, finite minds indict the Father and His Son for murder on the basis of these incidents, which are nothing more than circumstantial evidence. Are you willing to stand on a witness stand and claim that you believe God is guilty of murder on the basis of these scanty, fragmented, accounts? And remember that all throughout the Old Testament God is always taking the blame. Look at Isaiah 53:10. "Yet it pleased the Lord to bruise him; he hath put him to grief." The Father here claims to be hurting his own Son. Once you understand how God is always doing this throughout the whole Bible, you will begin to really understand the plan of salvation.

In the Most Holy place of the sanctuary, beyond the sacred veil, was the ark of the covenant. The word "covenant" simply means "agreement." God is saying, "I have agreed with my son that He will come and get you out of this terrible predicament you are in. If you will enter into this agreement with us, we will be able to carry out our rescue mission successfully. You will have new bodies again and a beautiful new earth again." And so the covenant is really God's promise to save us.

The ark of the covenant or agreement was the center of action and the real goal of this desert drama, for that is where the very presence of the Eternal God rested. Now, this little ark was 4 ft. 4 in. long and 2 ft. 7 in breadth or width and 2 ft. 7 in. high. It was made of shittim wood (Exodus 25:5) or acacia, a hard, durable, and close-grained wood, suitable for cabinet-work. The Father's presence was just above the ark. The whole box was to be overlaid with pure gold, including the lid to the box, which was called the "mercy-seat." It was also known as the covering, since it "covered" the ark or box. Exodus 25:10 Says the ark was 2 1/2 cubits long, 1 1/2 cubit wide and 1 1/2 cubit high. There were long cubits and short ones in Bible times. The measurements given above are based on Egyptian cubits and royal Egyptian cubits since Moses was educated in Pharaoh's court. Most people think of a cubit as 18 inches. The common Egyptian cubit was 17.7 and the royal was 20.6 inches which is what the above figures are based upon.

But, let's consider the covering or lid of the ark, which is called, "the mercy seat." It was also made of acacia wood and overlaid with pure gold, representing God's love, mercy and faith. But it means much more. It means that God is covering up for us. I mean he is taking the blame for us. Deuteronomy 10:5 tells us God commanded Moses to put the two tables of stone (Ten Commandments or law of God that he wrote with his own finger) inside of the ark. Paul confirms this in Hebrews 9:1-5. By Solomon's time only the Ten Commandments were in the ark. That law is what condemns us as sinners. It is like a mirror which points out our sins. It is God's perfect standard of obedience that no human in his own strength could ever keep after Adam fell and passed on to us his weak, fallen, degenerate and disobedient nature. We are not born sinners, but we have a natural inclination and leaning toward it which is impossible to resist, therefore every man has sinned. But through Jesus we can become obedient. But it is only because our wonderful Heavenly Father has taken the first step toward us that we have hope, for we are not naturally attracted to our Heavenly Father. We have a fallen nature which must be exchanged for the divine nature of Christ, who is the express image, of the Father. It is not natural for us to love. No, it is natural for us to hate. It is not natural for us to want to give. It is natural for us to take. If we are raised by godly parents who teach us the truth of God's law we are most fortunate, but even in the most religious homes there are rebels. And even the children who are "righteous" or "good kids" we find have a struggle. Some more and some less, but all have a struggle against sin. The Bible has declared that none are righteous, "no, not one." "For all have sinned and come short of the glory (character) of God." Romans 3:23 KJV.

And so we need mercy and God showed that he had given that mercy in the Most Holy place of the sanctuary, over the ...mercy seat. Here the blood of a bullock was to cleanse a priest of all sin before he was ready to make atonement for all the people. This young bull (Christ was a young man) was a sin offering for the high priest and for his whole house or family. Leviticus 16:11. This was the "day of atonement" or "yom kippur."

Then after atonement had been made with this "sin offering," for himself and his family, he was to offer a ram for a burnt offering. Verse 3. But the atonement for all of Israel was made with two goats. Lots were cast and one goat became the "Lord's goat," and the other became the "scape goat." Just as the bullock was killed and its blood sprinkled seven times over the mercy seat and also over the altar in the outer court, so the same thing was done with the Lord's goat. Then when Aaron came out of the most holy place and had made atonement for all of Israel, "Aaron shall lay both his hands upon the head of the (live) goat, and confess over him all the iniquities of the people of Israel, and all their transgressions, all their sins; and he shall put them upon the head of the goat, and send him away into the wilderness by the hand of a man who is in readiness. The goat shall bear all their iniquities upon him to a solitary land; and he shall let the goat go in the wilderness." Leviticus 16:21-22.

The goat which died would have to represent Christ who

made atonement for our sins. The scape goat (Azazel in the Hebrew) escaped alive. Now, who does this represent? It would have to represent the one who is responsible for all the evil that has gone on in the world since sin began. God is not responsible, so the live goat or scapegoat does not represent the Father or his Son. The goat that was slain represents Christ's death on the cross for us. He is willing to die that all of His creatures who will accept His death may live. This includes even Satan. This goat going into the wilderness alive is symbolic of Satan during the 1,000 years. All the saints are reigning with Jesus in the Father's house (John 14:1-3; Revelation 20:4-5) and all the wicked are dead. Only Satan and his angels are here roaming the earth. They cannot stand truth and righteousness, light and glory, so they stay here by their own choice, since it is more comfortable or perhaps I should say, less painful here on this earth than in any other place in the universe. In Greek mythology, Pan was a "god" of nature who had the legs and hips of a goat, but the arms and face of a man. Sometimes he even had the horns and ears of a goat. This was a representation of Satan, although the people thought it was one of the gods. Pan destroys the nature he is supposed to protect.

Someone may be asking, "will Satan and his angels be saved?" The Bible predicts that the devil will be "tormented" in the lake of fire "day and night" with all the wicked "forever and ever." Revelation 20: 10. This everlasting fire" is prepared only for the "devil and his angels." Matthew 25:41. The phrase "forever and ever" and "everlasting" again do not mean "without end," for the Bible teaches that Satan will come to an end. In fact he will be brought to "ashes," right here on the earth in the sight of all the righteous who are safe inside the city. Ezekiel 28:18.

The question is this: What does the word "ashes" really mean? Well, I have already explained that in an earlier chapter but it bears repeating.

"Among the ancient Hebrews, to put on sackcloth and ashes, or to lie in them, or to sprinkle ashes on the head was a token of grief and mourning , 2 Sam 13:19; Esther 4:1, 3; Job 2:8; Neh 9:1. To sit in ashes was also a sign of penitence Jonah 3:6; cf. Job 42:6." Bible Dictionary, page 82. Therefore, when we see the word "ashes" in Ezek. 28:18 we know this is a sign and prediction of a future event when Lucifer will be brought to "grief, mourning and repentance" in the sight of the whole universe. And, like the prodigal son, he will repent and be welcomed back with open arms because Lucifer is the first prodigal son and the last to finally come back home.

Sometimes when you first read a verse it may seem pretty harsh. It sounds like God is going to get even with the devil in the final day by destroying him with fire. But, is that really what God is saying here? No, it isn't, for we know the Father is not like that. Why? Because Jesus painted an altogether different picture of him. For example, let's read in just one place how Jesus pictured his Father.

"If a child asks his father for a loaf of bread, will he be given a stone instead? if he asks for fish, will he be given a poisonous snake? Of course not! And if you hard-hearted, sinful men know how to give good gifts to your children, won't your Father in heaven even more certainly give good gifts to those who ask Him for them?" Matthew 7:9-41. Living Bible.

IS GOD TO BLAME FOR LUCIFER'S FALL?

Now, we know Lucifer or Satan, as he is now named due to his own actions, was created by the Father in a glorious, pristine state-absolutely perfect. Ezekiel 28:15. It was Lucifer who made himself into what he is now-a devil. Isaiah 14:12-14. God is not to blame for Lucifer's original sin, his fall, for Jude 6 tells us he "left," heaven. Nor is God to be blamed for His final terrible suffering and death to self.

In fact, the Father has been doing all he can to protect and preserve Lucifer so he would not destroy himself or his evil angels. Why else would Satan bow down with all the rest of human race at the end of the 1,000 years? Philippians 2:10 and

Psalms 22:29 refer to this. And John the Revelator says this song will be sung, "Who shall not fear thee, 0 Lord, and glorify thy name? for thou art holy: for all nations shall come and worship before thee; for thy judgments (decisions) are made manifest." Revelation 15:4. James tells us that the devils even believe and tremble, James 2:19. They admitted Christ was the Son of God and worshiped him in fear, Mark 1:34, 5:6, 7.

We already know that the fire that destroys Satan comes from inside of the devil himself. God's fire always gives life. It does not destroy. Jesus said, "I am come to send fire on the earth . . ." And what was that fire? It was His eternal love, for on the day of Pentecost God's fire came on the disciples and they spoke in different languages about "the wonderful works of God." Acts 2:11. Ezekiel saw God's messengers as living creatures (beings)" which "ran and returned as the appearance of a flash of lightning." Ezekiel1:14. Daniel saw a "fiery stream" come forth from God's throne. Daniel 7:10.

The angel which rolled back the stone from Jesus' grave had a "countenance (face)...like lightning, and his raiment white as snow." Matthew 28:3. The soldiers evidently fainted "for fear of him," but they were not hurt in any way. Now, it is very significant what Luke says about Christ's transfiguration experience. "And as he prayed, the fashion of his countenance was altered, and his raiment was white and GLISTERING." Luke 9:29. It is very interesting that the word "GLISTERING" in-Young's analytical concordance to the Bible is from the Greek word exastrapto which means, "To flash as lightning."

What great meaning is now added to our Lord's words with this understanding. "For as the lightning, that lighteneth out of the one part under heaven, shineth unto the other part under heaven; so shall also the Son of Man be in his day." Luke 17:24. In Matthew 17:2 we read that Jesus' "face did shine as the sun," on the mountain. Jesus had promised the disciples that they would not see death until they "see the Son of man coming in his kingdom." Matthew 16:28. And so this was a little sample of the wonderful "fiery glory" Jesus will have when He comes to this earth again. This glory is His love and the wicked will not be able to stand it. They will pray for the mountains and rocks to fall on them, which proves His glory does not kill them. Revelation 6:16.

And so what we are saying is that the life-giving fire of God brings death to the person who rejects it. Not that God kills him. Oh, no, not at all. The person turns away from God's light and destroys himself. "0 Israel, thou hast destroyed thyself, but in me is thine help." Hosea 13:9. Judas is a prime example. He was not willing for Christ to cast the demon of greed out of him, so he sold his Lord for 30 pieces of silver and then went out and hanged himself. Matthew 27:5. He exchanged the fire of Christ's soul cleansing love for the fire of guilt, regret and age-lasting remorse. That my friend, is the fate of everyone who refuses God's life giving fire. You cannot ignore it, avoid it or resist it. It will either drive you to your knees at the foot of the cross or drive you to your grave as you wear yourself out trying to run away from it.

And did you know that God's love is in His Ten Commandment law. Yes it is and that law is implanted and imbedded in the very heart and being of every created being in the universe, including Lucifer (now Satan) and all of his evil angels. Why even the people who have never been taught about God, whom the Bible calls "Gentiles," have the law of God written in their hearts. The Bible tells us about it.

"For when the Gentiles who lack the Law do naturally practice it, they are for themselves a law, though they have none. They show that what the Law requires is written in their hearts, while their conscience also bears witness and their thoughts accuse or defend one another." Romans 2:14-15, ML Version.

Yes, it is true. The law of God, His very own fiery law is built in to everyone of us and was built into Lucifer himself in the beginning. The Father has been taking the penalty of that law upon himself all this time so as to shield Lucifer and all of his demons from suffering and death.

In the Garden of Eden the most beautiful of all of God's

creation was chosen to be a medium by which to speak to Mother Eve to tell her that nothing was wrong with God's creation. Ever since that fateful day the serpent has been the most degraded and despised, hated and feared creature in the animal kingdom. And yet, it was this very creature that became a symbol of God's redemptive power in the desert with Israel when Satan brought his fiery serpents of death into the camp.

"And Moses made a serpent of brass, and put it upon a pole, and it came to pass, that if a serpent had bitten any man, when he beheld the serpent of brass, he lived... And as Moses lifted up the serpent in the wilderness, even so must the Son of man be lifted up: That whosoever believeth in him should not perish, but have eternal life." Numbers 21:9; John 3:14, 15. My friend, that whosoever included Satan. That serpent showed how the Son of God was willing to go down to the very depths of sin and depravity ... yes even to the pits of hell itself to include his beloved Lucifer, the first and highest angel he had ever created. When Jesus was nailed to that cross on Golgotha's hill the eyes of the universe were drawn to Him. God was demonstrating his fiery love for all the universe to see. No one could avoid it. No one could escape it. Jesus' very words were fulfilled by it.

"And I, if I be lifted up from the earth, will draw ALL (men) unto me." John 12:32. The word, "men" is a supplied word and not in the original. Jesus said He would draw "all" to Himself and that *all* included Satan and his evil angels. Yes, they were drawn there too. They were there watching, for Satan was there leading the Jews to kill their Creator. And Jesus never once lashed out at any of them with a hateful word or look or glance. He showed His unchanging, eternal character of love is stronger than hatred, malice and death, for after He was dead and buried, He rose again. And His chief angel saw it all, but never repented. But all of these facts are stored in Satan's memory banks. He has been resisting them for centuries, yes millenniums now. And the more he resists these "fiery" reminders of God's great love for him, the more hatred builds up in his heart or mind. This hatred is the "fire" that will burst forth on that great final day of "decision" (judgment) when the Father reaches out to His beloved older boy to rescue him from the fiery self-destruction Satan is leading all the lost to bring upon themselves. God the Father, through his Son will arrest them from this suicide mission to remind them of the Father's great love. All of them will stand transfixed as they see in the heavens the history of God's love story. They will all bow down and admit God is right and they are wrong. The original Greek indicates that this will be a true conversion experience. It has to be, otherwise, it could not "bring glory to God the Father" to God the Father as Phil 2:10, 11 predicts that it will. Furthermore, no one can say or confess "that Jesus is Lord, but by the Holy Ghost." I Cor 12:3. Repentance includes change and reformation and the proof that this happens is that they all eventually will drink of the water of life and go into the city.

Neither can any human being change his words, habits, thoughts and lifestyle in his own strength. "Can the Ethiopian change his skin, or the leopard his spots? then may ye also do good that are accustomed to do evil?" Jer. 13:23. Jesus himself said, "without me ye can do nothing." John 15:5. But Paul said that through Christ he could do all things, Phil. 4:13.

Oh, how the Father's and Son's heart will be rejoicing as they see all the wicked lost outside the city bow and repent and change so they can join the rest of their brothers and sisters in the New Jerusalem. The fiery revelation of truth spoken of in Revelation 20:9, "and fire came down from God out of heaven, and devoured them," goes into even Satan's heart and he bows with all the lost. Does he accept it? Not on the first invitation. At first he resists God's love and all the hatred of the ages comes out. This leads him to his "death" for all the wicked are filled with the same hatred that motivates Satan and they all turn on him as he no doubt tries to convince them they can go ahead and take the city. Ezekiel 28:6-10 shows that the people will "kill" Satan by blaming him for all of their problems and loss, etc. His death will come from the midst of his own followers (who will turn on him) and his own fiery hatred in his heart.

Ezekiel 15:7 is explained by Song of Solomon 8:6 and Isaiah 9:18. What we are talking about here is the destruction of the carnal nature. Satan means "one who opposes or is against." The death and destruction of Satan is referring to that person or identity who has been an enemy of God. How does God destroy His enemies? By making them into His friends. And that is what will happen to Lucifer. Satan will die but Lucifer will be re-born in his original and renewed perfection and beauty. This will demonstrate the power and wisdom of God beyond any thing that has ever been done before. Rev. 15:1-4 proves this because it predicts all of God's creatures will be praising Him together when they finally see the completion of His creation.

Revelation 20:7-15 gives a clear picture of the final consuming of all the wicked outside of the walls of the New Jerusalem. The wicked of all ages are raised up to see the final and full display of God's eternal love. Do you think God is raising them up so he can make them suffer some more for their sins? Is that your idea of God the Father and His Son, Jesus Christ? Well, that is not the God that Jesus revealed in His beautiful life. Well, then why does God bring all the lost back to life? It is for the same reason that He has kept Lucifer and his angels alive for 6,000 years. He can't stand to let them go. Listen to this mighty Creator sob His heart out. "Oh, how can I give you up, my Ephraim? How can I let you go? How can I forsake you like Admah and Zeboiim? My HEART CRIES OUT WITHIN ME; how I long to help you!" Hosea 11:8. Living Bible. This is the Father's and Son's cry as they see all the lost outside of the city.

The Psalmist tells us what a wonderful relationship he had with his own son Absalom. But, this Psalm I am going to share has another setting in heaven between the Father, Christ, His Son and Lucifer, his highest angel. Oh, how They loved him. "For it was not an enemy that reproached me; then I could have borne it: neither was it he that hated me that did magnify himself against Me; then I would have hid myself from him: But it was thou, a man mine equal, my guide, and mine acquaintance.

We took sweet counsel together, and walked unto the house of God in company." Psalms 55:12-14.

Music is one of the main features in heaven. Ezekiel 28:13 tells us Lucifer had musical instruments built into him. Can't you see the Father and the Son singing trios and duets with their number one angel? Job 38:7 And imagine all the council meetings and talks they must have had together. If you were a father and had a son and he grew up and went bad would you give up on him? Not if you were a true father. And that is human love. And suppose the son cursed you and slandered you. You would only know that your son was sick and needed help. You would try and get him the best help the medical profession provides. That's human love. But let us suppose your son is put in prison on death row for murder and when you go to visit him to plead with him to give his heart to God he tells you he hates you and wants you to go away and leave him alone. Would you do it? Not if you really love your son. You would keep going back right up until the night of his execution. And even if he had rejected your love a thousand times before, you would still go that last night to make one last appeal. Your love for that boy is so great that you can't stay away. And that is only human love. How much greater is DIVINE LOVE? Isaiah 49:15, 16 tells us that God's love is greater than mother love which is often thought of as the highest form of love human beings can express.

It is almost impossible for most people to understand how God could love the devil, but He does. It is because we are so inclined to hate instead of to love. Nowhere in the Bible are we commanded to hate the devil. We are warned against his wiles and power to deceive, but I have never found a text that indicates I am to hate Satan. Jesus Himself even refused to "rail" or "accuse" Satan. Jude 9.

Jesus always treated Satan with dignity and respect. He even permitted Satan to carry Him up to the pinnacle of the temple, Matthew 4:5, so he could tempt Him to cast himself down to prove that the Father loved him enough to send an angel to catch him. I wonder what Jesus said to Lucifer when he was carrying Him up to the pinnacle of the temple and to the high mountain? Since Jesus is love I would imagine Jesus said, "Lucifer, I still love you. I want to help you. Won't you let My Father and me help you to change so you can come back home to heaven with us?" The Jews also had a tradition that said the Messiah would stand on the roof of the holy place. If Christ would have called to the priests below and then when He had their attention jumped down while they watched, it would have been a most impressive sight. But Christ resisted this temptation and Satan left him.

Paul tells us in 1 Corinthians 13:8 that "love never faileth." The word "faileth" in the original means "to cast away or drop or fall away." God is love and He never casts anyone away or falls away from anyone. Paul tells us that we should "covet earnestly the best gifts: and yet shew I unto you a more excellent way." 1 Corinthians 12:31. The love chapter, 1 Corinthians 13 follows. This love that Paul is describing says that it "beareth all things, believeth all things, hopeth all things, endureth all things." Verse 7. God the Father never stops hoping that His prodigal son, Lucifer, will come home.

GETHSEMANE

This love is the kind of love God wants us to have. This is the love Jesus prayed would be in us as He poured out his soul in Gethsamne. He actually sweat blood there resisting sin, Hebrews 12:4. "I made known to them thy name, and I will make it known, that the love with which thou hast loved me may be in them, and I in them." John 17:26. RSV.

WHAT IS THE LAKE OF FIRE?

And so the choice is ours, my friend. We can be inside loving everyone or outside hating and cursing everyone. That will truly be a "lake of fire" outside of the city as all the wicked begin turning on each other, blaming each other for being lost. Revelation 17:15 tells us that people represent or symbolize water. A lake is a body of water, therefore that lake of fire could represent all the lost outside of the golden gates of New Jerusalem turning the world into a blazing inferno with their words and actions. "So the tongue is a little member and boasts of great things. How great a forest is set ablaze by a small fire! And the tongue is afire - The tongue is an unrighteous world among our members, staining the whole body, setting on fire the cycle of nature, and set on fire by hell." James 3:5-6.

And that is exactly what is going to happen. God is preserving this earth and its atmospheric heavens from blazing into a deadly inferno that would destroy every human being on planet earth right now today, 2 Pet. 3:7. But after the 1,000 years Satan will have complete control of the wicked and will inspire them to create weapons of destruction that will make today's arsenals look like cap guns and fire crackers in comparison.* I want to be safe inside the city, not on the outside when that day comes. It is the Father's will for all of us to be inside the city with Him. The suffering the wicked will have to endure in this age and the age to come, after the 1,000 years, will be terrible. But it will be neccessary to bring them to repentance because He does not want one single angel or person to perish, in this age or the age to come. The choice is up to us. I want to choose life. What about you? Jesus is that life.

***Even though the wicked will be permitted to manufacture these weapons of mass destruction, the Lord will not allow them to be used. See Psalm 7:13 and Psalm 21:11. "For they intended evil against thee; they imagined a mischievous device, which they are not able to perform." After they view the movie in the sky they will all bow down, drop their weapons and repent and confess. Phil. 2:6-11.**

CHAPTER 23

THE UNFATHOMABLE DEPTHS OF THE FATHER'S LOVE

The gospel story of Jesus Christ and His Father is so deep and mysterious that the Bible tells us that even "the angels desire to look into" its unfathomable, unspeakable depths. I Peter 1:12. The prophet Isaiah foretold the sufferings of Christ and wrote up the account as if the Father was the one who was hurting and killing his own son. Listen: "Yet it pleased the Lord to bruise him; he hath put him to grief." Isaiah 53:10.

Someone may immediately ask, "Do you mean to say that it was God's will for his own Son to suffer and die on that terrible cross?" The answer has to be, "Oh, no. It was not the Father's perfect will that His Son die, but it was his permissive will. It was not God's will for His Son to die. Never. But it was His ultimate and perfect will for all men to be saved and the Father could not save even the ones who might desire to be saved unless His Son died, for it took the cross to open our blind eyes and break our hardened hearts." That is how terribly malignant sin is. But not only did Jesus show that He was willing to give up his eternal existence for us, the Father was too, for "God was in Christ, reconciling the world unto himself." 2 Corinthians 5:19. We know that all men will not be saved in this age, for they do not choose to be saved, but God's will is that no one perish in the ages to come for the Lord is going to bring them to repentance. 2 Peter 3:9. But that will not happen until after the 1,000 years or millennium. That was why the Father was willing to suffer in and through His only Son. It was to win back all of His lost creatures, not only in our age but in the ages to come. And in this endeavor, He will be totally successful as He predicted in John 12:32: "And I, if I am lifted up from the earth, will draw all men to Myself."

WAS THE GIFT OF GOD'S SON A PAYMENT OR A GIFT?

Paul tells us, "Thanks be unto God for his unspeakable gift." 2 Corinthians 9:15. The gift of Jesus is so great words cannot express it. Even the articulate, brilliant apostle Paul was speechless in the light of such a glorious gift. How terrible then to think that God demands a repayment. And because we could not pay it back the Father required that his only Son become that payment. Don't you see what that makes the Father out to be in our minds? It makes Him a monster, an unforgiving dictator and tyrant. A blood thirsty ogre and sadist. But we know that is not what our wonderful Heavenly Father is like. He is none of these things. In fact He is just the opposite. Satan is the one who fits all those descriptions. He is the "angel of justice," who demands "repayment." Revelation 6:5.

When the Father gave His Son to the human family it was an irrevocable gift. The cross proves that He would not take him back, even though we abused and killed him. On the day of Pentecost, Peter, under the Spirit's influence said, "Him [Jesus] ... ye have taken and by wicked hands have crucified and slain." Acts 2:23. Yes, my friend the Grace of God is free, but the delivery of that gift is what is so very expensive. Satan intended to make an eternal gulf between the Father's throne and our minds and hearts, but instead the Father and Son have taken the cross and laid it across the chasm. God gave us His only begotten Son as a gift. We turned that marvelous gift into a sacrifice. The cross was our idea of what he demanded. It was not God's required repayment, for He has always been willing to forgive us. The cross forever proves that He loves us. It was the purchase price our carnal mind demanded that God pay to prove that He loved us. ***The alienation was in our minds, not in God's mind.*** Colossians. 1:21.

THE FATHER HAS EVEN BEEN SHIELDING LUCIFER FROM THE GUILT OF HIS CRIMES

We know that guilt and remorse will destroy a person. They can drive you to the grave. Insanity is often caused because of guilt. Some have suggested that mental illness is actually an escape from the pain of reality and God permits some minds to escape in this manner. But one thing is very clear from the Bible. God, through His Son Jesus, is even now shielding every human being and the evil angels as well. How else could they have stayed alive? How could Satan have lived this long even? There is only one answer. God has been taking the blame even for Lucifer (Satan) and all of his evil angels all these millenniums. But Ezekiel 28:6-10, 18 indicates that the fire of guilt and hatred has been building up inside Satan all of this time and will burst forth in that final day when all the lost will "gang up" on Satan and take away his power to deceive. "Yet he shall come to his end, and none shall help him." Dan. 11:45. He is going to be blamed for everything by everybody and God will be powerless in that day to protect and shield him anymore. "Therefore thus saith the Lord God; Because thou hast set thine heart as the heart of God; Behold, therefore I will bring strangers upon thee, the terrible of the nations: and they shall draw their swords against the beauty of thy wisdom, and they shall defile thy brightness. They shall bring thee down to the pit, and thou shalt die the deaths of them that are slain in the midst of the seas." Ezek 28:6-8.

Let us take a closer look at the word "seas." What is this referring to? Well, in prophecy the word "sea" represents people. Notice: "And he said to me, 'The waters which you saw where the harlot sits, are peoples and multitudes and nations and tongues.'" Rev. 17:15. The next point we need to deal with is the "death" of Satan (meaning adversary). How will he die? The answer is in the text itself. "Thou shalt die the deaths of them that are slain in the midst of the seas."

Satan is going to die the same kind of death that the wicked die. "They will bring you to the pit of hell and you shall die as those pierced with many wounds, there on your island in the heart of the seas." Ezek 28:8. In order to know how Satan will die we need to understand how all the wicked will die. This is explained in two ways. First of all, the new birth is a death to the old man of sin. So, we are not talking about a literal death of our physical being, per se, but a death to the old man of sin, which is the carnal self that exists and operates by virtue of and by the strength of the ego. Further down in this chapter we read in Ezek 28:18 that Satan will be reduced to ashes in the sight of the whole universe. Ashes is a symbol of sorrow, remorse, grief and repentance which reveals that Lucifer will be brought to repentance.

It was not until Jesus died upon the cross that the good or unfallen angels were able to see that Lucifer was wrong and the Father was right. In fact, all the unfallen worlds did not fully understand the deceptions of Lucifer until Jesus was nailed to the cross. Finally, they saw that Lucifer truly was Satan. Now, why could they not see it before? Because every person who had ever been hurt or killed in the past legally deserved to die. Why? Because they had broken God's law. But Jesus was in a totally different category. He who knew no sin became sin for us.

Jesus Christ came on the scene of this world in a human body and lived an absolutely perfect life and yet Satan did everything he possibly could to make His life miserable. He didn't deserve to be treated that way, for He had never broken the law. Here was a human being (actually God in the flesh) obeying the law both in the letter and in the spirit deserving Satan's admiration and respect and all he receives is hatred and ridicule, abuse and persecution. The angels stood aghast. They knew that human beings deserved to suffer and die, but not God's Son. He never had done anything wrong. And so Jesus' perfect life began to tear away the mask Satan had been wearing for 4,000 years. It was seen that God's law was holy, just and good and that it could be kept after all. Satan's charges were seen to be unjust, untrue and totally without foundation. But, the Father was reaching out to Lucifer with his arms of love through Christ.

"Oh, Lucifer, my beloved angel, don't you see how much I love my creatures? Don't you see how I am forgiving them and healing them? I can do the same for you. Oh please come back to me and let me heal you. Please don't break my heart anymore. I am longing for you to come home. Don't you see, if you come back then all of your angels will come too. Oh, please don't keep fighting me, for you are going to kill yourself."

IS GOD ABLE TO KEEP HIS OWN LAW?

But Lucifer (Satan) wouldn't listen. He was getting angrier every minute that Jesus was alive for Christ was proving Satan a liar before the universe. Satan was becoming desperate. He had to do something to cause Jesus to sin, if he could. He had to create circumstances which would be very trying to one's patience so that Jesus would show anger or impatience, which would be out of harmony with God's revealed character in the law of God. In other words, can God or will God be able to live up to His own law or is He a hypocrite who is only manipulating us with a law that He himself does not keep for He cannot keep it? This was the heart of the issue. Satan saw his disguise was being torn away. His mask was about to be taken off by Jesus' beautiful demonstration of love. The unfallen worlds and angels watched intensely as the controversy drew to a close.

Satan knew that Christ's death would fulfill all the types of the Old Testament. He had succeeded in turning Israel against the Savior in spite of all of the miracles. The sacrificial system was an object lesson of what the Messiah would do when He came as well as what would be done to Him. But this gory, terrible, bloodletting system of animal slaughter was not God's perfect will. He had just been putting up with it and using it as symbols of Himself and what they would do to Him and His son when He came in the flesh. Gal 4:4. And to make matters worse Israel had perverted it. Satan had taken advantage of this and no doubt told the universe that God actually enjoyed all this butchery and carnage. This was the kind of person Satan made the Father out to be, a tyrant and a monster. The devil told the universe that he was doing them all a favor in revealing the truth about the Father so they could be free from his despotism. From the doctrine of eternal hell-fire torture, we can see what the devil has told all the universe about the Father. "God is a sadist and the devil is his hit man to punish lawbreakers."

But when Christ began to teach and heal the people, the eyes of the universe began to be opened. Their sympathy for Lucifer was beginning to diminish. Listen:

"And the seventy returned again with joy, saying, Lord, even the devils are subject unto us through thy name. And he (Jesus) said unto them, I beheld Satan as Lightning fall from heaven." Luke 10:17-18.

Demon possession was rampant in the world when Jesus came. Satan was gaining more and more power over the minds and bodies of men. All of the misery of the world Satan had charged to the Father. And the Father took the blame for it. All of the universe looked on. And then Christ came and grew up. Never once did He sin. Finally He began His ministry of love and deliverance. Satan's angels were being cast out of the minds and bodies of human beings and the universe saw the divine image restored. Here was the very Son of God being kind to sinners whom Satan had said God hated and loved to torture. He said no one could keep the law and all who broke it were his prisoners. Isaiah 14:16, 17. By the doctrine Satan taught about eternal torture before the cross and also since the cross, we can see how Satan gained the ear of the universe. (See Luke 16:19-31. The Pharisees believed this and taught it.)

His argument probably went something like this: "Inhabitants of the universe, I regret to tell you that the Creator has a law that no one can keep. As proof that what I am telling you is true I ask you to behold planet earth. Here are these wretched creatures, formed in the very image of God the Father Himself and yet even they cannot keep this foolish and defective law. I tried to convince Him of this, but he would not listen. He refused to take me into his confidence before he created this fiasco he has named earth. Planet earth has become a living inferno. It is an everlasting hell. He seems to be sorry for the mess He has caused and has asked me to carry out his justice, so I am doing the best I can down here with the help of my faithful assistants who had the good intelligence to listen to me and join with me in my efforts to convince God the Father that he was wrong. But instead of listening to me, He and His Son made war against me and drove me out of heaven. He seems to be sorry about that too now and always takes the blame for everything. Even the prophets of Jehovah, as they are called, have even written down in their scrolls that God the Father is to blame for all the bad things that are happening down here on planet earth. I have outlined my plan for freedom, but every time anyone down here starts doing what they want to do and having some fun, God claims they are breaking the law and brings some disease or calamity upon them to 'teach them a lesson,' as he calls it. I expect Him to soon destroy the whole planet to coverup his big mistake. When he does that it will only confirm what I have said all along. Inhabitants of the universe, listen to me. Listen to me while you still have a chance. What is happening here on planet earth could happen on any planet. You could be next. Join me in protesting against this horrible injustice God calls 'THE LAW OF GOD.' It will lead to disaster if you try to obey it. Listen to me and my plan will set the entire universe free of the curse of the law. This is your true and only friend in the universe speaking, Lucifer, Son of the morning. Please listen, for I may only have a short time yet to help you, for God the Father is threatening to kill me. The prophets Isaiah and Ezekiel have foretold it. (Isaiah 14:12-20; Ezekiel 28:6-10, 18. If I die the universe will have no one left to save it. Listen to me and live."

Can you see how the unfallen worlds and many of the angelic host could be taken in by this subtle reasoning. But thank God only one-third of the angels followed Lucifer. None of the unfallen worlds listened to him. It was an angel of unbelievable power and intelligence that had rebelled against his Creator.

The Bible tells us how well endowed Lucifer was.

"Son of man, take up a lamentation upon the king of Tyrus, and say unto him, Thus saith the Lord God; Thou sealest up the sum, full of wisdom, and perfect in beauty. Thou hast been in Eden the garden of God." Ezekiel 28:12, 13.

Notice carefully: This is not a condemnation. It is a LAMENTATION ... a weeping. God is weeping and He is saying to the universe, "weep for Lucifer, for he is destroying himself. Oh, how I love him. Oh, how I long to save him, but he will not listen to me. How can I save my beloved Lucifer from certain death?"

Please also notice that the Lord God says to the "king of Tyrus," that he has been in the Garden of Eden. It is almost as if he were saying, "Lucifer, you have been in that beautiful Garden of Eden I created for Adam and Eve. Remember? You were there in it, Lucifer. I was hoping it might remind you of what heaven is like so you would come back home to me. Oh, Lucifer, please come back I miss you so!" Dear reader, can you imagine a Creator who could love like that? It is only as we look at Jesus that we can understand such love.

Then in Ezekiel 28:13 the Lord names all the various precious stones He "covered" his beloved Lucifer with. God is remembering how wonderfully and carefully He fashioned this highest of all angels. "Thou was perfect in thy ways from the day that thou wast created, till iniquity was found in thee." Ezekiel 28:15. This scripture alone clearly proves that the Creator was not responsible for Lucifer's defection or sin. God made a beautiful, sinless angel and that perfect angel turned himself into His enemy or Satan, which means adversary.

The rest of Ezekiel 28 tells how Lucifer fell because he became proud of his beauty and wisdom. Can you hear the emotion charged voice of God crying out to Lucifer all thru this chapter? Can't you hear His voice breaking as he cries out to Lucifer, "Thou art the anointed cherub that covereth, and I have set thee so." Verse 14. "Lucifer, I gave you the third highest position in the universe, right next to My beloved Son. And,

Lucifer, that job is still waiting for you. I did not demote you. I didn't kick you out. You left me. But, Lucifer, I want you back. I will forgive and forget. I am your Creator. Nothing is too hard or impossible with Me." Jeremiah 32:27; Matthew 19:26.

But Lucifer refuses. He won't come back. His heart is hardened against the Father. All throughout Ezekiel 28 and Isaiah 14 and in other places in the Scripture God first pleads and then he warns, "and I will destroy thee, 0 covering cherub." Verse 16.

We all have seen a little baby start crawling, away from its father or mother. And what does the parent do? A loving parent will call out, "Come back to daddy, baby, come back to daddy." Usually a child will stop a moment and look to see if daddy is coming -- if he really means business. Then most of the time the baby will just keep on crawling away. The parent will then stop pleading and warn it. "Come back to daddy, baby, come back. Baby get hurt. Baby going to cry." And this is exactly what God is doing here. First he pleads and then he warns Lucifer of the painful consequences that will result if Lucifer does not repent and return. But the amazing aspect here is that God claims to be the one who is going to do this to Lucifer, when it is obvious that Lucifer is doing it to himself.

We can see that now, as we look back, nearly 2,000 years this side of the cross, but the universe of unfallen angels and unfallen worlds could not see it. That was what the contest over Job was all about in the book of Job. Is it possible to keep God's law? Is it possible to be perfect? God claimed perfection for job but Satan denied these claims. The suffering of Job proved God's claims were correct. Job's faithfulness under mental and physical suffering, few have endured, vindicated God's character. Each of us has that same opportunity for every human soul is an actor on the stage of this world's history. We each are part of this great theatric production which has been running now for nearly 6,000 years. God is counting on each individual to play out his role faithfully, just as Job did. And just as surely as Job was faithful, so God can help us to be faithful until the end and thus demonstrate a facet of God's beautiful character that no one else can portray. No two people are exactly alike. Each one of us has something very special to tell the universe about God's character of love. If we let Him work in us and through us He will enable us to deliver the message. Only eternity will reveal the value of a soul's worth and how important we each are to God's plan.

"But, how can I do it?" you may be asking. Here is the answer in God's holy Word. "Looking unto Jesus the author and finisher of our faith; who for the joy that was set before him endured the cross, despising the shame, and is set down at the right hand of the throne of God. For consider him that endured such contradictions of sinners against himself, lest ye be wearied and faint in your minds. Ye have not resisted unto blood, striving against sin." Hebrews 12:2,4.

The Father knew there was only one way to open the eyes of the universe to the enormity of sin and its terrible consequences or penalty. That was to let Himself, through his only Son, suffer the consequences of disobedience and rebellion. He could have allowed Lucifer and his evil angels, who rebelled with him, one third of the host of heaven, to reap the results of their evil choice. He could remove His shield of protection from Lucifer and let him suffer all the guilt and remorse he will one day suffer. If He had done this, Lucifer and his angels would have perished very quickly. But this would have raised more questions than it would have answered regarding Lucifer's charges and allegations. So, there was only one way to reveal the truth. And so Jesus alone with His Father, in the Garden of Gethsemane, pleaded with the Father to let the cup pass from Him if the world could be saved any other way. But there was no other way. Jesus had to drink the cup. He had to demonstrate what will happen to each created being when the Father is forced out of the life. But there was much more than that.

WHAT WAS IT THAT HORRIFIED JESUS?

Jesus said, "Now is my soul troubled; and what shall I say?

Father, save me from, this hour: but for this cause came I unto this hour." John 12:27. Jesus can see what is just ahead. He is not afraid of the pain, but the thought of being separated from His Father fills Him with horror. We cannot fully understand that, for none of us has ever fully known the Father as Jesus did, but that is our wonderful privilege. But Jesus fully surrendered to the Father's plan and purpose and was willing to think only of saving us by glorifying His Father's name, verse 28. And then this important scripture follows: "Now is the judgment of this world: now shall the prince of this world be cast out. And I, if I be lifted up from the earth, will draw all men unto me." John 12:32. The word *"men"* is a supplied word and is not in the original. All of God's creatures in the universe, including even Lucifer and his fallen angels would be drawn to the cross to watch the Savior receive the full penalty of the law.

Satan sees that if Christ does not sin by showing impatience, anger, self-pity, forcing the Jews to acknowledge Him, or coming down off the cross and giving up, his argument against God's law will be proved false. Jesus kept that law perfectly. He didn't sin even by a look, a glance, a grimace, nor any kind of facial expression during all of the physical and verbal abuse He took from the rabble and priests as well as the soldiers. The greatest temptation was to use His divine power to release Himself or permit the guilt of their deeds to come upon His enemies. But He loved them too much. The Scriptures must be fulfilled so God's word and law would stand true. When Peter lashed out with his sword and cut off Malchus' ear, Jesus said to Peter, "Put up thy sword into the sheath: the cup which my Father hath given me, shall I not drink it?" John 18:11. "All they that take the sword shall perish with the sword. Thinkest thou that I cannot now pray to my Father, and He shall presently give me more than twelve legions of angels. But how then shall the scriptures be fulfilled, that thus it must be?" Matthew 26:52.

What scriptures did Jesus have reference to? It would have to be the Old Testament predictions of His sufferings. "But he was wounded for our transgressions, he was bruised for our iniquities ... and with his stripes we are healed. He was oppressed, and he was afflicted, yet he opened not his mouth: he is brought as a lamb to the slaughter, and as a sheep before her shearers is dumb, so he openeth not his mouth." Isaiah 53:5, 7.

Our Lord knew His own people would crucify Him before they did it. But Christ tried to prevent His own people from this act, for His crucifixion sealed their doom by hardening their hearts into unbelief. It also melted a few, but the majority were sealed into darkness, for that age, just as Satan and his angels are until the "Times of Restitution of all things." Acts 3:21. 2 Peter 2:4. They have rejected the light of truth and closed the door against themselves. Yet God claims to be the one who is responsible for their blindness. "And the angels which kept not their first estate, but left their own habitation, he hath reserved in everlasting chains under darkness unto the judgment of the great day." Jude 6. And so we see the Father taking the blame in the New Testament as well as the Old. God never changes. Amazing grace. It's always the same, always available. God has never rejected or cast away anyone. John 6:37. It is our hearts that are hardened against Him, not His heart toward us. Never, because His heart is always positive toward us. It is the darkness of our mind that prevents us from seeing the eternal light and glory of His love. The mystery of iniquity is how sin blinds and hardens our human hearts against such love.

CHRIST'S DEATH REVEALED THE FATHER

The Father was "glorified" in his Son's death in that it revealed what the Father is really like. The Bible predicted this all throughout the Old Testament, but the Jewish leaders could not see it. They could only see the dollar signs $$$ in the temple. Jesus gently rebuked two of His followers after His resurrection. "Oh fools, and slow of heart to believe all that the prophets have spoken: Ought not Christ to have, suffered these things, and to enter into his glory?" Luke, 24:25, 26. Then Jesus began at Moses and went through the prophecies of

Moses and all of the prophets and proved that He had fulfilled these scriptures.

Sin had even blinded Lucifer and turned him into a monster called Satan. He should have been able to have foreseen that Christ's death on the cross would completely expose him as a murderer before the universe. But his selfish mind could not conceive that the Father would not only be willing to let His Son die on the cross of Tammuz, an ancient Sumerian pagan deity, but the Father Himself would even be willing to die with His Son, even as Abraham died a thousand deaths in his heart as he climbed Mount Moriah. But how much greater was God the Father's sufferings!

Satan knows only force and so he reasoned that he would either force Christ to sin or force Him to abandon His plan to save the world and go back to heaven rather than take the chance to lose out on eternal life Himself. Satan figured he couldn't lose on those terms. He may have thought that if Christ refused to go through with His plan to let Himself be nailed to the cross that the Father Himself would come and execute His Son to prove that the penalty of the law was death. Here again, the devil was looking at God through his own selfish eyes. But the Father kept silence. He did not curse or yell at Lucifer. It is not His nature to expose embarrass or hurt anyone. Lucifer had imagined in his mind that the Father and Son were out to get him just as he was out to get Them. But he was wrong. They both loved him. The Psalmist describes Lucifer's thoughts, which are God's thoughts through David:

"Thou givest thy mouth to evil, and thy tongue frameth deceit ... these things hast thou done, and I kept silence, thou thoughtest that I was altogether such an one as thysef." Psalm 50:19, 21.

We know Lucifer's plans and methods as we look at the people he uses and destroys. Let's take Judas as an example. Judas figured that if Jesus was the Messiah he would have to become king. Therefore, it was only a matter of political maneuvering to bring Jesus to the throne. Judas reasoned that Christ was too timid and modest to assume His rightful position, therefore Judas would arrange a set of circumstances that would "force" Christ to assert His power and authority and take the kingdom by overthrowing His enemies. If Jesus could not do this then this would prove that He was not the Messiah, because the Messiah would be able to overcome His enemies. The only problem with this reasoning was that it was based on a false premise. That is, it was based on the premise that God uses force to gain the victory over His enemies, when the truth is that God never uses force. He uses truth, righteousness and love. He never forces anyone to do anything, even to love Him.

JUDAS WAS CONTROLLED BY LUCIFER

Lucifer's mind is revealed through Judas. Judas figured that he would bring Jesus of Nazareth to the acid test. If Jesus were really the Messiah He would act as he believed the Messiah should act and would be able to act under the circumstances Judas was going to set up with the priests. The Jewish leaders would also have to accept Him and Judas would receive all the credit for having carried out such a brilliant scheme to its successful conclusion. In either case, he would be thirty pieces of silver richer no matter what happened. He was sure he couldn't lose. His plan was fail safe. Such is the mind of man.

But this is not the mind of God. "Let this mind be in you, which was also in Christ Jesus: who, being in the form of God, thought it not robbery to be equal with God: But made himself of no reputation, and took upon him the form of a servant, and was made in the likeness of men." Phil. 2:5, 6. Lucifer (now Satan) did not think this way. He had never humbled himself for anyone since He fell from Heaven. It was foreign to him. It was repulsive to him. Lucifer did not realize that God was going to humiliate Himself like this. He could not imagine the King of the Universe doing such a thing, therefore it never entered his selfish brain to consider the possibility that God would go this direction. *Lucifer's mighty intellect was not capable of comprehending how*

God could win by losing. He could not conceive how God could be victorious in defeat. And yet Jesus had explained it so clearly just before His death. "Verily, verily, I say unto you, Except a corn of wheat fall into the ground and die, it abideth alone: but if it die, it bringeth forth much fruit." John 12:24. The Father was saying, I will live by dying. If you want to live forever, you must die with Me. This was not only stupid to Lucifer, it was insanity. He rejected it out of hand. And this was his downfall. This was what unmasked him at the cross.

By leading the priests and Roman soldiers to abuse the Savior as they did, Lucifer proved to the unfallen universe what he really was and he fell "as lightning from heaven." Luke 10: 18. Now, do you think that Lucifer would have done this if he had known that it would have such disastrous results to his "image" throughout the entire universe? Absolutely not, In fact the Bible tells us: "But we speak the wisdom of God in a mystery, even the hidden wisdom, which God ordained before the world unto our glory: which none of the princes of this world knew: for had they known it, they would not have crucified the Lord of glory." 1 Corinthians 2:7, 8.

Who are the real "princes of this world?" Why they are Satan's angels, "for we wrestle not against flesh and blood, but against principalities, against powers, against the rulers of the darkness of this world, against spiritual wickedness; in high places." Eph. 6:12.

When Ezekiel spoke about Lucifer under the title, "Prince of Tyrus," Ezek. 28, we know that He was speaking about Lucifer. And so we see that Lucifer, looking back on the cross sees what a terrible blunder he made in leading men to crucify Jesus. And I think the Jewish leaders probably realized they had made a terrible blunder too. Of course, they were not sorry for what they did, but only that it exposed them for what they really were. They were only sorry for the results, not for the sin of killing the Son of God. And yet did they kill him? Their intent was to kill him, and so it is written up that they did kill Him, but Jesus categorically stated, "Therefore doth my Father love me, because I lay down my life, that I might take it again. No man taketh it from me, but I lay it down of myself. I have power to lay it down, and I have power to take it again. This commandment have I received of my Father." John 10:17, 18.

THE DIVINE MIND REVEALED

And when Christ was upon the cross suffering all the rejection and the physical torture and pain the chief priests mocked Him with the scribes and elders. They said. "He saved others; himself he cannot save. If he be the King of Israel, let him now come down from the cross, and we will believe him. He trusted in God; let him deliver him now, if he will have him: for he said, I am the Son of God." Matthew 27:43.

Here again we see the vivid contrast between God's mind and Lucifer's mind, the divine mind and the carnal mind. The mind of self-sacrificing love and the mind of self-preserving, calculated, expedience, which is really hatred of others.

Lucifer knew he had to stop Christ somehow. If he could not force Him to desert humanity by turning the leaders of Israel against Him, then he had to somehow cause Jesus to break His Father's law. If he failed to do either of these, then he knew that all was lost. Up until Gethsemane Jesus had not made the final decision to die for humanity. But when he entered the garden, the iniquity of the world began to come upon Him and he could sense His Father's presence being pressed out of His life by all the sins that were being laid upon Him. Young's analytical concordance defines "Gethsemane" as from the Hebrew, meaning wine press and oil (farm). Since wine represents doctrines or teachings (Luke 5:38) and oil the Holy Spirit, Matthew 25:1-13, we can see that the Divine presence was being pressed out of the Savior's life.

All the sorrows and woes of humanity with their suffering, both mental and physical were being laid upon Jesus so he could "taste death for every man." Hebrews 2:9. This was not the death that we die in this life. Oh, no. It was the second death that

Jesus was experiencing for us. It began to weigh upon Him as he entered the garden. "And he ... began to be sorrowful and very heavy. My soul is exceeding sorrowful, even unto death: tarry ye here, and watch with me." Matthew 26:38.

WHAT WRUNG JESUS' SOUL WITH ANGUISH?

But it was the strange and awful sensation of not having the Father's presence with Him that wrung his soul with anguish. Jesus lived in the very light of God's eternal presence. He knew the true meaning of David's psalm, "Thou wilt shew me the path of life: in thy presence is fulness of joy; at thy right hand there are pleasures for evermore." Psalms 16: 11. Therefore, when the Father's Spirit began to be replaced by all the evil of the ages, Christ recoiled and drew back in horror. "And he went a little farther, and fell on his face, and prayed, saying, 0 my Father, if it be possible, let this cup pass from me: nevertheless not as I will, but as thou wilt." Matt 26:39. This was not a selfish prayer. Christ did not want his Father or any of the angels, unfallen worlds or even His disciples to see Him suffer like this.

Jesus prayed this prayer three times according to Matthew 26:39, 42, 44. Luke 22:42-46, tells of an angel coming to aid Him and how he sweat blood. "Striving against sin," is what Paul blames the blood sweating on, Hebrews 12:4. Mark records that Jesus "went forward a little, and fell on the ground, and prayed that, if it were possible, the hour might pass from him. And he said, Abba, Father, all things are possible unto thee; take away this cup from me: nevertheless not what I will, but what thou wilt," Mark 14:34-36. After each request He went to see if his disciples were praying with Him. He was so concerned that they not be shocked by what was happening to Him and what was going to happen. He wanted their faith to be strong, but instead of praying they were sleeping. And so they were unprepared to keep their faith when the mob came to arrest their Master. They only had the carnal weapons of man, not the spiritual weapons of God with which to fight the devil. As a result, they lost the battle and were scattered like sheep without a shepherd as had been predicted in Zech. 13:7. Even here God takes the blame for man's failure and sin.

At each step of the way toward the cross the Father and His Son were thinking only of their beloved creatures, not of themselves. Each time Jesus requested His Father to take away the cup of sin and woe from His lips he always added that submissive P.S., "Not what I will, but what Thou wilt." Mark 14:36.

"Oh, Daddy, please don't leave me. If you can think of any other way to save our beloved human family, please do it. But you know best. I submit my will to yours." This truly is "THE FAITH OF JESUS." When Christ prayed that prayer of submission, He gave up everything to the Father. He gave up His relationship in the past, in the present, which He had always enjoyed, and He even gave up any hope of ever having that relationship again. He gave up every right He had for us that we might live. It was the supreme demonstration of submissive love and total faith in the Father.

In His humanity he could not see through the dark tunnel of death. He went forward to the cross in complete submission to the Father's will. The white-hot love of Song of Solomon 8:6 was flashing out of Christ from one end of the universe to the other. "I love you, I love you, I love," he was saying. Now the supreme demonstration of that love was to be held up for all to see. Every created being God had ever created focused its attention on that lonely hill. It was as if the Father and Son together were saying, "Come and tear My flesh with your whips. Rip out My beard with your hands. Spit in My face. Place a crown of thorns on My royal brow. Strip Me naked and nail Me to this tree. Call Me cursed, lost and damned. Tell everyone I am a fake, a phoney and a counterfeiting blasphemer for claiming to be God's Messiah. Do all of this and more, but you can never make Me stop loving you. Because I LOVE YOU! I LOVE YOU! I LOVE YOU! I LOVE YOU! I LOVE YOU! I LOVE YOU! FOREVER AND EVER THROUGH ALL ETERNITY I LOVE YOU!" This my friend is the message of the cross.

It is an obsessive love that will never stop.

The submission of Jesus to the Father reminds us of Job's triumphant cry. "Though he slay me, yet will I trust in him." Job 13:15. Isaac had this same submission to his father Abraham. The Bible says, "God did tempt Abraham ... Take now thy son, thine only son Isaac whom thou lovest, and get thee into the land of Moriah; and offer him there for a burnt offering upon one of the mountains which I will tell thee of." Genesis 22:1, 2. James 1:13-17 proves that God does not test or tempt man to do evil. And yet God let this trial come upon Abraham. But did God do it? Was it His idea? No more than it was God's idea for Job to lose all of his property, his children and later to have boils on his body. No doubt God permitted Abraham to have a dream or a vision. The Lord permitted this test from Satan to be revealed to him, but God was not behind it anymore than He was behind the death of his own Son on Golgotha's hill. But true to His unchanging character and nature, He assumed the responsibility and blame for it. See also Matthew 4:1-3; Jeremiah 6:26, 27. The Father did not test His Son in the wilderness, but Satan took advantage of Jesus time of fasting and meditation. *See note on page 320.

Saul is a type of Lucifer. Once during an important battle he made a law that no one was to eat anything. "Saul had declared, a curse upon anyone who eats anything before evening before I have full revenge on my enemies." 1 Samuel 14:24. Living Bible. Now, Saul's oldest son was Jonathan, a very godly man. He had not heard of his father's oppressive law and ate some honey. It was due to Jonathan's bravery that the battle had been changed from defeat to victory. When Jonathan was told that he had broken his father's law he freely stated that he didn't think it was a very good law and wished that it had not been made. But Saul's pride was so great that he was willing to kill or sacrifice his own son to prove he was right. The reason for this was that Saul had tried to communicate or ask counsel of God to see if he should "go down after the Philistines? Wilt thou deliver them into the hand of Israel? But he (God) answered him not that day." 1 Samuel 14:37.

Because God would not or actually could not communicate with Saul due to his pride and rebellion (Isaiah 59:1, 2, Saul went on a "witch hunt." He was determined to find out who was responsible for breaking off his connection with God. Saul was too blind to see that he himself had forfeited the right to speak to God and Satan had taken control of his life. And so he called all the leaders together for a council to determine by lot who the "guilty" person or persons were.

Now, we need to examine those passages very carefully, for they reveal something we need to understand about how God operated in the Old Testament especially. The lot was cast and it finally fell on Jonathan. But, notice who is asking the questions. "And the people said to Saul, 'do what seems good to you.' Therefore Saul said, '0 Lord God of Israel, why hast thou not answered thy servant this day? If this guilt is in me or in Jonathan my son, 0 Lord, God of Israel, give Urim; but if this guilt is in thy people Israel, give Thummim.' And Jonathan and Saul were taken, but the people escaped. Then Saul said, 'Cast the lot between me and my son Jonathan.' And Jonathan was taken." 1 Samuel 14:40-42 RSV.

This whole religious procedure was only for the purpose of blaming someone else for Saul's failures and sins. He was not interested in God's glory, but only to "be avenged of his enemies." And yet through it all, Jonathan was faithful and submissive to both God and his backslidden father, King Saul. When Saul asks Jonathan what he has done his son respectfully admits that he ate some honey and resigns himself to be punished by death so his father's word and rule might be maintained. What loyalty. "I tasted a little honey with the tip of the staff that was in my hand; here I am, I will die." Ibid., verse 43. It was in Saul's power to pardon his son, if he chose, but he shows the murderous perversity that controls his life when he haughtily announces. "God do so to me and more also; you shall surely die, Jonathan." Ibid., verse 44.

But the people rescued Jonathan so he did not die. "'Shall

Jonathan die, who has wrought this great victory in Israel? Far from it! As the Lord lives there shall not one hair of his head fall to-the ground; for he has wrought with God this day.' So the people ransomed Jonathan, that he did not die." Ibid., verse 45.

Again we can see the mind of Lucifer as we look at Saul and study his words and his actions. We have already seen that God was not able to communicate with Saul because of his sin of pride. 1 Samuel 13:11-14. But when the lot was cast to determine who the guilty party was, the lot strangely fell upon Jonathan. But was Jonathan the one who had prevented God's voice from being heard? No. It was Saul. Why did the lot then finger Jonathan? There is only one sensible answer. Satan was permitted to control the lot and communicate with Saul, for Saul is the one who is praying to his god. But who is Saul's "god"? Why it is Satan or the devil. Jesus told the Jewish leaders that their father was the devil. John 8:44. Nothing would have given Satan more of an advantage over Saul and Israel than to have Jonathan killed. And if his own father performed the deed it would certainly lead Israel into confusion and chaos. But God overruled events by inspiring the people to save Jonathan.

There is a beautiful symbolism here that we should not miss. First of all, Jonathan is a type of Christ. He was submissive even to death, although he was falsely accused by Satan through Saul. What was his "sin?" He had tasted a little honey with the tip of his staff. "Then said Jonathan, My father hath troubled the land: see, I pray you, how mine eyes have been enlightened, because I tasted a little of this honey." 1 Samuel 14:29.

The rod or staff and the honey each have a special significance to the Great Controversy between Christ and Satan over the Father's law. Listen to what the Psalmist says about honey and the law. "More to be desired are they than gold, yea, than much fine gold: sweeter also than honey and the honeycomb. Moreover by them is thy servant warned: and in keeping of them there is great reward.... the commandment of the Lord is pure, enlightening the eyes." Psalms 19:10, 8. And in Psalms 23

David says "thy rod and thy staff they comfort me." Verse 4. The shepherd's staff was used to not only guide the sheep with one end, but to protect them from the enemy with the other which was often weighted with lead or iron. And that is just what God's law does. It guides us into paths of righteousness and protects us from our enemy the devil and his evil angels. Isaiah 11:1, Christ is God's rod.

Please notice also that Saul requested for the truth to be known. "Therefore Saul said unto the Lord God of Israel, 'Give a perfect lot.' And Saul and Jonathan were taken: but the people escaped." 1 Samuel 14:41. The margin translates, "give a perfect lot," as "Show forth the truth." The Bible says, "And the men of Israel were distressed (faint) that day: for Saul had adjured the people, saying, 'Cursed be the man that eateth any food until evening, that I may be avenged on mine enemies.' So none of the people tasted any food." Ibid., verse 24.

Satan has told the universe that God's law is a cursed law. He has declared that no one can keep it. He has said it is unfair and the Father only uses it to manipulate His creatures. Satan had even charged that God Himself could not keep it. That was why Jesus came and exalted the law and, never sinning once, proved Satan's charges false.

*Note: The Bible never identifies God as the "tempter" or "deceiver", nor the "destroyer." The Lord allows and permits Satan to tempt, deceive, and destroy but God never breaks His own law.

CHAPTER 24

A SPECTACLE FOR THE UNIVERSE

"Then said I, (Jesus) Lo, I come: in the volume of the book it is written of me, I delight to do thy will, 0 my God: yea, thy law is within my heart." Psalms 40:7, 8. "The Lord is well pleased for his righteousness' sake; he will magnify the law, and make it honorable." Isaiah 42:21. Cf. Matthew 5:17. When in His body of flesh, Jesus asked the Jewish leaders, "Which of you can truthfully accuse Me of one single sin? (They refused to answer Him for they knew He was telling the truth.) And since I am telling you the truth, why don't you believe Me?" John 8:46. In verse 44 he had told them that they were of their father the devil and his works they were destined to perform. But they only hated Him the more for saying it.

Our little planet is a spectacle for the universe. All of God's creatures are observing us. When we read that the "people escaped" when the lot fell upon Saul and Jonathan, we should not think only of the people who were in Saul's army that day. Oh, no. This is a cosmic controversy, friend of mine. Satan zeroed in on the one who was hurting his cause the most by his honesty, purity and faithfulness. And that was Jonathan. And so he let the lot fall upon Saul and Jonathan and then upon Jonathan. It reminds us of the two goats on the Day of Atonement doesn't it? Yes. And which goat had to die? The innocent One. Do you see how deep and far-reaching and symbolic each story in the Bible is? God put these incidents in His Word for a purpose, for not only planet earth but the whole universe escaped death through Jesus.

God didn't start the great controversy and He hasn't kept it going. Sin wasn't His idea. Satan is responsible for every minute of it. But the Father has had to let Lucifer prove his point, if he could. Notice what the people said to Saul when he suggested that they find out who was responsible for sin in the camp. "Do what seemeth good unto thee." 1 Samuel 14:40. The people here represent all the unfallen worlds and all the angels who have been watching planet earth since our Father created it. Lucifer charged God with keeping the universe in bondage through the law. Through Saul's words to the people (the unfallen worlds and angels) we know what Lucifer said. "Cursed be the man that eateth any food until evening ...." 1 Samuel 14:24. If Lucifer could keep everyone away from the truth about God long enough, darkness would come and no one would be able to see in the "evening," who was right and who was wrong. "Then Jesus said unto them, Yet a little while is the light with you. Walk while ye have the light, lest darkness come upon you: for he that walketh in darkness knoweth not whither he goeth." John 12:35.

Jesus told us that He is the light of the world, John 8:12, And His disciple John declared of him, "In Him (Jesus) was life; and the life was the light of men." John 1:4. Christ was also declared to be the WORD by the same author, John 1:1-3, 14. This Word was made flesh and demonstrated that God's WORD or HIS LAW was good.

The life of Jesus Christ showed that we could eat "honey" and "be enlightened," as Jonathan was. Jesus even declared that it was a matter of life or death. "I am that bread of life ... Verily, verily, I say unto you, Except ye eat the flesh of the Son of man, and drink his blood, ye have no life in you. Whoso eateth my flesh, and drinketh my blood, hath eternal life; and I will raise him up at the last day." John 6:48, 53, 54.

DON'T KEEP JESUS OUTSIDE

The word "meat" here means food as we see in other translations. "For My flesh is food indeed, and My blood is drink indeed. He who eats My flesh and drinks My blood abides in Me, and I in him." John 6:55, 56. RSV. God loves to speak to us in symbolic words. For example the name BETHLEHEM, the town where Jesus was born, was an example or symbol in a name as to what the Messiah would do. Bethlehem meant

"HOUSE OF BREAD." God is saying, "come and abide in My house (Jesus) and let Me feed you." You see when we go to God's house and find out what a wonderful person the Father is, we want Jesus and the Father to come and eat with us. When they come in we never want Them to leave. Zacchaeus had already "tasted" some of Jesus' flesh (John 6:53) and was rejoicing. "O taste and see that the Lord is good: blessed is the man that trusts in Him." Psalm 34:8. Zacchaeus was "chief among the publicans (tax collectors)." Luke 19:2. He had previously eaten some of Jesus' words that he had heard from others and now he ran ahead of the throng in Jericho and climbed up into a sycamore (fig) tree so he could see Jesus better since Zacchaeus was short of stature. Climbing the tree was an act of faith and symbolic of the "tree of life" from which he had already been eating, even Christ's words. It also could represent the crucifixion of self. Now, Jesus asks Zacchaeus if He might come home to His house, "for today I must abide at thy house." Ibid., verse 5. "Zacchaeus," Jesus was saying, "I just can't wait to tell you how much you mean to Me. I must come home and tell you today!" What a wonderful God we have! I hope that you will invite him to come home and have supper with you.

He is standing at the door of your heart, waiting for you to invite Him in to have supper with you, Revelation 3:20. Don't keep Him waiting outside. Jeremiah found that eating with God was necessary to sustain life. "Your words are what sustain me; they are food to my hungry soul. They bring joy to my sorrowing heart and delight me." Jer. 15:16. God's Word is also likened unto a "lamp" in Psalms 119:105 that guides our feet. But God Himself is called a lamp. "For thou art my lamp, 0 Lord; and the Lord will lighten my darkness." 2 Samuel 22:29. In the beginning of the creation of this planet God's "Spirit" moved upon "the face of the waters." We know that waters represent people, Revelation 17:15, and so the people or beings God moved upon must have been all the unfallen worlds as He created this earth. As they watched, "there was light." Genesis 1:1-5. God would bring light and truth out of the creation of planet earth. Our

Creator did not plan for sin to enter, but he foresaw it and made provision to meet the crisis by coming down to this planet Himself in the very person of His Son, who became the Lion of the Tribe of Judah. I Pet. 5:8 depicts Satan as a lion who is our "devouring adversary."

It is God's glory to show both His love and His gentleness and His strength by using lambs and lions. He also is able to overcome Satan's accusations without ever hurting, embarrassing or taking away Satan's free choice. Christ is the lion of the earth made new, not of this sinful earth.

Satan destroys himself and in the process provides proof that God is just. Samson even made a riddle out of it. "Out of the eater came something to eat. Out of the strong come something sweet." Judges 14:14 RSV. Samson's bride-to-be wept because he would not tell her the riddle.

He finally told her and she betrayed him and told her countrymen who then came to Samson on the seventh day and said, "What is sweeter than honey? What is stronger than a lion?" Ibid., verse 18. Although he failed to show forth God's true character, the Lord was still able to bring "honey" out of the lion's mouth. The life-God message is a very sweet message. "Out of the strong came something sweet." The truth of God is as sweet as honey to those who love him and know his true character.

After his fiancé (in the east they call a bride-to-be a wife before they actually live together as man and wife) betrayed his secret to her own people, Samson went back home. He was hurt and bitter. Later he came back and the father would not allow Samson to consummate the marriage because he had given his daughter to another man. Samson then destroyed the Philistines' corn, vineyards and olives. To get even, these heathen Philistines then "burned" Samson's ex-fiancé and her father with fire. All this happened because of a riddle that these heathen men could not understand or solve. But once it was told to them they turned "the truth of God into a lie." Romans 1:25. They used the secret to destroy instead of to give life. How many people and religious organizations and churches have used the name of God as a cover for their destructive activities? They think they are doing God service. John 16:2. But their ways are the ways of death. The final apostate church will be done in by those she has been using and they will "burn her with fire" Revelation 17:16, because her father is the devil (John 8:44) the same as the Jews. All of the wicked will have to go through the lake of fire due to their own wickedness and hatred for God and each other. They will be in that condition/situation as long as it takes for them to change. Mark 10:43-49. "Where their worm (sin) does not die, and the fire (of God's love) is not quenched." In the case of Saul of Tarsus it only took a few minutes in his own little private Lake of Fire. It took Nebuchadnezzar seven years. Dan. 4. Each person is different.

In contrast to the apostate church, whom Satan uses, God has His true bride He is preparing to marry. She is even now making herself ready by receiving the robe of righteousness Jesus is giving to those who will accept it. This robe is His very own likeness and character which comes only by an intense and diligent study of God's Word, the Bible. As Jesus is able to program our minds He is weaving our robe of righteousness around us in preparation for our wedding day. Rev. 19:7, 8.

Jesus claims that His church will be perfect, without any defect at all. The universe accepted the Father's claims for His Son. Jesus Christ, in a "sinful" body of flesh, perfected a character after His Father's likeness and proved Satan a liar. God's law of love was written in Christ's heart and this was the secret of His power and victory over sin and the devil. But, can sinful human beings keep the law too? Satan claims they cannot and therefore the Father has no right to allow them to go up to heaven or to inherit the new earth after the 1,000 years. The universe is again looking on to see if God can perfect His likeness in us just as He did in His own Son, even while He was trapped and encased in a body of flesh like our own. He received the approval of the heavenly council for Jesus. Will He receive it for us too? Will "It is finished" be pronounced in our favor too? Listen to what Paul says:

"Husbands, love your wives, even as Christ also loved the church, and gave himself for it; That he might sanctify and cleanse it with the washing of water by the word, That he might present it to Himself a glorious church, not having spot, or wrinkle, or any such thing; but that it should be holy and without blemish." Eph. 5:23-26. "Now ye are clean through the word which I have spoken unto you." John 15:3. " Sanctify them through thy truth: thy word is truth." John 17:17.

It was the Word of God that created the world in the beginning, John 1:1-3, Hebrews 1:1-3, Psalms 33:6, and it is by that same creative power of his Word that we are born again into his kingdom of grace now. "But whoso keepeth his word, in him verily is the love of God perfected: ... I have written unto you, young men, because ye are strong, and the word of God abideth in you, and ye have overcome the world." 1 John 2:5, 14.

God's Word in us is His divine power to preserve us until the resurrection. It is, in fact, the spark of life that will respond to the "breath of his mouth" which is the fire of His love, for His word is His law and His law is a fiery law of love. "Then said Jesus to them again, Peace be unto you: as my Father hath sent me, even so send I you. And when He had said this, He breathed on them, and saith unto them, Receive ye the Holy Ghost." John 20:21, 22.

On the day of Pentecost, the Holy Spirit was poured out in its fullness on them and it came in the likeness of "cloven tongues." Acts 2:3. This fire of God is what will bring each believing saint forth from his dusty tomb when Christ returns. This fire of his love is His law written in our hearts as it was written in the heart of Jesus. This fire in our heart is proof that we know Him, whom to know is life eternal, John 17:3, The word "know" has a connotation of the intimacy that is known only in the sacredness of the marriage relationship. "And Adam knew his wife; and she conceived, and bare Cain, and said, I have gotten a man from the Lord." Genesis 4:1. We can see that the word "know" is used here to describe the act of sexual union between Adam and Eve, which was legal and according to God's law, for God Himself had pronounced them man and wife. It is through this union that new life was brought forth to populate the earth.

How much more significant is the relationship that God wants to have with each of us in the Spirit! He seeks to plant the seed of his Son Jesus in our hearts so we may bring forth fruit (souls) to his kingdom. He wants to conceive His only Son in us so we may be with Him forever. Paul expresses it like this: "That I may know him, and the power of his resurrection, and the fellowship of his sufferings, being made conformable unto his death." Phil. 3:10. In order for Him to conceive His son in us, the Father must be married to us through His Spirit and the Spirit of His son. What a glorious experience this is. Only those of us who have been through it can really know. But the Father desires for every human heart to truly "know" Him in this same way, so when He calls us on that resurrection morning we will respond and come forth from the grave or we will be translated without seeing death, as was Enoch and Elijah.

"Verily, verily, I say unto you, The hour is coming, and now is, when the dead shall hear the voice of the Son of God; and they that hear shall live." John 5:25.

When Jesus cried out on the cross, "IT IS FINISHED," John 14:30, the Bible also says he spoke to His Father. "And when Jesus had cried with a loud voice, he said Father, into thy hands I commend My spirit: and having said thus, He gave up the ghost." Luke 23:46. Jesus had both the power to lay down His life and the power to take it up again. "No man taketh it from me, but I lay it down of myself." John 10:18. This was much different than the "forced" sacrifices of the heathen. It may be that Satan really believed that the Father himself would come and kill His only Son to prove the justice of his law. But the Father symbolically died with his Son. It was a voluntary action for both of them. I believe that the universal council saw the sufferings of Jesus and began to realize that the Father's law was just and right and true after all. They finally realized Satan was not only a liar but a murderer. They saw that Christ's life and his voluntary death demonstrated the power inherent in the law of God to both give life to those who keep it, but take it from those who break it. The law of gravity is a good illustration of how this works. If you obey the law of gravity you will live but if you brake or defy it you will suffer and possibly forfeit your life. This is an example of how the law of cause and effect works in the natural world. But there is also a law of cause and effect in the spiritual world as well. And it was this law which was demonstrated in the life and death of Jesus Christ.

Christ's death on the cross demonstrated this principle of life and death, of light and darkness. As the Creator He willingly gave up His life in order to absorb all of the punishment the human race deserves for breaking the moral law of right and wrong. This demonstration had to continue until the heavenly council were all completely convinced that all the charges Lucifer (Satan, the adversary) had made were false. It had to be a unanimous vote. Jesus had to suffer and die the second death the law requires of every sinner. He did this by being completely separated from His Father. The human language does not have the words to fully describe the intensity of His suffering.

That is why the anguished cry of God's son broke forth from his parched and bleeding lips, "MY GOD, MY GOD, WHY HAST THOU FORSAKEN ME?" Jesus had to experience what every lost soul will experience in that final day as they stand outside of the gates of the New Jerusalem. Even though the gates will never be closed, Revelation 21:25, they will not be able to enter at first, because they have unfitted themselves for such a holy place. They cannot stand the light and the glory of his pure and holy presence until they die that second death...the death of the self life, the ego. That is why there is a great gulf fixed. Like Esau, they cannot find any place for repentance in their hearts. That is, they are sorry for the results of their sins, but not for the sin itself.

"Follow peace with all men, and holiness, without which no man shall see the Lord. Looking diligently lest any man fail of the grace of God; lest any root of bitterness springing up trouble you, and thereby many be defiled; Lest there be any fornicator, or profane person, as Esau, who for one morsel of meat sold his birthright. For ye know how that afterward, when he would have inherited the blessing, he was rejected: for he found no place of repentance, though he sought it carefully with tears." Hebrews 12:14-17.

By Esau's own choice he "fixed a great gulf," between himself and the Father, just as the rich man did in the parable, Luke 16:26. Jesus bridged that gulf for us. He went to his death not knowing for a certainty that He would ever be able to come into His Father's presence again. It was by faith alone that he gave up his life, and went into the grave, believing He truly did have the Father's eternal spark of life still residing in him by which He would come forth from the grave.

WHAT IF JESUS HAD SINNED?

But, friend of mine, His love for us was so great that He was willing to give up His eternal existence if it meant that we could live. That is a love which all of the eons of eternity will not be able to measure. It is a great mystery we cannot fathom. We are mortal. When we die, our intelligence or mind or whatever you want to call that part of us that is able to think, dies too. The "spirit returns to God," Eccles. 12:7. This is true, but the spirit is not able to think. It is not the mind. It is not the soul. The soul is a combination of the spirit plus the body. Our breath or spirit is simply that "spark of life," that God gave to Adam when he created him.

Jesus Christ was with His Father, a Creator Himself. Now, the point is this. If Jesus had failed to perfectly obey his Father's law in the least particular and a taint of sin had been on Him, would He have been able to return to heaven in either a visible or an invisible form? I don't think so. We know He did have a body after His resurrection. It was an immortal body, as we shall have, Phil. 3:20, 21. But, what if Christ had sinned even once in his life or in the Garden of Gethsamane, when the test was the greatest? Or what if He had sinned while hanging on the cross by showing anger or self-pity or lashing out at His tormentors? That would have been a sin, and I do not believe that He would have been resurrected. That is the risk He took my friends. There are some things we do not know but I have wondered what would have happened to the spirit of the eternal God in Christ, that could not die, which had become stained and tainted with the foul miasma of sin. What would He have done? Where would He have gone? He would have forever been excluded from heavenly beings and the presence of His Father. Can you think of a greater loss? This truly would have been eternal torment. On this point, I believe that Satan has reversed the truth again. The doctrine of eternal damnation and hell is not what humans will suffer, but what our Lord Jesus Christ would have suffered if He had failed. And would not the unfallen worlds slowly, one by one, have fallen under the terrible shadows of Satan's delusions? It could have spread like a cancer throughout the universe. This is what Jesus died to prevent. I do not think that we are capable at this time, in this age, to fully understand or appreciate the risk He took in coming to our planet to redeem us.

Dear reader, Christ's victory is ours. "These things I have spoken unto you, that in me ye might have peace. In the world ye shall have tribulation: but be of good cheer; I have overcome the world." John 16:33. "For even hereunto were ye called: because Christ also suffered for us, leaving us an example, that ye should follow his steps: Who did no sin, neither was guile found in his mouth: Who, when he was reviled, reviled not again: when he suffered, he threatened not; but committed Himself to Him that judgeth righteously:" 1 Peter 2:21-23.

Have you committed yourself to the Father? Have you entrusted yourself completely into His hands? He is waiting for you to come to Him right now. Listen to this wonderful promise.

"Now unto him that is able to keep you from falling, and to present you faultless before the presence of his glory with exceeding joy. To the only wise God our Savior, be glory and majesty, dominion and power, both now and ever." Amen. Jude 24.

ESTHER WAS A TYPE OF CHRIST

Queen Esther's experience comes closest to what Jesus was willing to give up than any other story in the Bible. She had not been called in to see the king for thirty days. There was a law that you could not come into the king's presence without being called and if you went otherwise, the penalty could be death for the presumptuous offender, unless the king held out his "golden scepter." Esther 4:11.

Mordecai, her uncle, told her that if she did not attempt to save the Jews that deliverance would come from some other source. This is an amazing concept which some people believe indicates that the Father and His son had a secondary plan of salvation set up to save us even if Christ failed. There is no way to prove this, nor any other indication of it in Scripture, besides Esther 4:14. Esther is a type of Christ though. Her name means "star," from Ishtar, the Babylonian goddess of beauty and fertility. Jesus is the "morning star," Revelation 22:16. The symbolism reaches its apex of beauty in verse 16. "... and so will I go in unto the king, which is not according to the law: and if I perish, I perish." Esther 4:16.

We know that the king did hold out the golden scepter to Esther and she saved her people. The thirty days, the three days and three nights and the banquet are all no doubt types which have significant meanings and applications. But the most important symbolism we should see is that Jesus was willing to sacrifice Himself for us no matter what the cost. Even if it meant eternal loss and torment forever and ever or external extinction or exclusion of a nature we cannot comprehend, His love was so overwhelming He was willing to go all the way to the cross even in the face of such terrible consequences against Himself. Such obsessive love is beyond our ability to comprehend.

But in addition to this, Jesus was suffering the agony of

knowing that His Father was hurting and suffering with Him as all of the sins of the world were laid upon Him. The greatest suffering is mental and emotional suffering. To better understand this let us think of the suffering of Jacob when he was told that his son Joseph had been killed, probably by a wild animal. And think of Joseph's suffering of knowing that his beloved father was grieving for him without Joseph being able to communicate comforting words of hope and cheer. Joseph never knew if he would ever see his father's face again. Finally, when he revealed his identity to his 10 brothers, about 20 years later, the first question he asked was, "doth my father yet live?" Genesis 45:3. The love that Joseph had for his father was just as great as the love that Jacob had for Joseph, his beloved son.

JOSEPH WAS A TYPE OF CHRIST

Notice, that Joseph did not expose his brothers, but refrained from contacting His Father all those years He was in Egypt. He knew that any word from him in Egypt would expose His brothers as liars and bring upon them a terrible guilt and remorse that may have caused them to begin fighting among themselves, blaming each other even to the extent of murder. We know that Simeon and Levi were capable of this kind of anger. Genesis 49:5-7. So, he sacrificed his own desire to let his beloved Father know he was ok to protect and safeguard his brothers. This is the same way Jesus treated Lucifer and all of his evil angels who followed him out of heaven, Revelation 12:4. The Father took the blame for all that Lucifer did all through the Old Testament. This is the way He treated Judas as well, never once exposing him. We must remember, however, that when Christ came in the flesh, He could no longer cover up for Lucifer. It was at last time for Lucifer to be exposed as a liar and a murderer, John 8:44. But even this identification was, in and of itself, a tremendous appeal on Christ's part to His beloved Lucifer, for God never gives up hope, (1 Corinthians 13:7), God never closes anyone's probation. We each close our own probation, but God can't quit hoping that we will some day come back. He is the incurable lover.

Now, let us draw a parallel between this human drama of Jacob and Joseph and the Divine suffering of God the Father and God the Son as all the sins of the ages were laid upon Jesus, the Divine, innocent, holy and only Son of His Father. "For he hath made him to be sin for us, who knew no sin; that we might be made the righteousness of God in Him." 2 Corinthians 5:21. And verse 19 states that "God was in Christ, reconciling the world unto himself."

True, unselfish, Divine love always concerns itself with the welfare of others. Divine love is unselfish. It always puts itself last and others first. From the first to the last Jesus demonstrated this type of love. He did everything He could to prevent Peter from denying Him and Judas from betraying Him. He even requested that the disciples be allowed to run away when He was captured in the Garden of Gethsemane. He healed Malchus' ear when Peter cut it off with the sword. He told Peter to put away his sword to prevent Peter from being arrested, perhaps killed by the mob who had come to arrest Him. At His trial He tried to help Pilate. On the way to Calvary He stopped to speak to some women who were weeping for Him to warn them that they should weep for themselves for they would suffer terribly too, if they did not accept His salvation. On the cross He asked His Father to forgive his tormentors, provided a new son for His mother and promised the thief he would be in the kingdom (paradise) with Him.

Never once did Jesus think of Himself or His own welfare but sacrificed Himself to the ultimate limits of human suffering and degradation, so no one could ever again say God was selfish or was unwilling to sacrifice Himself. Is it not logical then that his cries to His Father were not selfish, but cries of concern for His beloved Father's welfare? They both knew Lucifer was destroying himself and the Jewish nation by crucifying Him. This was what broke the Father's and Son's hearts; this terrible weight of sin, the sin of rejecting their love. If

Christ had not prayed that they be forgiven, Satan, the avenging angel of justice, might have had the legal right to kill the Jewish leaders right then and there. In fact, it is possible that the guilt of the whole ordeal may have even caused Satan and his angels to self-destruct.

Jesus and His Father were dying for all of their creatures. It had been predicted that a "sword" would pierce through Mary's heart, Luke 2:35. This same "sword" was piercing the Father's and Son's hearts as they suffered an agony that is beyond our comprehension. The Psalmist pictures them requesting that the other be delivered from suffering. "Deliver my soul from the sword; my darling* from the power of the dog." Psalms 22:20. Sometimes the dog's bark is almost as bad as his bite. They suffered both the "bark" and "bite" of sin for us. *My only One.

As Jesus entered the garden of Gethsemane (meaning the oil press) His connection with the Father began to be broken up. The Bible says that He "began to be sorrowful and very heavy. Then saith He unto them, my soul is exceeding sorrowful, even unto death:" Matthew 26:37, 38. Then He prayed in verse 39, that if possible, the cup of death might pass from Him. This was not a selfish request. In fact, it was very unselfish. First of all, He did not want His Father to have to go through this terrible suffering with Him, for He knew His Father would suffer even more than He would. He knew the sight of His sufferings would cause His Father to "die" too, if only in a symbolical sense. Secondly, He did not want to cause any embarrassment to His Father in case He was not able to bear up under the terrible load of all the sins of the world. If He went through with it and was separated from His Father He did not know if He would ever be able to see His Father again. He knew this would crush His Father's heart, as much as, if not even more than His own.

Never before had the communication with His Father been interrupted or broken up. This He had never before experienced. As Christ looked down that long passageway or corridor of death He could not, at that time, see any light at the other end of the tunnel. He would have to go into that tunnel by faith alone, not knowing if He would ever come out alive or see His Father again. Luke 22:41-44 tells how he removed Himself "about a stone's cast," from Peter, James and John, so they would not have to see Him suffer. An angel came to strengthen Him so He could drink the cup and that is when He began to sweat blood. Who was this angel? Do you realize that there are only two angels who are identified in the Bible? Their names are Michael and Gabriel. I am going to go into this here because it opens up a door that will reveal even greater depths of the sacrifice and suffering of Jesus Christ, which simply means, "The anointed SAVIOR." First of all, Michael is first mentioned in Daniel 12:1, not only as a "Prince" but as "the great prince," which stands up for "the children" or the descendants of "thy people" which could only be referring to the children of Israel, which indicates that the 144,000 sealed in Revelation 7 truly are the direct descendants of the tribes of Israel there named and numbered.

Furthermore, Michael is also mentioned two times in the New Testament. And in both instances it is in connection with resurrecting the dead, something only Jesus was able to do as we know from the story of Lazarus in John 11, whom He raised from the dead after he had been in the tomb four days. An incontestable miracle. Only God, the Creator, has power over death. In Jude 9 we are told that Michael is an "archangel," who came to contend with the devil over the "body" of Moses. Since Moses appeared on the Mount of Transfiguration later on, Matthew 17:1-8, we can safely assume that Michael did indeed raise Moses from the dead after he was buried on Mount Nebo although his body nor his grave site were ever found. Deuteronomy 34:5, 6. For the final proof that Michael and Jesus are one and the same personage, let us read together I Thessalonians 4:16. "For the Lord Himself shall descend from heaven with a shout, with the voice of the archangel, and with the trump of God: and the dead in Christ shall rise first:" Once again we see that the Archangel, Michael, is raising the dead. And how does He raise them? With His voice. "Verily, verily, I say unto you, The hour is coming, and now is, when the dead shall hear the voice of the Son of God: and they that hear shall live." John 5:25. Beloved how did He raise Jairus' daughter from the dead? "He...took her by the hand, and called, saying, Maid, arise." Luke 8:54. In this same manner He called forth Lazarus from the grave. "He cried with a loud voice, Lazarus, come forth." John 11:43.

Now, let's go back to Jesus' praying in the garden, where he sweats blood, which we will deal with later. Our Lord is praying that the cup of death be removed from Him. "Father, if you are willing, take this cup away from me-but it is not my will, but yours, that must be done." Luke 22:42. The Amplified reads: "Not My will, but (always) Yours, be done." The footnote states the Greek is in the "present imperative." Peterson's "Message" in contemporary language reads: "Father, remove this cup from me. But please, not what I want. What do you want?" At this point I can almost hear the Father saying in Jesus' mind, "The demonstration is not over...it must go on my beloved Son...I am so sorry." Surely the Father must have been weeping. And then something happened that we have not fully understood which we must examine here more fully because it will open the door to a much greater revelation of Jesus' sufferings and what was going on behind the scenes, in another dimension we cannot see. As we know, angels are always with us but we cannot see them but now an angel appears which the disciples can see. "And there appeared an angel unto him from heaven strengthening Him." Who is this "angel?" Remember there are only two angels in the Bible who are named. Michael and Gabriel. And remember that it was Gabriel who worked with Michael in the book of Daniel and who was sent to announce both the birth of the John the Baptist and the Messiah to Zechariah and Mary. So, here we are at the most crucial and critical moment in the history of this planet. So, what angel would the Father send to help His beloved, only Son make it through this crisis? Gabriel, of course.

The "Message" reads "No one helps me in my fight against

these beings except Michael, your angel-prince." The NAS, considered by many scholars to be the most accurate translation says: "Yet there is no one who stands firmly with me against these forces except Michael your prince." Dan 10:21.

But who is this Gabriel? In order to answer, let's analyze this Scripture that will begin to unlock the mystery surrounding this mighty angel. "But I will shew thee that which is noted in the scripture of truth: and there is none that holdeth with me in these things, but Michael your prince." Dan. 10:21. There are two points from this text which are extremely important: 1. This mighty angel is telling Daniel that the only being high enough in rank to help me is Michael. The reason for that is Michael and Gabriel are both Archangels. There is no other angel equal in rank to them. They are the highest and most powerful. This means that in power and position or rank Gabriel and Michael are equal. If Michael is Jesus Christ, in His pre-existent state, then what does that tell you about Gabriel? It means that they are both deity. Compare the parallel description Daniel gives of Gabrielle in Dan 10:5, 6 with John's description of Jesus among the candlesticks in Rev 1:13-16 and you will see they are almost identical, like twins. In Dan 10 the colors are feminine colors.

Before we go to the second point let me explain something that most people don't know about Gabriel. Gabriel is actually Gabrielle. When you go to Strong's 1403 & 1404 you will see the name Gabriel also has a feminine form as we note in Strong's, starting at 1397. And then 1376, 1377 which means lady, mistress, queen. One researcher wrote me saying: "THE ROOT FROM #1397 IS #1403 AND #1404 AND #1376 WHICH LEADS YOU RIGHT BACK TO #1397. A RULE OF HEBREW IS TO TAKE ALL THE ROOT WORDS IN FOCUS OR ELSE YOU WILL MISS THE WHOLE MEANING OF THE WORD. THERE IS NO DOUBT THAT GABRIEL IS A (feminine) WOMAN NOT A (masculine) MAN. SHE IS OF AUTHORITY BECAUSE OF HER FATHER, JUST LIKE Y'HOSHUA IS OF AUTHORITY FROM THE FATHER WHO IS G-D THE FATHER

BLESSED BE HIS NAME. BARUK HASHEM!"

Now, point #2 is from the word "holdeth." Strong's 2388 refers you to #8628 which defines the Hebrew word "taqa" whose prim. root means to clatter, i.e. slap (the hands together),...by impl. to become bondsman by hand clasping (i.e. a hand shake or agreement), also "suretiship." So, Gabrielle is explaining to Daniel that no one else in all the universe had entered into an agreement or bondsman ship as she and Michael had and were standing alone in fighting against the enemy in order to preserve their Father's kingdom. This hit me so hard when I first realized what this really meant that I had to stop writing and take a break.

It made me weep when I realized that Michael and Gabrielle were the only ones who understood who Lucifer really was in his true character. The rest of the angelic realm and the unfallen worlds did not see it at that time. And then I realized why Jesus had to come to this earth in a body of flesh to reveal the truth about the Father as well as the real truth about Lucifer. It confirmed this most insightful statement: "Christ did not yield up His life till He had accomplished the work which He came to do, and with His parting breath he exclaimed, 'IT IS FINISHED.' John 19:30. The battle had been won....All heaven triumphed in the SAVIOR's victory. Satan was defeated, and knew that his kingdom was lost. To the angels and the unfallen worlds the cry, 'It is finished,' had a deep significance. It was for them as well as for us that the great work of redemption had been accomplished. They with us share the fruits of Christ's victory. Not until the death of Christ was the character of Satan clearly revealed to the angels or to the unfallen worlds. The archapostate had so clothed himself with deception that even holy beings had not understood his principles. They had not clearly seen the nature of his rebellion." Desire of Ages, pg 758.

So, why was it that no one else in the universe could see the sinful "nature" of Satan's rebellion? Because the Father was always covering up for Lucifer, always taking the blame for whatever He did. There is not one place in the OT where Satan is charged, blamed or given credit for destroying anyone, even though he was continually doing it, as in the case of Job. The Father always assumed the responsibility. That is why Jesus had to come in a body of flesh to reveal the real truth about the Father. He alone, with Gabrielle, understood who Lucifer really was from the very beginning of the Great Controversy, which is exactly what Jesus revealed to the Jews, explaining clearly that Satan was their Father, and that he was a liar and a murderer. "You have the devil for your father and you wish to practice the desires (lusts) of your father; he was a murderer from the beginning and he could not stay in the truth because there is no truth in him. When he tells a lie he talks naturally; for he is a liar and its father;" John 8:44. Modern Language Version.

"You give your mouth free rein for evil, and your tongue frames deceit. You sit and speak against your brother...These things you have done and I have been silent; you thought that I was one like yourself. But now I rebuke you, and lay the charge before you." Psalm 50:19-21. RSV.

Now, let us come back to the sufferings of Jesus which begin in the Garden of Gethsamane. Not only is the Father suffering with His only Son but Gabrielle is also suffering. Here is a quote from a letter I received from a Jewish scholar regarding Michael and Gabrielle: "Shalom Mike, I agree that Gabrielle is Y'shua's bride and sister. That is a common belief among the Jews that Gabrielle is female and Michael is male and are twins. I do believe that the Ruach Ha Kodesh (the Holy Spirit) is female and is the glory of G-d." You can verify this from Song of Solomon 4:9 and 5:1 where Christ in symbolism refers to his beloved as "my sister, my spouse." The second way you prove this is to look at the counterfeits in every culture. In Egypt you have Osiris and Isis. Webster's dictionary defines Isis thusly: "The goddess of fertility, sister and wife of Osiris, usually represented with a cow's horns surrounding a solar (or lunar) disk."

In the Babylonian culture you have Tammuz and his twin sister and wife Ishtar. "In Ezekiel's time the Tammuz cult had found entrance into Judah, and Hebrew women were weeping for that god at the temple gates (Ezek. 8:14);" Bible Dictionary, pg 1064. This cult was carried over into Greece and Rome finding its expression in their culture in the myth of Venus and Adonis. Today, Mary is the new Queen.

Next you have Diana, who was the Roman virgin goddess of the moon and of hunting, often depicted with many breasts and sometimes identified with the Greek Artemis who was the twin sister of Apollo. "A goddess worshiped at Ephesus (Acts 19:24, 27, 28, 34, 35), more or less equivalent to Cybele, or to Magna Mater, the Great Mother, one of the many forms of the mother goddess of the Orient." Bible Dictionary, 77. The point here is that where there are so many counterfeits there has to be a real, a genuine, an original from which these imitations and pretenders sprung. ***And Michael and Gabrielle are the original.*** So, that is the daughter. Then who is the Mother God of Israel who "brought them forth?" Song of Solomon 8:5 and Proverbs 8:22-30. Genesis 17:1 identifies her. "The Lord (Yahweh) appeared to Abram, and said unto him, I am the Almighty God; walk before Me, and be thou perfect." This is "El Shaddai," THE ALMIGHTY BREASTED ONE, a very clear reference to a female deity. There is much proof in Bible Commentaries and dictionaries and on the internet for those who wish to do a little research. The Shekinah glory is also a reference used to refer to the feminine face of Yahweh or God.

So, now we have three beings who are identified as suffering with Jesus in the final hours of His mission. His Father, to whom He is praying that the cup be removed, His sister-spouse, Gabrielle, who appears at His side; obviously she was there all the time throughout His entire life, but made herself known so the disciples could see her and then you have the Holy Spirit, the true Queen of Heaven.* Jeremiah 7 and 44 reveal the counterfeit Queen of heaven, whom the apostate Jews worshiped, an obvious counterfeit of El Shaddai. *See note on page 354.

And in the midst of this super natural suffering and agony, Jesus did not know if He would ever see any of His family again or if they were alright. Can you imagine the terrible suffering they were going through, especially Gabrielle? Try and put yourself in their places? How would you feel if it were your own son or brother or husband? He did not even know for sure if He would come up from the grave. If Christ had sinned in any particular, His sacrifice would have been marred or imperfect, and therefore, unacceptable. He would not have been able to come up from the grave on the resurrection morning, for the "wages of sin is death." Romans 6:23. "The SAVIOR trod the wine press alone, and of the people there was none with Him." (Isa 63:3) But God (Elohim in the plural, the God family) suffered with His Son. Angels beheld the SAVIOR's agony. They saw their Lord enclosed by legions of satanic forces, His nature weighed down with a shuddering, mysterious dread. There was silence in heaven. No harp was touched. Could mortals have viewed the amazement of the angelic host (they could not believe what they were seeing Satan do to Jesus) as in silent grief they watched the Father separating His beams of light, love, and glory from His beloved Son, they would better understand how offensive in His sight is sin. The worlds unfallen and the heavenly angels had watched with intense interest as the conflict drew to its close. Satan and his confederacy of evil, the legions of apostasy, watched intently this great crisis in the work of redemption. The powers of good and evil waited to see what answer would come to Christ's thrice-repeated prayer. Angels (good) had longed to bring relief to the divine sufferer, but this might not be. No way of escape was found for the Son of God. In this awful crisis, when everything was at stake, when the mysterious cup trembled in the hand of the sufferer, the heavens opened, a light shone forth amid the stormy darkness of the crisis hour, and the mighty angel who stands in the God's presence, occupying the position from which Satan fell, came to the side of Christ. (Gabrielle) The angel came not to take the cup from Christ's hand, but to strengthen Him to drink it, with the assurance of the Father's love." Desire of Ages 693. Jesus was assured that His Father was greater and more powerful than Satan and that if He would be willing to go through to the cross and die that His death would result in the total defeat of Satan and that the kingdom of this world would be given to the saints of the Most High. Daniel 7:13-15. He was reminded of Isaiah 53:11, which says that "He would see the travail of His soul and be satisfied." The same thing had happened just a few weeks earlier on the Mount of Transfiguration when Moses and Elijah appeared to Jesus, Matt. 17, Mark 9, Luke 9. "These men, chosen above every angel around the throne, had come to commune with Jesus concerning the scenes of His suffering, and to comfort Him with the assurance of the sympathy of heaven. THE HOPE OF THE WORLD, THE SALVATION OF EVERY HUMAN BEING, WAS THE BURDEN OF THEIR INTERVIEW." Desire of Ages, pg 425.

We know that God the Son and God the Father both are immortal. They cannot die. But Jesus took on a body of flesh so that he could demonstrate to us that God in the flesh could endure the temptations of man successfully without sinning. He did this. But, he also took on a body of flesh that we might witness his beautiful character in the flesh. That is, He demonstrated total love at all times even though encumbered with a temple or body of flesh just like we have. Because of this body He was able to "die" for us.

"LET THIS CUP PASS FROM ME"

When God the Son began taking upon Himself all of the sins of the world a terrible thing began to happen. The connection and communication He had always had with His Father began to be broken up. Jesus never had a selfish desire or wish in His life. He was always thinking of others. Therefore, as soon as this separation began, He started pleading with His Father to let the cup pass from Him. He was thinking primarily of the sufferings His Father and no doubt even the angels and the unfallen worlds would go through, much more than even his disciples, as they watched him suffer. He prayed that if the human race could be saved any other way than this, to let the cup pass away. It was not a selfish prayer. He did not want His Father or the God family or any of His creatures to have to endure the sight and sounds this cup of death would bring. What a loving Savior we have. And as I said, He did not want to take the chance of being eternally separated from His family.

But Jesus had to drink the cup so we could live. A demonstration had to be made that would break our hearts and open our eyes. Sin is so terrible that it caused the Father and Son to not be able to help or comfort each other during the most traumatic suffering either of them had ever endured. "For He (God the Father) hath not despised nor abhorred the affliction of the afflicted; neither hath he hid His face (the Father's face) from Him Jesus; but when He (Jesus) cried unto him, He (the Father) heard." Psalms 22:24. We will never know the suffering of the God family, especially, the Father and His Son endured for us that we might turn away from sin and come into the Father's heart.

Imagine how you would feel if your child were calling to you for help, but you could not respond, even though you wanted to. Neither could you tell your child that you wanted to come to his aid, but you couldn't. And how would you feel if you knew the greatest suffering the child was going through was his concern for your welfare? But it was impossible to get a message of any kind through. This is what God the Father and His Son endured at the cross. The static of sin was that heavy.

When Christ cried out with a heart that was breaking, "My God, My God, why hast thou forsaken me?" Matthew 27:46, He was only saying what He Himself had inspired the Psalmist to write in Psalms 22. But notice what else Christ said that either was not heard by the those at the cross or Jesus only thought these thoughts or said them so low that no one could hear Him. Jesus never had any selfish thoughts. That would have been sin and we know He never sinned. 1 Peter 2:22. He was always thinking of others. And He thought and talked to His Father more than anyone. They were always as One. So, who would He be thinking about most when the sins of the world began to interrupt and break up this communion He always had with the Father? We have always pictured God the Father as turning His back on His only and beloved Son. But that would have been impossible for even a human father to do in his human love. How much more impossible for God the Father to do such a thing, and yet that is the way we have thought of Him. How terrible!

Isaiah 53:3 tells us that "we hid as it were our faces from Him;" Yes, "we" did that to Him, but God the Father didn't. Jesus knew His Father would never turn away from Him in His hour of need, and so when that wonderful channel of communication began to be cut off by the static of sin, He could hear His Father's voice filled with grief and suffering and emotion. It was then that He knew His Father was suffering the same thing He was suffering. As He sensed the Presence of His Father being withdrawn from Him, Jesus' first thoughts were for His Father's welfare. He did not want His Father to suffer because of what was happening to Him, but obviously His Father was suffering. After many hours on the cross, Jesus cried out, "My God, My God, why hast thou forsaken me?" Matthew 27:46. We have always interpreted this to mean Christ was blaming His Father.

But notice what else the Psalmist predicted Christ would say, at least in His mind to His Father. "Why art thou so far from helping me, and from the words of my roaring?" Christ is here pictured as suffering such a magnitude of mental, emotional and physical pain that His words are like a roar, which would perhaps be something akin to groaning and writhing in supreme agony. He probably was only able to breath by pushing himself up with His feet since His diaphragm muscles were probably sore and starting to collapse. His breathing and speaking probably sounded like a roar. In other words, Jesus was calling out and groaning out to His Father, "Daddy, you are not helping me like you always have and usually do. Where are you? Are you alright Dad? Is anything wrong? Please answer me and tell me you are ok." Notice Psalms 22:11. "Be not far from me; for trouble is near; there is none to help." It is, as if Jesus is saying, "Father, please don't go away from me now, for I don't have anyone else to help me. No one understands, no one realizes but you, why this is happening." But His Father was unable to communicate as usual because the sins that had been placed upon Jesus were crushing both of them with excruciating agony and making it impossible to see or hear or sense each other's presence.

Can you imagine the mental torture and anguish this must have caused both of them? It is beyond comprehension. And what about his original divine mother El Shaddai? We hear a lot about Mary's suffering. But what about Jesus' Heavenly mother? And what about Gabrielle? Satan was right there, of course, to make it just as bad as he possibly could. Satan no doubt told Christ that now that He had taken all the sins of the world upon Himself that He would never be able to see His family again. As we have seen, Psalms 22:24 proves that the Father heard His Son's cries, but was unable to respond to Him because sin had made the gulf too wide. This is the horribleness of sin. Even though God the Father could not die, He was suffering just as much as if He could die, maybe more, for death is a sweet release. For six terrible hours this agony continued. Jesus did not know how His Father was. The Bible tells us that Jesus was nailed to the cross at the third hour or between 8:00 a.m. and 9:00 a.m. of the morning before the Sabbath, the 6th day or what we call Friday. Matthew 27:45 tells us that "from the sixth hour there was darkness over all the land unto the ninth hour." This was from noon til 3:00.

This darkness was caused not only by Satan, the ruler of darkness, and all of his demons gathered about the cross to try and make Jesus either sin or give up, but this darkness was an indication that evidently, nature itself was "groaning" (Romans 8:22), and sorrowing, in sympathy with its Creator, weeping and trying to hide, as it were, its face from the awful sight of the ordeal.

But, I believe the Father remained at the cross with His Son, hiding and veiling Himself in the darkness, so He could be just as close to His son as possible. He was suffering the same agony; maybe worse, that Jesus was suffering, for even a human father would suffer more than his son in a similar situation.

If Jesus could not communicate with His Father, how then did He know when to say, "IT IS FINISHED?" The only answer is that when the darkness lifted at the ninth hour (3:00 P.M.), Jesus knew that the heavenly council had voted in His Father's favor. They were at last convinced that the Father was not guilty of the crimes Satan had charged Him with down through the ages. They were also convinced that the Father was only love and His law was a perfect and eternal law of love that could be kept, for Jesus, in human flesh had kept it to give us an example, that we "should follow in His steps." 1 Peter 2:21; Romans 8:1-3; Hebrews 2:16-18.

Matthew 27:45, 46 tells us that "darkness was over all the land unto the ninth hour," which would be 3:00 P.M. The word "unto" in this passage and "until" in Mark 15:33 would indicate that at about 3:00 P. M., the lights came back on. The heavenly council were no doubt horrified to see the Father and Son go through so much suffering. They were probably even more horrified to see Satan and all of his devils persecuting God's dear Son. And finally, when Jesus cried out, "My God, My God, why hast thou forsaken me," the heavenly council surely must have cried out with one voice, "LET THE SUFFERING OF GOD'S DEAR SON CEASE. WE ARE CONVINCED THAT THE FATHER IS INNOCENT." And that is when a special contingent or army of holy angels came down and surrounded the cross, scattering the darkness caused by the evil angels because when those demon angels saw those angels coming with all their light and glory they knew that the heavenly council had voted a verdict of acquittal for the Father and His Son and the God family, and they left.

And that is why the darkness lifted. Jesus knew at that very moment that His work had been completed. And no doubt Gabrielle whispered in His ear.... "My darling, it is over. You have won. You can go to sleep now. I will see you in the morning." John 19:28 says, "After this, Jesus knowing that all things were now accomplished, (THE LIGHTS HAD COME BACK ON INDICATING A VERDICT OF ACQUITTAL HAD BEEN GIVEN), that the scripture might be fulfilled, (or thus fulfilling the Scripture), saith, I thirst." The soldiers offered Christ a potion mixed with vinegar or wine and myrrh before He was nailed to the cross at 9:00 A.M. and again just before He died at 3:00 P.M. Matthew 27:34, 48; Mark 15:23. Vinegar is from the Greek word "oxos." Textual evidence favors the reading "oinos" which is the general word for wine in the NT, instead of oxos, "vinegar." According to Rabbi Hisda (c. A.D. 309), "When one is led out to execution, he is given a goblet of wine containing a grain of frankincense, in order to benumb his senses" Talmud Sanhedren 43a, Soncino ed., p. 279. This was a merciful act to lessen the sufferings of the victim. Jesus refused this in order to keep his senses at all times so He would know when to say, "IT IS FINISHED." Neither did He believe in imbibing in fermented wine, according to His instruction to Solomon, Proverbs 20:1, as well as other places in the Scripture. What an example He has set for us in every facet of life. And even though He must have literally been dying from thirst from all the loss of blood and the exhaustion from the beatings and smashes in the face from the soldiers and rabble, and from two floggings (Matt, 27:26 and John 19:1), which may have been 39 each or 78 lashes in all, He still refused a drink so He could remain clearheaded to the end. The physical abuse He went through is beyond belief and the mental suffering was even worse.

Christ knew that the universal council had voted in His Father's favor. He knew at 3:00 P.M., JST, Jerusalem Standard Time, that the heavenly council had acquitted them of the false charges Satan had brought against Him and His Father. But, He also knew that this meant that the universe had rejected Lucifer completely. That is what Jesus meant when He had said earlier, "Now is the judgment of this world: now shall the prince of this world be cast out. And I, if I be lifted up from the earth, will draw all men unto me. This he said, signifying what death he should die." John 12:31, 32. The word "men" is supplied. In other words, by dying on the cross, Jesus would draw "all" the universe to Himself, to either accept Him and thus His Father, or to reject Him. Thus, after six hours on the cross, the heavenly council had seen enough and voted in favor of the Father and His Son ... to acquit them ... to pronounce them "NOT GUILTY," of the charges Satan had brought that they are killers, and unworthy of our trust, worship and love. But did Jesus know for absolute certainty that He would come forth from the tomb? Could He see through that dark tunnel of death to the resurrection morning? By faith alone He could but He gave up His life not knowing for sure whether he would come up from the tomb or not. All He knew was that He had finished what He had come to accomplish, which was to vindicate His Father's name before the universe of angels and unfallen worlds. Now, He could truly say, "IT IS FINISHED."

Forgetting Himself, He gave up His life and by faith yielded Himself up to His Father and bowed His head and died. How sad His breaking heart must have been to know that the universe had seen the very worst side of Satan. How terrible it must have made him feel to know that this was the only way the universe could learn the truth about His wonderful Father. He had not purposely exposed Satan or the Jewish leaders. In fact, He had reached out to save them, just as He had reached out to save Judas, and in the very act of trying to reach out and save them they had destroyed themselves by rejecting His love. This is what broke His heart. This was the terrible sword of sin and sorrow that pierced His heart and His Father's heart on the cross. The battle had been won.

But, did Jesus really know if His Father was ok or not? Had the suffering they had gone through done something permanent to His Father so He would never be able to see His face again? When Jesus took all the sins of the world upon Himself it was as if the Father had taken them upon Himself too. Did this cause damage to both of them of some kind that would never be able to be repaired? These thoughts and no doubt many others went through the Savior's mind. Perhaps even Satan threw them at Him to make His suffering greater and to try and make Him give up.

We do know that upon arising from the tomb Christ told Mary not to "cling" to Him for He had not yet ascended to His Father. Perhaps the first question Jesus asked the angel who rolled away the stone was, "Is my Father ok? Will I be able to see Him and talk to Him again?" What joy must have flooded His soul when the angel assured him that it was His very own Heavenly Father who had sent him to roll away the stone and call Him home again. How very eager Jesus must have been to once again see His Father's face and hear His wonderful voice. This is no doubt the very reason the angels were so eager to bear the news to earth and swarmed around the cross with their light and glory so the evil angels would leave. As soon as this happened, the lights came back on and Jesus knew that the heavenly council had voted in His Father's favor and that the entire universe was now safe. He then cried out in victory, "IT IS FINISHED!" John then tells us that "he bowed his head, and gave up the ghost." John 19:30. It was, as if, by an act of His own will that He yielded up His life. In fact, John records that Christ stated, "No man taketh it from me, but I lay it down of myself. I have power to lay it down, and I have power to take it again. This commandment have I received of my Father," John 10:18. Perhaps even here Christ and His Father were attempting to shield the Jewish nation as well as Rome from the terrible guilt of murder. When the Jewish leaders refused to admit their crime and continued their efforts to keep the truth from the people and began a cover-up as well as a program of persecution, it was then that they were told that they had indeed "slain," Acts 2:23 and "killed," Acts 3:15, the "Prince (or author) of life." This was no doubt stated so as to bring them to their senses regarding the enormity of their crime. And it had its effect, for Luke tells us in Acts 6:7, "And the word of God increased; and the number of the disciples multiplied in Jerusalem greatly; and a great company of the priests were obedient to the faith." But of course, the vast majority of the Jewish leadership and the people refused to believe, even to this very day.

It is most interesting that at the end of the world, at the seventh plague, "a great voice out of the temple of heaven, from the throne," will say again, "IT IS DONE." That will be the day the heavenly council will again vote in favor of Christ in the person of His saints. Again the heavenly council will vote, "let the suffering of Christ and His Father cease, for they are suffering again in the person of the saints, whom Satan is trying to destroy from off the face of the earth. We are convinced that God can dwell in man and renew His own image in fallen humanity. Let the suffering cease and bring the exiles home." May God grant us that wonderful day of deliverance very soon.

"DO NOT CLING TO ME"

After the resurrection, Mary Magdalene fell at His feet or grabbed Him in some way or other and He lovingly said to her, "Do not touch (cling to) Me, for I have not yet ascended to the Father." John 20:17. This is extremely exciting and significant in that it indicates here that Jesus' is saying that He has not yet been to see His Father in the throne room above to receive the official stamp of approval for the completion of His Messianic mission. What infinite love we see here as Jesus takes time to comfort Mary in her sorrow and to give her proof that He is alive and that her faith in Him was justified, for she was the only one who truly believed that He was going to die. Did she not anoint Him with the precious ointment before His death? Jesus told them at the time, she hath poured this ointment on My body, "she did it for My burial." Matt. 26:12.

Later Christ appears to His disciples and eats with them and even asks Thomas to touch His hands as well as His side for confirmation that He is truly alive. John 20:27. In fact, He was with them for "forty days," before He ascended to heaven again for a longer stay by His Father's throne. This indicates to me that Christ, who had not been "called" into His Father's courtroom for over thirty days, went up to see His Father by faith. He believed that He would be accepted. He could not live in His Father's presence if any taint of sin was upon Him. He went into His Father's presence and received the well done spoken to Him. The golden scepter of approval or acceptance was held out to Him signifying that our salvation was sealed forever. At the last day the wicked will also come up in the 2nd resurrection. In that great final day of reckoning or judgment (decision) when every soul on the wrong side of the walls of the New Jerusalem (outside) makes his final decision against God's plan of salvation through Christ, the wicked are going to make an attack against the city.

"And when the thousand years are ended, Satan will be loosed from his prison and will come out to deceive the nations which are in the four corners of the earth, that is, Gog and Magog, to gather them for battle; their number is like the sand of the sea. And they marched up over the broad earth and surrounded the camp of the saints and the beloved city; but fire came down from heaven and consumed them." Revelation 20:7-10 RSV.

The Bible tells us, "And as it is appointed unto men once to die, but after this the judgment." Hebrews 9:27 KJV. We know that the word "judgment" means "to decide for or against something." It does not mean to condemn, although the result of a decision can lead to condemnation. But many decisions lead to justification and life, not death. Jesus said that anyone who ever came to Him would not be cast out. John 6:37. He also said His Father was not going to judge the world, but had committed all judgment (discernment and decision) to the Son. John 5:22. Christ plainly stated that He had not come to judge the world, but to save it. He said that the words that He had spoken, "the same shall judge him in the last day." John 12:48.

MAN'S TONGUE WILL DESTROY THE WORLD

Furthermore, the Bible tells us, "by thy words thou shalt be justified, and by thy words thou shalt be condemned." Matthew 12:37. And to the unfaithful servant who had a wrong concept of God's character because he thought of God as harsh and unforgiving the Lord said, "Out of thine own mouth will I judge thee." Luke 19:22. God is going to let each man decide his own destiny by the words of his or her own mouth or tongue. "Ye shall conceive (imagine, think or express in words) chaff, ye shall bring forth stubble: your breath, as fire, shall devour you." Isaiah 33:11. James tells us "the tongue is a fire, a world of iniquity: so is the tongue among our members, that it defileth the whole body, and setteth on fire the course of nature; and is set on fire of hell." James 3:6.

Yes, my friend, it is man's own mouth or tongue that will destroy this old world with a fiery holocaust in this present age...the outer surface of this planet will be destroyed by man himself. And then after the 1,000 years all the weaponry of the ages will once again be in the wicked's hands as they assault the city to tear the Father and Son off the throne and enthrone themselves. But what a surprise meets them. Psalms 7:6-8 depicts God as arising and returning "on high." How shocked the wicked will be when they see the Lord go up in the air before their very eyes. The Bible speaks of the judgment taking place in the heavens.

"Our God shall come, and shall not keep silence: (he's going to wake up the dead) a fire shall devour before him, and it shall be very tempestuous round about him. He shall call to the heavens from above, and to the earth, that he may judge (decide for) his people. Gather my saints together unto me; those that have made a covenant with me by sacrifice. And the heavens shall declare his righteousness: for God is judge himself. Selah." Psalms 50:3-6.

God decides who shall come up in the first resurrection to meet Him in the air. This will be the first phase of the Second

Coming of Christ, or the Barley Harvest. This will be followed by the Wheat (144,000) and then the Grape, the one third of the human race, Zechariah 13:7-9. I Thessalonians 4:13-18. This decision will be challenged after the 1,000 years by the lost outside of the city as they come up to attempt to attack the city and tear the King and His Son off the throne, see Psalms 2:1-4. God's righteousness or His right dealing will be "declared" in the heavens and it will come down upon the wicked. This is the fire of His love. "See how much I love you." Because God never changes, He will be saying, "Oh, how can I give you up? How can I let you go?" Hosea 11:8. Will He not still be holding out His outstretched hand to them, weeping for them? Oh, yes. His love is for ever and ever. "Come to Me so I can heal you," he cries out to them.

To their shocked and astonished amazement, God is going to offer them to share His throne with him. "You do not have to take it by force. I have died that you might share it with Me and sit down with Me for all eternity." Listen.

"To him that overcometh will I grant to sit with me in MY throne, even as I also overcame, and am set down with my Father in his throne." Revelation 3:21. And in verses 10 and 20 he tells them that He permits rebuke and chastisement to come upon those He loves, but He wants them to be zealous and repent. He tells them that He is standing outside of the door of their hearts ready to come in if they will only let Him in. But they have closed the door tight. They, with Lucifer, like the older son, will not come in. They are angry and stay outside. They will not go inside of the City and join the celebration of the returned prodigal. They do not consider themselves prodigals, but hardworking sons who deserve to be rewarded with a golden city for all their labors. And if they are not given their due reward, they will take it by force.

Their mind is the mind of Hophni and Phinehas. They wanted to eat their meat or burnt offering before the fat (sin) was burned out first. "And if the man said to him, 'Let them burn the fat first, and then take as much as you wish,' he would say, 'No, you must give it now; and if not, I WILL TAKE IT BY FORCE." 1 Samuel 2:15, 16 RSV.

But, here the wicked are surrounding the city and they see that God wants to give the throne to them. They can't believe it. Satan has deceived them again. They see that their mental attitude toward God has unfitted them to dwell with Him. They hate and despise themselves, and their fellow human beings, especially those who led them into sin and deception and rebellion. But their greatest hatred is for Satan. This is when the "Lake of Fire" will begin. It will be a time of terrible suffering as they begin stewing in the juices of their own anger, remorse, guilt and hatred. This could go on for a very long time...whatever time it takes for them to repent and realize that God still will accept them. They are like the prodigal in the pig pen and until their moment of enlightenment comes that is where they will stay until they realize the gates are still open and they can go in if they are willing to repent.

The symbolism of God the Father giving up his throne for his wayward boy is found in the story of David giving up the throne and leaving the city of Jerusalem for Absalom. This story is found in 2 Samuel chapters 14-18. Joab found a way to have Absalom brought back and later Joab turns against Absalom just as the wicked will turn against Satan. But David represents the Father who weeps when he learns that his son is dead; His head caught in an oak tree, then Joab threw three darts into his heart and killed him. You may see for yourself the symbolism here. Jesus was crucified on a tree for us and the fiery darts of our sinful deeds pierced His sinless, innocent and sacred heart and killed him. If we do not accept His death for us, we will have to die ourselves. May God grant us grace today to repent and accept Jesus death for our reconciliation and his life for our salvation. Romans 5:10.

***Mary, the mother of Jesus, has been exalted today in the Catholic church to the status of the new "Queen of Heaven," which is false. The true queen of heaven and angel of mercy is a female deity. "The angel of mercy was then folding her wings to step down from the golden throne..." D.A. 578.**

CHAPTER 25

HOW WILL THE WICKED BE DESTROYED WHEN CHRIST RETURNS?

The Bible describes the coming of Jesus in many ways, but one of my favorite texts is found in 2 Thess. 2:8, "And then shall that Wicked be revealed, whom the Lord shall consume with the spirit of his mouth, and shall destroy with the brightness of his coming." This scripture has a dual or double application to both the Second Coming before the 1,000 years starts, which we believe will occur very soon, and also to the coming of Jesus after the 1,000 years. Another scripture Paul wrote in this same book says, "And to you who are troubled rest with us, when the Lord Jesus shall be revealed from heaven with his mighty angels. In flaming fire taking vengeance on them that know not God, and that obey not the gospel of our Lord Jesus Christ: who shall be punished with everlasting destruction from the presence of the Lord, and from the glory of his power; when he shall come to be glorified in his saints...." 2 Thess. 1:7-10.

Paul wrote this epistle about 54 AD, during the time when Rome was beginning to persecute Christians, so we may assume he had Pagan Rome in mind. It also applies to Papal Rome for it also killed God's people. But Satan is back of it all and so "that Wicked" basically applies to Satan and then in a secondary sense to anyone he uses to deceive and destroy God's work through His people. Jesus told the Jews that He had come to bring fire on the earth, Luke 12:49, therefore, Christ's Word, the Bible, is a "fiery" power that gives life to those who accept, and death to those who reject it. This helps us to clearly see then that the "brightness of His coming" is a development or a result of the spirit of His mouth which is simply His spoken and written word, not only in books, but especially in the lives of His people. John the Revelator pictures Christ as "smiting" the earth with a sharp sword that comes out of Jesus' mouth. Rev. 19:15. And Paul tells us that God's Word is "quick, and powerful, and sharper than any two-edged sword, piercing even to the dividing asunder of soul and spirit, and of the joints and marrow, and is a discerner of the thoughts and intents of the heart." Heb. 4: 12.

When we speak of fire, we are talking about the only kind of fire that we know of, which is a literal and tangible fire that we can see and feel. This is a destructive fire which consumes literally. But when the Bible speaks about God being "a consuming fire," is this the same kind of fire that we see and feel? Is God a physical, literal fire? Of course not, because this is a fire that is out of our realm of existence. It is from another dimension, as they say. On the day of Pentecost the "fire of God" fell on the 120 waiting, humbled, united believers, but that was not a literal, physical fire like you get when you strike a match and light your gas stove or wood stove or camp fire.

Oh, no! Listen to God explain it through Jeremiah. "Is not my word LIKE A FIRE? Saith the Lord; and like a hammer that breaketh the rock in pieces." Jer. 23:29. Notice, friend of mine, that God says his word is "like" a fire. He didn't say it was actually a fire, but like or similar to it. Was not this Moses' experience when he saw the burning bush? Yes it was. "And the angel of the Lord appeared unto him in a flame of fire out of the midst of a bush: and he looked, and, behold, the bushed burned with fire, and the bush was not consumed." Exodus 3:2. God's presence does not consume or destroy matter.

This is not fire as we know it. It is completely out of the realm of science, as far as man's knowledge and experience is concerned. Jeremiah explained it further when he said, "Then I said, I will not make mention of him, nor speak any more in His name. But his WORD was in mine heart as a burning fire shut up in my bones, and I was weary with forbearing, and I could not stay." Jer. 20:9. KJV The LB says, "His word in my heart is like a fire that burns in my bones, and I can't hold it in any longer." Jer. 20:9. LB. And John the Baptist was referred to by Jesus Himself as "a burning and a shining light:" John 5:35. We know John was Christ's forerunner, his herald or the one who paved the way by announcing that the Messiah was about to appear. And what would He do when He came. "He shall baptize you with the Holy Ghost, and with fire. Whose fan is in his hand, and he will throughly purge his floor, and gather his wheat into the garner; but he will burn up the chaff with unquenchable fire." Matt. 3:11, 12. And isn't that just what Jesus did? Yes, it is. The followers of Jesus received this "fire," of truth and righteousness, healing, mercy and love. This revived and empowered them to receive the Holy Spirit (God's fire) on the day of Pentecost. They went and preached the truth about Jesus and His Father everywhere. But, the Jewish leaders and people who resisted and rejected Jesus' "fire of love" were burned up by the hatred inside of them. This caused division among them and eventually led to the actual destruction and literal burning of Jerusalem in A.D. 70.

But did God do that to them? No. In fact, He did everything he could to prevent it from happening...to hold back the Destroyer (Satan, Rev. 9:11), but they would not listen. Their burning words of malice and hatred burned down their own city along with them. So it will be in the final day when Christ returns. "Even so the tongue is a little member, and boasteth great things. Behold, how great a matter a little fire kindleth! And the tongue is a fire, a world of iniquity: so is the tongue among our members, that it defileth the whole body, and setteth on fire the course of nature; and it is set on fire of hell." James 3:5, 6. That is why James 3:2 tells us that if a man does not offend in word the same is a perfect man and able to bridle the whole body. But only God can do this in us and for us as we surrender to Him, for the "tongue can no man tame; it is an unruly evil, full of deadly poison." v .8. Our precious Lord Jesus drank that deadly cup full of poison or fire of hatred for us. But, if we do not accept what He did for us in Gethsemane (oil press, Matt 26:36) and on Calvary, as well as what He is doing in the heavenly sanctuary above for us right now, then we will have to drink that cup of deadly poison ourselves, and it will kill us. That's what Obadiah meant when he said, "For the day of the Lord is near upon all the heathen: as thou hast done, it shall be done unto thee: thy reward shall return upon thine own head. For as ye have drunk upon my holy mountain, so shall all the heathen drink continually, yea, they shall drink, and they shall swallow down, and they shall be as though they had not been." Obadiah 15, 16. 306. And so we see, dear friend, that God destroys no man. Nothing bad ever comes from God. Why even our temptations do not come from God. "Let no man say when he is tempted, I am tempted of God: for God cannot be tempted with evil, neither tempteth he any man: But every man is tempted, when he is drawn away of his own lust, and enticed. Then when lust hath conceived, it bringeth forth death. Do not err, my beloved brethren. Every good gift and every perfect gift is from above, and cometh down from the Father of lights, with whom is no variableness, neither shadow of turning." James 1:13:17.

God does not kill us. It is our sinning that kills us, and the "wages of sin is death." Rom. 6:23. Jesus told the Jewish leaders that they would die in their sins if they did not believe in Him as the Messiah, John 8:24. He did not say, if you reject Me I will destroy you. They destroyed themselves. And so we see, dear reader, that when the Bible speaks of the "fire of God" as having destroyed someone we know that fire from God's person or His presence did not flash out and kill that person, for God is not a literal fire. What then is the source of the literal fire that destroyed people and animals in the Old Testament? Can we find a model that will give us a clue? Yes, we can. Listen: "And the Lord replied to Satan, 'You may do anything you like with his wealth, but don't harm him physically:'" Job 1:12, 13, LB. Many tragedies then struck Job's properties, one of which was fire falling from the sky. "The fire of God has fallen from heaven and burned up your sheep and all the herdsmen, and I alone have escaped to tell you." Verse 16.

The amazing thing that puzzles and baffles most people is the fact that the Father seems to be willing, even eager to take the blame. Notice: "...still he (Job) holdest fast his integrity, although thou movedst Me against him, to destroy him without cause." Job 2:3. Remember that this conversation is taking place before all the council of heaven. Doesn't this show the Father's infinite love for Lucifer? He is actually covering up for him in front of the heavenly council by taking the blame for the destruction of all of Job's property. But now he goes beyond that and seems to purposely be sending Satan out to hurt Job physically. "And the Lord said unto Satan, Behold, he is in thine hand, but save his life." Job 2:6. Now, who brought this literal fire down from the sky to kill the sheep and herdsmen? The messenger reported that the fire came from God. But which God? Satan is called "The god of this world.... 2 Cor. 4:4. And the simple truth of the matter is that Satan sent the fire which destroyed Job's property. And this is true in every instance in the Bible when fire destroys a person or anyone's property, for God never changes. We will deal more fully with this issue in chapter 27.

The Bible tells us in Rev. 13: 13 and 16:14 that Satan can bring fire down from heaven and work miracles. So the devil does have the power to bring fire down from heaven, and make it look like the Father did it. Obviously, this is what happened in Job's case. We have already seen from the Scriptures that "God's fire" is not a literal fire, as we know fire. Literal fire disfigures and destroys. This is not the work of our loving, heavenly Father, for only good gifts come from Him, James 1:17. Satan is not only our "adversary, the devil," I Peter 5:8, but God tells us he is the destroyer. "Their king is the Prince of the bottomless pit whose name in Hebrew is Abaddon, and in Greek, Apollyon (and in English, the Destroyer). Rev. 9:11. LB. Sin entered the universe at the time of Lucifer's defection and fall from heaven. This mastermind and genius of evil (genie means demon) began plotting the overthrow of God's throne right from the beginning. Jesus identified him as a killer, and liar. "He was a murderer from the beginning, and abode not in the truth, because there is no truth in him. John 8:44. Jesus is the truth. John 14:6. As soon as Adam and Eve sinned, Satan began working through the elements to deceive and destroy the human race. We know this from the parables Jesus told. "All these things spake Jesus unto the multitude in parables; and without a parable spake he not unto them: That it might be fulfilled which was spoken by the prophet, saying, I will open my mouth in parables; I will utter things which have been kept secret from the foundation of the world." Matt. 13:34, 35. Now, let us notice the parable which will give us valuable insight into our search for the one who has introduced fire and other harmful aberrations of nature. "The kingdom of heaven is likened unto a man which sowed good seed in his field: But while men slept, his enemy came and sowed tares among the wheat, and went his way. But when the blade was sprung up, and brought forth fruit, then appeared the tares also." Matt. 13:24-26. The servants could not understand how the tares were growing up when only good wheat was supposed to have been planted. The servants represent God's angels as well as human agents the Lord uses in His harvest field. Jesus gave a direct answer to their question as to who had planted the tares (noxious or poisonous weeds which look like or appear to be genuine plants or in this case good wheat). "The enemy that sowed them is the devil; the harvest is the end of the world; and the reapers are the angels. As therefore, the tares are gathered and burned in the fire; so shall it be in the end of this world. The Son of man shall send forth his angels, and they shall gather out of his kingdom all things that offend, and them which do iniquity; and shall cast them into a furnace of fire: there shall be wailing and gnashing of teeth. Then shall the righteous shine forth as the sun in the kingdom of their Father. Who hath ears to hear, let him hear." Matt. 13:39, 43.

We have already learned from Scripture that the word fire has a literal meaning and a symbolical meaning. The literal one is not from our God because He has nothing to do with literal fire. It did not exist before sin entered. It is one of Satan's noxious weeds or aberrations of nature. But, God claims that anytime anyone is burned with literal fire He did it to them, for He always takes the blame. That is not only His nature, but His character. The symbolical one is the fiery emotion of the mind, anger, hatred, envy, jealousy, remorse regret, etc. The "furnace of fire" is the same as the "FIERY OVEN" in Psalm 21:9. We find that in Ps. 21:8 it is the "right hand" of God which causes the lost or wicked to burn up inside like a "fiery oven." Throughout the Scripture from Exodus 15:6 to Deut. 33:2 to Psalm 98:1 to Isa. 48:13 to Heb. 12:2, we see that Jesus is the right hand of God. The expression, " Arm of the Lord, " also refers to Christ, Isaiah 52:10, 53:1. Jesus is God's "WORD," "HAND," and" ARM," to accomplish His holy will. And His will is always to save man, never to hurt him. As they reject Him they suffer terrible guilt. Isa. 31:9 indicates a fire is in Zion, where God's heart is. He loves His people with a love as hot as a furnace of fire. His heart is on fire with an eternal love for us. The very "flame of Jehovah." Song of Solomon 8:6.

In Hosea 7:6, 7 we see that God says, "For they have made ready their heart like an oven....in the morning it burneth as a flaming fire. They are all hot as an oven, and have devoured their judges: all their kings are fallen." Man's fire is hatred. God's fire is love. Notice that God says that "they," the people themselves had "made ready their heart like an oven." The heart is the same as the mind in the Bible. And so we see that the people are responsible for the anger, grief, remorse, regret, hatred and murder that burns within them. In the story of Calvary we can see clearly how it happens. Jesus pleaded with the Jews day after day to come to Him, but the more He loved them the more they hated Him. Finally He permitted them to stretch out His hands on the cruel cross. Still He was pleading for them, "FATHER, FORGIVE THEM; FOR THEY KNOW NOT WHAT THEY DO." Luke 23:34. The translators of the Authorized King James Version, KJV, 1611 were classical Greek scholars, and therefore not so familiar with the Biblical Greek of the New Testament. One particular facet they seem to always omit in their translation is the present indicative or active mood and the imperfect active mood. My Greek and Hebrew teacher at Bible college taught us this and it makes the Scripture more meaningful in many cases. For example, Luke 23:34 could be translated "FATHER, KEEP ON FORGIVING THEM, FOR THEY DO NOT KNOW WHAT THEY ARE DOING." And even the initial phrase of the text, "THEN SAID JESUS," could be translated, "THEN (or at that time) JESUS WAS CONTINUALLY SAYING, OR JESUS KEPT ON SAYING." If Jesus had not kept on praying this prayer Satan would have had a legal right to destroy everyone for they were killing their own Creator. Even Satan might have self-destructed with his angels if it had not been for Christ's continual prayer. Even though his people were rejecting eternal life, Jesus, by dying on the cross earned the legal right to plead that their lives be spared and protected from as much mental and physical suffering as possible.

Another case of the continuous action is John 13:23; 21:20, where John refers to himself as 'THE DISCIPLE WHOM JESUS LOVED." I will not take time to go into all of the Greek grammar to try and prove my point here, not that I am a Greek scholar, for I am not, but I did take three years of Greek under a brilliant teacher and am familiar enough to figure most of these out to satisfy myself, which I have already done. But, this favorite phrase of John takes on a brand new meaning when you translate it with the continuous action present indicative. "THE DISCIPLE WHOM JESUS KEPT ON LOVING OR CONTINUED TO LOVE." This immediately takes away the possible interpretation of Christ playing favorites. John was a disciple that did not always have a loving or lovable nature. A quick look at Luke 9:54 will prove that. Mark 3: 17 designates James and John as the "sons of thunder." They probably were sometimes loud, boisterous, uncompromising, headstrong, fiery and fighting fishermen. But Jesus "KEPT ON LOVING THEM ANYWAY."

Jesus clearly stated that the "HARVEST IS THE END OF THE WORLD." Matt. 13:39. He also said that, "In the time of the harvest I will say to the reapers, Gather ye together first the tares, and bind them in bundles to burn them: but gather the wheat into my barn." Matt. 13:30. Our objective is to discover how the wicked are destroyed when Jesus comes the second time before the 1,000 years begin. We have touched on aspects of this event in other places in this book, but each time we discuss it we will learn more details. By this time it should be crystal clear in your mind that the Hebrew prophets who wrote the Bible, under the inspiration of the Holy Spirit, always held God responsible for that which he permitted to happen. In other words, God always took the blame. This is clearly revealed on the cross when Jesus let them do anything they wanted to Him and then asked the Father not to punish them, but to forgive them. Since God never changes, we can see that He was doing in a body of flesh the same exact thing He had always been doing all through the Old Testament in a spirit form, as He led Israel through the wilderness and later in the Promised Land, as well.

"In all their affliction he was afflicted, and the angel of his presence saved them: in his love and in his pity he redeemed them; and he bare them, and carried them all the days of old." Isa. 63:9. But the very next verse seems to contradict this one because it says that He was turned "to be their enemy, and He fought against them." It is impossible to understand the Scripture with the carnal mind, for Paul tells us, "the carnal mind is enmity against God: for it is not subject to the law of God, neither indeed can be." Rom. 8:7. The law of God is a transcript of His wonderful character of love. Stony hearted readers of the law, like the Jews, will only see the letter of the law, which "KILLETH, BUT THE SPIRIT GIVETH LIFE." 2 Cor. 3:6. The fight of Isa. 63:10 is the battle for the mind. Jesus was fighting or wrestling with them to submit to His love. Jacob had this experience. He wrestled with Jesus or fought against God's efforts to save him, for if Jesus had "wrestled" in a physical sense he could easily have overcome Jacob. But God never uses force. He only uses the drawing power of love. Satan desired to destroy Jacob, but Jesus only let him touch Jacob's thigh and put it out of place. Christ took the blame for that even. It woke Jacob up to the fact that he was not wrestling with just a "man" although Christ had taken on or assumed a human form for the occasion, in order to assure him of His love and forgiveness. Satan was trying to destroy Jacob with a sense of guilt. The physical activity that night may have helped Jacob to release most of his tension so he would not have a nervous break down or go insane. In any event God was able to reveal Himself to Jacob in this most unusual circumstance and make it a beautiful lesson for all of us today. We can gird up the loins of our minds, I Pet. 1:13, and thus defeat Satan, by strapping on the sword of the spirit, Eph. 6:14.

Now, let us explain the "BINDING" of the tares of Matt. 13:30. The binding of the wicked is for the express purpose of "burning" them. Let's take the word "bind" first and notice how it is used in Rev. 20:1-3. Satan is pictured here as being cast into a bottomless pit, bound (past tense of bind) with a chain by the angel from heaven. He is supposed to stay in this pit for 1,000 years so he will not deceive the nations anymore for ten long centuries. Since Revelation is a book of symbols we should first look for a symbolical meaning of the actual events that will take place when Jesus comes the second time. The bottomless pit is simply this earth, for the word "pit" as used in the Bible means "the grave," although it is expressed in various terms. Let's notice the Hebrew parallelism of Isaiah 38:18. "For the grave cannot praise thee, death cannot celebrate thee: they that go down into the pit cannot hope for thy truth." Another text reads, "whose graves are set in the sides of the pit, and her company is round about her grave." Ezekiel 32:23.

So, we see that a "bottomless pit" is basically an endless graveyard, which is what planet earth has been for 6,000 years. The phrase is from the Greek, phrear tes abussou, "pit of the bottomless (place)," or "well of the abyss." The word "abussos" is used very often in the LXX to translate the Hebrew "tehom" which seems to represent the primeval ocean or "deep" of Gen. 1:2. Job 41:31 uses "abussos" to represent the sea in general and in Psalm 71:20, the depths of the earth. In Rev. 17:15 waters or sea represent peoples or nations. Since Satan is the "king" of the bottomless pit (Rev. 9: 11) and the "god of this world" (2 Cor. 4:4) it is only logical to conclude that Satan is the one who is making the people angry at each other so they go to war and kill each other. Christ calmed the sea and told His disciples to not be afraid. Psalm 46 tells us "we will not fear" even though the earth is removed and the mountains (governments) are carried into the midst of the sea;" v. 2. What this means to me is that no matter what Satan stirs the masses (sea) up to do, we do not have to be afraid, for God always has control. "BE STILL AND KNOW THAT I AM GOD." Ps. 46:10. We know that when Jesus comes the wicked are going to die by their own hands, for the Bible tells us, "every man's sword shall be against his brother." Ezek. 38:21. Compare also Zech. 14:13; Jer. 25:31-33. Christ will rescue His elected saints or church out of this final holocaust or suicide of the nations which is really what Armageddon is going to be. Notice that the word, "GATHERED" is used in Rev. 16:16 just as it is used in Matt. 13:40. But Rev. 16:14 reveals who is actually doing the gathering. Jeremiah 22:7.

EVIL SPIRITS ARE GATHERING THE NATIONS

"For they are the spirits of devils, working miracles, which go forth unto the kings of the earth and of the whole world, to gather them to the battle of that great day of God Almighty." Rev. 16:14. But true to form, God takes the credit or blame for this gathering in verses 15 and 16, because He is allowing Satan and his angels to do it.

THE FINAL SUICIDE OF THE NATIONS

Now, the result of this final suicide of the nations is that everyone but those who believe in Jesus will die. Jeremiah saw this terrible slaughter revealed to him in a vision over 600 years before Christ was born in Bethlehem. "O my soul, the sound of the trumpet, the alarm of war. Destruction upon destruction is cried; for the whole land is spoiled: How long shall I see the standard, and hear the sound of the trumpet? (He is no doubt given a vision of all the wars of the long centuries which builds up to the final battle of Armageddon). I beheld the earth, and, lo, it was without form, and void; and the heavens, and they had no light. (Here the earth is described in the same way Moses' pictures it in Genesis 1 before God created the earth in the beginning). I beheld the mountains, and, lo, they trembled, and all the hills moved lightly. (No doubt from all the earthquakes and volcanoes Satan will bring in the last days and hours before Jesus returns to rescue us). I beheld, and, lo, there was no man, and all the birds of the heavens were fled." Jer. 4:19, 20, 21, 23,-25; Isa. 14:12-17.

"THERE WAS NO MAN," the prophet said. Now, why wouldn't there be any "human beings," left on this earth? For man is a generic term here referring to people in general, or the universal race, which would include women and children as well as "men." The answer is so simple you will probably wonder why some people seem to make it so hard to understand. First of all, Satan will "gather" all the nations together to destroy them. God will try to prevent them from killing each other with a wonderful message of love through His final elect, but they will not listen and will pass a death decree against this chosen group who will stand up against the New World Order and expose it by preaching the truth about God. Rev. 2:10; Rev. 13:15. This will be a time of trouble for God's people, which will be similar to what Jacob went through at the ford Jabbok. The Bible calls this "THE TIME OF JACOB'S TROUBLE." The prophet described it like this: "Alas! for that day is great, so that none is like it: it is even the time of Jacob's trouble; but he shall be saved out of it." Jeremiah 30:7.

Jesus told us that the "harvest is the end of the world," Matt. 13:39. He also said that the wheat and the tares would "grow together until the harvest." But He also told us that the tares (wicked or lost) will be bound in bundles to be burned first. So, the "burning" of the wicked takes place before the "wheat" (righteous or saved) are gathered "into My barn." Now, where is God's barn? Jesus told his disciples, "In my Father's house are many mansions: if it were not so, I would have told you. I go to prepare a place for you. And if I go and prepare a place for you, I will come again, and receive you unto myself; that where I am, there ye may be also." John 14:2-3. The apostle Paul predicted this same event in these words, "For the Lord himself shall descend from heaven with a shout, with the voice of the archangel, and with the trump of God: and the dead in Christ shall rise first: Then we which are alive and remain shall be caught up together with them in the clouds to meet the Lord in the air: and so shall we ever be with the Lord." I Thess. 4:16, 17. Jesus warned us that there would be many deceptions in these last days just before He returned to take His people out of this world to the "FATHER'S HOUSE."

For decades now many people have believed in what is known in theological circles as the "Secret Rapture." The word rapture is not a biblical term. It is from the Latin and its essential meaning was a "a mercy rescue by force," as I understand it. Well, Jesus is coming to rescue his people at His Second Coming, but it will not be a secret coming. The Bible makes it very clear in the gospels as well Revelation 1:7; 6:14-17 that "every eye shall see Him" and "then shall all the tribes of the earth mourn, and they shall see the Son of man coming in the clouds of heaven with power and great glory." Matt 24:27-30. Jesus also compared His return to the lightning that shines from the east to the west. Jesus used the Harvest as a means of illustrating His planned return to this earth in the final age before the millennium. He said that the Harvest would be the end of world (age). Matt. 13:39. ***But the Harvest is not a one time event.*** It has three phases. The first phase is the Barley, a very short period of time, like one day. The second phase is the Wheat which takes forty days and then the Grape Harvest, which will take the rest of the last segment of time which will be three and one half years. So, there will be three phases of the harvest. There are precious promises to those who dedicate their all to Jesus Christ in this last hour of earth's history to vindicate the character of the Father. Luke 21:34-36, Malachi 3:16-18 and Revelation 3:10 are promises that the Elect will be translated at the time of death decree which will be passed against them.

There are actually at least 24 titles or designations for them which I refer to as the Barley to begin with. They are also called the "Watchmen on the Walls of Zion," who are not sleeping. In contrast the Ten Virgins are fast asleep until the midnight hour when the cry goes forth, "Behold the Bridegroom is coming." Jesus was a prototype of the Barley or first fruits and the 120 is a type of the 144,000 whom the Elect will go throughout the earth and select during a forty day period, the same as Jesus increased His disciples from 12 to 120 in forty days after His resurrection. The Remnant are those who will be hiding out for three and one half years from the face of the serpent, Rev. 12:14. They will comprise the grape harvest at the end of 3 1/2 years. They will be the one third of the human race who survive, Zechariah 13:7-9. But the rest of humanity, the two thirds, will die. I have written about this in-depth in other publications and made videos explaining it.

WHEN CHRIST STANDS UP FOR HIS PEOPLE

For then shall be great tribulation, such as was not since the beginning of the world to this time, no, nor ever shall be. And except those days should be shortened, there should no flesh be saved: but for the elect's sake those days shall be shortened." Matt. 24:21, 22. We know there have been times of tribulation for God's people in the past. Jesus predicted the fall of Jerusalem by Titus and gave instruction to His disciples so they could escape it, Matt. 24:15-20; Luke 21:20-24. In both of these chapters Jesus was speaking under the inspiration of His Father's Spirit, not only to the Jews of His day, but to the believers who would go through the dark ages as well. But, I believe his message has even a greater relevancy and application to our day.

The reason I say this is because of Daniel's prediction.

And at that time (when Satan has his final destructive machine completely set up to destroy God's people, Dan. 11:44,45) shall Michael stand up (this represents Christ standing up for his people to protect and shield them from Satan) and there shall be a time of trouble, such as never was since there was a nation even to that same time: and at that time thy people shall be delivered, every one that shall be found written in the book. And many of them that sleep in the dust of the earth shall awake, Some to everlasting life, and some to shame and everlasting contempt." Daniel 12: 1-2. Now, we have in this last Scripture the same description of trouble or tribulation as Jesus gave in Matt. 24:21, 22. But in Daniel's prophecy we see that He connects the resurrection with this time of trouble as well as the standing up of Michael which would indicate that He has completed a certain necessary work or made a decision and now is about to do something. The thing He is standing up to do is come to earth to rescue His "bride," who is about to be killed. Everyone has made a final and irrevocable decision for or against Him and He has only one thing left to do, and that is to claim His bride and leave the rest of humanity to do whatever they wish to do, for He created them with free choice. This will be the time of the "burning" of the wicked, which will be followed by the coming of the bridegroom (Christ) in the clouds of glory to catch up the quick and the dead, His mature church, Philadelphia. Rev. 3:7-12.

GOD MAKES HIS FINAL CALL

Remember that Jesus holds out his hand of mercy to the people by delivering a final message of love (His fiery law of love) to the world through His people, His Elect. This wonderful message of love is simply, "BEHOLD YOUR GOD." In other words, "LOOK AT OUR WONDERFUL SAVIOR JESUS." Isa. 40:9. Notice that when the wicked are cast "into a furnace of fire: there shall be wailing and gnashing of teeth."

Matt. 13:42. It doesn't say that their bodies are being consumed at this point in time, for this burning is a mental agony as they realize that they are fighting God Himself in the person of His saints. Gamaliel's counsel to the Jewish Sanhedrin is proof that He recognized this possibility. "And so my advice is, leave these men alone. If what they teach and do is merely on their own, it will soon be overthrown. But if it is of God, you will not be able to stop them, lest you find yourselves fighting even against God." Acts 5:39. This very truth was soon after displayed in the life of Saul of Tarsus, when the light of God's love shone on him and he submitted to it by saying, "Lord, what wilt thou have me to do?" Acts 9:6. Saul the "Christian killer" became Paul the Christian tiller, tilling the soil of human hearts and planting the seed of God's love in those hearts throughout the then known world. Jesus did not appear to Saul to hurt him, but to actually stop the pain of guilt and remorse in his mind which was "pricking his conscience" every day more and more. It was a fire inside of him that would eventually have burned him up completely if he had not surrendered to the light and voice of Christ's loving appeal. "Saul, Saul, why are you persecuting me? You are only hurting yourself." Acts 9:4; 22:6. LB This was actually a mini Lake of Fire for Saul, explaining what all the wicked will experience in the future until they also come to their senses and repent.

Judas heard this same voice of entreaty over and over again, but kept on rejecting it. Jesus revealed Judas' sinful plot at the last supper to the twelve without exposing or fingering him. It was, as if, Jesus was saying to Judas, "OH, JUDAS, PLEASE DON'T DO THIS TO YOURSELF. I LOVE YOU JUDAS. ABANDON YOUR PLANS AND LIVE." But Judas wouldn't listen. Jesus washed his feet and later whispered, as he handed him the "sop" (probably a crusty piece of bread dipped in honey), "He it is, to whom I shall give a sop (morsel), when I have dipped it." John 13:26. Only Judas heard Jesus say that for Peter had a sword and would not have let Judas escape from that upper room to betray Christ and the other disciples. "Now no man at the table knew for what intent he spake this unto him." Jn. 13:28. Can you imagine these rugged fisherman sleeping if they had known Judas was leading a mob to arrest their Lord and perhaps even them? I cannot imagine such a thing. They would have never let Judas out of that upper room if they had known. But, just as no one knew the wicked heart of Lucifer until the cross, so no one knew Judas' heart until he later cast down the thirty pieces of silver in the temple and said, "I have sinned in that I have betrayed the innocent blood. And they said, 'what is that to us? see thou to it:" Matt. 27:4. In other words, "We couldn't care less. That's your problem." Judas then went out and hanged himself. Can you imagine the guilt, grief, sorrow, self-Loathing and self-hatred Judas had for himself as he saw Jesus being so terribly mistreated and abused? Can you imagine the "FURNACE OF FIRE" that was burning inside of Judas during this time? It must have been terrible.

This is precisely what the wicked will go through who reject the SEAL OF GOD and accept the MARK OF THE BEAST. The Father's hand of love, even His only begotten Son, was reaching out to Judas to draw him back from the edge of the abyss over which he was about to plunge. But Judas wouldn't listen. That outstretched hand of love burned in his mind as he remembered Christ's many acts and words of kindness toward him. It all came down upon his head like "COALS OF FIRE." Proverbs 25:21, 22. "Thine hand shall find out all thine enemies: thy right hand shall find out those that hate thee. Thou shalt make them as a fiery oven in the time of thine anger: the Lord shall swallow them up in his wrath, and the fire shall devour them." Psalm 21:8, 9. Compare Malachi 4:1-3; Hosea 7:5-7. John the Revelator also saw the wicked "burning up" inside "as a fiery oven." He drew a word picture of the sufferings of those who would choose to worship the beast and his image by receiving the mark of the beast in his forehead or hand. "He shall be tormented with fire and brimstone in the presence of the holy angels, and in the presence of the Lamb: (God's presence is always with us (Ps. 139), always pleading. Was not Judas tormented in Christ's presence?) And the smoke of their torment ascendeth up for ever and ever: and they have no rest day or night, who worship the beast and his image, and whosoever receiveth the mark of his name." Rev. 14:10, 11.

WHAT IS THE LAKE OF FIRE?

This terrible mental suffering takes place before Christ comes for Rev. 19 gives more detail on this same event. In Rev. 14 they are still worshiping the beast, but in Rev. 19:19, 20 we see that the beast and all of his allies gather together to make war against Jesus. But the beast is "taken" and the beast and all of his worshipers are cast alive into a lake of fire burning with brimstone." A lake is a body of water and water represents people, Rev. 17:15. So, here we see a great mass of humanity "burning up" with hatred toward God and toward each other. "EVERY MAN'S SWORD IS AGAINST HIS BROTHER," and there is a world-wide slaughter. The masses of humanity who have refused the SAVIOR's outstretched hand of love now turn themselves into a sea of blood, Rev. 16:3. This is exactly what happened to the Jews inside of Jerusalem. They slaughtered each other without mercy. The blood of dead men was everywhere. This is the terrible future for every person who does not receive the outstretched hand of the SAVIOR. Oh, friend of mine, won't you let Him take you by the hand right now? You'll never regret that decision.

As a result of the wicked destroying themselves literally, just as Judas did, in order to escape the terrible burning in their minds, the earth is now empty of any living human beings, for all the righteous have been gathered into God's barn," or taken up to the "FATHER'S HOUSE." Satan is now left alone here on this earth for 1,000 years to argue and feud with his evil angels about what they should have done or could have done to win in their fight against God. Perhaps the greatest proof that Satan is an unrepentant, incorrigible sinner is the fact that after the 1,000 years he still seeks to destroy by deceiving the lost masses of humanity into thinking they can attack and overcome the Holy City, New Jerusalem. Another interesting aspect of Satan's personality, nature and character is that he is not able to rebuild the earth that he has destroyed. The ruined condition of planet earth is a mute reminder of what he really, truly is ...A WASTER, SPOILER AND DESTROYER. Exodus 12:23, Isa. 16;.4; 48:18; 54:16; John 10:10. The literal fire that the wicked used to destroy themselves with at the coming of Jesus is an aberration of God's original creation. Satan somehow has learned how to pervert nature against man by combining certain elements in a reverse manner so the new formula of elements caused a breakdown of life instead of a sustenance, as God originally intended. A good example of this is oxygen which, one chemist and scientist told an audience, is called the "SWORD" of the elements. I suppose that he meant by this that oxygen combines with other elements to cause a chemical breakdown in matter. I believe that God's original creation was easy to understand. It was in harmony with man. And man and his mind and body were in perfect harmony with nature as it came from the hand of God, its Creator. Satan learned how to distort the vibratory frequencies of man and animals, turning them against each other and themselves. Thus these distortions and perversions have caused nature to be out of harmony with itself and with man. Animals hunt and kill each other and so does man. But, let's come back to oxygen. According to Webster's unabridged dictionary.

"Oxygen is the most abundant of all elements. It occurs free in the atmosphere, forming one fifth of its volume. It is very active, being able to combine with nearly all other elements and is essential to life processes and to combustion." Now, I want you to think about that for a moment. Without oxygen, as we know it today, nothing can burn. In other words, without oxygen, as we know it today, literal fire could not exist

The reason I am making a point of this is that I want us to realize that fire as we know it today is a literal fire that can burn and devour and destroy. Oxygen, as it exists in our atmosphere, makes that possible. Therefore, I am convinced that the oxygen we have today is not the way God created it in the beginning. Something has happened to our air and to oxygen, as well as to all the elements. Before sin entered, there was no breakdown of matter. No bacteria, no rust, no mold, no waste, or destruction or death: This all came as a result of Adam's transgression. Let's take oxidation as an example of how our air has been changed. Oxidation is the union of a substance with oxygen. It is the process of increasing the positive valence or of decreasing the negative valence of an element ion. Oxidation is simply the process by which electrons are removed from atoms or ions. Oxidation is in a phrase, the scientific definition of how oxygen combines with other elements to break down matter. NO FIRE WITHOUT OXYGEN. Rust is a product or result of oxidation. Rust is the reddish-brown or reddish-yellow coating formed on iron or steel by oxidation. In botany rust is the name of any number of plant diseases caused by parasitic fungi. Rust is simply deterioration and spoilage. But it cannot occur without oxygen. According to the oxidation reaction theory, all matter or substance in the earth today breaks down because of or by a process known as oxidation. Time correlates with oxygen. There is no time without oxygen. Scientists measure time with or by radio active isotopes. Carbon 14 dating is based upon the half life of carbon 14 (C-14). It is by this dating method that scientists are able to determine the age of life forms from the past which only have part of their matter left, such as a bone from a dinosaur or a piece of wood or coal buried in the ground. Without oxygen this would not be possible.

The reason God is eternal is that everything in the universe, except for planet earth, is continually regenerating itself by virtue of the fact that it has a vital and unbroken connection with Him, the Creator. Only this earth measures everything by time. We count years by how long it has been since we were born. We know we are growing older by the wrinkles and gray hairs: Time is used to measure how long it takes for matter to deteriorate, rust or bacterialize and finally return to dust again.

Man would never have returned to dust again if Adam had not sinned. Adam and Eve did not know what death was. They had never seen it or experienced it. Even Lucifer, as far as we know, had not observed death. God was preserving him alive so he too could witness the results of his selfish sinfulness and rebellion.

Surely the Father's hope was that Lucifer would return once he saw how terrible a thing sin is. He would preserve the fallen angels and Lucifer himself alive without death. But He would allow death to come to Adam and Eve and their children, the creatures of His love, made in His very own image. Can you imagine the pain it must have caused Him? Revelation 13:8 tells us that Jesus Christ is "the Lamb slain from the foundation of the world." Our little world would become the eternal classroom and guidebook for the universe throughout the ceaseless ages of eternity. Why did the Father permit Lucifer to lead one-third of the angels astray? Jesus tells us that the devil was a murderer "FROM THE BEGINNING, AND ABODE NOT IN THE TRUTH, BECAUSE THERE IS NO TRUTH IN HIM." John 8:44. It had to be demonstrated to the entire universe that all life, light and power comes from the Father. Lucifer challenged this and only time would prove whether or not he was right or wrong.

It has taken nearly 6,000 years for this demonstration to be fully carried out. Every challenge and question Lucifer has raised has been answered in the life and death of Jesus, and today in His followers. The lord god of Eden told Adam and Eve in their garden home, "in the day that thou eatest thereof thou shalt surely die." Gen. 2: 17. This is the first death threat in the Bible. Paul tells us that the "fear of death" and even the concept of death itself, was brought in by the devil, Heb 2:14, 15, because our Heavenly Father is always and only a life God, never a death God. That is, beloved, although the Lord permits and allows death He is not the one who started or initiated it. There was a tree of knowledge of "Good and Evil" in the "midst" of the garden, Gen. 3:3. But, the TREE OF LIFE was also in the midst of the garden, Gen. 2:9. They may have been side by side. As it has turned out this tree has become the "Tree of growing up," because of all that the human race has learned since Adam and Eve ate of it. It was not His perfect will for them to learn the difference between good and evil in this fashion but He permitted it and the Great Controversy between and evil has ensued to this day. Why did God permit it? This is the question we are trying to answer. On that answer turns both the mystery of iniquity and the mystery of godliness.

The next natural question that comes, is: "Did God create evil then?" We can answer this by simply asking another question. Did God create Satan? The answer is, "no, He did not." He created a beautiful angel named Lucifer, but Lucifer turned himself into a devil or into Satan; the Adversary of God and man. "Thou (Lucifer) was perfect in thy ways from the day that thou was created, TILL INIQUITY (SIN) WAS FOUND IN THEE." Ezek. 28:15. And so we see that God did not originate or create evil, but He takes the blame for it, Isaiah 45:7, so we will not have to bear the guilt of sin.

Divine love and compassion mitigated, moderated, lessened or softened the results of sin, which is death. But with each passing generation, the result of that penalty has become more and more obvious and severe. When Adam doubted the goodness of His Creator and that all of God's trees were good he broke the light connection with Jesus, His Creator and his robe of light slowly began to fade and his whole nature began to fall and deteriorate. If they had been faithful to God and developed a perfect character like Christ, their Creator, they would never have witnessed the results of sin in their own bodies or in the creation they loved so much. But it was permitted for a purpose and a reason that is beyond our full understanding at this time.

As we look at Jesus we never see Him rejecting anyone, but we see the majority of the people rejecting Him. His hands were continually stretched out in love to all. Isaiah 9:12, 17, 21. "Him that cometh to me I will in no wise cast out." John 6:37. We again must realize that the "FIRE" which has been prepared for the devil and his angels is not only a literal fire, but a symbolic one as well. Furthermore, the fire spoken of here by Christ as having been "prepared for the devil and his angels," has not been prepared by God. We assume the text means that, for that is our carnal concept of God. Notice in Jere. 22:7 that God claims to be preparing "destroyers against thee, every one with his weapons:" God claims to be doing that which He is permitting. We see this in Matt. 13:30, where the householder (God) is instructing His servants (angels) to bind the tares in bundles to burn them. This "burning," is two-fold. First there is the mental suffering, as with Judas, and then secondly, comes the physical destruction as with King Saul and Judas, who both committed suicide. I Chron. 10:4, 5, 13, 14; Matt. 27:3-5. We must also realize and re-emphasize that when the Holy Bible speaks of God's fire, or the "fire of God," it is not speaking of a literal burning inferno like Nebuchadnezzar's fiery furnace, Dan. 3, but a non-literal fire like Moses saw on Mount Sinai. That fire did not require oxygen to burn, for the bush never burned up or consumed as it would have if oxidation or combustion had been occurring. There was no smoke. GOD'S FIRE represents truth, righteousness, holiness, purity and love. The giving of the law was another occasion when God's fiery presence was manifested in a loving attempt to draw his people into close fellowship with himself. Jesus Christ was and is the living personification and embodiment of this fire. In fact, He even described Himself in this manner.

Notice his words: "I have come to bring fire to the earth, and oh, that my task were completed." Luke 12:49. In the verses following, 50-53, He spoke of a baptism He had to go through, obviously a fiery baptism of persecution in the form of hatred, slander, malice, physical torture, total rejection by those He loved the most, and finally death, due to a broken heart.

But it was the FIERY LOVE, THIS WHITE HOT PASSION, Acts 1:3, that enabled Jesus to overcome and conquer the fire of Satan's hatred through the heart of carnal flesh. FOR YOU CANNOT KILL LOVE. And because God is LOVE, I John 4:8, and is also "harmless" (Heb 7:26) and therefore, does not destroy, the only kind of fire that could possibly come from Him, would be a loving fire of truth and righteousness.

DOES JESUS BRING DIVISION?

Therefore, the fire that Christ brings with Him when He returns, is not destructive in ITS INTENT, BUT IN ITS EFFECT. Why? Because of the way people will relate themselves to it. Jesus said, "Suppose ye that I am come to give peace, on earth? I tell you nay; but rather division." Luke 12:51. "I came not to send peace, but a sword." Matt. 10:34. Was it Christ's intent to bring "DIVISION" and "A SWORD?" No. But that was the effect of His first advent or coming. Why? Because men rejected Him and this rejection brought strife and division. It sometimes seems that wicked men are more united in carrying out their evil plans than the righteous. For example, while Moses was up on the mountain, receiving the Ten Commandments from God, Aaron was down below "leading" the people into apostasy. The people were more united in this apostasy than they ever had been or ever would be under Moses. And in the same way, the Jewish leaders and people in Christ's day were more united in their condemnation and crucifixion of Jesus than they had ever been before or ever would be again. And so, we see that Jesus, the Prince of Peace did not cause strife, division, war and bloodshed, but He claims to be causing it, for He always assumes responsibility or blame for whatever He permits. The sword in Matt 10:34 is equated with fire. Jesus guided Israel for 40 years with a cloud by day and a fiery pillar at night. Nehemiah 9:9-17 and I Cor. 10:4 tells us this was Jesus Christ revealing Himself to Moses and Israel. The Bible teaches us that fire is a revelation of God Himself, "FOR OUR GOD IS A CONSUMING FIRE." Hebrews 12:29.

Since God is love, then a revelation of God would naturally be a revelation of His character of love. Jesus is the Word made flesh and that we "beheld His glory (character) the glory as of the only begotten of the Father, full of grace and truth." John 1:1-3, 14. This revelation of His WORD OF TRUTH OR FIRE OF TRUTH saw its ultimate fulfillment in the person of Jesus Christ. The Bible abounds with references to God's Word being a light or a fire.

"Thy Word [Jesus] is a lamp [fire] unto my feet, and a light [fire] unto my path." Psalm 119:105. "In Him (Christ) was life; and the life was the light [fire] of man." John 1:4. Cleopas and his friend said, "Did not our heart burn within us, while He talked with us by the way, and while he opened to us the Scriptures." Luke 24:31, 32. Satan and Christ appeared to Abraham as a "SMOKING FURNACE AND A BURNING LAMP." Gen. 15:17. We know the lamp represents God's Word or Christ and I believe the smoking furnace represents Satan. God was appearing to Abraham to reveal a special message to him and Satan was right there to pervert it. The Burning Bush did not give off any smoke. See Rev. 9:2, 3. God's lamp (flaming torch) Gen. 3:24; Heb. 1:7, Rev. 1:14, was not literal fire. But the smoking furnace was. Jesus told his disciples, "I am the light (fire) of the world." John 8:12. If Jesus abides in our hearts, we too will be vessels and channels of His glory." Matt. 5: 14. The phrase "like fire" indicates that the presence of God had the appearance of fire to human eyes, but was not actually fire as we think of fire in a literal sense.

With this Scriptural understanding firmly implanted in our minds now, let us consider another fiery passage. "When the Lord Jesus shall be revealed from heaven with His mighty angels. In flaming fire taking vengeance on them that know not God, and that obey not the gospel of our Lord Jesus Christ: who shall be punished with everlasting destruction from the presence of the Lord, and from the glory of His power when He shall come to be glorified in His saints and to be admired in all them that believe (because our testimony among you was believed) in that day." 2 Thess. 1:8-10.

JESUS' FIRST FIERY COMING

We know that Jesus Christ is the total and absolute perfection of God's presence. That presence was revealed in a bodily, fleshly, human form almost 2, 000 years ago when Jesus came to earth. Jesus said that He had come to "BRING FIRE," on the earth and truly He did, for the demons screamed in terror and fright at His presence. Jesus was "REVEALED FROM HEAVEN" the first time in a body of flesh. But it didn't take place in just a day or a week or a month or even a year. No. It took about 33 years for the Father to fully reveal Himself to the Jewish nation at that time. "And the Word was made flesh, and dwelt among us, (and we beheld his glory, the glory as of the only begotten of the Father), full of grace and truth." John 1:14.

This is the way God revealed Himself to the world "IN FLAMING FIRE" at Christ's first advent. It was a PROGRESSIVE REVELATION of truth, righteousness and love lived out in the person of our beloved Redeemer. The Hebrew mind never writes in reference to time, for God is beyond and above time, space and matter. Throughout the Old Testament there are many "fiery" references to the coming of Christ which applied to both His first coming and His second coming in our day. Here is one. "Behold, he shall come, saith the Lord of hosts. But who may abide the day of his coming? and who shall stand when he appeareth? for he is like a refiner's fire, and like fullers' soap." Mal. 3:2, 3. That prophecy was written 400 years before Christ's first advent, but it applied to both of his appearances or advents. Compare it with Rev. 1:7. "For the great day of his wrath is come; and who shall be able to stand?" Now, let us look at two passages which will clearly reveal how the wicked will be burned up and destroyed when Jesus returns in the clouds of glory. Remember now and keep in mind the concept of PROGRESSIVE REVELATION. "But the path of the just is as the shining light, that shineth more and more unto the perfect day." Proverbs 4:18. Notice the phrase, "MORE AND MORE," indicating that the "SHINING LIGHT" was not revealed in an instant or in one single day. It took place over a period of time. And so it was with Christ's first advent and so it is and will continue to be with his second advent. God is pouring out his Holy Spirit on "ALL FLESH" today, Joel 2:28. That is, He is pleading with all people to come to Him. But this prophecy had an initial fulfillment on the day of Pentecost and lasted all the way through the early Christian dispensation until the apostasy or falling away (2 Thess. 2:3) Paul predicted. It is to have a much wider and greater fulfillment in our day. Some people believe it has already come and will continue until Jesus Himself appears in the clouds of glory to culminate and consummate THE BLESSED HOPE.

CHRIST'S FIERY LOOK OF LOVE

Let us now consider for a moment what we have learned so far. Christ's glorious and destructive coming does have an explosive end-point, but there is a progressive build-up to that dramatic moment. Let us look at what is transpiring on the stage of action right now that is leading us to this climatic end-time event. In Rev 19 we find another description of Christ's second coming to this earth with fire parallel to what Jesus and Paul described. "And I saw heaven opened, and behold a white horse; and He that sat upon him was called Faithful and True, and in righteousness He doth judge and make war. His eyes were as a flame of fire, and on his head were many crowns ...And the armies which were in heaven followed him upon white horses, clothed in fine linen, white and clean. And out of his mouth goeth a sharp sword, that with it he should smite the nations; and he shall rule them with a rod of iron: and he treadeth the winepress of the fierceness and wrath of Almighty God." Rev. 19:11-15.

The key phrases we should notice here are "HIS EYES WERE AS A FLAME OF FIRE." Once again the fire simile is used to describe His look of love. Then the phrase "HE HAD A NAME," tells us that He is revealing His character, for in verse 13, it tells us His name or title is "THE WORD OF GOD." And then verse 15 tells us that a SHARP SWORD, goes out of His mouth and this is also His Word. It is with this SHARP SWORD which is His "FIERY WORD" that He smites and burns up the nations. The phrase in verse 16, "KING OF KINGS AND LORD OF LORDS" reveals this august personage to be none other than the CREATOR GOD Himself, even our Lord Jesus Christ. When Jesus walked the earth in a body of flesh He sent seventy of His disciples all over the countryside to prepare the way for His coming, see Luke 10:1. Later on persecution caused His gospel message to be spread everywhere. Acts 8:1-4 tells about it. In the Old Testament God used angels to carry messages to human beings. How appropriate then for the final "LOUD VOICE," message or "LOUD CRY" proclamation of Rev. 14 and Rev. 18 to again be given by angels who are working with and through human beings as the angel Gabrielle worked through Daniel. An angel also worked through John the Revelator, Rev. 1:1.

Angels are called, "FLAMES OF FIRE," Heb. 1:7 and yet they are "MINISTERING SPIRITS," to us, Heb. 1:14. In Matt. 13 Jesus told His disciples "THE HARVEST IS THE END OF THE WORLD AND THE REAPERS ARE THE ANGELS." See also Rev. 14:14-20. Matt. 16:27 tells us Christ will come with the angels when He returns the second time to earth in "FLAMING" glory. 2 Thess 1:8. In Rev 19:14 Jesus is pictured as riding a WHITE HORSE. "And the armies which were in heaven followed Him upon white horses, clothed in fine linen, white and clean." Now, verse 8 tells us that the "FINE LINEN is the RIGHTEOUSNESS OF SAINTS." The armies in heaven would therefore be His translated people, (saints), riding horses, as if in battle. 2 Kings 2:11, 2 Kings 6:17. Rev. 6:1-8 describes four horses which represent the first four church eras or periods of church history after Jesus went back to heaven. When we piece these symbols together, we see a beautiful picture of Jesus using (riding) His saints (church(es) as vehicles to give or sound out a last warning message to the world.

Furthermore, Psalm 34:7 and Psalm 91:11, 12, indicate God protects His people (church(es) through the holy angels.

From the information we now have we can see that God always reveals Himself to the people on this planet through fiery experiences. This explains why the final message and Christ's glorious return are spoken of in these terms, consistent with the manner of his dealing with people in the past. The life of Christ and His first advent serves as a model for His second coming. Therefore, there is a parallel between His first coming and His second coming. Just as His first coming took about thirty-three years to take place, so His second coming is also a progressive revelation of His fiery character of love through the Holy Spirit in His final chosen people as they give the loud cry ...BEHOLD YOUR GOD! At the close of the period of Jesus' first coming He died. The cross marked the end of the era of His first coming. It appeared that the church had died with Christ. But the resurrection brought it to life and vitality again. And so it is with the second coming. The church is about to experience persecution as they demonstrate the Father's true character of love in their lives. The same love, patience, meekness, dignity and grace that shone in the SAVIOR's face as He stood on trial before the rulers, Herod and Pilate, will again shine through the lives and faces of the waiting saints in this last hour of earth's history. The destruction of Jerusalem followed 40 years after Christ's death on Calvary.

Jerusalem is a symbol of the impending destruction that will fall upon the whole world because of their rejection of truth and their persecution of God's people. But as the world dies in their sins, as did the Jews, John 8:24, God's people will be raised a victorious church as they meet their Lord in the air. I Thess. 4:13-18. The Bible declares that God will "consume" Satan and of course, all of his followers by the "BRIGHTNESS OF HIS COMING." 2 Thess. 2:8.

Let us notice now how this actually took place. When Jesus arrived on the scene in Bethlehem, the Jews were in a very serious state of apostasy. God had not been able to speak to them for over 400 years. Malachi was their last prophet. However, there was a little glimmer of hope left. They had not completely separated themselves from God by joining up with Rome, but as the "BRIGHTNESS" of Jesus' character-glory shone on them they began to resist its glorious rays and forced themselves into the arms of Rome and full apostasy. The Father did not intend for this to happen, but this was the result or effect of His efforts to reach out and bring them to Himself. It broke His heart. Their rejection of Him brought them under the shadow of the Golden Roman eagle who then swooped down in 70 A.D. and destroyed them. They were destroyed by the BRIGHTNESS OF HIS COMING which they rejected. "OH ISRAEL, THOU HAST DESTROYED THYSELF;" Hosea 13:9. Even now in our day, history is about to repeat itself. The world today is in a terrible state of apostasy similar to the days of Noah when the wickedness of man was great in the earth, and that every imagination of the thoughts of his heart was only evil continually. Gen. 6:5. The "BRIGHTNESS" of the Father's and Son's character glory is even now beginning to be revealed in the earth. It will become brighter and brighter as the darkness of apostasy and rebellion of church and state increase in their hatred and antagonism toward the final Elect and their message.

The world's rejection of the Father's love will drive both religious and secular elements in society to separate themselves from God's protection. THE BRIGHTNESS OF CHRIST'S CHARACTER GLORY today will again destroy them as it did the Jews, but not in the sense that God is smashing them with his fists from heaven. This is never God's method of dealing. His nail-pierced hand of mercy is held out to save, never to hurt. As they move away from it, instead of toward it, they are left to themselves and the unrestrained forces in man and nature will destroy them as it did in the days of the flood. This same character glory, which is driving them to self-destruction, is the very means by which God hopes to save them and would save them, if will they relate themselves to it properly and accept it. But if they reject His love, all that God intends for their salvation will be turned for their destruction because of their own perverse and stubborn will. The very weapons they prepare to destroy God's people with will be turned upon themselves for their total annihilation.

"And I will call for a sword against him throughout all my mountains, saith the Lord God: every man's sword shall be against his brother." Ezek. 38:21; Zech. 14:13. "He made a pit, and digged it, and is fallen into the ditch which he made. His mischief shall return upon his own head, and his violent dealing shall come down upon his own pate." Psalm 7:16. The physical means by which Satan was able to destroy the Jewish nation was the Roman armies. This was the shadow to which they had run for safety which led to their destruction. Darkness hates light and seeks to hide from it. "And the light shineth in darkness; and the darkness comprehended it not." John 1:5. "Walk while ye have the light, lest darkness come upon you: for he that walketh in darkness knoweth not whither he goeth." John 12:35. "And they shall look unto the earth; and behold trouble and darkness, dimness of anguish; and they shall be driven to darkness." Isa. 8:22.

GOD'S PEOPLE BLAMED

The seven last plagues, which men will bring upon themselves, will be the means by which Satan will destroy this final generation on planet earth. But even while they die men will be cursing God instead of repenting. "And men were scorched with great heat, and blasphemed the name of God, which hath power over these plagues: and they repented not to give him glory." Rev. 16:9. This text proves that God never gives up in His loving efforts to draw the sinner to Himself by repentance. Repentance is still available to the sinner at this point, but they refuse it again. "AND THEY REPENTED NOT TO GIVE HIM GLORY." The word "GLORY" here means "character." The wicked still refuse to acknowledge and receive God's true character, which alone will fit them for heavenly citizenship.

God has "power" (control) over the plagues, but He is not bringing the plagues. In fact, He is trying to save mankind from the worst effects of that which he is bringing upon himself by his rape and abuse of nature through avarice, greed and self-aggrandizement. The plagues are simply an ecological rebellion or kickback of nature itself against man's terrible abuse of it, during the last few decades especially. Pollution of all kinds in the air, water and man himself with all types of man-made chemicals will have its sure result during the seven-last plagues. But instead of accepting responsibility for what they have done, man will blame God for the plagues. Our very atmosphere is ready to ignite into flames. Only God is preventing this. 2 Peter 3:7, 10, 12.

A death decree will be passed against God's people who refuse to acknowledge, join and bow down to the NWO beast system Rev. 13:15. Just as the Jews sought to blame Jesus for their troubles with Rome, so the leading men in authority in our day will blame God's people for the plagues and all other problems in the earth. It will be declared that we must die in order for the world to be saved. Notice the parallel in Jesus' life and death. "He stirreth up the people, teaching throughout all Jewry, beginning from Galilee to this place." Luke 23:5. "Then gathered the chief priests and the Pharisees, a council, and said, What do we? for this man doeth many miracles. If we let him alone, all men will believe on him: and the Romans shall come and take away both our place and nation." John 11:47, 48. Then Caiaphas, the high priest stated prophetically, "Ye know nothing at all, nor consider that it is expedient for us, that one man should die for the people, and that the whole nation perish not." John 11:50.

Thus it has been recorded and history is about to repeat itself in the person of Christ's final Elect who will reflect His very likeness in this last hour of earth's dark and bloody history. "For, behold, the darkness shall cover the earth, and gross darkness the people: but the Lord shall arise upon thee, and his glory (character) shall be seen upon thee." Isa. 60:2. Jesus will arise and cover our nakedness with His Holy and Righteous character within and without. Jesus was able to overcome the hatred of men in His hour of trial through the white hot passion of His Father's eternal love. Acts 1:3; Song of Solomon 8:6, 7. This will be the very same experience of all who trust in the Lord Jesus. Listen: "He that overcomes, the same shall be clothed in white raiment; and I will not blot out his name out of the book of life, but I will confess his name before my Father, and before his angels... because thou hast kept the word of my patience, I also will keep thee from THE HOUR OF TEMPTATION, which shall come upon all the world, to try them that dwell upon the earth. Behold, I come quickly: hold that fast which thou hast, that no man take thy crown. Him that overcometh will I make a pillar in the temple of my God." Rev. 3:5, 9-12. Yes, the final elect will overcome and get the victory, just as Jesus did, by trusting in the Father's love. Satan will not be able to overcome them. "Now unto him that is able to keep you from falling, and to present you faultless before the presence of his glory with exceeding joy." Jude 24.

"Husbands, love your wives, even as Christ loved the church, and gave himself for it; That he might present it to himself a glorious church, not having spot, or wrinkle, or any such thing; but that it should be holy and without blemish." Eph. 5:25-27. What a glorious promise of victory for all who trust in the Father's love even as Jesus did. We may lose everything in this life. We may even be put to death as was Jesus, but we will have a part in the resurrection and come forth from the grave just as Jesus did. It may appear that Satan has almost won in this final conflict, but out of the darkness will shine forth the glorious, saving message of God's eternal love. This is truly the power of His resurrection that Paul spoke of which each of us may claim by faith right now. "That I may know him, and the power of his resurrection, and the fellowship of his sufferings, being made conformable unto his death; If by any means I might attain unto the resurrection of the dead." Philippians 3:10, 11.

CHAPTER 26

THE ANIMAL SACRIFICE SYSTEM

How the animal sacrifice system of the old testament began seems to be one of the most fascinating mysteries in religious history. In order to understand any mystery in the great controversy between good and evil, we must go to the cross and stand in its light and glory.

When Jesus died on the cross, the veil in the temple that separated the holy place from the most holy place was torn in two from top to bottom just as Jesus' flesh was ripped and torn from his head to his feet, Matt. 27:51. His tearing was total and complete so that our healing might be total and complete. "With his stripes we are healed." Isaiah. 53:5.

The Bible tells us God never changes, Mal. 3:6. The question we must answer then, is, whose idea was it to kill poor, dumb, innocent animals, if God does not kill? The answer will be clear enough for those who wish to believe. As we have seen throughout this book there has been a progression of thought and information leading us to more and more understanding about God's true character of love. The prophet Daniel predicted that in the last days this would happen. "But thou, O Daniel, shut up the words, and seal the book, even to the time of the end; many shall run to and fro, and knowledge shall be increased." Dan. 12:4. Many believe this is referring to the increased knowledge in science and industry such as the invention of the telephone, electric lights, automobiles, airplanes, radio and TV, etc. But what this is referring to specifically is an INCREASE IN KNOWLEDGE ABOUT GOD, OUR HEAVENLY FATHER. Dan 12:3, 10 refer to the "Wise," who will be shining "as the brightness of the firmament," and will be the only ones who "understand," or know what is going on in the last days. This is one of the 24 designations I spoke of in chapter 25. The Wise and the Elect are titles for the same group of people, the Barley. Jesus called them the "righteous" who at the time of the Harvest would "shine forth as the sun in the kingdom of their Father." Matt 13:43. So the spiritual journey of God's people is one of progressive joy, understanding and increased knowledge about our wonderful heavenly Father. "But the path of the just is as the shining light, that shineth more and more unto the perfect day." Proverbs 4:18.

As we find out more and more truth about God we will also discover the truth about Lucifer, the fallen angel who is our sworn enemy, the devil. Jesus revealed to the Jews that he was their real father. "You are of your father the devil; and it is your will to practice the lusts and gratify the desires [which are characteristic] of your father. He was a murderer from the beginning, and does not stand in the truth, because there is no truth in him. When he speaks a falsehood, he speaks what is natural to him; for he is a liar [himself] and the father of lies and of all that is false." John 8:44. Amplified.

Most Christians today know very little about their enemy the devil and that is why he has been able to wreak havoc in the church and the world because he is always posing as an angel of light. We know from Zechariah 3:1-3, that wherever the Lord is, Satan is right there on the scene to resist, oppose and slander everything our heavenly Father is trying to do for us. His hatred knows no bounds. "Then the guiding angel showed me Joshua the high priest standing before the Angel of the Lord (Christ), and Satan standing at Joshua's right hand to be his adversary and to accuse him." Amplified.

We know from the first two chapters of the book of Job that Satan claims to be the representative from planet earth who is "going to and fro on the earth, and from walking up and down on it." Job 1:7. I Peter 5:8 expands our knowledge on this point by explaining that Satan truly is our "adversary" who like "a roaring lion, walks about, seeking whom he may devour."

2 Corinthians 4:4 refers to Satan as the "god of this world" who has "blinded the minds of them which believe not, lest the light of the glorious gospel of Christ, who is the image of God,

should shine unto them." We know that Satan's goal is to be worshiped by the entire world, which would mean that he must deceive everyone into thinking that he himself is God. And this will be part of the final deception when he finally sits in the "temple of God, showing himself that he is God." 2 Thess. 2:4. But it is all for the purpose of destroying as many people as possible. Jesus revealed that this has been his modus operandi from "the beginning." If this be true, then we should be able to discover something in the Garden of Eden where Adam and Eve first fell, because that is where all the trouble in the world began in the first place.

Beginning in 1992 the Lord led me to research and write an article about the "THE BROKEN AND FORGOTTEN LAW OF GENESIS ONE." Other articles followed which expanded on this theme and have been printed in a 101 page book (8 1/2 x 11) I have entitled ***"The Mystery of God's Will Revealed in the Plan of the Ages,"*** now in its third edition. In chapter 5 of this book I included an article entitled, "UNDERSTANDING THE REAL TRUTH ABOUT EDEN AND GOD'S ETERNAL PLAN." All of this knowledge has come to me since 1982, when the first edition of "INTO THE FATHER'S HEART," was first published, so that is the reason I am including as much of this information in this updated and revised edition you now have in your hands. A knowledge of God is ongoing and progressive as one writer has so eloquently expressed it: "In every age there is a new development of truth, a message of God to the people of that generation. The old truths are all essential; new truth is not independent of the old, but an unfolding of it. It is only as the old truths are understood that we can comprehend the new. When Christ desired to open to His disciples the truth of His resurrection, He began 'at Moses and all the prophets' and expounded unto them in all the scriptures the things concerning Himself.' Luke 24:27. But it is the light which shines in the fresh unfolding of truth that glorifies the old." Christ's Object Lessons, pg 127.

Acts 3:21 tells us that before Jesus can return there must be a "restitution of all things," or a restoration of a knowledge of God that has been lost since the days of Adam when he and Eve fell, not only losing their robe of celestial light, righteousness and innocence, but of the true knowledge of God's love. And that is why Jesus had to come to restore this knowledge to us. "And this is life eternal, that they might know thee the only true God, and Jesus Christ, whom thou has sent." John 17:3. He came to show the mercy and love of the Father which Adam and Eve lost. But why did they lose it? Because they became afraid. But why were they afraid? Ah, that is the question which will unlock the mystery of the animal sacrifice system, the theme of this chapter.

Here is a text which will help us in our search for the truth. "For I desired mercy, and not sacrifice; and the knowledge of God more than burnt offerings. But they like men have transgressed the covenant: there have they dealt treacherously against Me." Hosea 6:6, 7. The phrase "like men," in the marginal reading reads "Like Adam." We know that Adam was the first man to begin killing animals. But why? If the true God never commanded any animals to be slaughtered where did the idea come from? Jeremiah 7:21, 22 clearly tells us the true Lord never spoke such a command to kill or sacrifice His own creation. And Jesus said that His sheep hear His voice. So, that leaves only one voice left which would be that of the fallen angel, Lucifer or Satan.

And that is the voice Adam listened to in the Garden who caused him to become afraid. "And he (Adam) said, I heard your voice in the garden, and I was afraid, because I was naked; and I hid myself." Gen 3:10. What was it that caused Adam to be afraid of God in the first place? The answer is found in Gen 2:17 where the "Lord God" threatens Adam with death if he eats of the tree of knowledge of good and evil. Right there is where the "fear of death began." But who is this "Lord God" who made a law that they were not allowed to eat of one of the trees? Paul tells us: "That through death He (Jesus) might destroy (render powerless) him that had the power of death, that is the devil; and deliver them who through fear of death were all their lifetime subject to bondage." Hebrews 2:14, 15.

We need to realize that all laws are not from God. Some laws are bad. And this was a bad law. Paul calls it the ***"Law of sin and death."*** "For the law of the Spirit of life in Christ Jesus has made me free from the law of sin and death." Rom 8:2. Ok, let's go back to square one. God created the world in six days and pronounced His work very good. Gen. 1:31. He also gave Adam and Eve (both of them) "every tree" along with all the herbs for food. He gave them dominion over all the earth. He withheld nothing. And then it says that He rested on the 7th day Sabbath and blessed it. Gen 2:1-3. This is the first version of the creation story. Let me also mention that throughout the Bible there are "couplets," which means two versions of the same story. You will find this in Genesis 15 and 17 as well as in the Chronicles where many of the stories recited in 1st and 2nd Samuel are repeated with some variations and differences. For example, you have the story of David numbering Israel in 2 Sam 24:1 where it says the Lord moved (incited) David to number Israel (take a census to see how many men were eligible to go to war against David's enemies). But when this same story is repeated in I Chronicles 21:1 you find that it says "Satan stood up against Israel, and provoked David to number Israel." The first account is recorded about 1035 BC and the second one 500 years later, in the days of Ezra, about 535 BC. So, here we have, in the last book of record of the Old Testament, a final interpretation of this remarkable incident and the inspired author of this history sees that the Lord who "moved or incited David" was not the true Lord, but was in fact the devil or Satan, the adversary lord god Yahweh. An incredible difference to be sure, which opens up a window into what is going on behind the scenes. It reveals that there are two Lords operating in the Old Testament but one of them is an impostor, a counterfeit, gestapo, pretender lord or god.

And that is precisely what we have in the book of Genesis. Two versions of the same story. In the first version God creates everything in an orderly fashion. Adam and Eve are spoken into existence on the sixth day together, at the same moment in time. But in the second version there is a counterfeit "Lord God" who creates Adam first and then puts him into some kind of sleep or trance similar to what was done to Abram in Gen 15. Eve is brought forth from one of Adam's ribs thanks to a quick surgical procedure. This pretender lord god is also an Indian giver, taking back one of the trees and then threatening Adam with death if he eats of it. If you believe God does not destroy you would immediately be able to detect this deceiving lord god as an impostor.

When we come to chapter 3 the true character of this imposter lord god is fully revealed. No Hollywood movie or fairy tale has ever been able to compete with this ageless story of what we know as the "Temptation and Fall." But who is the tempter? Remember that Ezekiel 28:13 reveals that Lucifer (under the title here as the King of Tyrus) was in the Garden of Eden, not as a serpent, but as the deceiving, counterfeit lord god. Now, let's deal with the serpent first.

By all accounts I have ever read about this serpent, it was the most intelligent and loveliest of all the creatures God had made. So, let's be clear about one thing. The serpent was not an evil creature before the fall. It was in fact, the most beautiful creature of all. The question we must answer is, who is using this creature as a medium to speak to Eve? Is it the devil as we have always thought, or could it be that God Himself chose to speak to Eve in this manner. Did the Lord ever do this any other time?

Yes, as a matter of fact, he did in the days of Baalim "speaking with a voice of a man, restrained the madness of the prophet." 2 Peter 2:16; Numbers 22:30. But let us examine the evidence regarding the true identity of the voice behind the serpent. What did the voice using the serpent as a medium ask Eve? This is crucial because the old English here is not very clear. "Yea, hath God said, Ye shall not eat of every tree of the garden?" This question was designed to elicit a response from Eve regarding what she believed. The being using the serpent is trying to determine if Eve believes that the law of Gen 2 is a valid law or not. Here is another version: "Why hath God commanded you, that you should not eat of every tree of paradise? And the woman answered him, saying: of the fruit of the trees that are in paradise we do eat: But of the fruit of the tree which is in the midst of paradise, God hath commanded us that we should not eat; and that we should not touch it, lest perhaps we die. And the serpent said to the woman: No, you shall not die the death." Gen 3:1-4. Douay Version, 1609.

What this being wants to clarify is if Eve believes that the lord god of Gen 2 is the same as the God of Gen 1. If Eve believes the same voice spoke both laws then the being behind the voice knows that Eve (and Adam) have been deceived. Why? Because the true God told Adam and Eve together, in Gen 1, that all the trees were very good and that they all belonged to them. Now, they have been told that one of the trees is not only suddenly "off limits" but that there is now a death penalty in effect for anyone who dares eat of this tree. No wonder they became terrified and ran for their lives. No wonder their connection with the throne of God was broken, shedding them of their beautiful robe of light, leaving them shaking and shivering in fear, hiding in the bushes wondering when this angry lord god would strike them dead for eating of the fruit of the "forbidden" tree. But who was it that forbade them to eat of it? Was it the true God of Gen 1 who gave them all things? No. Our heavenly Father is not an Indian giver god. So, the law forbidding Adam and Eve to eat of that tree was from Satan, the false lord of Eden, who created the "Law of sin and death" out of thin air. See Rom. 8:1-3.

Now the being speaking through the serpent is ready to reveal the truth to Eve about God's creation, confirming that it is good and nothing is wrong with the fruit of the tree. The true God of creation never made any such tree as a "tree of the knowledge of good and evil." That is not mentioned at all in Genesis 1. All of God's trees were totally pure and good. There was no evil in them. Then the "voice of truth" tells Eve there is a "god" or "ruler" (one claiming to be god or Yahweh Elohim) who does not want you to eat of this tree he has put off limits and pronounced evil, because if you do eat of it you will find out he has lied to you because you will not die, for there is no death in God's creation. "O taste and see that the Lord is good: blessed is the man that trusts in Him." Psalm 34:8. And when you eat of this fruit and nothing bad happens you realize that this so-called "God" has lied to you. Your "eyes will be open to the truth." And you will then be able to know the difference between good and evil, which the true Lord wants us to know so we will not be deceived, which is precisely what Paul teaches in Hebrews 5:14.

The early Christians taught that the voice using the serpent was a feminine being. "Then the Female Spiritual Principle came [in] the Snake, the Instructor; and it taught [them], saying, "What did he [say to] you [pl.]? Was it, 'From every tree in the Garden shall you [sing.] eat; yet-from [the tree] of recognizing evil and good do not eat'?" The carnal Woman said, 'Not only did he say 'Do not eat,' but even 'Do not touch it; for the day you [pl.] eat from it, with death you [pl.] are going to die.'"

"And the Snake, the Instructor, said, "with death you [pl.] shall not die; for it was out of jealousy that he said this to you [pl.]. Rather your [pl.] eyes shall open and you [pl.] shall come to be like gods, recognizing evil and good. And the Female Instructing Principle was taken away from the Snake, and she left it behind merely a thing of the earth." "Adam, Eve and the Serpent," page 67, by Elaine Pagels, of the religion department at Princeton University. It is my belief that this female instructor was the Shekinah glory, daughter of the most high God, Gabrielle, mother of Eve. *See Additional Note #31.

What convinced me more than anything else that the gestapo "lord god" of Eden was Satan is when he turned the pure air of Eden blue with curses upon the serpent, Eve, Adam and even the ground of the earth itself. He also said that he would put "enmity" between the serpent (Holy Spirit) and the woman (church). The true God never puts enmity between people. In fact, Jesus came to destroy or remove the enmity. Eph. 2:15, 16. This is the work of Satan, the fallen angel, our deadly foe. Neither does the true Lord cause the earth to bring forth "thorns and thistles." That is also the work of the devil. If you wish to go into more depth on this topic you may read my articles on God's Last Call web site at: www.godslastcall.org and order my books which are listed in my quarterly newspaper.

We know that it was Satan who degraded that once beautiful serpent to what has become, to most people, one of the most loathsome, feared and hated creatures in the animal kingdom. It certainly wasn't God's idea. No. The Bible tells us that the serpent represents Satan, Rev. 12:7-9. Besides, God only gives good gifts to us, James 1:17. But we must remember that there are two serpents in the Bible. The one representing goodness and truth is the one which is above the ground, as in Numbers 21:6-9, on a pole which the true Lord commanded Moses to make so the people could look at it and be healed. We know the true God would not command Moses to make a symbol of the devil to look at to be healed. Nor would Jesus tell Nicodemus that He was going to become the serpent again in John 3:14 to bring healing to all who would look at Him as they did in Moses day. When the serpent is up off the ground in the tree or on a pole or in Moses hand, as in Pharaoh's courts, it represents the healing power of God, but when it is crawling around biting people it represents Satan.

We know that the tree of knowledge of good and evil could not have been God's original idea to tempt Adam and Eve, for the Bible tells us God does not mix good with evil. Only good comes from God. Evil comes from Satan. Furthermore, James 1:13 tells us God does not tempt anyone with evil. Why then would He need a tree in His garden with evil in it? Since God created everything in the garden perfect and very good, then the tree of knowledge of good and evil was not God's idea. This perfect tree was used and perverted by the "ENEMY" just as he perverted himself and cursed and degraded the innocent serpent. He did this also with the good wheat field. Matt. 13:28 tells us that Jesus recognized the enemy's hand in perverting his wheat field. "Sir didst not thou sow good seed in thy field? From whence then hath it tares? He said unto them, 'AN ENEMY HATH DONE THIS:'" Isn't this exactly what happened in the Garden of Eden? Yes, it is. God created a beautiful garden and Satan sowed his tares or seeds of evil. After Adam and Eve fell, he was able to not only pervert God's good trees, but to even plant his own evil trees. Jesus commented on this by saying, "Every plant, which my Father hath not planted, shall be rooted up. Let them alone: they be blind leaders of the blind. And if the blind lead the blind, both shall fall into the ditch." Matt. 15:13. Compare Ps. 7:15. The thorns and briars and all hurtful and noxious plants are from Satan. God never created any such thing.

From the very inception of Satan's rebellion the Father's policy has been to give each creature free choice. This free moral agency is never rescinded or taken away, for God doesn't take back his gifts. "For the gifts and calling of God are without repentance." Rom. 11:29. Another translation uses the term "IRREVOCABLE," (MLT) and the LB says, "For God's gifts and his calling can never be withdrawn; he will never go back on his promises." God's gifts are His blessings. Under inspiration Balaam said, "...He hath blessed; and I cannot reverse it." Num. 23:20: Compare also Ps. 89:34, Mal. 3:6, Heb. 13:8. When we apply this principle to God's loving character we can see that God is forever the same. He has never been anything but pure, total love. It is impossible for him to kill just as it is impossible for him to lie. Heb. 6:18. God never uses force or coercion. He doesn't have to, for man always proves God just no matter what device man may scheme up to evade God's loving commands and warnings which are for our own best good.

When Adam and Eve ate of the fruit, which in and of itself was not harmful, they thought they had done something wrong and reacted accordingly. Adam believed Satan's lie that there was death in the tree and became afraid. This caused Him to distrust His Maker. Eve fell into the same trap. It was then that their connection with God was broken and they lost some kind of light, heat or radiance which clothed them. Their fear led to distrust and lack of faith, which extinguished that light because it broke the electrical light connection in their brain by which God had infused His very life and presence into their minds and bodies.

Christ came to re-light the fire of His Father's love in man's heart, which the doubt and disobedience of Adam had extinguished. Paul tells us the kind of body we will have in the resurrection, Philippians 3:20, 21. It will be a glorious body just like Jesus had, and still has, after He arose from the tomb. When Jesus arose from the dead, He no longer needed earthly garments for the Bible tells us he had very neatly laid them aside, Luke 24:12; John 20: 5-7. Yes, He arose with that glorified, heavenly body, which could be handled and touched, and could even eat food, Luke 24:36-43. And it is this very "same" Jesus which angels told the disciples would come again in the clouds of glory, Acts 1:9-11. Furthermore, this "same" Jesus appeared to John on the Isle of Patmos and notice how John describes His appearance. "...His countenance was as the sun shining in his strength." Rev. 1:16. This description is similar to Luke's account of the transfiguration when "His countenance was altered, and his raiment was white and glistering." Luke 9:29.

After the resurrection Jesus had that inner glow from His Father's throne of glory which actually seemed to radiate out from His face and body. But, Jesus veiled this glory from His disciples so they would be able to stand in His presence. Moses had to veil his face when he came down from the mountain, Exodus 34:25-33. Moses was not even aware that his face shined. These scripture references give us an idea what kind of body we will have in the resurrection. Paul calls the resurrection body a "spiritual body," I Cor. 15:44. Nevertheless, it is a real body that can be seen, felt and eat food. But there will be no bodily wastes as we have now, since the food will be completely assimilated or digested and turned into energy. The metabolism will be perfect and complete. All things will be made new again as God made them in the beginning. Eden will be restored. "And thou, O tower of the flock, the strong hold of the daughter of Zion, unto thee shall it come, even the first dominion; the kingdom shall come to the daughter of Jerusalem." Micah 4:8; See also Isa. 30:26 where it indicates the sun will be seven times as hot as it is today and the moon will be as hot or bright as our sun is today.

Before they sinned they were polarized naturally toward the Father, drawn to His throne of mercy and love by the bright beams of glory which emanated forth from His eternal presence. But as soon as they believed the words of the serpent, which was Satan, their polarity was reversed and they were now drawn to him. They would now be susceptible to his suggestions and under his control to do his bidding unless something was done to interfere with his plans. Since Lucifer (Satan) himself was a created being (Ezekiel 28:15) he would not fully realize the ultimate consequences of what he was doing. The on looking universe, also filled with created beings, would need a demonstration to fully understand the malignity of sin, which was simply the transgression of God's eternal law of love, which issued from His very heart.

God had declared that the "WAGES OF SIN IS DEATH," Rom, 6:23. Satan challenged this before the universe. He was claiming that God was a liar. Because God's very nature is love, He could not allow his creatures to bear the penalty of the broken law, which was eternal death. Therefore, a plan was devised whereby the Creator Himself would take the full penalty of the law, that is, suffer the physical and mental and emotional consequences of the law Himself. By doing this He would be able to shield the creatures and creation of His love from the penalty of the law long enough so they could see what sin will do and choose to listen to Him instead of to Satan, if they so desired. He would not force them. He will not force us today, for He has too much love and respect for our individual freedom.

Adam and Eve's minds were completely darkened and alienated from the Father's love. They hid from Him because their minds were now under the influence and control of the evil one. In a sense they didn't even have the power of choice anymore. Their brains had somehow been short circuited and they were unable to think straight. The electrical connection or light connection they had with their Creator was burned out perhaps like an alternator and the battery could not be recharged.

Adam and his wife Eve were now basically puppets on a string. They were like robots or automatons with no power to choose for themselves. Satan manipulated them at his will and fancy most of the time. But the Father set in motion a plan that would help them to resist Satan's power so they could call upon their Creator, if they chose. A promise was made that Satan's control over them would eventually be completely broken through Jesus' death on calvary.

Satan's power to deceive would be taken away by the life and death of Jesus. The woman represents the church, or God's people who keep the law through His power. Jer. 6:2; 2 Cor. 11:2. The following Scriptures speak of Christ and His people "bruising" Satan under their feet and putting "all enemies under His feet." Rom. 16:20; I Cor. 15:25. Ephesians 6:15 and Rom. 10:15; Isa. 52:7 speak of the feet as being "shod with the preparation of the gospel of peace," and of "beautiful... feet...that preach the gospel of peace." This makes it crystal clear that the taking away of Satan's power to deceive and lead people astray is accomplished by the preaching of the gospel to the world. When evil men resist and reject the message they are only destroying themselves by doing so in the process.

Let us prove this to ourselves more clearly as we read another prophecy. "For behold, the Lord cometh out of his place to punish the inhabitants of the earth for their iniquity: the earth also shall disclose her blood, and shall no more cover her slain. In that day (the day of Christ's return) the Lord with his sore and great and strong sword (the Bible or Word of God through his people) shall punish leviathan the piercing serpent, even leviathan that crooked serpent; and he shall slay the dragon that is in the sea." Isa. 26:21; Isa. 27:1.

Satan is leviathan, the crooked serpent and the dragon. Rev. 12:7-9. These passages and the interpretation we have put on them is consistent and in harmony with the way we have been interpreting God's dealings with Lucifer and all of his followers throughout the great controversy. It is the light of God's loving and eternal word that will destroy Satan and all of his hosts, and this light emanates from the law of God which is a transcript of His very character. It is the light from this law, which is the very mind of the Father and His Son, that must shine into our hearts and lives to reveal our defects of character so we may, through His power, overcome every sinful trait and tendency. When we refuse to be drawn to Him, we die in our sins. Jn. 8:24.

Light has ever been a symbol of the Divine presence. "The Lord is my light and my salvation; whom shall I fear? the Lord is the strength of my life; of whom shall I be afraid?" Psalm 27:1. "Arise, shine; for thy light is come, and the glory of the Lord is risen upon thee." Isa. 60:1. Notice the word glory is used here in connection with the command to arise and shine. This is an end time prophecy which is coming to pass right now, for verse 2 speaks of the darkness that will envelope the earth at the very time this message will be given; which of course will only make it shine with even greater radiance and giving it more visibility than ever.

Our wonderful heavenly Father is the source of all light. That is the reason why only the Son of God, who stood in the light of His Father's eternal presence could reconcile us to the Father's throne from whence flows all life and light and love. Jesus was symbolized by the ladder (Gen. 28:12) which connected heaven and earth. John the beloved said of him; In Him was life; and the life was the light of men." John 1:4. Additional texts to look up on the subject of light and life in Christ are: John 5:24-26; John 6:35; 6:40; 6:51; 6:53; 6:63; 8:12; Rom. 5:10; Col. 3:4; 2 Tim. 1:10.

Soon after Adam and Eve sinned, their beautiful robe of light began to fade and they realized that they were naked, Gen. 3:7. They had listened to the wrong voice and their light began to go out. As soon as they believed the lie that something was wrong with God's creation, something happened to them. An inner glow in them was extinguished which before had radiated an aura of light out from their bodies and formed a beautiful and holy robe of light around them so they didn't need clothing. This would also explain the radiance in Moses' face when he came down from Mount Sinai, Ex. 34:30, and Jesus' experience when he was transfigured, Matt. 17:2. "And his face did shine as the sun, and his raiment was white as the light." Jesus was the second Adam to re-connect us to the Father's throne.

Just as soon as Adam and Eve broke the covenant of Gen 1 by doubting God's love and harmless character, they blew all their fuses and circuits, breaking their electrical or light connection with God, and the light in them began to fade out until they realized they no longer had a robe of light and were "naked." The message to the Laodicean church is very interesting at this point. Christ is rebuking them in love and trying to convince them that they are "wretched, and miserable, and poor, and blind, and naked:" Rev. 3:17. And then He begins to give His Father's heavenly counsel to them. "I counsel thee to buy of me gold tried in the fire, that thou mayest be rich; and white raiment, that thou mayest be clothed, and that the shame of thy nakedness do not appear; and anoint thine eyes with eye salve, that thou mayest see." Rev. 3:18.

Whenever angelic or heavenly beings visit the earth men are afraid. John the Baptist's father, Zacharias, is one example (Luke 1:12) and the shepherds are another, (Luke 2:9). The Bible says the Shepherds were "sore afraid." Why this fear? Man in his pre-fall state, with the light of God's presence shining in him, was in perfect physical, mental and spiritual harmony with his Maker. He was on the same frequency. His electrical vibrations were on the same wave length and rhythm as his Creator. There was no fear or incompatibility. There was no decay, no corrosion, no dust, no deterioration or death. But just as soon as Adam ate of that fruit of the tree of knowledge of good and evil in the midst of the garden, and believed that there was something wrong with it, when there was nothing wrong at all (that was the lie that broke his light connection with the Father's throne) their bodies began changing from an anionic state down to a cationic state.

The very matter of their beings began to break down, deteriorate, decay, grow old and die. But was God responsible for this? No. Satan did it, but man cooperated and sin entered our world. In order to understand this more clearly, let us again go to the life of Jesus. He took on a body of flesh like our own and lived a perfect life of obedience to the Father's will. That perfect will is expressed in the perfect law of God, Ps. 19:7. "The law of the Lord is perfect, converting the soul." It is the perfect law of life and love from our loving Father above. By placing that law in our hearts, He is placing His very own character in our minds. This is what happened in the life of Jesus so we would have an example to follow. His reward on that resurrection morning was a new body; an anionic physical being that was not subject to time, space or matter. This is the kind of body Jesus regained and reclaimed for us through his perfect life of obedience. Phil. 3:20, 21 and I Cor. 15:35, 44—'53. This is what Adam had before his fall. And this is also the same kind of body we will have at translation or on the resurrection morning, if we are obedient to the Father's law through the power of Christ's overcoming spirit of love. The law broken by Adam, but kept by Christ.

As we look at Jesus' life we see Him cleansing the temple of animal sacrifices. Never once did he tell a person to go to the temple and kill an animal to wash away or cleanse himself of his or her sins. In fact, He cleansed the temple at the beginning of his ministry as well as at its close. The only time Jesus ever told anyone to follow the law of Moses was in Mark 1:44, and this was not to receive forgiveness, but to receive the priest's official recognition so that the leper could return to society. It was also a witness to the priests that Christ was the Messiah. The law of Moses included the "eye for an eye and tooth for a tooth," regulations along with the animal sacrifices. Did our Lord Jesus Christ really give these laws or did He only give the Ten Commandments? Let us seriously consider this question. If Jesus never changes, why then did he abolish this whole system of animal sacrifices?

Is it possible that this whole carnal system of ordinances was not God's perfect law, but His permissive will and law, until Christ Himself should come in the flesh to fully demonstrate the Father's heart of love?

Notice what Christ said in the sermon on the mount. "Ye have heard that it was said by them of old time... Thou shalt not kill, and whosoever shall kill shall be in danger of the judgment; BUT I SAY UNTO YOU, that whosoever is angry with his brother without a cause shall be in danger of the judgment (condemnation of self)...Ye have heard that it hath been said, 'an eye for an eye, and a tooth for a tooth:' BUT I SAY unto you, that ye resist not evil: but whosoever shall smite thee on thy cheek, turn the other also. And if any man will sue thee at the law, and take away thy coat, let him have thy cloak also." Matt. 5:21, 38-40.

HE WAS BEATEN BEYOND RECOGNITION

At his trial, Jesus lived out these principles as He let demon-possessed human beings spit in his face, pluck out his beard, hit him on the head to drive the thorns deeper into his skull, say untold words of ridicule, slander, abuse and hatred beyond computation until his Divine heart of love broke in two. The Bible had predicted, "I gave my back to the smiters, and my cheeks to them that plucked off the hair: I hid not my face from shame and spitting." Isa. 50:6. Matthew 27 :29-31 records the fulfillment of this prophecy. Isaiah also predicted that his face would not even be recognized because of all His sufferings. "His visage was so marred more than any man, and his form more than the sons of men." Isa. 52:14.

CHRIST WAS REDUCED TO HUMAN RUBBLE

The mental agony Jesus endured in the garden not only forced blood from his pores, but must have also twisted and disfigured his face so even His disciples could barely recognize Him. And why would the women of Jerusalem be weeping for

Him? Was it not because he looked so terrible? His head must have been swollen in many places and his face puffed out of shape from mental agony and physical abuse. He was simply beaten beyond recognition. It was a miracle He could even stand up, let alone try and shoulder his cross. His body was a heap of human rubble. There was probably not a square inch on his body that was not cut, torn, lacerated and bleeding. Oh, friend of mine, He did it for you; He did it for me. What have you done for Him?

Our precious Lord Jesus endured all of this to demonstrate three things. 1) That you cannot kill or quench His love no matter what you do or say to Him. 2) That the sin in our hearts is a terrible malignity that will destroy us. 3) That the law of God is a transcript of His eternal character of love and can never be changed. But more than that the law of God is simply God's will and love for us expressed in human terms, written on tables of stone, for our hearts are like stone toward Him in our carnal state. Therefore, only as we become Christ-like and receive His divine nature are we able to realize that the real "law of God," is a relationship between the Father and ourselves and when we come into His presence we no longer need a rule book, because we can look into His face and immediately know what is right and what is wrong and we would never, ever be able to see Him have a hurt or disappointed look on His face, therefore we would always be doing His will for we desire only His presence and His smile. This truly is heaven. "Thou wilt shew me the path of life: in thy presence is fulness of joy; at thy right hand there are pleasures for evermore." Psalm 16:11.

WHAT WAS IT THAT JESUS CHRIST NAILED TO HIS CROSS?

God's perfect and holy, Ten Commandment law, a transcript of His very likeness and being, and an expression of His ultimate reality was not what Jesus nailed to the cross of Calvary. This law can never be done away, abolished or abrogated. This law was placed inside of the golden ark of the covenant, (Deut.- 10:5; Heb. 9:4), which is a representation of the believer and is symbolic of the believer's conscience, for this is where God seeks to write His law of love Jer. 31:33.

This is the same law that was given on Mt. Sinai or Horeb. "These words the Lord spake unto all your assembly in the mount out of the midst of the fire, of the cloud, and of the thick darkness, with a great voice: AND HE ADDED NO MORE. And he wrote them in two tables of stone, and delivered them unto me." Deut. 5:22. The Lord only spoke Ten Commandments. "AND HE ADDED NO MORE." The complete and perfect will of God was embodied in that law which was all He gave.

Where then did the law of "enmity" come from? Who gave the law that Jesus abolished "IN HIS FLESH?" when He died on the cross? Ezek. 20:21-26 tells us that God "Gave them ...STATUES that were not good, and judgments whereby they should not live." In other words God had to give or allow them to have their own desire. Cf. Ps. 78:29-31. It was given by someone who is "against" us. The Father and His Son have never been "against" us, but always for us. "What shall we then say to these things? If God be for us, who can be against us?" Rom. 8:31. There you have it. No matter how many people may be against us, God will always be for us. And His love and protection is greater than all of their hatred and enmity .

Paul tells us that we must "wrestle...against principalities, against powers, against the rulers of the darkness of this world, against spiritual wickedness in high (heavenly) places." Eph. 6;12. He specifically states that we are not wrestling with "FLESH AND BLOOD," and so we know that our enemy is Satan the destroyer. And yet God's holy angels, nor Christ Himself ever bring "railing accusation(s) against them before the Lord." 2 Pet. 2:11; Jude 9. God is never an accuser, never a destroyer. He is never against anyone, but always for all of His creatures, even Lucifer (Satan) and all of His hosts. Yet, He holds them in check so as to protect us from them and them from destroying each other. It takes the divine nature of Jesus to understand such love.

Although we have Moses' testimony that he never added anything to the Ten Commandments, there is further proof from the Scripture that God did not speak the animal sacrifice system on Mt. Sinai nor any of the laws that were abolished when Jesus died on the cross. These were the laws that were put in the "side" of the ark, not inside. "And it came to pass, when Moses had made an end of writing the words of this law in a book... that Moses commanded the Levites ...take this book of the law, and put it in the side of the ark of the covenant of the Lord your God, that it may be there for a witness against thee." Deut. 31:24-26.

ANIMAL SACRIFICES WERE NOT COMMANDED BY GOD

Notice carefully, friend of mine, that it was "THIS BOOK OF THE LAW," that was a "WITNESS AGAINST," them. It was not God who was against them or even His Ten Commandment law that was against them, for it is the Ten Commandments that He seeks to write in our hearts, that is the Spirit of the law...His love, and which is a transcript of His very own character. No, the law of God is not "AGAINST" us, for God would not give us a law that would be against us, for Paul concludes about the Ten Commandments, "wherefore the law is holy, and the commandment holy, and just, and good. Was then that which is good made death unto me? God forbid. BUT SIN, that it might appear sin, working death in me by that which is good; that sin by the commandment might become exceeding sinful. For we know that the law is spiritual: but I am carnal, sold under sin." Rom. 7:12-14. But God's Ten Commandment law brings us to perfection when we let Him write it in our hearts, that is the true Spirit of that law, in Jesus, not the letter of it, for the letter kills but the Spirit (Holy Spirit) gives us life. Psalm 19:7.

Now let us take Jeremiah's testimony about the animal sacrifice system. "Thus saith the Lord of hosts, the God of Israel; Put your burnt offerings unto your sacrifice and eat flesh." (The LB says, "Away with your offerings and sacrifices.")

"For I spake not unto your fathers, nor commanded them in the day that I brought them out of the land of Egypt, concerning burnt offerings or sacrifices: But this thing commanded I them, saying, Obey my voice, and I will be your God, and ye shall be my people: and walk ye in all the ways that I have commanded you, that it may be well unto you. But they hearkened not, nor inclined their ear, but walked in the counsels and in the imagination of their evil heart, and went backward, and not forward." Jere. 7:21-24.

Notice carefully what God said here to Jeremiah for him to tell the leaders and the people of Jerusalem and Judah. "For I spake not....Nor commanded them....Concerning burnt offerings or sacrifices:" Jere. 7:22. And the time period was when God had brought them out of the land of Egypt. So, this is talking about the instruction given to Israel after they came out of Egyptian bondage and received the law at Mount Sinai. The record is clear. God did not speak or command Israel to kill animals.

When Jesus came to planet earth, He announced the principles of His kingdom with the now famous, "Sermon on the Mount," as recorded in Matthew 5. But on Mt. Sinai nearly 1500 years earlier, God had attempted to give the same sermon, but was not able to do so because of Satan's interference.

The darkness, lightning, thunder and earthquake at Mt. Sinai were not caused by God, but were reactions to His presence. In other words, Satan considered God's descent on Mt. Sinai as an invasion of his territory. Satan, the prince of darkness, brought these distortions and freaks of nature to upstage God and confuse the people about God's real personality and character. Yes, Satan brought those quirks of nature to slander the Father's and Son's beautiful name. He also brought the smoke, for God's presence does not give off smoke, for God's fiery presence is not a literal fire, as we know of and think of fire.

And yet God hid Himself in that darkness, as we read in Psalm 18:11, which is a description of what happened at Mt. Sinai. Compare 2 Sam. 22. In fact, we read that God came down and rode upon a cherub, and did fly." Ps. 18:10. Satan was the "covering cherub," Ezek. 28: 14. Did He allow Lucifer (Satan) to escort Him around in his chariot when God came down on Mt. Sinai? Preposterous?! Ridiculous?! Not necessarily. Read the account of Christ's temptations in Matt. 4 and you will see that Satan escorted Jesus to a "pinnacle of the temple," v. 5 and later "up into an exceeding high mountain, and sheweth Him all the kingdoms of the world", v. 8. I wonder what Jesus said to Satan as they rode around together? Do you think Christ perhaps told him how much He still loved Him? Do you think that perhaps He even appealed to Him to "get behind Him" as He did later, (Matt. 16:23), which could actually be taken as an appeal to become a follower and supporter of His Father's cause. Can you conceive of a God with that much love in His heart? I do not think Jesus or His Father have ever spoken roughly or harshly to anyone, even to Satan. Jude 9 indicates that Jesus refused to bring a "railing accusation" against Satan when He came to resurrect Moses from the grave. Friends, God's angels don't even bring "railing accusations" against leaders of evil in this world, according to 2 Peter 2:10, 11.

In other words, the angels do not go up before God's throne and tell all the bad things they can think of against the evil powers of this world. They bear the image and character of God. And to bring "railing accusations" against anyone is against God's nature and character. This means God's angels do not accuse or jeer or ridicule or make fun of anyone, even Satan, his angels or the evil men and women they victimize. So, when God came down on Mount Sinai, He treated Lucifer (Satan) with the same dignity, love and respect with which He had always treated him, for God never changes. Lucifer was the first created being. Ezek. 28:3, 4 indicates he had no equals. He was the highest of all the angels. He was the leader and commander of all the angels in heaven, and still leads and commands the one-third of the heavenly host who followed him out of heaven to this earth to set up his base to try and reach the rest of the universe. The cross stopped him from reaching the unfallen words. Oh, how he has broken his Creator's heart. And so, God came down on Mt. Sinai and spoke His perfect will in the form of Ten Commandments. These ten words or laws were written with God's own finger on Two Stone Tablets which Moses brought down from the mountain. The record declares, "And He added no more." Deut. 5:22. Does this mean that God didn't say anything else? It means that He did not speak anything else to the multitude. But Moses went up into the thick darkness and received what has been called, "the law of Moses." This was the "added law" which contained all of the instructions for killing animals and regulating the children of Israel's day by day lives and activities. In many respects, these laws were much more humane than any laws that had ever existed before, and the health code of Moses probably surpasses many codes in our present world society. But, we know that when Jesus came He abolished the animal sacrifice system and stated on the Mount of Olives that we are to love our enemies instead of exacting an eye for an eye and a tooth for a tooth. Even the permission to eat the clean animals was not God's perfect health code, for He desired for them to eat a vegetarian diet similar to Daniel and John the Baptist. So, the question we must try and solve is, who really is the author of the animal sacrifice system?

We know God was in the darkness that Satan and his angels brought, for God only brings light, because "in Him is no darkness at all." I Jn. 1:5. The universe is looking on. They are watching to see what is going to happen. Are Lucifer's charges against God and His law true or not? In Exodus 19 we see that God successfully brought Israel out of Egypt in spite of Satan's efforts to keep them enslaved through his servant, Pharaoh. Now, as they came to Sinai, God came down on the mountain to reveal to Israel His beautiful and perfect character of love, just as Jesus did later on the Mt. of Olives.

"And Moses went up into God, and the Lord called unto

him out of the mountain, saying, Thus shalt thou say to the house of Jacob, and tell the children of Israel; ye have seen what I did unto the Egyptians. (Here God takes the blame for what Satan did to the Egyptians during the 10 plagues) and how I bare you on eagle's wings, and brought you unto myself. Now therefore, if ye will obey my voice indeed, and keep my covenant, then ye shall be a peculiar treasure unto me above all people: for all the earth is mine: and ye shall be unto me a kingdom of priests, and an holy nation. These are the words which thou shalt speak unto the children of Israel. Exodus 19:3-6.

Nothing is said here about killing animals or exacting an "eye for an eye or a tooth for a tooth," for God clearly stated that He "spake not....nor commanded them in the day that I brought them out of the land of Egypt, concerning burnt offerings or sacrifices. Jeremiah 7:22.

And of course, Jesus, on the Mt. of Olives said, "Ye have heard that it hath been said, Thou shalt love thy neighbor, and hate thine enemy. BUT I SAY UNTO YOU, LOVE YOUR ENEMIES, bless them that curse you, do good to them that hate you, and pray for them which despitefully use you, and persecute you; That ye may be the children of your Father which is in heaven." Matt. 5:43-45. What Christ is really saying here is: "I never gave that law in the first place. That isn't the law my Father and I gave. That is not how we operate at all. This is what you have Heard, But I Say Unto You....Love Your Enemies."

When Moses told the leaders of Israel what God had offered and promised, they quickly agreed to His offer to become His "peculiar treasure....above all people....a kingdom of priests and an holy nation." This really sounded great! Just think....from slave to God's special priests....His own treasure above all people in just a few short weeks! Who wouldn't agree to such a bargain? "Of course, of course, Moses," they chimed, "go tell the Lord that we will be happy to accept His covenant or agreement. All that the Lord has spoken we will do. We'll do anything He says. Just get us over into that land flowing with, milk and honey....that promised land."

But, they did not understand God's true character of love. Actually, for a few exceptions here and there throughout the Old Testament, I do not believe anyone fully understood the truth about God's character until Calvary. Even the holy angels nor the unfallen worlds comprehended it all until Jesus was crucified. I Peter 1:12; Rev. 12:10-12. Remember, beloved, that it was not until the death of Christ that the character of Satan clearly was revealed to the angels or to the unfallen worlds.

And, because they did not understand God's character they could not understand what it meant to be His special people. The Lord wanted them to be a nation of priests to represent His true character, not only to this world, but to the universe. "But ye are a chosen generation, a royal priesthood, an holy nation, a peculiar people; that ye should shew forth the praises of Him who hath called you out of darkness into his marvelous light." I Peter 2:9. Here are some related texts you may study. Deut. 7:6; Isa. 62:12; I Thess. 5:27~ Rev. 20:6. This last text shows how God's original plan will finally be realized.

You can imagine how angry and upset Satan must have been about God's offer to Israel. If the Lord is successful with His plan Satan will be completely exposed to the universe. He will be proved wrong. God is about to lead a whole nation of people into perfect obedience to His law, the very law Lucifer (Satan) challenged in heaven and has said all along is faulty and cannot be kept. If Israel learns about God's true character of love, they will be empowered to keep His law and Satan will be exposed as a liar before the universe.

Satan must therefore, by some means try and stop this plan. Now, remember that God is continually covering up for Lucifer or Satan. He did this all throughout the Old Testament. It was not until Jesus allowed Satan to "bloody" him up that the universe lost their sympathy for Satan. Christ indicated that Satan would be cast out at the same time He was "lifted up" or crucified, John 12:31, 32. Christ drew "all" of the evil angels of Satan and, of course, Satan himself, to the cross. That's why there was so much darkness there.

The same is true about Mt. Sinai. Satan and all of his hosts of darkness were there to interfere, interrupt, pervert, confuse, and disrupt the service God was attempting to hold, to prevent Israel and all the universe from understanding the real truth about the Father's and Son's beautiful character.

Now, we notice in Exodus 19:10-13 that special instruction was given to Moses to protect the people from being hurt by Satan. They were warned not to come up into the mountain on pain of death. Notice in verse 16 that "on the third day in the morning that there were thunders and lightnings, and a thick cloud upon the mount, and the voice of the trumpet exceeding loud; so that all the people that was in the camp trembled."

Satan brought the darkness and the thunders and lightning and thick clouds, (Ps. 18:11, 12, Prov. 25:14, Joel 2:2, Jude 12) but God was in the darkness with Lucifer and His evil angels. And God let everyone think He was doing it. A trumpet announced that an important event was about to take place. Notice that God spoke to John the beloved on the isle of Patmos with "a great voice, as of a trumpet," Rev. 1:10. We know this was Jesus from the description given and also from v. 18, which tells us that He who was dead is now alive. We know also that the dead in Christ will arise from the grave when Jesus descends "with a shout, with the voice of the archangel, and with the trump of God: and the dead in Christ shall rise first, I Thess. 4:16, 17.

Next, we read in Exodus 19:18, "And Mt. Sinai was altogether on a smoke, because the Lord descended upon it in fire: and the smoke thereof ascended as the smoke of a furnace, and the whole mount quaked greatly." Did God bring this smoke? Let me answer that question with a Scripture and then you decide for yourself. Ok? "And he opened the bottomless pit; and there arose a smoke out of the pit, as the smoke of a great furnace;" Rev. 9:2. Who is the king of this bottomless pit? "And they had a king over them which is the angel of the bottomless pit, whose name in the Hebrew tongue is Abaddon, but in the

Greek tongue hath his name Apollyon." Rev. 9:11. The marginal reading defines Apollyon as "a destroyer."

Remember also that the animal sacrifices Abraham offered were divided or cut into pieces and a "smoking furnace (Satan) and a burning lamp or flaming torch (Christ) passed between those pieces." Gen. 15:17. Compare also Heb. 1:7; 12:29; Ps. 119:105; Song of Solomon 8:6. Next we notice that while the voice of the trumpet continued and increased, Moses spoke to God and "God answered him by a voice." The trumpet was a call to assemble around the base of the mountain so all of Israel could hear God speak His law or covenant (contract) and also to confirm the leadership of Moses in the minds of the people, Exodus 19:9. The Lord knew that Israel could not be blessed without first knowing His true character. They would not be able to fully appreciate all the good things He wanted to give them. His blessings would be turned into curses unless they first understood what He was really like.

It is true that the voice of the trumpet was loud, but I do not believe that was what frightened the people. No. It was the smoke and darkness, the lightning and quaking of the mountain that scared them. God does not bring these things. He does not try to scare people. His love "casts out fear." I John 4:18. Satan brought these aberrations of nature in reaction to Christ coming down on Mt. Sinai to reveal His true character. God's voice is as the voice of "many waters," like a soothing voice of an angel, John 12:28-30. Cf. Heb. 12:18-24.

Next, God warns Moses to keep the people from breaking through the boundaries he had set up at the base of the mountain. The Lord was so concerned for the people's safety that he insisted that Moses go back down the mountain and charge or warn the people again not to "break through unto the Lord to gaze, and many of them perish. And let the priests also, which come near to the Lord, sanctify themselves, lest the Lord break forth upon them;" Exodus 19:21, 22.

The expression or phrase, "break forth," is very important, for it identifies the "Lord" or "God," who would kill anyone who disobeyed. The god of "breaking forth," is "Baalperazim," Lord of breaches. This is how Uzzah died, 2 Sam. 6:8. Isaiah 28:21 refers to Mt. Perazim, the mountain of "breaking forth," when all the wicked will die in the final day because of God's "strange act." His strange act has been explained already, in part, but for emphasis let us say that God's strange act is simply when He permits the wicked to see themselves as they really are without any restraints. This leads them to self-destruction or suicide. Saul and Judas are examples. And yet, we know God did every-

In Exodus 19:20–24 Jesus warns Moses that another Lord is appearing in the mounain as "Lord." He commands Moses to go back down to the base of the mountain and warn the people not to come up in to the mountain to gaze upon this lord or they will "break forth upon them," vs. 24. The phrase, "lest he break forth," proves Christ is not talking about Himself, for "he" is in the 3rd person singular instead of in the first person singular, "lest I break forth," etc. Ex. 20:3 shows how Jesus speaks in the first person when he is referring to Himself. See also Exodus 24:12.

thing He could to save them from killing themselves. God has always covered up and restrained the wicked. In the final day He no longer does this. This is a strange act for God. To those who say that God's strange act is when He kills them in the final day, I would simply ask, what is so strange about God killing them if in fact you believe He has been doing that all along anyway? Besides that, the "god" who acts "strange" or "different" is another god, truly a "stranger," for the true God never changes.

We know Baal represented Satan. Baal Peor was Lord of the opening. Baal Perazim was Lord of the breaches and Baalzebub was Lord of the flie. Maggots, as we know, are most often found feeding on the flesh of dead and decaying animals or man. They hatch into flies. Satan is the lord of death. He is the death god. Jesus is the life God. Baal or Baalim means master, possessor or husband. Satan wants to get married to us and be our master, lord and husband. How thankful we can be that Jesus has a prior claim upon us by virtue of creation and now a second claim by virtue of His redemptive act at Calvary. Psalm 2:12 is an invitation to get married to Jesus, signified by "Kissing the Son." The Pharisees accused Christ of casting out devils by the power of Beelzebub (Baalzebub) the prince of the devils, Matt. 12:24. So, Baal or Baalim was a title for Satan. Therefore, the god of breaking forth, Baalperazim, is Satan. Pharez, one of the illegitimate twin sons of Tamar, by Judah, was given his name because he tried to come out of his mother's womb ahead of his brother, Zarah, meaning dawn or day star, which represents Christ.

The midwife rebuked Pharez by trying to push ahead of his brother. "How hast thou broken forth? this breach be upon thee: therefore his name was called Pharez. And afterward came out his brother, that had the scarlet thread upon his hand: and his name was called Zarah." Gen. 38:29, 30. The midwife had tied a scarlet thread around his hand when he was about to be born, so she would know which was the older of the two. But then Pharez pushed himself ahead. These twins are used to symbolize the great controversy between Christ and

Satan. Satan is always trying to push himself ahead of Jesus by "breaking forth."

And so we see that even at Mt. Sinai Satan is trying to upstage the Lord with lightning, thunder, darkness, smoke and earthquakes. But God is finally able to speak His perfect law to the people as recorded in Exodus 20:1-17. This was all God spoke to the multitudes. These ten laws were written on two tables of stone, but the additional law was recorded in a book and placed on the outside of the ark. Deut. 31:26. But the Ten Commandments were placed inside of the ark, which represents our heart or mind or conscience. Exodus 25:16; Deut. 10:5, Ezek. 20:24-26.

Moses then went into the darkness, "where God was," Ex. 20:21. Satan was there too, but as an "angel of light," to deceive as much as God would allow him to deceive. Satan was permitted to insert his ideas into the "added laws," which the people had been living by all along since Adam and Eve fell. These laws included the animal sacrifice system which Jesus abolished by nailing them to His cross. They also included the laws which said, "ye have heard that it hath been said, an eye for an eye and a tooth for a tooth;" Christ abolished this and other laws by saying, "but I say unto you, that ye resist not evil; but whosoever shall smite thee on thy right cheek, turn to him the other also." Matt. 5:39. The reason Christ gave this more perfect law was so we could become "perfect even as your Father which is in heaven is perfect." Matt. 5:48. Paul tells us to "overcome evil with good." Rom. 12:21.

We can do this by heaping fire on the heads of those who are trying to do evil to us as Proverbs 25:21, 22 instructs. That fire is the fire of God's love. We show it by giving food and drink to our enemies. James also tells us to "resist the devil and he will flee from you." James 4:7. But we are only able to resist by "submitting ourselves to God," as the first part of the verse tells us. So when Jesus said we are not to "resist evil," he simply meant that we are not to fight back and exact "a tooth for a tooth and an eye for an eye," because He never gave that law in the first place. And if God didn't give it to Moses, the "angel of light," in the darkness must have been permitted to give it to Moses. But God was right there to guide Moses and make sure that even that which was not His "perfect" will would be as humane as possible until Christ Himself should come in the flesh to show us that perfection of character He was not permitted to explain at Sinai, due to the hardness of the people's hearts. For, Satan can only deceive those who are carnally minded and living after the flesh, as Israel was at that time. But in spite of all the problems that God encountered, He was still able to get enough of His message through to the people so that there was always a "remnant," who were left to carry on the truth. And now, finally, at the close of time, when the world is coming to an end, He is again speaking to our hearts about His true character, through all the thunders, lightning, smoke, earthquakes and fire of Satan. See Additional Note #30.

THE MELCHIZEDEK PRIESTHOOD IS GOD'S PERFECT WILL

The laws prescribing animal slaughter were not God's perfect will. We will discover this as we proceed and learn God's perfect will which Paul explains in detail in the book of Hebrews regarding the Melchizedek priesthood. This is in direct contrast to the system which had existed from the days of Adam when Satan himself put it into Adam's mind that he should kill animals in order to get his sins forgiven. The whole system was based on fear because Satan is the prince of fear. God's "perfect love," will "cast out fear." I John 4:18. Satan controlled mankind so fully through this animal slaughter system that he was even able to lead them to sacrifice their very own children.

When Israel came to Mt. Sinai, God came down to meet with them so they would understand His true character. But, because of their unbelief and desire to work their own way into the land of Canaan, Satan was able to give them what they really wanted. Moses' understanding of God's character was also progressive. I don't believe that he fully understood, at this time, God's "holy, harmless and undefiled," nature and character, but it was progressively revealed to him. See Exodus 34:4-9. When Moses came down from the mountain his face "shone," Exodus 34:29. But Moses was not aware of it. The people were so afraid of Moses that he had to put a veil over his face to speak to them. The Israelites had hard, stony hearts filled with fear. That is why they could not understand God's true character of love. Jeremiah lamented this and God prophesied through him that the covenant that was made at Sinai was not really "HIS COVENANT." Notice what God says here. "Behold, the days come, saith the Lord, that I will make a new covenant that I made with their fathers in the day that I took them by the hand to bring them out of the land of Egypt; which my covenant they brake, although I was an husband unto them, saith the Lord: But this shall be the covenant that I will make with the house of Israel; After those days, saith the Lord, I will put my law in their inward parts and write it in their hearts; and will be their God, and they shall be my people:" Jeremiah 31:31—33.

THE KILLER PRIESTHOOD

Paul quotes this passage from Jeremiah in Hebrews 10:16. In fact, the whole book of Hebrews is an explanation as well as an appeal to God's people in all ages to come into the Father's heart through the priestly ministry of Jesus who was a priest "forever after the order of Melchisedec," which priesthood is "holy, harmless, undefiled, separate from sinners, and made higher than the heavens;" Hebrews 7:21, 26. The "changing" of the priesthood Paul is referring to in Heb. 7:12 is basically a change from the Levitical priesthood, which was a killer priesthood, to the Melchizedec priesthood, which was a life-giving priesthood through Jesus Christ, our Lord. This meant that a transfer had to be made by all true believers of their allegiance from the Jewish system of animal slaughter to the life-giving priesthood of Christ. It also meant that all of their time, talents and material possessions, which especially had to do with tithes and offerings were now to be given to those priests (preachers) who, like Paul, were preaching the truth about the Father in His Son Jesus Christ. This did not need to be done arbitrarily, for the Jewish nation was basically destroyed in A.D. 70 by Rome. That same kind of transfer is going on right now in the Christian era without any special announcements. God's true, blue, believers are silently and quietly withdrawing their support from the killer-priesthood to the life-God priesthood of Christ Jesus again today, by supporting those ministers and ministries who are teaching that the Father and Son are life-Gods, not death-Gods.

Let us go again to Mt. Sinai and see how the killer-God priesthood was set up. Paul tells us in Galatians 3:19 that the Law of Moses, in which the sacrificial system is found, "was ordained (arranged throughout or prescribed) by ANGELS in the hand of a mediator go between) or by the disposition arranged by, instituted by ANGELS." Acts 7:53. Now, we must remember that all of the angels, both good and bad, holy and unholy, belong to God by right of creation. So, when we speak of angels having a part in the giving of the law at Sinai, let's remember that God's angels were there as well as Satan's angels. Let us also realize that even God's holy angels did not fully understand, at this time (Mt. Sinai) the nature of Satan's rebellion. It was only when Jesus Himself came and let Satan inspire wicked men to bloody him up that these holy angels began to see the real truth about Satan and about God.

That is why Paul referred to these ordinances "as a shadow of things to come," Col. 2:17. What is it that causes a shadow? Someone is standing in the light, but not properly reflecting that light. That is what Satan did at Sinai. But God overruled Satan's hellish machinations and maneuvers and made those shadows point to what Satan would actually do to God's only Son, Jesus. The Father was warning Lucifer that he would do this, but he would not listen. God built the whole sanctuary service around the killing of innocent animals to make it mean something and point forward to the cross.

Paul further cautioned, "let no man beguile you of your reward (that is of Christ, Gen. 15:1) in a voluntary humility and worshiping of angels, (in ceremonies to demonstrate piety and outward holiness) intruding into those things which he hath not seen, vainly puffed up by his fleshly mind." Paul goes over this again in Gal. 4:8. "Howbeit then, when ye KNEW NOT (were not married to Christ, Gen. 4:1 and John 17:3), ye did service (were a slave) unto them (these evil angels) which by nature are no gods." Here in Gal. 4:8 Paul is referring to the law of Moses (Gal. 4:4) as the "weak and beggarly elements" (Gal. 4:9) of bondage to angels through observing "days, and months and times, and years." The question is, which angels prescribed or arranged throughout the law of Moses as a remedy for transgressions? There's a hint or clue to this hidden fact in Gal. 3:20. Notice: "Now, a mediator is not a mediator of one, but (contrariwise) God is one." The "but" in this verse is the key; it means "the opposite is true." It denotes a distinction that is in reference to the mediator, that mediator (go between) for these angels was not God, our wonderful, heavenly Father. "Oh, no," Paul is saying here. "On the contrary. In fact the very opposite is true." Who then is the "go-between or the "mediator" for the evil angels?

"PAUL'S ANSWER"

Paul answers this question in this way. "For although there may be so-called gods (that is idols) in heaven or on earth-as indeed there are many 'gods' and many 'lords'-yet for us there is one God, the Father, from whom all things, and for whom we exist, and one Lord, Jesus Christ, through whom are all things and through whom we exist." I Cor. 8:5, 6. Yes, friends, Paul is right. Satan and all of his hellish legions consider themselves gods and almost every heathen religion worship Satan's demons in one form or other in their pagan religious ceremonies. Satan and his devils consider themselves "the gods of this world." And since the majority of the population of this planet have been deceived into paying homage to Satan, the Bible itself acknowledges that Satan is indeed the "god of this world" who "has blinded the minds of them which believe not, lest the light of the glorious gospel of Christ, who is the image character of God, should shine unto them." 2 Cor. 4:4. It is a sad fact that when we "know" or are "married" to evil, we have our eyes closed to THE ONLY GOOD ONE, which is God, our Father and Jesus His Son. Matt. 19:17. All who reject Jesus Christ as their SAVIOR and Lord have by that very choice become slaves to Satan and reap the fruits of it. Stephen refers to the results of such a choice in his speech recorded by Dr. Luke, Acts 7:38-43. Satan and his evil legions want us to share their fate of being estranged from the Presence of the Lord. Misery loves company. The way to avoid that is to come to Jesus and give your heart to Him.

Once a person makes that decision it will not be so difficult to understand where the law of Moses came from. This problem is directly related to man's inherently evil nature, Jer. 17:9, Rom. 8:7. We are born, legally speaking, creatures of justice, devoid of understanding with regard to God's infinite grace and mercy. We are born with an innate desire to "get even," and "stand up for our RIGHTS." In Rev. 6, the beloved John saw "a black horse; and he that sat on him had a pair of balances in his hand." Rev. 6:5. That black horse certainly does not represent Christ and His love, truth and mercy. No, it represents Satan's "Justice" for he is the angel of justice. The angel of "getting even." The angel of "an eye for an eye, and a tooth for a tooth." Matt. 5:38. Jesus contradicted this law by saying, "But I say unto you, That ye resist not evil: but whosoever shall smite thee on thy right cheek, turn to him the other also." v. 39. In the days of Job, Satan said to God, in controversy over Job's loyalty to the Lord, "Skin for skin, yea, all that a man hath will he give for His life." Job 2:4. Sounds familiar somehow doesn't it. "Eye for eye, skin for skin." A frightening voice from the past is identified. It is Satan, the angel of justice. See Exodus 21:23-25.

SPIRITUAL THINGS MUST BE SPIRITUALLY DISCERNED

The problem with regard to understanding where the Law of Moses came from is directly related to our carnal way of reasoning. Spiritual things must be spiritually discerned. The Law of God is spiritual, but we tend to desire a carnal law that will enable us to "do" some kind of "work" which will justify our carnality, for our pride and ego refuses to admit there is absolutely nothing we can do to merit salvation. Man would much rather kill an animal than kill his ego or pride. To accept God's sacrifice instead of something we have done means to surrender our will, ourselves.

Our hunger is for justice, but our real need is for mercy or God's grace, for if we received "justice," than we should all be left to ourselves to self-destruct (die by our own hand or the hand of another). Our only hope is God's mercy. The law of Moses meets the requirements of our desire for "justice." But it is only GOD'S PRESENCE in us that can ever fulfill our need for mercy. That is why Paul said, "Christ in you, the hope of glory." Col. 1:27. The law of Moses' had in it a carnal method or way for carnal man to justify himself and thus relieve his guilt which he has incurred by transgression of God's law of love, the Ten Commandments. In this system man would be able to put the blame on innocent animals. The only problem with the whole system was that man would never find out the truth about God. And thus carnal, sinful, guilty man would never be able to become perfect like His Creator. That is why Paul tells us that this terrible system of animal slaughter could never bring anyone to perfection, Hebrews 7:11; 10:1, "For if that first covenant had been faultless, then should no place have been sought for the second. For finding fault with them, he saith, Behold, the days come, saith the Lord, when I will make a new covenant with the house of Israel and with the house of Judah." Heb. 8:7, 8. Friend of mind, God is a perfect God. He never makes mistakes. He never has to change, Mal. 3:6. Can't you see that if

God had been the one who had given that animal slaughter system that He would not have had to abolish it? But Paul tells us that God wants to write His laws in our hearts," so He can be our God. Heb. 8:10. The guilt we incur by sinning can never be cleansed from our minds by killing animals. Paul tells us that there was no perfection in this system. So, why was the system allowed to be set up in the first place? God permitted it in order to let men see what they really were in their minds-brute beasts. Solomon tells us we die like the beasts, Eccles. 3:18, and Rev. 13:18 speaks of men in the end time receiving the mark and the number of the "beast," which is sun worship in the 666 beast system. That is where the whole world is headed today, friend.

Under the law of Moses you received speedy punishment for any transgression. Paul tells us that the "word spoken by angels was steadfast," (of force, firm, cannot be broken), and every transgression and disobedience received a just recompense of reward." Heb. 2:2. In other words if that law "spoken by angels" and not by God, for God only spoke the Ten Commandments, Deut. 5:22, could not be broken without suffering a consequence, how much more certain is our punishment, if we break the law that God Himself spoke! "How shall we escape if we neglect so great salvation;"? Paul asks us. Now, beloved, let us use the spiritual discernment that God has given us. If God only spoke the Ten Commandments and the animal sacrifice system was a system that God never required or desired and if that terrible system of animal slaughter and "an eye for and eye and a tooth for a tooth" was abolished by Jesus because He never gave it in the first place, then who are these "angels" who spoke or gave this covenant of animal slaughter which God said was "faulty" Heb. 8:7. God's angels are "holy," Matt. 25:31 and keep His holy law,. Psalm 103:20. But, Satan's angels are called "devils" Matt. 25:41. God charges these evil angels which "sinned" with folly. "Behold, he put no trust in His servants; and His angels he charged with folly." Job 4:18, It makes sense to me that sinful, wicked, foolish angels would be capable of inventing such a system of animal slaughter, for the Bible tells us that

Satan is a destroyer and that his angels are "destroyers." Psalm 78:49. The law of Moses did not have the character of God in it, for it was put on the outside of the ark, Deut. 31:26, not on the inside of the ark, as was the Ten Commandments, which truly is a transcript of God's very character, which He seeks to implant in our conscience, which was symbolized by the ark. Heb. 9:4. What a tremendous compliment and tribute it is to the wisdom and love of God that He Was able to preach the gospel through this terrible system of carnage and slaughter. In fact, Paul even tells us that the sacrificial system of killing animals was nothing but "sacrifice to devils." I Cor. 10:19-21.

SATAN DISGUISES HIMSELF AS AN ANGEL OF LIGHT

In the thick darkness that Satan brought at Mt. Sinai, God permitted this animal slaughter system to become part of the Mosaic law which was later abolished at the cross. Someone may ask, "Why would Moses write down laws that were from Satan?" The answer is that Satan disguises himself as an "angel of light," 2 Cor. 11:14. "For such are false apostles, deceitful workers, transforming themselves into the apostles of Christ. And no marvel; for Satan himself is transformed into an angel of light. Therefore it is no great thing if his ministers (men and angels) also be transformed as the ministers of righteousness; whose end shall be according to their works!"

In other words, Moses, nor even the good angels necessarily saw anything wrong with these laws, inasmuch as the people were so unruly and hard to deal with. Besides God is not saying anything against Lucifer. Christ nor His Father would not expose Lucifer (Satan), but tempered these carnal laws with mercy as much as they could. They gave additional laws (good laws) and built the sanctuary service around the animal slaughter system to counteract its baleful influence, as well as, to point forward to Christ's bloody ordeal in the garden and on the cross.

There were many things in the law of Moses that were

good. A person has to use spiritual discernment when he goes through the first five books of Moses and tries to decide which laws were given by God and which were the devil's idea. Remember that God covered up for Lucifer by saying that He gave all the laws, just as He covered up for Him by saying that He killed every person whom Satan murdered. Through Ezekiel, God tells us that He gave "statutes, and shewed them my judgments, which if a man do, he shall even live in them." Ezek. 20:11. The next verse speaks of the Sabbaths which God said were a sign of sanctification between Him and His people. But in verse 25 God tells us that He "gave them also statues that were not good, and judgments whereby they should not live;" Obviously, these "bad" laws that God "gave" to them would be referring to the killing of animals and those other laws such as an "eye for an eye," and so forth. I do not believe that Moses or the holy angels really were able to discern all that was transpiring at this time. It took centuries of observance and finally the death of God's own Son to fully reveal the insidious treachery involved in Satan's clever chicanery and subterfuge. Only the Creator Himself could unveil Satan's masterful deceptions in a loving manner in harmony with His eternal character of love. Imagine! God used Lucifer's own system to make an appeal to Lucifer Himself and to warn him what his final end would be. Listen to this passage in 2 Sam. 14:14. "Neither doth God respect any person: yet doth he devise means that his banished be not expelled from him." And the Modern language says, "God, however, does not sweep away life, but rather takes measures so as not to keep the banished away from Himself." Isn't that just what God has done all through the great controversy? He has continually devised means whereby Lucifer and his angels could constantly be observing the plan of salvation first hand. God is truly infinite both in His love and wisdom. Eph. 3:9-11.

Even now God is forming His Elect. And when the special number He has chosen fully understand who He really is and what He is really like Jesus will be able to say again, "It is done or It is finished." Rev. 16:17. I believe that many who have died in past generations will be saved without the full knowledge of God's character, because they lived up to all the light that they had in their time. If we live up to what we do know, God counts us as perfect. But, if we fail to do what we know is right, then we have sinned, James 4:17 tells us. Out of this final generation God will have a nation of people, scattered all around the globe, who will stand true to His Ten Commandment law, the Sabbath especially, even though we be threatened with death. ***We will not hate our enemies, but will pray for them. This will be the final demonstration of God's love. It will prove that the same character perfection the Father manifested in His Son can be manifested in humanity.*** In actuality, this final remnant is on trial before the universe along with Christ and His Father. We have been called upon to prove that which has never been fully proved before in the history of the world, except in rare cases here and there, such as Job and Daniel, Enoch and Elijah. Never before has an entire nation of human beings been fully exposed to the onslaughts of Satanic fury as we will be in this final hour of earth's history. Whether we realize it or not, we have been called upon to pass a test that former generations were never called upon to endure. Is it not for their sakes, as well as for Christ's and the Father's sake that we prove faithful? Indeed it is! What a sacred responsibility and privilege we have. May God grant us what we need to pass the test Satan will bring upon us, for only as Christ lives within us will we ever make it. Christ told the Jews that He had not come to destroy the law or the prophets, but to fulfill that law, Matt. 5:17-19. In other words He had come to give it the full and true meaning He wanted to give at Sinai because Lucifer (Satan) interfered and because Israel's heart was not able to receive it. In reality, Jesus gave the same law on the Mt. of Olives that He had given on Mt. Sinai. Only, this time Satan was not allowed to pervert it with his distortions of nature. Just as the people wanted a king over them in Samuel's day in place of God's loving leadership through Samuel, so Satan led the people at Sinai to reject Moses' and God's loving character. Satan, as an angel of light, was permitted in the thick darkness to insert his ideas into the "added law" Moses wrote down. As you read through the laws of Moses in Exodus, Leviticus, Numbers and Deuteronomy, you can see much good counsel and common sense. Most of our modern laws are based on the laws of Moses. But it was only through the teachings of Jesus that we realize that the added law was for the carnal heart, not for the spiritually minded who truly want to be like their Father which is in heaven. May God help us to not only see this spiritual law of Christ, but to receive it into our hearts and live it, for it is the Ten Commandment law God spoke from Sinai. The Father wants to number us among His faithful Elect in this final hour.

There is much more evidence and we will look at it, but before we do that, let us consider the terrible slander that has been leveled against the Father's name. It is incredible. Notice what Jesus said regarding His Father's love for animals. "Are not two sparrows sold for a penny? And not one of them will fall to the ground without your Father's will." Matt. 10:29 RSV. Yes, our heavenly Father adores each one of His creatures. He guards them with loving care. Jesus went ahead to emphasize the Father's infinite love for us. "But the very hairs of your head are all numbered. Fear ye not therefore, ye are of more value than many sparrows." Matt. 10:30, 31. Does not such love call forth a response from your heart, dear one. Oh, how the Father's heart yearns for you to commit yourself to Him just now. Don't delay. Come to His open and yearning arms of love right now, today.

Now, let us consider further proof that our Heavenly Father isn't the author of the animal sacrificial system, nor did He ever require it. "Sacrifice and offering thou didst not desire; mine ears hast thou opened: burnt offering and sin offering hast thou not required." Ps. 40:6. Again we see that God did not desire or require that animals be killed for the forgiveness of sin. The phrase, "mine ears hast thou opened:" also helps us to see that even Jesus' understanding of His mission developed gradually as He grew in "wisdom and stature," Luke 2:52. In Exodus 21:2-6 we read about the practice of "opening" or piercing (opening) a servant's ear which indicated to the public at large that he had voluntarily given himself to His master as a slave forever. This was the dedication Jesus made both to His Father and to us. He loved us so much that He was willing to humble Himself not only to become a slave but to be nailed to the cross as the chief of sinners.

Jesus referred to Hosea 6:6 twice in Matthew's gospel Matt. 9:13 and 12:7. He asked them to study carefully what Hosea meant, *"I will have mercy, and not sacrifice."* Jesus also connected this important study with the temple and the Sabbath, two of the most controversial doctrinal subjects in the religious world today, the sanctuary and the Sabbath. Is it possible that a true understanding of these two subjects is impossible until we comprehend the truth about the animal sacrifice system? It would seem so. Here are some more scriptural proofs that God did not require animals killed to appease His "wrath." "I will take no bullock out of thy house, nor he goats out of thy folds ...Will I eat the flesh of bulls, or drink the blood of goats?" Psalm 50:9, 13. Now notice what God really wants from His people. "What I want from you is your true thanks; I want your promises fulfilled. I want you to trust me in your times of trouble, so I can rescue you, and you can give me glory." Ps. 50:14, 15. Please notice the phrase, "AND YOU CAN GIVE ME GLORY." The word glory means character. God wants us to come to Him as we are so He can cleanse us and make us clean and whole. He wants to give us the "FLESH AND BLOOD" of His dear Son to eat. John 6:48-58. Jesus Christ is the Father's glory or the complete and perfect representation of the Father's character. Unselfish, self-sacrificing love perfected. This "DIVINE NATURE" is what the Father wants to give each of us through His only begotten Son. Unless we receive it we will not survive the end of this world.

Throughout the centuries God has remained silent and taken all the guilt and blame. He is still doing that today and would continue to do it if it would do any good, but when he sees that mankind is about to destroy itself, He must intervene. True love can not stand by and not try to save life. And so, since the birth, life and death of His only Son, the Father has been revealing Himself more and more. Christ's spotless life of purity is the greatest rebuke the world has ever had. Satan could not take it and had to kill him. And yet Christ's death revealed God and Satan even more. Satan is the accuser of the brethren (Rev. 12:10) and leads men to speak against each other. God is grieved over this.

"Thou sittest and speakest against thy brother; thou slanderest thine own mother's son. These things hast thou done, and I kept silence; thou thoughtest that I was altogether such an one as thyself: but I will reprove thee, and set them in order before thine eyes. Now consider this, ye that forget God, lest I tear you in pieces, and there be none to deliver." Psalm 50:20-22.

God is pleading with us here, for we all have gone aside and "become filthy." Psalm 14:3. Here God claims to be the one who tears the unrepentant sinner "to pieces." Is that really the way God is or—is He taking the blame for what Satan and man do to other people and themselves? He is taking the blame, for that is His nature and His character to conceal and cover up for us, Proverbs 25:2.

Let us go on to more proof that God did not ask Israel to kill animals. "For thou desirest not sacrifice else would I give it: thou delightest not in burnt offering. The sacrifices of God are a broken spirit: a broken and a contrite heart, O God thou wilt not despise." Psalm 51:16,17.

This next Scripture will make more sense and take on a new meaning now, for we can see that even though God never "desired" man to offer Him the blood of animals as an propitiation for sin, the Father accepted this carnal and yes, we could even call it, "slanderous," type of worship. God was willing to be worshiped at this level and on this basis until His only Son would come and reveal the real truth about Him. But by the time Jesus came, Israel had sunk so low that God would have to use an extraordinary method to reach them.

Even in Isaiah's day God tried to tell them that to "kill an ox is as if he slew a man;" and to "offer an oblation," was like "swine's blood." God said Israel had chosen "their own ways." He said they delighted in abomination. Isa. 66:1-4. In verse 1, he seems to indicate He did not even want them to build Him a temple. He was hoping to dwell in their hearts.

They were under the control of the "DEATH GOD," Satan, who was their father, Jn. 8:44. There was only one thing left to do. Jesus would have to become a "human" sacrifice and let the leaders and people, under Satan, slaughter Him as they would a helpless lamb. Jesus pleaded with His Father to find another way, if possible, and to let the cup pass from Him, so They would not have to be separated, but there was no other way for the human race to realize how terrible sin was. It would take this terrible crime of killing the very Son of God to break their hearts and open their eyes. He had known it from the beginning and inspired the prophets to write about it. And yet divine love and infinite purity shrank from such a demonstration.

WAS IT GOD'S PERFECT WILL THAT HIS ONLY SON DIE?

"All we like sheep have gone astray; we have turned every one to his own way; and the Lord hath laid on him the iniquity of us all. He was oppressed, and he was afflicted, yet he opened not his mouth: He is brought as a lamb to the slaughter, and as a sheep before her shearers is dumb, so he openeth not his mouth." Isaiah 53:6, 7. Was it God's will that His dear Son suffer and die like that? Listen to what the Bible says, "Yet it pleased the Lord to bruise Him; He hath put Him to grief." Isa. 53:10. Notice that the Father here is actually taking the blame for the suffering of His only Son. He always takes the responsibility upon Himself to protect and shield us from the guilt and remorse of sin.

No, my friend, it was not the Father's perfect will that Jesus suffer and die on the tree, but it was God's perfect will that all men be saved. And all men could not be saved unless Jesus suffered and died like He did. It took that much to wake man up to the enormity of sin. So God permitted the animal sacrifices, which He never commanded, to become a symbol, a shadow and a type of what Satan would eventually do to Christ Himself. But God had nothing to do with starting the animal sacrifice system. And He had to let them kill Him to stop it. All the types of the sanctuary service pointed to this terrible slaughter of God's dear Son.

"But now in Christ Jesus ye who sometimes were far off are made nigh by the blood of Christ. For he is our peace, who hath made both one, and hath broken down the middle wall of partition between us; Having abolished in his flesh the enmity, even the law of commandments contained in ordinances: for to make in himself of twain one new man, so making peace;" Eph. 2:13-15.

In Saul's day the prophet Samuel made this significant statement. "Hath the Lord as great delight in burnt offerings and sacrifices, as in obeying the voice of the Lord? Behold, to obey is better than sacrifice, and to hearken than the fat of rams. For rebellion is as the sin of witchcraft, and stubbornness is as iniquity and idolatry." I Sam. 15:22.

And listen to Isaiah's testimony. "To what purpose is the multitude of your sacrifices unto me? saith the Lord: I am full of the burnt offerings of rams, and the fat of fed beasts; and I delight not in the blood of bullocks, or of lambs, or of he goats. When ye come to appear before me, who hath required this at your hand, to tread my courts?" Isaiah 1:11, 12. God is asking, "WHO HAS REQUIRED THIS AT YOUR HANDS?" It was not our wonderful Heavenly Creator. He is not that kind of a person. There is only one person in the universe whom God has designated as a "murderer and a liar," (John 8:44) and that is the Devil or Satan. Isaiah 27:1 calls him, "Leviathan, the piercing serpent, even leviathan that crooked serpent." Isn't it interesting that the first part of "Leviathan," is "LEVI" the tribe that was designated to kill the animals for the temple service?

"Simeon and Levi are brethren; instruments of cruelty are in their habitations. O my soul, come not thou into their secret; unto their assembly, mine honor, be not thou united: for in their anger they slew a man, and in their self-will they digged down a wall. Cursed be their anger, for it was fierce; and their wrath, for it was cruel: I will divide them in Jacob, and scatter them in Israel." Gen. 49:5-7.

The natural inclination of Simeon and Levi was to be cruel. They enjoyed hurting people and animals. This is the curse of the sinful, carnal nature that Adam has passed on to the human family. Only by partaking of the Divine nature can we overcome this tendency. The expression, "digged down a wall," literally means, "they hamstrung an ox." Evidently Simeon and Levi mutilated some cattle in this way just out of meanness. This attribute of their character made them both unfit for any kind of leadership position.

Jacob put a curse on their anger, not on them. Jacob was trying to warn his sons that their children and grandchildren would suffer as a result of their evil traits of character if they didn't change. It wasn't something God was going to do to them, but what they were doing to themselves. But, true to form, God claims to be doing that which man does to himself. God always shields us from the guilt.

The second time Moses numbered Israel the tribe of Simeon had become the smallest and weakest of all the tribes with only 22,200 (Num. 26:14). The father's sinful characteristics seemed to have been passed on to many of his descendants causing them to almost be phased out. Yet, the tribe of Simeon was envisioned as the ideal Israel in Canaan in Ezek 48:24 and in Rev 7 we see that the Lord will perfect 12,000 of them to be one of the 12 tribes composing the 144,000 revealing the power of God to perfect the weakest and most perverse of his children.

God was able to bless Levi by bestowing on this tribe the Aaronic priesthood. They were scattered throughout Israel into

48 cities Joshua 21:1-42. At Sinai Levis' descendants stood alone for the truth when the rest of the tribes bowed down to the golden calf. This is indicated by Exodus 32:26 when "all the sons of Levi," came to Moses when He made a loyalty call. They became the executioners of the ones who persisted in worshiping the golden calf and thereby earned the right to execute the office of the priesthood in the temple. This was the Levitical or Aaronic priesthood. But when Christ came, he abolished this system, for it was a killer priesthood which did not represent His true character of love. It was had been an expression of His permissive will, not His perfect will.

"Wherefore when he (Christ) cometh into the world, he saith, Sacrifice and offering thou wouldest not, but a body hast thou prepared me. In burnt offerings and sacrifices for sin thou hast had no pleasure...Then said he, Lo, I come (in the volume of the book it is written of me,) to do thy will, O God." Heb. 10:5-7. Jesus was the first human being in a body of flesh to completely obey the Father's law without once sinning or acting selfishly, thus proving Satan's charges about the law completely false. Jesus brought in a new and better kind of priesthood. A temple of heart-service where God Himself dwells in the human heart and every believer is a priest, offering up thanksgiving and praise to the Father for all He has done for Him. "He taketh away the first, that he may establish the second." Heb. 10:9. Compare Rev. 20:6. The law of priesthood was changed from Levi to Melchisedec. From this time forward, the tithe was to go to those preachers (PRIESTS) who were teaching the truth about God. Thus the tithe was transferred from the Jewish priests to the Christian ministers. In this last hour of earth's history God is inspiring His people to give their tithes and offerings to the life-giving message of the Melchisedec priesthood, not to ministers who are teaching that God is a killer.

The Levitical priesthood did not make us love God more. No, it made us afraid of Him, for the human heart feared a God who required such blood and carnage. But under the

Melchisedec priesthood we can draw nigh unto God without fear. "Yes, the old system of priesthood based on family lines was cancelled because it didn't work. It was weak and useless for saving people. It never made anyone really right with God. But now we have a far better hope, for Christ makes us acceptable to God, and now we may draw near to him." Heb. 7:1-19. LB.

Jesus was not a priest who took a sword and killed animals or human beings. He was after the order of the Melchisedec priesthood. "For such an high priest became us, who is holy, harmless, undefiled, separate from sinners, and made higher than the heavens." Hebrews 7 :26.

In chapter 4 of Hebrews Paul makes a stirring appeal to our hearts to come boldly into the very presence of God to "OBTAIN MERCY, AND FIND GRACE TO HELP IN TIME OF NEED." Hebrews 4:16. We are to come BOLDLY UNTO THE THRONE OF GRACE." Just think of what that means. It means, dear friend, that you don't have to be afraid of God. Our HEAVENLY Father is a kind, understanding, wonderful, compassionate and loving God who wants to help us. He will never, ever hurt us. Jesus had to let us bruise and batter and bloody Him up in order for us to realize that God would never hurt or harm anyone, no matter what they do to Him. He had to go through all of that in order to establish the Melchisedec priesthood.

Jesus assured us that the Father loves us just as much as He, Himself does, but because we are so blind, stubborn and stiff-necked, we had to have a demonstration before we would believe it. "Jesus answered and said unto him, If a man love me, he will keep my words and my Father will love him, and we will come unto him, and make our abode with him..... For the Father himself loveth you, because ye have loved me, and have believed that I came out from God. I came forth from the Father, and am come into the world: again, I leave the world, and go the Father." John 14:23; 16:27, 28.

WHAT IS IT THAT BRINGS ETERNAL LIFE?

The final prayer of Jesus before he went to the cross is recorded in John 17. In this chapter you will find some of the most moving and magnificent phrases in all English literature or any literature in the human language, as far as I am concerned. It is a knowledge of God, a knowledge of the Father Himself, as revealed in His only Son, Jesus Christ, that will bring salvation to any human heart. "And this is life eternal, that they might know thee the only true God, and Jesus Christ, whom thou hast sent." John 17:3.

Through the prophet Hosea's tears we can see into the Father's broken and bleeding heart. Just as Gomer broke Hosea's heart again and again, so Israel broke God's heart continually all through out the OT. And finally when Jesus did come in the flesh, they rejected His wonderful love again and nailed Him to the tree. They were blind to what they were doing and to what God was really like.

"For I desired mercy, and not sacrifice; and THE KNOWLEDGE OF GOD MORE THAN BURNT OFFERINGS. But they like men (Adam) have transgressed the covenant: there have they dealt treacherously against me." Hosea 6:6,7. One paraphrase says, "I DON'T WANT YOUR SACRIFICES-I WANT YOUR LOVE; I DON'T WANT YOUR OFFERINGS- I WANT YOU TO KNOW ME." LB. And that is just what Jesus said salvation was—KNOWING THE TRUTH ABOUT GOD. John 17:3. Jesus demonstrated it. The incredible truth is that from the very beginning the Father has only wanted us to come into his transforming, renewing presence so He could make us well again. But our darkened minds have been so alienated from Him that we could not understand that. Col. 1:21. Satan told Adam and Eve that God would never forgive them. So when the Father came looking for them they hid from Him. Their minds were now under the control of Satan and he is the one who put it in their minds to kill animals in order to get back into the good graces of the Father.

Thus Satan was able to establish the concept of substitution in order to be ransomed or reconciled with God. This is a pagan concept. But even though this is not the real truth about God, He has dealt with us on our terms and definitions, not His definitions, for we would not listen to Him. The Father has always wanted to forgive us without a substitute, but our darkened minds could not comprehend that kind of love and forgiveness, so God has permitted us to pervert "the unspeakable gift" of His Son, 2 Cor. 9:15, into a substitutionary human, blood sacrifice. But, in this last hour of earth's history He has promised that "the times of restitution of all things," would come when the "times of refreshing" would arrive just before Christ returns, Acts 3:21, 19. This is no doubt the "mystery of godliness," that will be finished in this last hour of earth's history. And it definitely is connected with the revelation of God's true character of love.

God came down to our level so He could bring us up to His level. The substitutionary covenant says that God, in giving Christ's blood to buy our freedom, was simply supplying what He Himself demanded, for did He not say, "WITHOUT THE SHEDDING OF BLOOD THERE IS NO FORGIVENESS OR REMISSION OF SINS?" Hebrews 9:22; Lev. 17:11. Who was it who brought up the idea that the law demanded a blood payment or atonement? If God is not that kind of a person, then Satan had to be the one who dreamed the whole scheme up to slander the Father's name before the angels and the unfallen worlds. We can see from the story of the prodigal son that God does not demand repayment before he will forgive. Therefore, the whole human race have been prisoners of a bloody concept of our Creator that has absolutely nothing to do with the truth about God, His law or His system of justice. The "alienation" was not in God's mind. Col. 1:21 makes it clear that we had separated ourselves from God.

God did not alienate or separate Himself from us. He has always wanted to take us back. But Satan lied, telling his angels and Adam and Eve that God didn't want us back. That is the reason our Lord had to let us bloody Him up before we could see and believe that He would never hurt us. That is what it took to remove this terrible enmity and lie from our minds. The alienation was not on God's part. Listen: "And you, that were sometime alienated and enemies in your mind by wicked works, yet now has He reconciled." Col 1:21. Please notice beloved that the separation and alienation between God and man is because of what was in man's mind. *"And I will put enmity between you and the woman, and between your seed and her seed;"* Gen 3:15. This was spoken by the "death god" of Gen 3.

Now, Friends, let's talk about forgiveness. There are two distinct ways of dealing with a debt. Either it is paid or it is forgiven, one or the other. It never requires both. Now, does the Bible teach us that God forgave us of our sins or that he demanded repayment from us or from anyone? If Jesus paid our debts, as all so-called Christian religions teach, why should God have to forgive them? Which concept does the Bible teach?...That God collected payment for our debt to Him through Christ's death or does it teach that God was able to forgive us our debts because Jesus' death opened our eyes to the fact that God never considered us in debt to Him in the first place? It teaches the latter concept, that there is no debt to pay.

You see, the idea of a debt that must be paid to be reconciled to God is man's idea that Satan placed in his mind after his light connection with His Creator was broken. And so the Lord had to work the entire plan of salvation around our concept of Him and what He required of us based on our confused and distorted understanding of Him. He put up with this all through the centuries and the record was never set straight until Jesus came and revealed the real truth about the Father. "Having the understanding darkened, being alienated from the life of God through the ignorance that is in them, because of the blindness of their heart." Ephesians 4:18.

The real truth about the Father is that He has been willing and ready to forgive us at any time, but Satan has placed these bloody stumbling blocks in our minds so that we were so afraid of God we could not come to Him until Jesus came and showed us what the Father was really like. Now, we can come boldly into the Father's presence and be renewed at any time we are willing to come to Him. Heb. 4:16. See also Micah 7:18, 19. I John 1:9.

The fear and enmity that Satan had put in Adam and Eve's mind was finally removed from humanity's ancestral, blood-line by Christ's death. This is really what was abolished and nailed to the cross. Paul explains it like this:

"But now in Christ Jesus ye who sometimes were far off [far off from God the Father and from the rest of the human family] are made nigh by the blood of Christ. For he is our peace, who hath made both one, and hath broken down the middle wall of partition between us; Having abolished in his flesh the enmity, even the law of commandments contained in ordinances; for to make in himself of twain one new man, so making peace; And that he might reconcile both unto God in one body by the cross, having slain the enmity thereby." Ephesians 2:1-16. "Blotting out the handwriting ordinances that was against us, which was contrary to us, and took it out of the way, nailing it to his cross; and having spoiled principalities and powers; he made a shew of them openly, triumphing over them in it." Col. 2:14, 15. Now, who are the "PRINCIPALITIES AND POWERS," that Christ "spoiled" and "made a shew of them openly." Eph. 6:12 tells us that they are "the rulers of the darkness of this world." Before the entire universe Jesus demonstrated the Father's love. He did this by letting wicked men, controlled by Satan and his demons, do anything they wanted to do to Him. But Jesus never reacted with anger or hatred. The white hot love that flashed from the Father through the Son on Calvary to the ends of the universe revealed for all eternity that God is total pure love. It also exposed Satan for what he was, a liar and a murderer, John 8:44. And Jesus never called Satan a liar or a murderer because he was mad at him. He had no bitterness or vindictiveness in his heart. No. All through the 0. T. the Father and His son had covered up for Lucifer but this had failed to bring him to repentance. So, now, in passionate, divine love, yearning and pity, the Father, through His Son begins to speak openly about Satan's true character. They do this, hoping that this loving revelation of Satan's heart and mind will bring him to a realization of his need to repent. "Oh, Lucifer, look what you have become—a liar and a murderer. Oh, please come back to Me." But, Satan wouldn't listen. He had hardened his heart against the Father's love. Yet the Father did not let him die, for the complete demonstration of the effects of sin was still future. This will take place after the 1,000 years when all the lost turn upon Satan and each other. Satan will be the last one to bow and confess before the Father's throne of Grace. Phil 2:10, 11.

In vision John saw them that "had gotten the victory over the beast, and over his image, and over his mark, and over the number of his name, stand on the sea of glass, having the harps of God." Rev.15:1-4.

Now notice what it is that this group says, "Great and marvelous are thy works, Lord God almighty; just and true are thy ways, thou King of saints...all nations shall come and worship before thee; for thy judgments are made manifest." Rev. 15:4. Please notice that little word "All." That is "muy importante," (very important) my friend.

In Phillippians 2:10, Paul tells us that "every knee" is going to someday bow down before God. Even Satan will bow down and confess and admit that the Father has always been righteous and just in all of his dealings with each one of His creatures, especially with Lucifer. Every question that has ever been raised in the great controversy between Christ and Satan has been fully, completely and satisfactorily answered. The universe is now forever secure from future rebellion. "What do ye imagine against the Lord? he will make an utter end: affliction shall not rise up the second time." Nahum 1:9. Never again will sin arise.

CHAPTER 27

A STUDY ON THE CONTRASTING PERSONALITIES OF THE TWO LORDS OF THE BIBLE. WHICH IS THE TRUE LORD AND WHICH IS THE FALSE LORD?

About 1968 I attended a meeting in Texas of a fellow evangelist who was preaching on end-time events. His text that night was from Matt. 24 where we find Jesus departing from the temple and walking up to the Mount of Olives. Jesus had just finished the most scathing denunciation of his career on the scribes and pharisees in Matt. 23. His final word was, "Behold, your house is forsaken and desolate -- abandoned and left destitute [of God's help]." I Kings 9:7; Jer. 22:5, Matt. 23:38. If you back up and read the whole chapter in a modern version the directness of Christ's words are incredible. And then, as if that were not enough, He told them that they would be held responsible and found guilty of every righteous person who had been martyred from Able to Zechariah. v. 35. How could this have happened to a nation of people who had been given more information about God than any other on the face of the earth? Jesus explained it to them: "Why do you not understand my language? It is because my revelation is beyond your grasp. Your father is the devil and you choose to carry out your father's desires. He was a murderer from the beginning, and is not rooted in the truth; there is no truth in him. When he tells a lie he is speaking his own language, for he is a liar and the father of lies. But I speak the truth and therefore you do not believe me." John 8:44, 45. NEB.

"If God was your father," said Jesus, "you would love me, for I came from God and arrived here. I didn't come on my own. He sent me. Why can't you understand one word I say? Here's why: You can't handle it. You're from your father, the Devil, and all you want to do is please him. He was a killer from the very start. He couldn't stand the truth because there wasn't a shred of truth in him. When the liar speaks, he makes it up out of his lying nature and fills the world with lies. I arrive on the scene, tell you the plain truth, and you refuse to have a thing to do with me. Can any one of you convict me of a single misleading word; a single sinful act? But if I'm telling the truth, why don't you believe me? Anyone on God's side listens to God's words. This is why you're not listening-because you're not on God's side." John 8:42-51. The Message Bible in Contemporary Language.

Jesus' dialogue with these blind Jewish leaders is recorded for us today upon whom the "ends of the world are come." I Cor. 10:11. These incredible statements were spoken by Him only after He had totally exhausted every other means of reaching their hearts and minds. It must have broken His own heart to have to speak so bluntly, and must have hit them like a bomb blast, totally blowing their minds. Were they aware that Satan was their father and that it was he whose voice they were listening to and following? Obviously not. They were totally blind to it just like their fathers were blind to the fact that the Lord spoke through Isaiah and Jeremiah and all the other prophets. Stephen spoke to that point very clearly in Acts 7 when he told them in verse 42 that God had to give up on their fathers and allow them to worship "The host of heaven," connecting it to the animal sacrifice system which even Paul in I Cor. 10 said was the worship of demons. And, of course, they stoned Stephen to death because of that and for quoting from Isa. 66 and then telling them that even though Solomon had built a marvelous temple, which King Nebuchadnezzar had destroyed in 586 BC, God does not dwell in temples made with hands.

Christ had reached a point of desperation, as it were, and was using the strongest language possible with the hope and intention of trying to shock the leaders of the nation into reality; to wake them up to the fact that they were facing total destruction, which eventually came in AD 70. "Little did the Jews realize the terrible responsibility involved in rejecting

Christ. From the time when the first innocent blood was shed, when righteous Abel fell by the hand of Cain, the same history had been repeated, with increasing guilt. In every age prophets had lifted up their voices against the sins of kings, rulers, and people, speaking the words which God gave them, and obeying His will at the peril of their lives. From generation to generation there had been heaping up a terrible punishment for the rejecters of light and truth. This the enemies of Christ were now drawing down upon their own heads. The sin of the priests and rulers was greater than that of any preceding generation. By their rejection of the SAVIOR, they were making themselves responsible for the blood of all the righteous men slain from Abel to Christ. They were about to fill to overflowing their cup of iniquity. And soon it was to be poured upon their heads in retributive justice." DA 618, 619. Everyone knew exactly what Jesus was talking about. The history of how king Joash had commanded that the prophet Zechariah be killed right out in public with the words of warning fresh on his lips, was well known. 2 Chron. 24:20. "His blood had imprinted itself upon the very stones of the temple court, and could not be erased; it remained to bear testimony against apostate Israel. As long as the temple should stand, there would be the stain of that righteous blood, crying to God to be avenged. As Jesus referred to these fearful sins, a thrill of horror ran through the multitude." DA 619.

Now, friends, it was on this very day, after speaking these solemn words that Jesus left the temple. "Pharisees and Sadducees were alike silenced. Jesus summoned His disciples, and prepared to leave the temple, not as one defeated and forced from the presence of His adversaries, but as One whose work was accomplished. He retired a victor from the contest." DA 620.

After His crucifixion and resurrection many who were awestruck by His words that day took their stand for the truth and became mighty instruments of the Holy Spirit to spread the message of salvation to all who would listen while probation lingered for this apostate people and nation until October 66 AD when the Roman armies came and surrounded the city. They withdrew a little later, which was the door of opportunity Jesus had predicted for His people to escape. No believer in His words died in the next siege that lasted until AD 70.

Our country and the whole world stand today in a similar circumstance as the Jewish nation at that time. The leaders who heard Jesus' words of warning that fateful day were shocked and filled with terror even though they tried not to show it. They could not imagine their magnificent temple lying in a heap of ruins. But now an unseen danger seemed to be threatening them. This foreboding of coming disaster had also affected the disciples. In an effort to call forth a more positive statement about the future the disciples pointed out to their Lord the strength, beauty and magnificence of the various buildings of the temple, as if to say, Lord, surely all of this will stand forever.

But Jesus had no encouraging words about the future. The Jewish nation had sealed its very own fate: "Do you see all these? Truly, I tell you, there will not be left here one stone upon another that will not be thrown down." Matt. 24:2. These words were not spoken privately so many no doubt heard Him. A little later, as He sat on the Mount of Olives, four of His disciples mustered up the courage to ask Him for more details of His prediction about the temple. "And as He sat on the Mount of Olives opposite the temple (enclosure) Peter, James, John and Andrew asked Him privately, Tell us when is this to take place and what will be the sign when these things, all (of them), are about to be accomplished?" Amplified Bible. Mark 13:3, 4. We have always assumed that all 12 of His disciples were with Him at this time but there were only four. It is possible that Jesus had invited them to be with Him for a special time of meditation, prayer and instruction. It is extremely important here that we notice the very first seven words that came out of Jesus' mouth. "TAKE HEED THAT NO MAN DECEIVE YOU." Matt. 24:5.

So, the leading sign of the end is DECEPTION. During the last year of his life, AD 66, Paul expanded upon this theme of deception to his young disciple, Timothy, from prison in Rome. "But wicked men and imposters will go on from bad to worse, deceiving and leading astray others and being deceived and led astray themselves." 2 Tim. 3:13. Amplified.

So, with all this information before us today, we are able to clearly see that Jesus Himself taught that Satan had been able to palm himself off to the leaders of Israel for centuries as their Father. They were convinced that Jehovah God was truly their heavenly father when in reality it was Satan.

REVEALING THE TRUTH ABOUT THE FALSE IMPOSTER GOD OF THIS WORLD

This study on the Two Lords is pivotal. You will either understand it and allow the Holy Spirit to expand your knowledge about God or you will go the other way. It is your choice. Matthew 7 contains Christ's concluding remarks of the Olivet discourse. And he saves His most important teaching to the last. In Matt. 7:13, 14. Jesus tells them there are two gates to enter in this life. A narrow gate which leads to eternal life and a wide gate which leads to destruction. And then in vs. 15 he warned them to "Beware of false prophets." He warned us because they may look like sheep but in their hearts and minds they are nothing but ravening wolves. So, how do you know the difference? "By their fruits you shall know them." Matt. 7:20.

In Galatians 5 Paul makes two lists. In the first he lists the "Works of the flesh." I find it most revealing that the first four are sexual sins: Adultery, Fornication, Uncleanness, Lasciviousness. These sins are also progressive, including homosexuality which Paul clearly condemns in Romans 1, yet almost all churches today have chosen to excuse homosexuality on the grounds that homosexuals are born that way and cannot help themselves. This is the doctrine of Babylon today and why John the Revelator calls for an exodus of her in Rev. 18:1-6, even stating that she (the church) "is fallen, is fallen, and is become the habitation of devils, etc." vs. 2. This is why Paul's next two listed sins are idolatry and witchcraft which has to do with evil spirits or demons. These two lead right into the next 11 which come as a result of allowing evil spirits to lead and control.

"But when you follow your own wrong inclinations your lives will produce these evil results: impure thoughts, eagerness for lustful pleasure, idolatry, spiritism (that is, encouraging the activity of demons), hatred and fighting, jealousy and anger, constant effort to get the best for yourself, complaints and criticisms, the feeling that everyone else is wrong except those in your own little group -- and there will be wrong doctrine, envy, murder drunkenness, wild parties, and all that sort of thing. Let me tell you again as I have before, that anyone living that sort of life will not inherit the kingdom of God." Gal. 5:19-21.

Now, in order to see how this deception (of demons) works we only need to read the life of Jesus in the four gospels. Here is the perfect Son of God going about doing good, healing all who were oppressed of the devil because His Father was well pleased with Him and guiding Him in all He did, Acts 10:38. But almost every time He healed someone the church leaders were trying to find a way to have him arrested, put on trial and crucified. In Matt 12:10-13 we read how Jesus restored a man's hand that was withered. You would think that everyone would be very happy about such a good work, and most of the "common" people were, but the leaders of the nation wanted to kill Him. Why? Because they said He had broken the Sabbath. But Jesus told them, "It is lawful (right or legal) to do well on the Sabbath days." vs. 12. "Then the Pharisees went out, and held a council against him, how they might destroy Him." Matt. 12:14.

Beloved, we have to stop and ask ourselves, What kind of insanity is this? These Jewish leaders prided themselves on being the best and most faithful law keepers in the world. Yet here they are seeking to break their own law by killing the Son of God. Let's listen to the clear reasoning of the Son of God. So, the question comes to us today, who is the "Father" of the churches today in our modern "Christian" world? And why are church leaders taking a wrong stand on abortion and homosexuality as well as other issues? Is it not because Satan is their father the same as he was in the days of Christ? Yet,

Satan has blinded them to this fact.

"My teaching is not Mine but His who sent Me. If anyone wills to do His will He will understand the teaching, whether it is from God or whether I speak from Myself....Has not Moses given you the Law? Yet none of you practices the Law. Why are you seeking to kill Me?" John 7:19. Now, the Pharisees listening to Jesus were shocked that He could read their minds. They knew immediately that they were in conflict with infinite power. "Like a swift flash of light these words revealed to the rabbis the pit of ruin into which they were about to plunge. For an instant they were filled with terror. ***They saw that they were in conflict with Infinite Power.*** But they would not be warned." DA 456. So, what did they do? They tried to cover up their murderous designs by accusing Jesus of being devil possessed. Incredible! In Matt. 12 the same issue is addressed by Christ when He told them that by accusing Him of casting demons out through the power of Beelzebub they were committing blasphemy against the Holy Ghost. Matt. 12:31, 32.

Jesus' dialogue with these blind Jewish leaders continued on through John 7 and 8 which I hope you will take time to read for yourself because of the incredible statement that Jesus makes to them after He has totally exhausted every other means of reaching their hearts and minds. It must have broken His own heart to have to speak so bluntly as to reveal that Satan was actually their father.

Now, having accepted this as a fact is it possible to find Scripture in the Old Testament which will reveal how Satan is identified as the imposter God, as both Jesus and Paul revealed? Yes, it is. Let us begin.

A CONTRAST AND CONTRADICTION OF THE TWO DIFFERENT PERSONALITIES BOTH CLAIMING TO BE "THE LORD."

PERSONALITY 1

"And again the anger of the LORD was kindled against Israel, and he moved David against them to say, Go, number Israel and Judah. For the king said to Joab the captain of the host, which was with him, Go now through all the tribes of Israel, from Dan even to Beersheba, and number ye the people, that I may know the number of the people." 2 Samuel 24:1-2

PERSONALITY 2

"And Satan stood up against Israel, and provoked David to number Israel. And David said to Joab and to the rulers of the people, Go, number Israel from Beersheba even to Dan; and bring the number of them to me, that I may know it." 1 Chronicles 21:1-2

PERSONALITY 1

"And Elijah answered and said to the captain of fifty, If I be a man of God, then let fire come down from heaven, and consume thee and thy fifty. And there came down fire from heaven, and consumed him and his fifty." 2 Kings 1:10 KJV.

PERSONALITY 2

"And when his disciples James and John saw this, they said, Lord, wilt thou that we command fire to come down from heaven, and consume them, even as Elias did? But he turned, and rebuked them, and said, Ye know not what manner of spirit ye are of. For the Son of man is not come to destroy men's lives, but to save them. And they went to another village."

Luke 9: 54-56 KJV.

PERSONALITY 1

"In the year that king Uzziah died I saw also the Lord (Jesus) sitting upon a throne, high and lifted up, and his train filled the temple. And above it stood the seraphims: each one had six wings; with twain he covered his face, and with twain his feet, and with twain he did fly. And one cried unto another, and said, Holy, holy, holy, is the Lord of hosts: the whole earth is full of his glory. And the posts of the door moved at the voice of him that cried, and the house was filled with smoke. Then said I, Woe is me! For I am undone; because I am a man of unclean lips, and I dwell in the midst of a people of unclean lips: for mine eyes have seen the King, the Lord of hosts." Isaiah 6:1-5. Note: There are three heavens and there are two thrones. The true Lord (Father & Son) sits on His throne in the third heaven, in the center of the universe surrounded by the two thirds faithful angels who remain loyal to their Creator. The false lord (Satan) sits on his throne in the first heaven (atmospheric heavens of this planet, earth) surrounded by the one third of the fallen angels who rebelled with him and left heaven. Here is a text which reveals him sitting on his throne.

PERSONALITY 2

"And he (the true prophet Micaiah) said 'Hear thou therefore the word of the (true) Lord (Jesus) I saw the lord (Satan) sitting on his throne, and all the host of heaven standing by him on his right hand and on his left. And lord (satan) said, 'Who shall persuade Ahab, that he may go up and fall at Ramoth-gilead?' And one said on this manner, and another said on that manner. And there came forth a spirit, (angel or demon) and stood before the lord (satan), and said, 'I will persuade him.' And the lord (satan) said unto him, 'Wherewith? (how?)' And he (evil angel) said, 'I will be a lying spirit in the mouth of all his prophets.' And he (lord satan) said Thou shalt persuade him, and prevail also: go forth, and do so.' Now therefore, behold, the lord (satan) hath put a lying spirit in the mouth of all these thy prophets, and the lord hath spoken evil concerning thee." Commentary: How do we know that this is the false lord sitting on his throne? Because the true Lord does not lie. "That by two immutable things, in which it was impossible for God to lie, we might have a strong consolation, who have fled for refuge to lay hold upon the hope set before us:" Hebrews 6:18; Numbers 23:19. And this "lord" is sending forth this evil angel to become a "lying spirit" in the mouth of 'all these prophets who belong to you.' Micaiah was the only true prophet of the true Lord. The rest were prophets of Satan. If a person cannot see this then what would ever persuade them? "And he said unto him, If they hear not Moses and the prophets, neither will they be persuaded, though one rose from the dead." Luke 16:31. And so Jesus rose from the dead but how many believe Him today?

WHO TOLD ABRAHAM TO OFFER UP ISAAC AS A HUMAN SACRIFICE?

"And it came to pass after these things, that God did tempt Abraham, and said unto him, Abraham: and he said, Behold, here I am. And he said, Take now thy son, thine only son Isaac, whom thou lovest, and get thee into the land of Moriah; (In Hebrew Moriah means, Jehovah provides) and offer him there for a burnt offering upon one of the mountains which I will tell thee of." Gen. 22;1, 2. Let us take the Scriptures as our guide as we seek to unravel this mystery. "Do not err, my beloved brethren. Every good gift and every perfect gift is from above, and cometh down from the Father of lights, with whom is no variableness, neither shadow of turning." James 1:16,17.

Would it be logical and fair to ask, "WAS THIS COMMAND TO OFFER ISAAC AS A HUMAN SACRIFICE A 'GOOD GIFT? Was it even a gift?" The answer has to be,

"NO." An unqualified and unequivocal, "NO." Secondly, "DOES GOD TEMPT PEOPLE?" What does the Bible say? "Let no man say when he is tempted, I am tempted of God, for God cannot be tempted with evil, neither tempts He any man:"

James 1:13. If God does not tempt us, who then does tempt us? I Cor. 7:5; Matt. 4:1; Mark 1:13; Luke 4;2, all tell us that Satan is the one who tempts us, not God. In Gen. 20, we find that Abraham lied about his wife in order to save his life. He broke the law. This would naturally give Satan, the accuser of the brethren, a chance to accuse Abraham before the heavenly council, just as he did Job. He probably said to God before the council, "Abraham is not fit to become the Father of many nations. He isn't even fit to live period, for he has broken your law. He deserves to die. He lied down in Egypt about his wife. The Messiah cannot come through his seed or line. He has disbarred himself by breaking your law." But, Abraham must have

repented of his sin, for God would not have blessed Sarah with baby Isaac if they had not repented.

The last and perhaps the most important point to consider in this story is the fact that it was God who told Abraham not to kill Isaac, Gen. 22:12. We know that God never changes, Mal. 3:6. ***It would be impossible for God to have told Abraham to kill Isaac and then for him to contradict himself by saying, "I changed my mind. Don't do it, Abraham."*** So, here again the Hebrew writer, Moses, under the inspiration of the Spirit put the blame on God for tempting Abraham. The command to sacrifice Isaac probably was given to Abraham in a dream or vision of the night, since God had spoken to Abraham before in visions, Gen. 15:1. The message apparently came that very night, as "Abraham arose up early in the morning, and saddled his ass and went unto the place of which God had told him." Gen. 22:3. Abraham did not seem to question or doubt that the message was from God, for he promptly obeyed. Paul says Abraham believed God could raise Isaac from the dead, Heb. 11:19, which suggests that Abraham did have an inner struggle over this great sacrifice he was commanded to make, even though human sacrifice was a common ceremony in Abraham's day.

Abraham probably did not question if the command to kill his own son was in accordance with God's character, because most old testament characters thought of Jehovah as a God who demanded sacrifice and blood in order to appease his wrath. Remember that Abraham was straight out of paganism. But, he probably wondered how God's promise to make Him a great nation could be fulfilled if Isaac was killed. But His loyalty to God was greater than his doubts and fears and this is what vindicated God's faith in Abraham before the heavenly council, just as Job's faith and loyalty had vindicated God before the same, council. Job 1 and 2. Abraham did not question God, but promptly obeyed. But whose idea was it? It was Satan's idea for Satan, not God, is the killer. Jn. 8:44. Nevertheless, God took the blame and permitted this satanic idea to be communicated to

Abraham. The voice sounded familiar. Could Satan, as an Angel of Light, been permitted to speak to Abraham? Yes, the very fact that a "horror of great darkness fell upon him" is proof enough since Satan is the ruler of Darkness, Ephesians 6:12.

The main issue here is: "WHOSE IDEA WAS IT ORIGINALLY TO KILL ISAAC?" THIS IS THE QUESTION WE ARE SEEKING TO ANSWER. We know the true Lord would never make such a suggestion, nevertheless, God took the blame for it before the universe to cover up for Lucifer just as He did in the case of Job. And remember that it was Satan who suggested that Job be tested, not the true Lord.

And the same is true in Abraham's case. But at the last minute, God stopped the sacrifice when Abraham's loyalty had been fully demonstrated before the universal council. ***If it had been God's original suggestion or idea for Abraham to offer up Isaac, then God would have been basing salvation upon our performance or works which is clearly condemned in the New Testament. Rom 11:6; Gal 2:16; Eph 2:8.*** It would have been, as if God had been saying, "Ah, let us see if Abraham is really worthy of my forgiveness, favor and my blessings. Well, he did what I said, therefore I will bless him." God's love and forgiveness is not based on our merit, works, performance or our goodness, for no one has ever been good enough. Therefore, no one has ever merited or earned His love, nor could they ever, if they tried. And many have tried. Instead, God's loving mercy and grace is based on our need, not merit. Why even the holy angels need God's love. God's loving forgiveness has flown freely and steadily out of his great and magnificent heart of love from the beginning, for God never changes. Many people erroneously believe that God the Father now loves us because of His son's death. They think the cross changed the Fathers mind toward us. But that is not true. God loved us before His only son died on the cross. "FOR GOD SO LOVED THE WORLD THAT HE GAVE." John 3:16. God the Father did not require the cross. God gave His only son as a gift. We turned that gift or perverted that gift into a human sacrifice. ***The cross is the price we made them pay to prove they love us.*** The Father loved us before Jesus died just as much as He did afterward, for He never changes. In fact, it was this love that motivated the Father to let His Son come to die for us so we might witness that mighty demonstration and be drawn to his great heart of love. The cross was not God's idea. No, it was Satan's idea which he planted in man's carnal mind after he sinned. Our darkened minds could not grasp the reality and magnitude of the Father's loving character. And so the cross on Calvary's hill became the vehicle through which the Father's heart was torn open and revealed to the universe. Golgotha's lonely hill became the stage upon which the Father acted out this unfathomable love through His only Son. We wrote the script for God and He and His son Jesus played the role. He let us do anything we wanted to do to Him so we could see once and for all that He would never ever hurt us. That's the price we made Him pay. But at the same time Judas demonstrated what happens to those who resist and reject that love. This is God's justice. This is His punishment, His judgment, if you please. Think of the two gardens, four millenniums apart in time. In the garden of Eden God was seeking man to rescue and save him. In the garden of Gethsamane man was seeking God to hurt and kill Him. The cross demonstrated that God's love and forgiveness has always been available. But our carnal minds could not see this truth "without the shedding of blood." Heb. 9:22.

The blood of animals and finally the blood of God's precious son was necessary to break our hearts and open our eyes so we could see that the path to the throne where the Father is seated has always been open. But our carnal eyes were blind to it. He has always wanted us to come to Him to receive His cleansing and healing touch. We see this clearly in the life and ministry of Jesus. Never once did he require anyone to go to the temple to sacrifice an animal before he could receive forgiveness. See Mark 2:5-12; Acts 10:38. In fact He cleansed the temple twice, once at the beginning of his ministry. John 2:13-17. And Luke 19:41-46, shows that He again cleansed it at the close of

His ministry. We see Isaiah the prophet called at a very tender age to be a prophet. How were his sins cleansed away? A coal off of the altar was taken and laid upon Isaiah's mouth and lips; "thine iniquity is taken away, and thy sin purged." Isa. 6:7. This "LIVE COAL" off the altar represents the love of God, Song of Solomon 8:6. God has three basic methods to cleanse us from sin. (1) Fire, (2) water and (3) blood, I John 5:8. Fire represents His cleansing love and its power to heal and restore the sinner to His favor. This was experienced by the disciples on the day of Pentecost, when they received the outpouring of the Holy Spirit or the very presence of God into their lives. This came in the form of cloven tongues of fire. This was a fulfillment of John the Baptist's prediction, "He shall baptize you with the Holy Ghost and with fire." Matt. 3:11; Luke 3:16.

Jesus represents all three of these elements. He claimed to be the "light (fire) of the world," John 8:12. He said he had come to bring "fire" on the earth-that is light, truth and righteousness, Luke 12:49. He told the woman at the well that if she would drink of the "water" (Himself) she would never thirst again, John 4:14. And in the last day of the feast of tabernacles Jesus declared to all the Jews, "if any man thirst, let him come unto me, and drink. He that believeth on me, as the Scripture hath said, out of his belly shall flow rivers of living water." John 7:37,38. And last of all, He told the Jews, "Except ye eat the flesh of the Son of man, and drink his blood, ye have no life in you." John 6:53. The Jews in the synagogue at Capernaum could not understand Him. They felt he was speaking against the law of Moses which prohibited them from drinking blood.

Jesus knew the prophecies predicted that he would be rejected and killed by his own people, Isaiah 53. He knew from Zech. 12:10; 13:16 and Ps. 22:16, that he would die by crucifixion. He knew Judas would betray Him. But Christ did everything in His power to prevent these events so as to save the Jews and Judas. For, by committing these acts, they were sealing their own doom. They were committing suicide. The cross of Christ is what destroyed them. They were slain by the blood that dropped from His sacred brow.

But, the cross is not what God did to His Son to pay our debt. Oh, no. The cross is the price we made the Father and Son pay to prove their love for us. Truly, they "bought us with a price." I Cor. 6:20. This was all prefigured in the story of Isaac. Now we can look back and see what it really meant. "Now all these things happened to them as examples... for our admonition." 1 Cor. 10:11.

WHO BROUGHT THE FIRE DOWN FROM THE SKY ON MOUNT CARMEL?

From what we have already learned in the Scripture, we know that the "FIRE OF God," is not a literal fire, for it does not consume literally. That is, it does not consume literally through oxidation. It does not burn up matter. But, the fire of God or God's fire, which is His loving presence, has the appearance of fire. The burning bush is a good example of this, for the bush did not "burn up," in the usual sense of the word. It was not "consumed." When Paul says, "our God is a consuming fire," Heb. 12:2, he is speaking in a spiritual sense, not a literal sense, otherwise, the 120 disciples in the upper room would have all been dead, literally consumed or burned up by the "tongues of fire," on their heads. Instead of being hurt, they were transformed into the likeness of Jesus in their attitude and demeanor. Consumed by His love, the fire of bitterness, hatred, envy, jealousy and striving against one another for the highest place was gone, burned out of their lives by the "fire" of His presence. They were all of "one mind." They were united in their purpose and desire to tell the world the good news of the gospel, that Jesus had risen from the tomb and truly was the Messiah, the Prince of Life. Having said this, we are now ready to go to Mount Carmel. What kind of fire was it that consumed the burnt sacrifice, the wood, the stones, and the trench? I Kings 18:38. This is literal fire that destroys and consumes matter. This is exactly the same kind of fire that fell in Job's day, and "burned up the sheep, and the servants, and consumed them." Job 1:16. And it was called by the only servant that escaped, "THE FIRE OF GOD."

This is the same, exact kind of fire that consumed the sacrifices of Abel, (Gen. 4) and Solomon (2 Chron. 7:1). This was real, literal fire that requires oxygen to burn. This is the same type of fire that destroyed Sodom and Gomorrah, Nadab, Abihu and the 250 princes, as well as the two captains and their companies of fifty soldiers who showed no reverence or respect for Elijah when they came to arrest him. I Kings 1:9-15. James and John thought this should also be done to the Samaritans who failed to show the proper respect and hospitality to Jesus. "And when his disciples James and John saw this, they said, Lord, wilt thou that we command fire to come down from heaven, and consume them, even as Elias [Elijah] did? But he turned, and rebuked them, and said, Ye know not what manner of spirit ye are of. For the Son of man is not come to destroy mens lives, but to save them. And they went to another village." Luke 9:54. Now, remember that Elijah is the "man of God" who took the sword and killed 450 prophets of Baal. Was this God's perfect will or His permissive will? In other words, was God pleased with this or was He just putting up with it? "And the times of this ignorance God winked at; but now commandeth all men every where to repent." Acts 17:30. The next verse indicates that the standard of righteous judgment is the Son of God, even Jesus Christ.

After Jesus came, lived and died and rose again, we have the perfect example of what God has always wanted us to be like. But, Elijah, did not live in Christ's day. When Peter took up the sword to defend His Lord, Jesus rebuked him. "Put up again thy sword into his place: for all they that take the sword shall perish with the sword." Matt. 26:52. Christ then told Peter that twelve legions of angels were available to Him at a moment's notice, should He but request their aid. If He was not calling upon them to deliver Him, why should He need Peter's help? It was not God's will for His Son to be delivered, for the demonstration had to be made in order for man's eyes to be opened and his heart broken to the reality of sin and its terrible consequences. "Ought not Christ to have suffered these things, and to enter into his glory?" Luke 24:26; Compare Acts 14:22; Heb, 5:8, 9. We are so pre-occupied with our own pain and sufferings here below, that we sometimes forget that God must still be suffering terrific mental anguish. In fact, the Bible indicates that He suffers with us even now through all of life's heart aches and tragedies. "In all their affliction he was afflicted, and the angel of His presence saved them: in His love and in his pity he redeemed them; and he bare them, and carried them all the days of old." Isa. 63:9. We already noticed that the servant blamed God for the destruction of Job's property. He called this fiery destruction, "THE FIRE OF GOD." But was this really God bringing down literal fire? No, it could not have been, for God never perverts His own creation and fire, literal fire, as we know it today never existed before sin entered, for it is destructive in its nature and there was no death or destruction before sin entered. Therefore, we must face the fact that the fire that consumed the animal sacrifices in the Old Testament was not from God. Therefore, they would have to be from Satan. Someone will surely ask, "Why would Satan bring fire down on Elijah's sacrifice and not on the sacrifice of His own prophets of Baal?" The answer is simple when you understand how God operates. Since He takes both the credit and the blame for everything that happens, God has the right and authority to say what will happen and what will not happen. Nothing takes place without His knowledge or will (2 Chron. 16:9). "For the eyes of the Lord run to and fro throughout the whole earth, to shew himself strong in the behalf of them whose heart is perfect toward Him." See also Heb.4:13.

Satan was prevented from bringing literal fire down for the priests of Baal to consume their sacrifice. This is axiomatic (obvious). God would not allow this. Satan wanted to do this very badly so he could prove that Baal was superior to Jehovah. Satan was really the god or deity behind or back of

Baal, the fire god.

The people's minds were in darkness. They had no true concept of God's love and forgiveness. Even Elijah did not understand the fullness of God's loving nature. But the Lord used Elijah on the basis of what He did know and understand. God always takes us where we are and brings us to where we should be. Even Elijah believed in a Jehovah God who consumed animal sacrifices and he challenged the priests of Baal on this premise. Remember that until Christ came and died even the holy angels and the unfallen worlds were still subject to Satan's visits, Rev. 12:7-13. Christ's perfect demonstration of the Father's true character in His life and death opened the eyes of the universe and Satan "AS LIGHTNING," fell from heaven. Luke 10: 17, 18. And so on Mt. Carmel, Satan could still bring fire down from heaven and consume the sacrifices of even those who thought Jehovah required this. Thus Satan could still make the Father and Son look like they were animal killers and required blood to pay for the sins of mankind. He was the one who had placed this false concept in man's mind after the fall and God allowed Satan to continue working through this system. Would Satan settle for this little of a control or this much control over the mind of God's creatures? Yes, he would. Why not? It was better than nothing. At least he still had his foot in the door to lead them back to Baal worship whenever he had the chance. And so God had to put up with this and took the blame for what Satan was doing until Jesus came and took the whole system away by allowing Himself to be nailed to the cross. Elijah lived in the Old Testament times of killing and slaughter. He lived in the time of God's permissive will, before Christ appeared 800 years later to show the Father's perfect will. Man has worshiped the death God long enough. The truth of God's loving character will smash every false idol in our hearts so we may become dwelling places for the living God, even a temple of His love. Just before Elijah was translated, God's true character was revealed to him. Elijah had run away to Mt. Horeb or Sinai, where the Ten Commandments had been given to Moses. God let a windstorm, an earthquake and a fire pass by

Elijah. But God was not in any of these destructive elements, for He never distorts his own creation. This is the work of Satan, the destroyer.... "A great and strong wind rent the mountains, and brake in pieces the rocks before the Lord; but the Lord was not in the wind: and after the wind an earthquake; but the Lord was not in the earthquake: And after the earthquake a fire; but the Lord was not in the fire: and after the fire a STILL SMALL VOICE. And it was so, when Elijah heard it, that he wrapped his face in his mantle, and went out, and stood in the entering of the cave. And, behold, there came a voice unto him, and said, What doest thou here, Elijah?" I Kings 19:11-13. It is most interesting that the phrase, "A STILL SMALL VOICE," is translated in the margin thusly: "THAT IS A DELICATE WHISPERING AS OF THE BREEZE AMONG THE LEAVES." That dear reader, is exactly how Jesus described the work of the Holy Spirit to Nicodemus, John 3:8. Elijah had become frightened and lost heart when Jezebel passed a death decree upon him for killing the 450 prophets of Baal, I Kings 19:1-3. This terrible work of killing had unnerved Him. It was not God's perfect will for Elijah to kill these priests. He was tired, exhausted and emotionally drained and when he heard a death sentence had been enacted against him, he temporarily lost his courage and faith in God's ability to protect him and he ran away to the wilderness. But God did not forsake Elijah. The Lord forgave Elijah, taught him His true character and translated him. What a lesson about God's love for those who will pass through the winds, earthquakes and fires of these last days when everyone is blaming God and His true SABBATH-Keeping people for all the destruction and aberrations of nature Satan will be bringing upon this planet. I want to stand faithful to God and proclaim His loving character so others will know that He is a life God, not a death God. Will you take that same stand too right now with me? God bless you my dear friend. Pastor Michael F. Clute.

CHAPTER 28

BEYOND THE SACRED VEIL OF THE TEMPLE

From the beginning the Father has always wanted to dwell in the human heart and soul. God's perfect will and His greatest desire has always been that man himself be His temple dwelling place.

But a barrier of doubt and distrust was erected in Adam and Eve's mind when they listened to the insinuations of Satan regarding the true character of God. Now, in a separated and sinful state, fallen from the sinless bliss of their garden home, they had forfeited God's wonderful Presence. It took the form of a glow of light that radiated from within their bodies, symbolic of their Creator's spirit in them. The departure of this aura or robe of light left them in a state of nakedness compared to what they had been accustomed to and they hid themselves from the Lord God of Eden, Genesis 3:6, cowering and trembling in fear. I have written more in depth on that topic in other articles which can be found on God's Last Call web site found at:

(http://godslastcall.org) And mankind has been hiding from God ever since. His stricken conscience will not allow him to come into the presence of a holy and sinless God. But, Jesus, the pure and holy, Son of god has brought us back into favor with our beloved Heavenly Father.

This Divine effort to restore His Presence in our minds has been going on now for over 6,000 years. Through numberless evidences of His Fatherly care, love and concern, the Father has tried to bind our human hearts to Himself. Through nature and the love that can exist between human beings in families and friendships, God has been continually attempting to let us know He is there, ready to help us any time we need Him. Psalms 50:15; Romans 10:8. But these evidences, as comforting and encouraging as they are, only give us a faint glimpse of the glory that exists beyond the sacred veil. The Father's great heart of love pulsates its message all throughout the universe. It is only on this planet that the meaning is garbled and perverted by the enemy.

Satan has led men to think of God as severe and unforgiving like a stern judge who only wishes to condemn them. He pictures Him as one who is watching with an exacting eye to discover the mistakes of each of us so he might have a reason to punish us with his "judgments." It was for this very reason that God's dear Son came to this dark earth to live, die and be raised from the dead.

In order for man to regain the lost estate of Eden, he must first regain the Presence of His maker in his mind. This could only be done through an educational process. God, the Teacher, and man the student. Jesus, in His great intercessory prayer in Gethsemane stated the solution in 21 brief words.

"And this is life eternal, that they might know thee the only true god, and Jesus Christ, whom thou has sent." John 17:3. This knowledge of God that Christ brought is a knowledge that every person must possess who desires and hopes to be in God's kingdom. This knowledge of God will change one's attitude toward God and thus toward his fellow man. It will fashion or mold a person into a brand new, happy, vibrant, and loving type of individual...the kind of person each of us wants to be but never imagines we can become. This wonderful knowledge and understanding of your heavenly Father will give you supernatural, spiritual power to become an over comer. It will actually recreate in your soul the image of God that Adam lost by doubting and disobeying God... "dealing treacherously with His Creator." Hosea 6:7.

Jacob had this experience when he wrestled with the angel, who was the Lord God of hosts (Hosea 12:4, 5), even Jesus Christ. Jacob's name meant "cheater" or "supplanter." Jacob overcame and got the victory by surrendering to God's will and received the victory. His new name, Israel, meant one who has overcome or prevailed with God. Eternal life can begin right now by receiving God's loving Presence into your life. A true understanding and knowledge of God's love is the beginning of eternal life. "And this is the record, that God hath given to us eternal life, and this life is in His Son. He that hath the Son hath life; and he that hath not the Son of God hath not life." 1 John 5:11, 12.

In order to make this knowledge known and available to man, God had to come down to our level. Paul describes this condescension in these graphic words. "Who being in the form of God, thought in not robbery to be equal with God: but made Himself of no reputation, and took upon Him the form of a servant, and was made in the likeness of men. And being found in fashion as a man, He humbled Himself, and became obedient unto death, even the death of the cross." Philippians 2:6-8.

Verses 10 and 11 go even further stating that because of this incredible demonstration of the Father's unutterable love every knee will eventually bow and every tongue will confess that Jesus Christ truly is Lord. And that this bowing down and confessing will "bring glory to God the Father." Vs. 11. Some people have interpreted this to mean that this will be a forced and/or fake conversion experience. That all the lost outside the gates of the New Jerusalem, after the 1,000 years, will just go through the motions but will not be sincere, i.e. not really mean it. And then God will have to burn them up with literal fire, Revelation 20:9.

Let us analyze the whole situation here logically and Scripturally. First of all, God never will force anyone to do anything they don't want to do. So, He is not going to force anyone to bow down before Him and confess the name of His beloved Son, for that would never "bring glory" to His name. Furthermore, we read in 1 Corinthians 12:3: "No man can say that Jesus is the Lord, but by the Holy Ghost." So, what other conclusion is there but that this confession and this bowing down before the throne of God is a true conversion experience. Actually it agrees with what Revelation 5:13 predicts, that ***"every creature which is in heaven, and on the earth, and under the earth, and such as are in the sea, and all that are in them, heard I saying, Blessing, and honor,***

and glory, and power, be unto Him that sits upon the throne, and unto the Lamb for ever and ever." Revelation 15: 4 says basically the same thing. And Paul also tells us "If any man's work shall be burned (up or lost) he shall suffer loss: but he himself shall be saved; yet so as by fire." 1 Cor 3:15. Eph. 1:10 also tells us that "all things" will eventually be "gathered together in one" and this will be the fulfillment of the "Mystery of His will." Then put with that 2 Peter 3:9 where we read that God does not "will" that any be lost. This is not just wishful thinking on God's part but careful planning from the days of eternity. If God "wills"* something that means a plan of action has already been set in motion from all eternity past and will be carried out exactly on time according to His perfect Divine will and pleasure. This is clearly stated in Daniel 4 in the confession of Nebuchadnezzar. That is why Paul says in Rom 11:26 that "All Israel will be saved." This is what Peter was talking about in Acts 3:21 regarding the Restitution or Restoration of all things which he said all the prophets had predicted from the beginning. Cf. Isaiah 40:5; Psalms 22:27-31. Ezekiel 16:53-55 even predict that Sodom will be restored along with Samaria and Jerusalem. And Ezekiel 47:1 and on go into detail about this rescue mission. There is much more proof if anyone desires to read about it on my web site at: http://godslastcall.org *God "intends" (original Greek) for all to be saved. 2 Peter 3:9.

So all this will result from Jesus' condescension to become one of us. When He at last sees the final result of His sacrifice Isaiah 53:11 tells us that He will "see the travail of His soul and shall be satisfied." How could He be satisfied with anything less than total success and victory? Of course, He couldn't.

The Bible calls this phenomenon of God descending into a human form, "THE MYSTERY OF GODLINESS." 2. Tim. 3:16. Peter spoke of it like this. "This salvation was something the prophets did not fully understand." I Pet 1:11-12, 22. Living Bible. But think of the price Jesus had to pay to make this knowledge available to us. When Christ died, the veil of the temple was torn into from top to bottom so we could see what

God is really like. That sacred veil represents Christ's flesh which was ripped and torn so we can see into the Father's throne room beyond the sacred veil. But it also represents the Father's heart, which was ripped open when His only Son suffered and died on Calvary.

Now, we can go into the Most Holy Place of the sanctuary, into the very presence of the Creator Father Himself, into His throne room without fear and make our petitions known. That is what Paul means when he says, "For we have not an high priest which cannot be touched with the feeling of our infirmities; but was in all points tempted like as we are, yet without sin. Let us therefore come boldly unto the throne of grace, that we may obtain mercy, and find grace to help in time of need." Hebrews 4:15, 16.

Sometime ago I was trying to make God more real to some friends of mine and I was given a special understanding of the problems the Father and Son have had in trying to communicate with people down here on earth. The Lord brought to my mind a story or parable that I finally wrote out to explain what the Lord has to go through in order to accomplish his mission of getting us into His throne room with Himself beyond the sacred veil. I will now share this story with you.

The Big Company

There was a big company with thousands of employees working for it in a big city. Now, the name of this big company was "OUR GOODNESS, INC." I know that sounds like an odd and weird name, but it advertises their product, which was "goodness." Yes, that's what I said. You heard me right. They manufactured goodness. You would be surprised how many people believed in their product and bought it. Why they were one of the wealthiest companies in the world. They had salesmen in every state in the USA and in almost every country in the world. This big company was known for their "goodness" all around the globe.

And they were always holding campaigns to spread the "good news" of their product into more communities and homes and to enlarge their smaller companies in every state and country into larger companies. And they were growing. But for all their labor, most of the members of this company didn't seem very happy. Their product just didn't seem to do much for them. I visited among them quite often.

I remember one time an older gentleman who had been with the company for more years than anyone could remember came in and gave a pep talk at one of their plants. His speech really upset a lot of people when he told them they had the wrong name for their product. He explained, "In the beginning when the big Boss upstairs started this company, it was called, HIS GOODNESS INC. and back in those days the workers were much happier, even though their sales volume was much lower and we had fewer and not so fancy of plants." Well, they just about ran him out of the plant that day, they were so angry. Before he left though, I talked to him out in the parking lot before he drove away. I asked him how and when the name of the company got changed from "HIS GOODNESS," TO "OUR GOODNESS." He told me it had happened at a stockholder's meeting many years ago. They had a committee meeting, he said, and they told the big boss upstairs they wanted to run the company themselves without His advice or interference. The Big Boss finally gave in and let them have their own way and little by little, things began to change. Then one day they had a committee meeting without inviting the Big boss, as He was rarely invited anymore anyway, and that was when they changed the name of the company. They borrowed lots of money and brought in a lot of outside experts and things just slowly but surely evolved into what they are today.

Then I asked him where the Big Boss was now and he said he still had His office in the same places as always...upstairs, beyond the veil. So, I asked him where that was and he invited me to come to work in the main plant. I had heard a lot of stories about the Big Boss and how mean he was and so naturally,

I was afraid.

He told me that I should meet the Big boss' Son and then I wouldn't be afraid anymore. This made me feel a lot better for I had heard a few things about him that were pretty nice, so I decided to go to work at the main plant. My first day on the job was very nerve racking. I was afraid I'd make a mistake of some kind and be dismissed. I heard all kinds of bad things about the Big Boss and how he could get you fired if things didn't go His own way. You see, even though they had changed the name of the company and were not doing everything like He wanted them to do, He still had a lot of power and they claimed that He often manipulated things around whenever He wished to do so.

There were all kinds of rumors floating around about Him. One had it that He was responsible for a number of the worker's deaths—workers who had gone against Him in the past. They had met with "accidents" no one could explain. They also said he had installed the one way glass all around the top of the walls to keep an eye on everyone. He was watching, they said, to see if anyone made a mistake so He could get them fired or at least demoted to a lesser position. Or if He didn't think they worked hard enough for the company and were sincere and dedicated enough, He could also arrange to have them fired.

Well, you can imagine what a nervous wreck I was working there that first week. The second week wasn't quite as bad, but I was still pretty shaky. Then one day, a very bright, cheerful and kind looking young man came up to my desk and said to me, "Hi, Joe." He greeted me with a smile and really seemed interested in me as a person. I was really shocked that He knew my name. Since I was very busy working at my desk processing "goodness" orders, I didn't know if I had time to talk to Him or not. "The Big Boss upstairs might see me and get mad," I thought. He must have read my mind for the next thing He said to me was, "Joe, don't worry about the Big Boss upstairs watching you. He's not out to get you or anybody else. I should know Joe, for the Big Boss is my Father, and He isn't bossy at all. You should not refer to Him as the Big Bad Boss, for He is your Heavenly Father and He loves you with an everlasting love."

I just about died right there on the spot when He said that. Oh, if there had just been a hole to crawl into somewhere under or near that desk. "Joe, the real reason I came to see you is because my Father and I were just talking about you this morning and He said He would love to meet you personally." "Meet me?" I somehow croaked out, hardly daring to look up. "Yes," Joe, "you," He replied with such a kind and loving voice. "I want you to meet my Dad. He's really a wonderful person. I know you would just love Him. I know there has been a campaign on to discredit Him Joe, but believe me, my Father has never hurt or killed one single person in this enterprise. Why I have been with Him right from the beginning when He formed this company and I know what He is really like. Actually, Joe, if you have seen Me and talked to Me, you may as well consider that you have seen and talked to my Dad. Look, Joe, there are a few people in this company whom I have persuaded to meet with my Father on a regular basis. We have group meetings with him and then he likes to talk to each person by Himself individually. He would like to explain to you the real purpose for which He created and formed this company in the first place. He's looking for sincere and conscientious people like yourself whom He can train through regular meetings with Himself and Me and then I will go out with you personally into all the world to teach others the real truth about My Father and His 'GOODNESS' which is His true character of love. You see, Joe, HIS GOODNESS was the original name of the company's product until they changed it to glorify themselves."

"Oh, Joe, My Father's original plan can change the world and make it a beautiful place in which to live. Everyone who will listen and cooperate will have a part in this new world in which there will be no more death, sickness, heartache or trouble of any kind. If people would only listen, but they have been deceived. The holocaust is coming, Joe. We don't have much time left to give the last warning message. Please, Joe, won't you come up and see Him with me right now? He is waiting for you. He asked me to come down here and invite you up for a personal get-acquainted interview."

By this time most of my fears had subsided and I was almost ready to go with Him when a very well dressed and handsome looking man I'd seen before walking around the plant, came over and whispered in my ear. "Joe, if you go with this charlatan to that so-called upper room He's telling you about you will never return. He and His Father are both liars. There is no 'upper room,' or 'sanctuary,' or 'Most Holy Place,' as They have stupidly called it, so don't let this sweet talking con artist trick you, Joe. The real group you want to join is my group right down here on this level—my level. Almost the whole plant and all the other plants around world belong to my group. Remember, Joe, the majority is always right."

Now, I was really confused. The Boss' son was standing there all the time, right by my desk. Was I ever embarrassed. But He didn't get a bit mad or upset. Finally, after the other fellow quit whispering in my ear, the son said, very quietly to me, "Joe, you are the only one who can decide. I'd love for you to come with me. Won't you please come?" I told him I would need time to think it over. So, he said, "fine, Joe. I'll be back next Monday morning at 10:00 a.m. and talk with you again."

After the Son left, this other fellow took me by my arm and almost dragged me out of my chair. "Come on Joe," He said, "I'm going to show you what a really cool plant we have here and how great our group is here on this level." He had a magnetic charm and a charismatic type personality that just seemed to leave you no choice in the matter. It was a little frightening, but I just didn't seem to have the will to resist. He took me all through the plant, and it was a beautiful place. Then we went to this meeting. At the meeting there were lots of people and they were all talking and seemed to be very excited over the company and their jobs. They were exchanging stories of how they had been able to sell more goodness orders then someone else and how they had started other plants in other states and countries and how they had received certain awards and certificates for all of their faithful service to the company.

It really did seem to be a well-organized company. I mean, I couldn't find anything wrong with it—except during the meeting someone got up and made a suggestion that the product name should be changed to "MY GOODNESS," from "OUR GOODNESS," for this was the day of originality and independence and everyone was looking out for number one (himself) these days. If we could appeal more to the individual's self-esteem, sense of dignity, pride, self-assertiveness, manhood (macho) and womanhood (wacho), the argument went, we could sell a lot more of our product and hasten our goal of converting the whole world to "Our Goodness." We just need to work harder and get the information out about "Our Goodness" and then the world will know. The speaker seemed to be very sincere and earnest. He concluded with an appeal to "finish the work before time runs out and the world destroys itself." Others said "amen" and still other workers arose and said, "friends, I believe the Holy Spirit is being poured out on us right now here in this meeting. We must all dedicate ourselves to get busy and work harder than ever or its going to be too late." Several "amens" rang throughout the auditorium as he sat down.

No sooner had they sat down than another person arose and stated that although the last speaker's suggestion seemed like a good one in theory, it wouldn't work for it would be too fast and too big of a change to start using a different name for the product. He was booed down and then a third speaker arose and said, "what we really need in this company is more respect. We need stricter rules to keep all the workers in line for there are too many trouble makers going around trying to introduce strange theories and doctrines to pervert the truth about our wonderful product, 'OUR GOODNESS.'"

Why some workers would even bring the Big Boss back into full power and that would be the end for all of us. We all know the Big Boss doesn't really care what we do or what happens to us, as long as we get our jobs done and the $money$ is there. So,

I suggest we make some more rules to get rid of these off-shoot, independent, heretic trouble makers. One of their most awful doctrines is that the Big boss never has nor ever will hurt or kill anyone. Now, we know that is not true. If people lose their fear of the big Boss, they will think they can do anything they want and this whole company will be ruined. The government will come in and take over because of all the chaos and confusion. So, we have to enforce law and order for ourselves, because this one truth about the Big Boss must not be changed. He does use force when He has to do so. He is above all law and does not have to keep the same laws we have to abide by. If He sees fit to destroy someone that is His business. He is the boss and we are not to question it. Anyway, we can't, so we might as well face it. If we just do what he says and keep in good with Him by obeying Him and making Him lots of money, He will not bother us." Many people were nodding their heads in approval but others were protesting. "Are you saying that He breaks His own law in order to uphold it?" one person asked? "That doesn't make any sense at all," another person said. "That would be hypocritical."

There seemed to be a lot of division and turmoil. Finally, someone called for a vote on the new name, "MY GOODNESS." Discussion ended and the new name, "MY GOODNESS," was voted in by a very narrow margin. There seemed to be quite a few pockets of resistance, but they fell silent as the LEADER who had led me in stood up to speak. "Now friends," he began in a very calming voice, "we must all work together toward the common goal of telling the world about 'YOUR GOODNESS.' As your LEADER, I expect loyalty and teamwork. Loyalty to me and this company. As long as you work hard for me and this great company we have built, I will work hard for you. The leaders I have selected are worthy of your trust. When we meet together and come to decisions we expect you to carry them out. I want you to accept these leaders as the very voice of God. Do what they suggest and all will be well and the company will prosper. Resist their authority and question them and you will only phase yourself out of the company and your retirement benefits. The prosperity of the company, its glory and honor insures that 'YOUR GOODNESS' will be known all throughout the world. Thank you my friends. Now, let's all go back to our jobs, and have a good day."

As I left the meeting hall that day, I was really confused. Whom should I believe? After much meditation and prayer and searching the Scripture, I decided that I would go with the Son and see where it led me. If at anytime I felt like I was in any danger, I would leave Him and get back to my desk processing goodness orders. Well, the next Monday, at 10:00 a.m. sharp, sure enough, here comes the boss' Son, just like He had promised. His handshake was firm and His smile was contagious. His whole being exuded warmth, love, and kindness, mercy and love. My fears subsided and a wonderful peace filled my soul. Psalms 16:11. It was as if I were in the very Presence of the Eternal God Himself.

Just as we were headed toward the stairway that leads up to the Big boss' upper room, the LEADER came by and whispered into my ear. "Don't go beyond the veil or you are a dead duck. No one has ever gone in there and come out alive except a special appointed one and he only goes in once a year. Just remember that if you expect to come back down here alive on my level." I was shocked and puzzled as to what he meant by the veil, and so I asked the Son and he said, "Come and I will explain it all to you when we get to My Father's outer office. You will understand in all good time. Don't be afraid. Trust Me and everything is going to be ok."

"Remember, I'll be with you at all times and will never leave you nor forsake you." Matthew 28:19, 20. These words calmed my nerves and we began the long climb up to the Father's upper room. "No wonder very few ever come up here," I said as we climbed the long, narrow, dark, stairway. "How far up is it to your Father's office?" I enquired. His only reply was, "we'll be there at the appointed time." He assured me. "But it's so dark," I said. "Just hold onto my hand, for I am the way the truth and the light of this world. John 12:46; John 14:6. I will lead you to the Father, whom to know is life everlasting." John 17:3.

On and on we climbed. It seemed we would never reach the upper room. I was getting weary, so he carried me up two flights of stairs and that rested me enough to continue on with Him just holding my hand. Finally, I saw a little glimmer of light at the top of the stairway and a door that opened. "All that enter that doorway must do so by faith alone. I will not force you to go in, but I will lead the way so you may follow me." "Come," He said in a kind voice, "let us go on. The appointed moment is near."

My heart was pounding from climbing all those steps and my throat was dry. I was really scared to go through that door. But He went on in and encouraged me to follow Him. Soon we were both standing in a large beautiful room. It was one of the most unusual and yet one of the most gorgeous rooms I'd ever been in. The interior decorator must have really been inspired, whoever he was. There was a candlestick on the west side and some freshly baked bread of some kind on the north side and some incense burning on the south side that was the most pleasant aroma I had ever experienced. He explained in great detail what it all meant and then he said, "My Father is waiting for us just beyond that sacred veil." It was one of the most beautiful curtains I had ever seen. The colors were just out of this world. The son asked me, "Joe, are you afraid to go in?" "Yes, I am. I don't really think I have the courage to do it just now." "Joe," he said, "I will go in first and show you that there is nothing to be afraid of. Ok?"

His face was radiant with excitement and His voice was musical like the voice of many waters. Revelation 1:15. He walked over to curtain, lifted it up, bent over and walked in. He was in their for several minutes and I wondered if he would ever come back out. Finally, the curtain raised and He returned to be with me. His face was radiant with a beautiful glowing light. The whole room seemed to be filled with a lovely bluish and greenish-golden haze that was very soothing to my troubled nerves and spirit. His lovely voice brought me back to the purpose for which we had come. "Joe," he began. "My Father is longing to meet you. He wants you to come in. Don't be afraid. Joe, do you believe in Me?" He asked me kindly. "Oh, yes, you are very nice," I replied. "Well," He said, "if you have seen Me, you have seen my Father. We are one. Come, Joe, He is waiting for you. I cannot lift the sacred veil for you. You alone must do that. No one can do it for you. Meeting my Father is an individual matter."

"Just go over and lift the veil, Joe, as I did, and take a peek inside. I know you will like it." And so, slowly, I edged toward the curtain. But all the stories I had heard about the big bad boss upstairs came rushing into head again and I retreated to the farthest corner of the outer office trembling all over. But, with much pleading and encouragement the Son persuaded me to try it again. He sure was patient with me. And so once more I slowly went over to the curtain and lifted the veil just a little and peeked inside.

The room was so beautiful I could scarcely believe it, let alone describe it. All the colors of the rainbow were in there and in the midst of the room was the most gorgeous, most beautiful throne decked with all kinds of precious and rare jewels.

And on this throne sat a majestic personage that I knew must be the Father—THE BIG BOSS. He sure did look like the Son all right or rather the Son looked like Him. Anyway, they looked just like each other, is what I mean. And He was smiling at me. I was so elated I dropped the curtain and danced around the room. At last I knew the truth. "THE BIG BOSS REALLY IS A WONDERFUL AND LIVING PERSON!" He isn't like they said at all. He is a kind, loving person, just like His Son. John 14:6-9; Revelation 21:3, 4; Revelation 22:3, 4.

Then I went over and lifted up the curtain again. This time the Father not only looked at me and smiled again, He also motioned with His hand to come on in. I was so startled that I dropped the curtain again and began to weep for joy. The Son said, "Joe, what's the matter?" He's ... He's...smiling ...at...me!

And He just motioned for me to come on in. I can't believe it! He actually wants me to come into His very throne room—into His very Presence. Who am I to be so honored and privileged?

"Joe," the Son said, with a patient and kind smile, "let's go in together." And so He lifted the curtain and went in first and I lifted it myself and went in after Him. The Father stood up and extended his arms to me and said, "Come here to Me my son. I want to talk to you. I have been waiting for this special moment from the day you were born." I could hardly believe it was happening to me, but now He was talking to me again. "Joe," He said, as He took me in His warm and loving arms and embraced me with a kiss, He had the same musical voice of His son.

But now He was speaking to me again. "My Son and I are so thrilled to have you in our company. We are so thankful you have joined us here beyond the sacred veil." The Son had now taken a seat beside His Father and the Father said to him, "Son, please take off your gloves so Joe can see your hands." I had been wondering why the Son always wore those beautiful white gloves. But now I understood why. His hands looked like they had been pierced with a big nail or spike or something. They were deep, but somehow beautiful scars. And a light seemed to shine forth—like rays of the sun or bright beams of light. Habakkuk 3:4; Zech. 12:10; 13:6; Psalms 22:16.

Now the Father was speaking to me again. "Joe," He began. "My beloved and only begotten Son here has tried through the years to convince my many workers that I am not the kind of person their LEADER (the one they have chosen to rule over them) has told them I am. John 8:44; Rom 6:16. Well, they have treated him pretty bad and roughly. Once they even crucified Him. But we have forgiven them and a few have repented and come to Me and learned the truth. Yes, my Son died, but I have raised him from the dead and now He is alive forever more and has the keys of hell and death." Revelation 1:18.

"But Joe," He continued, "time is running out. And that is why it was important for you to come with my Son and Me here in our upper room, beyond the sacred veil. In the days ahead—-and those days are upon us already—there will be no place to hide but in My presence here in this Most Holy place. No one in the world will be able to survive the coming Time of Trouble unless he knows the real truth about Me and comes here to be with My Son and Me, just as you did. Each person must come here and receive the special unction of My Spirit My Son and I are going to give to you right now, so you will be able to survive the coming holocaust."

And then He told me all things about myself (John 4:29; 8:29, 38), and asked me if he could adopt me into His royal family (1 John 3:1-3), for I was born an orphan. I gladly accepted and then He breathed on me His Spirit (John 20:22) and programmed my mind with light, truth, peace and love that will carry me through to the end. All my sins and fears of the past were gone. He said that from now on I would daily and hourly, minute by minute, second by second live with Him in His very presence by faith and this would be my safety and salvation in the days ahead. Psalms 34:7.

He explained many other things I cannot tell you. Words would fail me to tell you what I learned, but I would only encourage you to also go up to the upper room with the Son. He will teach you along with His Father how to process "HIS GOODNESS" orders and how to avoid the LEADER'S advances. He will also teach you how to help others to come to the upper room and receive the unction of His Spirit.

I know you would love to meet Him yourself. His name is Jesus and He is conducting daily tours to His Father's outer office and then on into the most holy place, beyond the sacred veil. Oh, here He comes now. Let me introduce you to Jesus, the Son of the living God, my blessed Redeemer, Savior and coming King.

CHAPTER 29

QUESTIONS & ANSWERS

WHO KILLED KORAH, DATHAN, AND ABIRAM?

Korah had become dissatisfied with his position. Did God tempt him to feel this way? No, for God never tempts anyone to do evil. James 1:13-15. So, we cannot blame God. Korah secretly opposed the authority of Moses and Aaron, and finally came out into the open with the bold design of overthrowing both the civil and the religious authority. Now, who leads out in all of these type of activities? JESUS OR SATAN? If we say Jesus does it, then God is guilty on two counts. First of all, He tempts and leads men to break a law He knows they, in their fallen condition, can't keep anyway. Thus, according to this logic, He will have a "legitimate" excuse or reason for killing them, thereby proving that He and His law are just and true. But, if we say that Satan is the one who leads them into these activities and God is the one who kills them, then we have an even greater problem, for God would not only be a killer, but a very sly, shadowy, sneaky person we can't really trust, for he has to get someone else to do the "dirty work," of tempting men to sin so he can prove his law just by destroying them. This concept is totally unacceptable and out of harmony with God's character, and therefore, must be rejected. But, this latter view is the one most people hold about God. Satan is the tempter, (Matt. 4:3, Jere. 6:26,27.) they say, but God is the destroyer. That is, most of the time. Oh, sometimes he uses Satan as a hit man, but only when it would look bad for Him to "do it," some reason in their carnal minds. In the Korah case, Satan led them into sin and rebellion, but God killed them with an earthquake which split open the earth. This is the fruit of such logic. Logic, which is only "carnal thinking."

We know Satan causes earthquakes by causing the earth to "tremble" and is the one who will destroy all the cities of the earth at the end of this age. Isaiah 14:12-17. See also Isaiah 28:2, 25:4, Psalm 86:14. "Tremble" in Isa. 14:16 can also be translated shake or undulate. "Raash" is the Hebrew word (Strong's concordance 7493) and means to shake: undulate or tremble through fear. It means to spring as a locust and locusts refer to demons in Rev. 9:7. When Satan and his demons fire out their fear, the earth trembles. This is what happened at Sinai when Jesus and His Father came down to give the Law. Satan was afraid and caused the mountain to tremble, not Jesus. Therefore, it is a terrible slander against the lovely character and name of Jesus to even think, much less say that Christ killed these people. The only answer left to consider is the right one. SATAN WAS PERMITTED TO TEMPT AND TO LEAD THESE REBELS INTO SIN BECAUSE THEY CHOSE TO FOLLOW THE VOICE OF SATAN, RATHER THAN THE VOICE OF GOD, AND GOD WAS FORCED TO "GIVE THEM UP TO THEIR OWN WILLS," Psalm 78:49. AND SATAN LED THEM ON TO DESTRUCTION.

Jesus told us that Satan has been a murderer from the beginning and abode not in the truth, because there is no truth in Him. John 8:44. Korah and his company were bitter about the sentence that they all must die in the wilderness. Satan tempted them to blame Moses and were thus led on to their own destruction. Miriam's leprosy came as a result of this same kind of jealousy, envy and murmuring. This was the cause of the fall of Korah, Dathan and Abiram. Numbers 12:8. Notice carefully verse 9. AND THE ANGER OF THE LORD WAS KINDLED AGAINST THEM: AND HE DEPARTED. GOD'S ANGER HERE IS THE SAME AS WRATH. It simply means He withdraws His presence to a certain degree and permits evil to have its way to the extent He has decided. Psalm 78:50. He (Jesus) made a way to His ANGER (desire). But, notice carefully, that the leprosy on Miriam did not come until after the Lord had departed. We all know who brings sickness and disease.

"How God anointed Jesus of Nazareth with the Holy Ghost and with power: who went about doing good, and HEALING ALL THAT WERE OPPRESSED OF THE DEVIL; for God was with Him." Acts 10:38.

The story of Miriam being afflicted with leprosy is indicated in Deut. 24:8 & 9 as an act which the "Lord"...did unto Miriam, a punishment for speaking against her brother Moses. But was it the true Lord who afflicted leprosy on Miriam? The answer is "No, He didn't." Remember that the Hebrew writers always made God responsible for that which He permitted to happen. Because He is the Creator He takes the blame for everything, good and bad. Isaiah 45:7. "How God anointed and consecrated Jesus of Nazareth with the (Holy) Spirit and with strength and ability and power; how He went about doing good and in particular curing all that were harassed and oppressed by [the power of] the devil, for God was with Him." Acts 10:38. Amplified Version. Whatever Jesus revealed the Father to be like in His life, while He was here on earth, is what the Father has always been like because God never changes. Psalm 89:34; Malachi 3:6; Heb 13:8; James 4:17.

Yet, Num. 12:10 proves God "DEPARTED before she was afflicted which proves the true Lord did not afflict her. When the twelve spies came back with an evil report (Numbers 13, 14) they refused to go up and God said they would have to die in the wilderness for not believing His promise. Satan cannot do anything unless he first gets God's permission. We must be careful how we ponder that, for it can be misconstrued. God allowed Satan and his angels to bring the "plagues" of sickness upon the ten spies. But true to His divine character, the Lord claimed that it was His doing, so that the people, in their ignorance, might revere and worship only Him and thus be saved from a similar fate. A correct understanding of God is progressive throughout history, as well as in each human life. Sometimes God permits us to misinterpret an event so as to awaken us to our danger. Thus we turn to Him out of awe and fear, Jude 23, but Jesus is always trying to bring us closer to Him to show us His true heart of love. Moses was blamed by Korah for all of Israel's problems, and his accusations seemed to unify the entire camp. Next, we see the Lord directing Moses to set up a meeting for all to see who was right and who was wrong. The Bible tells how God instructs Moses to separate himself along with Aaron, from among the congregation, "THAT I MAY CONSUME THEM IN A MOMENT." Now, someone will say, "now, how can you say God doesn't kill and destroy, when it clearly says here that God wants to 'consume,' them?" Here again, surface reading will cause a person to miss the true character of God. You must hunt and dig for "HIM" as for hidden treasure. He is the PEARL OF GREAT PRICE. God cannot save Israel from Satan's power to destroy them and the power of sin itself, to reap its natural result, UNLESS SOMEONE INTERVENES FOR ISRAEL. So, God here pictures Himself as about to "consume or destroy" the people (when He is only about to withdraw and let the people have their own way and thus be led by Satan to destruction). But, Jesus always takes the blame. Unless someone pleads for Israel, they are going to suffer and perish. Will Moses step into the breach and pray for rebellious Israel? Because God is not only Omnipotent, (all-powerful), but also Omniscient, (all knowing), He knew Moses' heart of love would intercede for rebellious Israel.

WHO IS REALLY SPEAKING HERE?

When we read a parallel account in Exodus 32:7-11 we see something very interesting. The voice that is claiming to be the "LORD" is actually Satan. How do I know this? 1. In v. 7, the voice lies by telling Moses he brought the people out of Egypt, calling them, "thy people." Moses rebukes this voice claiming to be the "lord" by telling him that they are His people and that He brought them out, not Moses. But the most amazing part of this story is that Moses has the temerity and audacity to rebuke this lord by telling him that his idea to kill the people is a very bad idea and will make him look bad and that he should "repent" of this evil which is a terrible idea in the first place. 2. In v. 9, the voice is accusing and condemning Israel and God never accuses or condemns. 3. The voice says, "Let me alone," which is a familiar phrase of Satan. Mark 1:24: Luke 4:34. 4. The voice says, he wishes to "consume" the people. God does not kill people. 5. The voice tempts Moses to become the leader of a great nation just like Satan tempted Jesus in Matt. 4:8 by offering Him "all the kingdoms of the world." Moses argued with this voice and interceded for Israel as a type of Christ.

Now we can see why Jesus said that we should pray for our enemies. Yes, our prayers for those who persecute and hate us will hold back the DESTROYER from afflicting and killing pre-

Moes does not realize that it is Satan who is tempting him to step aside so Satan can destroy the people, so Moses pleads with God not to destroy His own people. "Lord, you must not do this evil thing... you must not destroy your own people, for it will make you look bad." Exodus 32:11, 12. Paraphrased by the author.

Satan, claiming to be God, tempts Moses to let him destory Israel. "Let me alone, that my wrath may wax hot against them, and that I may consume them: and I will make of thee a great nation." Ex. 21:10.

Satan successfully tempts the people to put pressure on Aaron to make them a golden calf to worship. Once they have broken the first and second commandments, Satan then goes to Moses, posing as God, and tries to get Moses' permission to destroy the people. But Moses' love for the people is so great that he stands in the breach and offers his own eternal salvation, so they will not be lost. By doing this, Moses became a type of Christ. Exodus 32:7-14, 32.

cious souls for whom Christ died. This brings us now to the final showdown. Moses tells the people to get away from Korah, Dathan and Abiram. The majority of Israel obey the warning. Now, the DESTROYER is permitted to take over the remaining rebels and do with them as he wills. God knows ahead of time exactly what Satan will do and communicates this information to his servant. Moses then relays it to the people: "Hereby ye shall know that the Lord hath sent me to do all these works; for I have not done them of mine own mind. If these men die the common death of all men, or if they be visited after the visitation of all men; then the Lord hath not sent me. But if the Lord make a new thing, (margin says, CREATE A NEW NATION), and the earth open her mouth, and swallow them up, with all that appertain unto them, and they go down quick into the pit (grave or opening in earth. Not hellfire); then ye shall understand that these men have provoked the Lord." Numbers 16:28-30. The following verses show how this actually happened... "AND THEY PERISHED FROM AMONG THE CONGREGATION." Paul says they were "destroyed of the destroyer." I Cor. 10:9,10. Satan is the DESTROYER. He is the one who causes earthquakes. So, my friend, please don't tell me God split the earth open here. He didn't do it.

When Jesus told Moses he was going to make "a new thing," he did not mean that He was going to kill people in a NEW WAY He hadn't used before. This is absurd. God is not like that. He meant instead, that He was about to permit the leaders of this rebellion to die and Israel would have to choose some brand new leaders. It would in a sense be a NEW NATION, in that the new leaders would be new men appointed by God, through Moses. Satan works through accident, war disease or a natural calamity such as lightning. Today Satan is often pictured with a pitch-fork in his hand. That actually is a bolt of lightning and used to be drawn as such, a bolt of lightning with three forks to it, but has now become a pitch-fork to imply Satan is pitching people into hell-fire. The pagans used to pray to Satan, "0 thou who controls the lightning. 0 thou all powerful destroyer, have mercy on us as we sacrifice to you." Satan is the one who brings hail and other types of storms. Psalm 78:47-49. Remember that the 7th plague is hail! In the case of the 250 princes, God controlled and permitted these events. Now, pay close attention to the next point. Where is Satan during all of this death and destruction? Why He is right next to Jesus....at his right hand, doing his best to pervert and twist everything He can. We see this in Zech. 3:1, where Satan is accusing Joshua the high priest, the same as he accused Job.

It was not God who hurt Job. No, my friend. it was the DESTROYER, Satan. And it was not our Precious, Holy, JESUS who flashed fire out and killed these 250 princes. How do I know that? First of all God's law says, "THOU SHALT NOT KILL." Christ kept the law perfectly when He was on earth, showing that it was a perfect law. He demonstrated His true character then and for all eternity, past and present. He is always like that. He never changes. Heb. 13:8; Mal. 3:6. Secondly, let us notice what the Lord was doing while Satan was accusing the 250 princes of sinning and telling God, "I have a right to destroy them. They have sinned." What was Jesus doing then? He was seeking to save them from the DESTROYER by offering them forgiveness. Amazing! Jesus doesn't bring Wrath. He saves us from it. "We shall be saved from wrath through Him." Rom. 5:9. Praise God! And yet, God here again permits Satan to slander His name by making it look like fire is coming from Jesus. Yet Christ says, "I did it, worship only Me or you will die too."

Did Moses and Aaron kill the 250 princes? No, they did not. Moses and Aaron stood as God's visible representatives to give His word and show His power and authority over all events, people and nature. God said they would die if they did not repent. He, alone, had the power of life and death in his hand....not Satan. Satan never could harm them, unless God permitted it, therefore, it is blasphemy to attribute to Satan or Moses the power to decide whether or not these men live or die. Only the CREATOR HAS THE RIGHT TO DECIDE and carry out such a decision. Satan can only do what God permits. Look at Job's case for proof. Jesus alone, with His Father and the Holy Spirit, had the power to let them die if they did not repent or to save them from Satan and themselves, if they didn't. God was in control of the situation, not Moses, nor even Satan. Since Satan, himself, could not kill unless God "decided" (judged) it to be so, Satan could not kill them, so it was the "judgment of God" (HIS DECISION ALONE) that killed the 250 princes. But, what was the decision? And this is the key to this whole question and scenario.

It was a decision to let these men reap the full result of their own choice. God let them go. He decided to let them go their own way and do their own thing; This is called God's wrath in the Bible. This is how God destroys. "Destroy thou them O God. Let them fall by their own counsels." Psalm 5:10. This was God's JUDGMENT, and it was delivered by Moses and Aaron in the name of God. Yet, the people sinned by not giving God reverence when His power was so signally manifested. The people sinned by saying that Satan was the one in control of life and death, when it was the Creator.

This was blasphemy because they rejected God's efforts to save them from destruction, which He was only allowing, and therefore controlling, but not bringing. The true legalist will make the same mistake at the TIME OF TROUBLE when he charges God and His people with the plagues. They will be blaspheming God's Holy name then too. And men were scorched with great heat, and blasphemed the name of God, which hath power over these plagues: and they repented not to give him glory. Rev. 16:9. They do not give God credit for being the LIFE GOD and reject His SIGN {Sabbath Day, 7th day} which shows His true character as life-giver, not life-taker. They do not give Him GLORY or CHARACTER. That is, they do not assign to Him His rightful place as CREATOR and REDEEMER and thus they are perishing. Actually, the plagues should cause them to repent and ask forgiveness, but like Pharaoh, their hearts are just more hardened with additional evidence.

QUESTION: IF GOD DOES NOT DESTROY PEOPLE, HOW THEN DID THE PEOPLE IN THE DAYS OF NOAH DIE? How do you explain the plain Word of God, which says, "And it repented the Lord that he had made man on the earth, and it grieved Him at His heart"? And the Lord said, "I will destroy man whom I have created from the face of the earth both man, and beast, and the creeping thing, and the fowls of the air; for it repenteth me that I have made them." Gen. 6:6,7.

ANSWER: Jesus' comment on the flood is significant: "The flood came, and destroyed them all." Luke 17:27. Matt. 24:39 says the same thing will happen again when Jesus returns, only the destruction will be by fire this time instead of by water. It is SIGNIFICANT THAT CHRIST DID NOT BLAME HIS FATHER OR HIMSELF FOR DESTROYING THE PEOPLE, but simply blamed the event itself as the cause of their death. The flood is an example of how God permitted the people, under the leadership of Satan, to run this planet according to their own will. Satan had kept telling the universe that if he were in charge of planet earth completely, things would be much better. So, the Lord permitted Satan to do just that. Of course, he fouled things up so badly that the flood came and Satan himself thought he was going to be destroyed in the warring elements. Patriarchs & Prophets, pgs 99, 100. The word "repent," means to sigh deeply, or sorrow. Now, just what actually caused the vapor envelope to collapse upon that ancient race is not totally clear, but, we do have some evidence that is most interesting. There are two concepts I have at this time, and yet they could be fused into one, for it is possible that not only did man bring upon himself some type of nuclear holocaust, it also seems that Satan has in the past been permitted to cause astral CATASTROPHES. Jesus has told us Noah's day is a model for our day. Just how similar conditions are today with what they were then, we cannot know for sure, but today man is again about to destroy himself with his own greed, selfishness and so-called scientific advances. Is it possible that a similar situation developed in Noah's day? We must consider the possibility. Jesus said there would be a parallel between the days of Noah and our day. Matt. 24:37.

Are we, as a modern counterpart of the people in Noah's time, about to repeat history? It would seem so. Who is destroying our civilization today? God or man? Man is doing it, not God. If we can't blame God today for man's death, why blame God for man's death at the time of the flood?

In his book, "Malfunctions of Nature," Edward F. Bowman, of Kansas City, has suggested that a major planet in space 28 exploded. He says there is no proof that this happened, except that there is no planet in space 28, according to Bode's law. He says that for years the empty space where planet 28 should have been, remained a mystery. Since 1801, astronomers have been sighting what seems to be fragments of an exploded planet. To date, several thousand have been located and named. Some are 500 miles across, others smaller. They are called Asteroids and are baby planets which are simply parts of a regular planet that once exploded. Since God created a perfect universe of harmony and order, it does not seem logical that exploding planets would be part of his modus operandi.

But Satan, as the "Prince of the Power of the Air," (Eph. 2:2) could cause such an explosion, if God permitted him to do it. The disintegration of planet 28 might have been the beginning of a chain reaction, causing a shift in the magnetic force field, and thus setting off earthquakes on planet earth, which may have detonated certain nuclear devices that race had manufactured. Or it is possible that the disaster worked in reverse order-planet 28 exploding and some of the other planets fragmenting to a degree as a result of an upheaval on planet earth and her one moon, due to some kind of detonation on this earth, which set the whole thing off. Since astronomy and physics are out of my specific areas of concentration, I will not theorize further. However, I would like to quote Mr. Bowman. He suggests that the Lord allowed Satan to explode planet 28 for reasons we cannot fully understand. "He (God), to be fair with Satan, allowed him to retain some of his powers (Eph. 2:2), so Satan, therefore, may have destroyed the planet in question, by (causing a cosmic cloud to alter earth's balance in space) explaining to his fallen angels that his controversy with the Creator was justified, otherwise God would have prevented him from upsetting or meddling with natural laws. Satan does many things which appear at the time to be victories for him, by trying to cover up God's works and hiding them from view, but in the long run, God reverses and uses the same covering up to preserve them." Page 23. Ibid. Actually, Satan lost none of his powers when he left heaven. But, Job 38:11 and Mal 3:11 show that God has put a limit on Satan's power to destroy. See also Job 1 and 2.

As a final answer to this question, I will quote from Job. "Hast thou marked the old way which wicked men have trodden: Which were cut down out of time, whose foundation was overflown with a flood:" This is a direct reference to the deluge in Noah's day, written about 828 years after the flood which said unto God, depart from us: and what can the Almighty do for them? Job 22:15-17. See also, Isa. 59:19, Luke 6:48,49. The next two verses indicate that God blessed these people in spite of their rebellion, just as He is doing today. But, this shows that the people before the flood told God to get lost. "GET OUT OF OUR LIVES AND LEAVE US ALONE," they defiantly shouted. We hear the echo of their voices today in our world. This is "GOD'S WRATH," when He has to let them go their own way and do their own thing. It would seem then, that the flood was simply a result of man coming under the complete control of Satan, who brought destruction upon them with the deluge in Noah's day.

How did it happen? By accident or design? We do not know for sure. Anyway, the Lord took the responsibility for it. Satan no doubt feared for his own existence and actually, if God had not protected him and his angels, perhaps they too would have perished, for they were compelled, to remain in the warring elements. Since God never uses coercion, force or acts arbitrarily, it was circumstances which compelled Satan to remain in the flood as he feared for his life. Have you ever thought of it in that way, giving God the credit for saving his life? It seems that we always want to perpetuate the concept of a hateful God, bent on killing and destroying people, instead of the loving God who is always seeking to "save" us. It is also interesting to note an ancient tradition which has been passed down for centuries. It says that the gods long ago decided to bring a flood upon the earth and then screamed for their lives when it came, as they thought they would die too.

QUESTION: What do you think of Immanuel Velikovsky's theories, regarding astral catastrophism. Do you think it answers any questions on this subject?

ANSWER: Velikovsky wrote "Worlds in Collision" and "Ages in Chaos," while Patten, more recently, has authored "The Long Day of Joshua, and Six Other CATASTROPHES," as well as a work on the flood and ice age. These men may vary somewhat from Edward Bowman's idea, but not perhaps as much as we may think. Although I do not claim to be an expert in any sense of the word, I see possibilities in all three theories or ideas. For example, Bowman is talking about a planet exploding, which originally occupied space 28. Fragments of that planet may very well have passed by our planet and caused terrible magnetic upheavals, resulting in the flood. Is it even possible that part of that planet became Venus, which passed by our planet after it fragmented and then began orbiting the sun? Velikovsky believes Venus is a chunk of Jupiter, due to an explosion long ago. Patten agrees with Velikovsky in general, but says he believes that Mercury's "flyby" caused the flood, or at least its proximity was the cause of gravitational dislocations on our earth, which caused earthquakes and tidal waves. He believes that it also supposedly caused one of Mercury's ice moons to be pulled into our atmosphere and destroyed the water shield or vapor envelope, which protected the antediluvian world and caused the earth to have a very even and beautiful temperature similar to a tropical climate. The resultant ice-dump on both poles buried man and animals alike. Patten says this was caused by the fly-by of Mercury. Velikovsky Spoke about the fly-by of Venus, causing the Exodus catastrophe, whereas Patten says Mars was the cause of the ten plagues upon Egypt.

Personally, I have come to believe that none of these astral events were necessary for God to have permitted the ten plagues upon Egypt or for even the flood to have occurred. Man today could bring earthquakes upon this planet without the help of a "fly-by," but that doesn't mean we won't have some astral catastrophes in these last days, just as they may have had them in the past. But, referring to the ten plagues upon Egypt again, the frogs, flies, lice and many of the other plagues could have come as a result of an ecological imbalance caused by man himself and/or Satan, who, as we know has the power to bring plagues and sicknesses of various sorts. But, God has to withdraw His hand of protection before these aberrations of nature can occur. Look at the leprosy on Moses' hand. I believe God simply withdrew his protection from that portion of Moses' body and the disease immediately manifested itself. Isn't the same thing true of Miriam? See Numbers 12. God permits, prevents, directs and determines in the affairs of men and nations. Don't each of us carry germs in our bodies which, if God withdrew His protecting hand, would spring forth in horrible disease and destroy us? Absolutely! By holding or withdrawing, preventing or permitting, God can and does control the whole universe. But, He never brings evil directly. Our main interest and purpose in examining certain ideas and theories about the flood and other past catastrophes is simply to consider alternate possibilities which enable us to see that God is not arbitrary in his dealings with men or angels and that Jesus, nor His Father directly destroyed the earth with a flood. It was an aberration of nature, caused by the great enemy of God for selfish and sinister motives beyond our understanding, for Satan was enjoying the antediluvian world. The people were his puppets and play things, you might say. He simply over or underestimated the results of this manipulation and things got beyond his control. As God withdrew everything just blew up in his face. But, true to His nature, he did not accept the blame for what he had caused, but blamed Jesus, his rival for our affections, allegiance and worship. Finally, man made disasters, as well as, Satanic disasters on the earth and in the heavens may both take place in this end time simultaneously. Matt. 24, Lk. 21.

The prophet Isaiah has additional testimony regarding the flood of Noah. "For a small moment have I forsaken thee; but with great mercies will I gather thee. In a little WRATH I hid my face from thee; but with everlasting kindness will I have mercy on thee, saith the Lord thy Redeemer. For this is as THE WATERS OF NOAH unto me: for as I have sworn that the waters of Noah should no more go over the earth; so have I sworn that I would not be wroth with thee, nor rebuke thee." Isaiah 54:7-9 .

We have already discussed astral catastrophism and man made nuclear explosions as possible explanations for the flood disaster. I have tried not to be dogmatic in this area, due to the fact that we are over 4,300 years removed from that incident. But, I have this additional concept to share, which is perhaps the most uncomplicated theory of them all.

It simply says that God withdrew Himself from the Antediluvian world but "For a small moment..." Isa. 54:7, which was right after He shut the door of Noah's Ark. Without God's hand over and under and in nature, everything began falling apart. Seven days later, the rain began to fall. The water envelope or vapor shield around the earth had seven days to cool down, due to the sun being toned down seven times and the moon being extinguished, Isa. 30:26. Since this Scripture promises that God will recreate the earth or "bind up the breach of his people and healeth the stroke of their wound," Cf. Mal. 4: 1, 2, we may safely assume that the sun was seven times as hot before the flood as it is today and the moon was a blazing orb as hot as our present sun. One Creationist scientist suggests that the sun had only 14% of its lighting and heating capacity, after the flood which would figure out to be but 1/7th.

After seven days, the force of gravity began to pull down the condensed droplets of water, which were previously held together by the chemical action of the suns rays which were seven times hotter and caused the vapor envelope to remain in a non-congealed "steam" or misty vapor state, which served to moisten the earth, Genesis 2:6, in some manner, so rain, as we know it, wasn't necessary. As the Lord removed His Presence, by popular demand of the Antediluvians, (God's Wrath), this whole watering system began to fall apart. Satan, probably led the people to try and break into the ark, but they could not. Noah had followed God's instruction, and was safe. So, it will be in this our day, when probation closes. God is giving us the "materials" (gifts) we need to construct our ark of safety so we can survive in that evil day...even the seven last plagues. The gifts are 1) The Holy Spirit, which abides in our hearts and leads us to 2) Prayer and 3) study the Holy Bible and then 4) share what we have learned about Jesus and His love. As we do these things, we are constructing our "ark of safety," which will carry us through the final holocaust of destruction, so we will be among the Elect, who will be "alive and remain," to be translated at Christ's return. I Thess. 4:15-17. Our "ark" of safety is the Character of Jesus formed within us.

Perhaps someone will ask how the fountains of the great deep were broken up at this same time. It would seem that some kind of terrific shaking and violence would be necessary for such an event to occur. If the Lord permitted the earth to be tilted at this same time, that would account for it. Or it might have been part of the events that transpired once He removed His protecting hand.

The mystery of Golgotha explains all other mysteries. In the light that shines from Calvary we can see the real truth about God. The Father and the Son are total love. God the Father did not bring the flood. His creatures rejected him and chose the rulership of Satan. As soon as the majority of His creatures again chose Him as their ruler, He re-asserted His power over creation. That is, when the people of the antediluvian world no longer existed (expired in the flood), God regained His right to rule His creatures on planet earth by a majority vote—that is by Noah and his family's vote. Thus God stepped in and controlled planet earth again. If God had not done this, the earth no doubt would have been completely destroyed. Throughout the great controversy, God has always controlled the elements. That is, even though Satan has been permitted to use the elements of fire, wind and water against us, from time to time, God is still in control. It was not until the New Testament that Satan's power to use these elements of nature to destroy was revealed. "The prince of the power of the air ...that now worketh in the children of disobedience." Ephesians 2:2.

God has set boundaries for Satan, and these he cannot cross, unless we ourselves permit him by breaking the law. The law of God is our protection. On Mount Sinai God gave this beautiful transcript of His own character in the midst of a fireworks that had never been seen before. There was a thick cloud all over Horeb (Mt. Sinai) and lightnings flashed from the cloud. (Satan uses clouds to come between us and God Job 36:32). These lightnings were not permitted to hurt or injure or kill anyone. Christ was in that thick cloud of darkness, using it to veil His glory from the people so as to protect them. Jesus was coming onto Satan's territory, and Satan was contesting every inch of "his" ground. Christ used the darkness, but did He bring it? "God is light, and in Him is no darkness at all." I John 1:5. Yes, Satan did everything possible to make God's law seem very fearful and frightening. If the people accepted the law as a beautiful token of God's love and protection, Satan could never touch them. He has always sought to represent Jehovah as harsh and unforgiving. Satan has ever been at the side of Christ to twist and distort His beautiful character. When fire flashed out and destroyed the rebels at the rebellion of Korah, Satan made it look like Jesus did it. Few can comprehend this. But, remember that Satan is ever at the side of Christ to destroy any who disobey. "And he shewed me Joshua the high priest standing before the angel [Christ] of the Lord, and Satan standing at his right hand to resist him." Zech. 3:1.

Imagine it! Think of what Jesus and His Father and all the Holy Angels have to put up with and endure. Satan was in the sanctuary too! Psalm 74:3-8. If the high priest had one unconfessed sin on his heart or made one mistake while in the most holy place of the sanctuary, he was immediately struck dead by Satan, the legalist, who is fighting for his "legal right" to destroy us every time he gets a chance. Do you see how important it is to stay close to Jesus and claim His blood over you at all times? And do you see the importance of not blaming God for Satan's works? For example, just as Satan killed Job's children and his livestock, so Satan put Jacob's hip out of place when Jacob refused to yield to Jesus. Satan claimed the right to destroy Jacob because of his sin, but Jacob claimed the blood of Christ. Because Christ knew that it would motivate Jacob to plead for the assurance of God's mercy and forgiveness, Jesus permitted Satan to put Jacob's hip out of joint. Satan pointed to the unprotected hip of Jacob and asked Jesus, "may I touch him here?" Because Jacob did not have his "sword" strapped on his hip, Satan was allowed to hurt his hip. Instead of causing Jacob to give up, this suffering only caused him to pray harder and completely yield to God's will for His life and prevail.

QUESTION: According to your concept, God did not destroy Sodom and Gomorrah. I would like to be able to explain this to my friends who believe in a destructive God. Can you help me?

ANSWER: Let us read the Scriptures on this first. Then the Lord rained upon Sodom and upon Gomorrah brimstone (sulphur) and fire from the Lord out of heaven. Gen. 19:24. The first thing we must remember is that God always takes the blame or credit for all disasters in the Bible, sometimes even in the New Testament. The seven last plagues are an example. We have already gone into great detail to show that Satan is behind all the aberrations and quirks of nature: Satan is always eager to use the elements to destroy. I simply see the destruction of Sodom and Gomorrah as an example of such an occasion he was permitted to bring fire down upon these people he had led into sin and rebellion. God held His hand over the situation and controlled it, permitting Lot and his family to be extricated barely in time before Christ commanded His angels to withdraw and destruction to come in the form of fire from the sky. Satan is called the "PRINCE OF THE POWER OF THE AIR." Ephesians 2:2. To be consistent with Bible exegesis, we would have to admit that Satan could be the destroyer here just as he was in the days of Job. If we say that Satan brought the fire in Job's case, but not in the case of Sodom and Gomorrah (God got the blame both times, by the way), we are immediately contradicting a number of basic Scriptural principles on the character of God, i.e. Psalm 89:34; Mal. 3:6; Heb. 13:8; James 1:17. God does not change...EVER. It is Satan who would have us to believe God is fickle, unreliable, and unworthy of our faith and trust.

It is through the life of Jesus that we see this is a lie. God is true. He is trustworthy. One of the main reasons people fall for false religions is because Satan tells them they will be "as gods." They will be above all law. They will become a law unto themselves. Therefore, he paints a picture of deity as the ultimate playboy, doing whatever He likes whenever He likes; "There are no rules and regulations to hinder you. No laws to get in your way from carrying out your 'holy' thoughts and your 'perfect' ideas. After all, once you are a god, you are infallible." Thus, Satan sells the idea that Jesus can do what he wants when he wants. If things get out of hand, there is no need to worry, for Jesus can kill anyone he wishes anytime they get out of line. "Zap! Kill them with fire from the sky! That will show the rest of the world what kind of a person I am and they better watch their step."

The overwhelming majority of Christendom believe in this kind of Jesus. Is it any wonder that the world is in the mess it is in! Christ came to change this false concept of God and His ETERNAL LAW OF LOVE. Let us look at another Scripture and see if it will shed any light on what happened at Sodom and Gomorrah. "For the punishment of the iniquity of the daughter of my people is greater than the punishment of the sin of Sodom, THAT WAS OVERTHROWN AS IN A MOMENT, AND NO HANDS (THE HANDS OF THE ANGELS) STAYED ON HER." Lamentations 4:6. I was on the way to a place to speak and was impressed to pray about this question, as I was not sure how to answer it at that time. My mind immediately remembered this Scripture and when I looked at it, I saw the phrase *AND NO HANDS STAYED ON HER*, as the key to what had happened there. Psalm 91:11,12 prove that God protects us by the "hands" of the holy angels. Let us put with that this verse. "Hurry to escape there, (Angel telling Lot to go to Zoar) for I CAN DO NOTHING UNTIL YOU HAVE REACHED IT." Gen. 19:22. Holy angels had been commissioned to hold back the DESTROYER until Lot's family (the only righteous ones in the city) were safely out of town. When God's angel said he could nothing, he simply meant that he was not allowed to command the angelic host to withdraw and permit Satan to rain down fire. What other explanation can one give and still be in a harmony with the life of Jesus revealed in His perfect life? The most logical explanation is that Satan brought fiery bolides from the sky to ignite the very combustible asphalt and tar (pitch) pits in this area. Gen. 11:3. 14:10. Deut. 29:23. "Slime" is mineral pitch, asphalt or tar which is very combustible. In Job's day we have an example or model as to how Satan can destroy with fire, "THE FIRE OF GOD IS FALLEN FROM HEAVEN," Job 1:16. We know that this was not GOD'S FIRE, but Satan's fire, literal or real, sent by permission of God, Job 1:12. This was not merely a lightning storm. But some greater form of destructive fire. Job 37:3 shows us that the writer knew what lightning was, as opposed to fire.

Patten refers to this experience as having been caused by bolides and meteorites which came into our atmosphere by the fly-by of Mars. That is, some of the debris from this passing planet fell to earth. Unless God directed it to hit out in the desert, harmlessly extinguishing itself. Satan, as the prince of the power of the air could guide it to hit anything he wished. This type of destruction was going on in a regular cycle. Because Jesus, as Creator, has all power and all authority over all creation He claimed to be the one behind all of these disasters. Thus by taking the blame in this manner, He often was able to gain the worship of peoples who otherwise would never have worshiped Him but would have instead worshiped Satan and been destroyed.

Another interesting point we should not overlook is that this disaster occurred during the daytime (Gen. 19:23), perhaps, to prove to the heathen in other parts of the earth that the sun god had no power to deliver them. See *LEGENDS OF THE JEWS*, by Louis Ginsberg, Vol. 1, pg. 256. Why would Satan destroy his own? 1) He could blame it upon God. 2) He also garnered more souls into his lost net. 3) He could use this experience to show that God's law cannot be kept. That it is unfair , and when a person breaks it, God simply destroys him. This is Satan's favorite modus operandi. I should mention in closing, that some have suggested that these people destroyed themselves with an atomic explosion, when God withdrew his power of protection. I have no proof that this theory is right or wrong. In this situation I simply view Patten's idea as more plausible.

QUESTION: Do you believe all the people in Sodom and Gomorrah and the flood are lost for all eternity?

ANSWER: I believe God already knows who among the dead are saved or lost for the age in which they lived. But, it only seems logical that many of the people who died in the time of the flood were children who did not have a chance to decide one way or another. The same may be true of Sodom and Gomorrah. The children of Korah were not destroyed with him, (Numbers 26:11). So it would seem that God does not make a final decision about one's salvation on the basis of who your father or your mother might be. Only God knows how the children would have turned out, therefore, only He has the right to decide their destiny. No one is "lost for all eternity." I have explained universal restoration already, and the ages. Who will have to go through the lake of fire is a decision made only by the Creator.

QUESTION: How do you explain the death of Uzzah?

ANSWER: Let's read the Scripture. "And the ANGER OF THE LORD (key phrase) was kindled against Uzzah; and GOD SMOTE (key phrase) him there for his error (his error was rashness or presumption, Psalm 19:13); and there he died by the ark of God." 2 Sam. 6:8. The key phrases are above, as I have indicated. What do they always mean? Psalm 78:49 tells us what anger means—W-R-A-T-H. And the wrath of God is always when He withdraws. Mark 3:5 also indicates God's anger can mean "emotion," or "desire." See Strong's. Thus, God's withdrawing caused Uzzah's death. That is, God let Uzzah alone and gave him over to his "own counsel," (Psalm 5:10) and Uzzah was destroyed by Satan in a way we cannot know or completely understand, for Satan is the destroyer. He simply forfeited the protection of the Holy Spirit in his life and when that was no longer active in his behalf, he committed a presumptuous act which carried the death sentence. Ps. 19:13, 2 Sam. 6:8. The "breach" upon Uzzah was caused by Satan, who is the God of breaking forth. Job 16:14, Eccles. 10:8. "Hedge" equals the law of God or His covenant. A breach implies the breaking of that covenant.

God judges us each according to our knowledge of right and wrong. The Philistines didn't know any better, so they placed the ark upon a cart drawn by oxen, but the Israelites had in their hands God's sacred instruction which they had neglected to follow. "To him that knoweth to do good and doeth it not, to him it is sin." James 4:17.

In case someone wants to insist that God certainly did kill Uzzah, let me encourage you to keep in mind the principles you must work from at all times. God is always the same. He doesn't change. Whether Satan did this directly or indirectly, it is still his fault, not God's fault. By that, I mean that Satan has murdered all the evil angels, even though they are still alive. Jesus called him a "murderer from the beginning." Jn. 8:44. So, when God removed His protection from Uzzah, he could have dropped dead due to the lack of God's life support system keeping him, alive or he could have died as a direct result of Satan killing him in some way we do not understand. It is also possible that Uzzah died because he knew he had broken a law which demanded the death penalty. The mind is a powerful thing. If he believed he was going to die, and his mind accepted it, then he willed himself to death. Either way, it is sin which kills and Lucifer (Satan) started the whole sin scene in the beginning. I, myself lean towards the idea that Satan destroys directly more often than indirectly. Also, remember that Satan makes thousands of mistakes. He is so very anxious to kill, when it would do him more good not to kill, that he hurts his own cause. He is not as clever as he wants you to think he is. And, since God is always taking the blame, he can safely hide behind that no matter whether his actions are in his favor or against him. God never puts the finger on him in the OT, except in the book of Job, and even there, He claims that what is happening to Job is His fault. Job 2:3. Yet, Satan betrayed himself with his own words.

In further answer to this question about Uzzah, let us consider how God "punished," the Philistines, when they looked inside the ark and treated it disrespectfully. It may give us insight into the question of Uzzah's death. Since we cannot see the play and counter play of holy and unholy angels behind the scenes, it is impossible for us to fully understand just how God "uses" people like we use them. We do it to save ourselves and bolster up our pride and our position, whereas, God "uses" these to save us from as much pain, hurt and sorrow as possible. God may have 1,000 ways to solve a problem, but He will always choose that one way which will bring us the least amount of harm and the most amount of joy. God is like that. Isn't He beautiful! Yes, He is

The main reason we do not see how beautiful Jesus is, is because the prince of the power of the air, even Satan, has blinded our eyes. 2 Cor. 4:4. Now, let us notice how God uses the ark to impress the Philistines that he is a God over all their gods. First of all, their god Dagon, had fallen upon his face to the earth before the ark of Jehovah. No human life was destroyed by its fall. The ark of God's presence was then placed by itself in a building. Now, who brings sickness and disease? Why, it is Satan. Acts 10:38. Luke 13:16. James 1:17 also tells us God only brings "GOOD AND PERFECT GIFTS." Therefore, any kind of sickness or accident or calamity is from another source. The disease of the Philistines was EMERODS. A Bible dictionary defines Emerods thusly: "The Hebrew Techorim, some form of Tumors, probably 'Hemorrhoids.'" It could also have been cancer.

Even though the Philistines did not follow the health laws God had given to Moses, the Lord was protecting them from these diseases, to a high degree. But, now that they were forfeiting that protection, by not respecting the ark of God's eternal presence, they were permitted to suffer the consequences of that irreverence. In addition to not eating the right diet, these people also deified sex and dedicated themselves to every kind of immoral sexual perversion (known and unknown to man), all in the name of religion. Emerods could also have been some sort of social disease we have not heard of today. Whatever it was, God did not bring it, but simply permitted it in order to impress upon the Philistine nation that His power was greater than Dagon's.

QUESTION: If God doesn't destroy and kill at any time, how do you explain the 10 plagues of Egypt in Moses' day? How did they happen?

ANSWER: First of all, let us define the word "plague." PLAGUE. (Heb. generally, maggephah and makkah; Greek, mastix, 'A lashing," 'tonnent,' 'suffering,' plague, blow, stroke, wound, misfortune : generally, in Scripture, a divine visitation as punishment for sin, usually a virulent disease or a catastrophe resulting from the unusual operation of the forces of nature, as the ten plagues upon the land of Egypt (See Exodus 9:14). Notice carefully how "disease" is included in this list. If Jesus doesn't bring disease, why should he bring anything else? Can we logically assign such terrible deeds to Him, the "Meek and lowly One?" Whoever would bring such disasters upon human beings would have to be a horrible, sadistic monster. Let us now settle one thing in our minds. God permits, and this power to let things happen is spoken of as "HIS JUDGMENTS." But it never happens unless man already has chosen to forsake God. The Lord always holds His hand over the situation and controls everything, and yet He is not the one responsible for the disaster. He is not bringing it.

What happened in Egypt, long ago, will happen again in our day. If we can learn who brings the seven last plagues, we will know who brought the ten plagues of Egypt. Since we have already discovered that Satan is allowed to destroy the earth in the last days when God withdraws His protection (called the Wrath of God), we know that God is not the one who brings the seven last plagues, nor is He the one who brought the ten plagues of Egypt. Right? Right! We know the Bible says God hardened Pharaoh's heart. But did God actually - do that? Obviously God did not cause Pharaoh to reject him. God is not like that, for Jesus is not that way. It simply tells us that the same love that melted and moved Moses' heart to obey God, hardened Pharaoh's heart to disobey Him.

God cannot and will not interfere with our free choice, but He hangs in there to the very last minute, saying "Oh, why will you die, O house of Israel?" Ezek. 18:31. Most people will not realize it, but the prophet of God just told us how men who reject Jesus in the last hour will destroy themselves in the final end, for GOD DESTROYS NO MAN. James 1:17.

God has "power over," or "control over," the plagues, Rev. 16, in the last days. The magicians didn't have any power except what Satan could give them, which was basically a power of deceptive imitation. After the third plague, God was withdrawing his power over certain aspects of nature Satan had not yet studied and learned the secrets of yet. Satan has studied long and hard to learn how to manipulate nature against us. At that time he did not have the power or knowledge to do the things he can do today. God was forced to allow certain ecological laws to be broken by the ongoing erosion of the sin factor that Satan set in motion when he rebelled in heaven. When Adam and Eve set that sin factor loose on earth, the same thing began happening here. God holds it back as long as He can, but when man continues to go deeper into sin God is forced to withdraw his power. An example of what I am saying is found in Moses' experience when he put his hand inside of his robe and then withdrew it all infected with leprosy. Did Satan do that? Possibly, but God simply showed Moses that He had control over all things and when He withdraws His protecting hand over any portion of man's body or over any part of nature, sin, sickness, heartbreak, disaster and calamity of every description breaks loose. Satan is the author of all sickness.

Just as in the flood Satan feared for his own life, for things were out of his control, so in the 10 plagues of Egypt Satan, after the 3rd plague, was scratching his head, so to speak, as far as imitating these signs and miracles. This does not rule out the possibility that Satan was also causing destruction in ways we may not be aware of, for as long as Jesus was taking the blame and credit for it all, what did he have to lose by killing a few more Egyptians? Psalm 78:40-51 proves Satan and his angels brought the 10 plagues on Egypt.

What happened in Egypt will soon happen in America and around the World. Egypt rejected God's protection when she refused to listen to the prophets God sent and even began persecuting the Lord's chosen nation, Israel. The plagues that fell upon Egypt are an example of the kind of destruction Satan will again be allowed to bring when Jesus leaves the most Holy Place of the heavenly sanctuary.

God is not the destroyer, but permits him to work his will out in the lives of those who choose to serve the evil one rather than Jesus. We are even now nearing the time of the NATIONAL SUNDAY LAW, and this will begin to fulfill prophecy.

Unless you realize that God punishes by withdrawing his protective restraints, you will believe (with the rest of the world) that God is the one who is destroying the earth. Now, most Sabbath keepers do not realize that there will be much destruction before the seven last plagues. These will not come until everyone has made a final decision and closed his or her probation. We close our own probation, you see, by rejecting the truth about God, that He is not a killer or a destroyer. Because most professed Sabbath keepers believe that God does destroy and kill they will join the ranks of Sunday keeping people who will persecute God's true Elect believers, who are giving the final message about God's character and how we must come out of Babylon in order to be like Jesus. But, because these nominal believers have not studied and prayed for "refreshing from the Lord," when their lamps begin to go out they will realize they are in serious trouble. In the parable of the Ten Virgins, the five foolish virgins go back to those who "buy and sell." But, who is "buying and selling?" And what are they "buying and selling?" In Isaiah 55;1 we read the invitation of Jesus to "buy" salvation from Him free of charge. All it "costs" us is the surrender of our entire will. So, the five foolish virgins are simply looking for some more of God's Holy Spirit (the oil) to help them understand what is going on in the world. They are confused. They realize they do not have spiritual understanding for they have not studied the Word of God. When they ask the five Wise Virgins for some of their "oil," the five Wise tell them that their oil is not transferable. Character cannot be passed on to someone else. Each person must receive Christ's character from Him alone. It is a personal matter and intimate relationship that one must have before you can receive that extra oil which will take you INTO THE FATHER'S HEART. But; because the five foolish virgins have rejected Jesus' true character they see Him as a destroyer, not a life giver. Evidently, the five foolish virgins go to those who are still allowed to "buy and sell," (dispense salvation, see Rev. 13), and they receive, evidently, some kind of "light" but when they come back to the wedding, the DOOR IS SHUT. Did Jesus shut the door in their faces?

No, Jesus never shuts the door in anyone's face. They have closed the door of their own heart by believing the false teachers who are telling them that God is the one who is bringing the "judgments" upon the earth and that the only hope of the world is to keep Sunday. This is their new "light" from those who "buy and sell," but it is a false light. Thus many professed Sabbath keepers will join the ranks of Sunday persecutors prior to the seven last plagues falling, as they have slowly come to the same conclusion that the BEAST BELIEVERS HAVE COME TO. And what is that? Simply, that Lucifer is Jesus and the true day is Sunday. These five foolish virgins look at the earthquakes, tornadoes, tidal waves and astral catastrophes as "acts" of God. They think God is bringing these aberrations of nature as a punishment upon the earth for not keeping Sunday holy. Through the lying wonders of Spiritualism, the majority of the members of the church will begin keeping Sunday. When Satan appears as Christ, these same ex-Sabbath believers will be the leading persecutors of God's people. They will lead out in the death decree. WHY? Because THEY REFUSED TO BELIEVE THE TRUTH ABOUT GOD'S WONDERFUL CHARACTER OF LOVE. "And for this cause God shall send (He still is taking the blame for everything) them strong delusion, that they should believe a lie." 2 Thess, 2;11. This final delusion has two parts: First, it is a lie about God's character. Satan (claiming to be Jesus) tells the multitudes in many different ways that God is a violent God of destruction and no doubt demonstrates it in various ways, using much "magic" and great scientific wonders to convince (deceive) the masses. When they are finally persuaded to believe the lie, that he is Jesus, he then tells them he has changed the day of worship from Saturday to Sunday. This is the final delusion that will take the world and most of the church captive. How terrible! How sad! It will be a long night of weeping for God's people.

QUESTION: I agree that God allows Satan to bring many disasters, but don't you agree that God's angels also destroy on occasion? Isa. 37:36 tells how the Angel of the Lord killed 185,000 Assyrian soldiers in one night.

ANSWER: The "KILLER-GOD" advocates like to use this story as the final and ultimate, conclusive proof that God does indeed destroy, at least through His angels, and at least once in a while (when things get out of hand!). But, here again, if we are merely "surface readers," we will miss the real meaning behind the words. Furthermore, we will be isolating a few sentences out of context, which are not really saying what you think they are saying. The 185,000 died of a plague. See 2 Kings 19:35, margin.

Who destroyed the firstborn? Was that Jesus? Or was it one of His angels? Exodus 12:23 clearly reveals two distinct personalities, and Jesus is not the "DESTROYER," in that verse. The destroying angel of Egypt was a "DESTROYING ANGEL" of Satan, permitted by the Lord. When the angel withdrew, destruction in the form of a plague or sickness of some kind came. God's angel "destroyed" the firstborn by allowing Satan to kill with a plague. Could God have prevented Satan from killing the firstborn? No, He couldn't and be true to His nature and His policy of free will and free choice among His creatures. God can only have the authority to protect us as we yield ourselves to Him and obey, in as far as we understand His commandments. When man refuses God's overtures in his life, as Pharaoh did, the Lord cannot interfere with the ultimate outcome of his choice. All who refused the blood of Jesus in Egypt experienced death in their homes. The same is true all through history and especially today. God can no more interfere with a man's choice than He can lie or steal or kill or break the Sabbath. God is amenable to His own law. He is answerable and legally responsible to the laws He Himself has set in motion. Would you want any other kind of a God to run this universe?

Jesus does not change. He never contradicts Himself. His so-called "changes" are only in response to man's acceptance or rejection of Him. For example, if He had a blessing in store for us, but we disobeyed, and broke fellowship with Him, He would not be able to go ahead and bless us as He had planned. He did change, but because of us. A better word might be ADAPT. He adapted to accommodate us so we would not die. But, throughout history, God's Modus operandi has always been the same, therefore, the way he dealt with Moses and Pharaoh would be the same way He would deal with David. Now, let us notice the "firstborn," scripture again, and compare it with the "NUMBERING," Scripture of David's time. For Jehovah will pass through the land and kill the Egyptians; but when he sees the blood upon the panel at the top of the door and on the two side pieces, He will pass over [THE MARGINAL REFERENCE SAYS: 'HE WILL PAUSE AT THE DOOR OF THAT HOME AND NOT PERMIT THE DESTROYER TO ENTER] that home and not permit the destroyer to enter and kill your first born. Exodus 12:23 LB. The Hebrew word used here for the noun "DESTROYER," is "SHATACH," which means to mar or corrupt and is never an attribute of God in the Bible inherently, but is only, and always an Assigned Attribute. That is, the Bible writers assumed God did what He did not prevent, and the Holy Spirit inspired them to write it this way, so God would remain sovereign.

The Bible makes a clear distinction between Jesus, the SAVIOR and Satan the Destroyer. Notice also, that Moses points out two distinct personalities involved in the death of the first born. Jehovah is the first personality who is preventing the second personality, THE DESTROYER, from entering the houses where the blood is on the door. Do you have the LAMB'S BLOOD

ON YOUR HOUSE? ON YOUR FAMILY? ON YOURSELF?

MANY TIMES GOD IS BLAMED FOR CAUSING THINGS WHEN HE ONLY PERMITS THEM. IN THE ANCIENT HEBREW LANGUAGE OF THE OLD TESTAMENT, THERE WERE NO CAUSATIVE VERBS. CONSEQUENTLY, THE TRANSLATION FROM HEBREW TO GREEK, AND THEN FROM GREEK TO ENGLISH SUBTLY CHANGED THE MEANING OF THE PASSAGE. AND IN THAT TRANSLATION (or transition) THINGS THAT WERE PERMITTED BY GOD CAME OUT AS BEING CAUSED BY GOD. GOD DIDN'T HARDEN PHARAOH'S HEART, HE ALLOWED PHARAOH TO HARDEN HIS OWN HEART. HE GAVE PHARAOH A SITUATION WHERE HE COULD HARDEN HIS (OWN) HEART.

Now, in the case of David numbering Israel, I Chron. 21:1, says, "Then Satan stood up against Israel, and provoked David to number Israel." BUT LET US COMPARE 2 Sam. 24:1, which says, "AND AGAIN THE ANGER OF THE LORD WAS KINDLED AGAINST THEM TO SAY, 'Go, number Israel and Judah.'" So, we see here again God giving little clues for those who really want to know what He is like. Only those who truly want to know the truth that God does not destroy will see and understand these truths. Jesus said, in connection with the future destruction of cities which had rejected Him, "But I say unto you, that it shall be more tolerable for the land of Sodom, in the day of judgment (decision), than for thee." Matt. 11:22. (Now notice how the next verse ties in.) At that time Jesus answered and said, I thank thee, O Father, Lord of heaven and earth, because thou hast hid these things from the wise and prudent, and hast revealed them unto babes. Even so, Father: for so it seemed good in thy sight. All things are delivered unto me of my Father: and no man knoweth the Son, but the Father; neither knoweth any man the Father, save the Son, and He to whomsoever THE SON WILL REVEAL HIM." Matt. 11:25-

27. Next follows the famous invitation of Matt. 11:28-30. So, we see that only as we "COME UNTO JESUS," will we truly understand the Father.

Because of His sin, David, had to choose which punishment Israel would receive. He wisely asked God to choose for him, and the Bible says, So, the Lord sent a pestilence upon Israel. 2 Sam. 24:14, 15. But which "Lord" sent this plague? We know the true Lord does not send disease and sickness. This plague caused the death of 70,000 men, and perhaps others beside, for the word men is used here, due to the fact that women were not often counted in those days. Next we see how God pictures his authority over all the events of planet earth. I Chron. 21:16. And David lifted up his eyes, and saw the angel of the Lord stand between the earth and the heaven, having a drawn sword in his hand stretched out over Jerusalem. This also happened to Balaam in Numbers 22:22-35. This clearly shows that God has the power to permit destruction, as in David's case, or to prevent it, in Balaam's case. The same experience happened to Moses on his way from Midian to Egypt, because of his neglect to circumcise his son. The Bible in Exodus 4:24-26, states that God appeared to Moses, as if He (God) were going to kill him. Moses' wife, Zipporah, "took a flint knife, and cut off the foreskin of her young son's penis and threw it against Moses' feet, remarking disgustedly, 'what a blood-smeared husband you've turned out to be.' Then God let him alone." Exodus 4:24-26, LB. Circumcision was the sign of allegiance Jehovah had given to Abraham.* Evidently, Moses had put off or neglected circumcising his child due to his wife's resistance and protests. Moses' life would constantly be in danger while he was in Egypt. God could protect him only if he fulfilled all of his known duties, for the Bible tells us that "the angel of the Lord encamps around those that fear him." Psalm 34:7. And James says that "to him that knoweth to do good (God's will) and doeth it not, to him it is sin." James 1:17. Therefore, Moses' sin was a sin of omission. Satan knew that Moses had failed to obey this law, which was a token of his allegiance to Jehovah.

Therefore, Satan, the original legalist, had a "legal right" to kill him, which he tried to do, but God intervened and saved Moses' life. But the Hebrew writer penned the incident as if God was the one who tried to kill Moses when it was really Satan, for God always took the blame for what Satan did, in the Old Testament especially. Moses' wife thought it was the true Lord who was trying to kill him and immediately obeyed the letter of the law by circumcising her child. At that point, Satan no longer had a legal right to put Moses to death. He had no case against him, and was obliged to let him go. This is another classic example where God is held responsible for what He permitted but was not actually doing.

QUESTION: But, why should God have to be bound by or amenable to His own law and keep His own commandments? He is the Creator and is above and apart from His own law, isn't He? He can do whatever He wants, can't He? He doesn't have to keep His own law if He doesn't want to, does He? Of course, I know He expects us to, or He will destroy us. Please answer my questions. I am somewhat confused.

ANSWER: First of all, because God's law or commandments are a transcript or reflection of His character, which is His glory. He could no more break His own law than He could change His law or character.

Furthermore, this is precisely what Lucifer originally charged. He accused God of asking the angels to do what He Himself was not willing to do. Jesus Christ came to this dark earth to disprove these charges. He kept His own law, showing that God is not above it or apart from it, but that He and the law are inseparable. Then said I, [Jesus] Lo, I come: in the volume of the book it is written of me. I delight to do Thy will, O My God: yea, thy law is within my heart." Psalm 40:7, 9. This proves God, through His son, obeys the law, just as He asks us to do. There is no hypocrisy here. Satan said God was selfish, and arbitrary, and would never forgive anyone who broke His law. He said that God would vindictively kill and destroy any person or angel who broke the law. Has God ever killed any angel? Of course not. Not one single evil angel has ever even been threatened, let alone hurt or killed. The demons of Satan have been brain washed to believe that God is going to kill them. Notice what the demons said to Jesus: "Let us alone; what have we to do with thee, thou Jesus of Nazareth? Art thou come to destroy us? I know thee who thou art, the Holy One of God." Mark 1:24. It is truly amazing that the demons acknowledged Jesus as the Son of God, but the Jews rejected Him. Jesus came and showed us the true nature of His Father's law and of the Father Himself. Praise God!

QUESTION: If God does not bring sickness and disease, how did Moses get leprosy on his hand when he placed it inside his robe or cloak, next to his chest?

ANSWER: This is a very good question, for it answers several matters at once. This miracle or wonder was given Moses to show him and the elders of Israel, as well as Pharaoh, that God was superior to all their gods (demons) and He had control over or power over all sickness and disease. We know that Satan is responsible for starting sickness and disease and for spreading it. Acts 10:38. But he is on a dead end street, for although he is perverting his God-given powers to hurt and destroy, he has no power to create life. He can't bring back to life all the people he has killed. He cannot create new tissue in a person who has his hands and feet eaten away with a cancer or with leprosy. He has no power to reverse what he has done and restore mankind. He can change matter from form A to form B, paper to ashes, but he cannot change the ashes back into paper. Only God can do that. He cannot give life, nor sustain it. It is true that he can remove, to a great extent, evidently, a disease he himself has caused, as far as sickness is concerned. He does this to deceive, however, not to help anyone. His only purpose is to obtain a stronger hold on a person's life, so he can cause them more misery and draw their friends and loved ones into his trap.

And so it is, that only the Creator can control everything. In this way God can claim to be able to "bring" or "send," sickness, disease and calamity by simply withdrawing the restraints He constantly maintains against evil in its ongoing progression to final destruction. If God, in His great mercy, had not resisted and restrained evil, Satan and his angels, along with all of mankind would long ago have destroyed themselves. This will finally be demonstrated after the 1,000 years, when God lets them alone completely.

QUESTION: Do you think some of the plagues in Egypt were caused in this way?

ANSWER: I answered this question in part, but I will elucidate some more here. It is very possible that this would explain how even Satan was seemingly baffled by the plagues or "miracles of Moses." However, we cannot be sure about this, as Satan is a wily foe. He would gladly have destroyed all of Egypt, if God permitted him to do so, with the knowledge he had thus far attained and was using to destroy throughout the earth, in as far, as God was permitting him to destroy. Thus, he would be able to perpetuate his claim that God is a killer. Of course, Satan, the deceiver, has been, and still is, to a great extent, able to make it look like God is doing it. How he does this, we do not know. Until the death of Christ, even Holy Angels, did not fully understand his true character and nature. See Psalm 78:41-51.

And so, the magicians were not able to duplicate the plagues, after the third one. Either God would not allow Satan to duplicate them or Satan was unable to do so. Or, Satan wanted to make it look like he could not do it, so as to put all the blame on God. It is not clear, but very complex, and not really possible to analyze as well as we would like. Donald Patton, believes that the plagues were caused by an astral catastrophe. He says earth's atmosphere was bombarded by cosmic dust and debris from a passing planet. This might account for the waters turning red, due to some cosmic-like dust particles colored red. He and Velikosvky try to show from history that Egypt was only one of the nations hit by this disaster. They say this and other catastrophes related to this, threw the ecological balance out of whack and each plague followed. If this is true, then it could be part of the explanation. If so, it just means God knew beforehand the precise second each particle of dust and debris would enter the atmosphere and controlled and regulated each plague, so as to save Egypt from the worst effects of it. This demonstrated His power over all the aberrations of nature, which Satan caused by his original sin, as well as, by his present ongoing power to manipulate nature against us. The more Satan can cause mankind to reject God, the more authority he has to destroy, as God is forced to withdraw His power to restrain and protect those who have broken the law and despised HIS EVERLASTING COVENANT. It is possible the water turned into a blood-like substance, and that Satan did it both times. Exodus 7:17,22; Psalm 78:44.

QUESTION: Why hasn't God made the issues clearer so we can understand everything better? Why is it all so mysterious and complicated?

ANSWER: We must remember that God's program has been a progressive one. Each generation has revealed more of the character of God, as well as, the character of Satan. In the OT it was "God for His people." When Jesus came, it was "God with us," and since the cross, it has been, "God in His people." Christ has come closer and closer to us in each succeeding age, until now He can fully possess us, (get married to us) if we let Him. God permitted the race to become weaker so we would sense our need of Him more. The issues are becoming crystal clear in this last hour of earth's history; No one need be deceived. Remember also that man's mind is carnal. Jer 17:9,

Rom. 3:10, I Cor. 2:9-15.

QUESTION: If God is always loving and kind, why did He put a mark on Cain? Wasn't that unfair?

ANSWER: The mark on Cain was for Cain's protection, not to hurt him. Gen. 4:9-15. Notice, that Cain is blaming God for what He brought upon himself. This has always been the way Satan and all of mankind has operated, yet God still loves us and helps us. He never gives up, but always takes the blame for us. Cain's mark could have been the "guilty look," on his face since he would not repent. He truly was a man marked with "regret, hatred, remorse and every evil trait."

QUESTION: Why does God say He has "reserved" the evil angels "in everlasting chains under darkness unto the judgment day?" Jude 6.

ANSWER: It simply means that God has never revealed the full enormity of their guilt to the evil angels, so as to not interfere with their free choice. And also to keep them from destroying each other as they will finally do, Dan. 2:44, 45. And even in the final day, the full revelation is done in love to bring them to repentance and restoration, which will finally be achieved.

Remember that the day of judgment is the final day of decision. When God gives the panoramic view in the final day (after the 1,000 years) as the hosts of Satan come against the city to destroy God and His people, every evil man and woman, and every evil angel will finally see the whole truth they refused to acknowledge before. This will cause a terrible burning inside of them as they are forced to face the straight truth. They are bound by the chains of their own hatred and deceit, which Satan has led them to. (Prov. 5:22; Ps. 7:16; Ps 149:79) They still believe the original lie told by Satan, "God is selfish. "God will kill you. You better not trust Him, or He will destroy you. No one can keep His law anyway. He just made that up to keep us under his control and have an excuse to kill us when we break it." These lies will be allowed to be unmasked and proved false. The suffering will be the most painful and intense ever experienced up to that time but that is what it will take to bring the wicked to total repentance and restoration.

QUESTION: You say that God is always the same and never changes. I agree with that, in part, but I don't agree that God doesn't get angry, because He says, "you must not exploit widows or orphans; if you do so in any way, and they cry to me for my help, I will surely give it, and my anger shall flame out against you, and I will kill you with enemy armies, so that your wives will be widows and your children fatherless." Exodus 22:22-24 LB. We also know that Moses became angry once on Mt. Sinai and was excused and that Jesus got angry at least twice in the NT. Once in Mark 3:5 and later when He drove out the money changers, on two occasions. How can you explain that?

ANSWER: Your misunderstanding of these Scriptures and incidents stem from the fact that you do not understand the "ANGER" OR "WRATH" of God. Psalm 78:49 is the key text on this, as well as Rom. 5:9 and other Scriptures which explain God's wrath, such as Romans 1:18, 24, 26. God's anger or wrath is simply when He can no longer legitimately or lawfully protect the sinner from the destructive power of sin and Satan and the evil angels who are always lurking by eager to destroy the minute God gives them a chance. Now, in the case of Christ in the temple, we know that He never touched anyone with that whip of cords He made. This was only symbolic of His authority over the situation and over all mankind. It was a parallel to the sword He held over Jerusalem in David's day. It represented His right to act as God, for He was and is God. He did not cast the people out, but commanded that their animals and money (ill-gained) be taken out. They loved the money more than Him and so they went with the $$$$. He actually said, "TAKE THESE THINGS HENCE." John 2:16. Psalm 5:4; Jer. 7:11,

John 10:1, 10. It was a conviction of their sins that made them leave, but "The blind and the lame came to him in the Temple; and he healed them." Matt. 21:14. Don't you imagine some of the moneychangers needed some physical, as well as spiritual healing too? But, their pride and unbelief kept them away. Compare Hosea 11:4, Eccles. 4:11, 12. Cords represent His "binding" love. See also Psalm 2:1-3.

Now, let's read Mark 3:5. "And when he had looked round about on them with anger, being grieved for the hardness [blindness or stubbornness of their hearts] He saith unto the man, 'stretch forth thine hand.' And he stretched it out: and his hand was restored whole as the other." I think we have some real insight into the true meaning of Christ's anger in the whole Bible here. His anger is equated with grief. If anger in the OT means God's withdrawing, so Satan can fill the vacuum (or the results of sin taking over), and thus destruction come, it would mean the same thing in the NT, for Jesus has never changed. Hebrews 13:8. In each instance, it would mean "Divine Grief." Jesus was not mad or angry. He was hurt. He was grieved. Christ showed in His face a look of sorrow, hurt and disappointment, which comes over from the Greek, as anger, but is actually grief, and desire and deep emotion and longing. "Oh, if you could only understand what I am trying to do here and how much I love you." It probably was similar to the look Christ gave Judas in the garden when Judas betrayed Him with a kiss. Later, He gave Peter the same kind of look. Judas hanged himself and Peter repented.

It actually is a key to the "divine heartache," which Jesus, His Father, and all the angels have been suffering, since the controversy began. It tells me God can be hurt and that we should always be careful not to add to His grief by willful disobedience. In all we do and say, we should be sure that we are pleasing Him and not wounding Him, crucifying Him afresh by our sinful attitudes of pride or envy or malice or any such thing. The Greek word in this case is Orge {Or-gay}, and means to stretch oneself out to another or reach out after, long for or after, to covet after or desire. It comes from the Greek word Oregomai. The verb form means "desire," as a person reaching forth to another person to help them. It also means an excitement of the mind, which could be indicative of tremendous passion or love. i.e. violent passion which is justifiable and synonymous with "anger, indignation, vengeance, wrath." AMAZING!!! AMAZING LOVE!! See Strong's concordance, Greek Section in back, page 52, Ref. 3709.

QUESTION: Who struck Zacharias dumb? Luke 1:11-22,64?

ANSWER; The power to speak is a gift from God, as is all of life. Zacharias' lack of faith was sin, "FOR WHATSOEVER IS NOT OF FAITH IS SIN." Rom. 14;23. Unbelief kept Israel out of Canaan land for nearly 40 years, Heb. 3;19. The wages of sin is death - Rom. 6:23. But Jesus took that penalty upon Himself. He took the blame. Because of that, Zacharias was not struck dead, but as in Numbers 12, Miriam received leprosy, because of her sin of murmuring against Moses. God did not bring the leprosy, and God did not strike Zacharias dumb. He simply withdrew his power and Zacharias could not speak. Sometimes Jesus spoke to or commanded the spirits to depart from people. When God withdraws His power, this is Satan's opportunity. In Mark 9:25 Jesus commanded a deaf and dumb spirit (angel of Satan or demon) to "come out of him, and enter no more into him." Since Satan is the cause of all sickness and disease and all malfunctions of the body, we can safely assume he is behind people who are deaf and dumb from birth or from any other cause. When Nebuchadnezzar lost his power to reason (Dan. 4) and ate grass for seven years, that was Satan's work. He lost his power to think correctly because of pride and unbelief. Zacharias' problem was not as severe, but from the same source. Zacharias was filled with fear due to his unbelief. The spirit of fear comes from Satan. Luke 1:12, 2 Tim. 1:7.

QUESTION: Pastor Clute, I believe what you teach about God's character, that He is not a killer or destroyer. But how do you explain some of the verses in the Bible, the Old Testament especially, which plainly state that God kills? For example, Deuteronomy 32:39: "See now that I, even I, am he, and there is no god with me: I kill, and I make alive; I wound, and I heal: neither is there any that can deliver out of my hand." And also this one: "The Lord kills and makes alive: he brings down to the grave, and brings up. The Lord makes poor, and makes rich: he brings low and lifts up." I Sam 2:6. "Blessed be the Lord my strength, which teaches my hands to war, and my fingers to fight:" Ps 144:1.

ANSWER: First of all let's find out who is speaking here. In the first text it is Moses. "And Moses spake in the ears of all the congregation of Israel the words of this song, until they were ended." Deut. 31:30. And then the entire 32nd chapter of Deut. follows, including this text in which he states his belief and opinion that it is God who kills and makes alive. Did Moses understand God's character? No, he did not. This is very clear by the following statement he and Aaron made to Pharaoh: "And they said, The God of the Hebrews has met with us: let us go, we pray thee, three days' journey into the desert, and sacrifice unto the Lord our God; lest he fall upon us with pestilence, or with the sword." A modern version says: "Lest He strike us with either disease or death." Exodus 5:3. We have already learned in this book that even the angels did not fully understand the issues of the Great Controversy clearly until the death of Jesus. So, knowledge and understanding is progressive. That is why we call it "progressive revelation." Now in the second text from I Sam 2:6 we find that it is Hannah who is the author of these words in her prayer of thanks to God for giving her the baby Samuel. Once again, this was her understanding of God in that era of history, that God kills. In my reading of the bible I have found only two texts in the Old Testament which reveal God does not destroy and both of them are in the last part of the Old

Testament Canon. Here they are: "I will not return to destroy Ephraim: for I am God, and not man; the Holy One in the midst of thee." Hosea 11:9. 740 BC. And then in 397 BC we read in Malachi 3:6: "For I am the Lord, I change not; therefore ye sons of Jacob are not consumed."

Let us read this with clarity of mind. God is telling the men of Judah the reason that they were still alive is because He is not a destroyer, and that He never changes. Amen to that. And then in the same chapter we read this verse in which the Lord reveals that the one who does destroy is another entity. "And I will rebuke the devourer for your sakes, and he shall not destroy the fruits of your ground:" Malachi 3:11.

QUESTION: Pastor Mike: You state that there are two Lords in the Old Testament, the true and the false. Why then is it so hard to understand this topic?

ANSWER: This is a very good question. One of the main reasons is that the title Satan appears in only four occasions throughout the entire Old Testament. This should stimulate more interest and investigation into this topic. I Chron 21:1; Job 1 & 2; Psalm 109:6; Zechariah 3:1. Early in my writing career on this topic of the character of God, beginning in April & May of 1977, I realized that the Lord had done a masterful job of covering up for Satan's activities in the Old Testament by taking the blame or responsibility for all the Devil was doing in his career as the Tempter and Destroyer of planet earth. The book of Job is a perfect example and exhibit A. It is only when we come to the New Testament, especially the life of Jesus, and later the writings of the converted Saul of Tarsus, aka, Paul, that we see Lucifer exposed for the evil, fallen angel that he actually is.

John 8:44 is the classic text most theologians use. "You are of your father the devil... (Christ said to the Jews) ...he was a liar and a murderer from the beginning." John 8:44. Wow! Nothing like that was ever stated in the OT...but it was hinted at in Job and also in Isa. 14, for example, and Ezekiel 28....but usually in, shall we say, somewhat of a hidden and mystical type of Hebrew symbolism. But Jesus and Paul came right out in the open and boldly pointed Satan out as the destroyer of all mankind from the beginning.I Cor 5:5; I Cor 7:5; 2 Cor 2:11; 11:14; 12:7; I Thess 2:18; 2 Thess 2:9; I Tim 1:20; I Tim 5:15. Satan is also mentioned in seven texts in Revelation.

In the classic work on the life of Christ, "Desire of Ages," pgs 758 & 759 the author states that it was not until the trial and crucifixion of Jesus Himself that the holy angels came to realize the enormity of Satan's apostasy, fall and evil nature and character. What this tells us then is that from the beginning Lucifer was able to mask and cover up his terrible sins and destructive deeds...making it look like the Creator Himself was doing the destroying, as in the flood, for example and Sodom and Gomorra, the death of Uzzah and even in the NT the death of Annias and Saphira in Acts 5:1-11. To this day most Christians believe that God killed this lying pair in order to scare the young church into honest obedience. But in Acts 10:38 we read that it is Satan who oppresses and makes people sick, etc. But until one studies the Two Lords on level three of the character of God message, you cannot fully understand how Satan has been able to successfully masquerade as an "angel of light." "And no marvel; for Satan himself is transformed into an angel of light." 2 Cor 11:14. So, how can we detect the deceiver in his disguise? Only by a lot of prayer and diligent study and by learning to recognize the true Voice of the Lord in our daily walk. Satan speaks to us all the time, claiming to be the true Lord. And half the time people listen to him and follow his voice, thinking it is the true Lord. Go to my web site and study on the articles on the Impostor God and learn how to tell the difference. Here is the web site: http://godslastcall.org

Here is an e-mail I wrote on March 17 of 2004 in answer to a question a lady had about one of my articles regarding the two Lords in the book of Genesis: Here is the question and my answer follows:

Pastor Clute:

In light of your article about the two Lords in Genesis 1 and 2 how do you explain 2 Corinthians 11:3 and I Tim 2:14 where Paul states that Eve was the one who was deceived by the serpent?

Dear Sister L.

I just rec. your letter this a.m. and will respond briefly. There is a theological assumption, based on 2 Tim 3:16 that "all Scripture" is infallible. But let us check this out. Look at vs 16 and you will see that the verb "is" is indeed a supplied word which changes the meaning of the text when we read it minus the "is"...note: "All scripture given by inspiration of God, and profitable for doctrine, etc."

Therefore, all of the texts, i.e. every single text in the 66 books are not necessarily inspired by our wonderful Creator who is totally holy, harmless and undefiled (Hebrews 7:26) but instead, often by the carnal thoughts of men, such as you can and do find in some passages, such as in the book of Job with Job's "friends" who are spouting off their own ideas and philosophies and Solomon who was very negative in his book, Ecclesiastes, where he says that everything is "vanity" and in "much wisdom is much grief; and he that increases knowledge increases sorrow." That is not correct. Everything is not vanity in this life and the more wisdom and knowledge you can gain the better off you are. He just used his knowledge and wisdom in a selfish manner and it made him very unhappy and a broken man. This is not to say that there is not a lot of good in the three books he wrote, for the book of Proverbs and Song of Solomon are full of God's wisdom. However, what I do believe is that the life of Christ is our bench mark and everything must be measured against that. Even some of the Psalms are very violent in their words and suggestions re: God being a destroyer and a killer. Here is one example: "The righteous shall rejoice when he sees the vengeance: he shall wash his feet in the blood of the wicked." Psalm 58:10. "Arise, O Lord; save me, O my God: for thou hast smitten all mine enemies upon the cheek bone; thou hast broken the teeth of the ungodly." Psalm 3:7. And this one: "Happy shall he be, that taketh and dasheth thy little ones against the stones." Psalm 137:9. See also Psalm 68:23. "That thy foot may be dipped in the blood of thine enemies..." Obviously, these Psalms do not represent the mind and character of Christ we see portrayed in the New Testament. Thankfully, most of the David's Psalms are filled with hope and inspiration. What we must have is the Spirit of discernment as we read the Word of God in these last days as we are striving to understand and form the character of God in our lives so we can survive the final days of this age.

This is especially true in regard to all of the killings of the OT, supposedly commanded by God Himself, which we know is completely out of harmony with the Divine Character our Beloved Redeemer revealed in His life. Even Mel Gibson's film reveals Jesus never hurt or killed anyone...never spoke a harsh word or retaliated against anyone at any time.

So, to assume and believe that the Apostle Paul had the final and last word on God's holy character, when he Himself was a very legalistic Pharisee at one time and killed many people, etc. and declared before He died (and after he wrote all of his works) that he had not yet reached perfection; To assume that every word Paul wrote is infallible is assuming too much. The only words that are infallible are those of Jesus Himself, the perfect Son of God, and what we read in the NT re: what He told Nicodemus about Himself and the serpent. John 3:14-16. This is a very important key to unlocking the mystery of the serpent. Also check out Numbers 21:9 where the Lord told Moses to put the serpent on the pole and when they looked they were healed. Why would God use the serpent as an instrument of healing if it was indeed a symbol of Satan? And why would our precious Lord even refer to it as such Himself, comparing it to Himself in His coming sacrifice on the tree? These are compelling arguments which have convinced me. If you would like to receive a free gift package send me your snail mail address and I will send you some back issues of my paper with two books I just republished. May the Lord bless and keep you is my sincere prayer for you. Your friend always in the Lord Jesus. Pastor Mike Clute.

QUESTION: Why did Jesus give His disciples fish? In John 21 we read that Jesus cooked some fish for His disciples on the sea of Galillee. How do you explain this?

ANSWER: Christ in both the O.T. and N.T. always met the people at the point of their needs. Fish was a major staple of the people's diet and was one of the clean foods allowed by the Law of Moses in Lev. 11. In this last age, when sickness and disease is rampant upon both man and beast, it is no longer safe to eat flesh food. There is an abundant testimony and evidence to prove the validity of this position. Mad cow disease is but one example.

*See Additional Note #32 on page 551: ***"How and when did the rite of circumcision begin?"***

CHAPTER 30

ADDITIONAL NOTES

#l-Just as Christ was not appreciated by the Jews in their day, because He had no "form nor comeliness; and when we shall see him, there is no beauty that we should desire him." Isa; 53:2. So, today, our wonderful heavenly Father is not valued or appreciated in the character message, for we do not go deep enough. The sanctuary had many colors, such as blue, purple, scarlet and white and silver and gold. But, the covering of the sanctuary itself was of badger's skins, which was not an attractive color, a dark, close to black color. So one had to go into the sanctuary itself, to appreciate its beauty and understand its meaning. David wrote: "Until I went into the sanctuary of God; then understood I their [the wicked] end." Ps. 73:17.

So it is with the Father. Until you see inside of His heart and know His real character, you cannot understand how He will finally deal with sin and sinners in the end time. When the wicked see the beauty and holiness and love and purity of Christ and the Father at the end of the world, in the final judgement after the millennium, it will be such a "burning" revelation to them that they will not be able to resist His love. The Bible tells us that "Every knee shall bow and every tongue confess." Phil. 2:10, 11. Let us go into the sanctuary today and learn the truth about God and receive His character now, so we may dwell with the devouring fire ...and with everlasting burnings ...thine eyes shall see the king in his beauty [and live, not die, if you are like Him]. Isaiah 33:14,17.

#2- The cleansing or justifying of the sanctuary in heaven is symbolic of the cleansing and sanctifying experience in the believer here below in this age. We will not be lost in this age, because we have sins on the books in heaven. We will be lost because there is still sin in our hearts. It is only on the books because it is in the heart, in the mind of believer who has refused

God's salvation. But each of us may be cleansed today. Even now, through the blood of Jesus, we can be made whole. As the "abomination that maketh desolate" moves forward in our midst, let us stand firm "in the (most) holy place." Matt. 24:15. A fuller understanding of the sanctuary message is necessary for us to become like Jesus and stand through the last days of this eon or age before Jesus comes and the 1,000 years begins. It has everything to do with understanding the character of God. The final atonement and perfection of the believer is being debated today, but not experienced. The Lord will demonstrate His perfection of character in each believer who submits to His love. The sanctuary message proves God does not destroy, but gives life. Life from above: from the sanctuary, where Jesus intercedes for us. Even the scapegoat going into the wilderness to die "alone" shows that God does not kill Satan. The sins that are laid upon him separate him from the life giver. It is his own sins that unfit him to be restored in this age. But the great "Age of the Ages" is coming, after the 1,000 years, when he will be fully converted and restored to the Father's throne. That is an important and vital meaning of the symbolism of the scapegoat.

#3-Luke 11:52 is a woe upon the legal experts of the gospel. The "lawyers" of the gospel are forever arguing and explaining, but never teaching the Truth; which is Jesus: Because, THE TRUTH is not a set of beliefs or doctrines or rules and regulations, but the TRUTH IS JESUS CHRIST. While the ministers are debating, the people are perishing. Jesus said, "WOE UNTO YOU, LAWYERS for ye have taken away THE KEY [JESUS] of knowledge: ye entered not in yourselves, and them that were entering in ye hindered." The final message and its preachers will be opposed mainly by those who profess to know the law, but do not know Jesus. They will be our worst persecutors.

#4-Luke 12:10-The reason the Holy Spirit does not forgive when it is sinned against is because the person will not ask to be forgiven. This simply means that once a person shuts out the voice of God from his or her mind for the last time, there is no more help or hope. Here again God takes the blame and says "I left you. I rejected you. I won't help you anymore, for you have rejected my Spirit. Now you have had it." That is the way some people interpret it, but that is not the way it is. Unless you are really wanting to know what God is like, you will not find Him. You must "search for Him with all your heart." Jer. 29:13.

#5-In Ex. 28:39-43, we see God's specific instruction regarding the garments the priests should wear as they go into the sanctuary. Their naked bodies were to be covered. If they did not carefully obey, they could die. Would God destroy them or Satan? If the latter, it only proves that Satan was in the sanctuary at all times waiting for a slip-up so he could accuse them and receive permission (as he did with Nadab and Abihu) to destroy them. It only proves the Divine protection of the Law of God and how important it is to obey it in letter, as well as in Spirit.

#6- The curse of God is simply the absence of His Holy Spirit in the life. It is refusing to let God direct your life so you will receive His blessings instead of the devil's curses. Proverbs 5-6 are two chapters young men should read carefully. They speak of the results of unfaithfulness.

Today, it could also apply to young women who get involved with other women, as well as men, so it is for both sexes. See Romans 1:18-28. But in Proverbs 5:11, we read of one of the results of sexual waywardness (promiscuity or licentiousness). "Lest afterwards you groan in anguish and in shame, when syphilis [literally disease] consumes your body." The word consume does not necessarily mean to "burn up" with literal fire, but also has the meaning of disease. Take for example, this verse: "Before Him (Jesus at His coming) went the pestilence, and burning coals (or diseases)* went forth at His feet." Habakkuk 3:5. *Marginal reading.

#7-The "DAY OF VENGEANCE," is when God permits the accounts to be settled. Every man's sword will be raised against his neighbor, and God can no longer protect or restrain. In Solomon's writings again, he warns men against going out with another man's wife, as the man will get even at all costs. For "JEALOUSY IS THE RAGE OF A MAN: (whose wife has been stolen or slept with) THEREFORE HE WILL NOT SPARE IN THE DAY OF VENGEANCE." Proverbs 6:34.

#8-On Zechariah 14:12 we have additional information regarding the plague which will destroy the people who gather themselves to fight against Jerusalem (God's People) in this age. "Their flesh shall consume away while they stand upon their feet, and their eyes shall consume away in their holes, and their tongue shall consume away in their mouth." KJV. The next verse says, "THEY WILL BE SEIZED WITH TERROR, PANIC-STRICKEN FROM THE LORD [notice how God gets the blame here], and will FIGHT AGAINST EACH OTHER IN HAND-TO-HAND COMBAT." v. 13. NOW IN THIS SAME CONNECTION, NOTICE THIS EXCERPT FROM THE BOOK, "THE ATOM SPEAKS," which is out of print now, as far as I know, but the author quotes from a John Hershey's work called "HIROSHIMA." Here is the account of what people looked like after the atom bomb went off in this Japanese city in 1945. "Mr. Tanimoto found about twenty men and women on the sands pit ...they were too weak to lift themselves (into his boat). He reached down and took a woman by the hand, but her skin slipped off in huge, glove-like pieces: He was so sickened by this that he had to sit down for a moment. Then he got out into the water and, though a small man, lifted several of the men and women, who were naked, into his boat. Their backs and breasts were clammy, and he remembered uneasily what the great burns he had seen during the day had been like: yellow at first, then red and swollen, with the skin sloughed off, and finally, in the evening, suppurated (cracked and oozing pus) and smelly. With the tide risen, his bamboo pole was now too short and he had to paddle most of the way across with it. On the other side, at a higher spot, he lifted the slimy living bodies out and carried them up the slope away from the tide. He had to keep consciously repeating to himself 'these are human beings.' It took him three trips to get them all across the river. When he had finished, he decided he had to have a rest, and he went back to the park. When he had penetrated the bushes, he saw there were about twenty men, and they were all in exactly the same nightmarish state: their faces were wholly burned, their eye sockets were hollow, the fluid from their MELTED EYES HAD RUN DOWN THEIR CHEEKS. (They must have had their faces upturned when the bomb went off. Perhaps they were anti-aircraft personnel). Their mouths were a mere swollen, pus-covered wound, which they could not bear to stretch enough to admit the spout of the teapot. So Father Kleinsorge got a large piece of grass and drew out the stem so as to make a straw, and gave them all water to drink that way. One of them said, 'I cannot see anything.' Father Kleinsorge answered, as cheerfully as he could, 'there's a doctor at the entrance to the park. He's busy now, but he'll come soon and fix your eyes, I hope.'"See also Joel 2:30 for a reference to the atom bomb in end times.

#9-Read through I Kings 22 carefully and you will see how God deals with the angels: He lets them have a part in his "JUDGMENTS," or His decisions. See verses 19-23. These angels who withdrew from Ahab so he would be deceived by the false prophets of Baal are called "lying Spirits," but we know God's angels do not lie. Neither do they steal or kill. They obey God's laws. Ps. 103:20. Notice also, that Ahab was given about 3 to 31/2 years to repent after chapter 21, where it is recorded how he stole Naboth's vineyard and had him killed through the treachery of his wife, queen Jezebel. There is your state power: Ahab, the king, letting the church (woman or Jezebel, false religious system or Baal worship or Beast system, Rev. 17, 18) carry out its murders with the states approval. It ends in death for both the church and the state. But, God did not kill Ahab. He was destroyed, as was Jezebel, by their own people who turned against them. God's angels withdrew their protection, and allowed the "lying spirits," of Satan to move in and deceive Ahab and thus lead him on to destruction. In other places they are referred to as "destroying" angels. Psalm 78:49. By withdrawing, as they did in Micaiah's day. Study the parallels in the life of Jesus, regarding the 3 1/2 year periods, and in the book of Revelation re: the time of His return. God will reveal to you what He wants you to know, if you seek Him in humbleness and contriteness of heart. See I Thess. 5: 1-6. Although we will not know the exact time of Jesus' return, we can know the season, just as Jesus knew when His ministry was to begin when He learned that John the Baptist was preaching at the Jordan river. The Father will announce the day and hour of His son's return. Matt. 24:36.

10-Notice some additional places and situations in which God takes the blame. Ezekiel 14:9-God says He deceives false prophets and then destroys them just as in case of the 450 prophets of Baal on Mt. Carmel with Elijah. Ezekiel 20:25 tells us God gives people "bad" or "not good" judgments and statutes. What it means is that whatever God allows or permits the people to have, because they demanded it, the Lord says that He gave it to them. He is accepting the responsibility for letting them have what they demanded. i.e. divorce laws; laws for making war; laws for having a king, laws for eating flesh food. He gave them a "bad" king-Saul, but actually it was a man "after their own heart." David, however, was a man after God's own heart. Ezekiel 5:13 shows Jesus' love. "Mine anger (withdrawing) shall be accomplished, and I will cause my fury to rest upon them, and I will be comforted: and they shall know that I the Lord have spoken it in my zeal, ..." In His zeal to save them and show them His matchless love. Haggai 2:22 shows how God destroys by permitting people to kill each other, Cf. Jer. 25:31-33. In the book of Zephaniah, even though the Lord is warning the people that He is the one who is killing them, He also tells the "meek" to seek Him, so they might be hid in the day of the "Lord's anger." Zeph. 2:3. And in Nahum 1:1-3 God tells us about His "burden," for Nineveh. Just think of it. God had a burden for a great city. Strong's 4853. The Hebrew word is "Massa." It means to have a desire. Do you have a desire for any cities? A desire for them to know God and His salvation? Do you

desire for them to have a better way of life and to be saved when Jesus comes again? The Bible tells us that God is "jealous, and the Lord revengeth;" He is also "furious." Oh, friend, can you see how God hides His true character in all of these adjectives which describe what He permits and takes the blame for, in order to shield us, as well as Satan and the evil angels? Can't you see that? "THE LORD IS SLOW TO ANGER, AND GREAT IN POWER, AND WILL NOT AT ALL ACQUIT THE WICKED: THE LORD HATH HIS WAY IN THE WHIRL WIND AND IN THE STORM, AND THE CLOUDS ARE THE DUST OF HIS FEET." Nahum 1:3. Through it all, God works out His will. He knows all things ahead of time—Isaiah 46:9, 10. Nothing takes Him by surprise. Everything that happens is not God's will, but nothing can happen to defeat His will. He has His own way in the end, the way He planned it from the beginning, by absorbing all of our sorrow and pain on the cross. He never interferes with anyone's free moral agency or choice, and yet He always does everything just right and perfect. And someday all will bow down and admit He was absolutely right in the way He did it. See Phil. 2:10 and Rev. 15 and 16. Do you realize that everything is happening just as it should? And that at any given time in the history of the universe, everything is happening just as it should? In the final analysis this will be understood perfectly, Jer. 23:20, Gen. 49:1. ISN'T JESUS WONDERFUL!!

#ll-The Jews multiplied animal sacrifices, instead of humbling their hearts in repentance for their sins. A great system was developed over the centuries and became a most lucrative business for the Jewish hierarchy. The Pharisees feared Christianity would do away with this system. So, it is today. Many leaders fight the truth about God's love, for the people would become revived and give Jesus their time and talents in service to Him for humanity, in ways the church leadership does not approve of, (such as going out on your own as a radio preacher, or a lay-worker evangelist, etc.) In order to make money off of the people, the leadership in times past, as well as today, must make up hundreds of rules, regulations and policies, which do not lead us to love and adore our Creator, but maintain our loyalty and allegiance to the organization. Sin is not rebuked from the pulpit, but the people are many times led to believe that God will be pleased with them if they give large donations. The impression is left that this will make up for the lack of personal labor for souls, and strict obedience to the law of God. Thus man again has a vast monetary system built on the guilt and disobedience of the people.

#12-How does God make war? Rev. 19:11, 15, shows that God makes war with His Word, which comes out of His "mouth," which is His Holy Word. Beloved, there is a spiritual warfare we must fight in this life if we are to overcome and receive the character of Christ. Listen to this excellent quotation, from one who knew the SAVIOR intimately, as to how Christ's beautiful character was formed while on earth. "We are forming characters for heaven. No character can be complete without trial and suffering. We must be tested, we must be tried. Christ bore the test of character in our behalf that we might bear this test in our own behalf through the divine strength He has brought to us. Christ is our example in patience, in forbearance, in meekness and lowliness of mind. He was at variance and at war with the whole ungodly world, yet He did not give way to passion and violence manifested in words and actions, although receiving shameful abuse in return for good works. He was afflicted, He was rejected and despitefully treated, yet He retaliated not. He possessed self-control, dignity, and majesty. He suffered with calmness and for abuse gave only compassion, pity and love. Imitate your Redeemer in these things. Do not get excited when things go wrong. Do not let self arise, and lose your self-control because you fancy things are not as they should be. Because others are wrong is no excuse for you to do wrong. Two wrongs will not make one right. You have victories to gain in order to overcome as Christ overcame. Christ never murmured, never uttered discontent, displeasure, or resentment. He was never disheartened, discouraged, ruffled, or fretted. He was patient, calm, and self-possessed under the most exciting and trying circumstances. All His works were performed with a quiet dignity and ease, whatever commotion was around Him. Applause did not elate Him. He feared not the threats of His enemies. He moved amid the world of excitement, of violence and crime, as the sun moves above the clouds. Human passions and commotions and trials were beneath Him. He sailed like the sun above them all. Yet He was not indifferent to the woes of men. His heart was ever touched with the sufferings and necessities of His brethren, as though He Himself was the One afflicted. He had a calm inward joy, a peace which was serene. His will was ever swallowed up in the will of His Father. Not my will but Thine be done, was heard from His pale and quivering lips.

We long and pray that the grace of God may come into your hearts. We want you to make an entire surrender to God...May God help you to walk humbly and carefully is our prayer." Letter 51a, 1874. EGW.

#l3-Jeremiah 23:19, 20, tell us that the "anger" of the Lord will be understood in the last days. The anger of the Lord shall not return, until He has performed the thoughts of his heart: (holy thoughts) in the latter days ye shall consider it perfectly." Jer. 23:20.

#l4-Because of Christ's suffering and death, even those who refuse his salvation are being protected. God's love is unconditional. Because of this, He loves every human being the same whether they believe in Him or not. He therefore has a legal right to make life as painless as possible for each of His creatures and He loves to do it for each of them, hoping that they will eventually repent and accept His salvation. And even if they don't and are lost (for this age) the sufferings He and His Father went through will make their final death less painful. This is part of the mystery of His love which is in keeping with His Eternal plan of the ages.

15-Neither God the Father, nor His Son nor the Holy Spirit have ever once hurt or killed an evil angel, including Satan himself, the chief of the devils. Why then should we blame the

God family for the death of any human beings? Are you willing to indict God for murder on the basis of circumstantial evidence? Satan and his angels are much more guilty than we and therefore, should by all rights be the first to be killed, not us, yet none of them have ever been hurt or killed!

#16-Christ is our "burden-bearer." David tells us, "Cast thy burden upon the Lord, and He shall sustain thee: He shall never suffer the righteous to be moved." Ps. 55:22. And Peter tells us, "Casting all your care upon Him; for He careth for you." I Pet. 5:7. Isaiah says, "Surely He hath borne our griefs, and carried our sorrows:" Isa. 53:4. Jesus rode upon a donkey or ass when He entered Jerusalem, Matt. 21:1-9. If Christ came to reveal the Father, and we are to pray now to the Father, in Jesus' name, then truly it is the Father who bears our burdens in His Son's name. As we think about the symbolism of the donkey or ass, we can see that this donkey fitly represents the Father as our burden-bearer. We might even paraphrase Paul's love chapter thusly; at least verse 7 of I Cor. 13. "The Father beareth all things, hopeth all things, endureth all things." Surely the Father's name has been slandered more than we could ever know. It is said that in the Satanic mass of witchcraft ceremonies that the leader is supposed to lean over and expose his buttocks so the participants might give him what is called the "kiss of shame." There is an expression which is actually dirty American slang or even cussing. It is the expression people use when they become angry at someone and tell them to "kiss my donkey," only they don't say donkey. Do you see, dear heart, how this reflects directly upon the Father's name and character? He is our donkey, our burden-bearer and such an expression is a slander against Him. How very careful we should be not take His name in vain, even to the extent of saying "gosh," or "golly," or "gee-whiz," or "jeez," etc., for all of these are corruptions of God's name and we thus are taking his name and character in vain and breaking the third commandment.

#l7-Kiss the Son, lest He be angry and ye perish from the way, when His wrath is kindled but a little. Blessed are all they that put their trust in Him." Ps. 2:12. This verse sounds like Jesus is going to get mad and kill us if we don't "Kiss" Him. But is this what it means? Of course not, for it would be out of harmony with the Jesus of the New Testament and we know that God never changes, Mal. 3:6 and Heb. 13:18. What the Father is really saying here is, "Come and get married to my Son, Jesus. For if you don't marry Him, He will be forced to give you up to your own thoughts and ways, You will force Him out of your life and break His heart and mine too. Oh, Please don't do this to us and to yourself. You will destroy yourself and perish along the roadside of life all alone and lonely." God's anger and wrath is when He is forced to permit Satan to have an influence and/or an effect upon our minds and bodies which very often leads to sorrow and sickness and death. God does not smite people on the cheek bone or break their teeth, (Psalm 3:7), but He permits Satan to do that and then takes the blame for it. Cyrus "smote" Babylon and yet God called Cyrus His "ANOINTED." See Isa. 45:1.

#18-In Ezek. 9, God is pictured as commanding both the sealing and the slaughter of the people in Jerusalem. Because the good and bad angels both belong to God He can speak as if His "permission" to destroy is a command when in reality they are only being allowed to destroy because God has been forced out of the wicked people's lives. Proverbs 8:8 proves that God cannot speak death. James 1:17. But as usual, He accepts the responsibility for it.

#19-Satan, not God, destroyed the Egyptian army in the Red Sea by bringing "a strong east wind." Exodus 14:21. In Exodus 10:13 Satan brought the plagues of locust with an east wind. Hosea 13:15. We see an "east wind," drying up the spring. In Habakkuk 1:8, 9; the Chaldeans are compared to the "violence" of the "east wind." Rev. 9:3, 7, 11 identify the locusts and their "king." Locusts clearly represent evil angels there. I Kings 19:11 tells us God was not in the violent wind that "rent the mountain." Satan opened up the Red Sea as a trap to destroy Israel when he saw the "pillar of the cloud" protected Israel. But

God used the east wind for a way of escape and let Moses think the wind was a divine act. When Satan saw he could not kill Israel in the sea he began to attack the Egyptians as God had not commanded them to go into the sea. Satan inspired them to go for the wrong reason so he would have a legal right to destroy them.

THE BIG DOUBLE CROSS

Satan is a double crosser. He is a liar, swindler and a deceiver. He breaks his promises and finally destroys all who serve him.

That is precisely what he did to the Egyptian army. The following Scriptures not only reveal his modus operandi but also show God delivers His people. Isa 10:20; Psalm 17:13; Psalm 35:5, 6; Psalm 83:14, 15; Psalm 143:3. God's "destroying wind" is Satan. Psalm 78:26 & Hosea 12:1. Satan knew very well God's power and that he would not be able to stop God's plan to deliver Israel.

"About six hundred thousand on foot that were men, beside children. Exodus12:37. "So were all those that were numbered of the children of Israel...from twenty years old and upward...Even all they that were numbered were six hundred thousand and three thousand and five hundred and fifty." Numbers 1:46; 3:39. The margin says that this would be a population of about 2,450,000. Even if there were only four to a family that would make over 2 million souls. Satan decided that if he could not hurt or kill the Israelites, he would gladly destroy as many Egyptians as possible with the ten plagues. Exodus 12:23 clearly shows that it was the "Destroyer," (Satan), who killed all the first born with plague #10. If he could lead the whole Egyptian army (600 chariots plus horses and men) with murder in their hearts to pursue after Israel, he would have a "legal right" to destroy them. And that is exactly what he did. He knew that if he could entice Pharaoh to pursue Israel, with murder in his heart he would have a legal right to destroy the whole army. See Obadiah 15; Isa 14:17; Jer 6:26, 27; 2:30. Actually, the very day that Pharaoh threatened Moses' with death, Exodus 10:28, Satan had a legal right to kill Pharaoh and all of his people. But the Lord only allowed the first born to die whose parents did not put the blood on the door posts. As soon as Israel left Egypt Satan inspired Pharaoh to chase after him to either re-capture and/or kill as many of them who resisted. But the Lord opened up the Red Sea with a "strong East Wind." Exodus 14:21. I Kings 19:11-13 proves that God does not bring the "wind." The East Wind is always a destructive force in the Bible. Ex 10:13; Hosea 13:15; Hab 1:9. And so the East wind which opened the Red Sea for Israel's deliverance and escape became a tomb for Pharaoh and his army. The DOUBLE CROSS was successful.

#20- In I Sam. 8:6, Satan put the idea into the people's minds to cry out for and demand a king like the heathen nations around them. God permitted them to have King Saul. Neither Samuel nor the people in those days fully understood God's character. When Satan was permitted to bring thunder (Psalm 78:48, I Sam. 12:17) even Samuel thought God was doing this. The holy angels themselves did not understand fully under how Satan operated until Jesus came in the flesh. The prophets' understanding of God's nature was progressive. Samuel cut

King Agag in pieces with the sword. God did not tell him to do it. He just thought God was that kind of a person, the same as Elijah did. I King 18:40.

#21-The carnal mind is enmity against God. Rom. 8:7. It does not "know" God, whom to know is "life eternal," John 17:3. The carnal mind wants justice; and desires to "get even," and demands "its rights." By contrast, the spiritually minded person knows only mercy. He does not try to get even or stand up for his rights. He doesn't "resist" those who would persecute him, James 5:6. He "turns the other cheek," Matt. 5:39, loves his enemies, does good to those who hate him and prays for them. Matt. 5:44. ***The angel of justice, Satan, is the god of get even,*** who always carries a grudge and never forgives or forgets anything. But, Jesus is the angel of mercy who forgives all freely and never keeps record of any wrongs. The record is only in the minds of those who are carnally minded, Col. 1:21.

#22-What Satan fears most in the great controversy is "flesh mediums." That is, human beings who will communicate God's true character of love to the universe by the way they live. When Satan saw Jesus come in the flesh, he knew that his kingdom was being threatened and in deep trouble, and attempted to kill Jesus by destroying all the little babies at Bethlehem. Matt. 2:16-18. That was just the beginning of Satan's war against Christ while He was on earth.

#23-Abraham, Job and all the patriarchs of the Old Testament knew God only as a monarch or king, not as a loving father, until they experienced Him. Abraham learned this through his temptation to sacrifice Isaac. Job may have learned of God's mercy and love after his pride was broken and he prayed for his friends. Job 42:10. The Old Testament patriarchs had faith in God and His justice as a king and judge. God was just, no matter what He did, because He was the supreme ruler and no one had the right to question his authority. They had absolute faith in God on this level of comprehension and understanding, but Jesus showed us that God is not just an "angry judge" who always does right. He is also a loving Father who never gets angry, and lets us judge ourselves. John 12:47, 48. We have the privilege of knowing the Father as Jesus did. This is called the "faith of Jesus." Rev. 14:12.

#24-Re: The Restoration of the Defiled Temple. Recently a doctor friend called and talked to me about the "daily" of Dan 8:13, 14. He said he had learned that the word "sacrifice" was a supplied word. As a result of his call I began reading those two verses and praying for understanding. Slowly, the Lord has answered my prayer. My understanding of it now is that Christ is the first saint and the second saint must be Gabrielle. The question that came to my mind was: "Why would the second saint be asking 'How long?'" Then, it occurred to me that Gabrielle and Michael are on a need to know basis and only knew what the Father revealed to them. The reason I say this is because before Jesus returned to heaven He told His disciples, "It is not for you to know times or seasons which the Father has put in His own authority." Acts 1:7. NKJV. "But of that day and hour knows no man, no, not the angels of heaven, but my Father only." Matt 24:36. The word cleansed can also be translated "Justified" or "Vindicated" "Restored," or "set Right." Then I thought about the basic or real meaning of the sanctuary. Jesus and the Father are our sanctuary or temple, our safe dwelling place. "He that dwells in the secret place of the most High shall abide under the shadow of the Almighty." Psalm 91:1. In Judges 13:18 the angel said his name was "Secret" or "Wonderful." Christ is the wonderful numberer of Daniel and Revelation.

So, if it is the "Temple" which is to be restored and vindicated, and God is our temple and we are His temple and abiding place, as Jesus prayed in John 17 "You in us and we in you" then the restoration or cleansing of the Temple is simply the vindication of God's name and character, which has to do with answering all the charges Satan has made against God's name, character and government, i.e. all the lies he has told which has caused the sanctuary or temple to be defiled, dirty and in need of cleansing.

So, when God's name is totally cleared by restoring the image of Himself in His people, and they become as one, then the sanctuary will truly be cleansed, vindicated and restored. mfc.

I sent the above letter to a fellow researcher on Dan 8:14 and he replied that he agreed with me and had believed the same thing for the last 20 years.

#25-When the Lord told Moses to "set bounds," Exodus 19:16-25, to keep the people from breaking through, He was simply warning them that Satan, the "lord of breaches, " would have a legal right to kill them if they came up into the thick darkness where "god was." Now, if Christ had been the one who would "break forth" upon them, then He should have said, "lest I break forth upon you." But, He didn't, for it was Satan He was trying to warn them against, i.e., the "god of breaking forth." Paul tells us there are many "lords" and many "gods." I Cor. 8:5. Many evil angels and men claim deity. I understand that in Britain all aristocracy is referred to as "Lord." Anyone who has ever been a Lord can still claim and use the title. And so, in the Old Testament, we find Satan, on occasion, assumed the title of Lord or God and spoke as if he were God, even to Moses as we have already seen in this book.

#26-I think that when you approach the subject/topic of Michael and Gabrielle like you would the topic of the Sabbath and/or State of the dead, God does not kill and other topics and just piece together little by little the evidence it is pretty clear that Michael and Gabrielle were twins ***"brought forth"*** together and that they became angels to try and help the angels understand what was going on with the creation of this world, etc. and to put down the rebellion of Lucifer. There is a teaching that Lucifer has a spouse also, and her name is Lilith. This is also the name of a night demon who kills babies. I don't know if is possible to prove that or not. Who knows if the angels have partners or not? Is it possible that the 7th commandment, forbidding adultery, has a wider application than we have realized? Luke 20:36 is referring to the saved being "equal to the angels," in the sense that they are no longer subject to death. This subject deserves a lot more study. The Father knew all things ahead of time. Jesus took it all by faith and believed the Father's word and obeyed Him in all things and desired to come and die for us. It was no doubt a terrible struggle for the Father to give up His son...so can you imagine the Father weeping and the Mother as well??? And what about His Sister Spouse? Was it Gabrielle in the Garden of Gethsamane who stood between Jesus and the mob as a bright light and they all fell back? I believe it was. She must have been dying a thousand deaths watching her brother-husband being so terribly treated and then on the cross all alone for six hours. That is really heart wrenching to say the least. I don't think we even know 5% of God's suffering or what really went on or what is going on even now. I think the only way for Gabrielle and Jesus to get back together is for her (Holy Ghost) to possess or inhabit the Elect and that is how she will finally get married to Jesus. Beloved, is it possible that this is what the wedding feast of the Son is all about? One person told me that the Wedding was when Jesus, the Lamb, becomes one with or married to the Holy Ghost. After much study and prayer on this thought I finally concluded that the marriage supper of the lamb is when the Holy Ghost totally possesses each human temple of the Elect as she has been doing slowly through the ages but will totally complete in this final age and that is when the church, as a corporate and mature body of believers will be ready for the wedding supper of the Lamb. The New Jerusalem, God's people, will become the bride of Christ. May the Lord help each of us to cooperate with the Lord by submitting totally to His will so this wonderful wedding may soon take place and we all can go home to heaven with Him.

#27-Satan's final effort to deceive and completely destroy the human race is soon to be manifested in a most dramatic fashion in this last age or eon before the return of our Lord Jesus Christ. Remember that the false always comes just before the true. In recent years new age type books have been published regarding the origin of the human race. The authors have attempted to prove that beings (gods, if you please) from outer space, other planets, far advanced in science and technology, have visited planet earth and started the human race with two beings whose progeny (offspring or children) now populate this planet. The Christian Bible in Genesis 1-3 calls these first two beings Adam and Eve. Although these New Age versions of earth's beginnings vary the one theme they do agree on is that planet earth was not created by God/Elohim/Jehovah/Yahweh or any other of the other various titles/names assigned to the Hebrew God of the Old Testament. They teach that mankind has evolved from this original species and that these gods from outer space, the creators, have visited this planet throughout history to check up on their creation to see how they are doing. These visitations have become more frequent since 1945 which was the advent of the atomic/nuclear age. These gods claim to be coming back to earth now to save mankind from destroying himself. One inspired writer exposed this end-time deception with these words: "Fearful sights of a supernatural character will soon be revealed in the heavens, in token of the power of miracle-working demons. The spirits of devils will go forth to the kings of the earth and to the whole world, to fasten them in deception, and urge them on to united with Satan in his last struggle against the government of heaven. By these agencies, rulers and subjects will be alike deceived. Persons will arise pretending to be Christ Himself, and claiming the title and worship which belong to the world's Redeemer. They will perform wonderful miracles of healing and will profess to have revelations from heaven contradicting the testimony of the Scriptures.

"As the crowning act in the great drama of deception, Satan himself will personate Christ. The church has long professed to look to the Saviour's advent as the consummation of her hopes. Now the great deceiver will make it appear that Christ has come. In different parts of the earth, Satan will manifest himself among men as a majestic being of dazzling brightness, resembling the description of the Son of God given by John in the Revelation. Revelation 1:13-15. The glory that surrounds him is unsurpassed by anything that mortal eyes have yet beheld. The shout of triumph rings out upon the air: 'Christ has come! Christ has come!' The people prostate themselves in adoration before him, while he lifts up his hands and pronounces a blessing upon them, as Christ blessed His disciples when He was upon the earth. His voice is soft and subdued, yet full of melody. In gentle, compassionate tones he presents some of the same gracious, heavenly truths which the Saviour uttered; he heals the diseases of the people, and then, in his assumed character of Christ, he claims to have changed the Sabbath to Sunday, and commands all to hallow the day which he has blessed. He declares that those who persist in keeping holy the seventh day are blaspheming his name by refusing to listen to his angels sent to them with light and truth. This is the strong, almost overmastering delusion. Like the Samaritans who were deceived by Simon Magus, the multitudes, from the least to the greatest, give heed to these sorceries, saying: This is 'the great power of God.' Acts 8:10. But the people of God will not be misled. The teachings of this false Christ are not in accordance with the Scriptures. His blessing is pronounced upon the worshipers of the beast and his image, the very class upon whom the Bible declares that God's unmingled wrath shall be poured out." "The Great Controversy Between Christ and Satan." Pages 624, 625. Most UFO researchers date the beginning of these outer space manifestations in the year 1947 when a pilot reported seeing saucer like aircraft in the Pacific Northwest in the vicinity of the state of Idaho. He referred to them as "Flying Saucers" and the name stuck. Scientists have referred to them simply as Unidentified Flying Objects. The military has denied their existence from day one. Several books by Christian and non Christian writers alike have clearly shown that there is a definite link between these so-called space beings and the occult due to the fact that their communications are the same, such as automatic writing, use of the Ouija board, channeling messages through human beings while in a trance like state and so forth. Because of the tremendous amount of publicity via literature and Hollywood movies, sightings and abductions, there has been a paradigm shift in public opinion from outright skepticism and unbelief to curiosity and a desire to know more about this modern day phenomenon. When the world comes to its final crisis Satan will be ready to manifest himself as the Christ who has come to save the world. That time is not far distant, but at hand.

#28-SEVEN LEVELS OF THE CHARACTER OF GOD:

1. "Beloved, let us love one another: for love is of God; and everyone that loveth is born of God, and knoweth God. He that loveth not knoweth not God: for God is love." I John 4:7-8. Therefore, if God is love, "GOD DESTROYS NO MAN." COL 84. MAN DESTROYS HIMSELF AND SATAN DESTROYS. Texts to look up & Read: Malachi 3:6: Hosea 11:8, 9; John 10:10; I Cor 10:10; Luke 13:15; Acts 10:38; Hebrews 7:26. There is no text in the four gospels which states that Jesus ever hurt or killed anyone, which proves what He is really like. Pure logic tells us if He never killed or destroyed while He was here with us for 33 years, which is the fullest revelation of who God the Father really is, then it stands to reason and logically proves that He has never hurt or killed anyone, because God never changes. Mal 3:6; Ps 89:34; James 1:17; Heb 13:8. Finally, God does not break His own law. It is impossible for God to lie, Hebrews 6:18, which is #9, "Thou shalt not bear false witness." #6 says, "Thou Shalt not Kill or murder." In the original the Hebrew word translated "kill" is the same as the one translated "murder." God does not break His law in order to uphold His law. He is not a law breaker. Therefore, God does not kill. "God Destroys no man." COL 84.

2. GOD DID NOT COMMAND THE ANIMAL SACRIFICE SYSTEM OF THE OLD TESTAMENT BUT ONLY PERMITTED IT. Matt 9:13; Matt 12:7; Hosea 6:6, 7; Psalm 40:6-8; Amos 5:24; Deut 22:5; Isaiah 1:10-12; Isa 66:1-4;

Jeremiah 7:21, 22; I Cor 10:18-21.

GOD PERMITTED IT BUT DID NOT COMMAND IT AND WHEN JESUS DIED HE ABOLISHED THE WHOLE SATANIC SYSTEM WHICH OFTEN LED TO CHILD SACRIFICE AND THE SACRIFICE OF VIRGINS.

3. THERE ARE "TWO LORDS" IN THE OLD TESTAMENT. THE WORDS LORD AND GOD ARE ONLY TITLES AND ARE NOT GOD'S TRUE NAME. SATAN OFTEN WAS ALLOWED TO ASSUME THOSE TITLES OF LORD AND GOD AND IN THE NAME OF GOD COMMANDED ISRAEL TO SLAUGHTER AND KILL, ETC. THAT IS WHY JESUS SAID TO THE JEWS IN JOHN 8:44, "YE ARE OF YOUR FATHER THE DEVIL." BECAUSE THEY ATTRIBUTED AND BLAMED THE TRUE GOD, JESUS CHRIST AND HIS FATHER, FOR WHAT SATAN WAS ACTUALLY DOING. JESUS TOOK THE BLAME ON CALVARY AND FORGAVE THEM ALL ANYWAY. IN GEN. 22 ABRAHAM WAS COMMANDED TO GO AND KILL HIS ONLY SON, ISAAC AS A HUMAN SACRIFICE. Which Lord do you think would ask a father to kill his own son? Satan is the god of this world: 2 Cor 4:4; Eph 2:2; 2 Sam 24:1; I Chron 21:1; John 8:44. Exodus 19:18-25; Ex 24; Ex 32:1-14.Gen 22:1-3.

#4- Universal Reconciliation or Universal Restoration or Universal Salvation: Rev 5:12; Rev 15:1-4; Psalm 22:26-29; 2 Peter 3:9; Phil 2:5-11; Eph 1:9-12; Eph 3:9-11; I Cor 3:10-15; Rev 21:25. The gates of the city, New Jerusalem, never close.

#5- The Harvest Principle. Jesus told the parable about the wheat & the tares in Matt 13 and explained that the Harvest is the "End of the World." There are three phases of the harvest. 1. Barley. 2. Wheat. 3. Grape. This harvest will take place during the last 3 years of this age. The Barley is another name for the Elect, Matt 24:24. There are at least 24 names or designations for this group.

#6- This level deals with the female image of God. I have not written very much on this yet as it is still in the process of being revealed. See Additional Note #26.

#7- This last level deals with the final transformation and translation of God's Elect at the close of the first three and half years of this age. The Elect will be translated at the time of the death decree which is explained in Revelation 11, 12, 13 and 14 as well as Dan 11 and 12.

#29-Many people believe that God the Father planned the death of His son. But let's find out whose idea it really was. "Christ's betrayal, trial, and crucifixion were all planned by the fallen foe. His hatred, carried out in the death of the Son of God, placed Satan where his true diabolical character was revealed to all created intelligences that had not fallen through sin. The holy angels were horror-stricken that one who had been of their number could fall so far as to be capable of such cruelty. Every sentiment of sympathy or pity which they had ever felt for Satan in his exile, was quenched in their hearts. That his envy should be exercised in such revenge upon an innocent person was enough to strip him of his assumed robe of celestial light, and to reveal the hideous deformity beneath; but to manifest such malignity toward the Divine Son of God, who had with unprecedented self-denial, and love for the creatures formed in His image, come from heaven and assumed their fallen nature, was such a heinous crime against heaven that it caused the angels to shudder with horror, and severed forever the last tie of sympathy existing between Satan and the heavenly world (3SP 183, 184)." 5BC 1149, 1150.

#30-Now, we are ready to go back to Mt. Sinai to learn more about the Ten Commandment law that was given by the hands of angels. The first time God appeared to Moses in the burning bush, Ex. 3:2, the Bible says that the bush was not consumed by this fire. When Jesus appeared among men the only kind of fire he taught and spoke about was the fire of His love and truth that burned in the hearts of men. But when the law was given Deut. 5 tells us that "the mountain did burn with fire," which seems to indicate a literal fire because the elders spoke to Moses about it they were so afraid. "We have seen this day that

God doth talk with man, and he liveth. Now therefore why should we die? for this great fire will consume us: if we hear the voice of the Lord our God any more, then we shall die." Deut. 5:23-25. So, it would seem that both kinds of fire were in the mountain...the literal kind from Satan and the non-literal kind from Jesus. Certainly the voice that spoke and the smoke and the lightnings and shaking of the mountain was not from Jesus because Isa. 14:16, 17 identify Satan as the one "that made the earth to tremble, that did shake kingdoms?" Paul even confirms this in Hebrews 12:18-24 where he contrasts the law given at Sinai with the peaceful kingdom of Mt. Sion. "For you are not come unto the mount that might be touched, and that burned with fire, nor unto blackness, and darkness, and tempest...so terrible was the sight, that Moses said, I exceedingly fear and quake: But you are come unto mount Sion, and unto the city of the living God, the heavenly Jerusalem, and to an innumerable company of angels,...And to Jesus the mediator of the new covenant." When God speaks it is with a still small voice, very quiet and humble.

The voice that thundered out the Ten Commandments was not a still small voice. It was very frightening. All of Israel were totally terrified. No wonder the Jews in Christ's day did not accept Jesus as the Messiah. How could this man be the God of Israel? He is too quiet and humble. We want the thunderous God of Sinai with all of its power, glory, fear and bluster and with all of its signs and wonders. But Jesus was there in the mountain with Moses and Satan the same as He was with Elijah later on. In Exodus 24 we gain some more insights about this same mountain top experience. Notice in vs. 1 that the true Lord tells Moses to come up "unto the Lord," but to "worship ye afar off." Jesus did not want them to get too close to this Lord because this God is a killer. John 8:44.

This was the same warning Jesus had given Moses in Ex. 19:21. "And the Lord (Jesus) came down upon Sinai, on the top of the mount:...And the Lord said unto Moses, Go down, charge (order or tell) the people, lest they break through unto the Lord (Satan) to gaze, and many of them perish, And let the priests also, which come near to the LORD, sanctify themselves, lest the LORD break forth upon them." Moses argues with Jesus on this point so Jesus again tells Moses: "let not the priests and the people break through to come up unto the Lord (Satan) lest he (Satan) break forth upon them." Ex. 19:24. Then in Ex. 23:20, 21 Moses is warned again about this Angel that was to "keep thee in the way...Beware of him, and obey his voice, provoke him not; for he will not pardon your transgressions: for my Name is in him. But if thou shalt indeed obey his voice, and do all that I speak;" v. 22. Ok, here we have the key point in all of this explanation about the law given at Sinai. Even though the voice that was bellowing out these Ten Laws was not the actual voice of Jesus Christ, as we know Him in Matt. 5, speaking in a very kind and loving tone of voice (remember God never changes, Mal. 3:6) God intended for the children of Israel to understand that this was His voice and His law that He was ordaining. Now there is another key word. Everything that God "ordains" is said to be from Him. We are told that "God ordained the thorn and the thistle." "Steps to Christ," page 1. He also "ordained" the animal sacrifice system which was not His perfect will which He did not speak at all. But He allowed it and permitted it and claimed that it was His law for whatever He allows He claims to be doing. "Obey his voice, and do all that I speak." Ex. 23:22. This is obviously why Jesus had to come in a body of flesh so that all of mankind, the angels, fallen and unfallen, as well as all the inhabited universe could see and hear theunvarnished, total, perfect will of God the Creator so no created being could ever have any doubts about His true character. And it was all planned out ahead of time down to the smallest detail.

In Exodus 24:1-18 we have another example of the two laws. From vs. 1-11 you have the animal sacrifice system...the ceremonial law. In vs. 9-11 you have a being appearing to them claiming to be God. Of course, Moses and everyone obviously thought this was the true God. But because the true God was invisible at this time the being that appeared to them was the pretender God...the imposter God. But He was allowed to do it for that was the true God's will for Israel at that stage. He was also involving Lucifer (Satan) in the symbols pointing to the coming of the Redeemer. Because the Bible tells us that Jesus never gives up hope... "Beareth all things, believeth all things, endureth all things and hopeth all things," Jesus was obviously hoping that Lucifer would have a change of heart somewhere along the way. Of course, we know He didn't. Neither did Israel. In fact, their hearts only became harder with every animal they slaughtered. This is a most fascinating aspect of God's character. That He is always hoping against hope that people will do the right thing. This is brought out in Isa. 63. Read the whole chapter. "For He said, Surely they are my people, children that will not lie: so he was their Saviour. In all their affliction he was afflicted, and the angel of His presence saved them: in His love and in His pity He redeemed them; and He bare them, and carried them all the days of old. But they rebelled, and vexed His Holy Spirit: therefore He was turned to be their enemy, and He fought against them." Isa. 63:9, 10. Notice that Jesus claims to be their enemy even though it was Satan who was their enemy...He is always a friend to sinners. And it says that He fought against them. Again He takes the blame for Satan fighting them but you could also say that He was resisting them, as He resisted Balaam on his donkey.

In Ezek. 20:24, 25 we find God saying that because they did not execute His judgments and despised His statutes, and had polluted His Sabbaths, and went after idols He allowed them to receive bad laws. But notice how He says that He gave it to them Himself. "Wherefore I gave them also statutes that were not good, and judgments whereby they should not live; And I polluted them in their own gifts, in that they caused to pass through the fire all that openeth the womb, that I might make them desolate, to the end that they might know that I am the Lord." "Thine own wickedness shall correct thee, and thy backslidings shall reprove thee:" Jer. 2:19.

We are now ready to go to the Mount of Olives with Jesus as He announces the laws of His kingdom or government. Matt. 5 records not only the Beatitudes but the ushering in of God's perfect law in the flesh through the first perfect medium, Jesus Christ. This was the beginning of the fulfillment of the promise of Jer. 31 that God would write His perfect and ultimate covenant in our hearts. The concepts Jesus spoke revealed for the first time in the history of the world the great depth and breadth of the love of God. "Blessed are themerciful: for they shall obtain mercy." Matt. 5:7. "Blessed are the pure in heart...blessed are they which are persecuted..." Such an idea had never been expressed before. "Blessed are ye, when men shall revile you, and persecute you, and shall say all manner of evil against you falsely, for my sake. Rejoice, and be exceeding glad: for great is your reward in heaven: for so persecuted they the prophets which were before you." vs. 7-12. No man had ever spoken such beautiful words before.

Now let's notice v. 17. "Think not that I am come to destroy the law, or the prophets: I am not come to destroy, but to fulfill." There are basically two schools of thought on this verse. The first simply explains that Jesus did indeed fulfill the law of Moses, which included the Ten Commandments, by nailing them to the cross. But when He rose from the grave on the first day of the week, He reinstated nine of the commandments, except the fourth one (Sabbath), which He replaced with Sunday. Of course, I do not believe this theory.

The second theory is that Jesus abolished all of the law of Moses except for the Ten Commandments, which was never part of the ceremonial law in the first place. Therefore, He did not abolish or do away with the Sabbath, which is a memorial of Creation. I have always basically agreed with this second theory even though I have never felt it totally answered the objections of the critics. But up to now it has been adequate, mainly because the Ten Commandment law was placed inside of the ark, representing the mind/conscience. But now with a greater understanding of the four levels of the character of God we can give a much better answer without sacrificing any of our beliefs. We are simply expanding on it which is what present truth does...it is a dynamic that never stops progressing.

Let me use another illustration. The old model T Ford was glorious in its time. But the day came when the model A came out and later on even newer models each a little better than the one before. And each new model had a glory of its own but the newer ones were somehow always more glorious causing the former models to "fade away."

And that is how Paul explains the "glory" of the law of Moses which he calls the "ministration of condemnation or death." vs. 7, 9. He is clearly talking about the Ten Commandments because it was the only one written in two tablets of stone. In our eagerness to defend the Sabbath commandment we have fallen into a serious error of trapping ourselves into the same legalistic administration the Jews of Christ's day trapped themselves into by refusing to move into the heart of Jesus where the original "law of God" resides in all of its blazing glory. "For if the ministry of condemnation has glory, much more does the ministry of righteousness abound in glory. For indeed what had glory, in this case has no glory on account of the glory that surpasses it." 2 Cor. 3:9, 10. People today are no longer driving model T Fords. Why? Because they have something much more "glorious."

Now, let's go to 2 Cor. 3, where Paul clearly teaches that the Ten Commandments was the "ministration of death, written and engraved in stones," simply because the law can never save us. Furthermore, he tells us that this "ministration of condemnation" v. 9 (although glorious in its day) has been "abolished." This is the KJV and I believe the word "abolished" does not give the correct rendering of Paul's meaning. I like the NAS better which uses the phrase "fading away." This correlates with what Jesus said in Matt. 5:17. "I did not come to abolish, but to fulfill." The KJV uses the word "destroy" instead of "abolish." What did Jesus mean when He said that He did not come to "destroy" the law? This is where an understanding of the original Greek word is so important. "Kataluo" is the Greek word Jesus used in Matt. 5:17. It means to literally destroy or dissolve or overthrow. Jesus said that was not what he had come to do. Instead he said that He had come to "fulfill" (Greek is Pleroo) meaning to "level up, finish, complete, fully preach, perfect." Of course, this is just what Jesus did. How appropriate and fitting that He was a carpenter who knew how to level, plumb and square which was just what He did with the law in stone. This brings to my mind a prophecy of Isaiah in which all wrongs would be made right and all problems would be solved... everything would be made perfect, before and during the coming of the Messiah. "The voice of him that crieth in the wilderness, Prepare ye the way of the Lord, make straight in the desert a highway for our God. Every valley shall be exalted, and every mountain and hill shall be made low: and the crooked shall be made straight, and the rough places plain: And the glory of the Lord shall be revealed, and all flesh shall see it together: for the mouth of the Lord hath spoken it." Isa. 40:3-5. This was also a prophecy of the work of John the Baptist as a forerunner of the Messiah. Yet, even John the Baptist did not understand the nature and character of the Messiah...His real mission and work. John tried to bring a revival of true godliness to Israel, to prepare their hearts to receive the message and work of the Messiah. And that is our work today as well. What a difficult and almost thankless task it seems to be at times. Yet, how exciting it is to see the character message developing year by year and the power it has to change lives in those few who do accept it.

Another illustration the Lord brought to my mind today to help me understand how He has been perfecting His true law of love in our hearts from the very beginning is that of a picture puzzle. We all have put a puzzle together at some time or other in our lives. I remember the ones I used to help my grandpa put together back in Indiana when I was about nine or ten years old. How exciting it was to see the picture developing little by little. It usually took us several days to put one together so we had time to guess and wonder what it was because some of them didn't have the picture on the top of the box or the box had been lost. But that is a good illustration of how the story of the Great Controversy is slowly being understood as one generation after another keeps putting more and more of the pieces of the puzzle together. And here we are now, the last generation putting the final pieces of the puzzle together...seeing the complete character of God in the face of Jesus Christ.

#31-Hi Pastor Mike,

In my devotions today, I noticed a similarity between the words of the Lord God of Gen. 2, 3 and the words of King Saul in 1 Samuel 14: 24-29, 37-39, 43, 44. These verses tell us that King Saul was acting under Satan's deceptions of pride and self glory. Saul says, "Cursed be the man who eats food before evening, and until I have avenged myself on my enemies." Jonathan did not know of it and ate some honey and his eyes were enlightened. But the people would not eat for they feared the oath. When God did not answer Saul's inquiry or prayer he became enraged and said, "If this sin is in Jonathan my son, he shall surely die." When the lot points to Jonathan, Saul says, "You shall surely die."

Now compare this spirit and words with the Lord God of Gen. 2 and 3. Genesis 2:17. "...for in the day you eat from it, you will surely die." Gen. 3:2, 3. Eve says to the serpent, "From the fruit of the trees of the garden we may eat, but from the fruit of the tree which is in the middle of the garden, God has said, 'You shall not eat from it or touch it or you will die.'"

After the Lord God confronted Adam and Eve about eating His forbidden Fruit, He says to the serpent, "Because you have done this, Cursed are you more than all cattle..." To the woman he said, "I will greatly multiply your pain...and your husband will rule over you." And to Adam He said, "Cursed is the ground because of you...both thorns and thistles it will grow for you...for you are dust, and to dust you shall return."

This tells me that the Lord God of Gen. 2 and 3 and King Saul have a similar spirit of threatening people with death and cursing them. This leads me to believe that this Lord God is actually the fallen angel Lucifer pretending to be God. And the innocent, and harmless serpent is used by Jesus to break Satan's power over the holy pair. It's too bad they lost faith in God when they ate the fruit. Romans 14:23. "But he who doubts is condemned if he eats, because his eating is not from faith; and whatever is not from faith is sin."

Both of these stories have to do with the death threat from eating good food that has been cursed by the "Lord God, or King." Also notice James 3:9,10. "With our mouth we bless God our Father and then we curse men made in the likeness of God. From the same mouth come both blessing and cursing. My brethren, these things ought not to be this way." NAS Bible.

So I thought you would be interested in these findings. God bless you always. Del.

#32-***How and when did the rite of circumcision begin?*** First of all, Jesus clearly stated that circumcision was "of the fathers," predating Moses. We know that God never changes but here is a law which was reversed by the Jerusalem council in 52 AD. Acts 15:1-29 is a detailed account of this council at which Peter testified that the Holy Spirit had been given to the Gentiles the same as to the Jews. The reason this council was held was because some believers from Judea were teaching that unless you were circumcised you could not be saved. Peter answered this argument by saying: "And He (Jesus) made no difference between us and them, but cleansed their (Gentiles) hearts by faith [that is, by a strong and welcome conviction that Jesus is the Messiah]...Now then, why do you try to test God by putting a yoke on the necks of the disciples, such as neither our forefathers nor we [ourselves] were able to endure? But we believe we are saved through grace of the Lord Jesus, just as they are." James then made a speech concluding: "Therefore, it is my opinion that we should not put obstacles in the way and annoy and disturb those of the Gentiles who turn to God." Acts 15:19. Amplified Bible.

We know that God never changes, therefore, He would not give this law of circumcision and then lead the early church to abolish it. "The Holy Spirit saw good not to impose the ceremonial law on the Gentile converts, and the mind of the apostles regarding this matter was the mind of the Spirit of God." Acts of the Apostles, page 194.

So, how did circumcision begin? It is first mentioned in Gen 17:10 as a token of the covenant between God and Abram. The question we must ask is "which GOD" told Abram to mutilate his body in this way? And why would God need to give him two tokens of the same covenant? The first covenant the Lord gave to Abraham was based on a change of his name from Abram to Abraham, meaning "father of nations." This was a very simple, faith covenant that God would keep His word and bless Abraham with many children. But the carnal heart is always seeking some kind of works of the flesh that they can perform, and Satan is always waiting nearby to give it to them. Paul tells us that Abraham was commended by God for his faith before he was circumcised. So, he did not need this extra proof. The "lord" who spoke to Abram in Gen 17:9 was lord Satan, the god of this earth.

Earlier in Gen 15:1-6 God had promised that his children would be as numerous as the stars of heaven. But in v 8 we see that later on Abraham's faith wavered and he demanded a sign, which was a sign of doubt and unbelief. So, lord Satan was allowed to step in and give Abraham the carnal sign of killing animals or blood sacrifice, Gen 15:7. And he (lord Satan) said unto him, I am the Lord that brought thee out of the Ur of the Chaldees..." He was then instructed by lord Satan to sacrifice some animals. As a result of this betrayal of trust Satan was permitted to bring a "horror of great darkness upon him." v 12. Abraham was shown the terrible things Satan would do to his seed. In v 17 the "smoking furnace" represented Satan and the "burning lamp" (flaming torch) was Christ, Psalm 119:105. Just as soon as the words of doubt came out of Abraham's mouth, Satan had a legal right to assert himself and give Abraham the sign he wanted. We know from Isaiah 1:10-12 and Isaiah 66:1-4 and especially Jeremiah 7:22 that God never gave the animal sacrifice system in the first place. "For I spake not unto your fathers, nor commanded them in the day that I brought them out of the Egypt." Paul also tells us that the Levitical law was not perfect and was therefore changed to the Melchisedec priesthood. He says in Hebrews 7:16-22 that this law was not only a carnal commandment but that it was weak and unprofitable but that Jesus was made a surety of a better testament or covenant. What an honor and privilege we have of working together on this project and mission.

#33-In his second letter to the church at Thessalonica, the Apostle Paul warned that just prior to the second appearing or coming of Jesus Christ there would be a great deception. "Then before the Lord returns, the wicked one who is doomed to be destroyed will appear. He will brag and oppose everything that is holy or sacred. He will even sit in God's temple and claim to be God. Don't you remember that I told you this while I was still with you?" 2 Thess. 2:3-5. CEV. The NAS reads, "so that he takes his seat in the temple of God, displaying himself as God."

This was written about AD 60 to 65 before Paul's death at Rome, and before Jerusalem was destroyed in AD 70. So, Paul probably believed it would be the temple of his day at Jerusalem where Satan would appear. So, in order for his prediction to come true in our day, a new or third temple will have to be built in Jerusalem. When this new temple is built and they start up the animal sacrifice system again, we will know that the time for Satan's appearance, as "the Christ," is near at hand. We also will know that the time for the appearance of the true Christ will be near because the counterfiet always comes just before the true, the real and genuine. I believe this will happen very soon.

In this book, I have referred to a seven-year period, which is devided into two 3 1/2 year segments. If you would like more information on this last seven year period, please write to me.

Thank you, my friend for your prayers and donations of love to help me keep on keeping on. If you would like to read this entire article, please go to GLC web site at http://www.godslastcall.org

SCRIPTURE INDEX

JOB

PSALMS

JEREMIAH

TOPICAL SUBJECT INDEX

Pastor Clute has also made many videos, sermons and interviews on the various topics of God's character. To obtain a list of all these videos and other materials on God's true character of love and to receive his 24 page quarterly newspaper, write to:

God's Last Call Ministries
P O Box 473
Woodburn, OR 97071

Buy this book in quantity and save money.
Special quantity prices:
1-5.....................$6.95
6-15...................$5.95
7-20...................$4.95
21-34.................$3.95
35 or more........$2.95

Please send me _______ books. I am enclosing my check or money order for $___________.
Please add $2.95 for postage and handling.

NAME____

ADDRESS____

CITY_________________________ STATE______ ZIP_____________

Make checks payable to God's Last Call Ministries.
Allow 2 - 3 weeks for delivery.

Other books by Michael F. Clute:

The Wonderful Truth About Our Heavenly Father, $12.95

Studies on the Character of God, $10.95

The Mystery of God Revealed in the Plan of the Ages, $10.95.

Would Jesus Kill A Little Sparrow? $10.95

Walking In the Light, (autobiography) $12.95

APPENDIX

COMING TO THE WORD OF GOD AS A LITTLE CHILD: REALIZING WE KNOW NOTHING AS WE OUGHT TO KNOW IT

In the year 1893, Alonzo T. Jones, a famous theologian and orator gave a series of lectures on what he called "THE THIRD ANGEL'S MESSAGE." It was based on chapter 14 of the Apocalypse or Revelation in which John described three angels flying in the midst of heaven giving three distinct messages. In #1 of this series, Jones, after some introductory comments about coming to the meeting to hear and learn things they had not heard before said, "It is very easy to hear things we never thought of before, but we do not always learn what we hear; but I suppose we have come expecting to learn things we never thought of before. It is simply saying we have come expecting the Lord to give us new revelations of Himself, of His word, and of His way altogether. I have come for this." Although I have had this 173 page document for years, I had never taken time to read any of it, so I began at page one and was surprised at the insights I received. For example: "This text is good advice for us all: '***Verily I say unto you, whosoever shall not receive the kingdom of God as a little child, he shall not enter therein.***' Mark 10:15. Thus we have come to learn of the kingdom of God, to receive things of the kingdom of God, things new and old, old things in a new way, and new things in a new way; whosoever shall not receive it as a little child shall not enter therein; cannot have it. Hence, we are all to come here and to sit down at the feet of Christ, looking to Him as our teacher, expecting to receive what He has to tell us, coming as a little child. Because, not only is this text here which speaks thus about those who would receive the kingdom of God, but in Matthew it is put in such a way as to cover all the time after we receive the kingdom of God from the first. 'At the same time came the disciples unto Jesus, saying, Who is the greatest in the kingdom of heaven? And Jesus called a little child unto him, and set him in the midst of them, and said, Verily I say unto you, except ye be converted, and become as little children, ye shall not enter into the kingdom of heaven.'" Matt. 18:1-3.

Let me stop here and say that Jones was not addressing novices who had no knowledge or understanding of the Bible. They were mainly pastors and general conference leaders who truly believed that they "had the truth of God already." He is trying to help them to see that there is more for them to learn. But in order for them to learn more of God's truth, because truth is always progressive and ongoing, they needed a more receptive attitude, e.g., like that of a little child. But, like the Pharisees and Scribes in the days of Christ, they were not willing to humble themselves, and as a result, most of them lost the blessing. Present truth is active and ongoing... it is alive and active, operating in the eternal NOW. In other words, what we know today is for today but tomorrow is a new day. Almost all denominations have stagnated in their creeds, beliefs and doctrinal points they believe in and have set in concrete. Any new ideas are called heresy and false doctrine. Jones was a pioneer who believed in progressive revelation. Let us continue on in his lecture.

"Now if any one should say that the other text refers to any who are receiving the kingdom of God for the first time and admit the truth that they can receive it only as a little child, confessing that they know nothing of it themselves, and cannot bring themselves to a knowledge of it, this verse shows that it goes beyond that, and the idea goes with it even after we have received the kingdom of God; for in order to be converted we are to be as a little child, receive the kingdom of God as a little child, allowing that we know nothing of ourselves, no wisdom of our own. It is not our own wisdom that can make it plain to us, or that can open the way by which we can understand it all right as it is. We must leave all our wisdom out in order to gain it, and by being converted become as a little child. 'Except ye be converted and become as a little child, ye shall not enter the kingdom of God.' What kind of children are mentioned? (By Jesus) *Little children.*" (What Christ was talking about is toddlers... say from the age of 1 to 3 or 4, maybe 5 at the most.) "'Little children have not much pride of opinion of their own. Grown up ones are not so ready to learn. Then this is spoken as giving us a model and example as to how we are to come to the word of God to learn.'"

In other words, as a little child is before his father and mother... very open minded and totally ready to listen and learn. And now Jones goes even further with some strong admonition from Paul.

"There is another verse that tells us the same thing and perhaps in a more forcible manner. 'And if any man think that he knoweth anything, he knoweth nothing yet as he ought to know it.' I Cor 8:2. How many people does that include? 'Any man,' all of us that have come here. Any one then who has come here, will it refer to us as personally as that? Every one. Any one of us then who have come here, that thinks he knows anything, how much does that cover? Thinks he knows how much? Thinks he knows what? -- ***'Anything.'*** Does that cover all things then? Yes sir. Then the text covers all people and all things that may be known. Then if any one of us thinks he knows anything, what does he know? How much does he know? ***He knows nothing yet as***

he ought to." (One might think that he would be satisfied with sharing that much of a straight testimony... but Jones continues on. Notice how he keeps on driving this theme home until there is absolutely no possibility that anyone present could miss the point he is trying to make... namely, that we do not know anything when we come to the Word of God. And if we think that we do, we are very mistaken and have a closed mind).

"Well then, we will all assent that that is true, shall we? Just set that down for yourself. If you came here thinking you knew something, you must decide you do not know that as you ought to know it. Then shall we come to this study in that way? Shall we all come to this study tomorrow, next day, each time we come here, and just settle it in our minds that we do not know anything as we ought to know it? I do not care if it is the oldest minister in our ranks; he must come and say, 'I do not know anything yet as I ought to know it; teach thou me.' And we will learn; every one that comes to this house that way will learn something every lesson he hears. And this includes that same oldest minister in the ranks; he will learn more than any of the rest of us, if he sits down like that. But how long a time does that text cover? How long will it remain there? Will we go beyond that time during this institute, think you? No sir. Very good then, we have that settled, for the whole institute, if we thought we knew anything. There are some things we thought we knew pretty well; if there is one thing we thought we knew, just put it down, we don't know anything. We are always learning the most out of those texts that we already know best. Don't forget that. We are always learning the most out of the texts with which we are already the most familiar. Then don't you see that any one who takes any text or thought, and studies upon it for a long time, and thinks he has got all the thought out of it that is in it, he just shuts himself off there? When he says, 'Now I know it,' he shuts himself off from learning what is really in that text."

And then in the last paragraph I will refer to Jones speaking of God's "eternal purpose" in every single text of Scripture which have an eternal depth. And this is very true beloved as I have learned over and over again as I have gone to the original text of Hebrew, Greek, even Spanish at times, and other languages as well. There is always a greater depth than we realized... always and forever. It just never stops. That is why it is called the Eternal Word of God. Pray as you read it and the Lord will give you new thoughts and understanding each time you read it.

Your friend,
Pastor Mike Clute

In 1979 I attended some meetings in which some important messages were recounted and explained regarding the true meaning of some lectures given in 1888. I was also given a pamphlet in which the views of speakers in 1888 were compared with the popular evangelical view of the day. For example: "The popular view said that God will torture the lost in an everburning hell." The contempary SDA view says, "God will torture and destroy the lost in hell-fire that annihilates... that they don't burn forever." But the 1888 view was ***"God destroys no man; every man who is destroyed will destroy himself."*** Sin, not God, destroys the wicked. "The second death is a merciful thing to end their real misery." Although this theology did not embrace Universal Restoration, it was the beginning of the character of God message which we find in 1900 in the book, "Christ's Object Lessons," pg 84, "God destroys no man." But before the message even had a chance to get off the ground, it was rejected by the leadership of the church at that time. The church and world had to wait almost 90 years until 1977 to hear this message as it should have been given in the 1880's. Here is one example of one of the speaker's lectures given in 1895.

Alonzo T. Jones wrote: "Jesus Christ, our Conqueror, the conqueror in our behalf, came into this land of the enemy, fought our battles, went into the stronghold of the enemy; then brought forth the captives and led them in triumph upon high to His own glorious city. Now 'thanks be to God which always causeth us to triumph' in Christ. 'In Him we triumph over this illegal power. And in this triumph over Satan there is displayed before the assembled universe the power of right as against might.'"

Now note: "The power of right as against might can never use any might! Do you not see that in that lies the very spirit that is called Non-resistance of Christians, that is, the very spirit of Jesus Christ, which is non-resistance? Could Christ use might in demonstrating the power of right as against might? No.

"For Satan to maintain the power of might as against right, might must be used at every opportunity; because that is the only weapon he can use to win. In Satan's cause, the right has only a secondary consideration, if it has any consideration at all. But on the other hand, the power or right as against might, is in the right, not in the might. The might is in the right itself. And he who is pledged to the principle of right as against might, and in whom that is to be demonstrated, can never appeal to any kind of might. He can never use any might whatever in defense of the power of right. He depends upon the power of the right itself to win, and to conquer all the power of might that may be brought against it. That is the secret. Then don't you see that that explains in a word why it is that Christ was like a lamb in the presence of this might that was brought against Him? He had nothing to do with using any might in opposing them. When Peter drew the sword, and would defend Him, He said, 'Put up your sword; he that taketh the sword shall perish by the sword.' Consequently, when tempted and tried as He was, when He was spit upon, when they struck Him in the face and on the hand, in all His public ministry His hand was never raised to return the blow. Not even the impulse to make any such motion was ever allowed. Yet He has our human nature, in which such impulses are so natural. When we get hold of that, all things will be explained as to what we shall do here, there, or the other place. We are pledged to allegiance to the power of right as against might; the power of love. And Jesus Christ died as a malefactor, abused, tossed about, mobbed, scoffed, spit upon, crowned with thorns, every conceivable, contemptible thing put upon Him, and He died under it, in His appeal to the power of right as against might. And that power of right has moved the world ever since, and it is to move the world in our day as it never has been moved before. Just as soon as God can get the people who are professedly pledged in heart to that principle, and who never expect to appeal to anything other than the absolute principle of the right, and to which we are pledged, then we shall see, and the world shall see this power working as never before." 1895 G. C. Lectures. Page 31, Lesson 22. By Alonzo T. Jones. This statement alone shows that the concept of ***"God does not kill"*** was a very special part of the 1888 message of Righteousness by Faith. In fact, based on the many writings published in the years following, such as "Desire of Ages," 1898, and "Christ Object Lessons," 1900, God's character, that He does not destroy, was the very heart of the message.

ABOUT THE AUTHOR

Michael F. Clute, was born in Anderson, Indiana, Jan 21, 1938. His mother, a devout Christian herself, raised him to believe in the Lord and he has been giving his personal testimony about Jesus, holding Bible studies and preaching since the age of ten. He was a Pastor-Evangelist until 1970 at which time the Lord called him to found God's Last Call Ministries, a non-denominational ministry.

If you would like to have a private study or seminar in your area, please contact him at GLC (God's Last Call), Box 473 Woodburn, OR 97071; or by e-mail. Below are some excerpts from His life story, "WALKING IN THE LIGHT," which will give you some insights as to how the Lord has developed the character of God's message in his life. ("Walking In the Light," 1992.) E-mail addres: mclute777@aol.com

CHAPTER 14

MEMORIZING IN PSALMS LEADS TO A DISCOVERY OF GOD'S CHARACTER MESSAGE

On the final weekend of a camp meeting in Oregon, July 17, 1976, I was in the big tent listening to my favorite preacher, HMS Richards talk about how one of his former teachers had memorized the book of Revelation after he had retired. He was up in his 70's but the Lord gave him the mental strength and capacity to do it. I was very impressed and began thinking about what part of the Bible I should start memorizing. As I drove home with my three children that night, the Lord impressed upon my mind the importance of understanding the Psalms better. I already knew Psalm 1 by heart so decided to start working on Psalm 2 the very next day. It turned out to be one of the most difficult tasks I had ever undertaken. It just didn't make any sense, especially the last part where it talked about ***"kissing the son lest you perish in the way when His wrath is kindled but a little."*** V. 12. I didn't like that picture of Christ. That wasn't the God Jesus had revealed in the New Testament. I continued on memorizing Ps 3 and 4 without any further understanding. But Psalm 5 was where I got the break through. ***"Destroy thou them, O God; let them fall by their own counsels; cast them out in the multitude of their transgressions; for they have rebelled against thee."*** Psalm 5:10.

As I kept going over this verse again and again it finally stuck in my mind. And then a wonderful thing happened. The light came on. All of a sudden I understood how God destroys. ***"Let them fall by their own counsels."*** Immediately I thought of what Paul says in Rom. 1 about God giving up on people and letting them go. "Wherefore God also gave them up to uncleanness...for this cause God gave them up unto vile affections...God gave them over to a reprobate mind..." Rom. 1:24, 26 and 28. As I continued to repeat this verse over and over my mind began to grasp the meaning more clearly just as the pieces of a giant puzzle fall into their respective places. I thought of how God claimed that He had hardened proud Pharaoh's heart when Pharaoh actually, had hardened his own heart. God didn't do it. He just assumed the blame because He is the Sovereign Creator. Then it dawned upon my mind... "God doesn't destroy." He simply takes the blame for everything that He allows to happen. But He is not the destroyer. Then I remembered what EGW says in COL, page 84. ***"God destroys no man."***

Suddenly my mind flashed back to the year 1969 when Elder M. D. Lewis had been permitted to speak at a worker's retreat one night. Elder Lewis had talked to many of the ministers about this subject and they seemed to be split about 50/50 down the middle, as to whether or not God destroys. There must have been at least 50 pastors present. Elder Lewis used a chalk board that night. He had been a professor of religion at Keene when the Lord revealed to him that ***"God does not destroy."*** He shared with me the following: "There can be no more conclusive evidence that we possess the spirit of Satan than the disposition to hurt and destroy those who do not appreciate our work, or who act contrary to our ideas." "Desire of Ages," 487.

Some leaders and pastors disagreed with Elder Lewis and he finally was asked to resign. But they made a big mistake because they took him out of the college and put him into pastoral work where he had direct access to all of us ministers. Elder Lewis was one of the most brilliant Bible scholars in Hebrew and Greek the church has ever seen. So, when he got up to speak that night I was all ears. When he explained how the Law of God is a flaming fire that destroys the wicked who break it, and this fire is not literal but symbolic of God's love, and also how it is sin in a man's heart that eventually destroys him, I was convinced that he was right. So, on that July summer day in 1976, all this began flashing through the memory banks of my mind along with this new information. The lights were really coming on and the darkness was fleeing away.

Then the Lord began to speak to me directly in my mind. First of all He said, "Michael, if you will stop telling your sob story and start telling My sob story things will go a lot better for you." I was embarrassed and ashamed. It was true. I was always telling everyone who would listen to all of the troubles and problems I had been through since GLC Ministries began in 1970. It felt good when someone felt sorry for me. This is what the Lord was referring to when He said I should stop telling "my sob story." I understood that part of it, but what I didn't understand was "His sob story." So I asked the Lord, in my mind, "What is your sob story Jesus?" Then, he said to me, "Michael, they nailed me to a cross." And I said, "Oh, I know Lord. It was terrible. If I had only been there I would have tried to help you." And then He said to me, "But, Michael, that's not all they have done to me. The worst thing is that they say I kill people, and I have never hurt or killed anyone in the entire history of the universe since I created it." When I heard and understood this I was so shocked I could hardly think, let alone speak. Finally, I began trying to put it altogether, piece by piece. All of the Scriptures I had read over and over again began to make sense. A very beautiful and logical concept was beginning to form in my mind about my Creator God I had worshiped and adored since childhood and now was trying to serve as a minister. It was so exciting.

According to most theologians, past and present, God is the one who puts sickness and disease upon people. He also kills and destroys. However, they also say that this same God sometimes heals people. And the devil sometimes kills. So, in essence what the preachers are saying is that God destroys just like the devil, only when God does the killing it is justified and when Satan does the killing it is not justified. The only problem with that line of reasoning is that it makes Christ out to be a hypocrite. Why? Because in John 8:44 Jesus told the Jewish leaders, "Ye are of your father the devil, and the lusts of your father ye will do. He was a murderer from the beginning, and abode not in the truth, because there is no truth in him. When He speaketh a lie, he speaketh of his own: for he is a liar, and the father of it."

So, what right would Jesus have to call Satan a liar if in fact Jesus Himself kills and destroys? Of course, He would have no right at all. As the truth slowly began to sink in I began to see the evil immensity of the terrible slander that had been brought against the Name and Character of God through the centuries. In fact, from the beginning of time. I was so angry and upset I just began weeping as I walked around the room. The enormity of the nature of this crime was just beyond belief. But what could I do? I was only one person. Who would believe me if I began preaching that ***"God does not kill?"*** Yet, I knew the record had to be set straight. I knew the Lord had spoken to me in an audible voice in my mind again, as He had done in the past. But I needed more proof before I could begin trying to explain it to others. I began memorizing in the Psalms on July 18th. On Aug. 14th I noted that I was starting on Psalm 6. So, evidently from July 18th until a few days before I preached on "GOD'S WRATH" on Aug. 7th, I had memorized up to Psalm 5:10 and had my breakthrough in the understanding I just wrote about. The pastor of the Mc Minnville and Sheridan churches, Dallas Dahl, asked me on the previous Tuesday afternoon if I would speak at the SDA McMinnville on Aug. 7th. I still have that original sermon on cassette tape, #724, "The Wrath of God." So, sometime between Tuesday, Aug. 3 and Friday Aug. 6th, I prepared the sermon which I put in my second book, "The Wonderful Truth About Our Heavenly Father," on page 363 and 364, as an exhibit in the appendix.

The timing of that first invitation to preach on God's character was Providential. I began receiving more and more invitations to preach on this subject right after the Lord led me into an understanding of his character of love. I preached at Grand Ronde, Hopewell, Newberg, Lincoln City and a number of other churches in the area during this same period of time. But the first time I spoke on the subject was Aug. 7th, 1976. I typed out the introduction word for word because I didn't want to take the chance of forgetting or leaving out an important thought or text. I was also very nervous because I didn't know how this subject was going to be received. But, no matter what the consequences might be, I was willing to begin preaching the truth. I just wanted to make sure that the message was delivered in the most factual, tactful, appropriate and acceptable manner possible so God's Name would be glorified. The sermon went very well and I was happy with the delivery and outcome.

At the close of my sermon I made this statement. "We, God's professed people, don't burn the wicked for eternity. We just cook them for a little while." I paused for a moment to let that thought sink in. There was a slight ripple of laughter in the audience. I then told the congregation that I could not accept that kind of God and concluded my remarks. As I shook hands with the people as they filed out of the church that day no one complained or became angry with me. In fact, one man, a doctor, as I recall, winked at me, as if to say he understood what I was trying to say. However, two ladies let me know they didn't like my remark about cooking the wicked at the end of the world. They thought it was sort of a "put down of the whole church." I told them I was sorry if my choice of words had offended them but that I had a burden to help people become more aware as to how they are coming across to the world.

I told some of the people on the way out that I would be giving more information the next time I was scheduled to preach, which would be Sept. 18th. Little did I realize the mental anguish and suffering I would go through during the next 30 days. The Great Controversy is hastening on to its final, climatic, show-down and we have a rendezvous with destiny. Up to this time I did not realize what all was involved in this message of God's Wrath and His character. But I was soon to find out. Sabbath, 9-18-76. On the way to the McMinnville SDA Church 9:15 A.M. "Have prepared second sermon on the 'Wrath of God.' The Lord has revealed many new, precious truths to me about the character of God and His love and His dealings with humanity. Elder Morris Lewis has greatly inspired me in this study." Elder Lewis lived in Keene, Texas. I kept in touch with him by phone and he would always answer my basic questions but I could never get him to answer a letter. The main problem I ran into in my preparation for my second sermon on the "Wrath of God," was the death of the first born. This is what I had told some of the people I was going to preach on. But when I finally sat down to begin my study I immediately ran into a serious problem. God Himself claimed that He was the very One who killed the first born in Exodus 12:12. "For I will pass through the land of Egypt this night, and will smite all the first-born in the land of Egypt, both man and beast; and against all the gods of Egypt I will execute judgment: I am the Lord." My heart just sank. I was not only shocked but upset at myself for promising to preach on this particular subject because now that I read that text I had no explanation why God would plead guilty or confess to something He did not do. In my heart I still believed the basic concept but knew that I had no logical explanation why the Bible was written in this fashion. A lot of thoughts began running through my head...like, "maybe I am not totally right on this. Maybe God does kill sometimes for reasons we cannot understand." At this point I began trying to think of some way out of my dilemma. If I am wrong then I am going to have to go back there and tell these people I made a mistake. I will have to say, "sometimes God does kill. I was wrong about this folks. I'm sorry." This was very upsetting to me. I was almost in a state of panic. "How could this be? I asked myself. I am sure the Lord has led me this far. What am I going to do now?" Finally, I began to pray and the Lord impressed me to read "Patriarchs and Prophets," page 279. So, I did and here is what I found. ***"The Israelites obeyed the directions that God had given... The Father and priest of the household sprinkled the blood upon the doorpost, and joined his family within the dwelling... Fathers and mothers clasped in their arms their loved first-born as they thought of the fearful stroke that was to fall that night. But no dwelling of Israel was visited by the DEATH-DEALING ANGEL. The sign of blood-the sign of a Savior's protection–was on their doors, and the DESTROYER entered not."***

At the time I read this I was sitting outside under an English walnut tree on the farm at Sheridan. Tears rolled down my cheeks as I realized Jesus was not the one who killed the first born. If I had just kept on reading I would have found out that verse 23 clearly states that it was the DESTROYER who killed the first born but it was the LORD (Jesus), the true Lord, who "suffered" or allowed "the destroyer" to kill the Egyptian firstborns but was not allowed to hurt or kill the Israelite's first born. I also called Elder Lewis a little later and he explained to me that the Hebrew word for "Destroyer" is SHACHATH. He said that whenever you see that word Destroyer in the Bible it always is referring to the Devil, never to the Lord.

He also explained that the scripture declares that God "hardened" Pharaoh's heart when in reality Pharaoh hardened his own stubborn heart. He pointed out that in 2 Chron. 10:4, 5 the Bible declares that King Saul committed suicide but in verses 13 and 14 it says that ***God killed Him.*** Then he explained to me that Psalm 78:49 clearly points out that it was the "evil angels" who brought the plagues upon Egypt. Then he quoted EGW. "Angels are sent from the heavenly courts, not to destroy, but to watch over and guard imperiled souls, to save the lost, to bring the straying ones back to the fold." "Review & Herald," May 10, 1906.

He also quoted "Education," pages 144, 145 which states that the Law of God itself destroys the sinner. "It bears witness against him at the judgment. A quenchless fire, it consumes at last soul and body." And finally he quoted his favorite: ***"God does not stand toward the sinner as an executioner of the sentence against transgression; but He leaves the rejecters of His mercy to themselves, to reap that which they have sown."*** Great Controversy, Page 36. Elder Lewis knew the Spirit of Prophecy backwards and forwards, upside down and inside out and the true interpretation of the words and their meaning. I thank God for such a man who was there to help me in my hour of need. As I look back at it all I see how the Lord was leading me at the very beginning of my journey in this message. The research, prayer and study I did in preparation for this sermon was a critical and major pivotal point in my life. It was during this 30 day period that the message of God's true character actually crystallized in my mind. There was no going back for me. I knew there were many unanswered questions but I had faith that God would eventually supply the answers to those questions as I continued to research, dialogue and study. And that is precisely what has happened.

As I went to church that fine summer day I was still recovering from the effects of a cold. I had sprayed some decongestant up my nose so I could breathe. This had the effect of making my mouth dry. As the usual custom is, a little before 11:00 A.M. I went into the back room with the pastor and elders where the order of service was explained and any last minute announcements were handed to the pastor. One of the elders, a professional man, who should have known better, did not like or agree with self-supporting work and verbally attacked me. This made me even more nervous and upset than I already was so that when I got up to preach I was not able to think clearly and keep my thoughts organized. My mouth went dry and I could hardly speak. I asked for a glass of water. This same elder must have felt sorry for me because he was the one who brought me a glass of water.

One of my strongest arguments was based on a statement found in "Christ's Object Lessons," page 84. I was so flustered by the unkind and unchristlike treatment of this elder that I could not remember where that statement was. I thought it was page 42 but when I turned to page 42 I could not find it. I was very embarrassed and even ashamed. I felt stupid. In listening to this talk again, Cassette Tape #731, I heard myself say "Maybe it is on page 84," which of course it was. I must have turned to page 84 but for some strange reason did not see it. So, I had to give up trying to prove that the statement actually existed and go to the next point. Actually, I think that the sermon made a better impression and was more effective because the audience sympathized with me more than if I had come across as a know it all and so sure of myself. I think I had more credibility. So, I don't feel so badly about that sermon anymore. What happened after the sermon was over was even more interesting.

A young college student, about 19, took a "Great Controversy" from the church library and walked up the aisle of the church while the congregation was still filing out. With a loud and angry voice he began reading from page 614. "A single angel destroyed all the first-born of the Egyptians and filled the land with mourning. When David offended against God by numbering the people, one angel caused that terrible destruction by which his sin was punished. The same destructive power exercised by holy angels when God commands will be exercised by evil angels when He permits. There are forces now ready, and only waiting the divine permission to spread desolation everywhere." GC 614. I have answered and explained the true meaning and interpretation of this quote many times through the years not only in my books but also in newspaper articles.

After the sermon about 10-15 people showed up to ask questions and receive more information. There were no more hecklers or protesters. But there were some sincere questions which I tried to answer to the best of my limited ability at that time. One young lady, Pam, in her mid-20s all of a sudden covered her face and just began sobbing uncontrollably. It took about five minutes for her to calm down. Pam was an attractive lady who was married to a nice fellow named Rick, who was a paraplegic. When I asked Pam why she was crying. she said, ***"I thought God hated me. But now I realize He loves me and it just overwhelms me."*** This is a very common positive result of this message. It releases people from their fear of an angry God so His love can flow into their heart. If we do not resist the Savior's love we will be drawn to Him just as naturally as flowers are drawn to the sunlight.

Meanwhile I continued memorizing in the Psalms, which was a real blessing, but also a stress because it is completely turning my theological world upside down as I learn that God does not kill, never has and never will.

In addition to everything else I was doing was now added the burden of trying to write out these new ideas so people could study it for themselves. I had a number of requests for my sermons to be put into print. My usual response was something like, "Well, I haven't written anything on it yet but when I do, I'll let you know." Meanwhile, the Lord was gently urging me to write but I didn't really want to write anything on this yet because it is not only a very controversial subject but it will require a lot more study and research...something I have very little time to do. So, I basically tried to tune the Lord's voice out of my mind and politely asked Him to give me a break. "Lord, if I put this concept into print now it will destroy the ministry." That's when the Lord spoke to me again and said, ***"Michael, if you will write a book on my true character I will open every door for you."*** That just about blew my mind. Instead of hurting the ministry, the character of God message would move it forward and bless it. That was enough motivation for me to begin writing, although I still didn't have enough time and I wasn't feeling very well anyway. As it turned out the Lord did open all the doors after I began publishing the first manuscript, "DOES GOD KILL PEOPLE?"

CHAPTER 16

WORK ON FIRST MANUSCRIPT OF GOD'S TRUE CHARACTER OF LOVE BEGINS

"Tuesday, April 19th, 1977 at 8:00 P.M. I went into my headquarters in McMinnville today and worked a little on the manuscript. Got 21 pages done. It really tired me out... just ran out of strength. Nervous exhaustion. Rested a little Friday and Saturday and got sick at my stomach Saturday night. I was in bed Sunday and Monday. Still tired today, but some better. Had worship with kids this morning. Showed them how to clean the toilet, etc." Then I listed all the things

I had to do for the next two days, which is too much to repeat here.

The donations were down that month and I had a hard time trying to raise the funds to keep going. But my strength was returning as I recorded that I was able to do 25 sit-ups and 15 push-ups and ran about a mile and read the Bible. On April 29th I wrote: "Was up until 12:00 Wed. night. Got to farm and bed at 12:30 A.M. Last night, I was here until 11:00 P.M. and to bed about 11:30. Am up to page 40 on book. Have made good progress. God has helped me tremendously. But am very tired this A.M. Must make up two newsletters and then go to the talk show. It is 8:30 A.M. Only God can preserve me. I have been memorizing Psalm 16. ***'Preserve me O God for in thee do I put my trust.'*** Can say almost the whole thing perfectly now."

Throughout my life God has performed many miraculous healings in my body when I was really sick. Some of these occasions were more dramatic and noticeable but most of the time it was a quiet, simple recovery which could be easily discounted. No matter how it came I always gave God the credit and praised His holy Name. I recorded such an event on April 30, 1977. "Sabbath. Farm at Sheridan. God performed a miracle yesterday and helped me to get to feeling lots better." Later I went into Portland to do the talk show. "Memorized Psalm 16 (finished it) on the way in and repeated it on the talk show and got through it without any mistakes. Talked on Astral catastrophes from Patten's book, 'The Long Day of Joshua and Six Other Catastrophes.' Also a quote from the beginning of Velikovosky's book, 'World's In Collision.' Was a good program although I did not receive any calls and usually didn't ask for them when I was presenting new material." After the talk show I called Elder William Pennick, (now deceased) pastor of the Sharon Church in Portland (The Black Church) to see if he was going to be on the program on next Thursday. He said he had talked to the Conference President, who said it was "ok" with him. I was rather amazed that he had given his ok. It was a miracle. The Lord truly is in control, moving this message forward.

On Sunday, May 8th, 1977 I recorded that my assistant and radio announcer, Gary, told me Chester was leaving to go up into the state of Washington to see his son. He told Gary he could not accept the "new light" regarding "God Does Not Kill." Even before I finished the rough draft manuscript last Wednesday night, Chester wrote up or typed up a rebuttal to disprove my book and gave a copy to Gary and me. Sharon and Gary stood firm against Chester and argued in favor of the ***God's Wrath*** Concept. In fact, Sharon even went beyond what I had ever heard her state before and said, 'I believe God has given Bro. Mike this special light to preach to the world.' Gary said basically the same thing. But Chester has stood adamantly against this, even refusing to read the manuscript. Most of the time when she verbalized her feelings about what I was doing it was more of a critical nature... to help me improve, which was often helpful. So, I was pleasantly surprised when she stood up for God's character. Up to that point I didn't really know how she felt. She had no desire to be out in front where people could see her. I almost always had to plead and beg her to come on the radio program or talk show. She didn't like the call in talk show because she liked time to think things over before she gave an answer. She admired me because I could think fast on my feet and make decisions quickly. She had always had a real hard time making decisions about almost anything. So, we complimented each other quite well in this regard. I think she liked the idea of a non-destructive God for her relationship with God, like so many people, had always been somewhat tenuous which I think is more or less characteristic among people who had traumatic experiences in their childhood, such as rape or sexual abuse. Nor did she receive the love she needed as a child from her mother. I have found this makes it difficult for people to make a full and unconditional surrender to God.

Also on May 8th I wrote: "For the past 4 weeks I have let everything go to complete this most important manuscript the Lord Jesus has given me on the 'Wrath of God or the Truth About God's Character.' On May 3rd, 1977, God helped me to complete the last section of this most important thesis. Never was I so 'bugged' by the Lord's Spirit to write something as I was on this manuscript thesis. First, I wrote out about 39-40 pages by hand and then let it set for a long time, it seems. Finally, I began typing it out, page by slow and painful page as the Lord led me into a different aspect of the work (message)... to correlate God's character with Righteousness by Faith."

Before I continue quoting I need to explain something I didn't write about in my diary. When I finally got the time to begin typing out the pages I had written out in longhand I set them by the typewriter up stairs in my new headquarters in McMinnville. I looked down at the first page and was about to begin typing out what I had written when the pages fell down on the floor. I started to reach down and pick them up when the Lord gave me this incredible thought...this first line to begin the book. "And we have known and believed the love that God hath to us. GOD IS LOVE; and he that dwelleth in love dwelleth in God, and God in Him." I John 4:16.

So, I immediately began typing out this text and the words the Lord brought to my mind to expand upon it. I ended up doing about two pages. It was really exciting because I could sense and feel the power of God's Holy Spirit coursing through my mind as I wrote out these thoughts. I entitled the first chapter "The Correlation of God's

Law of Love with Righteousness by Faith." When I had exhausted that first idea the Lord gave to me I again began to reach down and pick up the pages. Suddenly, I received another "flash from the throne" memo, as it were... this really great idea. Once again I typed out another few paragraphs and pages. If you asked me if I ever ended up typing out any of the handwritten pages I would have to tell you that I honestly don't remember. Hopefully, I did. But that is the way almost all of my writing and speaking, both in public and on the radio has been done... by direct inspiration or revelation. From the mind of Jesus to my mind. I know some people may think that is quite an audacious (bold, daring, presumptuous) statement to make but it is the truth. I have learned to recognize the voice of my precious Lord Jesus very well and He is more precious to me than anything this world has to offer. And He protects and guides me each and every moment and second of each day. His presence with me each day is the light and joy of my life and I feel His power coursing through my mind and voice when I speak to others about Him. It is truly an awesome experience. It is also a cleansing and molding experience, into the likeness of Jesus as in the face of Jesus Christ you behold the Eternal Father.

As you continue reading how the character message developed day by day in 1977 and on up to the present time you will see a progression in my own understanding and character development, as well as a greater ability and inclination on the part of people to understand the message as they are drawn to the uplifted Savior who died and yet lives for them. The Holy Spirit is truly being poured out on all who will receive it. "And I, if I be lifted up from the earth, will draw all men (men is a supplied word not found in the original) unto me." John 12:32. Jesus draws ***all*** to Himself who do not resist Him just as the flowers turn naturally to the sunlight we turn to the sunlight of His love.

Today is Sunday, June 26, 1994, as I write this. 2:55 P.M. I am in the back of my Bible Book Store here in the little city of Newberg. The light is off in the front of the store but on back here where I have my office. In spite of that a young couple just came in looking for some music cassette tapes. I had a good talk with them, played them some music which they purchased and then I gave them my 20 second Bible study on the two Lords from 2 Sam. 24:1 and 1 Chron. 21:1. The woman understood it immediately and then the man did too. I showed them my two books and they both wanted to read them. This has been happening more and more each day lately but it was very difficult back in 1977 as you will notice as we go along.

Let us now go back in time again, 17 years ago, to May 8th 1977. "I really began typing the manuscript out about 4/14/77, but I had begun writing it out in long hand on March 29th or so." I kept telling the Lord I didn't have the time to do it. So, after I got down really sick with a cold again and was trying to recover the Lord gently spoke to me again, saying, "Well, Michael, you now have time to do what I have been asking you to do." That's when I gave in and started writing. I ended up with 59 pages of single spaced-typed pages 8 x 11. It took more mental and emotional strength from me than any one single project I can ever remember doing in all the days of my past life. Yet, I have never been more aware of the closeness and holiness and preciousness of God's presence as I have in these past few weeks. It was terribly tiring and draining to have to stop so often to erase and "white out" my mistakes. But God helped me make it, although I often became impatient to "get it explained," so the people would know. But Satan was very angry with me and attacked me in different ways. But praise the Lord He has always helped me to triumph over all these attacks and gain the victory for our Blessed Redeemer. That first manuscript was completed on Wednesday May 11, 1977, exactly 7 years from the very day GLC ministries began on Wednesday May 13, 1970. The second manuscript, entitled, "The Final Absolute: Ultimate Truth About God," (85 pages) was completed on January 4th, 1979. The third one, "Into the Father's Heart," (85 pages) was finished in Aug 1981. The Lord led me to combine these three manuscripts, plus some extra materials, into one 412 page paper back which was published in June of 1982 (50,000 copies). And now, 23 years later, the volume you now hold in your hand has finally been re-published, revised and updated.

If the messages in this book have been a blessing to you please share it with others. You may order more copies from GLC Ministries, PO Box 473, Woodburn, OR 97071 (see page 584). Back issues of "God's Last Call" newspaper are also available as well as many video and audio tapes on God's Character. May the Lord richly bless and keep you as you continue to study and share with others that we all may be ready for His soon return. Your friend and brother in Christ, our Lord; Pastor Michael F. Clute. August 2005

God's Last Call website:

www.godslastcall.org